Tort Law Textbook

Tort Law Textbook

SECOND EDITION

John S. Hodgson MA, LLM, Solicitor

Principal Lecturer in Law, Nottingham Law School, Nottingham Trent University

and

John Lewthwaite LLB, LLM, ACIS

Former Senior Lecturer in Law, Nottingham Law School, Nottingham Trent University

OXFORD
UNIVERSITY PRESS

OXFORD

UNIVERSITY PRESS

Great Clarendon Street, Oxford OX2 6DP

Oxford University Press is a department of the University of Oxford.
It furthers the University's objective of excellence in research, scholarship,
and education by publishing worldwide in

Oxford New York

Auckland Cape Town Dar es Salaam Hong Kong Karachi
Kuala Lumpur Madrid Melbourne Mexico City Nairobi
New Delhi Shanghai Taipei Toronto

With offices in

Argentina Austria Brazil Chile Czech Republic France Greece
Guatemala Hungary Italy Japan Poland Portugal Singapore
South Korea Switzerland Thailand Turkey Ukraine Vietnam

Oxford is a registered trade mark of Oxford University Press
in the UK and in certain other countries

Published in the United States
by Oxford University Press Inc., New York

British Library Cataloguing in Publication Data

Data available

Library of Congress Cataloging in Publication Data

Data available

Typeset by Newgen Imaging Systems (P) Ltd., Chennai, India
Printed in Great Britain
on acid-free paper by
CPI Bath Press

ISBN 978-0-19-928764-2

10 9 8 7 6 5 4 3 2 1

John Lewthwaite dedicates this book to Judy, his wife, to Alistair, his son, to Christopher, and to the memory of his parents, Jessie and Albert.

John Hodgson would like to dedicate this book to Tamara, Thomas and Kristina.

■ PREFACE

Tort law continues to throw up new areas of interest and concern. At the moment one focus is on employers' liability for non-physical injury. Bullying and harassment at work appears to be 'the new rock 'n' roll'. The decision in *Majrowski* v *Guy's and St Thomas's NHS Trust* [2006] UKHL 34 has confirmed that in principle harassment by managers may be undertaken in the course of employment (as explained in *Lister* v *Hesley Hall Ltd* [2001] UKHL 22) and therefore attracts vicarious liability. In *Green* v *DB Group Services Ltd* [2006] EWHC 1898 an employee recovered some £800,000 from her employer on the basis of vicarious liability for harassment by a group of colleagues. Other claims for work-related stress have also occupied the time of the courts—*Barber* v *Somerset County Council* [2004] UKHL 13 and *Hartman* v *South Essex etc. NHS Trust* [2005] EWCA Civ 5. This no doubt reflects the realities of life in a nation where we have far more office wallahs than coal miners.

Causation issues are an endless source of interest. In *Gregg* v *Scott* [2005] UKHL 2 a majority of the House of Lords appear (the judgments of the majority are almost opaque) to have held that, following *Hotson* v *East Berkshire Health Authority* [1987] 2 All ER 909, reducing a chance of survival from 42% to 25% by delaying a diagnosis does not cause any harm, because on the balance of probabilities there was going to be a bad outcome anyway. Presumably reducing the chance from 51% to 49% produces full liability!

For many years there has been a chorus of criticism of the conservatism of the English judiciary in applying the *Bolam* test to issues of advice and guidance, so that the test was what a competent doctor would have explained, not what a reasonable patient wanted to know. See *Sidaway* v *Bethlem Royal & Maudsley Hospital Governors* [1985] 1 All ER 643. In *Chester* v *Afshar* [2004] UKHL 41 another bare majority of the Lords redressed this grievance with a vengeance. They were entirely correct to say that that the patient was entitled to advice and warnings which a prudent patient would need in order to make an informed decision and that the surgeon was open to censure if he did not provide this. However the evidence was that the claimant, although she would not have had the operation immediately, would have had it later. Her complaint was that, although the operation was competently performed, she had suffered a side effect. This was a risk she would equally have run at a later date. In compensating her for the result of the side effect the majority are perpetrating a dangerous nonsense.

The continued interventions of the judges in the law of tort are both a delight and a frustration. As the barrister said when the five foot judge emerged from the limousine at the Crown Court, 'these little things are sent to try us'.

John Hodgson and John Lewthwaite
Nottingham Law School, 2007

■ OUTLINE TABLE OF CONTENTS

■ DETAILED CONTENTS

■ ACKNOWLEDGEMENTS

Grateful acknowledgement is made to all the authors and publishers of copyright material which appears in this book, and in particular to the following for permission to reprint material from the sources indicated:

Blackwell Publishing: extracts from *Modern Law Review:* T. Hill: 'A Lost Chance for Compensation in the Tort of Negligence by the House of Lords' (1991) *MLR* 511; and W. Scott: 'Causation in Medico-Legal Practice—A Doctor's Approach to the Lost Opportunity' (1992) *MLR* 521.

Cambridge Law Journal: extract from 'Remoteness of Liability and Legal Policy' from (1962) *Cambridge Law Review* 178.

Jordan Publishing Limited: extract from *Family Law Reports* (FLR).

Incorporated Council of Law Reporting for England and Wales, Megarry House, 119 Chancery Lane, London WC2A 1PP, www.lawreports.co.uk: extracts from *King's Bench Reports* (KB), *Queen's Bench Reports* (QB), *Appeal Court Reports* (AC) and *Weekly Law Reports* (WLR).

Informa Professional a division of T&F Informa UK Ltd: extracts from *Lloyds Law Reports* (LLR) and *Medical Law Reports* (MLR).

News International Newspapers Ltd: extracts from *Faulkner* v *Chief Adjudication Officer* from *The Times*, 8 April 1994, copyright © *The Times* 1994.

Oxford University Press: extracts from B. S. Markesinis and S. F. Deakin: *Tort Law* (OUP, 1994); M. Napier and K. Wheat: *Recovering Damages for Psychiatric Injury* (Blackstone Press, 1995), and D. Howarth: *Textbook on Tort* (Butterworths, 1995).

Reed Elsevier (UK) Ltd trading as LexisNexis Butterworths: extracts from M. A. Milner: *Negligence in Modern Law* (Butterworths, 1967); and extracts from *All England Law Reports* (All ER), *Industrial Law Reports* (ILR), and *Road Traffic Reports* (RTR).

Sweet & Maxwell: extracts from Sir J. W. Salmond and R. F. V. Heuston: *The Law of Torts* (20th edn., Sweet & Maxwell, 1992); K. M. Stanton: *The Modern Law of Tort* (Sweet & Maxwell, 1994); T. Weir: *A Casebook on Tort* (Sweet & Maxwell, 1992); and P. H. Winfield and J. A. Jolowicz: *On Tort* (14th edn., Sweet & Maxwell, 1994).

Tottel Publishing: extract from M. Khan and M. Robinson: 'What is a responsible group of medical opinion?' (1995) *Professional Negligence* Vol. 11 No. 4.

Every effort has been made to trace and contact copyright holders but this has not been possible in every case. If notified, the publisher will undertake to rectify any errors or omissions at the earliest opportunity.

TABLE OF CASES

■ TABLE OF STATUTES

■ HOW TO USE THIS BOOK

This book will give students of tort law a clear and accurate introduction to the subject. Our aim has been to make the material as accessible as possible for those students coming to the subject for the first time. To this end we have included a number of features throughout the text to allow for interactive use of the book by students, in testing their knowledge and checking their understanding.

Cases and Materials

The Online Resource Centre that accompanies this book features additional cases and materials that complement the textbook. These resources can be downloaded free of charge, and can be used either as material for independent study, or integrated into your institution's existing virtual learning environment.

To access the online cases and materials:

1. Go to [**www.oxfordtextbooks.co.uk/orc/hodgson2e/**]
2. Click on the 'Cases and Materials' link
3. Login using the following details:

   username: **tortlaw2e**

   password: **materials**

Wherever there are cases or materials relating to the text, the Online Resource Centre symbol appears in the margin of the textbook.

Chapter Objectives

Each chapter opens with a set of objectives to help students identify the areas they should understand by the end of the chapter.

Question boxes

Questions are included throughout the text to encourage students to engage critically with the issues discussed. They also provide a useful means for students to test their knowledge while reading the chapter or during the revision process. Where the Online Resource Centre contains cases or materials relating to a question the ◉ symbol will appear in the question box.

Exercise boxes

Brief exercises are also included for students to test their understanding of the issues raised throughout the text, and to encourage deeper reading and analysis of cases. Where the Online

Resource Centre contains cases or materials relating to a exercise the ◕ symbol will appear in the exercise box.

Chapter Summaries

Chapters end with a summary of the main issues discussed in the chapter. This is not intended as a substitute for reading the chapter, but rather as a section to refresh the student's memory on the key issues discussed.

Further Reading

Sources recommended in the text for additional reading help the student to understand the important issues, and encourage a broader knowledge of the subject.

Assessment Exercises

Each chapter ends with an 'Assessment Exercise' that asks a question or sets up a scenario for the students to assess and answer using the knowledge gained through reading the chapter. Full specimen answers to the Assessment Exercises appear in the Online Resource Centre.

■ INTRODUCTION

Definition

In modern society it is inevitable that some people will be harmed or annoyed by the activities of others. This may take the form of physical injuries; loss of or damage to property; diminution in the value of one's property, because of the disruptive pursuits of the person next door; or injury to one's personal or business reputation.

The law of tort governs the question of whether the injured party, the claimant, may sue the party responsible for the injury, the defendant (sometimes called the tortfeasor—the 'maker of a tort'), to recover compensation for his loss, and, if so, how. Essentially, 'tort' is merely a collection of wrongs, to be resolved between the parties involved—i.e. civilly rather than criminally. Indeed both tort and wrong actually both mean something twisted—compare 'torsion' and 'wring'. In our context this means something untoward, and the only real difference in meaning between tort and wrong is that all torts are legal wrongs, thus excluding those wrongs which have no legal consequences, such as breach of social etiquette.

English law has traditionally concentrated on punishment for and redress in connection with such legal 'wrongs' i.e. 'wrongful behaviour' is emphasized, rather than the type of interests deserving protection. 'Fault' is the basis of much of the law. It is concerned with the readjustment of those losses that are bound to occur in society. In the words of Lord Denning ' . . . the province of tort is to allocate responsibility for injurious conduct'. English law was historically little concerned with abstract definitions of rights, preferring to concentrate on concrete cases where wrongs may have been caused.

Winfield defines tortious liability as that which 'arises from the breach of a duty primarily fixed by the law: this duty is towards persons generally and its breach is redressible by an action for unliquidated damages' (i.e. an amount to be fixed by the court having regard to the harm proved to have been caused by the evidence). Tortious liabilities exist by virtue of the law itself and are not dependent upon the agreement or consent of the persons subjected to them. It is this lack of agreement or consent which distinguishes tortious from contractual liability. Also crucial to Winfield's definition is the fact that the primary duty is towards persons generally. The breach of this duty gives rise to a remedial duty owed to a specific person or persons.

Tortious liability and other branches of law

The law of tort must not be considered in isolation: its role complements that of other branches of law.

> We do not live in a world governed by the pure common law and its logical [*sic*] rules. We live in a mixed world where a man is protected against injury and misfortune by a whole web of rules and dispositions, with a number of timid legislative interventions. To attempt to compensate upon the basis of selected rules without regard to the whole must lead either to logical inconsistencies, or to over- or under-compensation.
>
> (Lord Wilberforce in *Jobling* v *Associated Dairies* [1981] 3 WLR 155, 159)

Tortious liability and crime

Here there is a close relationship, for the two branches were originally one 'and now in their maturity they are not entirely divided' (*James on Torts*). Both deal primarily with wrongs done to people or their property. However:

(i) Crimes are generally the more serious wrongs for which the State, rather than the injured victim, takes legal action. Not all forms of tortious liability are trivial, however, and some wrongs (e.g. assault and battery) are both tortious and criminal.

(ii) Tortious liability is governed by civil procedure in a civil court; crime by criminal procedure in criminal courts.

(iii) Traditionally, the object of a criminal court is to punish the guilty, and deter others. The object of tort is to compensate the victim. However, criminal courts have wide powers to order a convicted person to compensate his victim (Powers of Criminal Courts (Sentencing) Act 2000, s. 130ff) and there are a number of occasions on which the courts have power to award punitive damages in tort: *Cassell* v *Broome* [1972] AC 1027. Tort undeniably contains elements of retribution and deterrence. Injunctions (restraining orders) are also available in tort.

Tortious liability and contract

Here, too, the same incident may give rise to proceedings in tort or contract, not only in cases of common callings (where a trader had to deal with 'all comers': e.g. bailees, innkeepers, etc.) but also generally, as where a developer negligently builds on unsuitable land: *Batty* v *MPR Ltd* [1978] QB 554 (CA), a dentist negligently extracts a tooth: *Edwards* v *Mallan* [1908] 1 KB 1002, or a solicitor omits to register a land charge in time: *Midland Bank Trust Co* v *Hett, Stubbs and Kemp* [1979] Ch 384. See also *Tai Hing Cotton Mill Ltd* v *Liu Chong Hing Bank Ltd* [1986] AC 80; *Henderson* v *Merrett Syndicates* [1994] 3 All ER 506 (HL). In some cases the contractual duty is to take reasonable care and such cases of 'contractual carelessness' may be authorities in the tort of negligence, and vice versa, as the ingredients of the duty are the same, or very similar.

In principle, however, the differences are said to be:

(i) in tort the duties owed are fixed primarily by the law, but in contract by the contracting parties;

(ii) in tort the duty is towards persons generally, whereas in contract it is towards a specific person or persons.

There are also important practical differences such as those relating to limitation of actions (the time limit for bringing claims).

Tortious liability and trusts

In this case the two categories are mutually exclusive, for if a civil injury is a breach of trust or other merely equitable obligations it is no concern of the law of tort. However, equitable **remedies**, such as injunctions, may be available in tort.

Tortious liability and restitution

Winfield's view is that in tort, but not in restitution, the remedial duty (i.e. the duty to compensate) always springs from a primary duty of some kind. It usually results in a liability to pay unliquidated damages—i.e. damages which are assessed on the basis of the court's conclusions as to the loss suffered by the successful claimant. In restitution, which concerns the reversal of transactions or events which result in one person being unjustly enriched by receipt or retention of money or property, the claimant usually claims liquidated damages (i.e. a specific sum representing the money in question or the value of the property) and the only duty on the defendant is to pay that sum.

Tortious liability and bailment

> A bailment is a delivery of goods (to the bailee) on a condition, express or implied, that they shall be restored to the bailor, or according to his directions, as soon as the purpose for which they are bailed has been completed.   (Winfield) (e.g. hiring out, storage, repair)

There is much academic controversy as to whether bailment is part of the law of tort, or the law of personal property. Winfield suggests that an action in bailment is akin to an action in contract if the bailment was created by contract, but to an action in tort otherwise. In any event the rules as to the burden of proof differ as between tort and bailment: *Port Swettenham* v *WU* [1979] AC 580 (PC).

Tortious liability and State or other provision

The relationships between, on the one hand, awards of damages in tort and, on the other, compensation through Income Support and other Social Security provisions, occupational sick pay and pensions, private insurance and criminal injuries compensation, etc., are complicated and are described in the 'Pearson Report' (the Report of the Royal Commission on Civil Liability and Compensation for Personal Injury, 1979, Cmnd. 7054; Vol. 1, pp. 27–45; Vol. 2, pp. 16–17). See also **Chapter 13**.

The basis of liability in tort

One action for breach of contract has much in common with the next: there will in both cases have been offer and acceptance, consideration (usually), intention to create legal relations, etc. But can this be said of a tort action? Salmond's view was that there are many individual torts, one very different from the next, outside which liability does not exist. In particular, one who has suffered damage which does not fit into one of the recognized tort categories has no remedy. Thus, for example, in *Mayor of Bradford* v *Pickles* [1895] AC 587, the defendant interfered with the claimant's water supply (which reached the claimant by percolation under the defendant's land), in order to persuade the claimant to buy the defendant's land. Held: the claimant had no remedy, as there was no right to receive water in this way, in contrast to the right to receive a flow of water from a river or stream. *Bradford* v *Pickles* was applied by the Court of Appeal in *Stephens* v *Anglian Water Authority* [1987] All ER 379. Slade LJ said:

> As the law stands, the right of the landowner to abstract subterranean water flowing in undefined channels beneath his land appears to us . . . to be exercisable regardless of the consequences . . . to his neighbours. Whether or not this state of law is satisfactory is not for us to say.

If on account of the negligent act of the defendant, the claimant suffers financial loss unaccompanied by any physical injury or damage, the claimant will usually not recover: *Spartan Steel* v *Martin* [1973] QB 27.

This situation used to be called '*damnum sine injuria*' in Latin, 'damage without a legal wrong', and you will still meet the phrase in some legal texts.

On the other hand, for Pollock and Winfield there was a Law of Tort rather than a Law of Torts. They felt that the fact that there was no case in which an action had been refused on the sole ground that it was new indicated a general theory of tortious liability (as evidenced in *Hunt* v *Damon* [1936] 46 TLR 579). Although it is true that novelty is no bar to an action (see *Pasley* v *Freeman* [1789] 3 Term Rep 51 and *Rookes* v *Barnard* [1964] AC 1129), it should be noted that Salmond's view was that a number of separate torts existed, not that their number was finite; and, further, although the courts have created new torts, they do not appear to do so upon any single general principle. In modern times it is doubtful that a wholly new area of tortious liability could be opened up by judicial decision; certainly in any area where rights under the Human Rights Act are at stake, a defendant could argue that any decision based on a new principle was not 'prescribed by law' as required under the Act. This expression has been said on many occasions by the European Court of Human Rights to require a law that is known, clearly established, and publicly available.

Furthermore, it will appear from an examination of those criteria of liability which most frequently appear in torts that there is no one criterion which is invariably present in every tort. The factors to be examined are: damage, fault, wrongful motive, and ability to bear the loss.

The causing of damage

At first sight this might appear essential to every action in tort, but some torts, such as trespass and libel are actionable without proof of damage: they are said to be actionable per se. These are said to be cases of *injuria sine damno*; there is a legal remedy without proof of actual harm—the reverse of *damnum sine injuria*.

Conversely, it is not for every item of damage suffered that the claimant may recover from the defendant. The claimant must first show that the defendant's conduct 'caused' the damage and that the damage was not too 'remote'.

Fault

Salmond says that 'reason demands that a loss should lie where it falls, unless some good purpose is to be served by changing its incidence'; and he thought that a sufficient purpose was the punishment of him who caused the loss, provided he was at fault, i.e. had acted deliberately or negligently. However, there are serious objections to the role of 'fault' as a basis of tortious liability:

(i) 'The real wrongdoer hardly ever pays for the damage he does. He is usually not worth suing. The payer is either his employer or his insurance company' (Devlin: 'Law and Morals', p. 18).

(ii) In some torts liability is imposed regardless of any fault: strict statutory duties, e.g. Part I Consumer Protection Act 1987; conversion of goods; some aspects of nuisance, e.g. *Rylands* v *Fletcher* liability. Fault attaches to behaviour. Strict liability attaches to the nature of the activity involved.

(iii) Even where 'fault' is relevant to the question of liability, it is usually judged objectively rather than subjectively (e.g. the 'reasonable man' test in negligence, under which, for instance, a learner driver can be held to the standard of an experienced driver).

(iv) Damages in tort are supposed to compensate, rather than punish. But contrast the views of those who consider punishment to be integral to the law of tort, e.g. as in 'Assault on the Law of Tort': 38 *MLR* 139.

 (v) A scheme of compensation based on tort, i.e. one which is essentially fault-based, will compensate only those claimants who can identify a tortfeasor (defendant). Not only may that present a problem for the claimant: the ability to pay the compensation will depend on the defendant's resources, though insurance funds are often (sometimes compulsorily) available to cover the liability. In contrast to this approach no-fault liability aims to compensate all victims of accidents. Since 1974 in New Zealand it has not been possible to sue in tort for death or personal injury. In that country the state administers a comprehensive system of compensation for this type of damage caused by 'accidents' (medical accidents and intentional acts are included).

The New Zealand scheme is financed by vehicle drivers (via their vehicle registration fee and a levy on petrol) for road accidents; by employers and the self-employed (via payments into a special fund) for work-related accidents; and by providers of healthcare services (again via payments into a special fund) for medical accidents. Funding for other accidents comes from general taxation.

Due to the escalating costs of that scheme, however, the Accident Insurance Act 1998 [New Zealand] has reduced the level of benefits payable: only lost earnings are now generally recoverable. Pain and suffering and other non-financial losses are no longer compensated; though some accident victims can claim a disability allowance.

The Pearson Report proposed similar changes for English law relating to road accidents, (funded by a tariff on petrol). The Medical Defence Union in 1989 suggested such a change in relation to claims concerning medical accidents. A limited statutory scheme has recently been introduced for some claims against the National Health Service, but this changes procedures more than the substantive basis of the claim.

Another alternative to the tort system has been proposed, namely, 'first party insurance'. Under a 'first party' insurance scheme each individual would take out insurance against suffering harm. (This is in contrast to the familiar 'third party' insurance, which covers liability for harm caused to others by the insured person.) In effect, each citizen would take out a form of personal accident insurance.

(vi) The cost of recovering damages in a system of compensation based on fault must also be borne in mind. According to the Pearson Report, in 1977/78 it cost at that time 85p to deliver £1 in damages.

In 'Access to Justice' (final report) 1996, Lord Woolf criticized the civil justice litigation system as being too expensive: ' . . . Costs often exceed the value of the claim . . . too slow and too unequal . . . a lack of equality between the powerful, wealthy litigant and the under-resourced litigant . . . ' According to the report the system was also too uncertain in terms of forecasting length of time on cost as well as being incomprehensible to many litigants. The imbalance between cost and amount of damages (also known as 'winnings') awarded was most marked where the award was small. His Lordship also said: ' . . . the present system provides higher benefits to lawyers than to their clients . . . '. As a result of this report the 'Woolf reforms' were introduced, for example 'fast-tracking' of certain claims and, in relation to personal injury cases resulting from road traffic accidents, a system leading to fixed costs.

Finding the money to fund litigation is a problem for many. Historically, trade unions have bankrolled their members; some insurance policies provide a certain amount for legal expenses, for example motor insurance policies; membership of organizations such as the Automobile Association, which is another form of motor insurance, for breakdowns, confer some legal support; and the State has provided legal aid and advice since 1949. State aid is now much reduced, however. As part of the cut-backs in this area conditional fee agreements (sometimes referred to as 'no-win, no fee' agreements) between solicitors and their clients have been introduced. See the Access to Justice Act 1999.

It remains to be seen whether these reforms will deliver a better and fairer system of justice.

To explore this topic further, see 'The Damages Lottery' (Atiyah—Hart Publishing, 1997).

Motive

The general rule, laid down by the House of Lords in *Mayor of Bradford* v *Pickles*, is that the defendant's motive is irrelevant: it will not turn a lawful act into a tort; nor will a good motive excuse tortious conduct. There are, however, some exceptions:

(i) An improper motive may be relevant, for example in cases of nuisance (e.g. by noise).

(ii) Damages may be increased in certain circumstances if the defendant acted with an improper motive.

(iii) Motive may also affect the award of a restraining order.

Ability to bear the loss ('loss distribution')

'Recent legislative and judicial developments show that the criterion of liability in tort is not so much culpability, but on whom should the risk fall': per Denning LJ in *White* v *White* [1950] pp. 39, 59. The argument runs that in most cases losses are actually borne by those best able to bear them, i.e. employers, insurance companies (whose function it is to bear them), and the State (through national insurance schemes), and that this is appropriate. In *SCM Ltd* v *Whittall* [1971] 1 QB 336, 344, Lord Denning MR said: 'The risk should be borne by the whole community ... rather than rest on one pair of shoulders.' The advantages of this approach seem to be that the community which enjoys the benefits of industrialization compensates its victims; that the victim is certain to be paid; that the payer is not left destitute; and that the administrative cost of the system is less than that of the tort system (see Ison, 'The Forensic Lottery', 1967). See also *Nettleship* v *Weston* [1971] 2 QB 350.

Insurance clearly plays a significant part in the development of tort law, but its precise role is a matter of debate. Lord Denning, for example, evidently regarded its presence and availability as a means of developing loss distribution within the law of tort. The traditional view, however, is that insurance should not affect liability. Thus, for example, in *Hunt* v *Severs* [1994] 2 AC 350, Lord Bridge said that in assessing damages it was not relevant that the defendant was covered by insurance.

It is certainly no defence for a defendant to plead that he/she was uninsured at the time of the accident or was otherwise without the means to meet the cost of a judgment.

However, as Hedley ('Tort' 3rd edn) puts it, at p. 9: 'Issues such as insurance and funding of tort actions were rarely discussed publicly, either in the law reports or in academic circles.

Academics and judges pretended that the law of tort floated freely, with no need for support. This was always nonsense, of course, and is today acknowledged as such.'

It is a fact of life that a claimant must, for all practical purposes, find a wrongdoer (defendant) with deep pockets. Many people choose to take out liability insurance, fortunately for some claimants. For example, household insurance which covers occupiers for liability to entrants and others, as well as providing cover for damage caused by the holder's children and pets. Manufacturers insure against any liability caused by their products. Professionals insure against liability: for example, medical doctors insure through the Medical Defence Union or the Medical Protection Society. At this point you may care to note the doctrine of 'subrogation' (substitution) which, in the context of insurance, means that an insurer is subrogated to the rights of the insured on paying his claim. In some instances the law requires insurance to be taken out, for example, the Employer's Liability (Compulsory Insurance) Act 1969 (5.6.8) and third party liability under the Road Traffic Act 1988. In relation to traffic accidents where insurance is compulsory, but none has been taken out or is invalid or the driver is of the 'hit and run' variety, claimants may bring an action against the Motor Insurers' Bureau. This body is maintained by the insurance companies and regulated by an agreement between the Bureau and the Secretary of State for the Environment, Transport and the Regions. The Bureau is funded by a levy on motor insurance premiums. Where owners or drivers cannot be identified claimants may apply to the Bureau under a separate (untraced drivers) agreement for compensation for personal injury only.

Those persons suffering from criminal injury generally may apply for compensation under the scheme administered by the Criminal Injuries Compensation Authority. Where a victim dies because of criminal injury only funeral expenses are payable to his estate, although partners, parents, and children of the deceased may claim in their own right. Additional compensation is payable to persons who were financially dependent on the deceased. Amounts payable to the victim and qualified claimants cannot exceed £500,000 in total. Some defendants are 'well-heeled': some employers fall into this category and are worth suing vicariously (see 8.4), public bodies and government departments have funds available (sometimes backed by insurance); the National Health Service funds its own cases, through the NHS Litigation Authority.

See also (1995) 58 *MLR* 820 (Stapleton).

The Human Rights Act 1998

This Act provides a framework for the adaptation of English law to meet the requirements of the European Convention on Human Rights (ECHR). It could well prove to be the catalyst for a radical change in the general nature of English law, including the law of tort. Tort law, in common with other branches of law, must, as a result of this Act, be compatible with the ECHR.

It was the case that before 2 October 2000, the date on which the Act came into effect, 'incompatibility' could be pursued in the European Court of Human Rights (ECtHR) in Strasbourg (see, e.g., *Osman* v *UK*, referred to at 1.5.1). The ECHR was ratified by the United Kingdom in 1951, and the individual right of petition was recognized in 1966. Now that the Act is in force, however, it is no longer necessary for claimants to take their cases to the ECtHR: breaches of the ECHR can be pursued in English courts.

In essence, the Act provides that any body exercising a public function, and this will include the courts, must perform that function in a way which is compatible with Convention rights.

It follows from this requirement that English courts must give effect to Convention rights and take into account the case law of the ECtHR.

An action for damages may be brought under the Act where such a body fails to observe its statutory duty. Although an award of full compensation is possible, it is not a statutory requirement (nor is it required by the ECtHR's case law) that such compensation be paid. Guidelines for awards in such cases were set by the Court of Appeal in *Anufrijeva* v *Southwark LBC* [2003] EWCA 1406. For an example of a successful claim under this head see *van Colle* v *Chief Constable of Hertfordshire* [2006] EWHC 360 (QB) (1.5.1).

The Act requires both primary and subordinate legislation to be interpreted and applied ('So far as it is possible to do so … ' s. 3(1)) in a way which is compatible with Convention rights. However, incompatible primary legislation (and incompatible subordinate legislation) cannot be declared invalid by the courts; though a declaration of incompatibility may be issued.

It is to be noted that the Act is aimed at public bodies, and is therefore **directly** enforceable against them, i.e. the Act provides a new remedy against public authorities (including quasi-public bodies exercising public functions), which do not act in a way compatible with the Convention. Where a private person or organization (including a quasi-public body acting in a private capacity) is sued, however, the Act can have an **indirect** effect, because the court must, in the proceedings, ensure compatibility with the Convention rights via appropriate interpretation of the law (statute, common law, and equitable rules).

Thus, the 1998 Act applies to **every** case involving Convention rights, whether civil or criminal, whether the parties are private persons or public bodies, whether the case is brought under statute or the common law. In each case the court must ensure compatibility with Convention rights—subject to provisions of legislation which are incompatible with the Convention, i.e. the courts may be prevented from ensuring compatibility by such legislation (though it may issue a declaration that the legislation is incompatible with the ECHR).

It is in this process of ensuring compatibility with the Convention, that the court must take into account any relevant ECtHR case law.

In s. 11(a) the Act provides that a person is not prevented, by relying on a Convention right, from also claiming any other common law or statutory right that he or she may have: i.e. non-Convention rights will exist side-by-side with Convention rights. Thus, a litigant will be able to claim the stronger of the available rights, where that is appropriate. It may be, for example, that a particular statutory or common law right is more extensive than the relevant Convention right; and vice versa. See *Marcic* v *Thames Water Utilities* [2003] UKHL 66.

Section 11(b) of the 1998 Act says that a person who relies on a Convention right is not thereby restricted in his or her right to make any other claim or bring any other proceedings. Under the Act (and the Convention) only 'victims' can make claims. This applies whether a person is bringing proceedings under the Act itself or relying on Convention rights in any other proceedings: s. 7. A 'victim' is someone who has been directly or indirectly affected personally by the infringement of the Convention. Section 11(b), therefore, provides the means to someone who is not a 'victim' to make a claim under some other legal provision alongside a claim under the Act.

It is important to remember that if a litigant decides to bring an action solely for a Convention remedy, an action under the Act can only be brought against a public authority. 'Convention arguments' can, however, be employed in other proceedings—even where the defendant is a private individual or body, as the court is itself a public body and bound by the Convention rights.

As we have already seen, the Act may also impose limitations on the ability of judges to make major changes to the law, as the ECHR lays great stress on the rule of law, including that part of it which states that the law must be known, accessible, and reasonably certain. In neither respect does the ECHR prevent either the incremental development of common law rules through new case law or the developing interpretation of statutory rules to meet changing social conditions: *CR* v *United Kingdom* (ECtHR, 1993).

You will find the Human Rights Act 1998 and the relevant provisions of the ECHR in *Cases and Materials* (10.1).

European Union Law

Today this is also an important source of law, and has already had considerable influence on the development of tort law in particular. Strictly, the law relevant in this situation is law of the European Community (EC) or 'community law'; the EC is the original component of what is now a European Union (EU) with a broader political, but not legal, dimension. The EC/EU can have direct influence on English law: e.g. Part I of the Consumer Protection Act 1987 is the result of an EC Directive on liability for defective products. EC/EU law may also have an indirect effect on national law (in our case UK law) via case law from decisions of the European Court of Justice (ECJ), holding that some breaches of community law are actionable in the national courts of member states of the EU. This is primarily a form of 'breach of EC/EU statutory duty' by either the state or private individuals to whom the law applies. See *Factortame* [1997] EWHC Admin 755.

It is important to **distinguish** community law, and the ECJ, from human rights law emanating from the ECHR and decisions on those rights of the ECtHR.

Studying tort law

General considerations

These are points which you always need to have in mind; they are aspects of the subject which may crop up at any time in your studies:

- **Negligence** is a pervasive theme—it gives its name to the most significant tort in practice, and describes the behaviour necessary to attract liability in some other torts as well.

- **Defences** and remoteness of damage are often relevant, but not necessarily immediately apparent.

- Some cases turn on whether the action has been brought in time under the Limitation Acts.

- Are you dealing with one or more parties, and if several, are they acting together or separately?

- Employers may be vicariously liable for the acts of their employees without being at fault themselves.

- What is the injury complained of—personal injury, property damage, or economic loss? The law treats them differently. It also has special rules for claims involving death (e.g. Fatal Accidents Act 1976).

- Did the defendant act intentionally/carelessly/ 'without fault'?

- Does the claim relate to a positive act (sometimes called misfeasance) or an omission to act (or non-feasance)? Liability for non-feasance is, in general, more difficult to establish. A defendant's deeds and words may be treated differently.

- Is there a direct or consequential link between the defendant's behaviour and the claimant's damage? Is the result something that could have been expected and/or avoided? A defendant cannot be responsible for unlimited liability.

- Does the claim arise from a pre-existing relationship, or a 'one-off' accidental coming together?

The importance of fact, proof, and evidence

If, as Maine said, substantive law was in the early days 'secreted in the interstices of procedure', it is no less true today that under the guise of procedure courts are able to shift imperceptibly into forms of liability without fault, whilst speaking the language of negligence. In the tradition of the common law, effect is frequently given to policies without mentioning them or, perhaps, even recognizing them . . . [C]ases which explore some of the problems of proof in negligence actions . . . also provide further material for a study of the basic objectives and policies of loss—shifting or loss distribution. Further, difficult problems of proof are a salutary check on the naive but common belief of students that 'black letter' law is more important than the facts to which it must be applied.

[Wright: Cases on the Law of Torts—section on 'Proof of Negligence: *res ipsa loquitur*'.]

Again, to quote the same learned author:

The study of torts . . . is really a study of fact situations. After a comparatively short period of time a student should have no particular difficulty in understanding basic principles. The real problem is in working out solutions or rules for individual cases. This problem of knowing 'how far to go', or 'where to draw the line', is one which will face the practitioner or judge throughout his entire career. Students approaching law with the notion that they can collect and state 'rules' which will solve all problems may be disconcerted by the seeming hopelessness of discovering a 'rule' which will automatically resolve a problem in the law of torts. Judgment is the important quality. It will be gained only through close study of the cases and constant practice in tackling problems.

As Lord Mansfield put it, in another context, in *Fisher* v *Prince* (1762) 3 Burr 1364: 'The reason and spirit of cases make law; not the letter of particular precedent.' This is true of the law generally; it is especially true of the law of tort as a whole, dependent as it is on such a vast body of case law. The 'law' is often found by reading 'between the lines' of the 'black letters' of the law.

In other words—cases, whether in practice or in a problem question, are fact sensitive and must be seen in their context. Wider implications (e.g. cost to society) and policy considerations must also be kept in mind. These will change over time, so older cases may be less reliable and helpful.

General technique in answering questions

- Do not rewrite the questions or rephrase them as a narrative by way of introduction to the answer. The examiner knows the question, though you must assume he/she knows nothing, or at least very little, about its subject-matter. Avoid verbiage and padding; these only waste time and may reveal your confusion.

- Aim at clarity of presentation by making your points clearly, concisely, and in logical sequence. Your memory sequence may be from cases to principle but your answering sequence must be from principle to cases. Argue legal principles; cases illustrate and show the source of the principles sometimes even where statute is involved.

- Your answer is not improved by making it look like an extract from a casebook. It is better to set out the legal principles involved before mentioning the name of a case than to quote one case after another without properly extracting the legal principles. Even less impressive is the mere naming of a string of cases. In any event, do not quote masses of cases. Practice directions require counsel in real life to concentrate on principle and keep down the number of authorities quoted.

Answering problem questions

The mnemonic 'IPAC' is a useful guide in dealing with these questions which appear in every law examination paper.

Identification (I)

The first step is to make sure you recognize the areas of law concerned; this involves setting out the legal issues arising on the facts given.

Principles (P)

Set out the relevant principles as they emerge from cases and/or statutes. Try to include all aspects of the law that appear pertinent, not those which merely rest on the narrow base of the question. Unless the problem clearly resembles a decided case, it is not generally advisable to set out all the facts of that case, a brief outline of the facts and the *ratio decidendi* suffices. The mere citation of case names will gain you nothing in marks and may even result in your examiner forming the impression that you have simply crowded your memory with case names without understanding the decisions.

Application of principles to the problem (A)

(i) make sure you fully understand the facts, seeking out any 'traps' or red herrings, and also what is implicit or understated;

(ii) analyse these facts and select those which have legal significance, i.e. the 'material' facts;

(iii) compare the facts with similar cases where this may illuminate your argument;

(iv) remember that there may be missing information about material facts; you then have to deal with alternative possibilities.

Conclusion (C)

Draw a conclusion (bearing in mind what the question calls for: e.g. if 'Advise A' then advice is required) but accept and indicate that there may be one or more alternative solutions which you should discuss. It is often the weaker student who expresses his or her views most dogmatically. A good student perceives the subtleties and uncertainties of the law.

Express your conclusion tentatively. There are rarely any certainties in law, and problem questions are invariably based on undecided or ambiguous principles or rules of law.

Legal terminology

Law has its own language, as you must have noticed. You will soon pick up the commoner terms, but you should use a law dictionary for the less familiar ones. There has recently been a modernization of legal vocabulary due to the Woolf reforms. Most importantly 'claimant' has replaced 'plaintiff', although some judges have been slow to adopt the new terminology. This is only the latest in a series of reforms, and technical language has also changed more gradually over time. Older cases will contain many strange terms, generally obsolete and of no current significance. This applies particularly to the use of 'law French', which was the general language of the law until the eighteenth century, but now survives only in isolated phrases. Latin was also in common use both to define legal concepts and in the form of quotations from the Latin authors whom the judges had all studied at school. We are now encouraged to avoid Latin where we can, but some expressions will remain, either because they have entered ordinary English (e.g. prima facie) or because they have no straightforward translation (e.g. *ratio decidendi*).

Further Reading

Atiyah, P.S., *Accidents, Compensation and the Law*, 6th edn (P. Cane), London: Butterworths, 1999.

Deakin, S., Johnston, A., and Markesinis, B.S., *Tort Law*, 5th edn, Oxford: Clarendon Press, 2003, Chapter 1.

Hepple, Howarth, and Matthews, *Tort: Cases and Materials*, 5th edn, London: Butterworths, 2000, Chapter 1.

Lunney, M and Oliphant, K., *Tort Law: Text and Materials*, 2nd edn, London: Longman, 2005, Part 1.

Weir, T., *Tort Law*, 2nd edn, Oxford: Oxford University Press, 2006, Chapter 1.

Williams, G., *Learning the Law* 13th edn, London: Sweet & Maxwell, 2006.

1 Negligence I: duty and breach

1.1 OBJECTIVES

By the end of this chapter you should be able to:

1 State the basic requirements for liability in the tort of negligence

2 Account for the degree of overlap between the three elements of liability

3 Explain the significance of the term 'duty of care' and the role played by **policy** in determining its existence

4 Account for those areas of potential liability which are of a contentious nature

5 Explain the significance of the term 'breach of duty'

6 Demonstrate familiarity with the mechanisms whereby the courts determine the requisite standard of care appropriate to the circumstances of each case

7 Explain the significance of *res ipsa loquitur* in relation to the establishment of a breach of duty

1.2 Introduction

We begin our study of the law of tort with negligence because in practice it is the source of most litigation due to its wide jurisdiction and its capacity to expand to meet changing social circumstances (as Lord Macmillan put it in *Donoghue* v *Stevenson*, 'The categories of negligence are never closed').

In the law of tort the word 'negligence' has two meanings: first, a descriptive meaning, synonymous with 'carelessly'; for example, one person may negligently libel another, the relevant tort being defamation (see **Chapter 12**), and negligence is a form of 'interference with goods' for the purposes of the Torts (Interference with Goods Act 1977 s. 1(c)) (see **Chapter 10**); secondly, it is a specific form of liability, which originated as such early in the nineteenth century. In its modern form, it dates from *Donoghue* v *Stevenson* [1932] AC 562 (see *Cases and Materials* (9.1)). It is negligence in the second sense which is the focus of this chapter.

As a tort, negligence is said to consist of three elements:

(a) a legal duty;

(b) a breach of that duty;

(c) damage suffered as a consequence of that breach.

However, these elements **overlap**: as the cases are examined in more detail, you will see that the courts often regard them as interchangeable concepts. The main issue is determining when there will be liability and the judges tackle it in a pragmatic fashion. In *Lamb* v *Camden LBC* [1981] QB 625, Lord Denning reminds us that we are not dealing with watertight compartments. His Lordship points out that duty, breach, and damage 'continually run into one another'; they are also 'devices' used by judges to control liability.

You may be surprised to learn that in *Hedley Byrne* v *Heller* [1964] AC 45, Lord Pearce said that he often found it useful to start with 'damage' and work his way back to 'duty'. In this chapter we examine each element separately, but throughout your study of the topic it is important that you bear in mind the preceding observations.

1.3 **Duty**

This is probably the most significant of the control devices referred to above.

The claimant must prove that a duty of care was owed by the defendant in the circumstances of the particular case. This issue raises points both of 'law' and 'fact'. This means that first a duty must exist in principle, and then the claimant must seek to justify the application of the 'law' to the actual 'facts' of the case. It is worth noting here that defendants can have two bites at the cherry—they can deny that a duty exists in principle, usually by seeking to 'strike out' a claim (i.e. have it dismissed) on the basis that it does not disclose a claim known to the law. If they fail at this stage they can still argue that the claimant has not established a claim on the facts. Since it can be quite cost-effective to argue a case on an application to strike out (or the claimant's equivalent procedure, application for summary judgment on the basis that there is no possible defence) many of the cases we consider are of this kind.

The law will recognize a duty of care in negligence only where the relationship between the parties is seen as giving rise to that duty: there can never be a duty 'in the air', so to speak. As Lord Keith put it in *Yuen Kun Yeu* v *A-G for Hong Kong* [1988] AC 175, '. . . otherwise there would be liability in negligence on the part of one who sees another about to walk over a cliff with his head in the air, and forebears to shout a warning'. Each case must therefore be examined in the light of its own facts, but in general terms the 'duty criteria' namely, 'foreseeability', 'proximity' and 'just and reasonable' may be more easily established where the parties already stand in some relationship to each other. This could be the case where there is a contractual or statutory relationship between the parties, or where they are fellow users of the highway or have some analogous relationship.

A claimant will have greater difficulty where the case is of a novel nature, that is, is what lawyers call 'a case of first impression'. Here, the argument must be based simply on the applicability of the 'duty criteria' to the facts of the case.

Today, a legal duty of care in negligence must satisfy the 'neighbour' principle originally formulated by Lord Atkin in *Donoghue* v *Stevenson* (see *Cases and Materials* (9.1)). He said (at p. 579 of the law report):

> You must take reasonable care to avoid acts or omissions which you can reasonably foresee would be likely to injure your neighbour . . . ['neighbours' being]: persons who are so closely and directly affected by my act that I ought reasonably to have them in contemplation as being so affected when I am directing my mind to the acts or omissions which are called in question.

? QUESTION 1.1

Consider this definition carefully. Is a defendant to be liable merely on the basis that his victim was 'foreseeable' in the circumstances?

The Atkin 'test' has always seen foreseeability as a necessary requirement in the 'duty' equation, but very rarely, if ever, has it been regarded as a sufficient determinant of liability, otherwise there might be unbridled expansion of liability. To the requirement of 'foreseeability' the courts have since 1932 added the requirement of 'proximity'. More recently it has also been hed that it must be 'fair, just, and reasonable' to impose liability. Together, these requirements can be said to comprise the 'neighbour' test, although some judges insist that it is 'proximity' which is synonymous with 'neighbourhood'. It is probably impossible to offer a completely satisfactory explanation of the expression 'proximity': all we can say is that it seems to mean some sort of 'nearness' between the parties; this could be physical proximity, in terms of spatial and geographical limitations; or legal proximity in that, for example, a contractual relationship might already exist between the parties.

For example, in *Watson* v *British Boxing Board of Control* [2001] QB 1134 (CA), the claimant, a boxer, sustained brain damage in a boxing match and produced evidence to the effect that his injury would have been less serious if he could have had immediate medical attention at the ringside. A duty of care by the Board was found to exist: injury was foreseeable, the Board's licensing system for boxers created proximity; and it was just, fair, and reasonable to impose a duty.

In *Alcock* v *Chief Constable of South Yorkshire* [1992] 1 AC 310 Lord Oliver said (at p. 411) '. . . the concept of proximity is an artificial one which depends more on the court's perception of what is the reasonable area for the imposition of liability than upon any logical process of analogical deduction'.

A Canadian judge, MacDonald J, made much the same point when, in *Nova-Mink* v *Trans-Canada Airlines* [1951] 2 DLR 241, he said (at p. 254):

> When . . . a court holds that the defendant was under a duty of care [it] is stating as a conclusion of law what is really a conclusion of policy as to responsibility for conduct involving unreasonable risk . . . There is always *a large element of judicial policy and social expediency* involved in the determination of the duty problem, however it may be obscured by the traditional formulae.

(By 'traditional formulae' the judge meant the familiar concepts of foreseeability and proximity.)

> **?** **QUESTION** 1.2
>
> In the quotation from *Nova-Mink* what do the words in italics mean?

A court will first determine what is good public policy in relation to the scope of a proposed duty of care before reaching a decision on the facts of the case.

In *Sutradhar* v *Natural Environment Research Council* (2006), *The Times*, 7 July, Clarke LJ, dissenting in the Court of Appeal [2004] EWCA Civ 175, said proximity was 'a convenient shorthand term for a relationship between two parties which would make it fair and reasonable that one should owe the other a duty of care'. He said that a duty of care might be too onerous if it renders a claimant liable for an indeterminate amount of care for an indeterminate time to an indeterminate class of people. As a matter of policy, however, it might be fair to impose a duty of care on a defendant who voluntarily exercises professional skills if that duty arises from another pre-existing duty, for example in contract, or perhaps if a duty of care would promote some socially desirable objective.

The House of Lords ([2006] UKHL 33) confirming the majority decision in the Court of Appeal, was unanimous in rejecting the claimant's appeal. He was a Bangladeshi who had brought an action in negligence against the Council whose predecessor had been commissioned by the Bangladeshi government to research the provision of safe drinking water supplies. The predecessor had issued a report into its findings and the claimant had alleged in his pleadings that the Bangladeshi health authorities' failure to take steps to see that his drinking water was not contaminated by arsenic had been induced by this report. The defendant Council claimed they were not in a proximate relationship with the claimant therefore he had no arguable case. Lord Hoffmann described as 'improbable' the argument that the Council, through its predecessor, had owed a duty to the population of Bangladesh not to publish a report which had implied, 'by what it had not said', that the survey 'shared the conventional wisdom about arsenic at the time: that its presence was so unlikely that it was not necessary to test for it.' The claimant had, in effect, argued his case not on any positive duty to act; rather, he emphasized the element of misrepresentation arising on the facts and claimed that the law had developed from the *Caparo* test, relying on Hobhouse LJ's judgment in *Perrett* v *Collins* [1998] 2 Lloyd's Rep 255. Lord Hoffmann declined to comment on that judgment but appeared to acknowledge that it was arguable now that liability for negligent misstatements could be subsumed 'together with other conduct causing physical injury under a single principle'. However, 'that principle was not that a duty of care was owed in all cases' where 'it was foreseeable . . . that someone might suffer physical injury . . .' Proximity was also necessary. His Lordship understood this to mean some 'control over and responsibility for the potentially dangerous situation'. This element was absent in the present case: there was no proximate relationship with the source of danger, that is the supply of drinking water in Bangladesh. It was also necessary to consider the question of cost. A trial of this action, which would involve examining the water resources programme in Bangladesh over several years, 'would be an enormous and expensive undertaking'. Apparently, other Bangladeshis wished to pursue similar actions. This decision is also of importance in relation to **Chapter 3** (3.5).

In *Peabody Donation Fund* v *Parkinson* [1985] AC 210, Lord Keith said that the Atkin test should not be treated as if it were definitive; in all cases, as well as establishing both foreseeability and proximity, it must also be just and reasonable to impose a duty. You should also consider the view expressed by Lord Goff in *Smith* v *Littlewoods Organization* [1987] AC 241 (at p. 248): '. . . the broad principle of liability for foreseeable damage is so widely applicable that the function of the duty of care is not so much to identify cases where liability is imposed as to identify those where it is not . . .'

1.3.1 The neighbour test as a general principle of liability

 EXERCISE 1.1

What points are being made by Lord Reid in *Dorset Yacht* and Lord Wilberforce in *Anns*?

Home Office v *Dorset Yacht Co. Ltd* [1970] 2 All ER 294 (HL)

LORD REID:
In later years there has been a steady trend towards regarding the law of negligence as depending on principle so that, when a new point emerges, one should ask not whether it is covered by authority but whether recognised principles apply to it. *Donoghue* v *Stevenson* [1932] AC 562 may be regarded as a milestone, and the well-known passage in Lord Atkin's speech should I think be regarded as a statement of principle. It is not to be treated as if it were a statutory definition. It will require qualification in new circumstances. But I think that the time has come when we can and should say that it ought to apply unless there is some justification or valid explanation for its exclusion. For example, causing economic loss is a different matter; for one thing, it is often caused by deliberate action. Competition involves traders being entitled to damage their rivals' interests by promoting their own, and there is a long chapter of the law determining in what circumstances owners of land can and in what circumstances they may not use their proprietary rights so as to injure their neighbours. But where negligence is involved the tendency has been to apply principles analogous to those stated by Lord Atkin: cf. *Hedley Byrne & Co. Ltd* v *Heller & Partners Ltd* [1964] AC 465. And when a person has done nothing to put himself in any relationship with another person in distress or with his property mere accidental propinquity does not require him to go to that person's assistance. There may be a moral duty to do so, but it is not practicable to make it a legal duty. And then there are cases, e.g. with regard to landlord and tenant, where the law was settled long ago and neither Parliament nor this House sitting judicially has made any move to alter it. But I can see nothing to prevent our approaching the present case with Lord Atkin's principles in mind . . . I would dismiss this appeal.

Anns v *Merton London Borough Council* [1978] AC 728

LORD WILBERFORCE:
Through the trilogy of cases in this House—*Donoghue* v *Stevenson* [1932] AC 562, *Hedley Byrne & Co. Ltd* v *Heller & Partners Ltd* [1964] AC 465, and *Dorset Yacht Co. Ltd* v *Home Office* [1970] AC 1004, the position has now been reached that in order to establish that a duty of care arises in a particular situation, it is not necessary to bring the facts of that situation within those of

previous situations in which a duty of care has been held to exist. Rather the question has to be approached in two stages. First one has to ask whether, as between the alleged wrongdoer and the person who has suffered damage there is a sufficient relationship of proximity or neighbourhood such that, in the reasonable contemplation of the former, carelessness on his part may be likely to cause damage to the latter—in which case a prima facie duty of care arises. Secondly, if the first question is answered affirmatively, it is necessary to consider whether there are any considerations which ought to negative, or to reduce or limit the scope of the duty or the class of person to whom it is owed or the damages to which a breach of it may give rise . . .

Lord Reid in *Dorset Yacht* and Lord Wilberforce in *Anns* regarded the Atkinian formulation as a statement of principle. The importance of this from our point of view is that the foreseeability test was raised to a greater prominence with regard to the general development of the tort of negligence; the Atkinian test was regarded more in terms of *ratio* than *obiter*. In particular, Lord Wilberforce seemed to suggest that a claimant who established an Atkinian relationship with the defendant would also have established a prima facie duty of care in law; in other words the claimant would have succeeded in establishing a presumptive duty of care and the court would look to the defendant to provide a convincing argument against the imposition of a duty. You can read a further extract from *Dorset Yacht* in *Cases and Materials* (1.1.1). The following cases are examples of this approach: *Ross* v *Caunters* [1980] Ch 297; *JEB Fasteners* v *Marks Bloom* [1983] 1 All ER 583; *Junior Books* v *Veitchi Co. Ltd* [1983] 1 AC 520. These cases are discussed in 3.4 and 3.5.

1.3.2 **Reaction**

This revised approach, represented by the 'Wilberforce test' from *Anns* v *Merton* and the 'Reid approach' in *Dorset Yacht*, became the subject of much criticism. Lord Keith in *Peabody* said he was concerned that the Wilberforce approach might lead to a situation in which the authority of common law precedent could be undermined.

In *Leigh and Sillavan Ltd* v *Aliakmon Shipping Co. Ltd* [1986] AC 786, Lord Brandon said that Lord Wilberforce's view was intended to be applied only in novel situations and not across the board in negligence so as to influence areas where clearly established authority can be found.

 EXERCISE 1.2

What is the point being made by Lord Keith in *Yuen Kun Yeu* v *A-G for Hong Kong* [1987] 2 All ER 705 (PC)?

Their Lordships venture to think that the two-stage test formulated by Lord Wilberforce for determining the existence of a duty of care in negligence has been elevated to a degree of importance greater than it merits, and greater perhaps than its author intended. Further, the expression of the first stage of the test carries with it a risk of misinterpretation. As Gibbs CJ pointed out in *Council of the Shire of Sutherland* v *Heyman* 59 ALJR 564, 570, there are two possible views of what Lord Wilberforce meant. The first view . . . is that he meant to test the sufficiency of proximity simply by the reasonable contemplation of likely harm. The second view, favoured by Gibbs CJ himself, is that Lord Wilberforce meant the expression 'proximity or neighbourhood' to be a composite one, importing the whole concept of necessary relationship between plaintiff and defendant described by Lord Atkin in *Donoghue* v *Stevenson* [1932] AC 562, 580. In their Lordships' opinion the second view is the correct one. As Lord Wilberforce himself observed in *McLoughlin* v *O'Brian* [1983] 1 AC 410, 420, it is clear that foreseeability does not of itself, and automatically, lead to a duty of care. There are many other statements to the same effect. The truth is that the trilogy of cases referred to by Lord Wilberforce in *Anns* v *Merton London Borough Council* [1978] AC 728, 751, each demonstrate particular sets of circumstances, differing in character, which were adjudged to have the effect of bringing into being a relationship apt to give rise to a duty of care. Foreseeability of harm is a necessary ingredient of such a relationship, but it is not the only one. Otherwise there would be liability in negligence on the part of one who sees another about to walk over a cliff with his head in the air, and forbears to shout a warning. . . .

In view of the direction in which the law has since been developing, their Lordships consider that for the future it should be recognized that the two-stage test in *Anns* v *Merton London Borough Council* [1978] AC 728, 751–2, is not to be regarded as in all circumstances a suitable guide to the existence of a duty of care.

Lord Keith said the Wilberforce test in its second stage was too vague and ineffective as a control mechanism. Its terms of control were of an 'indefinable' nature. His Lordship thought it preferable to develop new duties incrementally and by analogy with established categories of duty. Indeed, the Wilberforce test had been 'elevated [in later cases] to a degree of importance greater than it [merited]'.

It was held in *Yuen Kun Yeu* that the Commissioner of Deposit Taking Companies in Hong Kong had not voluntarily assumed responsibility to members of the public who had invested in companies he had admitted to the official register. It was not reasonable for the investors to rely on mere registration of the companies as proof of their financial probity: thus the relationship between the parties was insufficiently proximate. ('Assumption of Responsibility' is discussed in **Chapter 3**.)

Lord Bridge in *Curran* v *NI Co-Ownership Housing Association Ltd* [1987] AC 718, said that *Anns* v *Merton* represented the 'high-water mark' of a trend in the law of negligence towards the 'elevation' of the Atkinian principle into one of general application from which a duty of care could always be derived unless there were clear countervailing considerations to exclude it. 'The trend should be resisted.'

1.3.3 *Caparo Industries plc* v *Dickman* [1990] 1 All ER 568 (HL)

Caparo is the current leading authority on the general issue of 'duty of care'. Having dismissed the 'Wilberforce test', it now provides the template for the application of the general conditions which determine the existence of a duty of care in all cases of negligence. *Caparo* suggests that searching for a single 'test' is a fruitless exercise, yet later authority has interpreted it as laying down a three-stage 'test' for determining a duty of care, that is, not only must there be 'foreseeability' and 'proximity'; it must also be 'just and reasonable' to impose a duty in the circumstances of the case. It is arguable, however, that each requirement overlaps with the others: they cannot be seen as forming discrete conditions of liability. Lord Bridge put it as follows:

What emerges is that, in addition to the foreseeability of damage, necessary ingredients in any situation giving rise to a duty of care are that there should exist between the party owing the duty and the party to whom it is owed a relationship characterized by the law as one of 'proximity' or 'neighbourhood' and that the situation should be one in which the court considers it fair, just and reasonable that the law should impose a duty of a given scope upon the one party for the benefit of the other. But it is implicit in the passages referred to that the concepts of proximity and fairness embodied in these additional ingredients are not susceptible of any such precise definition as would be necessary to give them utility as practical tests, but amount in effect to little more than convenient labels to attach to the features of different specific situations which, on a detailed examination of all the circumstances, the law recognizes pragmatically as giving rise to a duty of care of a given scope. Whilst recognizing, of course, the importance of the underlying general principles common to the whole field of negligence, I think the law has now moved in the direction of attaching greater significance to the more traditional categorization of distinct and recognizable situations as guides to the existence, the scope and the limits of the varied duties of care which the law imposes. We must now, I think, recognize the wisdom of the words of Brennan J in the High Court of Australia in *Sutherland Shire Council* v *Heyman* (1985) 60 ALR 1, 43–44, where he said:

> It is preferable, in my view, that the law should develop novel categories of negligence incrementally and by analogy with established categories, rather than by a massive extension of a prima facie duty of care restrained only by indefinable 'considerations which ought to negative, or to reduce or limit the cope of the duty or the class of person to whom it is owed'.

One of the most important distinctions always to be observed lies in the law's essentially different approach to the different kinds of damage which one party may have suffered in consequence of the acts or omissions of another. It is one thing to owe a duty of care to avoid causing injury to the person or property of others. It is quite another to avoid causing others to suffer purely economic loss . . .

 See also *Cases and Materials* (1.1.2) and also 3.5.7, where *Caparo* is discussed in more detail.

The main message from *Caparo* is that the law must be developed within an incremental framework; that is, in general the law should develop on a case-by-case basis. The scope of a duty of care can be widened only through the process of reasoning by analogy to existing authority, and 'foreseeability', 'proximity', and the question of whether or not it is 'just and reasonable' to impose a duty of care in the circumstances of the case are factors for general guidance only.

? QUESTION 1.3

Can you see a practical disadvantage to this approach?

If there is no general principle, a litigant with a 'novel' claim who asks: will it succeed?, is likely to be told 'perhaps, but it depends on whether the House of Lords thinks it is an incremental extension of this or that decided case'. In other words, there is considerable lack of certainty, which can be resolved only by litigation to the highest level. If there is some agreed principle, it can at least be applied by the trial judge.

Cases involving personal injury and/or actual damage to property will rarely, if ever, cause difficulty in terms of the establishment of a duty of care. This was the position taken by Lord Denning in *Nettleship* v *Weston* (see 1.7.1.3) and Lord Oliver in *Caparo*.

1.3.4 **Reactions to** *Caparo*

The House of Lords in *Marc Rich & Co.* v *Bishop Rock Marine* [1995] 3 All ER 307, held that the three-stage test must be applied in all difficult cases regardless of the type of damage suffered. Their Lordships said there was no logical distinction between 'physical' damage and so-called 'pure economic loss': in both types of case, damages could only be awarded in terms of financial compensation. Another decision of the House of Lords, *Page* v *Smith* (see 4.3.7) has arguably diminished the distinction between 'mental' and 'physical' damage. 'Pure economic loss' is discussed in **Chapter 3**.

This approach was also adopted in *Islington Borough Council* v *University College London Hospital NHS Trust* (2005), *The Times*, 28 June, where a patient had been injured by medical negligence. She subsequently received free care from the local authority. Her damages did not include the cost of this, as she had not borne it. Buxton LJ, delivering the judgment of the Court of Appeal, said that the council proposed a 'pioneering' method of moving these costs of care from the local authority to the defendant, by using the law of negligence to give it a direct claim against the defendant. His Lordship said the action raised some novel questions: not only was it a claim for 'pure' economic loss (see 3.2) that fell outside the normal range of cases arising from a direct relationship between claimant and defendant, it took the law of negligence into areas that it had not previously entered. He went on to say that the council claimed for the direct infliction of financial loss arising from the hospital's negligent treatment of the person to whom the council had provided assistance. His Lordship said that this was an area into which the law would not easily enter. The council had to establish the existence of a duty directly owed to it by the hospital, and it could only do that by satisfying the three *Caparo* criteria. As far as 'foreseeability' was concerned, the level of certainty required for an outcome to be deemed, after the event, to have been foreseeable was largely 'a matter of impression' and, just as in *Jolley* (see 6.5.5.2) the precise manner in which the injury would occur did not have to be foreseeable. So it was enough for the hospital to have institutional knowledge that some persons with the patient's disability would fall into the category of a person requiring local authority care and would not be able to pay for it. On that basis, it was reasonably foreseeable that the circumstances of this would occur; it was difficult, after coming to that conclusion, to see how the relationship between the parties failed through lack of proximity. The stumbling block, for the council, was satisfying the requirement of 'just, fair, and reasonable' said his Lordship. These words were not to be read literally nor solely in the context of the relationship between claimant and defendant in this case; wider issues of policy might have to intervene. The court held that there was no identifiable public policy allowing the claimant to succeed in this case. Only Parliament could fill the gap in the law, if one existed. In this case, as in many other post-*Caparo* decisions, there is much stress on the determining influence of public policy and relatively little on the role of an 'incremental' approach in the settling of 'duty' issues in negligence; yet a case-by-case development of the law was seen as the way forward in *Caparo* itself.

In *Norwich City Council* v *Harvey* [1989] 1 All ER 1180 a sub-contractor damaged a building under construction by negligently setting fire to it. There was a network of contracts and the building owner accepted responsibility for fire damage in the main contract and insured against it. The insurers claimed in tort against the sub-contractor. May LJ said that the main contract itself did not assist the defendants, and went on:

> In my opinion the present state of the law on the question whether or not a duty of care exists is that, save where there is already good authority that in the circumstances there is such a duty, it will only

exist in novel situations where not only is there foreseeability of harm, but also such a close and direct relation between the parties concerned, not confined to mere physical proximity, to the extent contemplated by Lord Atkin in his speech in *Donoghue v Stevenson* [1932] AC 562. Further, a court should also have regard to what it considers just and reasonable in all the circumstances and facts of the case.

In the instant case it is clear that as between the employer and the main contractor the former accepted the risk of damage by fire to its premises arising out of and in the course of the building works. Further, although there was no privity between the employer and the sub-contractor, it is equally clear from the documents passing between the main contractors and the sub-contractors to which I have already referred that the sub-contractors contracted on a like basis . . .

Accordingly it was not fair, just, and reasonable to impose liability.

> **?** **QUESTION** 1.4
>
> In *Marc Rich and Co. AG* v *Bishop Rock Marine Co. Ltd* [1995] 3 All ER 307 a ship sank, and the persons liable to pay for some of the cargo were out of pocket, as it was being carried at their risk, and had not been fully insured, as it should have been. A surveyor employed by a classification society, which is 'an independent and non-profit-making entity, created and operating for the sole purpose of promoting the collective welfare, namely the safety of lives and ships at sea', had surveyed the ship after it had been damaged and found it fit to sail. The cargo owners sued the classification society in tort. The case was heard on a preliminary question of whether a duty of care was owed. What do you think the result was?

The majority of the House of Lords, while finding that there was foreseeability and proximity—if you are surveying a ship and get it wrong it is foreseeable that it will sink and that the cargo owners will be affected—it was not fair, just and reasonable. Classification societies were part of a system, and the main means of securing compensation was through contract, either carriage at the carrier's risk, or insurance if it was at the owner's risk. To make them liable was to require them to insure, and create extra costs. Only those who had failed to protect their interests through insurance would be interested in a claim, and it was unreasonable to disturb the whole system for their benefit. (See *Cases and Materials* (3.1.5).)

1.3.5 **Some conclusions**

On first acquaintance, the notion of 'duty' in the present context suffers from a lack of definition in terms of form and content. There is no magic formula which will enable you instantly to recognize this somewhat amorphous concept. A duty will not appear simply as a result of someone chanting 'foreseeability, proximity and just and reasonable' as though those expressions formed some mantra (see *Winfield*, Preface to 14th edn).

'Foreseeability' is sometimes said to be an issue of fact (the so-called 'factual duty') in that the court at this stage is questioning whether the claimant has been unreasonably put at risk by the defendant; that is, this is an enquiry into probability. One should always be aware of the influence of policy considerations. The enquiry into 'foreseeability' is not always the simple 'factual' exercise that it appears to be: foreseeability is a plastic concept which can be used by the courts to achieve normative ends.

In practice, 'foreseeability' embraces both 'fact' and 'law', concepts which are themselves 'adaptable' when used by a skilled and creative lawyer or judge. However, the legal, policy issues generally arise at the 'proximity' and 'just and reasonable' stages of the enquiry.

'Proximity' is generally more difficult to pin down than foreseeability, yet it lies close to the heart of the modern tort of negligence. It is a companion of foreseeability; the two notions must not be regarded as synonymous. Indeed, 'proximity' is meant to signify something more than mere closeness in terms of temporal or spatial relationships, though these factors of time and space are often of great practical significance. In some cases proximity may be established, at least partly, by reference to statutory and contractual relationships existing between the parties.

In essence, 'proximity' describes (it does not define) the legal relationship existing between the parties once foreseeability has been established. Lord Atkin, in *Donoghue* v *Stevenson* itself, put it in the following terms:

> Acts or omissions which any moral code would censure cannot in a practical world be treated so as to give a right to every person injured by them to demand relief. In this way, rules of law arise which limit the range of complainants and the extent of their remedy.

He made it clear later in his speech that the general governing factor in this context would be the 'neighbour principle'. We must, however, be careful to separate the 'foreseeability' element in the neighbour principle from the 'proximity' element: the notion of neighbourhood in Lord Atkin's sense is made up of these two elements.

In *Caparo*, Lord Oliver regarded 'proximity' as something which could not be defined: it was, in his Lordship's opinion, 'a description of circumstances from which pragmatically the law concludes that a duty of care exists'. In other words, a court uses 'proximity' merely to describe a conclusion which the court has reached on the basis of appropriate considerations; that is, 'proximity' cannot indicate what the court's conclusion should be.

Caparo appears to base considerations pertinent to 'proximity' upon the incremental approach. With regard to novel situations, their Lordships approved the approach advocated by Brennan J in *Sutherland Shire Council* v *Heyman* (see the extract from Lord Bridge's speech above). 'Proximity' is established by referring to, and applying, existing case law.

At the proximity stage it is clear that legal policy will play a leading role. The manipulation and application of existing case law is a creative process: the court must decide whether or not to extend/adapt the law to meet new demands. If a new case is 'on all fours' (that is, in all relevant respects alike) with previously decided authority, the result may be more predictable but there is often argument about the applicability of an earlier authority to the facts of the new case. The precise scope of the earlier authority may be debatable because the judges in that case may have disagreed or a judgment may be somewhat obscure or did not consider factors which the later court regards as crucial to the issue.

In short, the application of the established law is invariably not straightforward: a position highlighted when a case is presented for consideration which is at the opposite end of the spectrum from the 'all fours' case, that is, it is a novel case, a case which earlier authority has not yet resolved at all. Here the court must decide whether to extend the existing law to an entirely new situation. Cases involving 'pure' economic loss, public authorities, psychiatric damage, and omissions, for example, have in the past three decades been prominent in this context.

It is to the 'fair, just, and reasonable' stage of the enquiry that such a case must normally be taken. The resolution of the case will depend on what might be called considerations of pure policy. Considerations of fairness, justice, and reasonableness apply to all cases, however: they are not applied exclusively to the novel situation. Indeed, the House of Lords in *Marc Rich and Co.*

AG v *Bishop Rock Marine Co. Ltd* (see 3.5.13) said that every case, whatever the nature of the damage involved, had to satisfy the 'fair, just, and reasonable' test. Even where 'proximity' is clear, an inference of duty may be rebutted by use of the 'fairness' test.

What you have just read is an attempt to describe the formal state of affairs in relation to the duty of care problem. You must take this formal approach yourself when the question of whether or not there was duty of care arises. In practice, however, the matter is less clear-cut.

Lord Oliver, in *Caparo* said: 'The three requirements of proximity, justice and reasonableness, and degree of foreseeability might be regarded as facets of the same thing.' Lord Bridge, in the same case (see 3.5.7) described the three stages as 'labels' rather than as definitions. Foreseeable risk was the predominant factor in the decision of the Court of Appeal in *Margereson and Hancock* v *J W Roberts Ltd* (1996), *The Times*, 17 April. Over a number of years the appellants, who used asbestos in their manufacturing processes, deposited a great deal of asbestos dust outside their factory. As young children both claimants (they were now of late middle-age), played in and with the dust. The claimants, now suffering from mesothelioma (a form of lung cancer almost invariably caused by exposure to asbestos), successfully claimed damages in the tort of negligence: the appellant argued that the potential dangers from exposure to asbestos did not come to their knowledge until 1933. The court, in dismissing the defendant's appeal, found that sufficient, material, knowledge was common long before that date and the test to be applied here was whether the appellants should have reasonably foreseen a risk of some pulmonary (i.e. lung) injury, not necessarily mesothelioma.

A sense of judgment is the only 'answer' here; this will develop only with time and perseverance. Your sense of judgment will develop in a gradual and incremental way, once the whole of negligence, including established areas of liability, for example misstatements, has been considered.

Look back on this topic after reading **Chapters 3** and **4** and think a little about the matter. The cases discussed and referred to in those chapters will help you in gaining insight and a feeling of 'judgment'.

 You can read extracts from Weir's casebook and Howarth's textbook in *Cases and Materials* (1.1.2).

 EXERCISE 1.3

Do you think there might be any particular problems with the 'duty' issue?

Problems are likely to be encountered in relation to cases involving liability in contract and tort (see 1.4), the liability of public bodies (see 1.5), omissions, 'pure' economic loss, 'nervous shock' (psychiatric harm), and the unborn child (see 1.6).

1.4 Liability in contract and tort

In *Tai Hing Cotton Mill Ltd* v *Liu Chong Hing Bank* [1986] AC 80 (PC) Lord Scarman said, obiter:

> Their Lordships do not believe that there is anything to the advantage of the law's development in searching for a liability in tort where the parties are in a contractual relationship . . . their Lordships

believe it to be correct in principle and necessary for the avoidance of doubt to adhere to the contractual analysis.

Traditionally, a claimant who has a contract with the defendant has often been able to choose whether to sue in contract or tort: the choice would depend on which cause of action gave the better result. For example, the rules governing remoteness of damage differ between the two causes of action; different limitation periods apply; and contributory negligence is not a defence in contract.

The courts have been less willing in some instances to allow claimants this freedom, insisting that the law of tort cannot be used to create liability where none exists in contract. *Greater Nottingham Co-operative Society* v *Cementation Piling and Foundations Ltd* [1989] QB 71 (CA), which is examined at 3.4.2, is a case in point.

In *Henderson and Others* v *Merrett Syndicates Ltd and Others* [1994] 3 All ER 506, however, it was held by the House of Lords that a pre-existing contractual relationship between the parties did not of itself preclude a concurrent liability in tort. A claimant in such a case could choose which remedy produced the best results, unless the contract provided otherwise.

Lord Goff said that the *Tai Hing Cotton Mill* case was concerned only with the question of establishing a duty wider in scope than provided for by the terms of the contract between the parties. Lord Scarman's dictum did not apply to a duty in tort which was coterminous with the pre-existing contractual obligation. *Henderson* is considered in more detail in 3.5.8.

 EXERCISE 1.4

Consider *Johnstone* v *Bloomsbury Health Authority* [1991] 2 All ER 293. Why was an action brought in tort rather than in contract?

The claimant argued that the specific term in his contract, requiring him to work up to 88 hours a week (on average) was excessive and injurious to his health. This term, he said, should be read subject to his employer's common law obligation (see **Chapter 5**) to safeguard his health from reasonably foreseeable risks. It was argued that the employer could demand only those hours of work which did not conflict with the employer's common law duty: this duty requires the employer to take account of the needs of the *individual* employee. Here, said the claimant, the hours of work required were injurious to *his* health.

The Court of Appeal, on balance, accepted the claimant's argument though only Stuart-Smith LJ fully agreed. Browne-Wilkinson LJ was reluctant to see such obligations as a mixture of contract and tort, but agreed that the obligation to safeguard the employee's health did, in the circumstances, override the specific contractual requirement. Leggatt LJ did not at *all* agree that 'tort could trump contract': he regarded the case as turning entirely on the terms of the contract of employment. On the facts, the defendant was not in breach of contract and that ended the matter.

The claimant sued in tort to enlist the employer's common law duty of care (see 5.5) which contains an obligation to safeguard the employee's health, something to which his contract of employment made no specific reference.

Today, the demarcation between contract and tort is much less distinct than it used to be (if it was *ever* that clear). Furthermore, as you will read later (3.5.10.2), negligence liability has been developed to such an extent in *White* v *Jones* [1995] 2 AC 207 that considerable inroads have been made into the doctrine of privity of contract. (See also the Contracts (Rights of Third Parties) Act 1999.)

1.5 **Public bodies and negligence**

Public authorities do not enjoy a general immunity from suit in negligence, but on the whole the courts have traditionally taken a cautious approach to the development of the law in this context. The reasons for this include:

(a) the fact that public duties are often involved;

(b) Parliament has given the authorities concerned a considerable amount of statutory discretion to formulate policies and the courts are reluctant to interfere with this discretion;

(c) there is sometimes a statutory remedy available, such as a right of appeal; and

(d) the courts have developed remedies against public bodies by means of judicial review.

Judicial review is available to challenge the legality of decisions made by public bodies in purported exercise of their statutory powers. It is governed by s. 31 of the Supreme Court Act 1981 and RSC Order 53, and its availability may influence the court's decision on the liability of public bodies in negligence.

   The issue in the law of tort is whether public bodies should be governed by the same criteria as other defendants in terms of liability in the tort of negligence. In *Dorset Yacht* and in *Anns* it was said that to find a public body liable for the negligent exercise of its statutory powers two factors had to be established, in addition to the usual requirements for the tort of negligence:

(a) an *ultra vires* (this means 'beyond the powers of') exercise of the power in question; and

(b) the existence of a decision taken at the 'operational' rather than the 'policy-making' level.

One fertile ground for attacking a decision of a public body as *ultra vires* is 'Wednesbury unreasonableness' or 'irrationality': see *Associated Provincial Picture Houses Ltd* v *Wednesbury Corporation* [1948] 1 KB 223; and *Council of Civil Service Unions* v *Minister for the Civil Service* [1985] AC 374.

   You will find it instructive to read the extract from the speech of Lord Diplock in *Dorset Yacht* (*Cases and Materials* (1.1.1)), Lord Keith in *Rowling* v *Takaro Properties* [1988] AC 473 (PC), Lord Hoffmann in *Stovin* v *Wise* [1996] 3 All ER 801, Lord Browne-Wilkinson in *X* v *Bedfordshire County Council* [1995] 3 ALL ER 353 (HL) and Lord Slynn in *Barrett* v *Enfield LBC* [1999] 3 WLR 79 (all *Cases and Materials* (1.2)).

? **QUESTION** 1.5

Consider the difference between 'operational' and 'policy-making' decisions. Is it (a) understandable; (b) useful?

A decision arrived at by a public body within the terms of its statutory discretion is, according to this approach, a decision taken at the policy-making level. A decision taken in the context of implementing a policy is made at the operational level. In broad terms, a policy decision will involve the allocation of resources (which may be scarce in some instances). No doubt in most cases 'allocation of resources' will mean 'spending money'.

Haydon v *Kent County Council* [1978] QB 343 (CA), is a good example. Could the claimant succeed against the defendants for the consequences of their failure to grit footpaths in icy weather, the claimant having slipped and suffered personal injury? In essence, a public spending decision was involved: the council had decided to give priority to gritting the highways in preference to treating footpaths. The council's decision was regarded as coming within the ambit of the council's statutory, discretionary, policy-making powers, so was not amenable to an action in tort. This matter would, the court said, have to be pursued by means of judicial review. (If the council had decided to spend money on gritting footpaths, it would have been an operational error to have performed the task negligently.)

This distinction between decisions taken at the policy and operational levels, is given too much weight by some authorities. In *Rowling* v *Takaro Properties* [1988] AC 175 (PC), Lord Keith warned against over-reliance on the distinction. He advocated an essentially pragmatic approach in cases involving negligence by public authorities. His Lordship took a similar approach in *Murphy* v *Brentwood District Council* [1990] 2 All ER 908 (HL).

In *Lonrho plc* v *Tebbitt and Another* [1992] 4 All ER 280, it was held that a negligent decision given by a minister of the Crown which is categorized as an operational rather than a policy decision may give rise to a private law duty of care. The question of whether a duty of care in fact exists will depend on the facts determined at the trial.

The House of Lords in *X* v *Bedfordshire CC*, also accepted as legitimate an argument based on the distinction between 'policy' and 'operational' decisions.

Street (11th edn) suggests that a distinction can be made between 'decision-making' and 'implementation' cases. The former involve the actual use of the statutory discretion; the latter are concerned with the manner in which the discretion is performed.

In *Cocks* v *Thanet District Council* [1983] 2 AC 286 (HL) a further distinction was drawn. It was claimed that a local housing authority was in breach of its duty to provide accommodation to the claimant under the terms of the Housing (Homeless Persons) Act 1977 (see now Housing Act 1996). The court said there now existed 'a dichotomy between a housing authority's public and private law functions'. The question of whether the claimant satisfied the statutory conditions for eligibility was a public law issue and subject to challenge via judicial review. The authority's obligation to provide accommodation once the conditions were satisfied was, on the other hand, a matter of private law and thus susceptible to challenge via an action in tort.

1.5.1 **The police**

In *Calveley* v *Chief Constable of Merseyside* [1988] 3 All ER 385 (CA), Lord Donaldson MR said that the relationship between an investigating officer and a police officer under investigation, the subject matter in *Calveley*, is not dissimilar to the relationship between an adjudication officer and a claimant. In the performance of their duties, both the investigating officer and the adjudication officer derive their authority from, and are controlled by, statute. Both are performing non-judicial duties, but duties calling for judgment and due regard for rights.

In both cases there are statutory routes of appeal backed up by the public law supervisory function of the High Court (judicial review).

In *Hill* v *Chief Constable of West Yorkshire* [1989] AC 53 (HL), it was found that the police did not owe a duty of care in relation to the conduct of an investigation into the murders by the 'Yorkshire Ripper' (Peter Sutcliffe). The claimant was the mother of the last victim who, it was alleged, would not have died at the hands of Sutcliffe had the police exercised an appropriate degree of care. The court said that foreseeability of harm was not of itself sufficient to form the basis of a duty of care. As Lord Keith said:

> It has been said almost too frequently to require repetition that foreseeability of likely harm is not in itself a sufficient test of liability in negligence. Some further ingredient is invariably needed to establish the requisite proximity of relationship between the plaintiff and defendant, and all the circumstances of the case must be carefully considered and analysed in order to ascertain whether such an ingredient is present. The nature of the ingredient will be found to vary in a number of different categories of decided cases.

It was found in *Alexandrou* v *Oxford* [1993] 4 All ER 328 (CA), that the police were not liable for negligence to individual members of the public who suffered loss through the activities of criminals. In order to create a duty of care in such circumstances there must exist some 'special relationship' between the police and a member of the public. Thus, when an occupier of premises installed a burglar alarm system which was connected to a police station, that did not of itself create a 'special relationship' between him and the police. The claimant's loss in this case had not been caused directly by any act or omission on the part of the police; it had been caused by burglars. According to Glidewell LJ it was not sufficient for a claimant, seeking to establish that a defendant owed him a duty of care to see that he did not suffer loss through the activities of another person, to show only that the loss was foreseeable; it must also be shown that he had a special relationship with the defendant. In some cases, for instance, the police might owe a contractual duty to an occupier in such circumstances. In the present case, however, the communication with the police was by a 999 call and any duty owed was to the public at large and was not redressable in negligence.

In *Osman and Another* v *Ferguson and Another* [1993] 4 All ER 344 (CA), however, there *was* close proximity between the claimant and the police, creating a 'special relationship' between all parties, yet the court decided that public policy dictated that no duty of care in negligence to individuals sprang from that relationship. The court applied *Hill*.

However, in *van Colle* v *Chief Constable of Hertfordshire* [2006] EWHC 360 (QB) a successful claim was made in respect of the death of a witness at the hands of the defendant in the case, where the police officer in the case was aware of the serious threat posed to the witness, and could and should have taken protective measures. The claim was brought specifically under s. 7 of the Human Rights Act, relying on a failure to protect the right of the witness to life under Art. 2 of the ECHR, and his right to private life under Art 8. Cox J applied *Osman* v *United Kingdom* [2000] 29 EHRR 245, in which the European Court of Human Rights had found that the public policy argument in *Osman* v *Ferguson* was inconsistent with the positive obligation of the police to protect life where 'the authorities knew or ought to have known at the time of the existence of a real and immediate risk to the life of an identified individual or individuals from the criminal acts of a third party and . . . failed to take measures within the scope of their powers which, judged reasonably, might have been expected to avoid that risk.' The defendant's argument that *Hill* should be applied was rejected.

In *Ancell and Another* v *McDermott and Others* [1993] 4 All ER 355 (CA), it was alleged that as a result of the alleged negligence of other parties diesel fuel was present on the highway, and the police were aware of this fact. The first and second claimants were passengers in a car driven by the first claimant's wife; the car skidded on the diesel fuel and collided with another vehicle. The two claimants were injured and the first claimant's wife was killed in the accident.

It was held that the police were under no general duty of care to protect or warn road users in respect of hazards discovered by the police in the course of carrying out their duties on the highway, because it would be against public policy to impose a duty in the absence of exceptional circumstances creating a special relationship between the police and the claimants where the danger had been created by other persons for whom the police were not responsible.

The Court of Appeal in *Swinney* v *Chief Constable of the Northumbria Police* [1996] 3 All ER 449, distinguished *Hill* on grounds of proximity. In *Swinney* the claimant supplied certain information to the police in strict confidence. This information concerned the identity of a well-known violent criminal suspected of killing a police officer in a 'hit and run' driving incident. There was a clear risk of violence against the claimant should her identity become known to the suspect or his associates. Despite all this, the police recorded the claimant's details in documents which they left in an unattended police car, from which the papers were stolen. As a consequence the claimant was subjected to a sustained campaign of threats of violence, from the suspect and his associates, and she was so terrified that she suffered psychiatric damage and had to give up her business.

In preliminary proceedings the court refused to strike out the claimant's action in negligence against the police: it was held that there was a case to answer at full trial because the circumstances created a sufficient degree of proximity between the parties. The claimant's daughter in *Hill*, it was said, had not been at special risk because she was one of many women at risk in the area, whereas the claimant in the present case was in singular danger should the confidential information she had supplied 'fall into the wrong hands'. In short, the police had taken on special responsibility for the claimant's safety. In terms of public policy, a duty of care imposed on the police in this case would, in effect, secure confidential information and encourage other informants to help the police.

However, in *Cowan* v *Chief Constable for the Avon and Somerset Constabulary* [2002] HLR 44 (CA), the general reasoning in *Hill* was followed. The police were present at the illegal eviction of the claimant by his landlord, though they did not know that the landlord was acting illegally at the time (he was later found guilty of committing an offence under the Protection from Eviction Act 1977). The claimant argued that the police owed him a duty of care to prevent the eviction, but his claim was rejected because the police did not have any general duty to individual members of the public when performing their duties and the mere presence of the police at a particular scene did not establish legal proximity with members of the public who could have crimes committed against them. The police had often to act quickly when called upon and it would be against public policy to burden them with the obligation of minutely assessing the legal situation before responding.

In *Waters* v *Commissioner of Police of the Metropolis* [2000] 4 All ER 934 (HL), it was held that a statement of claim by a policewoman alleging that the defendant had been negligent in failing to prevent her victimization by fellow officers raised an arguable case which should not have been struck out. Lord Slynn, delivering the decision of the House of Lords, said: 'At the heart of her claim lay the belief that the other officers had reviled her and failed to take care of her because she had broken the team rules by complaining of sexual acts by a fellow officer.'

It was clear, or at least arguable, he continued, that duties analogous to those owed to an employee were owed to officers in the police service; s. 88(1) of the Police Act 1996 should be borne in mind. This results from the fact that police officers are not technically employees, so the usual employment rules do not directly apply. The complaints procedure under the Police (Discipline) Regulations (SI 1985/518) might or might not in particular cases constitute a sufficient remedy but its existence did not of itself rule out the possibility of a claim in negligence. The main question was whether it was plain and obvious that no duty of care could be owed to the claimant by the defendant on the facts alleged or that such facts could not amount to a breach of that duty.

If an employer knew, or could foresee, that acts being done or that might be done by employees might cause physical or mental harm to a fellow employee and he did nothing to prevent them when it was in his power to do so, it was arguable that he might be in breach of duty to that employee. If the sort of sexual assault alleged by the claimant was alleged by a police officer, whether it had happened or not, and the officer persisted in making complaints about it, it was arguable that it could be foreseen that some retaliatory steps might be taken against her and that she might suffer harm as a result.

On the authorities, it could not be said that it was plain and obvious that no duty of care could exist, that the injury to the claimant had not been foreseeable and that the acts alleged could not have been the cause of the damage. That left the question on which the Court of Appeal had decided against her: were there reasons of public policy why such a claim should not be entertained by the court?

His Lordship said that it had been accepted by the courts that the police might not be sued for negligence for their activities in the investigation and suppression of crime (see *Elguzouli-Daf* v *Commissioner of Police of the Metropolis* [1995] 1 All ER 833), and the Court of Appeal in the present case had taken the view that the decisions of the House of Lords in *Hill* v *Chief Constable of West Yorkshire* [1989] AC 53 and *Calveley* v *Chief Constable of Merseyside Police* precluded a duty of care for policy reasons. He concluded:

> Neither of those cases was conclusive against the plaintiff. The failure to investigate the assault on her would not alone constitute a viable cause of action, but her complaints went much wider and she was not in any event suing as a member of the public.
>
> Accordingly, her main claim for breach of personal duty should not be struck out. Although her other claims might be more difficult to establish, they also should not be struck out.

This case illustrates the operation of the employer's special duty of care (5.6) in connection with the provision of competent staff. Today the claim might well be brought in harassment; see 11.7.3.

The Privy Council, in *A-G of British Virgin Islands* v *Hartwell* [2004] 1 WLR 1273, held that a police authority owed the public at large a duty of care to see that any officer entrusted with a gun was a suitable person to be entrusted with such a dangerous weapon, in case by any misuse of the gun the officer inflicted personal injury, whether accidentally or intentionally, on other persons.

In *Brookes* v *Commissioner of Police for the Metropolis* (2005), *The Times*, 26 April, the claimant reported to the police a racial attack on himself and a friend, who sustained fatal injuries. The Court of Appeal had held that it was reasonably foreseeable that inappropriate treatment of the complaint by the police would aggravate the claimant's post-traumatic stress disorder, therefore the police could be liable in negligence.

The House of Lords, however, unanimously agreed that the police owed no such duty and the claim in negligence should be struck out. Lord Steyn referred to the 'framework' of the principles stated by Lord Bridge in *Caparo* ('fair, just, and reasonable'): the issues involved in the present case had to be resolved within this framework. He also referred to *Hill* and pointed out that since that case there had been decisions affecting its reasoning in part. Following *Z* (1.5.3), he said, it would be best to regard *Hill* in terms of the 'absence of a duty of care' rather than 'blanket immunity'. His Lordship went on to say that with 'hindsight' not every observation in *Hill* could now be supported; today a more sceptical approach to the carrying out of all public functions was necessary. He said that it was desirable that police officers should treat victims and witnesses properly and with respect, but the 'core principle' of *Hill* had remained 'unchallenged in domestic and European jurisprudence for many years' and to convert ethical values into general legal duties of care on the police towards victims and witnesses would be going 'too far'. The prime function of the police was the preservation of the Queen's peace. A retreat from the principle of *Hill* would have detrimental effects for law enforcement. The legal duties proposed by the claimant would 'tend to inhibit a robust approach in assessing a person as a possible suspect, witness or victim and lead to an unduly defensive approach in combating crime'. Where other, specific, torts were inapplicable against the police an aggrieved citizen might have to be content under 'the constantly improved' police complaints procedure. His Lordship did point out, however, that the liability of the police was 'not set in stone', that the present case concerned a striking-out application, and that each claim of negligence against the police would have to be considered and determined as it occurred.

In *Elguzouli-Daf* v *Commissioner of the Metropolis and Another; McBrearty* v *Ministry of Defence and Others* [1995] 1 All ER 833 (CA), it was held that the Crown Prosecution Service did not owe a duty of care in negligence to individuals it prosecuted unless its conduct indicated that it had assumed responsibility for a competent prosecution in the case of a particular defendant.

? QUESTION 1.6

Please consider briefly other possible reasons for not imposing a duty of care on the police to a member of the public or a police officer under investigation.

Lord Donaldson in *Calveley* identified another reason, that is, the public interest in the free and fearless investigation of such complaints. He agreed with Lord Keith's observation in *Hill* that while the existence of such a duty in relation to some activities might be in the public interest because it might lead to higher standards of care, this could not be said of police activities. It was also Lord Donaldson's opinion that if the investigating officer were to owe a duty of care to a police officer under investigation, it might be argued that he should owe a similar duty to the person who had complained about the officer, and whose complaint had led to the investigation in the first place. If such a person was convicted in a criminal court he might appeal against conviction and sue in negligence the investigating police officers should the appeal fail.

The decision of the Court of Appeal in *Calveley* was upheld on appeal ([1989] AC 1228).

🚶 EXERCISE 1.5

Please read the extracts from *Rowling, X* v *Bedfordshire CC* [1995] 3 All ER 353 and *Stovin* v *Wise* [1996] 3 All ER 801 in *Cases and Materials* (1.2).

In one sentence identify the common factor in all three cases.

The common factor is that the claims for damages in negligence were all made against public bodies, in relation to the exercise of powers rather than duties, and where a significant element of the complaint was that policy making had been inefficiently undertaken. (*Stovin* v *Wise* also places some emphasis on the notion of 'particular and general reliance'.)

1.5.2 Other public bodies

In *X* (above), it was found unanimously that a breach of statutory duty did not of itself create a cause of action in private law (tort). Such a cause of action might well arise where the traditional conditions for the common law action for breach of statutory duty were met (see 7.3) for example, where there was an allegation of abuse against someone appointed by the local authority to care for a child. There might also be the possibility of *vicarious* liability on the part of an authority in an appropriate case.

If an allegation was made of a careless exercise of a statutory duty, the claimant would have to show that a duty of care in negligence arose in *those* circumstances. An exercise by a public authority of its statutory discretion at the policy-making level was not actionable at common law. Their Lordships said that it was neither just nor reasonable to 'superimpose' a common-law duty of care on a local authority in relation to its performance of statutory duties to protect children, otherwise the system set up to protect children at risk would be upset.

Professionals retained by local authorities to advise them did not owe any duty of care to the children involved; nor was any such duty owed to their parents.

Stovin v *Wise* [1996] 3 All ER 801

S was injured when W turned right, across his path, at a road junction where visibility was restricted by a bank of land. Accidents had occurred at the junction in the past, but not often enough to warrant giving the site the title of an accident 'blackspot'.

Nevertheless, the council got in touch with the owner with a view to removing the bank, and eventually asked for permission to enter on to the land to do the necessary work. Neither party took the matter any further and the bank remained in place. The accident occurred nearly a year later. S sued W in the tort of negligence, and W (or rather her insurance company) joined the council as third party, claiming negligence and breach of statutory duty in failing to take reasonable steps to remedy a known road hazard. Both the court at first instance and the Court of Appeal found that the council owed a duty of care in negligence to road users, superimposed on its statutory obligations, and assessed its share of blame for the accident at 30%.

The council did not dispute its negligence (via its surveyor) but claimed that it did not owe a duty to take care on the facts in the first place. In the House of Lords, a majority found in favour of the council.

It was found that since the council had only a statutory power to act, and was not under a duty to act, it was to be presumed that the legislature had not intended to give individuals the right to sue in the tort of negligence, or for breach of statutory duty, in the circumstances of this case. Liability arises only where there is evidence available of administrative 'irrationality' (*Wednesbury* 'unreasonableness'), in other words where a failure to exercise the statutory power was *ultra vires*, **and** there are exceptional reasons for imposing liability in tort for the omission to act. According to Lord Hoffmann, exceptional reasons would only exist where there was general reliance on the part of the public that the power would be used.

To some extent *Stovin* v *Wise* follows the traditional line of reasoning that liability for omissions (failure to act)—particularly where the defendant is a public body exercising statutory powers—should be imposed only in limited circumstances. In *East Suffolk Rivers Catchment Board* v *Kent* [1941] AC 74 (HL), the Board was somewhat slow in repairing a breach in river banks caused by natural flooding—the work took 178 days when it should have taken 14 days. The Board had a statutory power, not a duty, to carry out such works: the claimant, whose land had been flooded, sued in negligence on the basis that the defendant Board, having voluntarily taken on the work, was under an obligation to carry it out with due diligence. It was held that the Board was not liable because it owed no duty to act in the first place, and its failure to act speedily had not added to the damage which would have been suffered by the claimant in any event even if the Board had decided not to act.

In *Capital and Counties plc* v *Hampshire County Council and others* [1997] 2 All ER 565 (CA), the Court of Appeal heard several appeals together because they all raised a common issue of public and legal importance, that is, the question of whether a fire brigade could be liable in the tort of negligence for a fire the brigade had attended in response to an emergency call. In other words, the question for the court to consider was whether a fire brigade owed a duty of care to the owners/occupiers of buildings damaged or destroyed by fire. It was held that a fire brigade is not under a common-law duty to answer a call for help and is not under any duty to take care to do so. If firefighters fail to turn up or fail to turn up in time because they have carelessly misunderstood the message, got lost on the way, or run into a tree (for example), they are not liable.

The court then considered the question of whether a duty of care is owed by a fire brigade to the owner/occupier after arriving at the scene of the fire. It was held that the fire brigade does not enter into a sufficiently proximate relationship with the owner or occupier of premises merely by attending at the site and fighting the fire, even though the senior officer actually assumes control of the operation.

With regard to a fire brigade's statutory duties under the Fire Services Act 1947, although a breach of statutory duty does not, in ordinary cases, give rise to any private law cause of action, a private law cause of action will arise if it can be shown, as a matter of construction of the statute, that the statutory duty was imposed for the protection of a limited class of the public and that Parliament intended to confer on members of that class a private right of action for breach of duty. On the facts no action for breach of duty lay under s. 13, Fire Services Act 1947. The duties laid down in ss 1 and 13 are in the nature of statutory provisions establishing a regulatory system or scheme of social welfare for the benefit of the public at large, conferring no right of private action. Accordingly, the West Yorkshire and the London Fire Brigade appeals, by the claimant owners/occupiers against the first instance decisions in favour of the fire authorities, were dismissed.

In the *Hampshire* case, following *Hill* v *Chief Constable of West Yorkshire*, the court found that there was no question that a fire officer, like anyone else, could be liable in tort to a person who is injured as a direct result of his actions or omissions. In finding the senior fire officer negligent in turning off water sprinklers (the building had its own fire prevention/containment system), the judge at first instance had found that no reasonably well-informed and competent fireman could have made such a decision. Although the defendant's fire expert said there were occasions when he had known sprinklers to be turned off, the judge gave unassailable reasons for not accepting the reasons which were given for turning them off in the instant case. The decision to turn off the sprinkler system had increased the risk of fire spreading, and the defendant fire authority could not show that the building would have been destroyed in any case, that is, without the fire officer's negligent action. Accordingly the appeal, by the fire authority, was dismissed.

Three further points may be made:

- the issues raised in relation to the action for breach of statutory duty are pertinent to the discussion in 7.4;

- the Court of Appeal considered the decision in *Stovin* v *Wise*, and applied the majority opinion in that case;

- this is a case in which a rescuer (albeit a professional rescuer) was found liable for making the situation worse.

The fire authorities were involved in another case, *Daly* v *Surrey County Council* (1997), *The Times*, 25 October. The claimant alleged that a fireman caused the death of her husband, a building-site foreman, by preventing colleagues of the deceased from trying to dig him free from a collapsed trench.

It was claimed that had the fire officer not prevented the site workers from continuing with their efforts to free Mr Daly, they would have reached him more quickly and his life would have been saved. The fire brigade, on the other hand, argued that (a) it owed no duty of care to the deceased, (b) there was no negligence on the facts, and (c) Mr Daly would probably have died anyway even if the construction workers' attempts had been allowed to continue.

May J found that there had been no breach of duty. His Lordship added, however, that Mr Daly had acted foolishly and that if the fire brigade had been negligent, any award of damages would have been substantially reduced because of the deceased's contributory negligence.

In *OLL Ltd* v *Secretary of State for Transport* [1997] 3 All ER 897, following *Capital and Counties plc* v *Hampshire County Council*, it was found that the coastguard service owes no private law duty to respond to an emergency call; nor is it liable if its response to such a call is negligent, although it might be different if it commits a positive act which directly causes greater injury than would have occurred if it had not intervened at all. The service is also not liable in negligence if it is guilty of issuing misdirection to other rescue organizations.

In *Kent* v *Griffiths* [2000] 2 All ER 474 (CA), it was held that an ambulance service owed a duty of care to a member of the public, on whose behalf an emergency telephone call had been made. The service could be liable in negligence where an ambulance did not arrive within a reasonable time in response to the call, unless there was a good reason for the delay.

? **QUESTION** 1.7

Why should the ambulance service be liable for delay where the fire service and police will not be?

Lord Woolf, MR, said that the defendant was providing a service under its duty laid down in National Health Service Act 1977, and ambulance staff should be treated no differently from doctors and nurses who provided health services under that Act, and who could be liable in the tort of negligence. His Lordship said that arguments against liability based on public policy were 'much weaker' in the case of the ambulance service than they were in the case of the police or the fire service.

The police, when protecting a particular victim of crime, were performing their general role of maintaining public order and reducing crime. The fire service would normally not only be concerned with protecting a particular property; it would also be working to prevent the further spread of fire, that is, protecting the public generally.

There could be situations where a conflict of interests between a particular individual and the public at large would arise but in this case the only member of the public who could have been adversely affected was the claimant: the ambulance had been called solely for her. In this case there was no question of an ambulance not being available or of a conflict of priorities. Having decided to provide an ambulance, the defendant was expected to offer a satisfactory explanation of its failure to attend within a reasonable time. On the facts, it took the ambulance 34 minutes to travel 6.4 miles; it should normally have arrived at least 14 minutes earlier, and the defendant was unable to give the court any good reason for this 'culpable' delay.

Lord Woolf referred to *Osman* v *UK* and said that courts in future might proceed much more on a case-by-case basis, where the defendant was a public body, paying less heed to the so-called public service 'immunity' which had developed as a result of the decisions in cases such as *Hill* and *X* (above).

In *Gorringe* v *Calderdale Metropolitan Borough Council* [2004] 1 WLR 1057, the House of Lords held, unanimously, that the duty imposed on the defendant by s. 41 (1) of the Highways Act 1980, to 'maintain the highway' did not include the provision of road signs or road markings containing information or warnings. The duty was limited to keeping the highway in a good state of repair. This decision is examined here because it was also held that there was no duty to provide signs or road marking in common law negligence. On this issue the claimant had argued that ss 539(2) and (3)(b) of the Road Traffic Act 1988 imposed an obligation on highway authorities to promote road safety and take appropriate steps, including the giving of information and advice, to prevent accidents and a duty was created at common law to exercise reasonable care in providing warning signs and road marking pointing to possible dangers, etc. As Lord Hoffmann put it, it was not suggested that such public duties 'expressed in the widest and most general terms' were enforceable directly by a private individual in an action for breach of statutory duty. His Lordship pointed to his own speech in *Stovin* v *Wise* in which he had said that if a statutory duty did not give rise to a private right to sue for breach it would be unusual if a right to sue in common law negligence arose in such circumstances. He found it difficult to imagine a case in which a common law duty could be founded simply on the failure, however irrational, to provide some benefit that a public authority had a power, or public law duty to provide. The public interest in local authorities taking steps to promote road safety did not require a private law duty to a careless driver (the claimant probably fell into this category since she crashed into a bus hidden from her view behind a sharp crest in the road until just before she reached the top when she had to slam on her brakes, skidding into the bus at 50 mph) or any other road user. At this point his Lordship referred to another of his speeches, in *Tomlinson* v *Congleton Borough Council*. Nor did it follow that authorities should be liable to compensate third parties whom careless drivers had injured. Drivers had to take responsibility for the damage they caused and compulsory third-party insurance was intended to ensure that they would be able to do so. In the 'difficult' case of *Bird* v *Pearce* [1979] RTR 369, the Court of Appeal had held that by removing lines indicating to drivers that they were entering a major road the highway authority had created a hazard. Lord Hoffmann, with whom the other members of the House agreed, expressed 'no view about whether that case had been correctly decided', but said he would accept the principle that if a highway authority conducted itself so as to create a reasonable expectation about the state of the highway it would be under a duty to ensure that it did not thereby create a trap for the careful motorists who drove in reliance on such an expectation. The council in this case was not alleged to have done anything to give rise to a duty of care. The complaint was that it had done nothing, and s. 39 of the 1988 Act had not created a common law duty to act.

This decision was followed by the Court of Appeal in *Sandhar and Another* v *Department of Transport, Environment and the Regions* (2004), *The Times*, 15 November. The claimant's husband had been killed when he lost control of his car on a trunk road. The car had skidded on frost or ice; the road had not been salted overnight nor on the previous day. In *Goodes* v *East Sussex County Council* [2000] 1 WLR 1356, the House of Lords had held that the duty to maintain the highway under s. 541 (1) of the Highways Act 1980 did not include a duty to prevent the formation of ice or remove an accumulation of snow on the road. However, this decision had been reversed by an amendment to s. 41(1A inserted by s. 111 of the Railways and Transport Safety Act 2003), but this amendment to the law came into force too late to be of any help to the claimants. They therefore sought to establish in the alternative to a statutory duty a relevant common law duty upon highway authorities. The court held that no such duty existed: *Bird* v *Pearce*, which the claimants had relied upon, had been doubted in *Gorringe* (above) and Lord Hoffmann in *Gorringe* expressed the limits of any principle which might be exemplified by *Bird*. The Court of Appeal in the present case held that the claimants had failed to establish a common law duty of care for two principal reasons: first, the defendant could not be taken to have assumed a general responsibility to all road users to endure that all or any trunk roads would be salted in freezing conditions. May LJ said it was the 'primary duty' of all road users to take care for their own safety and that of their passengers and other road-users; second, the case did not contain the necessary element of reliance. In the absence of reliance, and positive action by the defendant whereby it was taken as having assumed responsibility to the deceased, said his Lordship, the defendant could not properly be said to have created a trap. The defendant did nothing. If the deceased was not entitled to rely on the defendant to have salted the road the fact that the road was not salted was not to be regarded as a trap. The deceased was not entitled to assume the road had been salted and he had a primary duty to look after his own safety. The fact that Parliament needed to amend the law was an indication that, without legislation, the common law did not, without special circumstances, recognize such a duty. These cases, together with *Stovin* v *Wise*, are also relevant to breach of statutory duty (7.4).

The House of Lords was asked to consider some important legal issues affecting local authorities in *Barrett* v *Enfield London BC* [1999] 3 All ER 193 (HL). The claimant had been in care between the ages of 10 and 18 and sued in the tort of negligence for psychiatric and psychological difficulties allegedly caused by incidents occurring while he was in care. The Court of Appeal had decided that where a local authority takes a decision about the future of a child in its care which would in normal circumstances be taken by a parent, the authority does not owe a duty of care to the child.

The authority could, however, be vicariously liable where the decision concerned an 'operational' matter, for example, where a social worker was negligent in relation to an assessment of what action should be taken in relation to the child.

It was held by the House of Lords, however, distinguishing *X*, that whilst the exercise of a statutory discretion was likely to be non-justiciable, unless it was so unreasonable as not to be a real exercise of discretion (*Wednesbury* 'unreasonable') or there was a policy decision necessitating balancing different public interests (see *Stovin* v *Wise*), it was possible for a duty of care to arise in negligence where the claimant's claim concerned the way in which the discretionary statutory powers were exercised. A distinction was drawn in the present context between (i) a decision of a local authority about whether or not to take a child into care: this was non-justiciable unless *ultra vires* could be shown; and (ii) a decision concerning a child in care: this could give rise to a duty of care. The decision of the Court of Appeal was reversed. Lord Slynn was of the opinion that the 'policy'/'operation' level distinction used in earlier cases to distinguish between difficult levels of decision-making by public bodies was a useful aid in the judicial process.

You may care to contrast this view to that expressed on this matter by Lord Hoffmann in *Stovin* v *Wise*. There is an extract from Lord Slynn's speech in *Cases and Materials* (1.2).

In *Palmer* v *Tees Health Authority and Hartlepool and East Durham NHS Trust* [1999] Lloyd's Rep Med 351, the Court of Appeal struck out a claim for damages in negligence brought against hospital authorities by the mother of a child murdered by a psychopath who had been released from hospital. The psychopath was under the hospital's care from 1992 until being rehoused on the estate where the claimant lived. He abducted and murdered her daughter in 1994. It was held that since the psychopath had made no direct threat against the child or her family the hospital owed no duty of care to the child or her mother: there was a lack of legal proximity. A similar decision was reached in *Clunis* v *Camden and Islington Health Authority* [1998] 3 All ER 180 (CA). The claimant argued that a hospital was negligent in failing to provide him with appropriate treatment for his mental disorder, and sought damages for self-inflicted harm and an indemnity for damages the claimant had to pay to others because he had harmed them.

The Court struck out the claim for damages. Beldam LJ said it would not be just and reasonable to impose a common law duty of care on a health authority in relation to its statutory responsibility to provide aftercare. Nor would it be fair to hold the authority responsible for the claimant's actions. His Lordship said: 'The court ought not to allow itself to be made an instrument to enforce obligations alleged to arise out of the plaintiff's own criminal act.' This decision is also relevant to the general defence of 'illegality' (14.3.2).

In *K* v *Secretary of State for the Home Department* [2002] EWCA Civ 775, a citizen of another country with limited leave to be in the UK was held in custody under a deportation order after he committed a number of violent crimes. On his release he committed more serious crimes. The claimant, who was one of his later victims, argued that the Secretary of State was negligent in failing to deport the foreign national, but it was held that there was no private right of action in such circumstances.

In *W* v *Essex County Council* [2000] 2 All ER 237 the Ws fostered a 15-year-old youth and he allegedly abused the Ws' children. The Ws claimed that the defendant local authority and the social worker in charge of the case knew that the youth was an active sexual abuser. They claimed that they were told only that the boy could be a bully and a liar and that his father, a convicted paedophile, had abused him. They said they would not have fostered the youth had they known he had gone into care at the age of 12 after abusing his sister.

Hooper J held there was a case to go to full trial, on the basis (i) that a social worker placing a child with foster parents has a duty to provide them with such information about the child as a reasonable social worker would provide in the circumstances; (ii) a local authority is vicariously liable for the conduct of its social worker in this respect.

Their psychiatric damage was caused, said the Ws, not only by the discovery of abuse; they also felt guilty that they had, without knowing, harmed their children by bringing them into contact with an abuser.

This ruling gave the Ws' children permission to start full proceedings in negligence against the social worker and the council. His Lordship did, however, strike out the parents' claim for the post-traumatic stress disorder they developed after discovering the abuse because, like the parents in *Alcock* (see **Chapter 4**) who had not been at the football ground in that case, they were barred from claiming on the ground that they had not personally seen or heard 'a horrifying event'.

This decision was confirmed by a majority in the Court of Appeal. Stuart-Smith LJ, in his dissenting judgment, was of the opinion that the council's only duty was to do the best it could for the foster child.

In his Lordship's opinion local authorities and social workers 'might err on the side of caution', and might give too much information—'perhaps some of it based on rumour and hearsay'— to potential foster parents against the child's interest, should a duty of care in negligence be imposed. The abused children in this case could, he said, make a claim under the criminal injuries compensation scheme.

Judge LJ, delivering the majority judgment, however, said the local authority had introduced a 'potential menace' into the claimants' home. This case was different from other cases which had been struck out because here the victims were not children for whom the council had any care responsibilities. Indeed, for the benefit of the Ws' four children the council had accepted the express condition of 'no sexual abusers'.

Furthermore, if it were known that local authorities might withhold information from foster parents, they, the foster parents, 'might very well be discouraged from . . . offering to provide homes for children'. In the circumstances, the local authority had assumed responsibility for the accuracy of its positive assurance to the parents about G (the fostered boy in this case). The House of Lords upheld that decision and also allowed the parents' claim for psychiatric injury to go for trial on the basis that it was not clear that it was a case which should be dealt with on the basis of *Alcock*.

In *Phelps* v *Hillingdon London Borough Council, Anderton* v *Clwyd County Council, Gower* v *Bromley London Borough Council, Jarvis* v *Hampshire County Council* [2000] 3 WLR 776, it was held, at first instance, that an educational psychologist, employed by a local authority, owes a duty of care in negligence to a child whom he or she is assessing.

Two findings were made: (i) a psychologist who fails to diagnose dyslexia in circumstances where a competent psychologist would diagnose the condition will be negligent (*Bolam* applied); (ii) the local authority employing the psychologist is vicariously liable for that negligence (*X* v *Bedfordshire CC* followed).

Garland J said that children, and their parents, in normal circumstances have no access to educational psychological advice other than that provided by the local authority which runs both the school and educational psychological services and their reliance on this type of advice was so much the greater.

The Court of Appeal held, however, that the 'fair, just, and reasonable' (*Caparo*) test applied to employees of the local authority just as it did to the authority itself. The employees' only obligation was to their employers, not to the users of their services. Since the psychologist had not assumed a personal responsibility to the claimant, she owed no duty of care to the latter; consequently her employers, the local authority, could not be vicariously liable to the claimant. On appeal, the House of Lords rejected this argument and found in favour of the claimant.

The other cases before the House of Lords were, unlike *Phelps*, striking out cases, that is, it was only necessary for the court to decide whether there was a sufficiently arguable case to go to trial.

Anderton concerned a claimant who wanted access to her educational records so that she could try and prove that inadequate education had damaged her; *Gower* was a case in which the claimant had a progressive disease and he needed special equipment in order to communicate with other people: this was not provided and he claimed that his education had suffered, causing him psychological damage; in *Jarvis* the claimant had been correctly diagnosed with dyslexia (unlike *Phelps*) but the defendant had failed to give appropriate advice on the correct kind of school for him.

Their Lordships found in favour of all these claimants. It was held that a local education authority, through its employees, owes a duty of care in common law negligence to provide an education which is appropriate to a child's needs. The duty of care in each of these cases was owed by the teacher or educational psychologist concerned, and any liability of the education authority would be vicarious.

In *S* v *Gloucestershire County Council, L* v *Tower Hamlets* [2000] 3 All ER 346, the Court of Appeal found that striking-out applications concerning child abuse should be upheld in only the clearest of cases; in child abuse claims against local authorities there should be no blanket immunity. *X* v *Bedfordshire County Council* did not, the Court said, prevent all claims in negligence against local authorities for failing to prevent child abuse. Weak claims could, it was suggested, be dealt with by appropriate use of the *summary* judgment procedures available under the Civil Procedure Rules (that is, without a full trial of the issue) so satisfying Art. 6 of the European Convention on Human Rights.

The current Rules are more flexible than the earlier ones and allow the introduction of *evidence* at the striking-out stage.

In *A and B* v *Essex County Council* [2003] EWCA Civ 1848, the Court of Appeal held that there was in general no duty of care owed by an adoption agency or its staff in relation to deciding what information was to be given to prospective adopters. It would not be fair, just, and reasonable to impose a duty in such circumstances. There could be liability if they took a decision which no reasonable agency could take (this would require establishing 'irrationality' or *Wednesbury* 'unreasonableness') according to Hale LJ, who delivered the judgment of the Court. However, once the agency had decided, either in general or in particular, what information should be given there **was** a duty to take reasonable care to ensure that that information was both given and received. In the present case, said her Ladyship, there was a breach of **that** 'restricted' duty which had caused harm. Applying *Page* v *Smith* (4.3.7) that harm included psychiatric damage. With regard to the extent of that liability, the Court was of the opinion that Buckley J, at first instance, was correct in holding that there was a cut-off point when the adoption orders were made: by that time 'enough had happened' to enable the claimants to be able to make a decision for themselves.

Local authorities continue to face new challenges in the wake of *Barrett* v *Enfield LBC* and *Phelps* v *Hillingdon LBC*. In *Carty* v *Croydon London Borough Council* (2005), *The Times*, 2 February, the Court of Appeal held that education officers, employed to perform the statutory functions of local education authorities, were professional persons for whose negligence local authorities might be vicariously liable, just as the authorities might be liable for the acts and omissions of educational psychologists and teachers. It followed that where in the performance of those duties, an education officer entered into a relationship with, or assumed responsibilities towards a child with special educational needs, he might owe a duty of care to that child, depending on whether the matter was justiciable at all and whether it was fair, just, and reasonable to impose such a duty of care. Dyson LJ delivering the reserved judgment of the Court said the question of whether there could be a common law right to claim damages for breach of statutory duty did not admit of a blanket answer. The mere fact that an education officer had failed to make a formal reassessment of the claimant's needs under regulation 9 of the Education (Special Educational Needs) Regulations (S1 1983 No. 29) did not give rise to a private law claim for breach of statutory duty or negligence. Where, however, there was a relationship or assumption of responsibility (as set out above) a duty might arise, but would only arise in fact after consideration of the substance of the act or omission, and whether the subject-matter was justiciable, and whether it satisfied the three-stage 'test' laid down in *Caparo*. On the facts of the present case the Court was of the opinion that the judge at first instance had been right in finding that no breach of duty had occurred when the education officer failed to reassess the claimant's educational needs and to amend that statement of needs after the breakdown of the placement.

In *D* v *East Berkshire Community NHS Trust/MAK* v *Dewsbury Healthcare NHS Trust/RK* v *Oldham NHS Trust* (2003), *The Times*, 22 April, the Court of Appeal decided that a possible common law duty of care in negligence was owed by the doctors and/or social workers responsible to children who had been wrongly diagnosed as abused or mistakenly taken into care. In effect, the court lifted the long-standing immunity enjoyed by health and social work professionals. The Human Rights Act 1998 had superseded the decision in *X* v *Bedfordshire CC*. *X*, said Lord Phillips MR, had been 'significantly restricted' in its effect in any case by later cases such as *Barrett* v *Enfield Borough Council*.

X was now restricted to its 'core proposition': decisions by local authorities in the exercise of their statutory obligations whether or not to take a child into care were not reviewable by way of a claim in the tort of negligence. Where the interests of the child and the parents were potentially in conflict no duty of care in negligence would be owed to the parents (or carers, as the case might be).

Much of the argument in this case concerned the application of Arts 3, 6, and 8 of the European Convention on Human Rights. It was pointed out by Lord Phillips that s. 2(1) of the Human Rights Act 1998 required the court to 'have regard to' the jurisprudence of the Strasbourg court when dealing with a claim under the 1998 Act relating to action or inaction after October 2000 on the part of a local authority in relation to suspected child abuse.

His Lordship said factual situations could possibly arise where it was not 'fair, just, or reasonable' (*Caparo* v *Dickman*) to impose a duty of care in common law negligence, but each case must be decided on its own facts. No violation of Article 6 was involved in the application of the *Caparo* formula to individual cases. Any claim made under the 1998 Act itself would lie only against public authorities, not against the individuals employed by them.

Three sets of parents appealed to the House of Lords against the Court of Appeal's decision to strike out their claims. The House of Lords dismissed their appeals, ruling that parents who are wrongly accused of abusing their children cannot sue doctors and social workers who made the diagnoses even if they were negligent. The majority of their Lordships said that if a duty of care were owed to parents (or carers) in these circumstances it could conflict with that owed by doctors and social workers to the child and increase the risk that abuse would go undetected. Lord Brown acknowledged the 'legitimate grievances' of the parents, who were no longer suspected of abuse. But he said the price they paid in having their claims denied was a price paid 'in the interests of children generally'. All the parents claimed they suffered psychiatric illness as a result of their experiences, but this ruling allows compensation claims only by children who suffer from wrong diagnosis of abuse. Lord Bingham would have allowed the cases to go ahead to trial, arguing that the law should evolve to deal with contemporary problems. The Court of Appeal in *D* v *Bury Metropolitan Borough Council* and *H* v *Bury Metropolitan Borough Council* (2006), *The Times*, 22 January, held that a local authority which was investigating allegations of child abuse and which started care proceedings with regard to a particular child did not owe a common law duty of care to that child's parents in respect of psychological shock, upset, and resulting depression during the period of an interim care order or while investigations were continuing under the order. Furthermore, a child who had been removed from the care of his parents for a certain period and placed in a local authority's care under an interim care order could not claim damages from the authority where the removal had not caused him any identifiable harm nor any psychological harm while he was in foster care. Any damage suffered was transient and non-justiciable. (It should be noted that in the case of *H* the local authority had admitted that it owed a common law duty of care in principle to the child.)

Wall LJ, delivering the unanimous decision of the court, referred with approval to the speech of Lord Nicholls in *D* above in which his Lordship had emphasized that it was in the interests of public policy that care professionals should be free to exercise their functions without having at the back of their minds an awareness that if doubts about the injury or abuse proved unfounded they might be exposed to claims by a distressed parent.

In *Kane* v *New Forest District Council* [2001] 3 All ER 914 (CA), the claimant was hit by a vehicle which had come on to the highway from a footpath at a point where the sightlines were poor. The footpath had been constructed because the defendant council, as planning authority, had required it to be built and allowed it to open being fully aware that the sightlines were poor. The interesting question in this case was whether a planning authority could be liable in the tort of negligence for giving permission for a development which it knew, or ought to have known, would be dangerous without sightline improvements (road-markings etc.).

The council applied to have the claim struck out at first instance and succeeded, but the Court of Appeal said this was wrong: the claimant had a realistic chance of establishing his case, which was a strong one. It was said that it must not be assumed that planning authorities, even though they are exercising 'public interest' statutory functions, have a general immunity against claims in tort for negligently exercised planning decisions.

Stovin v *Wise* (*Cases and Materials* 1.2) was distinguished: the defendant council in the present case had 'created the danger' by 'requiring' the construction of the footpath (Simon Brown LJ), whilst the council in *Stovin* had only 'omitted' to reduce a pre-existing danger. The defendant, arguably, had a duty to take reasonable care to minimize the risk created by the construction of the footpath.

1.5.3 **Conclusions**

The decisions in *Osman* v *Ferguson* and *X* v *Bedfordshire CC* (and *M* v *Newham LBC*) have been subject to appeals to the European Court of Human Rights. In *Osman* v *UK* [1999] 1 FLR 193, the European Court held that the immunity of the police from compensation claims in their crime prevention and investigation roles violated the right to a fair hearing (Article 6 of the European Convention on Human Rights). The claimant was accordingly awarded £10,000 for this violation. The use of striking out applications to deny a duty of care in actions against public bodies has been questionable since the decision in this case.

In *X* v *UK* and *M* v *UK*, Registry of the European Court of Human Rights Press Release 624: 5/11/99, it was found by the European Commission of Human Rights that in both cases the claimants were denied a fair hearing (Article 6); in *X* the Council's failure to act subjected them to 'inhuman and degrading treatment' (Article 3); and in *M* there had been a violation of the guarantee of respect for family life (Article 8).

The European Court itself, in *Z* v *UK* (2002) 34 EHRR 3 (the later name for *X*), subsequently ruled that the local authority immunity relating to the delivery of statutory social services duties, as applied in *X*, amounted to a violation of the right to a fair trial under Article 6 and a violation of Article 13 (the need for an effective remedy). The applicants should have had the opportunity to argue their cases on the merits.

It is clear from this decision, however, that the European Court of Human Rights has not set its face against the adoption by English courts of legal rules rejecting actions such as the one brought in *Hill*; rather, the objection is to the adoption of a 'blanket' policy of immunity, say, for the police, which would be applied regardless of the circumstances of each case.

The Human Rights Act 1998 came into force on 2 October 2000. From this date English judges have had to take account of earlier decisions from the European Court of Human Rights. The existence of a duty to take care in negligence will in future depend in some circumstances on issues concerning human rights. The right to a fair trial, for example, has already influenced decisions on the immunity of public bodies. We have observed the decision in *Osman* v *UK*, and looking further ahead it is likely that the authority of *X* v *Bedfordshire C.C* will be weakened by this factor. Indeed, the decision in *Hall* v *Simons*, which has put paid to advocates' immunity (at least in part), must also have been affected to some extent by this consideration (see 1.6.5).

Many decisions affecting public bodies may have to be reassessed in the light of human rights' legislation. The courts will need to avoid the blanket immunity approach in favour of regarding a claimant as being entitled to having the merits of his or her case tried, unless there is a much stronger argument in favour of the defendant not owing a duty of care. The courts may have to develop a considerably more coherent and principled body of law governing the liability of public authorities; even decisions such as *Murphy* v *Brentwood DC* (discussed at 6.3.2) may have to be revisited, though that decision appears to rest primarily on arguments concerning 'pure' economic loss.

In *Barrett* v *Enfield LBC* and *Phelps* v *Hillingdon LBC* the courts have indicated more willingness to reject striking-out applications by public bodies claiming immunity from suit, quoting *Osman* in support of such an approach. It is possible to detect, in more recent cases, a movement away from the general approach to this matter adopted in *X* v *Bedfordshire CC*, that is, only in the clearest of cases will the striking-out application be used to decide the question whether it is fair, just, and reasonable to impose a duty of care on the defendant.

The *Osman* case also requires balancing the policy considerations behind an immunity against the requirements of an individual case in substantive law (that is at the actual trial of an issue) as well as at the procedural level.

It is the contention of some commentators that the effect of these recent decisions involving local authorities, particularly *Phelps*, is to diminish the role of the 'duty' control mechanism in limiting liability in such cases because the move away from any sort of blanket immunity for the authorities, in favour of looking at each case on its merits, militates against the use of this device. See, for example, Giliker and Beckwith, 'Tort' (2004). This may lead to an increased recourse to the other control 'devices', 'breach of duty', and 'causation'. If that is true of local authority cases it may also be true for cases involving public authorities generally.

1.6 Specific issues in relation to duty

1.6.1 Omissions

The common law traditionally distinguishes between liability for misfeasance and non-feasance (or positive act(s) and omissions to act): in general terms, there is a marked reluctance to impose liability for omissions. The following extract from the speech of Lord Goff in *Smith* v *Littlewoods Organization* [1987] 1 All ER 710 (at p. 729) makes this position clear:

> Why does the law not recognize a general duty of care to prevent others from suffering loss or damage caused by the deliberate wrongdoing of third parties? The fundamental reason is that the common law does not impose liability for what are called pure omissions. If authority is needed for this proposition, it is to be found in the speech of Lord Diplock in *Home Office* v *Dorset Yacht Co. Ltd* where he said:
>
> > The very parable of the Good Samaritan (Luke 10:30) which was evoked by Lord Atkin in *Donoghue* v *Stevenson* illustrates, in the conduct of the priest and of the Levite who passed by on the other side, an omission which was likely to have as its reasonable and probable consequence damage to the health of the victim of the thieves, but for which the priest and Levite would have incurred no civil liability in English law.

See also Lord Hoffmann in *Stovin* v *Wise* [1996] 3 All ER 801 in *Cases and Materials* (1.2). This distinction may, however, be of less importance in the future as a result of the Human Rights Act 1998.

> One might suppose that the requisite respect [i.e. the obligation to respect Convention rights] involved only refraining from invading the rights in question, but in fact the distinction between invasion and omission is occluded in that the obligation clearly extends in certain circumstances to the provision of positive protection against harm, such as child abuse or other criminal conduct (Weir, p. 15).

His Lordship is referring to the primary obligation imposed by the Act on public bodies to respect Convention rights. 'Convention arguments' can be used in other proceedings; indirectly, in this way, Convention rights may influence and shape the law of tort even where the defendant is some private person or body. It is a well-established principle of common law that there is no duty to be a 'Good Samaritan'. An adult who stands by and does nothing to help a drowning child commits no tort as long as the child is a stranger to her . . . pure omissions are not actionable at common law. Could the child's parents argue that the absence of any obligation to rescue the child violated his right of life (under Article 2)? Will long-established principles of common law have to be revisited and revised? (*Street on Torts*, p. 6).

1.6.2 'Pure' economic loss

See **Chapter 3**.

1.6.3 'Nervous shock'

See **Chapter 4**.

1.6.4 **The unborn child**

The Congenital Disabilities (Civil Liability) Act 1976 confers a limited right of action upon a child born disabled as a result of pre-birth injury, but this is restricted to claimants born after 22 July 1976, which is the date of the Act's commencement. A corresponding common law duty of care caters for claimants born before that date: *Burton* v *Islington Health Authority* [1992] 3 All ER 833 (CA). You will find an extract from the 1976 Act in *Cases and Materials* (1.3.1).

In *McKay* v *Essex Area Health Authority* [1982] 2 WLR 890, the Court of Appeal rejected, on grounds of public policy, a claim for 'wrongful birth' ('or life') by the claimant, who had been born disabled, allegedly as a result of the failure of a doctor to diagnose rubella in the claimant's mother when she was pregnant with the claimant. It was claimed that had the doctor not been negligent, the mother would have aborted the claimant, who would not then have been born in a handicapped condition. See, now, the 1976 Act (above). There is nothing to prevent parents suing doctors for failing to inform them that their children will be born handicapped, on the basis that otherwise an abortion would have been considered and carried out: *Rance* v *Mid-Downs Health Authority* [1991] 1 All ER 801.

1.6.5 **Advocacy**

In *Rondel* v *Worsley* [1969] AC 191, and *Saif Ali* v *Mitchell* [1980] AC 198, it was held that advocates (barristers and, possibly, solicitor-advocates) did not owe a duty of care to their clients for the way in which they conducted court proceedings and in respect of any pre-trial work tantamount to a preliminary decision affecting the presentation in court. This immunity was extended to solicitor-advocates by the Courts and Legal Services Act 1990, s. 62.

Barristers' immunity was justified on a number of grounds, for example:

(a) liability in negligence would unduly interfere with the advocate's duty to the court to act in the interests of justice (there must be no undue pressure on the advocate to 'bend the rules' in favour of his client);

(b) under the 'cab-rank' rule barristers, though not solicitor-advocates, must accept any client (assuming expertise on the advocate's part and the payment of a fee by the client);

(c) since a client would have to show that the case would have had a different outcome had the advocate not been negligent, there would, in effect, have to be a re-hearing of the case and this could bring the judicial process into disrepute—a disgruntled client should seek redress only via the system of appeal.

The House of Lords has now, however, reviewed the issue of advocates' immunity in *Hall* v *Simons* [2000] 3 WLR 543, although in strict terms it was not necessary to do so because the cases themselves (several, including *Hall*, were heard together) involved claims of negligence against solicitors concerning the settlement of claims.

It was the unanimous view that the immunity could not be justified in relation to civil cases. The divided loyalty, to clients **and** courts, and the threat of vexatious litigation arguments were now said to be outweighed by a judge's increased powers under the 'Woolf reforms' to manage civil cases much more efficiently. The other arguments were also dismissed as having no real weight in the debate about immunity.

In relation to criminal litigation, however, the House was divided. Four of the seven judges thought that the immunity should also be abolished in criminal cases. Three were in favour of retaining the immunity for criminal proceedings as it was in the public interest that the immunity should continue in criminal cases because of the particular emphasis on the adversarial process in that type of case. This left the advocate open to vexatious claims. 'Divided loyalty' arguments carried more weight in the context of criminal proceedings.

The duty is of course only one to take reasonable care in the circumstances, and the fact that the advice is given under pressure of time may affect the standards to be expected. In *Moy v Pettman Smith (Solicitors)* (2005), *The Times*, 4 February, the House of Lords found that advice by an advocate regarding acceptance or rejection of the offer of a settlement of an action, especially where it had to be given 'at the door of the Court', could not be reasoned with 'comprehensive precision' (Lord Carswell) and the advocate could not be expected to detail all the factors that might affect a decision. See also 1.7.1.3.

It should also be noted that advocates receive some protection from the principle of 'abuse of process', whereby the court may strike out an unmeritorious claim on the basis that to allow it to continue would be an abuse of the process of law. This principle is relatively readily applied to disgruntled litigants seeking to reopen the case by a collateral attack on the quality of representation.

In *Hunter v Chief Constable of the West Midlands Police* [1982] AC 529, it was found by the House of Lords that a claim brought against an advocate for the negligent conduct of a criminal case in which the client had pleaded guilty or been convicted, but had failed on appeal, would usually be struck out as an abuse of process. Public policy would not prevent a successful appellant from suing his advocate for negligence. A claim in a civil case will be struck out only where to allow it to proceed would either lead to manifest unfairness to the defendant (the advocate) or bring the administration of justice into disrepute. These cases come under the heading of 'collateral challenge' because they are attempts to establish a re-trial of issues which have been decided against the claimant.

1.6.5.1 Judges and witnesses

In English law, immunity 'from suit' (immunity from litigation) extends to these participants in the trial process. For example, a witness who commits perjury cannot be sued by the accused, even where the witness has set out to harm him or her.

1.7 Breach of duty

1.7.1 General observations

'Breach' is the essence of negligence; it describes the defendant's behaviour which actually injures the claimant and is often treated in practice as synonymous with 'negligence'. **This** is what most people would regard as 'negligence'. The question here is whether the defendant has measured up to the **standard of behaviour** in the particular circumstances of the case. The defendant's behaviour at the relevant time must conform in general to the standard of the hypothetical 'reasonable man'. The question posed by the law is 'What would the reasonable man have done, or not have done, in the circumstances of the case?'

> **?** **QUESTION** 1.8
>
> The standard of care is constant, though the actual 'quantum' or amount of care required varies from case to case. What do you think this statement means?

In formal terms the standard, of the 'reasonable man', is constant and objective, but in practice the relevant standard will have to be determined in **each** case, according to the **circumstances** of that case, judged in the light of the reasonable man test. The standard eventually set will contain subjective elements.

1.7.1.1 Capacity

The capacity in which the defendant was acting at the relevant time can be important. Say that the defendant was a competitor in a dangerous sport, such as motorcycle racing. He may owe a low quantum of care as a competitor going all out to win and as such he will be entitled to take risks which would not otherwise be justified, but that will not protect him from liability if his negligent act in fact arises from another capacity, that is his capacity as someone obliged to maintain his machine in a reasonably safe condition, as in *Harrison* v *Vincent* at (14.3.1.3).

1.7.1.2 Consent

A claimant's consent may affect the degree of care expected. In *Condon* v *Basi* [1985] 2 All ER 453 (CA), approving the approach taken in the Australian case of *Rootes* v *Shelton* [1968] ALR 33, the issue was the standard of care expected in a sporting activity in which the parties have agreed to abide by the rules of the game. In a game of football, for instance, 'serious and dangerous foul play' would be negligence, but that would not be true of every technical infringement of the rules because in the normal course of events accidental infringements of the rules are likely. In addition, according to Sir John Donaldson MR, more care is required in the Premier League than in a local league game.

In *Smoldon* v *Whitworth* [1997] PIQR 133, Curtis J applied *Condon* v *Basi* in finding the defendant, a referee in a rugby match, liable in negligence to the claimant who had been severely injured when the scrum, in which he was the hooker, collapsed upon him. His Lordship said 'the duty of referees is to exercise that degree of care for the safety of players which is appropriate in the circumstances.' In his Lordship's opinion the referee wears a 'preventive mantle'.

It was found that collapsing a scrum was contrary to the rules of the game and dangerous. In the particular game, a 'Colts' game, for players under 19 years of age and who were consequently not fully mature, the risk of injury was greater than it would have been in other circumstances. There was a finding of fact that the defendant did not fully understand the purpose of some rules and was thus poorly qualified to referee this match.

The Court of Appeal upheld this decision. It was emphasized that a referee owes a duty of care to his players; indeed the referee, the defendant, did not contest this issue. Thus, the case was argued on the content of the duty, that is the relevant standard of care.

Lord Bingham LCJ, giving the judgment of the court, said that since the game of rugby was involved, with all its dangerous consequences and fast-moving and competitive nature, the referee's job was 'difficult and demanding' and he could not reasonably be expected to be in 'all parts of the field at the same time'; furthermore, the job was usually, as in the present case, 'performed out of goodwill by a devotee of the game'. In such circumstances, said his Lordship: 'The threshold of liability is a high one. It will not easily be crossed.'

It was a 'Colts' game, involving young and inexperienced players. The defendant had been properly found to be in breach of his duty of care by failing to take appropriate steps to prevent a collapse of the scrum; and one of the players, the claimant, suffered spinal injuries of a kind that the rules of the game were designed to prevent; that is, the defendant was liable for the foreseeable result of his breach of duty, even though in statistical terms it was a very unlikely eventuality.

The defendant had also argued that the defence of *volenti non fit injuria* applied but the court rejected this plea. Although it was true that as a player the claimant had consented to the ordinary incidents of a game of rugby football of the kind in which he was taking part, it could not be said that he had consented to a breach of duty on the part of the very official who was duty bound to apply the rules of the game, which were meant to protect the claimant, and take reasonable care to see that those rules were observed by others. *Volenti* is a general defence in the law of tort (see 14.3.1).

In *Vowles* v *Evans* [2002] EWHC 2612, Morland J decided that as a matter of policy it was 'just and reasonable' to impose a duty of care upon an amateur referee at an adult rugby match in respect of the safety of the players. On the facts, the defendant (the referee) had not been negligent with regard to the control of set scrums or the general control of the game. He had, however, failed to enquire properly whether a player was suitably trained and experienced to play as replacement front row forward. In effect, the defendant left the decision whether or not to play 'non-contested scrums' to the teams themselves. During the course of a set scrum which collapsed, the claimant dislocated his neck and developed permanent incomplete tetraplegia. It was held that the defendant was in breach of his duty of care because he did not order non-contested scrums; his failure to do so was a material cause of the claimant's injury. This decision was subsequently upheld by the Court of Appeal, (2003) *The Times*, 13 March. Their Lordships said that the standard of care would depend on the circumstances, but the threshold of liability was high for a fast-moving game.

In *Blake* v *Galloway* [2004] EWCA Civ 814 (CA), the claimant had participated in 'good-natured horseplay' with some friends who were throwing pieces of bark chipping at each other. A piece of bark thrown by the defendant in the general direction of the claimant hit him in the eye, causing 'significant' injury. In an action for battery and/or negligence the defendant relied upon *volenti*, on the basis that the claimant had consented to the risk of being hit by the bark even if it was thrown without reasonable care. Dyson LJ said that people who took part in horseplay owed each other a duty of care not to cause injury, but what did that mean in context? His Lordship said no authority had been cited directly on this point, but he considered that there was a close enough analogy between organized and regulated sport or games and the horseplay involved in the present case for the application of authorities such as *Wooldridge* v *Sumner* and *Condon* v *Basi*. The only real difference was that there were no formal rules for horseplay, but his Lordship did not consider that to be a significant distinction. It was held, unanimously, that someone injured during horseplay with friends, as well as during an organized and regulated game, would not usually recover damages unless it could be shown that the injury was cased by a failure to take care amounting to recklessness or a very high degree of carelessness, or that it was caused with intent to harm. The claimant had failed to establish any of this and the defendant's appeal was allowed. On the issue of battery (see 10.4) the claimant, by participating in the horseplay, had impliedly consented to the risk of a blow on any part of his body, provided that the missile was thrown 'more or less' in accordance with the tacit understanding or convention of the game.

1.7.1.3 Experts

The foresight of the ordinary reasonable man is not appropriate where defendants actually possess or hold themselves out as possessing special skills or expertise. Defendants in such cases are judged by the appropriate professional or 'expert' standard of care which, in the medical context, for example, is known as the *'Bolam'* standard. As McNair J put it in *Bolam* v *Friern Hospital Management Committee* [1957] 1 WLR 582,

> [W]here you get a situation which involves the use of some special skill or competence, the test as to whether there has been negligence or not is not the test of the man on the top of a Clapham omnibus because he has not got this special skill. The test is the standard of the ordinary skilled man exercising and professing to have that special skill.

He went on to say

> . . . he [the defendant, a doctor] is not guilty of negligence if he has acted in accordance with a practice accepted as proper by a responsible body of medical men skilled in that particular art.

Accepted practice will, in the professions, depend largely on the particular profession's code(s) of guidance issued by its governing body. In the case of the medical profession the General Medical Council issues such guidance. In 1999, for example, the Council issued new guidelines on consent entitled *'Seeking Patients' Consent: the ethical considerations'*. These guidelines, coupled with the Senate of Surgery's guidance, contained in *'The Surgeon's Duty of Care'* (1997) have the potential, via *Bolam*, to lead to a 'duty to inform' on the part of doctors. See, however, the discussion on *Sidaway* in 10.4.3.4. In that case the House of Lords, by a majority, stopped short of imposing a full obligation of informed consent on doctors. Lord Scarman, in a robust dissenting judgment, did not agree. He argued that it was for the court to decide, via an objective test rather than the traditional *Bolam* test, what the doctor ought to have disclosed in the context of each case: see now *Chester* v *Afshar* [2004] UKHL 41, where a doctor was held liable for a failure to disclose a risk which ought to have been disclosed to enable the patient to make an informed and autonomous choice.

In *Matrix-Securities Ltd* v *Theodore Goddard (a firm)* (1997), *The Times*, 13 November, it was held that the duty of solicitors and counsel practising in a specialized field is to exercise such skill and care as would be exercised by a reasonably competent practitioner in the relevant sector, that is, the specialized field, of those professions. 'Field' in this context means area of work.

? QUESTION 1.9

What ought to occur to the 'reasonable man' in special situations?

A defendant who has claimed to possess some special skill or expertise will normally be regarded as having 'held himself out' as possessing that skill or expertise, and will be judged accordingly.

Cattley v *St John's Ambulance Brigade* (1988) QBD, unreported, but see 53 *MLR* 255, involved an allegation of negligence against two members of the St John Ambulance Brigade. The judge applied the *Bolam* test: 'has the defendant exercised the ordinary skill of an ordinary competent man exercising that particular art?' He found that a volunteer administering first aid would be negligent if he did not observe the standards of 'the ordinary skilled first aider exercising and professing to have that special skill of a first aider'. No negligence was found on the facts because the volunteers had observed the procedures laid down in the Brigade's *First Aid Manual*. This must be distinguished, however, from other situations, for example, where a layman renders first aid in an emergency. Such a person will not be expected to show the dexterity of a doctor as he is not holding himself out as possessing any special skill.

In *Wells* v *Cooper* [1958] 2 QB 265, a householder performing the ordinary household task of screwing on a door knob was expected to observe the standard of a 'reasonably competent carpenter', but was not required to exhibit the competence of a carpenter working in a professional capacity.

In *James* v *Butler* (2005), *The Times*, 19 May, a man who lost an eye when a rafter from the conservatory he was building fell on him was awarded damages against the neighbour who had agreed to help him. The defendant, who worked in the building trade, agreed to help the claimant construct a conservatory at his home for £300 over five days. The defendant thought he had screwed the rafter in place by hand before the accident but the Court of Appeal found that he had committed a breach of his duty of care. As Lady Justice Smith put it, 'The act of inserting and finger-turning the screw is so simple that it falls well within the capability of all but the most inexperienced of handymen.'

In *Phillips* v *Whiteley* [1938] 1 All ER 566, a jeweller who pierced ear-lobes was not regarded as having purported to be anything other than what he was. (But do you suppose that a jeweller piercing ear-lobes today would be expected to have an increased awareness of the risks of infection, for example, the HIV 'Aids' virus, through blood or other body fluids?)

You will not be surprised to learn that one who carries out electrical rewiring (*Green* v *Fibre Glass Co.* [1958] 1 QB 245) or electro-convulsive treatment (*Bolam* v *Friern Hospital* [1957] 1 WLR 582), will be expected to come up to professional standards even if he is not in fact possessed of them. In *Nettleship* v *Weston* [1971] 2 QB 691 (CA), however, it was held that a learner driver owed even to his passenger instructor the same degree of skill which would be expected from a qualified driver. In *Wilsher* v *Essex Area Health Authority* [1986] 3 All ER 801 (CA), it was held that an inexperienced doctor is expected to observe the standard of a reasonably competent doctor of the relevant grade. The standard of care was said to be related to the job undertaken, not to the individual's experience.

? **QUESTION** 1.10

What other considerations are to be taken into account by the reasonable man?

There is no exhaustive list of factors indicating breach of duty, but the cases do show that certain common factors are considered by the courts when setting the standard of care appropriate for the circumstances of the particular case. These factors are identified by most authorities (for example, *Street on Torts*, Chapter 13.2, 11th edn, 2003) as follows.

1.7.1.4 The usual practice in the trade, profession, or calling in question

If the defendant has followed the normal pattern of care to be expected in his trade or profession, this raises a presumption that there was no breach of duty. In *Morris* v *W Hartlepool Navigation Co.* [1956] AC 552, however, the claimant was injured because a ship's hatch was left open and unfenced at sea. The evidence showed that the normal practice had been followed. According to Lord Cohen (at p. 579) 'when the court finds a clearly established practice "in like circumstances" the practice weighs heavily in the scale on the side of the defendant and the burden of establishing negligence, which the claimant has to discharge, is a heavy one'. On the facts, it was held that the claimant had discharged this burden because the general practice was so manifestly unsafe and unnecessary.

In *Gold* v *Haringey Health Authority* [1987] 2 All ER 888 (CA), a doctor did not warn his patient of the failure rate for sterilization, but he was found not to be negligent although experts said they would have warned the claimant, because there was still a considerable number of doctors (possibly 50%) who would not have issued a warning.

Conversely, the fact that the defendant has not followed the normal practice is evidence, but not proof, that he or she was negligent.

There is an argument that the courts in some medical cases have given undue emphasis to the 'normal practice' factor, usually in favour of the medical profession. See the extracts from the journal, *Professional Negligence*, and Jones, *Textbook on Torts*, in *Cases and Materials* at 1.4.1.1.

The decision of the House of Lords in *Bolitho* v *City and Hackney and Hackney Health Authority* [1997] 4 All ER 771, is of some considerable importance. A boy aged two was admitted to hospital after an attack of croup. He suffered respiratory failure and a senior registrar was called on two occasions by the nursing staff, but she failed to attend. It seems that she 'bleeped' a junior doctor on the second occasion to go in her place, but he did not receive the message.

The boy suffered catastrophic brain damage, and died. Negligence, in failing to attend, was admitted, but legal liability for the brain damage and death was denied on the ground that there was a lack of causal connection between that negligence and the damage suffered.

There is nothing remarkable in such an argument, provided the defence can show that the patient would have died anyway (as in *Barnett*); the point about this case is the legal basis of the argument about causation. The defence used *Bolam* in this context: the '*Bolam* test', it was argued, was a determining factor in any decision on causative links, it was not restricted merely to the issue of breach of duty.

On the facts, the patient would probably have survived if he had been 'intubated' (i.e. if a tube had been inserted to provide a clear airway) and the question the court was asked to decide was whether the doctor would have intubated had she been in attendance. If the answer was 'no', her (admitted) negligence was not a cause of the death.

The doctor said she would not have intubated even if she had attended the patient, and used the *Bolam* test to justify her argument. Since the court was willing to accept this use of *Bolam*, legal argument then turned on the question of what a 'responsible body' of doctors would/would not have done in the circumstances.

Five medical experts gave evidence for the claimant to the effect that the child had been in such a state that total respiratory failure was inexorably developing; intubation was therefore recommended. The defence's three experts, however, disputed this by arguing that the risk of total failure was small; and the nurses' evidence also gave support to the defence. The notional decision not to intubate was therefore in accordance with a responsible body of opinion and not a breach of duty in itself. Thus, on the facts, the failures to attend and to intubate were not material factors and the claimant failed to prove causation.

Although the court accepted that *Bolam* could be used in this way their Lordships did say that judges must not simply accept the word of medical experts who give evidence for doctors that a particular course of action was acceptable. Lord Browne-Wilkinson, giving the judgment of the court, said judges have to be satisfied that the experts' opinion has a logical basis, that they have directed their minds to the risks and benefits of a particular course of action, and that they have reached a 'defensible conclusion'. On the facts, the court was satisfied that it was reasonable not to subject the child to such an invasive procedure as intubation bearing in mind the small risk of total respiratory failure.

It may be thought that the advice from the House of Lords to judges concerning their assessment of expert evidence might indicate a potential weakening of *Bolam's* grip, but their Lordships did also say that it will only be in rare cases that it will be correct for a judge to conclude that the views held by a competent medical expert are unreasonable.

In *Shakoor* v *Situ* [2000] 4 All ER 181, the defendant practised traditional Chinese herbal medicine. The claimant, one of his patients, suffered an adverse and unusual reaction to a certain remedy and subsequently died. At first instance it was decided that the defendant did not have to observe the standard of care of a reasonably competent practitioner of orthodox medicine. However, he did have to follow the standard of care expected of a reasonably competent practitioner of alternative medicine, and this meant that the defendant had to take into account the fact that alternative medicine was practised alongside orthodox medicine. Thus, he had to ensure that the alternative remedy had not been adversely reported upon in an orthodox medical journal.

The deceased's reaction, though rare, was considered to be a possibility in orthodox medicine, but a general practitioner of orthodox medicine would not have been negligent in failing to appreciate the risk. A practitioner of traditional Chinese herbal medicine was, therefore, only expected to observe the standards of a reasonably competent practitioner of that art.

On the facts, the defendant had not been negligent because the published discussions of the alternative remedy did not indicate to a sufficient degree that the remedy was too dangerous to prescribe. Thus the defendant had observed the standards of care required of such persons in the UK.

1.7.1.5 The magnitude of the risk

In *Bolton* v *Stone* [1951] AC 850, the House of Lords found that the risk of anyone outside a cricket ground being injured from within was so remote that the defendant was not liable in negligence. Only a handful of balls had been hit out of the ground over many years.

In *Hedley* v *Cuthbertson* (1997), *The Times*, 21 June, an experienced climber, assisting a relative novice for a fee of £50 was held liable for not using two ice screws in belays or setting up running belays. This was the 'universally accepted practice' in climbing, and there had to be 'overriding reasons' for departing from the normal safety measure. The threat of a rock-fall in this case was a real one, but it had been only 'slight' and did not justify the use of only one screw compounded by failure to install running belays.

1.7.1.6 Importance of the defendant's objective

If the defendant is under some compulsion, legal or moral, to act, say, in an emergency, he may be expected to be less careful than otherwise. In *Watt* v *Hertfordshire CC* [1954] 1 WLR 835 (CA) firemen, in a hurry to rescue a woman trapped under a vehicle, failed properly to secure a heavy jack on the back of their lorry, the vehicle properly equipped for such a task being unavailable. The jack slipped and injured the claimant, one of the firemen. In the circumstances it was found that the fire authorities had not been negligent. Lord Denning indicated that the decision might have gone the other way had the defendants been engaged in ordinary commercial pursuits.

1.7.1.7 The seriousness of any likely injury to the claimant

In *Paris* v *Stepney BC* [1951] AC 367, a one-eyed workman, engaged on work underneath vehicles, was blinded in his remaining eye by a metal splinter. The House of Lords held that though his disability, which was known to the defendant, his employers, did not increase the likelihood of injury, it made any such injury much more serious than in the case of an ordinary employee and negligence was found on the facts.

In *Morrell* v *Owen* (1993), *The Times*, 14 December, it was held that organizers of a sporting event for disabled persons owed a greater standard of care in the tort of negligence than would be the case in relation to organizing a similar event for able-bodied participants.

1.7.1.8 The state of technical or scientific knowledge

This factor played a very important role in *Roe* v *Minister of Health* [1954] 2 QB 66, in which the claimant was admitted to hospital for treatment, including a spinal injection of nupercaine. The drug had to be stored in ampoules kept in a sterilizing solution of phenol. Unknown to medical science generally, at that time, phenol could percolate through microscopic cracks in the ampoules. The claimant was injected with contaminated nupercaine and became paralysed from the waist down. It was held that the defendant was not liable for the actions of the doctors involved. As Denning LJ said: 'Nowadays it would be negligence not to realize the danger, but it was not then.'

In *Maguire* v *Harland and Wolff plc and Another* (2005), *The Times*, 27 January (CA), it was held that the claimant, a 67-year-old woman who died of mesothelioma after years of washing her husband's contaminated work clothes, was not entitled to damages from his former employer, the defendant. The court found that the defendant did not owe any duty of care to the claimant with regard to secondary exposure to asbestos, though the defendant accepted that they would have been in breach of duty to the claimant's husband had he suffered ill-health associated with exposure to asbestos. The decision turned on the issue of whether employers such as the defendant could, before 1965, have foreseen the risk of asbestos exposure to the families of their employees. By a majority the court found that it was not reasonably foreseeable that the claimant would incur any injury by coming into contact with asbestos at home. No one had identified any such domestic or secondary risk in published literature before 1965. Judge LJ said that when considering criticisms of actions and omissions forty years ago, one must be warned against the wisdom of hindsight, and recognize the potential unfairness of using knowledge accumulated during the last forty years which, by definition, was not available to the defendant. You should compare this case with the decision in *Margereson* (1.3.3 above).

1.7.1.9 The practicalities of taking precautionary steps

If safety measures are comparatively easy to take, the balance may weigh in favour, though not necessarily conclusively, of the claimant. In *Haley* v *London Electricity Board* [1965] AC 778 the defendant's servants 'roped off' a hole they had been digging in the road, blocking the entrance by a single bar, near the ground, to deter pedestrians. The claimant, a blind man, fell into the hole and was injured. It was held that because the presence of a blind person was foreseeable, and adequate precautions would have been simple to take, the defendant was liable. See also s. 1 of the Disabled Persons Act 1981.

In *Bolton* v *Stone* (see 1.7.1.5), there was a distance of one hundred yards between the claimant and the batsman, and a seventeen-foot fence in between. In view of the slight risk, it was difficult to see what further precautions could have been taken.

1.7.2 Some conclusions

It would be a mistake to conclude that the list of 'relevant factors' is exhaustive; and there may well be overlap between them. One important lesson which you should have drawn is that each case must turn on its own facts.

The following extract from Weir's *Casebook* is instructive in this respect:

This decision (*Qualcast* v *Haynes* [1959] AC 743), which emphasized the importance of the facts of the case in breach problems should deter counsel from citing decisions on breach as authority for the case in hand, and dissuade the student faced with a problem from hunting down cases 'on all fours', like a housewife seeking a matching thread in a haberdashery.

But the student may have to read a good many cases to gain vicariously the experience which lies at the root of sound judgment. Despite the best efforts of the higher courts, however, counsel (who are paid by the day) continue to cite enormous numbers of case (see *Lambert* v *Lewis* [1982] AC 225) and county court judges (who are paid to use their judgment) continue to apply decisions on breach as if they laid down fixed rules ('inching forward into traffic isn't negligence', *Worsfold* v *Howe* [1980] 1 All ER 1028).

Another effect of the principal decision [*Qualcast*] is to emphasize that the proper form of question, when one is dealing with breach of duty, is 'Did the defendant take reasonable care?' One must not pick on some feature of the defendant's acts and say: 'Was he under a duty not to do that?' (see also *A.C. Billings & Sons* v *Riden* [1958] AC 240, 264, per Lord Somervell of Harrow). Of course, the claimant must normally identify what it was in the defendant's behaviour that he finds objectionable—e.g. that he omitted to give a signal before turning right on the highway. But the question remains 'Did the defendant drive with reasonable care, considering that he gave no signal?' and does not become 'Was the defendant under a duty to give a signal?' Matters of detail are to be treated as part of the question of breach, not as raising sub-duties with a specific content.

? QUESTION 1.11

Two 15-year-old girls are using rulers as 'swords' during a school lesson. A piece of plastic snaps off one of the rulers and hits the claimant in the eye. What do you consider to be the appropriate standard of care for these circumstances?

According to the Court of Appeal in *Mullin* v *Richards* [1998] 1 All ER 920, the appropriate test to apply was 'would an ordinary, careful, and reasonable 15-year-old have foreseen that the game carried with it the risk of personal injury?' Apparently, the 'game' was common in the school and was not banned, nor had any warning of any danger been given. The Court concluded on those facts that the injury was not foreseeable. Perhaps, however, we should leave the last word on this issue with James (*General Principles of the Law of Torts*,

4th edn): 'To say that conduct is "careless" or "negligent" is not to define, but to evaluate it; and evaluation can only be made in the light of some measure or "norm" which the evaluator has in mind.'

1.7.3 Burden of proof of negligence on the facts

The burden of proving any allegation against the defendant lies on the **claimant**; the evidence being assessed on the so-called 'balance of probabilities' and not on the basis of beyond all reasonable doubt (the higher standard applied in criminal law).

 EXERCISE 1.6

Read the extract from s. 11, Civil Evidence Act 1968 in *Cases and Materials* (1.4.2), and in one paragraph describe the implications for the law of tort.

The Civil Evidence Act 1968, s. 11, reverses the common law rule that a conviction may not be used as evidence in civil proceedings. The effect of the section is that if a person is proved to have committed an offence, he shall be taken to have committed that offence until the contrary is proved. For example, proof of a conviction of an offence involving negligence places the burden of disproving negligence on the defendant.

? **QUESTION** 1.12

Consider the meaning of the maxim *res ipsa loquitur*.

In some cases a claimant cannot point exactly to the person(s) to blame for his or her injury; a typical example would be of a claimant waking up after an operation in hospital to find a swab inside his or her body. It is in such situations that a court might be persuaded, after the claimant has made out an outline or prima facie case, to infer negligence by the defendant, unless the defendant can offer an acceptable explanation of the circumstances. Such a situation is summed up in the maxim *res ipsa loquitur* ('let the thing/situation speak for itself'). As Lord Denning put it in *Roe* v *Minister of Health* [1954] 2 All ER 131 (CA): 'If an injured person shows that one or other of two persons harmed him, but cannot say which of them it was, he is not defeated altogether. He can call on each of them for an explanation.'

The claimant in *Scott* v *London and St Katherine Docks Co*. (1865) 3 H & C 596 (Court of Exchequer Chamber), was standing near the door of the defendant's warehouses when he was injured by some bags of sugar which fell on him. The judge at first instance had directed a verdict for the defendant on the ground that there was no evidence of negligence. The Court of Exchequer Chamber (the forerunner of the Court of Appeal) however, directed a new trial by relying on the doctrine of *res ipsa loquitur*.

Erle C.J. said: 'There must be reasonable evidence of negligence. But where a thing is shown to be under the management of the defendant or his servants, and the accident is such as in the ordinary course of things do not happen if those who have the management use proper care, it affords reasonable evidence, in the absence of explanation by the defendant, that the accident arose from want of care.'

In *Morris* v *Winsbury-White* [1937] 4 All ER 494, the defendant had operated on the claimant, and the post-operative treatment involved the insertion into his body of tubes and their frequent replacement. The tubes were originally inserted by the defendant during the operation but replacements were made subsequently by junior doctors and nurses. Sometime after his discharge from hospital a portion of a tube was found in the claimant's bladder.

In an action for negligence against the defendant, it was held that *res ipsa loquitur* did not apply because, in hospital, he was treated by numerous doctors and nurses and was not in the control or charge of the defendant for the whole period.

Since 1937, accounting techniques, and record-keeping generally have been greatly improved in the context of surgical and analogous procedures. Consequently the application of *res ipsa loquitur* in such cases is now unlikely.

In *Easson* v *London and North Eastern Railway* [1944] 2 KB 421 the claimant, aged four, fell through the door of a passenger train. At the time of the accident the train was seven miles from its last stopping place. It was held that *res ipsa loqitur* was not applicable because the defendants did not have sufficient control over the door at that time. Anyone in the train corridor could have meddled with the door.

In *Barkway* v *South Wales Transport Co. Ltd* [1950] 1 All ER 393 (HL), the claimant was injured when the bus he was travelling in burst a tyre, mounted the pavement and fell down an embankment. The tyre had burst owing to a defect in its wall which could not have been discovered beforehand. The House of Lords held that *res ipsa loquitur* did not apply here, because there was evidence of the circumstances of the accident, and a negligent system of tyre inspection at the defendant's garage.

A claimant who is able to present a partial account of what happened, however, is not prevented from relying on the principle of *res ipsa loquitur*.

Lord Porter said:

> The doctrine is dependent on the absence of explanation, and, although it is the duty of the defendants, if they desire to protect themselves, to give an adequate explanation of the cause of the accident, yet, if the facts are sufficiently known, the question ceases to be one where the facts speak for themselves, and the solution is to be found by determining whether, on the facts as established, negligence is to be inferred or not.

The claimant in *Cassidy* v *Ministry of Health* [1951] 2 KB 343 (CA), who was injured as a result of the negligence of hospital staff, could not produce evidence to show which member of the hospital staff had been negligent. However, it was held that in such circumstances, that is where the claimant cannot point to the particular servant who is in control, the principle of *res ipsa loquitur* will apply so as to render the employer vicariously liable.

In *Walsh* v *Holst & Co. Ltd* [1958] 1 WLR 800, contractors were carrying out work on a building when a brick from the building fell on and injured the claimant who was walking along the street. It was held that *res ipsa loquitur* did apply, so that a defendant's duty is so extensive that he is responsible for the negligence of an independent contractor. However, on the facts, it was held that the contractors were not liable as it was shown that they had not been negligent, having taken precautions.

In *Pearson* v *North-Western Gas Board* [1968] 2 All ER 669 (CA), the claimant's husband was killed and her home destroyed by a gas explosion. This was found to be due to a fractured main caused by a very severe frost. In such weather, the defendants had men standing by to deal with reports of gas leaks, but there was no way of preventing or predicting such an explosion. On this evidence it was held that, assuming *res ipsa loquitur* applied, the defendants had rebutted the presumption of negligence.

In *Widdowson* v *Newgate Meat Corporation* [1998] PIQR 138 (CA), the claimant, who suffered from a severe mental disorder, was injured in a road accident. At the trial of the action he gave no evidence, relying on *res ipsa loquitur*. In these circumstances the defendant called no evidence, claiming that there was no case to answer. The Court of Appeal held that where a judge could not find out what actually happened, because there was no evidence on which to form an opinion, *res ipsa loquitur* may apply. If the defendant cannot give a plausible explanation for what happened, the claimant is entitled to succeed.

Three conditions must be satisfied for the application of the maxim *res ipsa loquitur*. They are as follows:

(a) that the defendant had a right to control of the thing or event; and

(b) that the accident should be something which could not, in the normal course of events, have happened without someone's negligence; and

(c) that there should be no known facts on the basis of which the accident can be explained in terms of the negligence of the defendant, thus excluding the operation of *res ipsa loquitur*.

When the maxim does apply, and this is a matter of law for the judge to decide, we should assess its legal effect, that is, we have to consider here whether:

(a) any burden of proof shifts to the defendant; or

(b) the proof burden remains with the claimant. In this case, the formal burden would stay with the claimant, but the defendant would have to cope with the evidential burden. In other words a prima facie inference of negligence is raised by the claimant, which must be displaced by evidence adduced by the defendant. If the defendant's story is capable of belief, the 'ball' is back with the claimant, by analogy with a game of tennis, in which the ball is constantly moving between the players. Here, each player will be hoping that his or her opponent will be put 'on the spot' in dealing with the delivery.

EXERCISE 1.7

Read *Henderson* v *Henry E. Jenkins & Sons* [1969] 3 All ER 756 in *Cases and Materials* (1.4.2) and consider the following questions:

(a) Is an effect similar to strict liability achieved in some negligence cases by the use of *res ipsa loquitur*?

(b) Does it mean that a defendant can be found liable on circumstantial evidence?

(c) Does the formal burden of proof remain with the claimant?

> *Henderson* v *Henry E. Jenkins* & Sons [1969] 3 All ER 756
>
> An action in negligence was brought by the widow of a man who had been killed when the brakes on the defendant's lorry failed suddenly as it went down a hill. A pipe carrying hydraulic fluid for the brakes had corroded, causing a hole to form through which fluid had escaped. *That* part of the pipe could not have been seen without the whole of the pipe being removed. The action was brought against the owners of the lorry *and* their driver.
>
> Since the evidence showed that sudden, complete brake failure from corrosion was unusual the defendants claimed a 'latent defect' which would not have been discovered by the taking of reasonable care. They said they had followed usual practice by regularly inspecting only those parts of the pipe which could be seen without removing the pipe itself, and by doing this they were following the advice of the Ministry of Transport and the manufacturers of the lorry.
>
> The claimant's action was dismissed at first instance as was her appeal to the Court of Appeal. Her appeal to the House of Lords was successful, their Lordships finding that the defendants had not rebutted the inference of negligence. Although they had taken what appeared to have been reasonable steps in maintaining the vehicle they should, held their Lordships, have shown that there was nothing in the history of the lorry that would have caused the unusual corrosion, so requiring special inspection.

(a) It can be argued that the effect of the 'doctrine' of *res ipsa loquitur* is to produce in some negligence cases a form of strict liability. *Henderson* provides an example of such a decision.

(b) In effect, a defendant can be found liable on circumstantial evidence.

(c) It is said that the effect of the application of the 'doctrine' is that the claimant is entitled to judgment unless the defendant can exonerate himself. However, it is only a prima facie inference and if the defendant can produce some evidence to displace the inference the burden of proof remains with the claimant.

Henderson, however, is some authority for the proposition that the effect of applying *res ipsa loquitur* is to reverse the burden of proof. That is, the claimant, having made out a prima facie case of negligence, can expect the burden to pass to the defendant who will then be liable if he cannot prove that he was not negligent.

The Privy Council, in *Ng Chun Pui and Others* v *Lee Chuen Tat and Others* [1988] RTR 298, sought to clarify the status of the maxim. A motor coach, owned by D2 but driven by D1, left one side of dual carriageway, crossed the central reservation and collided with a public bus travelling on the other side of the dual carriageway. The claimants were injured in the accident.

No oral evidence was submitted by the claimants at trial and they relied merely on the fact of the accident (*res ipsa loquitur*). In this approach they were justified because in the ordinary course of events a well-maintained and properly driven coach would not collide with other traffic in the circumstances outlined. The claimants would be entitled to succeed in the absence of any evidence by the defendants.

In other words . . . according to Lord Griffiths '. . . the proper inference was that the coach was not being driven with the standard of care required by the law and that the driver was negligent.'

The defendants, however, did call evidence explaining how the driver came to lose control of the coach and this evidence was accepted by the trial judge but he found that because the claimants had relied on the doctrine of *res ipsa loquitur* the burden of disproving negligence remained on the defendants, and in the circumstances they had failed in their task.

The Privy Council said, in dismissing the claimants' appeal from the decision of the Hong Kong Court of Appeal, that it is not entirely correct to regard the burden of proof as shifting to the defendant on an application of the *res ipsa loquitur* maxim since it is up to the claimant to establish negligence on the facts and he must bear this burden throughout the case. The so-called doctrine of *res ipsa loquitur* is no more than a legal maxim to describe a state of evidence from which it is proper to draw an inference of negligence. In an appropriate case the plaintiff can establish a prima facie case by relying on the fact of the accident; if the defendant adduces no evidence, there is nothing to rebut the inference of negligence, but, if he does, that evidence has to be evaluated to see if it is still reasonable to draw the inference of negligence from the mere fact of the accident.

 See *Cases and Materials* (1.4.2) for extracts from the judgments in *Ward* v *Tesco Stores Ltd* [1976] 1 All ER 219 (CA) and commentary by Wright.

1.8 Damage

In common with many other torts, such as nuisance, negligence requires proof of damage. It is for the claimant to prove that he or she has suffered 'damage' *and* that that damage was caused by the defendant's tort(s). Causation is discussed in **Chapter 2**.

■ SUMMARY

- This chapter deals with two of the basic ingredients of the common law tort of negligence, 'duty' and 'breach'; the third ingredient, causation of damage, is dealt with in **Chapter 2**.

- All torts are composed of duty and breach; many of them also require damage and even where a tort is actionable per se (that is without proof of actual damage) for example, as in trespass to the person, actual damage will have to be established if the claimant wishes to receive compensation. Negligence, however, is of such an open-ended nature that special attention has to be paid to these elements.

- In cases where there is little, if any, established authority on the issues raised, the courts have to have some means of setting boundaries for duty situations: there can never be negligence 'in the air'.

- Since 1932, the 'neighbour test', based on reasonable foreseeability, has formed the basis for determining the existence of a duty of care in all cases, especially those involving novel situations. Foreseeability 'alone' has never been sufficient. 'Proximity' is also required; and policy has always played a crucial role in this context.

- Mainly as a result of the views expressed by Lord Reid in *Dorset Yacht* and Lord Wilberforce in *Anns*, 'foreseeability' was given a more prominent part to play; but a reaction set in to the more liberal approach that these opinions seemed to herald, chiefly because it was felt that insufficient emphasis was being given to established authority.

- Today, the three-stage '*Caparo* test' is in vogue for deciding whether a duty of care should be imposed.

- The main message emerging from *Caparo* is that a 'test' approach to the question of 'duty' is undesirable and should be avoided. If anything, *Caparo's* emphasis is on a 'just and reasonable'/incremental approach to the question of 'duty' or 'no duty'. The '*Caparo* test' referred to today is the creation of judges and lawyers, pursuing some element of 'certainty' in post-*Caparo* cases.

- Although the existence of a duty cannot be divorced from the facts of each case, that is, in formal terms a duty can only be owed to an individual claimant on the facts, the courts are also involved in making normative decisions, that is, imposing value-judgments.

- The right to life under the European Convention may at some time be used to challenge the common law's traditional approach to the question of liability for omissions.

- Once a duty of care is established the claimant must show that there has been a **breach** of that duty.

- The question of whether or not there has been a breach of duty turns on the relevant standard of care to be observed in the particular circumstances of the case.

- *Bolam* applies to the expert or professional defendant; in other cases the relevant standard is that of the hypothetical reasonable man: the question posed in each case is 'how would the reasonable man have acted in the circumstances?' Whilst this in formal terms consists of an objective approach to the problem, it is evident from the cases that subjective elements will inevitably influence any decision.

- As with the 'duty' issue in negligence, policy also plays an active role in determining the standard of care issues.

- The operation of the maxim *res ipsa loquitur* has been noted. This aids claimants in certain situations in getting cases off the ground. Without it they would not get very far at all because they are, in these special circumstances, unable to say precisely what went wrong and who is to blame. In a sense, claimants are enabled to set proceedings rolling merely by pointing a finger of reasonable suspicion at the defendant.

■ FURTHER READING

Cane, P., *Atiyah's Accidents, Compensation and the Law*, 6th edn, London: Butterworths, 1999.

Cane, P., and Stapleton, J., *The Law of Obligations: Essays in Celebration of John Fleming*, Oxford: Clarendon Press, 1998 (Weir, T., *The Staggering March of Negligence*, and Stapleton, J., *Duty of Care Factors: A Selection from the Judicial Menu*).

Convery, J., 'Public or Private? Duty of Care in a Statutory Framework—*Stovin* v *Wise* in the House of Lords' (1997) 61 *MLR* 559.

Craig, P. and Fairgrieves, S., *Barrett, Negligence and Discretionary Powers* [1999] Public Law 626.

Elliot, C. and Quinn, F., *Tort Law*, 5th edn, London: Longman, 2005, Chapter 2.

Giliker, P. and Beckwith, S., *Tort*, 2nd edn, London: Sweet & Maxwell, 2005, Chapters 2 and 5.

Harlow, C., *State Liability: Beyond Tort Law*, Oxford: Oxford University Press, 2004.

Harlow, C., *Understanding Tort Law*, 3rd edn, London: Sweet & Maxwell, 2005, Chapters 3 and 8 (especially pp. 140–50).

Hepple, Howarth, and Matthews, *Tort: Cases and Materials*, 5th edn, London: Butterworths, 2000, Chapters 2 and 5.

Jones, M., *Textbook on Torts*, 8th edn, Oxford: Oxford University Press, 2002, Chapters 1, 2, and 3.

Kidner, R., *Casebook on Torts*, 9th edn, Oxford: Oxford University Press, 2006, Chapters 4, 5, 7, 8, and 12.

Lunney, M. and Oliphant, K., *Tort Law Cases and Materials*, 2nd edn, Oxford: Oxford University Press, 2003, Chapters 3, 4, 9, and 10.

McBride, N.J. and Bagshaw, R., *Tort Law*, 2nd end, London: Longman, 2005, part II, pp. 51–238.

Markesinis, B.S. and Deakin, S.F., *Tort Law*, 5th edn, Oxford: Oxford University Press, 2003, Chapters 1 and 2 (pp. 65–162).

Murphy, J., *Street on Torts*, 11th edn, London: Butterworths, 2003, Chapters 1, 11, and 13.

Salmond and Heuston, *Law of Torts*, 21st edn, London: Sweet & Maxwell, 1996, Chapters 2 and 9.

Stanton, K.M., *The Modern Law of Tort*, London: Sweet & Maxwell, 1994, Chapters 1, 2, and 3.

Stauch, M., Wheat, K., and Tingle, J., *Sourcebook on Medical Law*, 2nd edn, London: Cavendish Publishing, 2002, Chapter 6.

Weir, T., *A Casebook on Tort*, 10th edn, London: Sweet & Maxwell, 2004, Chapters 1 and 2.

Winfield and Jolowicz on Tort, 16th edn, London: Sweet & Maxwell, 2002, pp. (v)–(ix) and Chapters 1, 2, and 5.

 CHAPTER 1 ASSESSMENT EXERCISE

1. '. . . the well known passage in Lord Atkin's speech [in *Donoghue* v *Stevenson*] should I think be regarded as a statement of principle. It is not to be treated as if it were a statutory definition. It will require qualification in new circumstances. But I think that the time has come when we can and should say that it ought to apply unless there is some justification or valid explanation for its exclusion.' (*Home Office* v *Dorset Yacht Company*, per Lord Reid.)

Discuss.

2. Mandy was driving her car home one night, when a tyre punctured as a result of an invisible structural defect in its wall. She attempted to change the wheel, but without success. Nick, a passing motorist, saw her plight and offered his assistance. He changed the wheel but forgot to tighten the wheel-nuts. As a result the wheel came off soon afterwards, the car crashed and Mandy was injured.

Advise her on any claim she may have in tort against Nick. Would your answer be different if Nick were an AA patrolman, whom Mandy had summoned to help her?

NB: **Two** questions are given here because questions on duty of care in negligence often take the form of essay questions; and **Chapter 1** covers breach of duty, as well as duty.

See *Cases and Materials* (1.6) for specimen answers.

2 Negligence II: causation and remoteness of damage

2.1 OBJECTIVES

By the end of this chapter you should be able to:

1 Explain the theoretical distinction between 'causation in fact' and 'causation in law'

2 Evaluate the so-called 'but for' test, particularly its utility in connection with the determination of 'factual' issues of causation

3 Describe the state of the case law on 'factual' causation and, in particular, explain the significance of the expressions (defences) *novus actus interveniens* and *nova causa interveniens*

4 Evaluate the 'tests' for determining issues of 'remoteness' of damage ('causation in law'); as well as the significance of the so-called 'egg-shell skull' principle

2.2 Introduction

It is convenient to deal with this topic immediately after studying the basic concept of the tort of negligence as most of the case law deals with issues arising in that form of liability. Furthermore, the establishment of damage is essential for liability in negligence. However, it is important to bear in mind from the outset that problems of causation and remoteness arise in all torts: they are not restricted to the tort of negligence. For example, exactly the same general rules apply in nuisance (see **Chapter 11**).

We will be examining in detail two topics in this chapter, viz. **causation** and **remoteness**. You may find it instructive to consider first the general nature of these topics.

In formal terms we need to distinguish between causation and remoteness. We should always remember, however, what Lord Denning has told us on several occasions, for example in *Lamb* v *Camden LBC* [1981] 2 All ER 408, that these two concepts cannot be separated in practical terms. In *Roe* v *Minister of Health* [1954] 2 All ER 131 (CA), he said:

> Duty, causation and remoteness, run continually into one another . . . they are simply three different ways of looking at one and the same problem. Starting with the proposition that a negligent person

should be liable, within reason, for the consequences of his conduct, the extent of his liability is to be found by asking the one question: Is the consequence fairly to be regarded as within the risk created by the negligence? If so the negligent person is liable for it: but otherwise not.

> **?** **QUESTION** 2.1
>
> What is the theoretical difference between causation and remoteness?

Causation refers to the chain of causation between the tort(s) and the damage; the claimant must establish an unbroken connection between his damage and the defendant's wrongful conduct. Causation is concerned with consequences and non-consequences in a factual sense.

In *Barnett* v *Chelsea Hospital* [1969] 1 All ER 428, a patient, the deceased, had been admitted to hospital with severe vomiting and the doctor concerned failed, negligently, to diagnose the man's condition. The medical evidence showed that the patient would have died anyway, from poisoning as a result of ingesting arsenic, irrespective of the negligence in diagnosis, which was not an operative cause of the death. (The decision is an example of the application of the 'but for' test, which we will return to later in this chapter.) In each case the basic issue to be determined is whether the defendant has materially contributed to the damage; his tort need not be the only cause of the injury.

Remoteness is relevant at the stage following the establishment of a factual connection between tort and damage. It is concerned with consequences; but these are said to be legal rather than factual. However, it is not always easy to draw a satisfactory distinction between 'factual' and 'legal' in this context. Remoteness is said to be concerned only with the question of which of the established consequences is to be the subject of compensation. In negligence, liability exists in general only for consequences of a reasonably foreseeable type or kind.

2.3 Causation

The courts claim to approach this matter in a pragmatic, common sense way; avoiding considerations of strict logic and philosophy. Policy often plays an important role in the determination of difficult issues.

The **'but for'** test is usually employed in the investigation of causative links between the tort(s) and the damage. This test involves asking the simple question: 'Would the claimant have incurred the damage "but for" the defendant's tort?' A negative answer to this question means that it is likely that the defendant's wrong factually caused the claimant's damage. If the damage would have been sustained anyway, irrespective of the defendant's wrong, there will be no liability. This test is a somewhat crude device and does not provide a satisfactory solution in every case.

> **?** **QUESTION** 2.2
>
> Can you think of any situations in which the 'but for' test might be an inadequate device for settling disputes concerning causative links?

Amongst such situations are the following:

First, where there are several concurrent causes of the damage, each of them being sufficient on its own to produce the end result. Here, the 'but for' test would cancel out each cause; in strict, logical terms the damage would have occurred irrespective of cause A, because the other cause(s) would produce the result; so it would be with cause B, etc.

In such a case common sense would be applied (see, for example, Stephenson LJ in *Knightley* v *Johns* [1982] 1 All ER 851, discussed at 2.4.2) and the court would assess the share of blame as best it could in the circumstances. If, for example, two causes could be identified in a particular situation, then, all things being equal, blame would be apportioned on a 50/50 basis. No doubt policy would be a factor to consider in such a context and, of course, each case will always turn on its facts.

Secondly, where there are successive acts/events causing damage. In *Cutler* v *Vauxhall Motors* [1974] 1 QB 418, the claimant grazed his right ankle in an accident caused by the defendants. The injury caused an ulcer to form and, because the claimant had been suffering for some time from varicose veins in both legs, an immediate operation was necessary. He claimed damages from the defendants for the pain and discomfort of the operation but the Court of Appeal held that since the claimant would very probably have needed a similar operation within five years in any case, the defendant's negligence could not be regarded as the cause of the operation.

However, in *Baker* v *Willoughby* [1969] All ER 1528, the defendant negligently injured the claimant's leg. He was later shot in that leg during a robbery and the leg had to be amputated and an artificial one fitted in its place. The House of Lords held that the second injury did not make the defendant liable only for the claimant's disability until the time the leg was removed. As a matter of policy it was found that there was causal connection between the defendant's negligence and the claimant's disability after the operation. If the first tortfeasor were released from further liability after the amputation and the second tortfeasor liable only for causing the removal of an already damaged leg, the claimant would receive less compensation than he deserved. It was decided that there was no practical difference between a permanently disabled natural leg (from the point of view of general disablement) and an artificial one. On that reasoning the defendant's liability was not decreased by the supervening act of X, whose own liability would be limited to the consequences of injury to an already disabled leg (here including the consequences of the necessary amputation). The person responsible for the supervening act was a bank robber, who could not be traced; even if found he might prove to be a 'man of straw' and unable to meet any judgment made against him.

A different approach was taken in *Jobling* v *Associated Dairies* [1982] AC 794, in which the supervening event was a 'natural' one, that is, a disease, which caused further injury to the claimant. The defendant was found liable by the House of Lords only up to the point at which the disease took over, when it effectively ended the claimant's working life. The court said that the later event must be taken into account in limiting the amount of damages awarded; the defendant was entitled to a 'discount'. In general, the courts make a deduction for the 'vicissitudes of life'; these vicissitudes cannot be ignored where they have occurred by the date of the trial.

See the extract from Hepple and Matthew's *Tort: Cases and Materials*, in *Cases and Materials* (2.1).

In *Jobling, Baker* was criticized in terms of its general approach, though it was not declared to be wrong on its facts. The law, it seems, may recognize a distinction between a supervening tort and a supervening natural event. In *Baker* and *Jobling* there were supervening events (or causes) to consider in each case and the court was of the opinion that justice and fairness would not be achieved were there to be a simple application of the 'but for' test to the facts. It is clear that a pragmatic and policy-based approach was taken by the courts in these cases. The same is true of *Cutler* except that the defendant's negligence brought forward a future possibility.

In *Murrell* v *Healy* [2001] 4 All ER 345 (CA), the claimant was injured in two successive car accidents (May and November 1995). It was held that where a claimant brings an action for two sequential torts the second tortfeasor (defendant) is liable only for any additional damage he or she has caused. This follows the basic reasoning in *Baker*, in which it was held that the first tortfeasor's liability was not reduced by the succeeding tort. The court also found that a claimant injured by a tort and suffering from an unconnected disease or condition making him or her unfit for work will have his or her damages for the tort reduced, applying *Jobling*, in which it was held that when calculating damages a court should consider what the claimant's life would have been like without any tort.

Performance Cars v *Abraham* [1962] 1 QB 33, illustrates a similar set of circumstances in which the 'but for' test was considered insufficient. There were two defendants in this case. The first one had negligently damaged the claimant's expensive car. Some time later the second defendant collided with the car and the question of his liability for a paint respray arose. The court found that since a respray was already essential because of the damage sustained in the first accident, the second defendant was not liable for this part of the claimant's claim.

2.4 Proof of causation

The legal burden of proof is on the claimant, on the basis of the balance of probabilities, that is it is for the claimant to show that it is more likely than not that the defendant's wrong caused the loss. As we have seen, this matter is usually resolved by use of the 'but for' test. This is a difficult issue where the damage might also be due to some other cause as well as the defendant's tort; indeed, the other cause may even be of a non-tortious nature. The claimant must prove that the damage is due, at least substantially or materially, to the tort.

McGhee v *National Coal Board* [1972] 3 All ER 1008

The claimant had contracted dermatitis through working in some brick kilns belonging to his employers. He claimed that they had been negligent in not installing shower facilities. The state of medical knowledge concerning dermatitis at the time meant that the court could not determine whether the taking of showers after work would have prevented the claimant from contracting the disease.

The lower courts found the employers to be in breach of statutory duty, by not providing adequate washing facilities, but said there was no tortious liability for the disease because the claimant could not show that the breach of duty had caused his injury. Nevertheless, the House of Lords held the defendants liable. The House refused to distinguish between materially increasing the risk of injury by failure to provide shower facilities and materially contributing to injury. (See *Cases and Materials* (2.2).)

? **QUESTION** 2.3

What do you think is the effect of this decision on the law in general terms?

This decision raised the possibility that there had been a change in the fundamental obligation placed on a claimant in such cases, from proof of factual causation to one merely of proving breach of duty. In view of the state of medical knowledge at the time, and the uncertainty of the cause, the 'but for' test was jettisoned and the court applied what might be called a 'probably for' test.

McGhee was applied by the Court of Appeal in two cases in 1987. In *Fitzgerald* v *Lane* [1987] 2 All ER 455, the difficulty in proving causation was not due to any deficiencies in the state of medical knowledge. The claimant was struck first by D1's car and then by D2's car while crossing a road. His damage included a neck injury. D2 claimed that the impact with his car was not a cause of the claimant's tetraplegia (the result of the neck injury). The claimant and D1 relied on *McGhee* and the question for the court was this: 'Had the impact with D2's car caused or contributed to the tetraplegia by inflicting a blow to an uninjured neck, or had it increased the harm to an already injured neck?' The Court decided that there was a clear risk of the claimant's head being harmed in a way which could result in tetraplegia. On the evidence, even if the neck was already injured through impact with D1's car, further damage 'must' have been caused by D2: there was a dented bumper and broken number plate.

Hotson v *East Berkshire Health Authority* [1987] 2 All ER 909

The claimant had an injured leg (an injury sustained in a non-tortious context) from which there was a chance (assessed by the trial judge as approximately 25%) of a full recovery. However, after negligent medical treatment for the injury the leg was permanently damaged. His claim against the Health Authority for loss of the chance of a full recovery was allowed by the trial judge and the Court of Appeal.

The House of Lords held, however, reversing the decision of the Court of Appeal, that there is no principle in tort which would allow a percentage of a full financial recovery based on probabilities. A claimant's claim could only be worked out on an 'all or nothing' basis. It was necessary to establish the claimant's status at the time of the negligence; in this case was he on the balance of probabilities a person already irretrievably damaged, or a person destined to recover? In view of the finding of fact on the likelihood of recovery, he clearly fell into the former category and therefore the negligence of the doctor was deemed not to be causally relevant.

You can read an extract from the speech of Lord Bridge in *Hotson* in *Cases and Materials* (2.2).

In *Kay* v *Ayrshire and Arran Health Board* [1987] 2 All ER 417 (HL), an overdose of penicillin was negligently administered to treat a child suffering from meningitis. He went into convulsions and suffered a degree of paralysis, but remedial treatment had a positive effect. However, on discharge from hospital he was found to be suffering from profound deafness. The defendants denied liability for the deafness, which they claimed was due to the meningitis; it was argued that the disease commonly had this effect. Medical knowledge indicated that deafness occurred in approximately one third of all cases of pneumococcal meningitis (the type contracted by the boy in the present case).

Lord Keith said that *McGhee* offered no assistance in the circumstances.

> Had there been acceptable medical evidence than an overdose of penicillin administered by lumbar puncture [as in the present case] was known to increase the risk that the meningitis, which the penicillin was intended to treat, would cause deafness the decision [in *McGhee*] would have been in point. It would be immaterial that medical science was unable to demonstrate the precise mechanism whereby the risk was increased.

There was no such evidence: on the balance of probabilities the deafness was caused by the meningitis.

In *Hill* v *William Tomkins Ltd* (1997), *The Guardian*, 18 October, the claimant, a farm worker, was found by Mrs Justice Smith to have suffered ill-effects from organophosphate poisoning via exposure to the insecticide 'Actellic D' in the course of his employment with the defendant. The defendant admitted that the exposure of the claimant to 'Actellic D' was tortious and that the claimant suffered an adverse reaction to it, but argued that the effects of that exposure were short-lived and that any long-term ill-health he had suffered, since 1993, had not been caused or contributed to by the exposure. However, her Ladyship said

> some of his continuing symptoms are attributable to that exposure. But some are in part attributable to psychological factors and have, at times, been exaggerated by him and his wife in description to doctors, and have also on occasions been affected by the frequency with which he has been examined by doctors . . . I think that there have been times when he has needed the wheelchair, but I think his acceptance of it owed more to psychological factors than physical ones. I think that by then he had begun to accept the role of a sick man.

In other words there was a serious doubt on causation in respect of much of the claim.

In *Wilsher* v *Essex Area Health Authority* [1988] 1 All ER 871 (HL), a prematurely born baby had developed a condition, typically found in premature babies who have been given too much oxygen, known as retrolental fibroplasia (RLF), which had had serious consequences for his sight. The Court of Appeal appeared to extend the decision in *McGhee*. Mustill LJ said:

> If it is an established fact that conduct of a particular kind creates a risk that injury will be caused to another or increases an existing risk that injury will ensue; and if the two parties stand in such a relationship that one party owes a duty not to conduct himself in that way; and if the first party does conduct himself in that way; and if the other party does suffer injury of the kind to which the risk related; then the first party is taken to have caused the injury by breach of duty, even though the existence and extent of the contribution made by the breach cannot be ascertained.

However, the House of Lords held that in cases of negligence it is for the claimant to establish causation. The two important points decided in this case were (1) that in law the trainee/learner medical doctor has to be judged by the same standard as that which would be applied to more experienced colleagues; and (2) that, contrary to the attempt by Peter Pain J in *Clark* v *MacLennan* [1983] 1 All ER 416 to allow it, a claimant cannot shift the burden of proof onto the defendant doctor (or the doctor's employer) merely by showing that a particular step in specific treatment which was designed to accept a risk, or to minimize it, has not been taken in the circumstances of the case. Therefore, even where the defendant creates the risk of a particular injury (and this amounts to a breach of duty) and the claimant suffers that injury, the burden of proof remains with the claimant.

In the opinion of Lord Bridge, *McGhee* did not lay down any new principle of law 'whatever'. On the contrary, it affirmed the principle that the onus of proving causation lies on the claimant.

It was found that *McGhee's* case was 'wholly different' from the present one in that in the former there was only one possible 'agent' which could have caused the claimant's injury; in *Wilsher* there were several possible 'agents' which could have caused the claimant's condition and a casual link was not established. A breach of duty plus injury could not raise a presumption of causation. Their Lordships allowed the authority's appeal against the decision of the trial judge (affirmed by a majority of the Court of Appeal) and ordered a retrial on the causation issue.

 EXERCISE 2.1

What effect did the decision in *Wilsher* v *Essex AHA* [1988] All ER 871 have on the ruling in *McGhee*?

McGhee may only be helpful to a claimant where a single 'agent' (per Lord Bridge) or cause is involved and the question is whether there has been a material increase in a clearly identifiable risk. In *Wilsher* five independent causes apparently contributed to the risk of the claimant's damage. The House of Lords was not willing to find the defendant liable merely because one of them was due to negligence. (This issue should now be examined in the light of *Fairchild* (below).)

Apportionment of blame

Closely allied to the question of causal connection is the matter of apportioning blame for the purpose of awarding damages where there are multiple causes/defendants. In *Holtby* v *Brigham and Cowan* [2000] 3 All ER 421 (CA), the claimant had contracted asbestosis while working as a marine fitter for 39 years. For roughly half that time he was employed by B, and for the rest of the time he was employed by other employers doing similar work in similar conditions. The claimant contended that he could recover all his losses from B; alternatively, he argued, once a claimant had proved that the defendant's conduct had made a material contribution to his disease, the onus was on the defendant to plead that others were responsible for a specific part of the injury. It was held, dismissing the claimant's appeal, that where a claimant suffers injury as a result of exposure to a noxious substance by two or more persons, but claims against only one of them, that person is liable only to the extent of his own contribution to the injury.

Fairchild v *Glenhaven Funeral Services Ltd and others* [2002] 3 WLR 89

At first instance in *Fairchild*, *Holtby* was distinguished by Curtis J because, unlike *Holtby*, there was no question of any cumulative effect flowing from breach(es) of duty by the defendants. Fairchild had worked on a number of sites, doing different jobs, over many years. He contracted mesothelioma, a form of cancer of the lung, which medical opinion accepts is caused in 90% of cases by exposure to asbestos fibres. Mesothelioma was said to be an 'all or nothing' disease: different from asbestosis or pneumoconiosis (other diseases of the lung), which are cumulative diseases, in that it requires asbestos fibres to 'hit' a cell in an appropriate way to cause malignancy.

Fairchild died from mesothelioma in 1996 and his widow brought claims against one of his former employers (exposure to asbestos fibres in employment) and two occupiers of premises (under the Occupiers' Liability Act 1957, discussed in 7.5) on which, it was claimed, the deceased was exposed to substantial quantities of asbestos fibres. The type of asbestos involved was not identifiable. The judge found against the claimant since it could not be established by her, on the balance of probabilities, which defendant if any, had caused or materially contributed to the deceased's fatal disease.

This was so even though it was clear that each employer was in breach of duty regarding protecting the deceased from exposure to the asbestos dust. It was not possible, on taking a 'but for' approach to the problem, to place the blame on any individual employer. A claim concerning the common duty of care arising under the 1957 Act was also decided in favour of the defendant:

CURTIS J: . . . There is no material [evidence] direct or by inference, upon which to make a finding that the Third Defendant *actually* knew of that risk [of exposure to asbestos dust] and I decline to do so.

His Lordship's judgment was upheld by the Court of Appeal.

The House of Lords, however, took a different view. Their Lordships held that in cases such as this justice required the Court to apply the *McGhee* test in favour of the claimant. In order to establish legal causation on the balance of probabilities it was enough for a claimant to show that each defendant's tort had materially increased the risk of injury; in this case from mesothelioma. The claimant here could sue any of the deceased's employers or any occupier of premises, as the case might be, notwithstanding that she could not prove which exposure had caused the damage. The House of Lords in *Fairchild* acknowledged for the first time that *McGhee*, and *Bonnington Castings* v *Wardlaw* [1956] AC 613 before it, were actually exceptions to the 'but for' test. You will find extracts from the speeches in the House of Lords in *Fairchild*, which is an important case, in *Cases and Materials* (2.2). These extracts are instructive on the issue of causation in cases where there are multiple defendants.

Bonnington Castings is referred to later on, at 7.3.1.1.

Fair shares

In *Fairchild* the claimant received full damages as did the claimants in *Bonnington Castings* and *McGhee*. This approach to the award of damages is consistent with the principle of joint and several liability (**see 13.4.8**). There is some considerable authority, however, for the proposition that the tortfeasor should be liable for damages only in proportion to the extent of his or her contribution to the claimant's injury. The 'proportional harm' approach to the award of damages, described by Weir, at p. 235, as 'revolutionary' and a 'novel doctrine', was adopted in

Holtby which was a case concerned with asbestosis. Asbestosis is a progressive disease and may be amenable to slicing into shares of blameworthiness but the proportionate harm approach has been taken in other contexts, for example *Hatton* v *Sutherland* [2002] ICR 613 (see 5.5) and *Barrett* v *Enfield LBC* [1999] UKHL 25; it was rejected in *Hotson* (above).

The doctrine of proportional harm has caused some disquiet, at least where it is universally applied. See, for example, McBride and Bagshaw at pp. 532–3. Weir, at p. 236, points to certain problems which may arise in this connection. He says that there is a danger of the 'egg-shell skull' rule (2.6.1) being jettisoned where, as in *Hatton*, a claimant's congenital condition is regarded as a contributing factor when awarding damages. He also argues that in some cases damage which is actually indivisible is often regarded as divisible and this may lead to problems where there are several defendants and apportionment on a 'just and equitable' basis is called for under the Civil Liability (Contribution) Act 1978 in respect of the 'same damage' '. . . where damage is divided there is no longer the "same damage" for the purposes of the [1978] Act'.

Fairness and *Fairchild*

Lord Hoffmann was one of the Lords of Appeal in *Fairchild*; he also delivered the majority judgment of the House of Lords in *Barker* v *Corus (UK) plc, Murray British Shipbuilders (Hydrodynamics) Ltd and Others, and Patterson* v *Smiths Dock Ltd and Another* [2006] UKHL 20. The claimants, all victims of mesothelioma, had had more than one employer over a number of years each one of whom had, admittedly, negligently exposed them to asbestos dust. Some of these employers, and their insurers, no longer existed at the date of trial and it was therefore crucial for the claimants to be able to seek full damages from any of the defendants under the 'joint and several' principle, especially since mesothelioma had until then been treated as an 'indivisible' disease. The claimants were successful at first instance and in the Court of Appeal but the House of Lords allowed the defendants' appeals and held that an employee who contracted mesothelioma after being wrongfully exposed to asbestos dust by more than one employer could recover only a portion of his or her damages from each employer, depending on the relative degree of contribution by that employer to the chance of the employee contracting the disease.

According to Lord Hoffmann, *McGhee* was a case in which there had been two possible causes of the claimant's dermatitis; one source was tortious but the other was not. The claimant was allowed to recover damages although he could not prove which source of risk (that is, which exposure) had caused the disease. He said that once one accepted that the 'Fairchild exception', based on *McGhee*, could operate even though not all the potential causes of damage were tortious, there was no logic in requiring that a non-tortious source of risk should have been created by someone who was also a tortfeasor. It should not matter, therefore, whether the person who caused the non-tortious exposure happened also to have caused a tortious exposure. The 'Fairchild exception' gave a cause of action against a defendant who had materially increased the risk that the claimant would suffer damage and might have caused that damage but could not be proved to have done so because it was impossible to show, on a balance of probabilities, that some other exposure to the same risk might not have caused it instead. For that purpose it should be irrelevant whether the other exposure was tortious or non-tortious, by natural causes, or human agency, or by the claimant himself. Those distinctions might be relevant to the attribution of responsibility but that was not so for the purpose of establishing a causal link between the defendant's conduct and the claimant's injury.

Fairchild only applied where the impossibility of proving causation 'arose out of the existence of another potential causative agent which operated in the same way, that is, the mechanism by which it caused the damage must have been the same.' His Lordship went on to say that consistency of approach suggested that if the basis of liability was the wrongful creation of a risk or chance of causing the disease the damage which the defendant should be regarded as having caused was the creation of such a risk or chance. If that was so it did not matter that the disease in question consisted of indivisible damage. In his Lordship's opinion chances were 'infinitely divisible' and different persons could be separately responsible to a greater or lesser extent for the chance of an event occurring. Treating the creation of the risk as the damage caused would involve quantifying the likelihood that the damage was caused by a particular defendant and it would then be possible to determine the defendant's share of the damage. However, it was necessary to ask whether the characterization of the damage in the present case as the risk of contracting mesothelioma was fair. The '*Fairchild* exception' was created because it would be unfair to leave a claimant in such a case with no remedy, but was it fair that the claimant should be able to recover in full from any defendant in such circumstances? Attributing liability according to the relative degree of contribution to the chance of the disease being contracted would, his Lordship said, 'smooth the roughness of the justice which a rule of joint and several liability created'. The justification for the imposition of joint and several liability was that if a person caused harm, there was no reason why his or her liability should be reduced because someone else also caused the same harm, but where liability was 'exceptionally imposed' because they might have caused harm, fairness suggested that if more than one person might have been responsible, liability should be divided according to the probability that one or other caused the harm. A defendant was liable for the risk of disease which he himself had created and not for the risks created by others, whether they were defendants, persons not before the court, or the claimant himself. Consequently, in cases which fell within the '*Fairchild* exception' the damage was to be apportioned amongst the persons responsible for the exposure to asbestos which created the risk according to their contributions to the risk.

Lord Rodger dissented. In his opinion the reasoning in both *McGhee* and *Fairchild* indicated the House's concern in maintaining a consistency of approach 'with the main body of law on personal injuries', but the 'new analysis adopted by the House in the present case would tend to maximize the inconsistencies in the law' by turning the '*Fairchild* exception' into an 'enclave where rules applied which had been rejected elsewhere in the law of personal injuries'. Inside this 'enclave' claimants would receive, for example, 60% of their damages if the court considered there was a 60% chance that the defendant had caused the injury and no other wrongdoer was solvent or insured. Outside the enclave, for example, claimants whose husbands were killed in an accident for which the only solvent defendant was 5% to blame recovered all their damages from that defendant. That was a form of 'rough justice [a reference to the principle of joint and several liability] where the law preferred, as a matter of policy, to place the risk of the insolvency of a wrongdoer or his insurer on the other wrongdoer(s) and their insurer(s)'; but now the House was deciding that the risk of the insolvency of a wrongdoer or their insurer would not fall on the other wrongdoer(s) and their insurer(s) and would be 'shouldered entirely by the innocent claimant'.

His Lordship said the desirability of the courts, rather than Parliament, throwing that lifeline to wrongdoers and their insurers at the expense of claimants was not obvious to him.

Speaking before their Lordships reached this decision, the solicitor for Mrs Fairchild said: 'What the House of Lords is being asked to do quite openly by our opponents is to change the law to save employers and insurance companies money . . .' (*The Times*, 2 May 2006).

This controversial decision will be reversed by s. 3 of the Compensation Act 2006.

The Act, which has retrospective effect, is due to come into force in early 2007. It will simplify claims for compensation by employees against their employers where mesothelioma is contracted as a result of the negligent exposure to asbestos in the course of employment. Where more than one employer is involved, as in *Barker*, the employee will be able to claim full compensation from any one of the responsible employers who can then claim against the other employer(s) for a sum proportionate to their share of the blame, and may be entitled to an indemnity from the State if the other(s) cannot be traced or has no assets.

2.4.1 **Loss of chance**

Hotson (above) involves the question of recovery for 'loss of chance'. In the context of the case this concerned loss of chance of medical recovery. (You can read extracts from articles by Dr T Hill and Dr W Scott in *Cases and Materials* (2.2).)

Hotson was reversed because the claimant had failed to discharge the burden of proof placed on him, that is, to show that there was a sufficient causative link between his condition and the defendant's negligence. The House of Lords left open the general question of recovery for loss of chance in tort.

In *Allied Maples Group Ltd* v *Simmons* [1995] 4 All ER 907, the Court of Appeal, in a non-medical context, held that where a claimant's loss flowed from the defendant's negligence but was dependent upon the hypothetical behaviour of some independent third person, issues both of causation and quantification of damages could arise. First, in terms of causation, the claimant had to prove that he acted to obtain a benefit or avoid a risk. He was not required to prove in that sense that the third person would have so acted. At the second stage it was then sufficient for the claimant to establish that there was a substantial chance (and not just a speculative one) that the third person would have acted in favour of the claimant. The assessment of a substantial chance was not a matter of causation, that is, an issue to be determined according to the balance of probability, it was a matter of quantification of damages: ranging from the barely real or substantial to the near certainty.

The court approved the following observation of Lord Lowry in *Spring* v *Guardian Assurance plc* (3.5.10.2 and 5.5):

> [O]nce the duty of care is held to exist and the defendant's negligence is proved, the claimant only has to show that by reason of that negligence he has lost a reasonable chance [of employment—this was a case of a negligent reference] which would have to be evaluated and he thereby suffered loss . . . He does not have to prove that but for the negligent reference [the prospective employers] would have employed him.

First Interstate Bank of California v *Cohen Arnold and Co.* (1995), *The Times*, 11 December, confirms that the evaluation of a substantial chance is a matter to be considered by the court when it is quantifying the amount of damages to be awarded. The defendant firm of chartered accountants reported negligently to the claimant bank that their client was a person of wealth. Consequently, the bank lent him a sum of money well above their normal lending for the particular type of deal. He defaulted on the loan and the bank lost heavily.

The Court of Appeal held, applying *Allied Maples*, that the judge at first instance, who had found that at the time the tort took effect the best price reasonably obtainable for the property was £3m, should have estimated the chance of selling it at that price in a falling market. That chance was two to one so the award would be reduced to £2m.

In *Equitable Life Assurance Society* v *Ernst and Young (a firm)* (2003), *The Times*, 10 September, the Court of Appeal allowed a claim by a company against its auditors for the loss of chance of sale of its business due to alleged negligence in the preparation of the company's statutory accounts to proceed. Brooke LJ said it was inappropriate to strike out a claim 'in an area of developing jurisprudence', because decisions on novel points of law should be based on actual findings of fact at the trial of the case.

In *Dixon* v *Clement Jones* (2004), *The Times*, 2 August (CA), the court drew a distinction between cases alleging professional negligence arising from a transaction or advice given by a professional person, and those arising from loss of the chance to litigate where the underlying litigation involved allegations of professional negligence. Questions of causation were relevant in the former, whereas in the latter the task of the trial judge was to evaluate the chance which had been lost, not to perform a trial within the trial to determine what the outcome of that litigation would be. Negligence had been acknowledged in that the claimant had lost her claim against accountants for professional negligence in the advice which they gave her over a business transaction, when her claim was struck out for failure by her solicitors to serve particulars of the claim. The question was whether the claimant had lost anything of value. The trial judge had found that the struck-out claim had some value, assessing the claimant's chance of success at 30%. The defendants, relying on the analysis in *Allied Maples*, which was a transaction claim and not a loss of litigation claim, said once the judge found that it was more likely that the claimant would have continued with her business project in any event, her claim was lost as a matter of causation. The court dismissed the solicitors' appeal on the reasoning that litigation concerning the loss of litigation was different from the transaction class of claim in *Allied Maples*, and so the claimant was not required to prove on the balance of probabilities that she would not have proceeded if she had had the right advice.

The Court of Appeal, in *Coudert Brothers* v *Normans Bay Ltd* [2003] EWCA Civ 215, had to consider a claim by the defendants that their own wrongdoing could break the chain of causation in a claim made against them by the claimant. The claimant lost its investment in a Russian company when a Russian court declared invalid its tender offering a five-year investment period when a maximum three-year term had been decreed by the Russian government. It sued the defendants for loss of chance and they claimed in relation to the assessment of the chance, that the transaction failed for a cause independent of the pleaded negligence, that is, the defendant's failure to seek anti-monopoly permission, which broke the chain of causation. If the claimant in the present case could establish that the defendant should have provided it with the chance (of winning the contract) could the defendant say in relation to the assessment of the chance that it should be reduced by their negligent failure to obtain anti-monopoly permission, because the intervening act gave rise to a separate cause of action in respect of which the limitation period had expired? The initial negligence had caused the loss of a chance. In the absence of authority directly on the point, the court appealed to public policy, where it was a principle that a person should not be entitled to rely on his own wrong (in this case a further act of negligence on the part of the defendant) in order to secure a benefit. Furthermore, it was not unfair to apply such a principle.

In *Gregg* v *Scott* [2005] 2 AC 176, the House of Lords arrived at a decision by a three to two majority, which has been the subject of some criticism. A negligent medical diagnosis failed to spot the claimant's cancer of the lymph gland and it was only discovered nine months later, decreasing his chances of survival. Had the correct diagnosis been performed, the claimant's chances of survival would, according to the relevant medical statistics, have been 42%. In the event, because the cancer was not picked up until after these crucial nine months, his chances of recovery had been reduced to 25%. Their Lordships, affirming the decision of the Court of Appeal and the decision of the judge at first instance, found against the claimant on the basis that his chances of recovery were less than 50:50 anyway. The recovery percentages were based not on any prognosis of the claimant's own condition but on the statistics of people with his disease. Lord Nicholls, who dissented, said the argument accepted by the majority was 'irrational and indefensible' and 'crude to an extent bordering on arbitrariness'. Lord Hoffmann, justified the majority decision by pointing to *Hotson, Wilsher,* and *Fairchild*. In the first two cases the House of Lords denied the claims for loss of chance, and in *Fairchild* the House of Lords had accepted that the disease had a determinate cause in one fibre or other but constructed a special rule imposing liability for conduct which only increased the chances of the employee contracting the disease. That rule was restrictively defined in terms which made it inapplicable to the current case. In his Lordship's opinion these cases showed that the law regarded the world as in principle bound by laws of causality. Everything had a determinate cause even if we did not know what it was. The law dealt with lack of knowledge by the concept of the burden of proof.

2.4.2 Intervening causes

A defendant may seek to establish a break in the chain of causation by introducing arguments based on a *novus actus interveniens* (act of a stranger) or a *nova causa interveniens* (intervening incident). The resolution of such an argument will depend on the facts and context of each case, as interpreted by means of such guiding principles as are available to the judges, and the requirements of policy.

In *Knightley* v *Johns* [1982] 1 All ER 851, the first defendant, Johns, had caused an accident in a road tunnel within which operated a one-way traffic system. A police inspector, who was in charge of the situation, realized that he had failed to close the tunnel to oncoming traffic and ordered two constables (one of whom was the claimant) to go back against the oncoming traffic in the tunnel to remedy his mistake. The claimant was injured when he collided with a car; the motorist was not negligent. In acting as they did both the inspector and the claimant had broken police standing orders. The claimant claimed damages from Johns, the police inspector and the chief constable (as being vicariously liable for the negligence of the inspector).

The Court of Appeal found that though the claimant had added to the danger by his behaviour, he had not acted in a wanton or foolhardy way and was not guilty of negligence; he was not responsible for his own injuries. On the issue of whether the inspector had been negligent, and whether that negligence was a *novus actus interveniens* (see below) breaking the chain of causation between Johns' negligence and the claimant's injuries the court held that:

(a) the inspector had been negligent;

(b) in considering whether a *novus actus interveniens* had occurred it was necessary to ask the question 'Was the damage the natural and probable, that is, reasonably foreseeable, result of the defendant's negligence?' Put another way, 'Was something similar likely to happen?' (not a mere possibility which would not occur to a reasonable man; or if it did would be discounted by him as being so remote that no precautions were required). If the answer was 'yes', no event in the sequence of events was a *novus actus interveniens*. Common sense, rather than logic would show what was and what was not reasonably foreseeable;

(c) the inspector's negligence in the present case was the real cause of the claimant's injuries; it was a new cause and not a concurrent cause with the negligence of Johns. It broke the chain of causation between the latter's negligent act and the claimant's injuries.

The inspector and the chief constable were liable to the claimant.

In these cases, said Stephenson LJ, it was always helpful, though not necessarily decisive, to determine which events were deliberate choices to do positive acts; which events were omissions or failures to act; which acts/omissions were innocent or mere miscalculations; and which acts/omissions were negligent. Deliberate/negligent acts were more likely to break the chain of causation than conduct which was not; positive acts would more easily break the chain than mere inaction; mistakes/miscalculations were more to be expected of human beings in a crisis.

The authorities suggest that in those situations where the supervening act/event is a 'natural and probable' consequence of the defendant's wrongful behaviour, the chain of causation is **not** broken.

In *Haynes* v *Harwood* [1935] 1 KB 146, Greer LJ said that a defendant may be liable for the consequences of the act of a third party where that act is 'the very kind of thing which is likely to happen if the want of care which is alleged takes place'.

The claimant in *Wieland* v *Cyril Lord Carpets* [1969] 3 All ER 1006, was unable to use her bifocal spectacles properly because of a neck injury caused by the defendant's negligence and as a result fell down some stairs, suffering further injury. It was held that the defendant was liable for the fall as well as the neck injury. The claimant had acted reasonably in descending the stairs in the circumstances: it was necessary that she should get on with her life and she had taken all possible care.

However, in *McKew* v *Holland* [1969] 3 All ER 1621, the claimant's legs were liable to give way without warning owing to an injury caused by the defendant's negligence. One day the claimant descended some stairs, felt his legs weaken, jumped to avoid a fall, and broke his ankle. The House of Lords found that the chain of causation was broken; the defendant was not liable for the broken ankle. The claimant had acted unreasonably in the circumstances and was the sole author of his misfortune because he had not taken all reasonable care in the circumstances.

? **QUESTION** 2.4

Is it possible to reconcile *Wieland* and *McKew*?

They are difficult cases to reconcile, other than on the basis that *McKew* is a classic case of contributory negligence (the partial defence under the Law Reform (Contributory Negligence) Act 1945). Perhaps *McKew* should have proceeded on this basis rather than on a finding that the claimant was wholly to blame for his own injury. Contributory negligence is examined in 14.3.4.

In *Lamb* v *Camden London Borough Council* [1981] 2 All ER 408, the defendants admitted nuisance and negligence by breaking a water main, which caused the claimant's house to be flooded so that it had to be vacated until it could be made safe. Squatters moved in and caused further damage to the property. The Court of Appeal held that the damage caused to the house by the squatters was too remote, so the defendants were not liable for it. Lord Denning said that although it might be arguable that the damage caused by the squatters was reasonably foreseeable (the trial judge had found the damage unforeseeable and too remote: no one familiar with the house and locality would have regarded such invasions as 'likely'), as a matter of policy it was not a recoverable form of damage; the claimant could have insured against such risks (so spreading the risk through the community). Watkins LJ thought that a 'robust and sensible' approach should be taken to such matters. Although the damage might be 'reasonably foreseeable' the approach he favoured would often produce an 'instinctive' feeling that the damage (as in the present case) was too remote. You will find an extract from the judgment of Scott J in *Ward* v *Cannock Chase DC* [1985] 3 All ER 537 together with extracts from Salmond and Heuston, and Weir's casebook in *Cases and Materials* (2.2.1).

Salmond and Heuston, *The Law of Torts*, describes the decision in *Lamb* as an illustration of 'Common Sense and the Law'.

2.4.2.1 Acts of third parties

The actions of third parties may be foreseeable and lead to liability on the part of the defendant. In *The Oropesa* [1943] P 32, the persons in charge of the defendant's ship were responsible, as a result of their negligent navigation, for a collision with another ship. The master of this other ship put to sea in a lifeboat to discuss the possibility of salvaging his vessel. This action was found to be reasonable in the circumstances and a foreseeable result of the collision. The personal representatives of the claimant, who was in the lifeboat and drowned when it capsized, recovered damages from the defendant in negligence.

In *Stansbie* v *Troman* [1948] 2 All ER 48 the claimant, a householder, employed the defendant, a painter. The claimant had to be absent from his house for a while and he left the defendant working there alone. Later, the defendant went out for two hours leaving the front door unlocked. He had been warned by the claimant to lock the door whenever he left the house. While the house was empty someone entered it by the unlocked front door and stole some of the claimant's possessions. The defendant was held liable for the claimant's loss for, although the criminal action of a third party was involved, the possibility of theft from an unlocked house was one which should have occurred to the defendant.

It has been held that a person whose tort creates a dangerous situation in the highway is not exonerated from liability for further consequences only on the basis that someone else comes along and negligently exacerbates matters.

? **QUESTION** 2.5

What sorts of fact might illustrate such circumstances?

You might have been thinking about the sort of circumstances that occurred in *Wright* v *Lodge and Shepherd* [1993] 4 All ER 299, where the Court of Appeal exonerated from blame, for subsequent events, the driver of a car who had negligently failed to get her car off the road when the vehicle broke down at night. The road was unlit, the weather was foggy, and the second defendant, a lorry driver, collided with the car injuring a passenger. Both the car driver and the lorry driver were found liable to the passenger; but the lorry driver alone was liable to other road users when his vehicle overturned on the opposite side of the dual carriageway. The court came to this second conclusion because the lorry driver was guilty of reckless driving, and this recklessness effectively broke the chain of causation (it was a *novus actus interveniens*) between the first driver's negligence and the injuries to the other road users. According to the evidence, this second batch of damages would not have occurred had the lorry driver been only negligent.

In *Rouse* v *Squires* [1973] 2 All ER 903, there was no liability because there was no relevant danger, where an obstruction of the highway was a danger only to a reckless driver.

Obstruction of the highway can in some circumstances create a public nuisance; see *Dymond* v *Pearce* [1972] 1 QB 496 (11.8.2.2).

? | **QUESTION** 2.6

What if the third party is not fully responsible for his or her actions?

Many decisions have turned on this factor. The defendant will be liable for damage caused by such a person in those circumstances where he should have reasonably foreseen the third party's lack of responsibility.

In *Shiffman* v *Order of St John* [1936] 1 All ER 557, children playing in Hyde Park pulled down a flagpole insecurely erected there by the defendants, injuring the claimant. The defendants were held liable in negligence to the claimant. Also, in *Thomas* v *Bishop* [1976] CL 1872, the defendant was held liable when a loaded pistol which he had put on top of a cupboard was obtained by a child of 2, who shot the claimant with it. It was found that the defendant ought reasonably to have foreseen that something of the sort might occur.

Consider the decisions in *Meah* v *McCreamer* [1985] 1 All ER 367 and [1986] 1 All ER 943. The claimant sustained head injuries in an accident caused by the defendant's negligent driving. As a result, he underwent a marked personality change and subsequently committed crimes of violence against several women. Prior to the accident he had had a history of petty crime and a poor employment record, but he had had a number of relationships with women and there was no evidence of his being violent towards them. The claimant argued that without the accident he would not have committed these offences because there would have been no personality change. There was medical evidence to the effect that the claimant was in any event a 'criminally aggressive psychopath' and that he was someone who had 'underlying tendencies to sexual aggressiveness', but the judge regarded him as a person who was not committed to violent crime prior to his accident. It was due to the accident that his inhibitions had been reduced and he had given vent to his feelings.

He was awarded damages for his imprisonment, subject to a discount for his free board and his poor employment record; and for his criminal tendencies, which would probably have resulted in him spending some periods in prison. His damages were also reduced for his contributory negligence in accepting a lift from the defendant, knowing him to be drunk at the time.

The claimant was later successfully sued in trespass to the person by two of the women he had attacked and, in the 1986 proceedings, he claimed from the defendant these amounts of money. This claim was unsuccessful, being too remote; it would also be contrary to public policy, said the judge, to allow such a claim.

In *Lawrence* v *Osborne* (1997), *The Times*, 8 November, the claimant, an accountant, suffered brain damage in a motoring accident caused by the (admitted) negligence of the defendant. The accident had not impaired the claimant's intelligence, indeed his intelligence had possibly been enhanced as a result of the incident, according to the evidence. What the accident had done, was to turn the claimant into a 'helpless flirt' who was unable to stop pestering women. In short, the accident had left the claimant with an impaired memory and a change of personality caused by damage to those parts of the brain governing behaviour, emotion, and control. He was now a voluntary patient whose financial affairs were administered by the Court of Protection.

According to May J:

> In so far as [the claimant's] present problems of disinhibition and temper are exacerbations of characteristics that he had before the accident, the essential difference is that before the accident they were under control and were not significant personal and social impediments, whereas now they are.

His Lordship awarded the claimant £950,000 in damages.

Cornell v *Green* (1998), *The Guardian*, 13 February, is a decision of the Court of Appeal to much the same effect. On this occasion, however, the accident left the claimant a 'better person' who was 'too nice' to be employable in his old job as an insurance salesman. The accident had robbed the claimant of his thrusting and aggressive personality, essentially of his cunning characteristics, which had made him so good in his job. Stuart-Smith LJ said that as a result of the accident the claimant was unemployable in 'a reputable sales force'. The court awarded the claimant damages totalling £320,000.

2.4.2.2 Acts of the claimant

 QUESTION 2.7

Would you consider it relevant that the claimant has committed suicide?

The authorities suggest that it is only another factor to weigh in the circumstances of each case.

In *Pigney* v *Pointer's Transport* [1957] 1 All ER 1121, the claimant committed suicide some years after he had received an injury to his head caused by the defendant's negligence. It was held that the suicide was the result of an acute anxiety neurosis and depression brought on by the head injury. Pigney's widow was successful in her claim against the defendants for damages for his death, because the original injury was still operating on Pigney. He was not entirely responsible for his actions. (In *McKew* v *Holland*, for instance, the original injury did not prevent the claimant from taking proper care of himself.)

In *Hyde* v *Tameside Area Health Authority* (1981), *The Times*, 16 April, Lord Denning denied that liability would lie for either an attempted or a successful suicide. He adopted a policy approach to the problem, basing his argument on the familiar 'floodgates of litigation' consideration and the fact that suicide is a crime in ecclesiastical law. Watkins LJ and O'Connor LJ, unlike Lord Denning, said they found it unnecessary to consider the issue of causation, though Watkins LJ thought the claimant's attempt at suicide was not foreseeable in the circumstances and O'Connor LJ said:

> I do not think that the fact that a patient commits suicide or attempts suicide will necessarily break the chain of causation . . . It all depends on the circumstances of an individual case. In the present case applying *The Wagon Mound* [below] I do not think that the injury . . . can be connected to the breach of duty suggested against the hospital.

It was decided that there was no breach of duty by the defendant authority.

At this point you should turn to 14.3.1.3 and refer to the decisions in *Kirkham* and *Reeves*. It would seem that in appropriately 'close', proximate, circumstances a defendant can owe a duty to a claimant to protect the claimant from injuring himself by informing a third party of the potential danger.

2.4.2.3 Duty approach

The problem of acts of a third party is sometimes treated as a duty issue. In *Perl* v *Camden LBC* [1984] QB 342, it was held that the defendant council did not in the circumstances owe a duty to the claimant to secure their premises to such an extent that thieves could not gain access via these premises to the claimant's dwelling. The court said that there was no special relationship as in *Dorset Yacht* (see 1.3.1), and *Stansbie* v *Troman* (2.4.2.1) was distinguished on the ground that in that case there existed a contract between the parties and there was an element of reliance by the claimant on the defendant.

A similar problem faced the Court of Appeal in *King* v *Liverpool City Council* [1986] 3 All ER 544. The claimant was the tenant of a council flat, and the flat directly above her was unoccupied. She informed the council, the defendants, of the unoccupied flat and the fact that it was not protected against vandals. Nothing was done and vandals entered the empty flat, ripping out water-pipes, etc. The claimant's flat was flooded. More complaints were made by the claimant and the defendants took some measures, but they were by no means extensive and vandals entered on two more occasions. There was more flooding of the claimant's flat. She claimed that the council had been negligent and were liable to her in both negligence and nuisance. It was held that since there was little that was available to the defendants in the way of effective deterrent measures, they owed no duty of care to the claimant. The court emphasized that there must be a duty in such cases to prevent harm from the actions of third parties.

In *Smith* v *Littlewoods Organization* [1987] 1 All ER 710, the House of Lords found that the owners of a disused cinema were not liable for damage to neighbouring properties caused by a fire started by trespassers at the cinema; on the facts, the owners had no knowledge of any fire risk arising from the state of the cinema. A duty of care to prevent that damage was the only duty alleged on Littlewoods and unless they were bound reasonably to anticipate and guard against that danger, they had no relevant duty of care requiring them to inspect the premises.

According to Lord Mackay, while it was probably the case that children might attempt to break into the cinema, that by no means established that it was a probable consequence of its being 'vacated and not lockfast' that it would be set on fire. No one anticipated any adverse consequences arising from the cinema. His Lordship drew a distinction between a fire hazard on premises and the 'ordinary case' of theft, where the thief used one set of premises to gain access to other premises from which he intended to steal; there was no similar hazard (to fire) on the first proprietor's land in such a case. Neighbours could take steps against theft in a way not possible with fire.

Lord Goff said there was no general duty of care to prevent third parties from causing damage, and there was nothing in the circumstances of the present case to put the defendants under any particular obligation. You can read an extract from his Lordship's speech in *Cases and Materials* (1.6.1).

In *Topp* v *London Country Bus Ltd* [1993] 3 All ER 448 (CA), an employee of the defendant left the bus he was driving at a bus stop outside a pub for about nine hours. The bus was unattended for all this time, was unlocked, and the ignition key had been left in place. Some unknown person drove away the vehicle and knocked down Mrs Topp, killing her. In an action in negligence brought by her dependants it was held that they had failed to establish proximity between the deceased and the defendant; nor was it just and reasonable to impose a duty on the defendant in these circumstances.

Smith v Littlewoods was applied, though distinguished on its facts, in *Clarke Fixing LMT* v *Dudley Metropolitan Council* [2001] EWCA Civ 1898 (CA). The defendant council had acquired land for development purposes. This land contained premises which were next to the claimant's premises. Trespassers frequented the council's premises and often started fires. On one occasion a fire got out of control and spread to the claimant's premises destroying them. The council was aware of the trespassing and of the fires being started. It was also obvious that there was a real risk of a fire spreading from one set of premises to the other, and it was held that the council had a duty to take preventative measures which included removing, at little cost, materials likely to catch fire. Having failed to take any such reasonable steps, the defendant council was found liable in negligence.

In *Gabriel* v *Kirklees Metropolitan Council* (2004), *The Times*, 12 April (CA), the claimant, aged 6, was walking past a building site owned by the defendant when he was hit in the eye by mud or stones thrown by children playing on the site. The council admitted that at the time the site was unfenced, partially excavated, and could have contained rubble. At first instance the claim was dismissed because the risk to the claimant was not foreseeable, the judge concluding that the council did not owe him a duty of care. The claimant appealed against that finding arguing, on the authority of *Smith* v *Littlewoods* and *The Wagon Mound (No. 2)* (2.5.1.4) that the rubble was a source of danger and that it was reasonably foreseeable that children would enter the site and might play in such a way as to cause injury. The court, in ordering a fresh trial before a different judge, said it was not possible to test the validity of the claimant's argument because the trial judge had failed to make any relevant findings of fact, such as the nature and extent to which rubble had accumulated, the general condition of the site, and its relation to the surrounding area. Nor were there any findings by the judge as to the council's knowledge and means of knowledge of the relevant state of affairs. Simply put, the court's conclusion was that the judge had no reasonable basis for arriving at her conclusions.

The claimant's own behaviour was at issue in *Chester* v *Afshar* [2004] UKHL 41. The defendant, a neurosurgeon, advised the claimant to undergo lumbar surgery. She consented and after the operation suffered partial paralysis. The trial judge found that although the defendant had not performed the operation negligently, he had not warned the claimant of the small risk of partial paralysis inherent in the operation. It was also found at first instance that, had she been warned, the claimant would not have consented to the operation taking place at that time but would have sought further advice before arriving at a final decision. Their Lordships, by a majority of three to two, confirmed both the decisions of the Court of Appeal and the judge at first instance in favour of the claimant. It was held that a patient whose doctor failed to warn her of an inherent risk in surgery when that risk materialized, satisfied the test for causation in negligence where she could prove that, had she been properly informed, she would not have had the operation which was in fact performed. Relying on the decision in *Sidaway* v *Bethlem Royal Hospital* (10.4.3.4), Lord Hope, delivering the majority decision, stressed the 'fundamental importance' of the patient's right to decide whether to accept or reject treatment proposed by a doctor. The scope of the doctor's duty was to inform the patient of the risks inherent in the proposed treatment so that her right to choose could be exercised. She had a right to be informed before giving her consent. The scope of the duty was not affected by the response she would have given had she been told of the risks. The function of the law, said his Lordship, was to protect the patient's right to choose; a doctor must, therefore, respect the duty to inform. But, asked his Lordship, how could causation be established when the patient would not have refused absolutely ever to undergo the operation if told about the risks but would have postponed her decision until later? The 'but for' test was 'easily satisfied' because the claimant would not have had the operation when she did if the warning had been given. But the risk was not created by the failure to warn, it was there already, it was inherent in the procedure involved; it was an inevitable risk. His Lordship said that a solution in the claimant's favour could not be based on conventional causation principles. On the contrary, the matter raised an issue of legal policy which a judge had to decide: whether justice required the normal approach to causation to be modified. His Lordship emphasized the subjective nature of the patient's right to make an informed choice as to whether and if so when and by whom to be operated on. He said patients might have and were entitled to have different views about those matters. The factors involved were of 'all sorts' and could include the patient's hopes and fears and personal circumstances and, 'above all', their own views whether the risk was worth taking. For some the choice might be easy, but for others it would be difficult, requiring time to think, take advice and so on. The 'normal' approach to causation would leave the patient who found the decision difficult without a remedy. Those who could not honestly say that they would not have had the operation 'once and for all' had they been warned would be discriminated against. The test of causation was satisfied, therefore, on policy grounds and justice required that the claimant be given the remedy she claimed. It is noteworthy that the claimant in this case had, unlike the claimant in *Sidaway* (10.4.3.4), actually enquired of the defendant as to the inherent risks of the operation. In *Sidaway*, Lord Templeman and Lord Bridge expressed the opinion that the defendant in that case would have been under a more onerous duty to inform the claimant had she made specific enquiries about the risks involved in her operation. *Chester* establishes that the duty to inform is of a subjective nature, assessed from the claimant's point of view.

However, in *Beary* v *Pall Mall Investments* (2005), *The Times,* 3 May, the Court of Appeal refused to extend *Chester* v *Afshar* to financial services mis-selling cases.

2.4.2.4 Intervening medical negligence

What we have to consider here is the issue of intervention: 'Does supervening human behaviour necessarily operate so to break the chain of causation?' In general terms it is likely that supervening negligence by a third party will be unforeseeable, and will break the causative link between the original wrong and the damage.

Problems are often encountered where later damage is inflicted by negligence: for example, where original injuries are aggravated or further (new) damage is caused by later medical negligence. In this situation the court must decide if the first cause was still operative at the time of the later negligence.

The House of Lords in *Hogan* v *Bentinck Collieries* [1949] 1 All ER 588, a case concerned with Workmen's Compensation Acts (now repealed) held, by a bare majority that medical negligence interrupted causation. Lord Normand said: '[However] an operation prudently advised and skilfully and carefully carried out should not be treated as a new cause, whatever its consequences may be.'

Lord Reid, however, dissented. In his Lordship's opinion later medical intervention should only interrupt causation if it exhibited a 'grave' lack of skill and care. This view may well represent the law today: see, for example, *Clerk and Lindsell on Torts*, 18th edn, 2000 (2–55). There is a general paucity of authority on the issue.

 EXERCISE 2.2

What guidance does the judgment of Beldam LJ in *R* v *Cheshire* [1991] 3 All ER 670 give on the issue of intervening medical negligence in the context of causation in the law of tort? He said:

Whatever may be the differences of policy between the approach of the civil and the criminal law to the question of causation there are we think reasons for a critical approach when importing the language of the one to the other. Since the apportionment of responsibility for damage has become commonplace in the civil law, judges have sought to distinguish the blameworthiness of conduct from its causative effect. Epithets suggestive of degrees of blameworthiness may be of little help in deciding how potent the conduct was in causing the result. A momentary lapse of concentration may lead to more serious consequences than a more glaring neglect of duty. In the criminal law the jury considering the factual question, did the accused's act cause the deceased's death, will we think derive little assistance from figures of speech more appropriate to conveying degrees of fault or blame in questions of apportionment. Unless authority suggests otherwise, we think such figures of speech are to be avoided in giving guidance to a jury on the question of causation. Whilst medical treatment unsuccessfully given to prevent the death of a victim with the care and skill of competent medical practitioner will not amount to an intervening cause, it does not follow that treatment which falls below that standard of care and skill will amount to such a cause. As Professors Hart and Honoré comment, treatment which falls short of the standard expected of the competent medical practitioner is unfortunately only too frequent in human experience for it to be considered abnormal in the sense of extraordinary. Acts or omissions of a doctor treating the victim for injuries he has received at the hands of an accused may conceivably be so extraordinary as to be capable of being regarded as acts independent of the conduct of the accused but it is most unlikely that they will be . . . It seems to us that [this case] demonstrates the difficulties in formulating and explaining a general concept of causation but what we think does emerge from this and the other cases is that when the victim of a criminal attack is treated for wounds or injuries by doctors or other medical staff attempting to repair the harm done, it will only be in the most extraordinary and unusual case that such treatment can be said to be so independent of the acts of the accused that it could be regarded in law as the cause of the victim's death to the exclusion of the accused's acts. Where the law requires proof of the relationship between an act and its consequences as an element of responsibility, a simple and sufficient explanation of the basis of such a relationship has proved notoriously elusive.

You will find that his Lordship emphasizes the different policies behind the criminal law and the law of tort. In the latter, it may be more likely that the chain of causation will be broken because the law is concerned primarily with liability to pay compensation, rather than with the question of deterrence.

The question to be answered in all these cases where the issue of intervening causes is raised is: 'What is within the scope of the risk created by the original defendant's negligence?'

2.4.2.5 Action taken by the claimant to minimize his/her loss

In general, it is unlikely that a claimant will break the chain of causation when performing their general legal obligation to **mitigate** the loss. *Spartan Steel & Alloys Ltd* v *Martin & Co. (Contractors) Ltd* [1973] 1 QB 27 supports this proposition but presumably the claimant's performance of this obligation will have to be reasonable in the circumstances. (*Spartan Steel* is discussed in 3.3.)

2.4.2.6 Reflex action

A 'natural' reflex action on the part of a third party or the claimant is probably something which a defendant will have to accept as 'likely to happen'. An early example from the cases is *Scott* v *Shepherd* [1773] 2 Wm Bl 892, in which the defendant lit a firework and threw it into a crowded market place where it fell on to the stall of X. X, acting instinctively to protect himself and his property, threw away the firework ('squib'), and it landed on Y's stall. Y reacted in similar fashion to X and the firework exploded in the face of the claimant, injuring him. The court found that there was an unbroken chain of causation between the defendant's act and the claimant's action.

In *Carmarthenshire County Council* v *Lewis* [1955] AC 549 (HL), a motorist swerved instinctively to avoid a young boy who dashed across the road after escaping from school as a result of the defendants' negligence. The motorist was injured, and received damages from the defendants.

The decision in *Lewis* was based on the special relationship that exists between a school authority and the children in its care. This relationship is something like that which exists between children and their parents, although a school authority will usually have a contractual, or statutory relationship with the child or his or her parents, as the case may be. Parents, teachers and school authorities, and social workers and social services authorities are expected to exercise the standard of care of the 'prudent parent' with regard to the behaviour of children in their care, and may be held personally, not vicariously, liable for that behaviour in appropriate circumstances.

This behaviour may, due to lack of appropriate control in the circumstances, be a causative factor in accidents affecting third parties, as in *Lewis*. It may also lead to liability on the part of the person in charge for theft and damage caused intentionally by the child. In *Vicar of Writtle* v *Essex County Council* (1979) LQR 656, a local authority, in its statutory capacity as social services authority, was found liable in negligence for theft and damage caused by a young person in its care. *Dorset Yacht* proceeds on similar lines. Note, also, *Jauffur* v *Akhbar* (6.5.1).

The 'person in charge' may also be liable where the child is injured, due to lack of adequate supervision. In *Barnes* v *Hampshire County Council* [1969] 3 All ER 746, a teacher, for whom the local education authority was vicariously liable, negligently allowed a young child to wander off into a nearby busy road, after classes had finished; as a result the child was injured.

The decision in *Kearn-Price* v *Kent County Council* [2003] EWCA Civ 1539 (CA), illustrates the point that decisions can turn on fine points of timing when questions arise as to whether a pupil is under the control of the defendant at the time of an accident. The claimant, a pupil at the defendant's school, was struck and injured by a football in the school playground, five minutes before classes commenced. The football was a full-sized one and balls of this type had been banned in the school, but the ban had not been rigorously enforced. Nor were any teachers in the playground at the time of the incident. It was held that the defendant had a duty of care to all persons lawfully on the school premises, even outside school hours. There was a breach of this duty because the ban had not been properly enforced.

In *Bradford-Smart* v *West Sussex C.C.* [2002] EWCA Civ 7, it was held that a school had a duty to prevent bullying on school premises, but not elsewhere. Garland J said that it would not be fair, just, and reasonable to extend the duty to situations outside school.

In English law, however, the issue of parental liability is a moot point. It is thought that the courts would, in general, be reluctant to find liability on the part of a parent in negligence for injury caused to a child through lack of adequate supervision, on the policy ground that such litigation would be harmful to the family relationship.

There are, nevertheless, some circumstances in which the law may allow claims; typically, these are situations in which there exists insurance cover. In *Parnell* v *Duguid* (1997), *The Guardian*, 22 July, a 13-year-old boy sued his mother for acute burns he suffered as a baby. He was burned after playing with matches when his mother, the defendant, left him in her car while shopping. Kay J approved a settlement of damages with the mother's insurers, but, while breach of duty was not admitted, it appears that the existence of a duty of care was not contested.

Occupiers' liability (6.5) is another area of liability in which insurance plays a very active role, and actions by children against their parents as occupiers of premises are unlikely to conflict with any policy concerning family relationships. Settlements with insurers are, in general, more likely than litigation.

At this point, you should look back to **Chapter 1** and the discussion on 'duty of care' and 'breach of duty' contained therein.

2.5 **Remoteness**

There are two main tests of remoteness which are applied in tort, namely direct consequences and reasonably foreseeable consequences.

 EXERCISE 2.3

Write down what you think each of these terms means and explain the essential difference between them.

2.5.1 Directness

In *Re Polemis* [1921] 3 KB 560 (CA), stevedores, who were servants of the defendant, negligently let fall a plank into a ship's hold containing petrol in metal containers. The impact of the plank as it hit the floor of the hold caused a spark, and petrol vapour was ignited. The ship was destroyed. Arbitrators found that the spark could not have been reasonably foreseen, though some damage was foreseeable from the impact.

The defendant was found liable because the claimant's loss was a direct, though not reasonably foreseeable, result. Unfortunately 'directness' was not defined, and there is still doubt as to whether 'direct' damage is confined to damage suffered by claimants which is foreseeable in a general sense, or to damage to the particular interest of the claimant which was likely to be affected.

Provided some damage is foreseeable, liability lies for all the natural and direct consequences flowing from the breach of duty. The decision is based on a broad approach to the definition of 'kind' of damage.

2.5.1.1 Reasonable foreseeability

In *The Wagon Mound (No. 1)* [1961] AC 388, the defendant carelessly discharged oil from a ship in Sydney Harbour, and the oil floated on the surface of the water towards the claimant's wharf. The claimant's servants, who were welding on the wharf, continued their work after being advised (non-negligently) that it was safe to do so. Sparks from the welding equipment first of all ignited cotton waste mixed up in the oil; then the oil itself caught fire. The claimant sued for destruction of the wharf by fire.

The defendant was found not liable in negligence, because it was not reasonably foreseeable that the oil might ignite on water in these circumstances. Damage by fouling was foreseeable; damage by fire (the case here) was not foreseeable. This approach was felt to be fairer to defendants, on the argument that the *Re Polemis* test was insufficiently precise and likely to lead to an unfair burden being placed on tortfeasors. Furthermore, it had the effect of ensuring that foreseeability governed all three stages of negligence.

The Privy Council said that in the tort of negligence *Re Polemis* was no longer good law, and liability would lie only for foreseeable damage of the kind or type in fact suffered by the claimant.

? **QUESTION** 2.8

Has the ruling in *The Wagon Mound* resulted in a big change in the law? You will recall that decisions of the Privy Council are, strictly speaking, of persuasive authority only in English law.

There will be practical significance in 'kind' or 'type' only if precision is required in their interpretation. The difference between *Polemis* and *Wagon Mound* must turn on how the two cases define 'kind of damage'. Some personal injury cases decided since 1961 suggest that the courts have not departed significantly from *Polemis*: a broad interpretation is given to 'kind' or 'type'.

In *Bradford* v *Robinson Rentals Ltd* [1967] 1 All ER 267, the claimant, an employee of the defendant, was sent on a 500-mile journey in a van with no heater in extremely cold weather, despite his protests. The defendant argued that damage by way of pneumonia or chilblains was foreseeable; but not the claimant's actual injury, which was frostbite. It was held that the claimant's injury was of a foreseeable type (injury from cold), so he succeeded.

A more precise approach was taken in *Tremain* v *Pike* [1969] 3 All ER 1303. The claimant, an employee of the defendant, caught leptospirosis (Weil's disease) through coming into contact with the urine of infected rats on the defendant's farm. It was alleged that the farm was overrun by the rodents because of the defendant's negligence.

Payne J said: 'This, in my view, was entirely different in kind from the effect of a rat bite or food poisoning by the consumption of food or drink contaminated by rats.' He went on to find that the claimant's damage was too remote. His Lordship evidently gave a strict interpretation to the words 'kind' or 'type'.

Although the decision in *Tremain* probably accords more with the letter of the law in *Wagon Mound*, in practice the approach taken by the judge in *Robinson* more accurately reflects the attitude of the courts to 'kind' or 'type'. *Tremain* is probably out of line with general authority. With regard to property damage (including pure economic loss) the position is less clear. According to Markesinis and Deakin (p. 189): '. . . the test of remoteness for property damage . . . is more strict . . . The precise limits to recovery can probably only be established on a case-by-case basis.'

Tremain might be decided differently today. In *Campbell* v *Percy Bilton* (1988), *The Guardian*, 17 February, it was held that where an employee of the defendants contracted Weil's disease through coming into contact with water infected by rats' urine (he was employed on a building site where he came into contact with pools of infected water in crevices in steel girders, etc.), he was entitled to damages in view of the incidence of the disease (it was greater than in 1969) and because of the available knowledge of this hazard in that particular working environment.

The court will assess the risk involved in each case. A broad view of fire risk was taken by Woolf J in *Salmon* v *Seafarer Restaurants Ltd* [1983] 3 All ER 729; and Lord Bridge in *Ogwo* v *Taylor* [1988] AC 431: '. . . [the claimant fireman] has no time to reflect on the precise nature and extent of the risks he is running'.

In *Crossley* v *Rawlinson* [1981] 3 All ER 674, it was found that an injury to a would-be rescuer was not foreseeable because the injury was suffered on the way to the dangerous state of affairs. In the court's opinion the claimant's injury had come about in an unforeseeable way.

The decisions on *Wagon Mound* seem to raise the question of whether quantum or amount of risk is relevant at the remoteness stage, as opposed to the duty stage, where it clearly is relevant; at the remoteness stage of the argument only foreseeability of consequences (not of risk) needs to be established. If it is relevant, and the cases suggest a positive answer, it might be claimed that the *Wagon Mound* test is one of risk or hazard rather than precise foreseeability of damage, and therefore more appropriate to the duty stage. However, since foreseeability is now relevant at each of the three stages of inquiry in negligence, perhaps the issue is only of academic significance.

2.5.1.2 The way in which the damage occurs

According to *Hughes* v *Lord Advocate* [1963] 1 All ER 705, the whole complex of events leading to the injury (which must itself be of a foreseeable 'type' or 'kind') does not need to satisfy the foreseeability test.

Post Office engineers left a hole in the road covered by a tent and marked by oil lamps. The claimant, a boy of 8, was badly burned when he entered the tent and dropped an oil lamp into the hole, which contained explosive gas. It was held that injury by burning (touching a hot lamp) was foreseeable, and injury by explosion was 'by burning'. Lord Guest said: '. . . it is sufficient if the accident which occurred is of a type which should have been foreseeable'. According to Lord Reid the 'precise concatenation of circumstances' need not be foreseeable.

This decision can be compared with the following:

Doughty v Turner Manufacturing Co. [1964] 1 All ER 98

The defendant's servant knocked a loose asbestos-cement cover into a cauldron of sodium cyanide which was at a temperature of 800°C. The claimant moved closer to see inside it, since there had been no reaction. A few minutes later there was an explosion and he was injured. In the event, he was not awarded damages.

It was held that only a splash was foreseeable: '. . . it would be quite unrealistic to describe this accident as a variant of the perils from splashing' (per Pearce LJ). An extract from the judgment of Diplock LJ can be found in *Cases and Materials* (2.3.1.2).

Doughty does not follow the *Hughes* line of reasoning: it appears to proceed on the same interpretation of *Wagon Mound* as *Tremain*. *Doughty* was decided at a time when asbestos was thought to be safe and unlikely to behave in this fashion and the decision might be different today. Consider, in this context, *Jolley* v *London Borough of Sutton*, discussed at 6.5.5.3.

Jebson v *Ministry of Defence* [2000] 1 WLR 2055 (CA) follows the reasoning in *Jolley*. The claimant, a soldier, was returning to camp with several colleagues in an army truck after 'a night out'. They were all somewhat the worse for drinking alcohol. He fell off the truck and into the road, after climbing on to the roof of the truck from the tailgate. At first instance it was held that the defendant was in breach of its duty to supervise the (drunken) soldiers; but the claimant's injury was too remote because it was not reasonably foreseeable that a soldier would try to climb on to the roof of the truck.

The Court of Appeal reversed this decision and held that the defendant ought to have foreseen that the soldiers would be returning in a drunken state and would be in 'high spirits' (*sic*). Thus, if the defendant provided transport for the 'night out', it should have taken reasonable care to see that the injury was not sustained through rowdy behaviour during the journey. Such behaviour, leading to personal injury, was reasonably foreseeable and the claimant's injury fell within the scope of the defendant's duty of care. The damage was not too remote, though it was found that the claimant's damages should be reduced by 75% for his contributory negligence.

2.5.1.3 Extent of harm

According to *Vacwell Engineering* v *BDH Chemicals* [1971] 1 QB 88, foreseeability as to extent of damage is not necessary. In this case it was held that an explosion was foreseeable in the circumstances and that that was sufficient for liability: it was irrelevant that the explosion that in fact occurred was unforeseeably large.

EXERCISE 2.4

Outline the case for and against the notion of reasonable foreseeability (as opposed to directness) in relation to remoteness of damage.

Reasonable foreseeability is a more flexible concept than that of directness, and helps the courts to arrive more easily at policy decisions. It is also said to achieve fairer results for defendants, where their liability depends on 'fault'. While this may be a desirable state of affairs in some respects, it is also the case that foreseeability entails a large measure of unpredictability. Its unpredictability in relation to the duty of care issue has been noted in 2.3. The role of the concept in connection with remoteness is, however, much more in the nature of a touchstone of liability than is the case with duty and is of much greater significance in the present context, because it determines more precisely the extent of the defendant's liability for what is by now his or her established negligence.

2.5.1.4 Relative nature of foreseeability

You may find the decision in *The Heron II* [1969] 1 AC 350 of interest in this context; indeed, if you have studied the law of contract you should remember the case as an important authority in that subject.

The House of Lords, in emphasizing the difference between the rules of remoteness in contract and in tort, gave to the word foreseeable a meaning different from probable or likely. Lord Reid said that the rule in tort imposes a much wider liability than that in contract:

> the defendant will be liable for any type [or kind] of damage which is reasonably foreseeable as liable to happen even in the most unusual case, unless the risk is so small that a reasonable man would in the whole circumstances feel justified in neglecting it.

'Foreseeability is a **relative**, not an **absolute** concept' [*emphasis added*]: *Winfield* p. 161.

 EXERCISE 2.5

Consider the extract from the speech of Lord Reid in *Wagon Mound (No. 2)* [1966] 2 All ER 709 at *Cases and Materials* (2.3.1.4). Write down a summary of its significance in relation to remoteness of damage.

Lord Reid considers that a risk is foreseeable to the 'reasonable man' even in what might seem to be 'improbable' cases, that it can be a 'real' risk for present purposes even though it is only a small risk. He also said the tort of nuisance, as well as the tort of negligence, was governed by the *Wagon Mound* test of remoteness. The House of Lords in *Cambridge Water Co.* v *Eastern Counties Leather plc* [1994] 1 All ER 53, confirmed Lord Reid's finding on nuisance (see 11.4.2.2). In essence, he reiterated this view on risk in *The Heron II* (above), though that case does not deal with the torts of negligence and nuisance: the point of debate concerned remoteness of damage in contract and tort generally.

Wagon Mound (No. 2) arose from the same facts as *Wagon Mound (No. 1)*, but the (successful) claimant was the owner of a ship damaged in the fire and different expert evidence on the causes of the fire was accepted.

2.5.1.5 The jurisdiction of reasonable foreseeability as a test of remoteness of damage

You should consider whether 'foreseeability' is restricted to the law of negligence as a governing factor in 'remoteness'. Its jurisdiction appears to extend beyond the tort of negligence.

The *Wagon Mound (No. 2)* (above) is authority for the proposition that the tort of nuisance is subject to the same test of remoteness as negligence, and the House of Lords has held in *Cambridge Water Co.* v *Eastern Counties Leather plc* [1994] 1 All ER 53 that this is also the case for liability arising under the rule in *Rylands* v *Fletcher*, which imposes strict liability at common law. (Nuisance and *Rylands* v *Fletcher* are covered in **Chapter 11**.)

> There now seems every likelihood that foreseeability will be held to be the test of remoteness in some other torts as well, whether or not it [foreseeability] is the test of liability'. (*Winfield* pp. 158–9).

It may not apply to deceit (*Winfield*, p. 289) or any tort where liability turns on proof of intention or recklessness; the action for breach of statutory duty may also be exempt from the influence of foreseeability. The position with the tort of defamation is not abundantly clear.

2.6 Sensitive claimants

> **?** **QUESTION** 2.9
>
> Do some claimants get special treatment? Can you think of a sensitive claimant?

2.6.1 Personal injury

Here we consider the effect of the so-called 'egg-shell skull' rule, that is the defendant must 'take his victim as he finds him'. According to this rule, once reasonably foreseeable damage occurs (of the right 'kind' or 'type') the defendant is liable for the full extent of that damage, even where that extent would not normally be expected.

In *Smith* v *Leech Brain* [1962] 2 QB 405, for example, approved in *Wagon Mound (No. 1)*, the claimant was splashed and slightly burned on the lip by molten metal, due to the defendant's negligence. Through the claimant's predisposition to cancer, the burn became malignant and the claimant died. The defendant was found fully liable, although a 'normal' person would not have suffered the cancer and death in those circumstances.

Again, in *Robinson* v *The Post Office* [1974] 2 All ER 737, the defendants negligently lacerated the claimant's leg, and a doctor was negligent in carrying out the test dose procedure for allergy reaction to anti-tetanus serum. As a result of the doctor giving the claimant an anti-tetanus injection, the claimant contracted inflammation of the brain, because he was allergic to the serum. The defendants were found wholly and solely liable for the claimant's damage, including the complications suffered as a result of the allergic reaction. It was shown that the claimant would have suffered the same harm whether or not the doctor had been negligent, and the defendants had to 'take their victim as they found him', with his allergy.

Consider the following observation of Eveleigh J in *Wieland* v *Cyril Lord Carpets* (see 2.4.2):

> I do not regard the *Wagon Mound* as dealing with the extent of the original injury or the degree to which it has affected the [claimant]. Still less do I regard it as requiring foreseeability of the manner in which that original injury has caused harm to the [claimant]. Indeed the precise mechanics of the way in which the negligent act results in the original injury do not have to be foreseen.

His Lordship is here affirming the 'egg-shell skull' rule and the validity of *Hughes* (see 2.5.1.2).

2.6.2 **Property damage**

In relation to property, to paraphrase Scrutton LJ in *The Arpad* [1934] P 189, if one injures a horse which happens to be the Derby winner one cannot claim that one thought it to be only 'an old nag'. However, *Winfield* (p. 164) says: [It is more uncertain, however] where the loss claimed is not 'intrinsic' [but is due to the fact that the claimant cannot, as a result of the damage,] **earn profits** [from the property] (*emphasis added*). There is authority going both ways, that is, that foreseeability is relevant and that it is not relevant in such circumstances.

In *Parsons* v *Uttley Ingham* [1978] QB 791 (CA), a contract case involving injury to pigs, and in which Lord Denning regarded the test of remoteness in contract as being the same as in tort, it was said that as long as some kind of illness/injury (to the pigs) was foreseeable it did not matter that it eventually took the form of an unforeseeably rare kind of illness/injury.

There is much disagreement with Lord Denning's view on remoteness in contract and tort. We can see that it does not accord with Lord Reid's view in *The Heron II* (see 2.5.1.4).

2.6.3 **Compensation**

In assessing monetary damages (that is, in awarding compensation), however, the court will take into account the fact that an 'egg-shell skull' victim is at greater risk from the ordinary vicissitudes of life than a 'normal' person, and might well award him or her less than would be given to a 'normal' claimant.

In calculating the amount of monetary compensation to which a claimant is entitled, the claimant's 'worth' or 'value' (the same is true of his or her property) cannot be subject to 'reasonable foreseeability' reasoning. Thus, it is a defendant's bad luck if he or she happens to injure the chairperson of a privatized utility (invariably a high-earner) rather than a vagrant.

2.6.4 **Impecuniosity**

In *The Liesbosch* [1933] AC 449 (see also 13.4.3.2), the owner of a dredger sunk by the defendant's negligence could not afford to buy a replacement, but had to hire one at extra expense. This extra expense was disallowed. It was not seen as a case of taking the claimant as he was (i.e. poor), but that the poverty was an extraneous and irrelevant coincidence. *The Liesbosch* has been distinguished by the Court of Appeal where extra cost was incurred in delaying repairs to a damaged car pending the approval of the claimant's insurer (in *Martindale* v *Duncan* [1973]

1 WLR 574) and to a damaged building where the delay was reasonable on commercial grounds (in *Dodd Properties (Kent) Ltd* v *Canterbury City Council* [1980] 1 All ER 928). However, in *The Borag* [1981] 1 WLR 274 (CA), the claimants incurred interest charges on overdrafts to provide a guarantee to secure the release of their ship which had been wrongfully arrested. The loss was held to be too remote.

It was also distinguished in *Perry* v *Sidney Phillips* [1982] 3 All ER 705 (CA). The claimant bought a defective house; and was also made redundant in his employment. He had put in an offer for the house subject to contract and satisfactory surveyor's report. The defendant surveyors had reported that the house was in a satisfactory state, but on the claimant moving in, various serious defects were discovered. The claimant obtained another surveyor's report, and estimates from builders for remedial work. He was involved in much expense and trouble.

Had the claimant done anything to mitigate his loss? Apparently he had not carried out any major repair work for several reasons: (i) he could not afford the expense (a second mortgage was not available); (ii) repairs might hide the serious defects; (iii) the intransigence of the defendants. He had, however, carried out a few small repairs himself and had obtained advice about a damp course and the eradication of woodworm, etc.

The defendants were held liable for the negligent performance of their contract to survey the house. Damages for inconvenience and vexation were included, though cost of repairs over and above the fall in value of the house (the claimant did not intend to effect the repairs) were not. In such cases a claimant is entitled, basically, to the difference between market value and what was paid for the house.

It was found that *The Liesbosch* did not apply to mitigation. In relation to mitigating his loss, the claimant had acted reasonably in the circumstances.

2.7 Intention/recklessness

Consequences (as opposed to acts) which the defendant intends or about which he is reckless may involve liability for more extensive consequences. In such cases it may be that the court will presume that the defendant intended the 'natural and probable consequences' of his behaviour. You may care to consider this point further when you encounter, for example, the ruling in *Wilkinson* v *Downton* [1897] 2 QB 57 (11.7.2.2).

■ SUMMARY

- 'Causation' and 'remoteness' are issues which may be of crucial importance in **any** context within which tortious liability is in question. In this book, however, they are dealt with immediately after the treatment of 'Negligence' because most difficulties are in practice encountered in this form of liability.

- In conventional, formal, terms 'causation' and 'remoteness' represent different stages in the process of linking the defendant's breach of duty with the claimant's damage.

- 'Causation' is all about the 'factual' link, that is there must be an unbroken chain of causation between breach and damage.

- Once that issue is settled, there remains the question about consequences in the 'legal' sense, i.e. 'is the defendant liable for all or only some or for none of the results of his or her tort?'

- The 'but for' test provides an answer to the problem of 'causation in fact' in straightforward cases, but in more complex situations the court must feel its way to a solution as best it can. It is said that the approach of the 'ordinary' person, possessing the virtue of 'common sense' is the one adopted by the courts.

- In general terms 'foreseeability' is the ruling factor in causation cases; this is clear from the authorities on *novus actus interveniens* and *nova causa interveniens*.

- The claimant must also be prepared to justify his or her case on the issue of remoteness of damage or 'legal' consequences, because a defendant will not necessarily be liable for all the consequences that flow from his or her tort.

- Here the *Wagon Mound* test applies, and a defendant will only be liable where the claimant has actually suffered damage of the 'kind' or 'type' which was reasonably foreseeable in the circumstances. The *Wagon Mound* test replaced the *Re Polemis* 'direct consequences' test, though that approach is probably still valid in some contexts, such as deceit.

- There is some controversy, at least in academic circles, concerning the difference between the *Polemis* and *Wagon Mound* tests. In practice, there seems little to choose between them bearing in mind the decisions in *Hughes*, the 'egg-shell skull' cases, and personal injury cases generally. There is room for debate as to whether the rather benign approach taken in personal injury cases to the exact requirements of 'kind' or 'type' applies to property damage.

- *The Liesbosch* says the 'egg-shell skull' rule does not apply to impecunious claimants but the rule has been qualified in more recent cases such as *Mattocks v Mann* [1993] RTR 13.

- In overall terms, policy plays a crucial role in all aspects of 'causation' and 'remoteness'.

■ FURTHER READING

Elliot, C. and Quinn, F., *Tort Law*, 5th edn, London: Longman, 2005, pp. 92–109.

Giliker, P. and Beckwith, S., *Tort*, 2nd edn, London: Sweet & Maxwell, 2005, Chapter 4.

Harlow, C., 'Understanding Tort Law', 3rd edn, London: Sweet & Maxwell, 2005, Chapter 4.

Harris, D., Campbell, D., and Halson, R., *Remedies in Contract and Tort*, 2nd edn, London: Butterworths, 2002, Chapters 19 and 20.

Hart H.L.A. and Honoré A.M., *Causation and the Law*, 2nd edn, Oxford, Clarendon Press, 1985.

Harvey, B. and Marston, J., *Cases and Commentary on Tort*, 4th edn, London: Longman, 2000, Chapter 5.

Hepple, Howarth, and Matthews, *Tort: Cases and Materials*, 5th edn, London: Butterworths, 2000, Chapter 6.

Jones, M., *Textbook on Torts*, 8th edn, Oxford: Oxford University Press, 2002, Chapter 4.

Kidner, R., *Casebook on Torts*, 9th edn, Oxford: Oxford University Press, 2006, Chapter 6.

Lunney, M., 'What Price a Chance?' (1995) 15 *Legal Studies* 1.

Lunney, M. and Oliphant, K., *Tort Law Cases and Materials*, 2nd edn, Oxford: Oxford University Press, 2003, Chapter 5.

Markesinis, B.S. and Deakin, S.F., *Tort Law*, 5th edn, Oxford: Oxford University Press, 2003, pp. 185–244.

McBride, N.J. and Bagshaw, R., *Tort Law*, 2nd edn, London: Longman, 2005, Chapter 30.

Morgan, J., 'Lost Causes in the House of Lords . . .' [*Fairchild*] (2003) 66 *MLR* 277.

Murphy, J., *Street on Torts*, 11th edn, London: Butterworths, 2003, Chapter 14.

Reece, H., 'Losses of Chances in the Law', (1996) 59 *MLR* 188.

Salmond and Heuston, *Law of Torts*, 21st edn, London: Sweet & Maxwell, 1996, pp. 521–40.

Stanton, K.M., *The Modern Law of Tort*, London: Sweet & Maxwell, 1994, Chapter 4.

Stapleton, J. *Unpacking Causation* in Cane, P. and Gardner, F. (eds) *Relating to Responsibility*, Oxford: Hart Publishing, 2001.

Weir, T., *A Casebook on Tort*, 10th edn, London: Sweet & Maxwell, 2004, Chapter 4.

Winfield and Jolowicz on Tort, 16th edn, London: Sweet & Maxwell, 2002, Chapter 6.

 CHAPTER 2 ASSESSMENT EXERCISE

David leaves an old paraffin lamp burning in his garden shed, where there is a strong draught. As a result fire starts, and spreads rapidly. This fire combines with another fire, the source of which is unknown, and the fire produced by this combination threatens Penny's house, which is located a quarter of a mile away. Penny is holding a garden party at the time, and a general panic ensues. Richard, the butler, drops a tray containing rare antique glasses, one of which cuts the arm of Ben, a haemophiliac, who bleeds to death before hospital treatment can be obtained. Penny's house is destroyed in the conflagration.

Advise David, on his liability in tort, if any.

See *Cases and Materials* (2.5) for a specimen answer.

3 | Negligence III: liability for pure economic loss/ negligent misstatements and services

3.1 OBJECTIVES

By the end of this chapter you should be able to:

1 State the law concerning claims for 'pure' economic loss in the tort of negligence

2 Explain and account for the evolution of the law regarding liability for negligent 'misstatements' and its apparent separation from the position concerning liability for negligent 'acts'

3 Explain and account for the decisions in *Hedley Byrne* v *Heller* and *Caparo* v *Dickman* and the special relationship requirement established in the former case, as interpreted in the later authority

4 Apply the law relating to third party claims in cases of negligent misstatement and explain the significance of the decisions in *Henderson* v *Merrett, White* v *Jones,* and *Spring* v *Guardian Assurance plc* regarding the relationship between contract and tort

3.2 Introduction

Historically, claims for 'pure' economic loss have generally been unsuccessful in the tort of negligence. The law of negligence in particular and the law of tort in general are mostly concerned with physical interference or loss and economic loss consequential upon that physical damage. However, 'pure' economic loss is recoverable in some torts, for example, deceit, conspiracy, and interference with contractual relations.

At common law the traditional position is that where negligence leads to so-called 'pure' economic loss, that is, financial loss which is not the direct result of physical loss, that loss may well not be recoverable. Consequential loss, that is, financial loss which is the direct result of physical damage (whether to person or property) is generally recoverable.

> **?** | **QUESTION** 3.1
>
> Is it the case that there exists a general rule, subject perhaps to exceptions, that damages for 'pure' economic loss cannot be recovered in the tort of negligence?

The answer to this question is as tentative as the issue is confusing!

In traditional terms the answer seems to be 'yes'. 'As a general rule pure economic loss is irrecoverable in the tort of negligence': Stanton (p. 332).

On this view of the law, it seems that to succeed in a claim for pure economic loss a claimant must bring his or her case within some recognized exception to the general rule, such as the liability imposed in *Hedley Byrne* (below). The authorities discussed in 3.2 certainly give considerable support to this view.

It is submitted that the true answer is 'no'. As Lord Oliver said in *Murphy* v *Brentwood District Council* [1990] 2 All ER 908 (a case which will be discussed in 6.3.2):

> It does not, of course, at all follow as a matter of necessity from the mere fact that the only damage suffered by a claimant in an action for the tort of negligence is pecuniary or 'economic' that his claim is bound to fail. It is true that, in an uninterrupted line of cases since 1875, it has consistently been held that a third party cannot successfully sue in negligence for the interference with his economic expectations of advantage resulting from injury to the person or property of another person with whom he has or is likely to have a contractual relationship (see *Cattle* v *Stockton Waterworks Co.* (1875) LR 10 QB, *SA de Rémorquage à Hélice* v *Bennetts* [1911] 1 KB 243). That principle was applied more recently by Widgery J in *Weller & Co.* v *Foot and Mouth Disease Research Institute* [1966] 1 QB 569 (see 3.3 for further discussion) and received its most recent reiteration in the decision of this House in *Leigh and Sillivan Ltd* v *Aliakmon Shipping Co. Ltd* [1986] AC 786. But it is far from clear from these decisions that the reason for the claimant's failure was simply that the only loss sustained was 'economic'. Rather they seem to have been based either on the remoteness of the damage as a matter of direct causation or, more probably, on the 'floodgates' argument of the impossibility of containing liability within any acceptable bounds if the law were to permit such claims to succeed. The decision of this House in *Morrison Steamship Co. Ltd* v *Greystoke Castle* [1947] AC 265 demonstrates that the mere fact that the primary damage suffered by a claimant is pecuniary is no necessary bar to an action in negligence given the proper circumstances (in that case, what was said to be the 'joint venture' interest of shipowners and the owners of cargo carried on board) and if the matter remained in doubt that doubt was conclusively resolved by the decision of this House in *Hedley Byrne & Co. Ltd* v *Heller & Partners Ltd* [1963] 2 All ER 575 where Lord Devlin convincingly demonstrated the illogicality of a distinction between financial loss caused directly and financial loss resulting from physical injury to personal property.
>
> The critical question, as was pointed out in the analysis of Brennan J in his judgment in *Sutherland Shire Council* v *Heyman* (1985) 60 ALR 1 is not the nature of the damage in itself, whether physical or pecuniary, but whether the scope of the duty of care in the circumstances of the case is such as to embrace damage of the kind which the claimant claims to have sustained (see *Caparo Industries plc* v *Dickman* [1990] 1 All ER 568).

In *Murphy*, Lord Keith expressed the contrary view to that of Lord Oliver, that is, recovery for pure economic loss is possible only if the claimant falls within some recognized exception (such as liability for negligent misstatement, discussed below) to the general rule, which forbids recovery. It is submitted that there is, in fact, little difference in substance between the views expressed by Stanton and Lord Keith on the one hand, and Lord Oliver on the other: once any 'exception' to the 'general rule' is recognized, the reality is that 'pure' financial loss is recoverable, albeit on a limited scale.

In relation to statements, the position is different. The two following cases illustrate two of the issues—what relationship is needed, and is the statement a response to a specific request for guidance.

In *Reid* v *Rush and Tomkins* [1989] 2 All ER 228 (CA), it was held that an employer owes no duty of care in tort to provide to his employee personal accident insurance covering special risks to the employee whilst he is working abroad; nor is there any duty to advise the employee to obtain for himself such insurance cover where the contract of employment contains no term to that effect. The common law could not devise such a duty which the legislature had not thought fit to impose and it could not be just or reasonable for the court to impose it. A court could not find a duty of care in negligence, although loss to the claimant was foreseeable, in a factual situation in which the existence of such a duty had repeatedly been held not to exist (see *The Aliakmon: Leigh & Sillavan Ltd* v *Aliakmon Shipping Co. Ltd* [1986] AC 786). An employer's duty, in the absence of some contractual term, was limited to the protection of the employee against physical harm or disease. This case is also relevant in **Chapter 5**.

In *Lennon* v *Commissioner of Police of the Metropolis* (2004), *The Times,* 25 February (CA), on the other hand, the claimant, a police officer, sought advice from a police personnel executive about his transfer to a job with another police force. As a result of relying on this advice the claimant lost certain financial entitlements in his new job. It was found that the executive officer had expressly assumed responsibility in a particular transaction, that is, the claimant's transfer, for giving him advice regarding a particular type of loss, that is the loss of his housing allowance, which he had expressly raised with her. The executive officer was not a professional person or a professional adviser, but she was in a managerial position and had access to the relevant technical knowledge. She had led the claimant to believe that he could leave it to her and rely on her to be responsible for handling the arrangements. She did not tell him that the matter was outside the area of her responsibility and that he should seek other advice. Mummery LJ, delivering the judgment of the court, said that though there was no contract between the police commissioner and the claimant, the relationship between them was analogous to a contractual one; and it was 'fair, just, and reasonable' to impose on the police commissioner a general duty of care to give advice to the claimant to protect him from economic loss. It should be noted that the commissioner was found vicariously liable here, for the negligence of the executive officer.

This chapter traces the development of the law regarding 'pure' economic loss in traditional terms, according to the vector of production; that is to say on the basis of whether the financial loss was caused by a negligent act or a negligent misstatement. Today, as we shall see later, the distinction between 'acts' and 'words' is of much less importance than it used to be; via an 'extended' *Hedley Byrne* principle the distinction has a reduced status in terms of legal significance.

3.3 Acts: the principle

In *Cattle* v *Stockton Waterworks* (1875) LR 10 QB 453, the claimant had contracted with a landowner to build a tunnel under his land and was unable to recover extra expenses incurred in finishing the work after the defendant had negligently flooded the land. The decision went against the claimant because his only loss was connected to his liability under the contract to finish the job on time. No tangible property of his had been damaged; nor had he suffered any personal injury. Any financial loss flowing from either kind of damage would have been recoverable.

This decision has been confirmed in a long line of later decisions, for example *SA de Rémorquage à Hélice* v *Bennetts* [1911] 1 KB 243, in which a tug company was unable to recover the towing fee lost when the defendant sank its tow; and *Weller* v *Foot and Mouth Disease Research Institute* [1966] 1 QB 569, where auctioneers failed to recover profits from cattle auctions cancelled owing to an outbreak of foot and mouth disease amongst cattle in the surrounding area caused by the defendant's negligence.

In *British Celanese* v *Hunt* [1969] 2 All ER 1252, the defendant negligently allowed metal foil strips stored on his land to blow on to a power line, cutting the supply to the claimant's factory. Machines were damaged and economic loss resulted. The claimant was awarded full damages because the economic loss flowed from tangible damage to property, in other words both the physical damage to the machines caused by molten metals solidifying therein, and the resultant economic loss, were recoverable. A similar decision was arrived at in *SCM* v *Whittall* [1971] 1 QB 337, where the defendant cut an underground cable supplying electricity to the claimant's factory.

 EXERCISE 3.1

Consider *Spartan Steel & Alloys Ltd* v *Martin & Co. (Contractors) Ltd* [1973] 1 QB 27. Where should the line be drawn for recovery?

The defendant negligently drove a power shovel through the cable supplying electricity to the claimant's factory, causing a fourteen-hour power cut. The claimant sought damages under three heads: (a) damages for the reduced value of metal which had to be removed from a furnace before it solidified and damaged machinery; (b) the profit which would have been made from that 'melt' had it been completed; (c) the profit from four other 'melts' which would have been made but for the long power cut.

The Court of Appeal, by a majority, held that only the first two heads were recoverable: the third was pure economic loss not flowing from the claimant's own physical loss. Lord Denning said this decision was dictated by policy: an admittedly arbitrary line had to be drawn somewhere, otherwise liability would rocket out of control. He pointed out that the claimant could insure against such a risk, so spreading the cost throughout the community. It would be an unfair burden to place liability on 'one pair of shoulders' in such circumstances. Edmund Davies LJ, dissenting, admitting that his view did not accord with tradition, said that he would have allowed the third head as well, since it was a foreseeable and direct consequence of the defendant's negligent act. (Lord Roskill in *Junior Books* (below) gave some support to this view.)

In *Londonwaste* v *AMEC Civil Engineering* (1997) 83 BLR 136, the claimant produced electricity from the burning of waste materials and lost profits because its operations had to be shut down when the defendants cut through an electricity mains cable while repairing a nearby road. The claimant recovered for physical damage to the power station but, following *Spartan Steel*, they could not recover for loss of income from the sale of electricity. Neither were they allowed damages for the costs of disposing of the waste materials. It was held that these losses were not the direct result of the physical damage to the power station, even though they did flow from the defendant's negligence.

In *Aswan Engineering Establishment Co.* v *Lupdine Ltd* [1987] 1 All ER 135 (CA), the claimants purchased some waterproofing liquid, 'Lupguard', from the first defendants and this was to be sent to Kuwait. The 'Lupguard' was supplied in plastic pails manufactured by the second defendants, but these pails proved to be incapable of withstanding the heat in Kuwait and much of the Lupguard was lost. The first defendants went into liquidation and the claimants sued the second defendants in the tort of negligence.

The second defendants were found not liable in negligence to the claimants because the damage suffered (the loss of 'Lupguard') was not reasonably foreseeable in the circumstances. Otherwise, according to Lloyd LJ, a duty would be imposed on manufacturers involving liability 'not far short of that of an insurer'.

Lord Diplock in *Lambert* v *Lewis* [1981] 2 WLR 713, said:

> where the economic loss suffered by a distributor in the chain between the manufacturer and the ultimate consumer consists of a liability to pay damages to the ultimate consumer for physical injuries sustained by him, or consists of a liability to indemnify a distributor lower in the chain of distribution for his liability to the ultimate consumer for damages for physical injuries, such economic loss is not recoverable under the *Donoghue* v *Stevenson* principle from the manufacturer.

His Lordship was referring to the so-called 'narrow' rule in *Donoghue*, which imposes a duty of care on manufacturers to their ultimate consumers. This branch of negligence is dealt with under Product Liability in **Chapter 9**.

The other judges in the House of Lords held, however, that such a loss may be recoverable. This decision shows how difficult it is to predict in advance how the courts will classify claims for financial loss.

In *Walkin* v *South Manchester Health Authority* [1995] 4 All ER 132 (CA), the claimant gave birth to a healthy child after a failed sterilization operation. She elected to claim only for economic loss, as she did not claim within the three-year period allowed for personal injury claims. This was arguably allowable as the normal limitation period for economic loss cases is six years. It was held that this pleading was in *substance* a claim for personal injury; the breach of duty in negligence that gave rise to personal injury also resulted in economic loss. No amount of special pleading could alter the substance of the claim, and a limitation defence succeeded.

3.4 *Junior Books* v *Veitchi*

 EXERCISE 3.2

Read *Junior Books Ltd* v *Veitchi Co. Ltd* [1982] 3 All ER 201 (HL); what was the outcome?

This decision establishes the principle that it is no longer a sufficient answer to a claim in negligence that the loss is 'purely' economic in nature and unconnected with physical damage, though because of the very high degree of proximity between the parties it is difficult to say how much further than that the decision takes us.

The claimants were having a building erected by X and it was necessary to include a special floor for the purpose of taking certain machinery. X contracted with the defendants, who were specialists in the work, for the supply of this floor at the request of the claimants who had been advised to do this by their architect. In relation to the claimants the defendants were subcontractors.

After the floor was completed it was found to be defective, although no damage to person or property was even imminent let alone caused by this defect. In other words, there was a defect of quality alone, the typical situation found in contract. The claimant's loss consisted of the cost of repair or replacement.

The House of Lords decided, in preliminary proceedings (no ruling on actual liability was made) that the defendants probably did owe a duty of care in the tort of negligence to the claimants; certainly there was a case to argue and the matter was referred back to the court of origin (in Scotland) for resolution of the issue.

No action was available in contract against X under Scots law, and the claimants' architect had not been negligent.

3.4.1 Post-*Junior Books* developments

In terms of conventional wisdom this decision had enormous implications. Was not the claimant's claim one for contractual liability, though framed in tort? It is as though the claimants had claimed a breach of warranty by the defendants, a warranty of care and skill (in England, though not in Scotland, it is possible to give effect to such a warranty by way of a collateral contract; see *Shanklin Pier* v *Detel Products* [1951] 2 KB 854). Lord Brandon, dissenting, certainly thought so. He pointed out the difficulties inherent in assessing the facts relating to quality in tort: unlike contract, the law of tort does not have a body of established criteria for tackling this problem.

The majority reasoning was based on the very special circumstances of the case. It was obvious that the parties were extremely close in terms of foreseeability and proximity. The claimant was claiming on an individual basis, not even as a member of a closely defined class of potential claimants.

The general interpretation given to this decision in later cases is a restrictive one. No doubt this reaction will not surprise you, in view of the cautious approach taken to the general development of the tort of negligence. *Junior Books* has been interpreted as turning on the claimant's reliance on the skill of the defendants.

The House of Lords in *Leigh and Sillavan Ltd* v *Aliakmon Shipping Co. Ltd* [1986] 2 All ER 145, held that a shipowner owed no duty of care to a buyer of goods which, it was claimed, had been damaged due to faulty storage while they were in the defendant's care; at the relevant time the buyer had neither title to, nor possession of, the goods. It was pointed out that there was already a settled line of cases on the point, and that authority should not be undermined by arguments based merely on foreseeability and proximity.

Doubt was expressed on the importance of reliance in limiting liability for pure economic loss in cases where there had been no express misstatement by the defendant. (We will see later that there may be liability for pure economic loss where the claimant has relied on a misstatement made by the defendant.) Effectively, the court refused to give the claimant a remedy in tort where none existed in contract.

In *Tate and Lyle v GLC* [1983] 1 All ER 1159, *Junior Books* was equated to a case in which damage to property had actually occurred, though this does seem difficult to accept. In *Junior Books* the floor had not been damaged; its quality was defective.

More recently, in *Bailey v HSS Alarms Ltd* (2000), *The Times,* 20 June (CA), a burglar alarm had been installed at the claimant's premises by X, who had sub-contracted the monitoring to the defendant. As a result of the latter's negligence in being slow to inform the police after the claimant's premises had been burgled property was stolen. It was held that HSS owed a duty of care directly to the claimant (X was insolvent) and this duty covered property damage and pure economic loss. You should keep this decision in mind when reading about *Henderson v Merrett* at 3.5.8.

3.4.2 **Contractual relationships**

The existence of a contractual framework underlying the issue of liability has been put forward in some cases as the reason for not allowing an action in tort.

In *Candlewood Navigation Corporation Ltd v Mitsui OSK Lines Ltd* [1985] 2 All ER 935, the Privy Council held that a claimant with no proprietary or possessory rights to goods, but only a contractual claim over them, could not claim damages in tort for economic loss suffered when those goods were damaged by the defendant. The law of tort could not be used, it was said, to provide a remedy where none existed in contract. Lord Fraser (who was in the majority in *Junior Books*) said that though *Junior Books* 'may be regarded as having extended the scope of duty somewhat' it was 'not in point' here.

 EXERCISE 3.3

Read this extract from the judgment of Goff LJ in *Muirhead v Industrial Tank Specialities* [1985] 3 All ER 750 and explain his view of *Junior Books*.

The facts of *Junior Books* [construction of a special floor, later found to be defective, for the claimant by specialist sub-contractors appointed at the behest of the claimant's architects] showed 'the parties had deliberately structured their contractual relationship in order to achieve the result . . . no direct liability inter se'. He thought it 'safest' to regard *Junior Books* as authority for liability on the basis of 'a very close relationship between the parties' on its particular facts, and chose not to stress the element of reliance emphasized by the other judges.

The Court of Appeal distinguished the present case from *Junior Books*. In *Muirhead* the claimants wished to keep live lobsters for business purposes, and bought from the first defendants a storage tank and some water pumps, one of which, supplied to the first defendants by the second defendants, proved to be unreliable because of a defective motor. As a consequence the claimants suffered 'pure' financial loss because they could not store the lobsters. They sued, successfully, the first defendants in contract but they went bankrupt and the claimants then sued the second defendants in tort. This claim was dismissed by the Court of Appeal because the loss was of a purely financial nature and arose only under the contract between the defendants themselves. *Junior Books* was said to have turned on special facts, the very close proximity between the parties and reliance by the claimant on the defendant.

In *Greater Nottingham Co-operative Society Ltd* v *Cementation Piling and Foundations Ltd* [1989] QB 71 (CA), it was held that the Society's claim in the tort of negligence for foreseeable economic loss caused by the mode of performance of the defendant's contractual obligations could not be sustained, because there was actual privity of contract between the claimant and defendant. This contract was silent with regard to the way in which the defendant was to carry out its work. Purchas LJ said there should be borne in mind the fact that the parties had an 'actual opportunity to define their relationship by means of contract and took it'. Woolf LJ indicated that 'for the time being at any rate' the courts were against any expansion of liability for pure economic loss beyond what was 'strictly required' by binding authority.

3.4.3 **General points**

Lord Goff in *Smith* v *Littlewoods Organization* [1987] 1 All ER 710 (HL) said: '. . . in *Junior Books* . . . some members of your Lordships' House succumbed, perhaps too easily, to the temptation to adopt a solution based simply on proximity'.

In **Chapter 6** (6.3.2) you will find a discussion of two important House of Lords cases, *D & F Estates* v *Church Commissioners for England* [1989] AC 187 and *Murphy* v *Brentwood District Council* [1990] 2 All ER 908. Their Lordships in these cases also regarded *Junior Books* as turning on its own facts, in other words liability was based on a relationship of a special nature.

It is submitted that the authorities on liability for pure economic loss inflicted by negligent acts do not demonstrate beyond doubt that recovery is denied in such cases because of a general rule to that effect. *Junior Books* is not said to be wrongly decided; rather, it is said to be of limited application, which is another matter. The courts are reluctant to impose liability for pure economic loss caused by acts, but a policy is not quite the same as a general rule, and a court should impose such liability where it is fair, just, and reasonable to do so.

3.5 **Misstatements and services**

Liability for negligently causing pure economic loss lies in ordinary common law negligence: it is **not** a separate tort. The usual requirements of duty, breach, and damage have to be proved. Special treatment is necessary because:

(a) the claimant must also establish extra factors under the head of 'duty';

(b) the cases are difficult;

(c) there is an overlap with the law of contract; and

(d) a duty regarding misstatements has only been recognized in principle since the decision of the House of Lords in *Hedley Byrne and Co.* v *Heller and Partners* [1963] 2 All ER 575.

The law of negligence in this respect has developed more slowly and restrictively than liability for negligence generally, although the original form of liability imposed in *Hedley Byrne* has been considerably expanded in scope since circa 1995, particularly, as we shall see, in the context of the provision of 'services'.

 QUESTION 3.2

What do you think may be the main reasons for this cautious development of the law?

There appear to be two main reasons:

(a) people are generally less careful in what they say than in what they do, particularly when expressing opinions on social or informal occasions, rather than in their business or professional capacity; and

(b) in the words of Lord Pearce in *Hedley Byrne* '. . . words are more volatile than deeds, they travel fast and far afield, they are used without being expended'.

3.5.1 Liability in other situations

Before we proceed to *Hedley Byrne*, you may care to note that economic loss caused by misstatements may be the subject of claims in other contexts: for example, where there is a fiduciary relationship (such as solicitor and client); and under statute; for example, the Misrepresentation Act 1967 (liability arises here in both contract and tort, see below).

The Financial Services and Markets Act 2000 imposes liability for loss caused by untrue or misleading statements made in connection with the 'listing particulars' or prospectus issued by a company concerning the issue of shares, debentures, or other securities. In such a case the defendant is obliged to show that he had reasonable grounds to believe that his statements were true or not misleading: a burden of proof favourable to the claimant.

 EXERCISE 3.4

Consider the Misrepresentation Act 1967, s. 2(1) in *Cases and Materials* (3.1.1). When may a claimant sue and what might be the advantages to him in so doing?

The cause of action conferred by the Act differs from the common law action under *Hedley Byrne* in that, amongst other factors, the claimant must have been induced by the defendant's misrepresentation to enter into the contract; the claimant does not have to establish a duty of care; and it is for the defendant to show that he believed on reasonable grounds that his statement was true, rather than for the claimant to prove negligence.

In *Howard Marine* v *Ogden* [1978] QB 574, it was held that s. 2(1) provides an action in tort for misrepresentation. However, the burden of proof is on the defendant to establish that he had reasonable grounds for making the representation. According to *Royscot Trust Ltd* v *Rogerson* [1991] 3 All ER 294, damages are assessed in tortious terms and remoteness of damage is determined as in the tort of deceit. This means that there is liability for all harm directly resulting. Foreseeability is irrelevant.

Where there are concurrent claims in tort and under the 1967 Act the defence of contributory negligence may be available: *Gran Gelato Ltd* v *Richcliffe (Group) Ltd and Others* [1992] 1 All ER 865.

3.5.2 Liability arising under *Hedley Byrne*

Hedley Byrne is a landmark decision in the field of pure economic loss. The case is still of central importance in this context.

***Hedley Byrne and Co.* v *Heller and Partners* [1963] 2 All ER 575 (HL)**
(*Cases and Materials* (3.1.2))

The appellants, an advertising agency, wished to know whether they could safely do work on credit for some clients. Accordingly, they asked their bank to obtain a credit reference from the clients' bank, the respondents. The respondents negligently supplied an arguably over-favourable reference, but they gave it 'without responsibility'.

The appellants were never paid by their clients, who became insolvent. They had been in a poor financial condition for some time and the respondent bank ought to have known of this situation. The appellants sued the respondents for negligence.

On the facts, their Lordships decided that the respondents did not owe the appellants a duty of care, because the 'without responsibility' disclaimer effectively acted as an exclusion of liability clause. It was their Lordships' opinion that without that statement there could well have been a duty to take care, even though the loss suffered by the appellants was purely of a financial nature.

Favourable reference was made in *Hedley Byrne* to a vigorous dissenting judgment of Denning LJ in *Candler* v *Crane Christmas and Co.* [1951] 1 All ER 426 (CA). According to his Lordship the defendants in that case, a firm of accountants, owed a duty of care in negligence not only to the client for whom they prepared accounts; they also owed a duty to any third parties they knew would be shown the accounts and who would be likely to rely on them. Since the accountants knew that the accounts were required in relation to a proposed sale of the company, this would include the prospective purchasers.

In strict terms, *Hedley Byrne* is authority only on the basis that it contains strongly persuasive obiter dicta; yet this view has for so long been taken as representing English law on the point that it would be pedantic in the extreme to insist that the case is not of binding authority.

> **? QUESTION** 3.3
>
> Is mere 'foreseeability' enough to determine liability for careless misstatements?

Any test will probably have to be based on very close proximity between the parties involved because of the fear of indeterminate liability, that is liability towards an indeterminate number of people, for indeterminate amounts of money. In *Hedley Byrne* the House of Lords came up with the idea of a 'special relationship'.

This requirement of a 'special relationship' has become an accepted feature of the law, as you will see. But it is at best a vague notion, as the various attempts to define it in *Hedley Byrne* demonstrate. It is more of a 'sum total of its parts' rather than a coherent 'whole'.

In the words of Lord Morris:

> If in a sphere in which a person is so placed that others could reasonably rely on his judgment or his skill or on his ability to make careful inquiry, a person takes it on himself to give information or advice to, or allows his information or advice to be passed on to another person who, as he knows or should know, will place reliance on it, then a duty of care will arise.

His Lordship went on to say that he thought a special relationship followed from proof that the defendant assumed responsibility for his advice. Lord Hodson agreed with him on this point.

Lord Devlin felt that a special relationship resembled a contractual relationship without any consideration. It is submitted that this 'definition' comes closest to the necessary relationship which must exist between the parties, though 'assumption of responsibility' is assuming an increasingly important role in more recent case law.

Denning LJ in the earlier case of *Candler* (above) might have been partly defining the special relationship when he said: '. . . it [the duty of care owed by the defendants in his opinion] appears to be limited to cases where the information or advice is given in response to an enquiry for the guidance in question'.

> **? QUESTION** 3.4
>
> What is the consequence of this view?

A negative view is that '[The special relationship signifies] little more than that the standard *Donoghue* v *Stevenson* foreseeability test cannot be used [in the context of negligent misstatements]' (Stanton, p. 341).

3.5.3 **Subsequent developments**

It is only by examining later cases, in which the courts have been given the opportunity to consider the ramifications of *Hedley Byrne*, that we can hope to draw a clearer picture of the law.

In *Mutual Life and Citizens' Assurance Co. Ltd* v *Evatt* [1971] AC 793, the majority of the Privy Council narrowed the ambit of 'special relationship' by confining it to cases where the defendant either was in the business of supplying information or advice, or had claimed to possess the necessary skill to give it and the preparedness to take care in giving it. It was held in this case that no duty of care was owed by an employee of a life assurance company in giving advice to a life policy holder about the wisdom of investing in a company associated with the employee's company.

There were two dissenting opinions in this case. They were delivered by Lords Reid and Morris (two of the judges in *Hedley Byrne* (above)) who argued for a wider duty than that suggested by the majority. They said that a duty existed not only in the circumstances stated by the majority, but also where advice was sought or given by someone in the usual course of business. Social and casual occasions were ruled out, as in *Hedley Byrne*.

In *Esso* v *Mardon* [1976] QB 801, both Lawson J at first instance, and the Court of Appeal, clearly preferred the reasoning of the minority in *Evatt*. M entered into a contract with E to lease a petrol filling station. He did so on the strength of a negligent misrepresentation by E's expert that the 'through-put' would reach 200,000 gallons per year, about double the realistic figure. M suffered considerable financial loss, despite all his strenuous efforts. The Court of Appeal held that E was liable to pay substantial damages, not only for breach of warranty but also in the tort of negligence, in respect of the loss suffered in the first year up to the renewal of the tenancy agreement (to which Lawson J had confined his assessment), the capital put into the business, the overdraft and loss of future earnings for a number of years.

In *Argy Trading Development Co. Ltd* v *Lapid Developments Ltd* [1977] 3 All ER 785, the defendant, who was the claimant's landlord, allowed fire insurance cover for the demised premises to lapse without informing the claimant. The defendant was found not liable because there was no 'holding out', no statutory duty, no sufficient business relationship between the parties, no 'financial interest' on the part of the defendant and no inquiry by the claimant coupled with advice or information given by the defendant; in short, there was no 'special relationship' between the parties.

? **QUESTION** 3.5

What are the main factors behind a special relationship?

The following are its main features:

(a) reliance by the claimant;

(b) gratuitous advice or information may lead to liability;

(c) assumption of responsibility by the defendant;

(d) the *Hedley Byrne* 'rule' encompasses statements/advice/notices/omissions, etc.

We will now examine the first three features in detail; the fourth feature is self-explanatory, though we ought to note that liability for **any** omission is always more difficult to establish than liability for a 'positive' act (see 1.6.1).

3.5.4 **Reliance**

The defendant must be someone on whose advice, skill, etc., the claimant can reasonably and foreseeably expect to rely. For example, in the Canadian case of *Klein* v *Canadian Propane* (1967) 64 DLR (2d) 220, it was held that advice given by the driver of a propane gas tanker as to the source of a gas smell was not such as to make him liable for the results of an ensuing explosion.

Again, the parties' relative position to each other may be a crucial factor. If the claimant has manifestly more skill or knowledge in the matter than has the defendant, it is less likely that the latter will owe any duty of care to the former.

 EXERCISE 3.5

What is the link between *Luxmoore-May* v *Messenger May Baverstock* [1990] 1 All ER 1067 (CA) and reliance? See the facts below.

It was held in this case that a provincial art valuer and auctioneer is not negligent merely because he does not notice the potential value of a painting (a 'sleeper') which later sold in London as an original Stubbs. The court found that the valuer's duty is to act with due diligence to give his honest and considered opinion on the sale value of the painting submitted to him. At first instance the defendants were found liable in negligence to the plaintiffs but the Court of Appeal reversed this decision. Slade LJ said that the nature of the defendants' duty was akin to that of general practitioners and the required standard of skill was not that of the specialist, i.e. the standard of the provincial auctioneer was to be applied in this case rather than that expected of one of the leading auction houses. Differing and even wrong views could be held without there being a breach of the practitioner's duty. The case should be approached according to the actual circumstances confronting the practitioners at the time 'rather than with the benefit of hindsight'. An exact science was not involved and it was a matter of opinion and judgment in such cases. '[T]he judgment in the very nature of things may be fallible and may turn out to be wrong.' The trial judge had demanded too high a standard of skill from the defendants; here the question was one on which many competent valuers and dealers could have held widely differing views.

Luxmoore-May indicates that a claimant may experience considerable problems in convincing the court of the appropriate standard of care which a defendant is expected to observe. In such a case it is also difficult to establish that there should be reliance.

Reliance is a factor which can arise in any context of misstatement; it can lead to problems of causation. In *JEB Fasteners Ltd* v *Marks Bloom and Co.* [1983] 1 All ER 583 (see 3.5.10.2), there was no evidence that the claimant had actually relied on the negligent statement, and as a result, it could not be shown that their losses were caused thereby.

3.5.5 **Gratuitous advice, etc.**

> **?** **QUESTION** 3.6
>
> Is there advantage in paying for advice?

In principle it does not matter that the advice or information is given free of charge, though it is always going to be easier for a claimant to establish the necessary relationship with the defendant where the latter is paid for his services, or at least has received some discernible benefit or advantage in the circumstances. Indeed there will often, but not always, be a contractual duty of care in such cases.

In *Chaudhry* v *Prabhaker* [1988] 3 All ER 718, the Court of Appeal held that the standard of care owed by an unpaid agent to his principal was an objective one, such as to be reasonably expected of him in all the circumstances. A friend was found liable for loss suffered when, in breach of his duty, he recommended to the claimant the purchase of a second-hand car which turned out to be both unroadworthy and valueless.

The defendant accepted that he owed a duty of care to the claimant, claiming only that he had discharged his duty by observing the standard of care required of him in law. The case proceeded on the basis that there existed a gratuitous relationship of principal and agent between the parties, so any question of liability arose in tort. The court accepted that liability could also arise under the *Hedley Byrne* principle: logically the standard of care expected in this context should be the same as that required of an unpaid agent.

May LJ, while concurring in the judgment against the defendant, said 'In the light of the more cautious approach taken in recent cases . . . [for example, *Yuen Kun Yeu*; see 3.5.6] it is doubtful whether the defendant's concession [as to the existence of a duty of care] has been rightly made in law'. He did not find 'entirely attractive' the proposition that one had to impose on a family friend a *Donoghue* v *Stevenson* duty of care.

> Neither can one apply the *Hedley Byrne* principle to the first defendant's answer to the claimant's inquiry about the car's history, since to do so would make social relations and responsibilities between friends unnecessarily hazardous. However, the concession has been made.

3.5.6 **Assumption of responsibility**

In *Lambert* v *Lewis* (above) it was found that a special relationship is not created between defendant and claimant merely as a result of the defendant having said something which he seriously intended another or others to act upon. Liability does not arise from a volunteered misstatement; the misstatement must be made in response to an inquiry from the claimants.

An 'assumption of responsibility' is required in all cases, to distinguish merely casual or 'social' advice (for example, a solicitor giving casual advice to a fellow-passenger on a train) from that given in a professional or business context. Even if advice or information is given in a situation which can be categorized as 'formal', however, it does not follow necessarily that an assumption of responsibility will be found.

In *Tidman* v *Reading Borough Council* (1994), *The Times*, 10 November, Buxton J held that liability under *Hedley Byrne* did not arise where council officials gave advice to a member of the public who had made an 'informal' inquiry about a matter concerning planning permission on land that he was trying to sell.

? QUESTION 3.7

What reasons do you think the judge gave for his decision?

His Lordship gave the following reasons:

(a) the council owed a public duty (under the relevant legislation) to apply the planning law; an overriding obligation to advise individuals would be inconsistent with the public interest;

(b) the claimant's approach to the council was by way of an informal telephone call; the advice was given on very little information available from the claimant. To impose liability in such a case would, in any event, deter local authorities from giving advice of this nature, and that would be contrary to the public interest;

(c) the claimant could be reasonably expected to seek independent advice before acting in such circumstances.

? QUESTION 3.8

Think back to *Hedley Byrne*. What did we say there was the basis of liability?

The basis of liability was a 'special relationship' and an 'assumption of responsibility', but there is some inconsistency in the cases concerning the **nature** of this assumption.

Some judges regard **voluntary** assumption of responsibility as a requirement for recovery of damages in every case of pure economic loss, see, for example, Dillon LJ in *Simaan General Contracting Co.* v *Pilkington Glass (No. 2)* [1988] 1 All ER 791. On balance, though, it seems that a defendant may be regarded in law (even though not in fact) as having assumed responsibility to the claimant. 'Voluntary' assumption is only a fiction, therefore, if this assumption of responsibility is deemed by law.

In *Yuen Kun-Yeu* v *A-G For Hong Kong* [1988] AC 175 (PC), Lord Keith said that liability depends not on 'voluntary' assumption of responsibility; it depends on a sufficient degree of proximity between the parties: thus voluntary assumption of responsibility is merely an example of a particular factual situation leading to 'proximity'. It is the directness and closeness of the relationship between the parties which is the crucial factor.

In *Banque Keyser Ullmann SA* v *Skandia (UK) Insurance Co. Ltd* [1989] 2 All ER 952 (CA) (*Westgate Insurance* in the House of Lords, below), it was accepted in the Court of Appeal that 'on appropriate facts', 'having regard to the special circumstances and the relationship between the parties' a defendant might be regarded in law (even though not in fact) as having assumed responsibility to the claimant. The court was much impressed by Lord Keith's opinion in *Yuen Kun-Yeu*. In this light, the voluntary assumption of responsibility is but one example of a factual situation giving rise to a direct and close relationship.

It was held that an insurer owes a duty of care to disclose to the insured the insured's brokers' dishonesty (known to the insurer) only where the insurer has voluntarily assumed responsibility to disclose and the insured has relied on that assumption of responsibility. (The duty of utmost good faith in the insurance contract cannot be used as a platform to establish a common law duty of care in such circumstances.)

According to Slade LJ it was not necessary in a claim for negligence for economic loss resulting from an act of an independent third party that the precise manner and means by which the loss was caused or the extent of a loss be foreseeable; it was enough to show reasonable foresight of the relevant kind of loss. A failure to speak (omission) was involved here, however, and, although in the opinion of the court a mere failure to speak was capable of giving rise to liability for negligent misstatement, there must be a voluntary assumption of responsibility together with reliance on it. In the present case both assumption and reliance were absent. In rare cases, because of special circumstances and the relationship between parties, the law might treat a defendant as having assumed a responsibility to the claimant even though there was no evidence of an actual assumption of responsibility and reliance by the claimant. But the defendant insurers did not fit into this category because it was a basic principle of the law of contract that there was no obligation to disclose a material fact during pre-contractual negotiations before entering into an ordinary commercial contract and this prevented a duty of care arising on the part of the insurers. To hold the insurers liable in negligence for their failure to disclose the third party's deception would be contrary to that principle of contract law.

In *La Banque Financière de la Cité* v *Westgate Insurance Co. Ltd* [1990] 2 All ER 947 (HL) the House of Lords dismissed the bank's appeal and held (confirming the decision of the Court of Appeal, though on other grounds) that there was no duty on the part of an insurer to warn an insured person that the latter's agent had committed a breach of duty in an earlier transaction. The insurer was not responsible for the agent's misconduct toward his principal in subsequent dealings; it followed that the insurers did not owe a duty to tell the banks in the present case that their broker had acted fraudulently with regard to the covering insurance for a loan.

 In *Smith* v *Bush; Harris* v *Wyre Forest DC* [1989] 2 All ER 514 (*Cases and Materials* (3.1.3)) Lord Griffiths said it was sufficient for the law to deem responsibility.

In *Smith* and *Harris* it was held that surveyors acting for mortgagees owed a duty of care to house purchasers, that is, the claimants, the mortgagors, who relied on negligent reports issued by the surveyors. In *Smith* the surveyor acted for a building society and his report was shown to the claimant. In *Harris*, the mortgagees were a local authority and the surveyor was a member of their own staff; his report was not shown to the claimant but the court said that he was entitled to assume from the local authority's offer of a mortgage that the property had been professionally valued. In both cases the claimant paid indirectly for the survey.

Their Lordships discussed the duty of care owed by a valuer to (a) the party instructing him (usually the mortgagee) and (b) any other party likely reasonably to rely on the valuation report (usually the purchaser). It was held that a dual responsibility exists in such cases.

It should be noted that the claimants had not employed independent surveyors to survey the properties. In many cases, however, it will be necessary to do this or at least opt for a full report on the structure from the building society surveyor, because mortgage valuations are of a cursory nature. The lender is interested in the property only to the extent that the resale value will equal the loan. In the present cases, however, the House of Lords said it was reasonable to rely on the basic reports (though they did not amount to full structural surveys) because the properties involved were of a standard nature and not expensive; it was common practice amongst buyers at this end of the housing market to rely simply on the mortgage valuation report.

According to Lord Templeman 'in both appeals . . . the existence of such a dual duty is tacitly accepted and acknowledged because notices excluding liability for breach of duty to the purchaser were drafted by the mortgagee and imposed on the purchasers'.

In this case a duty of care was found without any formal attempt to apply *Hedley Byrne*. There was, in any event, disagreement on the effect of that decision. While Lord Templeman and Lord Jauncey said that it was necessary for the defendant in such cases voluntarily to have assumed responsibility to the claimant, Lord Griffiths thought otherwise; according to him it was enough for the law to deem assumption of responsibility.

On the question of whether it was necessary to have a relationship equivalent to contract Lord Griffiths expressed no opinion, Lord Templeman and Lord Jauncey thought the answer was 'yes' and Lord Brandon and Lord Keith agreed with them.

The attempts to exclude liability were held, in each case, to be caught by sections 2(2) and 11(3) of the Unfair Contract Terms Act 1977. Under this Act, defendants acting in the course of business cannot exclude liability for negligence causing death or personal injury. In relation to any other damage, as in *Smith* and *Harris*, the test of reasonableness must be satisfied. Reasonableness is assessed on the facts of each case.

 EXERCISE 3.6

What general conclusions may be drawn from *Harris* and *Smith* about the circumstances in which the law will imply a duty of care?

It was said that the law will imply a duty of care where someone with a special skill is entrusted to exercise that skill and he knows, or ought to know, that reliance will be placed on his skill and judgment. Arguably, the decision in this case was not based on a simple application of *Hedley Byrne*; rather, it turns on its own special facts.

It is clear that 'assumption of responsibility' and 'reasonable reliance' lie at the heart of liability under *Hedley Byrne*. In *Lonrho plc* v *Fayed* [1988] 3 All ER 464, for example, the defendants (who were business advisers) were found not to have assumed responsibility towards their clients' business competitors for representations made by them, on behalf of their clients, to the Monopolies Commission.

In *Van Oppen* v *Clerk to the Bedford Charity Trustees* [1989] 3 All ER 889 (CA), it was held that a school had no general duty to take out personal accident insurance cover for its pupils or to advise parents of the desirability of such cover. Nor was there a duty to have regard to the economic welfare of pupils, arising naturally from the relationship of school and pupil. There was no evidence of a voluntary assumption of responsibility by the school; in any case there was no evidence that any parent had relied on the school. It might have been prudent to advise parents to insure, but all carelessness could not be elevated into a tort: there must be a legal duty not to be careless and it would be neither just nor reasonable to impose on the school a greater duty than that which rested on a parent. Compare the *Rush and Tomkins* case you read in section 3.2.

The relevant standard of care in such a case was that of the reasonably careful parent, subject to the conditions of school life and numbers of pupils involved. The question of whether a prudent parent had a duty to take out accident insurance was raised. O'Connor LJ thought that if a school decided that all pupils were to be covered by personal accident insurance under a block policy and then failed negligently to renew the policy, an injured pupil would have a good claim against the school.

> **?** **QUESTION** 3.9
>
> Do you think that the '*Caparo* test' (1.3.2) may be of especial importance in the context of negligent misstatement?

You will find that the answer is 'yes'.

3.5.7 *Caparo*

> *Caparo Industries plc* v *Dickman* [1990] 1 All ER 568 (HL) (*Cases and Materials* (1.1.2))
>
> *Caparo* is authority for the proposition that the parties must be very close together indeed before there can be any question of a duty of care arising from the facts: a high degree of proximity is required.
>
> The claimants were considering a takeover bid for a company in which they held shares and, as shareholders, they received a copy of the company's audited accounts. Acting in reliance on these accounts, which showed a profit made by the company, the claimants bought more shares in it and eventually took it over. It later emerged that due to the negligence of the defendant auditors, the accounts had been wrongly audited; the company had, in fact, made a loss.
>
> At first instance it was found that the defendants did not owe the claimants, as shareholders and potential investors, any duty of care. By a majority, however, the Court of Appeal found for the claimants. First, it was reasonably foreseeable that the claimants would rely on the audited accounts; secondly, there existed sufficient proximity between the parties and the defendants had voluntarily assumed responsibility directly to Caparo; thirdly, it was just and reasonable to impose a duty in this case. The duty was owed to the claimants only as existing shareholders in the company, not as potential investors and takeover bidders. The court clearly regarded 'special relationship' as inseparable from 'proximity' and 'justice'; 'reasonable reliance' did not alone define the 'scope' of the 'special relationship'; 'just and reasonable' was likened to the second stage of the Wilberforce test (see 1.3.2).

The House of Lords overturned the decision; it was found that auditors of a public company owed no duty of care:

(a) to a member of the public who relies on the accounts to buy shares (there was insufficient proximity because of the potential liability of the auditors); or

(b) to an individual shareholder in the company who desires to buy more shares (such a person is in no better position than a member of the public in the present context).

The auditors' statutory duty to prepare accounts was owed only to the shareholders as a body, to enable them to make informed decisions concerning the running of the company; the purpose of this duty, said their Lordships, was not to enable individual shareholders to buy shares with an eye on profits.

According to Lord Bridge, notions such as 'fair, just, and reasonable', 'neighbourhood' and 'proximity' are mere labels; they 'are not susceptible of any such precise definition as would be necessary to give them utility as practical tests'. He said:

> traditionally the law finds the existence of the duty in different specific situations each exhibiting its own particular characteristics. In this way the law has identified a wide variety of duty-situations, all falling within the ambit of the tort of negligence, but sufficiently distinct to require separate definition of the essential ingredients by which the existence of the duty is to be recognized.

His Lordship felt that the law has moved away from the difficulty of using a single general principle to determine whether a duty of care is owed and had

> now moved in the direction of attaching a greater significance to the more traditional categorization of distinct and recognizable situations as guides to the existence, the scope and the limits of the varied duties of care which the law imposes.

Lord Oliver felt that the most that could be attempted was a 'broad categorization of the decided cases according to the type of situation in which liability has been established in the past'; to pursue a general test of liability was to chase a 'will-o'-the-wisp'.

? QUESTION 3.10

How would you defend the action?

Approval was given by the House to the views of Brennan J in the High Court of Australia in *Sutherland Shire Council* v *Heyman* (1985) 60 ALR 1, where he rejected the use of Lord Wilberforce's two-stage test:

> It is preferable in my view that the law should develop novel categories of negligence incrementally and by analogy with established categories, rather than by a massive extension of a *prima facie* duty of care restrained only by indefinable considerations which ought to negative, or to reduce or limit the scope of the duty or the class of persons to whom it is owed.

As with all seminal cases it is necessary to examine subsequent case law to gauge the impact of the principal case (*Caparo* in this instance).

In *Al Nakib (Investments) Jersey Ltd* v *Longcroft* [1990] 3 All ER 321, it was held that while company directors owed a duty of care to those who bought shares in a rights issue after relying on the company prospectus, they did not owe any duty to shareholders or anyone else relying on the prospectus to buy shares in the company through the stock market. In other words, the duty was limited specifically to purchasers of shares in the particular rights issue.

A qualified approach to the establishment and terms of a duty of care can also be seen in *Mariola Marine Corp* v *Lloyd's Register of Shipping ('Morning Watch')* [1990] 1 Lloyd's Rep 547. The main issue here was whether Lloyd's owed a duty of care in negligence not to cause economic loss to persons (other than the owners of the vessel) foreseeably likely to rely on a survey of the *'Morning Watch'* before the ship was put on the market. Phillips J found against such a claim, because the main purpose of the classification of vessels for Lloyd's Register of Shipping was the physical safety of persons and property while at sea.

In *Morgan Crucible Co.* v *Hill Samuel Bank Ltd* [1990] 3 All ER 330, the court had to consider a take-over bidder's claim against the directors, advisers and accountants of the 'target' company, that financial representations made by the company to its shareholders during take-over tussles were misleading and negligent. It was claimed that the announcement of the bid distinguished the case from *Caparo*, and put it into the ambit of *Smith* and *Harris* (see 3.5.6). There was sufficient proximity between the parties.

 QUESTION 3.11

How would you decide this case?

Hoffmann J refused leave to amend the claimant's statement of claim, on the argument that the defence documents (like the audit certificate in *Caparo*) had a regulatory background, in the present case it was the *City Code on Takeovers, etc*. The purpose of the circulars issued by the defendants was to advise shareholders; they were not directed to bidders for the company. His Lordship felt that there was an even stronger case for denying a duty of care in the present circumstances than in *Caparo*, that is in a contested bid the interests of the shareholders and bidders conflicted.

On appeal, however, the Court of Appeal ([1991] 1 All ER 148) allowed modification of the claimant's statement of claim. It was found that the issue should be allowed to go to trial because there was an arguable case that the representations were made with a view to influencing the bidder's conduct, so creating a duty of care not to mislead the bidder.

In *Kuwait Asia Bank EC* v *National Mutual Life Nominees Ltd* [1990] 3 WLR 297 (PC), the court had to consider, in the context of the New Zealand rules concerning service of process outside the jurisdiction, the claims that a shareholder or other person who was concerned with the appointment of a director of a company owed a duty of care to the company's creditors, to see that the director acted diligently and competently. The Privy Council found against such a duty, and also said that a director does not owe a duty to creditors of the company merely because of his status as director, though a director could take on a special duty to creditors.

EXERCISE 3.7

Consider the decision in *James McNaughton Paper Group Ltd* v *Hicks Anderson and Co.* [1991] 1 All ER 134. What was the outcome of the case?

The claimants wished to take over a company and asked the defendants, who were accountants to the target company, to prepare some draft accounts of their clients' affairs as quickly as possible for use in the takeover negotiations. It was found that the defendants owed no duty of care to the claimants. The Court of Appeal regarded it as important that the claimants were experienced in business and, in any event, they could have brought in their own accountants.

Neill LJ said:

> . . . in England a restrictive approach is now adopted to any extension of the scope of the duty of care beyond the person directly intended by the maker of the statement to act upon it; and (b) that in deciding whether a duty of care exists in any particular case it is necessary to take all the circumstances into account; but (c) that, notwithstanding (b), it is possible to identify certain matters which are likely to be of importance in most cases in reaching a decision as to whether or not a duty exists . . .

- The purpose for which the statement was made and on which the claim was based: e.g. Was it made for the express purpose of being communicated to the advisee?
- The purpose for which the statement was communicated, e.g. for information only?
- The relationship between the adviser, the advisee, and any relevant third party.
- The size of any class to which the advisee belonged.
- The state of knowledge of the adviser (actual and attributed).
- Reliance by the advisee. Often, it would be useful to look at the matter from the claimant's point of view. In business transactions conducted at arm's length it might sometimes be difficult for an advisee to prove that he had been entitled to act on a statement without taking any independent advice or to prove that the adviser had known, actually or inferentially, that he would act without taking such advice . . .

? **QUESTION** 3.12

Briefly state the general effect of *Caparo* in relation to liability for statements.

As a result of *Caparo*, the scope of *Hedley Byrne* has been considerably narrowed. Mere foreseeability of reliance by the claimant is not enough; the defendant must be actually aware of:

(a) the claimant (either as an individual, or as a member of an identifiable class of persons, to whom the advice or information will be communicated);

(b) the purpose for which the advice or information has been sought; and

(c) the fact that the claimant is likely to rely on the advice or information for that purpose.

In *Barings* v *Coopers and Lybrand* [1997] 1 BCLC 427 (CA), Leggatt LJ described an auditor's duty in the following terms '[T]he primary responsibility for safeguarding a company's assets and preventing errors and defalcations rests with the directors . . . An auditor's task is so to conduct the audit as to make it probable that material misstatements in financial documents will be detected.'

You can read extracts from the judgments in *Gran Gelato Ltd* v *Richcliffe (Group) Ltd and Others* [1992] 1 All ER 865 and *Galoo Ltd (In Liq) and Others* v *Bright Grahame Murray (A Firm) and Another* [1995] 1 All ER in *Cases and Materials* (3.1.3).

In *The Law Society* v *KPMG* [2000] 1 All ER 515 (CA), a firm of solicitors employed the defendants to prepare a report for submission to the Society. The defendants, who were fully aware that the report would be submitted to the claimant, were negligent as they did not detect fraud on the solicitors' part. It was held that the defendants were liable for the Society's loss when it had to pay compensation to the defrauded clients of the solicitors.

The court found that it was foreseeable that loss to the compensation fund set up by the Society would occur should the accountants negligently fail to find irregularities in the solicitor's accounts; there was a sufficient degree of proximity between the claimant and the defendants; it was just, fair, and reasonable to impose a duty on the defendants on the facts because they were not under unlimited liability, that is, the compensation payable was limited to the amount of clients' money that had been lost because of the solicitor's fraud; and the time for claiming was limited in that annual reports were delivered, thus negligence in one year could be revealed by a proper report in the succeeding year.

In *Abbott* v *Strong* (1998), *The Times*, 9 July, A Ltd sent a circular to its shareholders inviting subscriptions for new shares (a 'rights' issue). Included in the circular was a profit forecast, supported by a letter from B, a firm of accountants, and the claimants (the shareholders) alleged that this forecast was misleading. The court had to decide whether B owed a duty of care to the claimants with regard to the advice given to A Ltd, that is a duty beyond that owed to the claimants flowing from the letter included in the circular. It was held that where X makes a statement or gives advice to Y, to help Y to make representations to Z, X does not owe a duty of care to Z where Z is unaware of X's assistance to Y.

In *Commissioners of Customs and Excise* v *Barclays Bank plc* (2006), *The Times*, 22 June, the claimant had been awarded asset-freezing injunctions against a certain customer's accounts held with the defendant bank and notified it accordingly. The defendant breached the injunctions by failing to stop money being taken out of the accounts and the claimant sued the bank in negligence. It was held by the House of Lords that the bank did not owe the claimant a duty of care in the circumstances. Lord Bingham, with whom the rest of their Lordships concurred, said there were three tests for determining liability in cases of pure economic loss, that is, (a) assumption of responsibility by the defendant; (b) the 'threefold test'(his Lordship said the 'fair, just, and reasonable' part of this test could be labelled 'policy'); and (c) the incremental test. The defendant had argued that test (a) was the most appropriate here and showed that no duty of care was owed in the circumstances and in any event the same conclusion could be drawn on application of either (b) or (c). The claimant's case was based on test (b) which showed that a duty was owed and in any event the application of either (a) or (c) achieved the same result. In his Lordship's opinion test (a) might well be sufficient where the 'paradigm situation [was] a relationship having all the indicia of a contract save consideration'; but it was not a necessary condition of liability. It was a first test which, if answered negatively, led to further considerations. It was to be applied objectively but the further removed it was from the behaviour of the actual defendant 'the less difference there was' between it and test (b). Test (b) itself gave no 'straightforward answer' to the question of whether or not a duty of care was owed in a novel situation. Test (c) was only helpful 'when used in combination with a test or principle which identified the legally significant features of a situation'. The closer the correspondence of the case being argued to a previously decided case in which a duty had been held to exist, the more likely it would be, following *Caparo*, that tests (a) and (b) would be satisfied.

His Lordship went on to say that the outcomes of the leading cases were 'in almost every instance sensible and just, irrespective of the test applied'. However, it was necessary to have a test of liability in negligence which 'any law of tort must propound if it is not to become a morass of single instances'. This 'concentrated attention on the detailed circumstances of the particular case and the particular relationship between the parties in the context of their legal and factual situation as a whole'. On the facts of the present case his Lordship said that it was not apt to apply test (a) because the bank had no choice in the matter being legally obliged to comply with the court orders; nor had the claimant relied on the defendant. Furthermore, reliance in law usually meant that 'if A had not relied on B he would have acted differently'. In the present case the claimant could not have done so because they had applied for the only remedy available in law. As for test (b), the foreseeability element was satisfied on the facts but proximity 'in the context of pure economic loss is notoriously elusive'. The parties here were only proximate in the sense that one had served a court order on the other party and that party was aware of the risk of loss to the other party if that order was ignored. The third ingredient of test (b), 'policy', had to be 'determinative' of the issue in this case. On that basis it was to be assumed, since the documentation of the court orders made no reference to any other remedy, that the only duty owed by the bank was to the courts. The customer of the bank in this case did not owe a duty to the party obtaining the court order because no duty was owed by a litigating party to its opponent and it would be 'strange and anomalous' if an action in negligence was allowed against 'a notified party who allowed the horse to escape from the stable but not against the owner who rode out on it'. Although, in principle, a tortious duty of care to the Commissioners could co-exist with a duty of compliance owed to the court issuing the orders, his Lordship said he was not aware of any case where a non-consensual court order ('without more') had been held to lead to a duty of care owed to the party obtaining the order. The claimant's argument 'involved a radical innovation' and 'it was notable that they had adduced no comparative jurisprudence' to support their argument. In 'the final analysis' it was 'unjust and unreasonable' that the defendant should, on being notified of an order it could not resist, be 'exposed to a liability which was in the present case for a few million pounds but which might in another case be for very much more'. The bank's only protection for that exposure, said his Lordship, was the claimant's undertaking to make good any loss which the court order might cause it: 'protection scarcely consistent with a duty of care owed to the commissioners but in any event valueless'.

This decision highlights the prolixity and circularity of the arguments employed in relation to the duty of care issue, particularly in the context of pure economic loss. Would it not be sufficient in all novel situations to argue simply on the basis of what is 'just and reasonable' in the circumstances of the case, subsuming the other 'tests'? This was the approach forced upon Lord Bingham in the present case. This decision is also of importance in the context of **Chapter 1** (1.3).

3.5.8 **Services**

In *Precis (521) Plc* v *William M Mercer Ltd (2005), The Times,* 24 February (CA), it was held that someone who made a negligent actuarial valuation report concerning pension funds of a company would only be liable for negligent misrepresentation to a purchasing company which, in reliance on the report, purchased the shares of the company on which the report had been made, where the compiler of the report had assumed responsibility in law. Arden LJ, delivering the judgment of the court, said the precise limits of the concept of assumption of responsibility were still in a state of development. Her Ladyship said there was no comprehensive list of guiding principles on the matter. It was necessary, therefore, to consider whether the circumstances of each case, as they arose, fell within the parameters of previous cases in which liability had been imposed. Assumption of responsibility did not depend on the terms of a private transaction between the claimant and a third party which was unknown to the defendant, therefore the fact that the provider of the information did not think he or she was assuming a duty of care was not a determining factor. However, continued Her Ladyship, when a court was seeking the true meaning of the exchanges between the parties it would apply the meaning which the parties might reasonably be supposed to have given to the words in the particular context in which they were used. It would not be fair, just, or reasonable to impose liability in the circumstances of the present case.

In *Henderson and Others* v *Merrett Syndicates Ltd and Others; Arbuthnott and Others* v *Feltrim Underwriting Agencies Ltd and Others; Deeny and Others* v *Gooda Walker Ltd and Others* [1994] 3 All ER 506 (HL), it was held that a *Hedley Byrne* duty arose on the facts because there was:

(a) an assumption of responsibility to provide professional/quasi-professional services; and

(b) someone who relied on those services.

The cases concerned the liability of managing agents at Lloyd's of London (the epicentre of the insurance business) to 'names' who were, at the relevant time, members of syndicates managed by the agents. Those agents gave advice to the 'names' on the risks involved in underwriting insurance and on questions concerning reinsurance.

It was said that the agents held themselves out as having special skills and the names relied implicitly on that expertise. Authority was given to the agents to bind the names to contracts of reinsurance, etc. The relationship between the parties (we must not lose sight of the fact that the parties were bound together by contract) was sufficient on its own to justify the imposition of a duty of care under *Hedley Byrne.*

We have already seen in 1.4 that this case is authority for the proposition that a pre-existing contractual relationship between the parties, at least in a case such as the present one where professional/quasi-professional services were involved, did not of itself preclude concurrent liability in tort. A claimant could choose which remedy produced the best results, unless the terms of the contract provided otherwise.

In *Henderson*, Lord Goff said that the law of tort provides the general framework for the law of obligations but the law of contract can be used to avoid or displace tortious obligations. Where, however, the parties have carried on business within the context of contract and sub-contract, that is where there is a contractual 'chain' which has been designed to prevent privity of contract arising between the claimant and defendant, the law can regard that 'chain' as being inconsistent with an assumption of responsibility, which can be used by the court to short-circuit 'the contractual structure so put in place by the parties'. In other words, the law of tort may be used, in appropriate circumstances, to create a relationship resembling a contract.

Henderson itself may be regarded as turning on its own special facts; it is the potential of the views expressed in that case which are of particular importance. Unfortunately, the speeches give little insight into when an assumption of responsibility will short-circuit a contractual claim. Lord Goff indicated that the court might well infer an agreement to exclude or modify tortious obligations in the case of an ordinary, everyday sub-contract in the building/construction context, but that is just about the limit of his specific guidance on this matter.

In *Henderson* the 'names' had a relationship with the managing agents, but the contractual framework was designed in such a way that the 'names' only had formal contractual rights against their own, members' agents; in turn, the managing agents were liable to the members' agents, under the terms of the sub-agency contract between the agents as a whole. Thus, in conventional terms, there was no privity of contract between the claimants (the names) and the defendants (the managing agents).

However, their Lordships regarded the facts as unusual, and took the view that in this case the agreements were neither inconsistent with the defendants' assumption of responsibility to the claimants, nor did the contractual framework provide for obligations which were less onerous than those provided for by the law of tort, that is the respective obligations were co-terminous. The claimants were free to choose whether to sue in contract or in tort. The key is the coextensive nature of the contractual and tortious obligations of the defendants.

Henderson is authority for the general proposition that the law of tort is not complementary to the law of contract: on the contrary, tort law is the fundamental one, although contract can be used, where appropriate, to modify tortious obligations. Tortious obligations stay in place unless they are so inconsistent with a contract that it can only be concluded that the parties intended to conclude or limit them. This might be the case where a contract laid down duties which were of a lesser nature than those provided for in the law of torts although, in the appropriate context (see above) an agreement would always have to be consistent with a defendant's basic tortious obligation of an 'assumption of responsibility'.

In *Welton* v *North Cornwall District Council* [1997] 1 WLR 570 (CA), it was held that where an environmental health officer negligently required the owner of food premises to undertake works which were unnecessary to secure compliance with regulations made under the Food Safety Act 1990, and the owner of the premises incurred substantial and unnecessary expenditure in carrying out the works, the local authority (the local food authority for present purposes) was liable for breach of its common law duty of care to the owner for the economic loss suffered.

The claimant took on the works because of the insistence of the officer, who knew that what he said would be relied upon by the claimant without independent inquiry. It was found that the fact that the relationship between the parties arose out of the purported exercise of statutory functions was no reason why the local authority should not be liable in the tort of negligence.

In *Williams* v *Natural Life Health Foods Ltd* [1998] 2 All ER 577 (HL), it was held that a director or employee of a limited company was not liable under *Hedley Byrne* unless it could be shown objectively that the claimant could reasonably have relied on an assumption of personal responsibility sufficient to create a 'special relationship' between the director or employee and the claimant. The claimants had taken out a franchise from the defendant company and suffered financial loss as a result of negligent advice given by the company in relation to financial projections about the likely future profitability of the shop.

The company went into liquidation and the claimants joined the second defendant, who was the managing director and principal shareholder. He was now the sole defendant in the action.

Lord Steyn, delivering the judgment of the House of Lords, said that *Henderson* v *Merrett* had decided that the *Hedley Byrne* 'assumption of responsibility' was not confined to misstatements; it might apply 'as the extended *Hedley Byrne* principle to any assumption of responsibility for the provision of services'. It was not enough to establish reliance, however, to show that there was a special relationship with a principal (the defendant company). Where an agent, an employee or director of the company in the present case) was sued personally there had to be a special relationship between that person and the claimant. His Lordship said that the 'touchstone of liability' was not the defendant's state of mind. The 'objective' test laid down in *Henderson* required that the main emphasis had to be on things said or done by the defendant in dealings with the claimant, though the 'impact' of this would have to be judged in 'its relevant context'. It was not a case of simple reliance in fact; it was a question of whether the claimant could reasonably have relied on the defendant's personal assumption of responsibility.

The defendant had owned and controlled the company which had held itself out as having the expertise to provide reliable advice to franchisees, and a brochure issued to potential franchisees had made it clear that the expertise came from the defendant's experience in operating his own shop. Those circumstances, however, were not enough to make the defendant personally liable to the claimants.

There had been no personal dealings between the defendant and the claimants: they had dealt in their pre-contractual negotiations only with the company, through Z, an employee of the company. The claimants had not known the defendant and had no material pre-contractual dealings with him.

More recently, in *Merrett* v *Babb* [2001] 3 WLR 1, the claimant applied for a mortgage to buy a house, and the defendant produced a valuation report for his employers who were valuers working for the mortgagees. The claimant was eventually given the report, though the defendant's name had been removed. Eventually defects appeared in the house which the defendant ought to have noticed, and because the valuers had become insolvent the claimant sued the defendant personally for negligent misstatement. It was found that the claimant had relied on the report although its authorship was unknown to her, but she had assumed (properly) that the person who had prepared the report must have been competent. In reaching this conclusion the majority of the Court of Appeal followed *Smith* v *Bush; Harris* v *Wyre Forest DC* (above). You will recall that that case probably turned on its own special facts; indeed, Aldous LJ, who dissented, pointed that out. Relying on *Williams* (above) he emphasized the absence of a reasonable reliance by the claimant in the present case on any assumption of responsibility by the defendant. '. . . [T]hose who have fallen into the trap of thinking that all pure economic loss cases where a defendant has been held to have owed a claimant a duty of care are *Hedley Byrne* cases cannot but think that there is some conflict between the decisions in *Williams* . . . and *Merrett* v *Babb*. There is . . . no conflict: the *Williams* case was concerned with when one person will owe another a duty of care under *Hedley Byrne*; the duty of care in *Merrett* v *Babb* arose under a completely different principle'. . . (That is, a principle imposing liability on a professional person (a surveyor in the instant case) who ought to know that someone who cannot afford a substantial financial loss is likely to suffer such a loss, should the professional be negligent in the discharge of his duties.)

3.5.9 Duty/Causation

In *South Australia Asset Management Corporation* v *York Montague Ltd and Others* [1996] 3 All ER 365 (sometimes known as *Banque Bruxelles Lambert SA* v *Eagle Star Insurance Co. Ltd.*) (HL), a valuer of real property negligently overvalued some premises and as a result a lender of money gave a loan on the security of that property. The lender could show that had the valuer performed his task properly, and correctly valued the property, the lender would not have made the loan.

The borrower defaulted and the lender sold the property, but in the meantime the property dropped in value because of the economic recession of the early 1990s. In an action for negligence and breach of contract, the court had to decide whether the claim for damages against the valuer would include the loss due to the fall in the market. Overturning a unanimous decision of the Court of Appeal, the House of Lords held that the valuer was liable only for that loss which was due to the overvaluation and not for that part of the loss which was due to the fall in property prices.

Lord Hoffmann, with whom the rest of the House agreed, drew an analogy with the fictitious example of a mountaineer suing his doctor where the doctor had negligently certified one of the climber's knees as fit for climbing and the climber suffered injury in a mountaineering accident, although the accident was not directly connected to the problem with the knee. In his Lordship's opinion, to find the doctor liable for that accident would offend 'common sense, because it makes the doctor responsible for consequences which, though in general terms foreseeable, do not appear to have a sufficient causal connection with the subject matter of the duty'.

Thus, the answer to this conundrum was not to be found in any analysis of causation, but in looking at the scope of the duty of care. In each case, a claimant must establish that the defendant owes a duty to him and that it embraces the kind of loss of which he is complaining.

Within the present context his Lordship drew a distinction between (i) a duty to provide information to the claimant in order that he could decide on a course of action, and (ii) a duty to advise a person as to which course of action he should take.

In (i) the duty would be limited to taking reasonable care to see that the information was accurate, and any negligence would result in liability for the foreseeable consequences of the information being wrong. Where (ii) applied, the defendant's duty would be to take reasonable care in considering all the potential consequences of the course of action, and liability would lie for the foreseeable consequences of the course of action taken by the claimant in reliance on that advice.

A valuer would normally come within the first category (though much might depend on the terms of the contract between the parties), that is he advises on the value of the property, knowing that this advice is likely to be relied on by the lender in deciding (a) whether to lend and (b) how much to lend. The valuer is not usually asked to advise whether to lend; indeed valuers would usually not be equipped to provide advice of that nature. This case can also be considered in the context of causation (2.4).

3.5.10 Three-party relationships

The problem here concerns those situations in which A makes a negligent misstatement to B who relies on it to C's detriment. At first sight this situation cannot easily be accommodated under *Hedley Byrne*, because liability arising from that authority is based on the claimant himself relying on the misstatement, and suffering a detriment in so doing.

For example, it is established law that a mortgagee owes to his mortgagor a duty to achieve a proper price for the mortgaged property when he exercises his power of sale when the mortgagor defaults. In *Parker-Tweedale* v *Dunbar Bank Plc (No. 2)* [1990] 2 All ER 588, the Court of Appeal held that this duty cannot be extended to a person known by the mortgagee to have a beneficial interest in the property. Nor can it be owed to a beneficiary of a trust of which the mortgagor was a trustee and the mortgagee knew this.

3.5.10.1 Statute

In *Ministry of Housing* v *Sharp* [1970] 2 QB 223, the defendant was required by statute to keep an official register of local land charges, and his servant negligently omitted the claimant's land charge from a list of charges relating to land about to be purchased. Consequently the claimant's charge was lost. The defendant was found liable for the claimant's loss (though the law was changed by the Land Charges Act 1972, s. 10(6)). The Court of Appeal regarded the case as consistent with the principle established in *Hedley Byrne*. The defendant made his statement not to the claimant, but to the purchaser, a third party.

Perhaps the decision is restricted to its own, statutory context; it does not fit into any established category of negligence. Lord Denning alone based his judgment squarely on the claim that *Hedley Byrne* applied in the circumstances. Salmond LJ thought that the principal case (*Hedley Byrne*) did not apply in the present context precisely, while Cross LJ was hesitant in finding for the claimant, but concurred.

Sharp was approved and relied upon by Megarry VC in *Ross* v *Caunters* [1979] 3 All ER 580, though it was held in this case that liability was more appropriately based on the broad principle laid down in *Donoghue* v *Stevenson* rather than on *Hedley Byrne*.

According to this approach *Hedley Byrne* was merely 'illustrative' of liability for 'pure' economic loss, that is, it was not 'definitive' of such liability, indicating that in the long term the law about misstatements might be assimilated into the general law dealing with negligent acts. His Lordship, however, relied heavily on the now discredited 'Wilberforce test' (see 1.3.2). (Arguably, the beginnings of that assimilation, albeit by means of a different route, may be observed at a later stage in our discussion.)

In *Ross*, solicitors, in breach of contract, negligently omitted to warn a testator that spouses of intended beneficiaries should not attest his will. They were found liable in tort to an intended beneficiary, with whom they had no contractual relationship, whose spouse had attested it with the result that the gift to that beneficiary was void. The judge said:

> There are at least two ways in which *Hedley Byrne* may be regarded. First, it may be regarded as establishing a special category of case in which alone, by way of exception from the general rule, purely financial loss may be recovered in an action for negligence. Second, it may alternatively be regarded as establishing that there is no longer any general rule (if there ever was one) that purely financial loss is irrecoverable in negligence.

? **QUESTION** 3.13

Could the negligence complained of in *Ross* be categorized other than in terms of a misstatement?

It would be more appropriate to regard the solicitors' negligence in *Ross*, at least from the claimant's point of view, as an **act**, that is a breach of contract to a third party.

We will return to *Ross* in 3.5.10.2 (below).

3.5.10.2 **Others**

The claimant in *JEB Fasteners* v *Marks Bloom* [1981] 3 All ER 289, was not an identified individual. Woolf J based his reasoning principally upon 'foreseeability', applying the dicta of Lord Wilberforce in *Anns*, and side-stepping the restrictive formula laid down in *Hedley Byrne*. *Hedley Byrne*, and subsequent authorities, were seen as merely illustrative and not definitive of liability for negligent misstatement. This reasoning is similar to that in *Ross*. The defendants in *JEB Fasteners* were company auditors, and had audited the accounts of a company which was now in financial difficulties. It was found to be reasonably foreseeable on the facts that these certified accounts might be relied upon by persons considering taking over the company. The court held that the defendant accountants owed a duty of care to the claimants, who had taken over the company.

The Court of Appeal at [1983] 1 All ER 583, however, found that the defendants' negligence, that is breach of duty, had not caused the claimants' loss sustained as a result of the takeover because the claimants' main purpose in taking over the company was to acquire the services of its two directors. The decision at first instance was reversed, but only on the issue of causation.

In *Lawton* v *BOC Transhield Ltd* [1987] 2 All ER 608, it was found that a special duty of care was owed where a reference was given by a former employer for a former employee who was on probation with his new employer. The defendant (former employer) knew or ought to have known that the claimant (former employee) would lose his new job if an unfavourable reference was given. There was said to be close proximity between the parties; *Hedley Byrne* was mentioned, but a *Ross* v *Caunters* approach was taken to the existence of a duty of care. (You will have noted that the reference was given to and relied upon by the new employer, to the detriment of the claimant.)

The defendant was found not liable on the facts because there was no negligence on its part, in other words, there was no breach of duty.

Spring v *Guardian Assurance plc* [1993] 2 All ER 273 (HL)

In *Spring*, the Court of Appeal overruled *Lawton*. It was held that a person writing a reference does not owe a duty of care in negligence to the 'subject of the reference'. It was said that the only duty to that person arises in the torts of defamation and malicious falsehood.

This decision was reversed by the House of Lords and the result in *Lawton* reinstated, though not on the same grounds. It was held that employers did owe a duty of care in relation to the giving of character references for past and present employees, but this liability was not based on grounds of mere foreseeability. While it is true that some of their Lordships (Lords Lowry, Slynn, and Woolf) relied on a general conception of negligence liability, *Hedley Byrne* was also applied (Lords Goff and Lowry). Others based their reasoning on the special duty of care owed by employers to their employees (Lords Goff, Slynn, and Woolf). Accordingly, we will return to *Spring* in 5.5. Lord Keith delivered a dissenting speech.

EXERCISE 3.8

Read the extracts from the speeches in House of Lords decision in *Spring* [1994] 3 All ER 129, *Cases and Materials* (3.1.4.1), and describe the outcome.

According to Jones (p. 65) 'The rather special facts [of *Sharp, Ross,* and *Lawton*] (involving reliance by a third party) make it difficult to derive any general principle from them . . .' Oliver LJ (in the Court of Appeal decision) in *Leigh & Sillivan Ltd* v *Aliakmon Shipping* (see 3.4.1) thought that '*Ross* [stood] on its own': damage resulted from a transaction with a third party, there was loss of expectation of profit to the claimant, and it was doubtful if there was any damage suffered by the third party (the testator). Goff LJ in the same case (in the Court of Appeal decision) 'assumed' *Ross* v *Caunters* was correctly decided.

In *Clarke* v *Bruce Lance and Co.* [1988] 1 All ER 364, the Court of Appeal refused to extend *Ross*, and found that a testator's solicitors did not owe a duty of care to a potential beneficiary under a will, to advise the testator that a particular transaction which the testator had entered into was likely to harm the potential beneficiary's interest. Reference was made to the decision in *Yuen Kun-Yeu* (see 3.5.6) and it was said that:

(a) there was a lack of close proximity between the claimant and the defendants;

(b) if the defendants owed a duty to a potential beneficiary of the property, it could not be owed to the claimant alone; it would be owed (per Balcombe LJ) to the whole indeterminate class of potential donees or beneficiaries;

(c) another effective remedy existed if the defendants were negligent in their advice to the testator, i.e. the testator (or his personal representatives, as the case might be) had a cause of action in contract. If the claimant also had a cause of action in tort, the defendants were at risk of having to pay damages twice over.

The Court of Appeal in *White,* however, affirmed the basic ruling in *Ross.*

White v Jones [1993] 3 All ER 481

In *White* the defendant solicitors were negligent in delaying the preparation of a new will to replace an earlier one which the testator had decided to revoke, and he died before the new will was prepared. The claimants received nothing under the first will, which was unrevoked and effective, but would have benefited under the proposed new will. The defendants were found liable in the tort of negligence to the beneficiaries, that is, the claimants. (See *Cases and Materials* (3.1.4).)

 QUESTION 3.14

What do you think the 'basic ruling of *Ross*' means?

It means that the Court of Appeal agreed with the learned judge in *Ross*, that the solicitors ought to be liable on the facts of that case, and that that was the position in the present case.

You will recall that the judge in *Ross* did not attempt to extend the principle of *Hedley Byrne* to the facts of the case before him, rather he found for the claimant on the basis of the ordinary 'neighbour' principle in *Donoghue* v *Stevenson*. In this approach he prayed in aid the Wilberforce test from *Anns* (see 1.3.2).

The Court of Appeal in *White* rejected the argument that *Ross* had been implicitly overruled by *Caparo* and *Murphy* v *Brentwood DC* [1990] 2 All ER 908 (HL) and found that *Ross* was correctly decided, because it was in a category of its own, a view suggested by Lord Oliver in *Caparo*.

In *White* the solicitors did owe a duty of care in negligence to the claimant, in that *Ross* could be extended incrementally to provide a remedy, otherwise a person who had suffered real damage, the beneficiary in such cases, would be without an effective remedy because of the doctrine of privity of contract. Only the testator or his personal representatives could sue on the contract for the will; or in tort as an alternative because a duty of care in negligence would be owed to the testator.

> The will takes effect upon the testator's death. The testator cannot sue. The executor cannot sue because the estate is not diminished by the negligence: it is only the distribution of the estate that is altered . . . the breach of [the duty of care owed to the testator] will result in an award of nominal damages in the sum of £1 . . . it seems just and reasonable that the law should provide a remedy . . . There is either a remedy in tort or there is no remedy. (Farquharson LJ in *White*)

In this way the testator's intention could be fulfilled.

All the judges in *White* went out of their way to make it clear that the ruling in that case was made to provide justice in a particular context. The decision is no authority for a general remedy against solicitors because they basically owe obligations only to their clients. The courts are extremely reluctant to open the door too far for claims regarding 'loss of expectation'.

Perhaps mindful of the potential dangers, of 'opening the floodgates', inherent in any extension of *Ross* v *Caunters*, the House of Lords declined to apply it on appeal in *White* v *Jones* [1995] 1 All ER 691. Their Lordships in fact found in favour of the beneficiary, as had the Court of Appeal, but disagreed with that court on the precise legal route leading to that conclusion.

? QUESTION 3.15

Can you think of any other way of finding for the beneficiary in *White*?

In the House of Lords any solution based on *Ross* was rejected; it was found that the defendant solicitors had 'assumed responsibility' under *Hedley Byrne* for their negligence, and that assumption of responsibility to the testator should be extended to include, as Lord Goff put it,

> the intended beneficiary [of the testator] who, as the solicitor could reasonably foresee, might, as a result of the solicitor's negligence, be deprived of his intended legacy in circumstances in which neither the testator nor his estate would have a remedy against the solicitor.

His Lordship said this approach not only produced 'practical justice' for the parties concerned; it also resulted in the following benefits:

1. There is no unacceptable circumvention of established principles of the law of contract.

2. No problem arises by reason of the loss being of a purely economic character.

3. Such assumption of responsibility will be subject to any term of the contract between the solicitor and testator which might exclude or restrict the solicitor's liability to the testator under the principle in *Hedley Byrne*, although such a term would be most unlikely to exist in practice.

4. As the *Hedley Byrne* principle is founded upon an assumption of responsibility the solicitor might be liable for negligent omissions as well as negligent acts of commission.

5. Damages for loss of an expectation are not excluded in cases of negligence arising under the principle in *Hedley Byrne* simply because the cause of action is classified as tortious. Such damages might in principle be recoverable in cases of contractual negligence and there is, for present purposes, no relevant distinction that can be drawn between the two forms of action.

His Lordship rejected the *Ross* v *Caunters* approach to the resolution of such a problem in the following words: 'an ordinary action in tortious negligence on the lines proposed in *Ross* v *Caunters* is inappropriate because it does not meet any of the conceptual problems which have been raised.'

It is submitted, with respect, that the view of the dissenting minority is to be preferred. To apply *Hedley Byrne* in such a situation, in which the key element of reliance (by the claimant) is missing, is to risk straining the notion of a special relationship to breaking point. On this view it would be far better and would accord more with principle to apply *Ross* to the present facts. In this way a special duty of care in negligence owed by solicitors to beneficiaries can be recognized and controlled. As Steyn LJ put it in the Court of Appeal:

> While I recognise that there may be difficult problems to be considered in future, it does not seem to me that *Ross* v *Caunters* created an uncontrollable principle. In my view the requirements of foreseeability, proximity and justice, which are needed to establish a duty, together with the concepts of breach, causation, loss and remoteness, are adequate to contain liability of the *Ross* v *Caunters* type within acceptable limits. And in my judgment the recognition of a duty of care in such a case, which involves very special considerations, will not assist arguments on the recoverability of other heads of economic loss. I would rule that *Ross* v *Caunters* was correctly decided.

 You can read more about *White*, and an extract from Weir in *Cases and Materials* (3.1.4.1).

In *Penn* v *Bristol and West Building Society and Others* (1995), *The Times*, 19 June, X owned a house jointly with his wife, the claimant, and, in collusion with the buyer of the property, forged the conveyance. It was found that this 'sham transaction' did not affect the beneficial joint tenancy of X and the claimant. Kolbert J held that X's solicitors, who had not taken steps to check whether they had the claimant's authority to act, were in breach of a duty of care in negligence owed to the claimant:

> Although the wife had never been a client of the solicitors she was reasonably within their contemplation when they received the title deeds, indeed she was necessarily within their contemplation, and her interest as co-owner was sufficiently proximate to the transaction in which they were engaged, concerning as it did her jointly owned home, for the solicitors to owe her a duty of care according to the principles enunciated by the House of Lords in *White* v *Jones* [1995] 2 WLR 187.

In *McCullagh* v *Lane Fox and Partners Ltd* (1995), *The Times*, 22 December (CA), a majority of the court found that (i) an estate agent who is negligent in stating the size of a property does not owe a prospective purchaser a duty of care, provided that the estate agent reasonably believes that the purchaser will not rely on his misstatement because the purchaser intends to obtain an independent property survey; and (ii) a duty of care does not arise later if the estate agent discovers that the purchaser has decided not to commission an independent survey, provided that the estate agent is still unaware of his 'innocent' (albeit negligent) misrepresentation.

Although Hobhouse LJ agreed that no duty of care arose on the facts, his reasoning was somewhat different. In his opinion, a duty of care could have arisen on the estate agent's part, once he became aware of the purchaser's decision to dispense with an independent survey and that he would then rely on the estate agent's misrepresentation, but on the facts of the present case the existence of a disclaimer (which satisfied the 'reasonableness' test in the Unfair Contract Terms Act 1977) prevented any such duty of care from arising. The existence of the disclaimer meant that the purchaser was prevented from believing that the estate agent was assuming responsibility for his negligent misstatement. His Lordship reviewed *White* v *Jones* and *Henderson* v *Merrett* and concluded that the principle to be applied is still to be found in *Hedley Byrne*. Under the principle laid down in that case, an agent can be as liable as his principal for a careless misrepresentation provided that the 'fundamental' elements of reasonable foreseeability, reliance, and assumption of responsibility can be established by the claimant.

In *Goodwill* v *British Pregnancy Advisory Service* [1996] 2 All ER 161 (CA), the claimant knew that her partner had had a vasectomy and did not use any form of contraception, becoming pregnant as a result.

It was held that she had no cause of action in negligence for financial loss against the person who performed the vasectomy. *White* v *Jones* did not apply. That decision, described by Peter Gibson LJ, who delivered the judgment of the court, as belonging to an 'unusual class of cases', produced a special remedy in tort to overcome 'the rank injustice' arising in the circumstances.

His Lordship concluded that the requirements of *Hedley Byrne*, as interpreted in *Caparo*, were not satisfied in the present case, that is there was no actual or inferential knowledge by the defendants that their advice 'when communicated to the claimant by her partner was likely to be acted upon by her without independent inquiry'. It was the *partner* who had been advised, and the claimant did not even have an existing sexual relationship with him at the time that the advice was given.

In *Harris* v *Evans (and the Health and Safety Executive)* [1998] 3 All ER 522 (CA), a striking out action, it was held that a health and safety inspector (and his employer vicariously) did not owe a duty of care in the tort of negligence to the claimant, who ran a bungee-jumping business.

The defendant gave advice (in accordance with his powers under the Health and Safety at Work Act 1974) to certain local authorities concerning the safety of equipment used by the claimant in his business, as a result of which the local authorities used their statutory powers (also under the 1974 Act) to prevent the use of this equipment. Consequently the claimant suffered 'pure' economic loss because of the loss of trade caused by this ban.

The court, adopting the *Caparo* incremental approach, said *X* v *Bedfordshire County Council* was the leading authority on the question of whether *Hedley Byrne/White* v *Jones/Spring* v *Guardian Assurance* applied in the present context. As in *X*, there was here a statutory scheme: the defendant advised the local authorities and they acted within the terms of the 1974 Act. It was implicit in the Act that economic loss might be caused when prohibition orders against the use of equipment were issued—whether by the local authorities acting on the advice of the defendant or by the defendant himself—and the Act itself provided remedies for the erroneous use of its powers by inspectors or local (enforcing) authorities.

Sir Richard Scott V-C, giving the judgment of the court, said that a further factor to be considered (as it had been in *X*, above) was whether the imposition of a duty of care in negligence on inspectors such as the defendant would 'engender untoward caution' on their part in the performance of their statutory duties. His Lordship said that had the defendant in the present case imposed some particular requirement which introduced 'a new risk or danger not present in the [claimant's] business activity as previously conducted' and this risk or danger materialized, causing damage to the business as well as physical damage to person or property, it was possible that that damage might be compensated via an action in negligence; but that was not so here: all that the alleged negligence of the defendant had done in the present case was to lead to statutory restraints being placed on the claimant's ability to carry on his business. That alleged negligence was not actionable, whether the notices had been issued by the inspector himself or by an enforcing authority acting on his advice. You will recall that the courts have now retreated from the restrictive approach in pleadings applications adopted in *X* (see 1.5). This decision is also relevant in 7.3.

In *Baker* v *Kaye* (1996), *The Times*, 13 December, it was held that a doctor who carried out a medical examination on behalf of someone's prospective employer owed a duty of care to the person he examined.

The prospective employee was not the doctor's patient, but the court took the view that the doctor assumed a duty of care to that person because he regarded himself as being under a duty to advise that person to seek medical advice if the examination revealed any illness. That produced a relationship of sufficient legal proximity, and it was 'fair, just, and reasonable' to impose a duty of care in the tort of negligence on the doctor. It may be thought that the decisive factor in this decision was the therapeutic nature of the responsibility assumed by the doctor towards the prospective employee.

However, this case must be considered in the light of the Court of Appeal's decision in *Kapfunde* v *Abbey National plc* (1998), *The Times*, 26 March. The claimant had applied for a job with Abbey National and, as part of the process of applying for the post, she had completed a questionnaire giving details of absences from work due to illness. A doctor, employed by the Abbey National as occupational health adviser, advised his employer that the claimant's medical history pointed to the likelihood of above-average absenteeism. As a consequence the claimant did not get the job.

As to the question of whether the doctor owed a duty of care in negligence to the claimant, the court identified the following factors as significant in this case: (i) the lack of any doctor/patient relationship because the doctor never saw Mrs Kapfunde; (ii) the lack of any legal liability on a potential employer to exercise skill and care in processing applications for employment; and (iii) the fact that the claim was only for economic loss, that is, salary and other benefits she would have enjoyed if appointed to the post.

The argument in this case centred on the duty of care issue and its attendant concerns of proximity, assumption of responsibility, and whether it would be just and reasonable to impose a duty in the circumstances.

Kennedy LJ referred to the decision in *White v Jones* which, in his Lordship's opinion, was not confined strictly to its own facts; but it had to be read in the light of *X v Bedfordshire CC*. The doctor's position in the present case could be compared with that of the social workers and doctors in *X*, or with that of a doctor conducting an examination for purposes of life insurance, except that the doctor here had made his assessment only on the basis of reading the claimant's completed questionnaire. His Lordship, referring to the speech of Lord Browne-Wilkinson in *X v Bedfordshire*, said that the incremental increase in the categories of negligence made in *White v Jones* was only small, sufficient to cover the facts of that case, but not sufficient to support the imposition of a duty of care in the circumstances of the present case.

There was no special relationship between the parties creating a duty of care. This was a better way of expressing the situation than to say there was insufficient proximity, but 'it amounted to the same thing'.

His Lordship also expressed the opinion that the judge in *Baker v Kaye* was wrong in finding that the doctor owed a duty of care to the claimant in that case.

In *Gorham v British Telecommunications Plc* [2000] 1 WLR 2129 (CA), *White v Jones* was applied in the case of an insurance salesman who had misrepresented the effect of moving out of a company pension scheme to a man who, acting on the salesman's advice, took out a personal pension plan. As a result of opting out of his employer's scheme he lost valuable benefits payable on his death to his dependants should he die whilst in service. His widow argued that these lost benefits were similar to a loss sustained by intended beneficiaries under a will, as in *White*. The court agreed with this argument, ruling that the insurance salesman had assumed responsibility to the deceased *and* his family.

In *Esterhuizen v Allied Dunbar Assurance plc* (1998), *The Times*, 10 June, it was held that the duty of care imposed on solicitors in *White v Jones* extended to persons other than solicitors who offered will-making services.

In *Cass Glyn v Frearsons* [1998] 4 All ER 225, a firm of solicitors negligently drew up a will by not checking whether certain real property was held on a joint tenancy or on a tenancy in common by a testator. The solicitors had not made sure that the property, which was intended for the claimant, a beneficiary under the will, would fall into the estate. (In the case of a joint tenancy a property goes to the surviving joint tenant on death. Under a tenancy in common the tenancy can be 'severed', that is split up into portions, with the testator's part going to the estate for distribution to the legatees. Since the property was held in this case on a joint tenancy it went to the surviving joint tenant and not to the deceased's estate, so the claimant lost his inheritance.) The solicitors were found liable under *White v Jones*.

The Court of Appeal in *Worby and Others v Rosser* (1999), *The Times*, 9 June was asked to rule whether a testator's solicitor owed a duty of care in negligence to the intended beneficiaries under a 1983 will, when preparing a 1989 will which affected their inheritances, to ensure that the testator had legal capacity to make the will and was not under the undue influence of another person. It was held that no duty of care was owed. In the event, the beneficiaries under the earlier will obtained their legacies; they brought the present action to recover their costs in successfully defending the earlier will in probate proceedings on the 1989 will.

In *Bank of Credit and Commerce International (Overseas) Ltd (in liquidation), BCCI Holdings (Luxembourg) SA (in liquidation) and Bank of Credit and Commerce International SA (in liquidation)* v *Price Waterhouse and Others and Ernst Whinney and Others* (1998), *The Times*, 4 March (CA), Neill LJ said that the leading cases involving accountants and other professional advisers for economic loss caused to persons other than their clients had followed three 'separate but parallel paths', viz.:

1. The 'threefold test' stated by Lord Griffiths in *Smith* v *Eric S. Bush* and considered in *Caparo* that raised three essential questions:

   (a) Was it reasonably foreseeable that the claimant would suffer the kind of damage which occurred?
   (b) Was there sufficient proximity between the parties?
   (c) Was it just and reasonable that the defendant should owe a duty of care of the scope asserted by the claimant?

2. The 'assumption of responsibility' test that was explained in *White* v *Jones*.

3. The adoption of an incremental approach, recognized by Lord Bridge in *Caparo* and which received further support in *Murphy* v *Brentwood District Council*. That approach ensured that developments in the law would take place in measured steps.

The fact that all those approaches had been used and approved by the House of Lords in recent years suggested that it could be useful to look at any new set of facts by using each of the three approaches in turn. If the facts were properly analysed and the policy considerations correctly evaluated the several approaches would yield the same result.

The general trend of the authorities made it clear that liability would depend not on intention but on the actual or presumed knowledge of the adviser and on the circumstances of the case.

3.5.11 Omissions and acts

There are two other special features of *White* to consider. First, the solicitors were negligent by way of omission rather than by way of commission (or positive act) because they failed to act in time. This problem can be accommodated under either *Ross* or *Hedley Byrne*.

As Steyn LJ said in the Court of Appeal:

> While as a matter of fact negligence in failing to act may often be more difficult to establish than negligence in the drafting or executing of a will, there ought in principle to be no distinction between commission and omission in this particular field.

The second factor causes more difficulty. The solicitors were guilty of breach of contract (to the testator) by failing to act; they did not utter a misstatement (or fail to warn) in classic *Hedley Byrne* terms. As a result of *White* it would seem that acts as well as misstatements are covered by *Hedley Byrne*. *Ross* did not raise the same problem because the decision in that case was based on ordinary *Donoghue* v *Stevenson* principles, whereas *Hedley Byrne* has invariably been regarded only as a misstatement case.

> **?** | **QUESTION** 3.16
>
> Can you see a way out of this difficulty?

Your attention has already been drawn to the views expressed in *Ross* and *JEB Fasteners* that *Hedley Byrne* can be viewed as authority for the proposition that there is no general rule against recovery for 'pure' economic loss in the tort of negligence; in other words, *Hedley Byrne* is not definitive of liability in this field, but is only illustrative of such liability. The decision in *White* seems to add strength to this argument, by applying *Hedley Byrne* to acts. If *Hedley Byrne* applies only to misstatements it might be a genuine exception to the so-called general 'rule', limited perhaps by the notion of 'assumption of responsibility'. (If, though, this 'assumption of responsibility' can be stretched as it has been in *White*, that would make it a control of dubious quality.)

In any event, earlier authority can be found for the view that *Hedley Byrne* applies to acts. The decision in *Junior Books* has been explained in terms of *Hedley Byrne* 'reliance' by Lord Bridge and Lord Keith in *Murphy v Brentwood DC*; and solicitors were found liable under *Hedley Byrne* for failing to register the claimant's interest in a piece of land as a land charge in *Midland Bank Trust Co. Ltd v Hett, Stubbs, and Kemp* [1979] Ch 384. Lord Keith said in *Murphy*:

> In *Pirelli General Cable Works Ltd* v *Oscar Faber & Partners (a firm)* (1983), it was held that the cause of action in tort against consulting engineers who had negligently approved a defective design for a chimney arose when damage to the chimney caused by the defective design first occurred, not when the damage was discovered or with reasonable diligence might have been discovered. The defendants there had in relation to the design been in contractual relations with the claimants, but it was common ground that a claim in contract was time-barred. If the claimants had happened to discover the defect before any damage had occurred there would seem to be no good reason for holding that they would not have had a cause of action in tort at that stage, without having to wait until some damage had occurred. They would have suffered economic loss through having a defective chimney on which they were required to expend money for the purpose of removing the defect. It would seem that in a case such as the *Pirelli General Cable Works* case, where the tortious liability arose out of a contractual relationship with professional people, the duty extended to take reasonable care not to cause economic loss to the client by the advice given. The claimants built the chimney as they did in reliance on that advice. The case would accordingly fall within the principle of *Hedley Byrne & Co. Ltd v Heller & Partners Ltd* (1964). I regard *Junior Books Ltd v Veitchi Co. Ltd* (1982) as being an application of that principle.

The Court of Appeal followed *Pirelli* in *Abbott v Will Gannon and Smith Ltd* (2005), *The Times*, 28 April. In this case the defective design had not caused any loss at the time when the work was completed. It would do so only when it manifested itself in some way which would affect the value of the building, measured either by the cost of repairs or depreciation in market value.

Lord Oliver in *D & F Estates* also suggested *Junior Books* can be seen as an application of *Hedley Byrne*:

> There is, therefore, a strong argument that *Hedley Byrne* has always had the potential as a form of liability not restricted to misstatements; that it opens up liability for pure economic loss in a general sense, being limited only by the requirements of the 'special relationship'. If *Junior Books* is to be explained in terms of *Hedley Byrne*, and if that authority applies to acts as well as misstatements, it is difficult to see *Hedley Byrne* as an 'exception' to a general 'rule'; indeed, it would seem to have the quality of a vector of change, of assimilating 'acts' with 'misstatements', of forming a 'general' 'rule' for liability for 'pure' economic loss.

3.5.12 Physical damage

In *Dutton* v *Bognor Regis Urban District Council* [1972] 1 QB 373 (CA), Lord Denning drew a distinction between 'the several categories of professional men'. A professional man giving advice on financial or property matters, for example an accountant, a banker, or lawyer, owed a duty only to those who relied on his advice and suffered loss as a result. However, a professional person advising on the safety of buildings, machinery, or materials owed a duty to all those who might suffer if his advice were bad. This is so not because the injured persons have relied on him, but because he knew, or ought to have known, that such persons might be injured if the advice were unsound. In *Dutton* a local authority building inspector was held to owe a duty of care to the claimant as a professional adviser, even though the claimant had not thought of it and had not directly placed reliance on his conduct. [The statutory context in such a case may be important.] The House of Lords overturned the ruling on the facts in this case in *Murphy* v *Brentwood DC* (6.3.2).

Liability for a careless misstatement resulting in physical damage was imposed in *Clayton* v *Woodman* [1962] 2 QB 533. An architect was found liable to a bricklayer for careless misstatements about how to conduct building work. The bricklayer suffered physical injury as a result of relying on the architect's assurances.

 EXERCISE 3.9

Read the decision in *Clay* v *Crump and Sons* [1964] 1 QB 533. What have you learned from it?

The owners of a building engaged demolition contractors to pull down the building and building contractors to erect a new one on the same site. An architect was employed to prepare plans and supervise the work. A wall on the site was also to be demolished but the owners asked the demolition contractors if the wall could be left intact on a temporary basis; they asked the architect for his opinion. Both decided the wall was safe. The foundations of the wall had been exposed and an expert could, with reasonable care, have seen that the wall was in a dangerous state. Neither the demolition contractors nor the architect had exercised due care and the building contractors merely assumed that the wall had been deliberately left standing and thus gave it only a cursory inspection. It was found that the architect and the demolition contractors knew, or ought to have known, that this assumption would be made in the circumstances. The wall collapsed, injuring the claimant, an employee of the building contractors. The architect, the demolition contractors, and the building contractors were all held liable in negligence to the claimant.

Although counsel for the architect based his argument partly on the reasoning in *Candler* v *Crane, Christmas and Co*, and *Hedley Byrne* v *Heller*, the court took the familiar proximity approach found in Lord Atkin's neighbour principle in *Donoghue* v *Stevenson*. In other words, the problem was seen in terms of the general neighbour principle rather than the 'special relationship' requirement in *Hedley Byrne* v *Heller*.

In *Clay* liability was imposed for a negligent misstatement causing personal injury in a three-party relationship, where someone else relied on the defendant's assurance to the claimant's detriment, on the basis of the *Donoghue* v *Stevenson* 'neighbour' principle.

There was very close proximity between a professional person, the defendant, and someone very likely to be affected by his careless assurances on safety matters, viz. the claimant. You might think that this separate strand of liability for careless misstatements causing physical damage could exist quite happily with *Hedley Byrne*, complementing that authority's jurisdiction in pure economic loss.

In *T (a minor)* v *Surrey County Council and Others* [1994] 4 All ER 577, *Hedley Byrne* was applied in a case of physical damage. The claimant, suing through his mother as his next friend, claimed damages in the following circumstances. His mother had been told by the local authority's child-minding adviser that there was no reason why she should not place her infant son, under one year old at the time, with X, who was a child-minder registered with the local authority under the Nurseries and Child-Minders Regulation Act 1948. A few months earlier, however, another young infant had been injured whilst in X's care, it was thought as a result of violent shaking, though X was not convicted of any offence and it appears that the local authority could not decide whether X was responsible. The child-minding adviser did, though, advise X that she should think about taking care of older children.

T's mother placed him with X and he subsequently sustained brain damage as a result of an incident similar to that involving the other infant. T, as claimant, sued the local authority for breach of statutory duty (failure to de-register X), negligence in failing to cancel X's registration, and the child-minding adviser's negligent misstatement. T also sued X for negligence, trespass to the person, and breach of contract.

It was held that the local authority was liable for negligent misstatement under *Hedley Byrne* because T's mother would not have put him into X's care had she known the full facts. X was also found liable under all three heads of T's claim.

 EXERCISE 3.10

Please read the extract from the judgment of Scott Baker J in *T*, and list from it four important features.

> In my judgment, the criteria for founding liability for negligent misstatement are met. Mr Bodycomb was at all times acting as the local authority's nursery and child-minding adviser. He was the only person employed in that capacity for the Ashford area. When he spoke to [the mother] on 25 August, he was consulted and speaking as a professional officer with special knowledge and responsibility. He knew, or ought to have known, that what he said would be relied upon. What he said related directly to the safety of the infant [claimant]. There was, in these circumstances, a special relationship of proximity between Mr Bodycomb and the [claimant]. I accept Mr Swift's submission that this case falls four square within the principle laid down in *Hedley Byrne & Co. Ltd* v *Heller & Partners Ltd* [1964] AC 465, but the [claimant]'s position is stronger in the present case because he suffered physical injury rather than mere economic loss.

The four important features of this case are as follows:

(a) there is no mention of assumption of responsibility;

(b) the point is not taken that it was not the claimant who relied on the misstatement, but his mother;

(c) the judge makes the point that it is easier to recover for physical damage than for economic loss;

(d) although the report does not say so, it is presumably the case that the local authority was found vicariously liable for its adviser's negligent misstatement. (Vicarious liability is covered in **Chapter 8**.)

The lack of attention to the question of assumption of responsibility is surprising in view of the importance attached to this requirement in other cases.

There is no discussion in *T* of 'third party' relationships arising under *Hedley Byrne*; in the past that has been a point of contention and the courts have had to find ways round the difficulty: for example, in *Ross* and *White*.

It is curious that the judge should consider a claimant to have a stronger case when claiming compensation for physical damage under *Hedley* Byrne rather than 'pure' economic loss. Is it not the case that this form of liability was developed specifically to meet claims for 'pure' economic loss?

The judgment in *Clay* was not cited in *T*, yet it provides a ready-made basis for finding in favour of the claimant; it suggests an approach which meets the difficulties suggested. *T* is yet another example of the extension of liability under *Hedley Byrne*, an expansion of jurisdiction which appears to be based solely on pragmatic considerations rather than on the basis of an orderly and principled development, in keeping with the incremental approach.

3.5.13 General

In *Burton v Islington Health Authority* [1991] 1 All ER 825, Potts J said different considerations arise where the loss is caused by physical damage. He queried Lord Bridge in *Caparo Industries plc v Dickman*.

> One of the most important distinctions always to be observed lies in the law's essential approach to the different kinds of damage which one party may have suffered in consequence of the acts or omissions of another. It is one thing to owe a duty of care to avoid causing injury to the person or property of others. It is quite another to avoid causing others to suffer purely economic loss.

And Lord Oliver in the same case:

> it is now clear from a series of decisions in this House that, at least so far as concerns the law of the United Kingdom, the duty of care in tort depends not solely on the existence of the essential ingredient of the foreseeability of damage to the claimant but on its coincidence with a further ingredient to which has been attached the label 'proximity' and which was described by Lord Atkin in the course of his speech in *Donoghue* v *Stevenson* [1932] AC 562 at 581 as 'such close and direct relations that

the act complained of directly affects a person whom the person alleged to be bound to take care would know would be directly affected by his careless act.' It must be remembered, however, that Lord Atkin was using these words in the context of loss caused by physical damage where the existence of the nexus between the careless defendant and the injured claimant can rarely give rise to any difficulty. To adopt the words of Bingham LJ in the instant case ([1989] QB 653 at 686): 'It is enough that the claimant chances to be (out of the whole world) the person with whom the defendant collided or who purchased the offending ginger beer.

. . .

Thus I proceed on the basis that the nature of the duty of care in cases involving physical injury and consequential loss remains as it was before the decisions of the House of Lords in *Caparo Industries plc* v *Dickman* [1990] 2 AC 605 and *Murphy* v *Brentwood DC* [1990] 3 WLR 414. In *Donoghue* v *Stevenson* [1932] AC 562 the foresight of a reasonable man was accepted as a general test as to whether a duty of care existed.

***Marc Rich Co. AG and Others* v *Bishop Rock Marine Co. Ltd and Others* [1995] 3 All ER 307**

See 1.3.4 and *Cases and Materials* (1.6) It was alleged that the defendant classification society had a duty of care to avert the consequences of the shipowners' breach of duty in operating an unseaworthy ship. The claimants also contended that where physical damage was involved it was incumbent on a claimant to show only foreseeability of damage; in other words, where only physical damage was involved it was not necessary in seeking to establish a duty of care, to satisfy the three-stage test (referred to in 1.3).

The court held that there is in principle no legal distinction between physical damage, whether to person or property, and pure economic loss. All claims for loss in negligence are matters of financial compensation and it followed that the three-stage test must be satisfied in all cases.

? QUESTION 3.17

How would you defend this action?

On the facts, the contracts of carriage imposed a non-delegable, contractual duty on the shipowners to exercise 'due diligence' to ensure the seaworthiness of their vessel. If a duty in negligence had been imposed on the defendants, it would be virtually identical to the duty owed by the shipowners (under the contract) but without the benefit of the protective provisions of the contract: so, it would not be 'just and reasonable' to impose a duty of care on the defendants in these circumstances. After all, there were no 'dealings' at all between the claimants and the defendants in this case. You can read extracts from the speeches of Lord Steyn, and of Lord Lloyd (dissenting) in *Cases and Materials* (3.1.5).

At first sight, *Marc Rich* suggests that at long last the courts have recognized the fact that there is no proper distinction between the different forms of damage. This decision has the potential for bringing *Hedley Byrne* closer than ever to *Donoghue* v *Stevenson*, particularly in the light of developments already discussed in this chapter. Past experience suggests, however, that the courts will continue to treat pure economic loss as a different form of damage. As Scott Baker J says in *T* '. . . the courts are more ready to find a duty of care owed where the consequence of a breach is personal injury rather than damage to property and still less mere economic loss'.

In *Reeman* v *Department of Transport* [1997] 2 Lloyd's Rep 648 (CA), it was held that a surveyor of fishing boats, whilst owing a duty of care in relation to physical loss, did not owe a duty with regard to 'pure' economic loss suffered by a potential buyer of a certified boat (or ship). This was the case even where the defendant knows that the vessel may be sold.

Marc Rich was distinguished by the Court of Appeal in *Perrett* v *Collins* (1998), *The Times*, 23 June. The claimant was a passenger in an aircraft owned, built and flown by D1 and he was injured when the plane crashed. D2 was an inspector employed by D3 (the statutory authority responsible for airworthy certificates). D2 had issued a certificate of fitness for flight under s. 3 of the Civil Aviation Act 1983, and the question for the court to decide was whether D2 and D3 could owe (this was a 'striking-out' application) the claimant a duty of care in negligence. It was held that a duty owed by D2 and D3 would not duplicate D1's liability, because D2's role was an independent and 'critical' one: the aircraft could not take off without a certificate from D2. A passenger in an aircraft was entitled to assume that it had met the appropriate safety standards and that those involved had taken proper care in discharging their obligations.

This decision can be compared with *Philcox* v *Civil Aviation Authority* (1995), *The Times*, 8 June (CA). It was held that an inspector owed no liability to the owner of an aircraft which was destroyed when it crashed, because it was members of the public, and not owners, who were protected by such inspections. The owner was obliged to ensure proper maintenance of his aircraft and the role of the inspector, and the CAA, was of a supervisory nature over owners; it was not an obligation to protect owners from their own failings. *Perrett* and *Philcox* are decisions relevant to the discussion in 7.4.

3.5.14 **Conclusion**

In *Henderson*, Lord Goff said that *Hedley Byrne* applied to the performance of duties other than the giving of advice or information, but the full implications of *Henderson* and *White* v *Jones* remain uncertain. For example, would *Junior Books*, if decided today, be based upon an 'assumption of responsibility' by the subcontractors? If so, would that be a more satisfactory way of circumventing the doctrine of privity than the utilization of the Wilberforce test? Is it acceptable to use *Hedley Byrne* to 'trump' privity's hand?

It is submitted that *Hedley Byrne*, so extended, has ceased to be an 'exception' to the general 'rule' concerning liability for pure economic loss in negligence. No longer restricted to liability for misstatements, it has metamorphosed into **the** all-embracing form of liability for negligently inflicted pure economic loss. This result may be welcome for three important reasons:

(a) it recognizes the illogical distinction between 'economic' and 'physical' loss (an illogicality emphasized in *Marc Rich*);

(b) it mitigates the often artificial distinction between 'acts', 'statements', and 'omissions';

(c) it further relieves, as did *Donoghue* before it, in relation to 'manufacturer' and 'consumer', the unfair results which can be caused by the doctrine of privity of contract.

There remain, however, a number of difficulties with this enlarged jurisdiction of *Hedley Byrne*:

Is it only **professional** acts which are caught by the requirement of an 'assumption of responsibility'? Is it merely a question of asking whether the defendant has 'engaged his professional responsibility' for the task in hand? It is uncertain whether, for example, in a situation similar to that in *Simaan* (below) there would be an 'assumption of responsibility' for a contractual obligation by A (subcontractor) (B is the main contractor with whom A has his contract) to C (the developer/owner of a building).

In *Simaan* (3.5.6) the defendant supplied glass panels under a contract to a subcontractor employed by the main contractor to install the panels in a building being erected for X. The main contractor, the claimant, suffered 'pure' economic loss when X rejected the panels as defective and withheld payments under the main contract. On the facts, the Court of Appeal thought it would be unjust and unreasonable to impose a duty of care in negligence on the defendant (in favour of the claimant) since to find for the claimant would not be in accord with the contractual arrangements which existed between the parties. The imposition of such a duty on the defendant would be tantamount to the imposition of a legal obligation on the defendant which the parties, via their contractual negotiations, had taken steps to avoid. See also the cases discussed in 5.4.2.

Secondly, it will be seen in 6.3, which deals with liability for dangerous premises, that developers, builders, etc., and local authorities, are not responsible in the tort of negligence for the provision of defective premises unless those defective premises cause damage to person or property. Professional people such as surveyors may be liable irrespective of whether damage is caused to other property, or to persons, by the defective structure. In other words, **their** liability, in tort, extends to defects in **quality**, which is in effect liability of a contractual nature, embracing as it does the cost of repair.

■ SUMMARY

- Liability for negligently inflicted 'pure' economic loss has always posed a difficult problem in the law of negligence.

- 'Loss of expectation', as it is sometimes called, is seen in traditional terms as more of a contractual problem.

- *Hedley Byrne*, however, changed all that. It can be seen as a bridge between tort and contract in that it recognizes a claim in tort for 'loss of expectation'. *White* may be seen as confirming this role for *Hedley Byrne*.

- By extending the scope of 'reliance' and 'assumption of responsibility', chiefly the latter, the courts have widened the jurisdiction of *Hedley Byrne* in recent times:
  - (a) it now encompasses 'acts', as well as misstatements;
  - (b) it embraces 'omissions', as well as 'acts';
  - (c) it covers three-party relationships;
  - (d) it may extend to cases of physical damage.

- *Henderson* and *White* v *Jones* are authorities for the proposition that 'assumption of responsibility', a concept of the law of tort, can be used to transcend the conventional tort/contract 'boundary'; to create a legal relationship equivalent to contract but without consideration (see Lord Devlin in *Hedley Byrne*) although the parties have refrained from entering into a formal contractual relationship. It may be thought that *White* v *Jones* goes further than *Henderson*, because there was no contractual chain in the former case.

- *Hedley Byrne* liability may be limited to negligent misstatements, advice, and the provision of services, though the notions of 'services' and 'reliance' may be capable of wider interpretation. Liability for defective products and premises in the tort of negligence are still, as far as 'pure' economic loss is concerned, governed by cases such as *Murphy* and *Aswan Engineering*.

- *Ross* and *Junior Books* represent an assault on the doctrine of privity of contract. *White* continues this attack, albeit from a different direction. It remains to be seen whether this develops into something more than a mere skirmish.

■ FURTHER READING

Allen, T., 'Liability for References: The House of Lords and *Spring* v *Guardian Assurance*' (1995) 58 *MLR* 553.

Cane, P., *Tort Law and Economic Interests*, 2nd edn, Oxford: Oxford University Press, 1996.

Cooke, R., 'An Impossible Decision' (1991) 107 *LQR* 46.

Craig, P.P., 'Negligent Misstatements, Negligent Acts and Economic Loss' (1976) 92 *LQR* 213.

Fleming, J.G., 'Requiem for *Anns*' (1990) 106 *LQR* 525.

Harlow C., *Understanding Tort Law*, 3rd edn, London: Sweet & Maxwell, 2005, Chapter 6.

Hepple, Howarth, and Matthews, *Tort: Cases and Materials*, 5th edn, London: Butterworths, 2000, Chapter 4.

Jones, M., *Textbook on Torts*, 8th edn, Oxford: Oxford University Press, 2002, pp. 58–100.

Kidner, R., *Casebook on Torts*, 9th edn, Oxford: Oxford University Press, 2006, Chapter 10.

Kaye, T., 'Acts Speak Louder than Statements, or Nine into One Will Go' (1995) 58 *MLR* 574.

Lorenz, W. and Markesinis, B., 'Solicitors' Liability Towards Third Parties' (1993) 56 *MLR* 558.

Lunney, M. and Oliphant, K., *Tort Law Text and Materials*, 2nd edn, Oxford: Oxford University Press, 2003, Chapter 8.

McBride, N.J. and Bagshaw, R., *Tort Law*, 2nd edn, London: Longman, 2005, Chapter 5.

Markesinis, B.S. and Deakin, S.F., *Tort Law*, 5th edn, Oxford: Oxford University Press, 2003, pp. 112–48.

Martin, R., 'Categories of Negligence and Duties of Care: *Caparo* in the House of Lords' (1990) 53 *MLR* 824.

Mullis, A. and Oliphant, K., *Torts*, 3rd edn, London: Palgrave MacMillan, 2003, Chapter 3.

Murphy, J., *Street on Torts*, 11th edn, London: Butterworths, 2003, pp. 206–17.

Salmond and Heuston, *Law of Torts*, 21st edn, London: Sweet & Maxwell, 1996, pp. 210–19.

Stanton, K.M., *The Modern Law of Tort*, London: Sweet & Maxwell, 1994, Chapters 14 and 16.

Weir, T., *Casebook on Tort*, 10th edn, London: Sweet & Maxwell, 2004, section 3.

Whittaker, R., 'Privity of Contract and the Tort of Negligence: Future Directions' (1996) 16 *Oxford Journal of Legal Studies* 191.

Winfield and Jolowicz on Tort, 16th edn, London: Sweet & Maxwell, 2002, pp. 93–118 and Chapter 11.

CHAPTER 3 ASSESSMENT EXERCISE

Doubledeal set up a tax consultancy service in 1985. The business has thrived. Apart from tax matters, Doubledeal has, over the years, given advice to his clients concerning investments. He admits that this policy has helped to expand his business.

Harold goes to Doubledeal to consult him about his tax problems. As a consequence of the advice given, Harold buys some rare works of art to escape inheritance tax. He also asks Doubledeal for his opinion as to the prospects of Unitechnics Ltd, a new company which has been set up to retrain displaced university staff. He invests £40,000 in Unitechnics Ltd, acting on Doubledeal's assurance that the company is in a healthy financial condition.

The conversation then goes on to more mundane matters, but just as Harold is about to leave, Doubledeal says: 'By the way, if you have any spare capital in these bad times, Ranchland Ltd (an American-owned real-estate firm operating in Snowdonia) is a good bet'. Two weeks later Harold invests £50,000 in this company.

Some weeks later, Harold learns that he has been wrongly advised concerning his inheritance tax position, and also that Unitechnics Ltd and Ranchland Ltd are just about to go into liquidation, having been in grave financial difficulties for six months. He also receives a bill from Doubledeal: 'For advice re Inheritance Tax'.

Advise Harold on any claim he may have in tort against Doubledeal.

See *Cases and Materials* (3.3) for a specimen answer.

<table>
<tr><td>

4

</td><td>

Negligence IV: nervous shock/psychiatric damage

</td></tr>
</table>

4.1 OBJECTIVES

By the end of this chapter you should be able to:

1 Explain the differences, if any, between 'physical' and 'mental' injury

2 Account for the distinction made in the cases between 'grief', 'sorrow', etc. and 'psychiatric injury' ('nervous shock')

3 Account for the categories of claimants entitled to recover damages

4 Assess critically the general nature of the 'special relationship' which claimants in this context have to establish, paying particular attention to 'foreseeability' and 'proximity'

4.2 Introduction

'Nervous shock' (that is the expression traditionally used by judges for what in medical language is more usually termed psychiatric damage), may be the subject of a claim for damages in its own right within the tort of negligence, although it may also be a component item in some wider claim for personal injury. 'Shock' is regarded in modern law as another type of harm to the person.

Lord MacMillan in *Bourhill* v *Young* [1943] AC 92 (HL) said:

> The crude view that the law should take account only of physical injury resulting from actual impact has been discarded, and it is now well recognized that an action will lie for injury by shock sustained through the medium of the eye, or the ear without direct contact. The distinction between mental shock and bodily injury was never a scientific one, for nervous shock is presumably in all cases the result of, or at least accompanied by, some physical disturbance in the sufferer's system.

 EXERCISE 4.1

Look up the words 'nervous' and 'shock' in a dictionary. Try to combine their meanings into a working definition. We will compare it with what the judges have said, at the end of this chapter (see 4.6).

4.2.1 **Intentional interference**

We should first distinguish liability arising under *Wilkinson v Downton* [1897] 2 QB 57, which is concerned with the infliction of intentional harm, including 'shock'. This is examined later, in the context of harassment (see 11.7.2). This chapter is concerned only with nervous shock inflicted negligently.

4.2.2 **Statute**

In *Glen and Others v Korean Airlines Company Ltd* [2003] 3 All ER 621, Simon J held that claims for psychiatric injury were recoverable as material loss or damage under ss. 76 (2) and 105 of the Civil Aviation Act 1982. See also 4.3.14 and 7.4.

4.2.3 **Grief, sorrow, and anxiety**

There is no liability in negligence for anxiety, grief, and sorrow, on their own, although the position is different in contract and in the tort of deceit. The Protection from Harassment Act 1997 (amended by the Serious Organised Crime and Police Act 2005) allows claims for 'anxiety': s. 3(2).

In *Hamilton Jones v David and Snape* (2004), *The Times*, 16 January, it was held that a mother who successfully made a claim in contract and tort against her former solicitors, alleging that their negligence lost her the custody of her children, was entitled under the contract to damages for 'mental distress'.

 These conditions may, however, be the subject of compensation in the tort of negligence where they result from some physical injury: *Kralj v McGrath* [1986] 1 All ER 54. (*Cases and Materials* (4.1.1).)

In the tort of negligence the courts look for medically defined damage. Lord Denning said this in *Hinz v Berry* [1970] 2 QB 40. Lord Bridge, in *McLoughlin v O'Brian* [1982] 2 All ER 298, favoured the expression 'psychiatric illness'; and in *Attia v British Gas* [1987] 3 All ER 455, Bingham LJ thought that the expression 'nervous shock' was misleading and inaccurate; he preferred 'psychiatric damage' because that term was more capable of embracing mental illness, neurosis, and personality change.

In *A and Others v P & O Ferries* (1989), *The Independent*, 5 May (arbitration proceedings concerning the *'Herald of Free Enterprise'* Zeebrugge ferry claims), post-traumatic stress disorder and pathological grief were acknowledged as recognized psychiatric illnesses. The arbitrators acknowledged that the 'odd legal phrase "nervous shock" did not connote shock in the sense in which it was often used in ordinary conversation'. Grief, distress, or any other normal emotion was not enough: a claimant had to establish a positive psychiatric illness.

Physical consequences of psychiatric damage are compensable: for example, see *Galt* (4.3.2).

4.3 **The legal cause of action**

Liability for psychiatric illness inflicted negligently has developed in a way analogous to liability for negligent misstatements. That is to say, the law has been applied over the years in a more cautious and guarded way than has been the case in some other areas of liability in negligence.

> **?** **QUESTION** 4.1
>
> Why has liability for psychiatric illness been approached in this way?

The reason for this caution has been the fear of bogus claims, based on the unreliability of medical evidence, and difficulties in proof of causation. However, as the medical profession has expanded its knowledge and expertise in this field, so the courts have in more recent times been more willing to expand legal liability for this type of damage. But the courts are still concerned to keep liability within what they would regard as reasonable limits. The 'floodgates of litigation' argument remains an important factor in this context, and many decisions can be explained satisfactorily only by reference to judicial policy.

4.3.1 **The history of the claim**

A claimant must establish the usual ingredients of the tort of negligence and meet a number of special requirements. We will examine these special conditions of recovery later (see 4.3.2 to 4.3.6.1), but first it will be instructive to have a brief look at the history of liability for 'nervous shock'.

In *Victorian Railway Commissioners* v *Coultas* (1888) 13 App Cas 222 (PC), a claim for shock was denied on the ground that the courts would be swamped by a flood of bogus claims; the medical evidence available was regarded as unreliable.

In *Dulieu* v *White* [1901] 2 KB 669, the claimant, a pregnant barmaid, suffered shock when the defendant negligently drove his horse-drawn van through the wall of a public house; she feared for her safety, but the van was halted before it could strike her. She did suffer a miscarriage, which was attributed to this incident. She succeeded when liability was recognized in cases of 'shock' suffered as a result of the claimant being placed by the defendant's negligence in a situation in which she feared for her **own** physical safety.

In *Hambrook* v *Stokes Bros* [1925] 1 KB 141, this basis of liability was extended. It was held that the claimant could recover because of fear for the safety of **relatives**. A mother (who was some four months pregnant) suffered shock after she saw a runaway lorry pass the spot where her children had just been walking, though she may not have feared for her own safety. Her daughter was in fact seriously injured. She subsequently died of complications of a haemorrhage and miscarriage. The Court of Appeal ruled that if her shock arose from what she actually saw (as opposed to additional information about her daughter relayed to her by bystanders) then in principle she could recover, as shock in these circumstances was natural and foreseeable.

In *Bourhill* v *Young* [1943] AC 92, it was held that the claimant must be in the 'area of risk', or 'disaster area'. The claimant, who was pregnant at the time, heard the sound of an accident caused by the defendant, who was killed in the incident. However, she saw nothing of the accident which had occurred about 50 yards away from her on the other side of the tram from which she had just alighted. She very soon afterwards made her way to the scene of the accident and suffered shock because of what she saw, and as a result had a miscarriage. Her claim for damages failed.

> **?** **QUESTION** 4.2
>
> Can you think of the reasons that led to this decision?

In the House of Lords, three judges said she was not entitled to recover because she was not within the area of impact. The other judges found against her on another ground, that is she had no relationship with the person injured in the accident and shock to her was not foreseeable. It was held that a pregnant claimant was abnormally sensitive to shock in such circumstances. Lord Porter said:

> The driver of a car or vehicle is entitled to assume that the ordinary frequenter of the streets has sufficient fortitude to endure such incidents as may from time to time be expected to occur in them, including the noise of a collision and the sight of injury to others, and is not to be considered negligent towards one who does not possess the customary phlegm.

In *King* v *Phillips* [1953] 1 QB 429, a mother, at home seventy yards from where a taxi was slowly backing over her child's tricycle, and who saw the tricycle under the taxi from a window was held to be outside the 'area of risk', even though she then went to the site of the accident, and her claim for shock was dismissed. The court concentrated on whether the driver owed a duty to the mother herself, rather than the relationship; in other words they followed *Bourhill* rather than *Hambrook*. Today, this claim might well have been successful, as an 'immediate aftermath' case: see *McLoughlin* v *O'Brian* (4.3.4).

4.3.2 Elements of the claim

In *Hambrook* the Court of Appeal said that a claimant must suffer, or experience, the shock by means of his or her own unaided senses: it is not enough merely to be told of an incident.

This requirement was confirmed in *Boardman* v *Sanderson* [1964] 1 WLR 1317, in which a father, out of sight, but within 'earshot' of a car backing over his son's foot, was allowed to recover from the driver, the defendant. However, it is not essential that the claimant sees or hears the incident itself: it is enough if he sees its immediate effects. The Court of Appeal distinguished *King* (above) on the ground that in the instant case the defendant knew of the claimant's presence in the vicinity; this meant there was a close proximity between the parties. A contention that it was necessary for the claimant to be actually on the scene at the time of the accident was rejected. The defendant owed a duty not only to the boy 'but [also] to the near relatives of the boy who were, as he knew, on the premises within earshot, and likely to come upon the scene if any injury or ill befell that boy' (Ormrod LJ).

The decision in the Australian case of *Benson* v *Lee* [1972] VR 879 is instructive. A mother recovered damages for shock suffered partly as a result of having been told of her child's death, and partly because of the effect on her of having accompanied the child in the ambulance to hospital. Lush J doubted whether the 'rule' that the claimant must perceive the accident had survived *Wagon Mound (No. 1)* [1961] AC 388 and argued that 'If within the limits of foresight something is experienced through direct and immediate perception of the accident, or some part of the events constituting it, which imparts shock, that is, I think, all that the law requires'.

In *S* v *Distillers Company (Biochemicals) Ltd* [1969] 3 All ER 1412 the claimant was the mother of a baby born deformed by thalidomide. The litigation was compromised (there were doubts whether the manufacturers were negligent in marketing the drug), but there was no doubt of the legitimacy of the mother's 'shock' claim. Hinchcliffe J said:

> So far as Mrs S.'s claim is concerned, it is plain that she suffered a grievous shock. For a happily married woman, it is difficult to comprehend any greater shock than seeing your child born misshapen and deformed. The fun and joy of motherhood is partially destroyed. Instead of enjoying and being able to show off the baby to your friends, there is a natural reluctance to do so. This has not been the sort of shock which has worn off like so many cases of shock that come before the courts; this is permanent. Ever since the birth Mrs S. has been depressed, anxious, and worried. She is daily reminded of her handicap. There is always a cloud over her happiness. She now has to take drugs prescribed by her doctor and she has a sense of guilt which makes it harder for her to recover, although heaven knows she has nothing to blame herself for.

? **QUESTION** 4.3

Is it possible that non-relatives may recover damages for psychiatric illness?

In *Chadwick* v *British Railways Board* [1967] 1 WLR 912, a serious train crash was caused by the defendant's negligence. The claimant suffered nervous shock from the horror of the incident after coming to render assistance. Walter J held the defendant liable because it was foreseeable that someone would suffer shock from the defendant's negligence; a duty was owed to rescuers; and shock caused by fear for the safety of others was remediable. The claimant had a history of psychiatric trouble, but the medical evidence showed that he had been cured of his previous illness.

In *Pearson* v *British Midland* (1998), *The Times*, 10 February, the claimant, who was the first person to rescue passengers from an air disaster, recovered damages for the 'recurring nightmare' which had blighted his life. The claimant suffered severe post-traumatic stress disorder (PTSD) for over six years after helping victims from the wreckage of the aircraft which crashed on to an embankment of the M1 motorway in 1989, killing 47 people. Out of the total award £17,000 was for general damages to compensate the claimant for his suffering. This award was in line with similar PTSD payments ordered by the courts, although previous awards were made to persons who suffered because they were accident victims or professionals called to the scene of the accident in the course of their duty. Claims by rescuers for psychiatric damage must now, however, be read in the light of *White* (4.3.8).

In *Dooley* v *Cammell Laird and Co. Ltd* [1951] 1 Lloyd's Reports 271, the claimant, who was an employee of the defendants, suffered shock when the sling on the crane he was working snapped and the load fell into the open hold of a ship. Some of his colleagues were working in the hold at the time, and he feared for their safety. He obtained judgment against his employer for breach of statutory duty; and against a second defendant, the owner of the defective sling, in negligence.

In *Galt* v *BRB* (1983) 133 NLJ 870, the claimant, a train driver, was driving his train when he came suddenly upon two fellow employees working on the track ahead, the train having just rounded a bend. He could not stop quickly and thought the men would be killed (in fact they managed to escape). He was awarded damages for nervous shock, and those damages included an award for increased injury due to a pre-existing disease, a symptomless condition which predisposed him to a heart attack (myocardial infarction) in such circumstances.

There was very close proximity between the parties in both cases; and in each instance the claimant was operating machinery which could have seriously injured the workmates who had been placed in danger. Claims for psychiatric harm by 'workmates' are now also subject to the ruling in *White* (4.3.8).

? **QUESTION** 4.4

What have you learned so far about the development of liability for psychiatric injury?

According to what we have read so far only those persons who can establish recognized psychiatric illness need consider legal action, if they can go on to show that they were in fear for their own safety or the safety of others, or they were seeking to rescue others. In each case they must show that they were also physically proximate and perceived matters with their unaided senses and not solely by reports from third parties.

4.3.3 Duty of care

The usual ingredients of negligence have to be established by the claimant and 'duty' is probably the main problem area here.

The *Bourhill* v *Young* [1943] AC 92 'phlegm and fortitude' approach, suitably adapted to meet the case of a person who can show some 'special relationship', as a test of reaction to circumstances may still hold good, as we will see later. The test of the susceptibility of a normal person has for long been regarded as the touchstone, although the reverse is probably true with regard to the nature of the accident itself. See also *Page* v *Smith* (4.3.7). In appropriate cases a duty may be owed to a claimant with peculiar characteristics, by analogy with *Haley* v *London Electricity Board* [1965] AC 778 (see 1.7.9).

The ordinary principles of liability for injury do not apply without qualification in this context.

? **QUESTION** 4.5

List the possible reasons for this state of affairs.

This state of affairs exists because of a number of factors:

(a) the risk of a great number of actions;

(b) the risk of fraudulent claims, though this may be of less importance today than in the past;

(c) the problem of putting a monetary value on such damage (see the *P & O Ferries* arbitration case at 4.2.3); and

(d) the difficulty in some cases of proving the link between the defendant's conduct and the claimant's shock.

To apply 'foreseeability' without qualification could produce what the courts might see as excessive litigation, although we will see later that two cases, *McLoughlin* v *O'Brian* and *Wigg* v *British Railways Board* have been influenced by *Anns*. It is foreseeable, for example, that the relations of an accident victim will be told of his death or injury, and that they may suffer shock simply on being given this news; but a claim for damages in such circumstances would be difficult to sustain.

In *Schneider* v *Eisovitch* [1960] 2 QB 430, the claimant and her husband were injured in a vehicle accident caused by the defendant's negligence. Upon recovering consciousness, some time later in hospital, she was told of her husband's death and suffered shock as a result. At first instance, it was found that she could add a claim for this damage to her claim for her physical damage.

? QUESTION 4.6

Can you think what the judge's reasons for giving this decision might have been?

The decision stands alone; it has not been overruled, but it is difficult to reconcile the ruling with later authority other than on the point that the claimant was herself injured physically in the accident itself, and it may be that the claim for shock was allowed to 'piggyback' on the claim for physical damage.

It seems that there must be some special limitation to the extent of liability for 'nervous shock', but there appears to be little agreement as to the nature and scope of this limitation. Winfield, for example, has suggested that there must exist some 'special relationship' in the circumstances of each case. Some judges have used the concept of remoteness of damage, for example Denning LJ in *King* v *Phillips*, but usually the concept of duty of care is more popular.

Few, if any, clear principles emerge from the majority of the cases. In *King*, Denning LJ suggested that had the claimant been physically injured she could have recovered damages. It does not follow that there is necessarily a duty not to inflict nervous shock merely because the claimant is within the area of physical impact; nor does it follow that a claimant's absence from that area is fatal to his claim for damages. The soundness of the 'impact theory', which we encountered in *Bourhill* v *Young* (above) may be doubted, particularly in view of the decision in *McLoughlin* v *O'Brian*, as we will see later.

In *King* v *Phillips*, Denning LJ said that the test adopted in *Bourhill* v *Young* (above) '. . . was not foreseeability of physical injury, but foreseeability of emotional shock'. This was approved by the Privy Council in *Wagon Mound (No. 1)*. In *Jaensch* v *Coffey* (1984) 54 ALR 417 (Australia), it was held that the specific illness suffered by the claimant need not be foreseeable. It was enough to show reasonable foresight of a recognized psychiatric condition brought on by shock. You should also consider the decision in *Page* v *Smith*, which is dealt with at 4.3.7. It was held here that foreseeability of psychiatric illness is not the correct test where the claimant is directly involved in the accident and well within the range of foreseeable physical injury. Here, the claimant is to be regarded as a 'primary' rather than a 'secondary', victim of the accident. The duty of care owed in such a context is the same duty not to cause 'personal injury', which applies in cases of physical harm. (This decision was applied in *Young* v *Charles Church*, 7.4.2.)

4.3.4 *McLoughlin* v *O'Brian* [1982] 2 All ER 298

The claimant was told at home that her husband and children had been seriously hurt in a traffic accident caused by the defendant's negligence. She went to the hospital to be with her family and saw each member in their injured state, before treatment; she was also told that one of her children was dead. Having witnessed this immediate aftermath of the accident she subsequently suffered nervous shock. At first instance it was held that no duty of care was owed to the claimant because she was not a reasonably foreseeable victim. The Court of Appeal held that the shock suffered by the claimant was reasonably foreseeable but public policy dictated that no duty of care was owed to her. However, the House of Lords rejected the policy argument and unanimously found in favour of the claimant. Liability was extended to the 'immediate aftermath' of an accident. It is instructive to examine the salient features of the speeches in this case. All their Lordships agreed that it was incumbent upon the claimant to establish that the shock which in fact she suffered was a reasonably foreseeable result of the defendant's careless driving. Lords Scarman and Bridge found that once causation was established (the defendants had admitted negligence) this was all that the claimant need show and that it was not for the courts to limit, on policy grounds, a right to recover for reasonably foreseeable damage caused by a defendant. Lord Scarman suggested that, apart from special cases, policy was not justiciable and it was the function of Parliament, not the courts, to set limits on grounds of policy. He thought that the result in the present case might be socially undesirable and there was a powerful case for legislation such as that enacted in parts of Australia, for instance section 24 of the Australian Capital Territory Miscellaneous Provisions Ordinance 1955:

(1) The liability of a person in respect of injury caused . . . by act, neglect, or default by which another person is killed, injured, or put in peril extends to include liability for injury arising wholly or in part from mental or nervous shock sustained by—

(a) a parent or the husband or wife of the person so killed, injured, or put in peril; or

(b) another member of the family of the person so killed, injured, or put in peril, where the person was killed, injured, or put in peril within the sight or hearing of that other member of the family.

However, Lords Wilberforce, Bridge, and Russell regarded policy as having a much more important role to play in judicial deliberations than that envisaged by the minority; reasonable foreseeability of shock to the claimant being a necessary, though not necessarily sufficient, condition of liability and policy may legitimately restrict the range of liability. Lord

Wilberforce did not employ his two-stage test: he argued for a 'logical progression' in the cases, that is he appeared to favour an incremental approach.

4.3.4.1 The decision

This decision emphasized certain 'boundaries' of the law, that is:

(a) no relief for mere grief or sorrow;

(b) no need to show direct impact or fear of immediate personal injury for oneself;

(c) shock suffered as a result of injury to, or fear for the safety of, a near relative was compensable;

(d) apart from *Boardman* v *Sanderson* (above) there was no English case in which a claimant out of sight and earshot of an incident involving a near relative had recovered damages for shock;

(e) a rescuer could recover damages.

4.3.4.2 The elements of a claim

The House of Lords said that three elements had to be considered:

'Class of persons'

The existing law recognized the claims of those with close family ties at one end of the range of protected persons and denied the claims of ordinary bystanders at the other end of the range. This was either because such persons were expected to show sufficient fortitude to cope with the ordinary vicissitudes of life, or because defendants could not be expected to compensate the world at large.

Proximity

On proximity to the accident, it was obvious that it must be close in both time and in space; it must be proved that the defendant's negligence has caused the nervous shock. The 'immediate aftermath' fell within the required degree of proximity.

Communication

As to communication, there was no case in which compensation had been awarded for shock brought about by a third party. The shock must come through sight or hearing of the event or of its immediate aftermath.

? QUESTION 4.7

Can you see a problem with this kind of limitation?

According to Lord Wilberforce the courts would have to consider at some time whether the equivalent of sight or hearing, for example 'simultaneous television', would suffice.

Lord Bridge said a defendant's duty must depend on reasonable foreseeability and must be adjudicated on a case-by-case basis. If asked 'where the thing was to stop' his answer would be 'where in the particular case the good sense of the judges, enlightened by progressive awareness of mental illness, decided'. His Lordship explained a hypothetical example of a hotel fire. He said it was logical to suppose that a mother who reads a newspaper report of a fire at a hotel where she knows her children are staying and who later learns of their death would have a claim against the person responsible for the fire: imagination rather than direct perception would link the defendant's behaviour and the shock for purposes of causation.

McLoughlin was an important influence in the Australian case of *Jaensch* v *Coffey* (1984) 54 ALR 417, in which the claimant went to hospital and there saw her husband in great pain from his injuries, both before and between emergency operations. She was awarded damages for shock.

4.3.4.3 **Nature of the accident**

It was also said in *McLoughlin* that the nature of an accident or its immediate aftermath, for example, its particularly horrific nature, may well be an important factor in these cases. Not surprisingly *McLoughlin*, like any other case, is a child of its era and the decision was no doubt influenced by *Anns*, though it is debatable whether it can be described accurately as an application of the 'Wilberforce test'. In *Wigg* v *British Railways Board* (1986), *The Times*, 4 February, the judge regarded *McLoughlin* as freeing the law from the shackles of policy considerations. He relied also on *Anns* and the 'Wilberforce test' in arriving at his decision.

The claimant, a train driver, succeeded in his claim for shock and trauma suffered when he came upon the body of a person very soon after it had been struck by an open door on the claimant's train as it left a station. He had left his cab to search for the victim. It was found to be reasonably foreseeable by the defendants that the driver would behave as he did, that there was a risk he might suffer nervous shock as a consequence, and that they were in breach of the duty of care they owed him. (The guard on the train had been negligent regarding the open door and BRB were vicariously liable for his negligence.)

His Lordship rejected the defendants' claim that it was not foreseeable that train drivers of reasonable fortitude would have suffered nervous shock (the claimant had had two previous experiences of death on the track in 1979 and 1980). It was also found that the claimant had done more than the ordinary disinterested bystander would have done: he had searched for and found the victim and offered him words of comfort as well as staying with him. Although the claimant could be described as a rescuer it was, said the judge, unnecessary so to find because the nervous shock suffered by the claimant was reasonably foreseeable.

4.3.5 **Property**

In *Attia v British Gas plc* [1987] 3 All ER 455 the defendants had a contract with the claimant to install in her house a central heating system. One day, whilst the work was being carried out, she returned home from a shopping expedition to find the house on fire; her home and its contents suffered severe damage for which the defendants admitted liability in negligence. Liability for the nervous shock she claimed to have sustained as a reaction to this event was denied and the matter became a preliminary issue for resolution by the court before the trial could proceed. The defendants claimed that as a matter of policy nervous shock caused only by damage to property could not be compensated. Further, the claimant's shock was not reasonably foreseeable in any event because it was not a direct consequence of the defendants' negligence.

The Court of Appeal said that provided there was 'psychiatric damage' (not merely grief and sorrow) suffered as a result of witnessing the destruction of property, for example one's home and possessions, damages could be recovered as long as the psychiatric illness was a reasonably foreseeable consequence of the defendant's negligence. The question of reasonable foreseeability was one of fact, to be resolved at the trial of the case.

The question of causation was not examined. It was also assumed that the claimant was a person of normal disposition or toughness ('the customary phlegm'). The court regarded the issue as one of remoteness of damage and, though it was not fantastic or far-fetched in the light of progressive awareness of mental illness to suppose that a person might suffer psychiatric illness from shock in the present circumstances, there was room for argument about whether the claimant's alleged damage was a reasonably foreseeable consequence of the defendants' (admitted) negligence. The court was not prepared to make a 'general *a-priori* ruling', to the effect that such a claim could never be a reasonably foreseeable consequence of someone's negligence, 'on such scanty material' (Dillon LJ).

The parties were not strangers to each other and the court approached the issue only from the point of view of remoteness of damage. It is true that the question of policy was also considered, but it is clear that the claim for nervous shock was allowed to proceed in a 'parasitic' form on the admitted duty and breach that the defendants owed to the claimant in respect of the damage to her home and possessions. The issue was remitted for trial and the judge awarded the plaintiff £16,409 damages for nervous shock and loss of earnings: *The Guardian*, 11 July 1989.

 QUESTION 4.8

Think of a special factor which might distinguish *Attia* from other authorities.

You might have thought about the possibility of a contractual relationship existing between the claimant and defendant. If you had done so you would have hit upon something which might well be a distinguishing feature of the case. The parties did have a contract and, while it is true this made no provision for the recovery of damages for shock, they were in very close proximity indeed. Deakin, Johnston, and Markesinis, at p. 107, suggest that *Attia* can be explained on the basis of an assumption of responsibility for 'psychiatric wellbeing'. The decision was not considered in *Alcock*, *Page* v *Smith*, or *White* and its legal validity must be questionable.

In *Perry* v *Sidney Phillips and Son* (see 2.6.4) the claimant was awarded damages for the worry and distress he suffered because of the physical inconvenience of living in a house with severe defects which the defendants had negligently failed to report.

All of what you have read so far must now be examined in the light of later developments.

4.3.6 *Alcock* v *Chief Constable of the South Yorkshire Police* [1991] 4 All ER 907

The court at first instance upheld claims by eight persons whose close relatives were victims of the Hillsborough football tragedy in April 1989. They witnessed the disaster unfold on television, knowing that their relatives were at the game.

It was held that watching live television coverage of an accident satisfied the requirement of 'proximity'. Siblings as well as parents were entitled to make successful claims; there was 'no basis in logic or law' why brothers and sisters should not be able to recover damages. Not all the victims died in the disaster: two were injured and one escaped unhurt. One claimant lost her case because she was the fiancée of the victim, and not a relative. Another succeeded who watched television in a coach parked outside the football ground as his son died; as did a claimant who was sitting in the stand above the Leppings Lane terrace, as his two brothers died.

Hidden J considered that a television viewer saw the same image that he would see if he were standing in the position of the camera, and would be aware that the pictures were coming live from Hillsborough football ground:

> Just as a store detective [watching on a TV monitor] sees goods put into the pocket and not in the basket, although he is not present at the scene, so does the TV watcher see the crowd surge forward in pen three of the Leppings Lane stand, though he is not present.

The defendants argued that a finding for the claimants would open the floodgates of litigation.

? QUESTION 4.9

What do you suppose the judge's reaction was to this claim?

Rejecting the claim that his ruling would open the floodgates for claims from the millions of people who watched the disaster on television, his Lordship said claimants had to meet three requirements: a medically diagnosed psychiatric illness ('post-traumatic stress disorder'); being at the match or witnessing it live on television; being a mother, father, brother, or sister of a victim.

Damages were claimed also by the families of three of the victims for pre-death suffering, under the provisions of the Law Reform (Miscellaneous Provisions) Act 1934. Hidden J rejected this claim. (Claims for this head of damages were successful in out-of-court settlements in connection with the disaster at King's Cross Underground station, which is referred to at 4.3.8, and the Zeebrugge disaster, which is referred to at 4.2.3.)

The Court of Appeal, however, limited liability to those persons in a parent–child relationship, which could include grandparents, and spouses. Even in relation to close relatives such as these, the court said liability does not extend to those who witnessed the events only by watching or hearing 'live' (or simultaneous) television broadcasts, or who identified a body in the mortuary afterwards. This was not regarded as coming within the *McLoughlin* 'aftermath'.

It was held that everyday simultaneous television broadcasts do not, because of the television industry's code of ethics, portray recognizable suffering in individuals; this form of communication did not satisfy the test of 'sight' or 'hearing' of the event or its immediate aftermath.

Parker LJ said: 'The vast majority of people do not suffer psychiatric illness from this sort of shock.' He thought that a television viewer was not sufficiently close and directly connected with the police negligence in this case.

According to Nolan LJ, nervous shock as used in the decided cases connotes a reaction to 'an immediate and horrifying impact' and this factor was missing in the present case. His Lordship did not rule out the possibility or recovery for **some** television viewers. He said:

> If a publicity-seeking organization made arrangements for a party of children to go up in a balloon, and for the event to be televised so that their parents could watch, it would be hard to deny that the organizers were under a duty to avoid mental injury to the parents as well as physical injury to the children, and that there would be a breach of that duty if through some careless act or omission the balloon crashed.

It is clear that his Lordship intended this to be only an example of a special 'live' broadcast that might be an acceptable means of communication of psychiatric illness.

Claimants, including rescuers, 'actively' involved in the event(s) need not, it was said, establish their relationship with the primary victim. Both Stocker and Parker LJJ explained *Dooley* (see 4.3.2) as turning on the fact that the claimant in that case took an active part in the course of events, because he was working the crane as an employee of the defendant at the time of the accident.

All this was accepted by the House of Lords, although a rather different approach was taken to the issue of qualifying relationships. Their Lordships adopted a more flexible categorization of those eligible to sue, though the formula which emerged from the House is still of a restrictive nature. The appeals of the relatives from the Court of Appeal decision were unanimously dismissed. Their Lordships applied the *McLoughlin* 'aftermath' test: the claimant must experience the incident or its immediate aftermath by seeing and/or hearing it. Throughout this case the Chief Constable admitted a duty of care and breach of that duty, but argued that this was owed only to those who died or were injured.

? QUESTION 4.10

Can you predict the reasons for this result?

It was held that a claimant who relied on shock suffered for the plight of others had to satisfy **two** basic conditions:

(a) it must be reasonably foreseeable that he or she would sustain psychiatric injury due to his or her close bond of love and affection with the victim; and

(b) there must be proximity in terms of time and space.

The House of Lords said that none of the claimants had witnessed the actual injury to their loved ones; seeing the disaster on a live television broadcast was not equivalent to being at the ground within actual sight or hearing of the event and its immediate aftermath. Watching such scenes on television could not in terms of law give rise to shock, though it might be different in medical terms. The court also rejected the claims of two persons who were actually at the event, namely a man whose brothers died and a man who lost a brother-in-law, because they failed to prove a sufficiently close bond with the victims.

It was held that in the case of parents and children or spouses there is a rebuttable presumption that the relationship between the victim(s) of the tragedy and the claimant(s) is of the closest bond of love and affection. It will be for the defendant to rebut this presumption. In the case of other relationships it will be for the claimant to establish love and affection.

There was general agreement that there was no need to limit a right of action to parents and spouses but, while Lords Ackner and Jauncey would require the claimant to establish a relationship akin to that of parent or spouse, Lords Keith and Oliver would merely require the claimant to establish close ties of love and affection. According to Lord Keith such ties may be stronger between engaged couples than others married for many years. Lord Oliver said that it would be 'inaccurate and hurtful' to suggest that grief was made any less real by a more gradual realization of loss, but the law should not be extended to cover such cases.

Alcock says that the shock must be the result of a sudden incident. There must be, as some judges put it, a 'shocking event' causing the immediate psychiatric illness: a gradual build-up of illness is not acceptable. It was also said by the House that attendance at a temporary morgue to identify a relative, no earlier than nine hours after the tragedy, was not participation in the immediate aftermath. None of their Lordships was prepared to rule out the possibility of a 'mere' spectator or 'bystander' recovering damages if the circumstances were sufficiently horrific.

4.3.6.1 *Alcock* and beyond

It is clear that the House of Lords in *Alcock* took a very cautious approach to the question of recovery for psychiatric injury. The incremental approach to the development of the law taken by Lord Wilberforce in *McLoughlin* was said to represent the law on shock.

In *McCarthy* v *Chief Constable of the South Yorkshire Police* (1996), *The Times*, 12 December, a half-brother of one of the Hillsborough victims who actually witnessed the incident in the football stadium, was awarded damages for his psychiatric damage because he established the strongest of ties of love and affection with the deceased.

Claimants must still exhibit sufficient 'phlegm and fortitude'; they must not be over-sensitive or receptive to shock. In *Bourhill* this test was applied to a bystander, but all claimants must clear this hurdle, although it may be that a mere witness may have to show a 'stiffer upper lip', that is such a person may have to be more robust in this respect than, for example, a close relative. The 'egg-shell skull' rule, however, applies to the extent of injury: that is, if the ordinary person would have suffered shock, the particularly susceptible person may succeed even though the consequences are more severe.

In *Malcolm* v *Broadhurst* [1970] 3 All ER 608, Lane J said: 'The defendant must take the wife [the claimant] as he finds her and there is no difference in principle [between] an egg-shell skull and an egg-shell personality.'

The claimant and her husband were injured in a car accident caused by the negligence of the defendant. She claimed damages for:

(a) her physical injuries;

(b) intensification of her pre-existing nervous condition (see the 'egg-shell skull' rule, above);

(c) her psychological injuries suffered because of her husband's injuries;

(d) loss of her wages flowing from (a), (b), and (c);

(e) loss of her wages caused by the termination of her husband's one-man business (which had employed her) due to his death from his injuries.

It was held that all were recoverable; (c) was recoverable because the damage was of a foreseeable type and 'the fact that it arises or is continued by reason of an unusual complex of events does not avail the defendant'.

In *Brice* v *Brown* [1984] 1 All ER 737, the claimant was severely neurotic and the court held that the defendant did not have to take her as he found her. The claimant and her young daughter were involved in a motor accident caused by the defendant's negligence. The daughter was only slightly injured, but the claimant suffered considerable psychiatric damage through fear for her safety. Applying the test of what would have been the reaction of someone of ordinary phlegm and fortitude, it was found that the claimant should recover nothing. If someone of ordinary phlegm would, in the circumstances of the case, have suffered shock the claimant would have been compensated for the full extent of her psychiatric damage, because she would have benefited from the application of the 'egg-shell skull' rule.

4.3.7 *Page* v *Smith* [1995] 2 All ER 736

 EXERCISE 4.2

Read the extracts from the speeches in *Page* v *Smith* in *Cases and Materials* (4.2.1). What was the outcome of this case?

Page v *Smith* [1995] 2 All ER 736 (HL) (*Cases and Materials* (4.2.1))

The claimant was involved, but not physically injured, in a traffic accident caused by the defendant's negligence. The claimant claimed that his myalgic encephalomyelitis ('ME') from which he had suffered for some 20 years, but which, at the time of the accident was in remission, had been aggravated by this incident. He claimed compensation for psychiatric damage.

The Court of Appeal dismissed his claim because it was not reasonably foreseeable that some-one of 'customary phlegm' would sustain any psychiatric injury due to a road accident in which he suffered no physical injury. A 'frightening experience' is not enough. In the House of Lords, however, it was held, by a majority of three to two, that foreseeability of physical harm was enough to enable a claimant, who was directly involved in an accident caused by the defendant's negligence, to claim damages for 'shock'. It was not necessary that the claimant should be physically harmed, and the duty of care extended to any injury sustained by the claimant; this would include psychiatric damage, which need not be foreseeable. The case was sent back to the Court of Appeal to determine the issue of causation, that is, did the claimant's experience in the accident cause his condition?

In *Page* v *Smith (No. 2)* [1996] 3 All ER 272, the Court of Appeal ruled that the test applicable in causation cases, determined on the 'balance of probabilities', was whether the defendant's negligence had caused or materially contributed to the development or the prolongation of the claimant's symptoms. A 'material' cause was one which was more than 'minimal' or 'trivial' or 'insignificant'. On the facts, the balance of medical opinion regarded the defendant's negligence as a factor that could have materially contributed to the re-emergence of the claimant's condition and 'converted it from a mild and sporadic state to one of chronic intensity and permanence' (Sir Thomas Bingham MR, with whom Morritt and Auld LJJ agreed). The court found that since the trial judge, who had listened to all the evidence, was satisfied on this issue it would not be appropriate to disagree with him.

In *McLoughlin* v *Jones* [2002] 2 WLR 1279 (CA), the claimant was convicted of robbery and spent several months in prison before new evidence resulted in his conviction being quashed. He suffered from depression as a result of his stay in prison and sued the defendant, his solicitor, alleging that he defended the claimant negligently. It was held that the defendant owed a duty of care to the claimant as a 'primary victim'. Brooke LJ said that the foreseeability of the 'reasonable man' in relation to 'duty of care' does not apply where the parties are in a contractual relationship, as in the present case.

The court found that the claimant, as a 'primary victim' was not affected by the 'reasonable phlegm and fortitude' test for sensitivity to psychiatric illness. (Hale LJ, in an *obiter dictum*, drew an analogy between McLoughlin's claim and that of the claimant in *Page* v *Smith*.)

The House of Lords approved and applied *Page* v *Smith* in *Simmons* v *British Steel Plc* [2004] UKHL 20, a case involving an industrial accident caused by the defendant's negligence.

Page v *Smith* was also applied in *Corr* v *IBC Vehicles Ltd* (2006), *The Times*, 21 April, an 'employment' case (see 5.3.1). The widow of a man who had committed suicide six years after suffering serious physical injury in an accident at work caused by the admitted negligence of his employer, the defendant, was awarded damages by the Court of Appeal for the consequences of the suicide. The deceased had developed post-traumatic stress disorder after several operations and this led to severe depression with suicidal tendencies; the court had to decide whether the suicide was too remote a consequence of the accident (see 2.4). Sedley LJ, delivering the majority decision, explained that in an action for negligence the question to be asked was not whether the particular outcome was foreseeable but whether the kind of harm for which damages were claimed was foreseeable; if it was, it then had to be decided whether the eventual harm was too remote on grounds of public policy. In the present case there was no other cause of the suicide but the depression and that depression was acknowledged by the defendant to be a foreseeable consequence of its negligence. Suicide was not an uncommon consequence of severe depression. His Lordship said that since the decision in *Page* v *Smith* the law of negligence did not distinguish between physical and 'psychological' injury. He emphasized that by imposing liability for the suicide in this case the court was not thereby imposing a duty of care on employers to anticipate and prevent suicide on the part of their employees. The claimant had not in any case argued for such a duty. Ward LJ, dissenting, said the question here was whether suicide was reasonably foreseeable at the time of the accident. On the facts it could not have been reasonably foreseen that the deceased, who at that time was a man 'happy in his life', would become so depressed that he would 'many years later kill himself'.

4.3.8 *White* v *Chief Constable of the South Yorkshire Police and Others* [1999] 1 All ER 1

Alcock acknowledged that rescuers may be in a privileged position with regard to claims for nervous shock, but it does not deal specifically with the position of professional rescuers, such as fire and police officers. The court left this point open.

In *Hale* v *London Underground* (1992) 11 BMLR 81, a fire officer, who had taken part in the rescue operations at the King's Cross fire disaster, was awarded damages for the psychiatric illness he suffered as a result of what he had experienced during that rescue. The defendants had admitted liability, but disputed the size of the damages. Other fire officers involved in this incident have received out-of-court settlements.

It was widely reported in early 1995 that fourteen police officers, present on the terraces of the football ground at Hillsborough, had reached favourable out of court settlements with the police authority's insurers for shock suffered during the performance of their duties at that event. These reports also indicated that some of the unsuccessful claimants in *Alcock* had been angered by these settlements.

In a consultation paper, published on 29 March 1995, the Law Commission recommended wider rights for disaster victims' families to claim damages for psychiatric illnesses, such as post-traumatic stress disorder, induced by their loved ones' deaths. It described the decision in *Alcock* as 'unnecessarily restrictive' and called for a new statute to clarify and liberalize the law. The Commission said:

> For the law to distinguish the claims for shock-induced psychiatric illness of one mother present at the scene of her son's death or its immediate aftermath from that of another mother who was not present at the scene but came across the aftermath several hours later, or who heard about the incident from a friend or saw it on television, might justly give rise to accusations of arbitrary and insensitive line-drawing.

The Commission also sought views on whether 'professional rescuers' should be entitled to compensation for psychological trauma. It expressed no view, but questioned whether there was any justification for distinguishing between physical and psychological injuries. It also noted that excluding professional rescuers would allow off-duty policemen and firefighters involved in rescues to claim, while barring those acting in the course of duty.

In *Scholfield* v *Chief Constable of West Yorkshire* (1998), *The Times*, 15 May, the claimant, a police officer, accompanied a colleague, X, to a house in which four guns had been found. X suddenly fired one of the guns into some bedding material but the claimant, quickly realizing what was about to happen, had moved to protect the persons who had reported the presence of the guns. The claimant later developed post-traumatic stress disorder and claimed damages from the Chief Constable as being vicariously liable for X's negligence. The Court of Appeal held that the relationship between the claimant and X, as colleagues engaged in the same task in the course of their employment, was sufficiently proximate to make the claimant a participant in the incident rather than a mere bystander. It was enough that she was involved in the event during which the negligent act took place: the claimant was directly involved in the incident and at risk of physical injury, as in *Page* v *Smith*. It was clear that X knew or ought to have known that the claimant was at risk of physical injury and that she might sustain psychiatric harm as a consequence.

In *White* six police officers brought test cases on behalf of twenty-three officers who played a part in the Hillsborough disaster, suffering severe psychological trauma as a result. The claimants were not on the terraces at the time, they dealt with fans on the pitch; they performed mouth-to-mouth resuscitation, sorted bodies on the pitch, and stripped bodies at the mortuary. They were not exposed to physical danger in the course of their activities.

Classing them as 'bystanders', the judge at first instance said that a bystander of a horrific incident was not entitled to claim damages for psychiatric damage. In any event, he said, police officers should be more able to deal with traumatic events than ordinary bystanders 'being persons of extraordinary phlegm'. It was also necessary to observe that an event might be less traumatic for someone who helped rather than watched it helplessly.

The House of Lords held, reversing the Court of Appeal, that police officers are not entitled to damages from their Chief Constable for psychiatric injury suffered as a result of assisting with the aftermath of a disaster in the course of their duties, either as employees or as rescuers. *White* is authority for the proposition that all claimants in cases of negligently inflicted psychiatric damage must satisfy the requirements of *McLoughlin*, *Alcock*, and *Page* v *Smith*. This means, in essence, that they must fall into one of the categories of primary or secondary victim. They will then be subject to the conditions of liability applying to each category. As you know, secondary victims can claim only in special circumstances. The claimants in *White* said they were entitled to claim simply because they were 'rescuers' and 'employees'. Earlier authority, including *Alcock*, supports the view that such persons may fall into special categories of claimant in the context of psychiatric injury, but *White* says rescuers, professional as well as voluntary, and employees must qualify as 'primary' or 'secondary' victims.

Only persons who are actually in danger of physical injury can call themselves primary victims: Lord Steyn referred to being 'objectively' exposed to danger **or** 'reasonably' believing oneself to be in that position. Others are only secondary victims and subject to the *Alcock* criteria. The claims in *White* failed because all the claimants were merely 'secondary' victims who did not satisfy *Alcock*. Lord Hoffmann, however, in an obiter opinion, suggested that an employee in the position of the claimant in *Dooley*, that is, who was an 'unwitting agent' in the incident who in some way participated or was implicated in the sequence of events, might still come within a special category of claimant unaffected by *Alcock*. His Lordship said that the *Alcock* control mechanisms were 'plainly' never intended to apply to all cases of psychiatric injury. You can read extracts from some of the speeches in *White* in *Cases and Materials* at 4.2.2.

In *Cullen* v *London Fire and Civil Defence Authority* [1999] PIQR P314, it was held, approving Lord Steyn's definition of a primary victim, and the view of Lord Goff to similar effect, also expressed in *White*, that it was arguable that the claimant firefighter could qualify as a primary victim if he satisfied the requirements set out by Lord Steyn and Lord Goff.

In the Scottish case, *Keen* v *Tayside Contracts* (2003), *The Times*, 27 March, it was held that the claimant, who had suffered post-traumatic stress disorder as a result of carrying out instructions from his employer, but did not sustain any physical injury or otherwise come within one of the exceptions recognized in *Alcock*, *Page* v *Smith*, and *White*, was a secondary victim so unable to receive damages for any negligence by his employer in giving those instructions. However, in another Scottish case, *Salter* v *UB Frozen and Chilled Foods Ltd* 2003 SLT 1011, the judge simply applied *Dooley*. The claimant was held to be a primary victim because he had been actively involved in the accident which had led to the death of his fellow employee, therefore he was not required to overcome the control mechanisms laid down by the House of Lords for secondary victims.

In *French* v *Chief Constable of Sussex* (2006), *The Times*, 5 April, a 'striking-out' case, the Court of Appeal dismissed the appeals of five police officers in their novel claim for damages for psychiatric injury from their employer. They were involved in events leading up to an armed raid which resulted in the fatal shooting of a member of the public; but none of them witnessed the shooting itself. Their claims were based principally on an allegation of 'corporate failure' on the part of their employer, that is a negligent failure to have in place a proper and effective system to deal with such an event as occurred in this case as a result of which the claimants became the subjects of unjustified disciplinary and criminal proceedings which caused them stress and resultant psychiatric injury. The court found that the case was subject to the ruling in *White*, that is liability for negligently causing some 'catastrophe' extended to secondary victims only where they suffered psychiatric injury as a consequence of witnessing the death or injury of 'loved ones'. In the present case the claimants were not secondary victims and their claims were therefore even more remote. Furthermore, to the extent that their claims were based on stress sustained at work, it had to be shown that the employer had notice of the claimants' vulnerability according to the principles laid down in *Hatton* v *Sutherland* [2002] ICR 613 (see 2.4). The claimants could not satisfy this requirement. Lord Phillips LCJ, delivering the judgment of the court, said the claims depended on showing that the chief constable should reasonably have foreseen the possibility of the alleged 'corporate failure' causing each claimant psychiatric damage. It was argued that the chief constable, in failing to give proper instructions to his employees, including the claimants, as to how they should perform their duties caused an 'untoward event' (the fatal shooting) which in turn led to disciplinary and criminal proceedings being brought against the claimants and this caused them stress leading to psychiatric injury. His Lordship found the reasoning of the judge at first instance in the present case 'compelling'. He had taken the view that if officers who had witnessed the shooting would have had no claim as secondary victims it necessarily followed that the claimants, who were more remotely affected, could have no claim. The Court of Appeal concluded that the claimants had no real prospect on the facts of establishing that it was reasonably foreseeable by their employer that they would suffer psychiatric injury in the circumstances. It would not be appropriate to extend the law of negligence by imposing on employers the duty of care postulated by the claimants. Apart from the issue of principle relating to remoteness of causation such an extension would be expensive in terms both of cost and police resources. The case was not even analogous to a 'stress at work' case (see 2.4).

4.3.9 Mere bystanders

> **?** **QUESTION** 4.11
>
> What do you see as the main problem in the way of recovery for bystanders?

Witnesses who are mere bystanders, in contrast to those bystanders who have a relationship with primary victims, have long been in a difficult position regarding claims for psychiatric injury. In *Alcock* such claims were not ruled out entirely, at least in those situations where the circumstances of the accident were particularly horrific. However, this requirement, of gruesome circumstances, indicates that these bystanders will more often than not be defeated in their claims for damages because of the 'phlegm and fortitude' requirement.

As Lord Keith said in *Alcock*:

> The case of a bystander . . . is difficult. Psychiatric injury to him would not ordinarily . . . be within the range of reasonable foreseeability, but could not perhaps entirely be excluded from it if the circumstances of a catastrophe occurring very close to him were particularly horrific.

Lord Ackner also observed

> while it may be very difficult to envisage the case of a stranger, who is not actively . . . involved in a disaster or its aftermath, other than in the role of rescuer, suffering shock-induced psychiatric injury by the mere observation of . . . injury of a third person . . . I see no reason in principle why he should not, if in the circumstances, a reasonably strong nerved person would have been so shocked.

In *McFarlane* (below) the court refused to define the word 'horrific' in the context of liability for psychiatric damage: Stuart Smith LJ pointed out that reactions to such events were 'entirely subjective'.

 EXERCISE 4.3

Read the extract from the judgment of Stuart Smith LJ in *McFarlane* in *Cases and Materials* (4.2.3). What does this case say about bystanders?

> **McFarlane v EE Caledonia Ltd [1994] 2 All ER 1 (*Cases and Materials* (4.2.3))**
>
> It was held, overturning the decision at first instance, that a worker, the claimant who witnessed the 'Piper Alpha' oil rig disaster from a rescue vessel, was not entitled to claim damages for psychiatric injury. He had completed his shift as a painter aboard 'Piper Alpha' and had returned to his quarters on the 'Tharos', which took part in the rescue operations, when the disaster occurred.
>
> The Court of Appeal rejected altogether the claim of a mere witness on the ground that a claimant, who is outside the recognized exceptions of the colleague or rescuer, must have ties of love and affection with the victim. This is inconsistent with obiter opinions expressed in the House of Lords in *Alcock*.

White confirms the requirement that a secondary victim can only establish reasonably foreseeable psychiatric injury where someone of reasonable phlegm and fortitude would so suffer, although this would not be the case where the claimant was unusually prone to such harm. It was pointed out, however, that this is not the same as the 'egg-shell skull rule', which was applied in *Page* v *Smith*. If someone of 'normal' qualities is likely to sustain psychiatric damage, it is irrelevant that the extent of the claimant's damage is made greater by some personal characteristic of the claimant. A claim will fail if the only reason for the **injury**, rather than its extent, is the claimant's particular characteristic.

4.3.10 **Aftermath**

The approach taken by the courts to the resolution of this issue is difficult to predict. In *Hevican* v *Ruane* [1991] 3 All ER 65, due to the defendant's admitted negligent driving of a school minibus the claimant's 'favourite' son was killed and 'shortly' afterwards the claimant was told that the minibus had been involved in an accident. He was taken to a police station where he was told of his son's death and then went to the mortuary where he saw the body. Medical diagnosis confirmed a 'continuing reactive depression'.

Mantell J found for the claimant although he was not present at the immediate aftermath of the accident; neither was it foreseeable 'that the nervous shock suffered by the plaintiff would result in continuing psychological illness such as continuing reactive depression'. It was found that the 'particular injury' need not be contemplated by a defendant, 'nervous shock' being foreseeable.

However, in *Ravenscroft v Rederiaktiebolaget Transatlantic* [1992] 2 All ER 470 (CA), the claimant's son was killed in a crushing accident at work and she was called to the hospital by her husband where he told her of their son's death. Imagining the extent of the injuries, her husband would not let her see the body. The family was described as 'very close indeed' and the claimant suffered a prolonged grief reaction—a prolonged depressive reaction—which was continuing at the trial. Ward J found for the claimant, the defendants having admitted that the son's death was their fault but contending that damages for the claimant's nervous shock were not recoverable.

The Court of Appeal overruled this decision because it was inconsistent with the opinions expressed by Lords Ackner, Keith, and Oliver in *Alcock*. This decision must cast doubt on the correctness of the ruling in *Hevican v Ruane*.

A restrictive interpretation of 'immediate aftermath' can be found in other cases.

In *Taylor v Somerset Health Authority* [1993] PIQR 262, the claimant's husband died in hospital as a result of the defendant's negligence; she was told of this and saw his body about an hour later. It was held that the claimant had not witnessed the immediate aftermath, as in *McLoughlin*, for the following reasons:

- she went to the hospital only to settle her mind;
- the visit was not to identify the body;
- her husband's body was not in an 'injured' state.

Again, in *Taylor v Shieldness Produce Ltd* [1994] PIQR 329, the claimants were told that their son had been involved in an accident and went to the hospital straight away, but did not see him. However, they followed the ambulance to another hospital where they caught a brief glimpse of him on his way to intensive care. They saw blood on his face. The father saw him afterwards in intensive care, and his mother saw him the following day. They stayed with him for two days, and then he died. The Court of Appeal said that the 'immediate aftermath' of this accident, which had happened at 10.45 a.m. on the day that the claimants were told of their son's involvement in it, could not be extended to cover the next two days while he was in hospital.

In *Sion v Hampstead Health Authority* [1994] 5 Med LR 170 (CA), the claimant's son was injured in a traffic accident and admitted to hospital, where he eventually died. The claimant's action for damages for abnormal grief reaction was struck out on the basis that he had not suffered sudden 'shock'. The claimant, who had alleged negligent treatment of his son, had stayed by the latter's bedside and watched him deteriorate slowly: in effect there had been a 'process' at work upon the claimant, from admission into hospital until perceived medical negligence after the inquest. His son's death was no surprise; rather, it was expected.

In *White*, Henry LJ, in the Court of Appeal, said:

> [W]hat matters is not the label on the trigger for psychiatric damage, but the fact and foreseeability of psychiatric damage by whatever process . . . Clearly the law should accept PTSD rather than exclude it whether it is caused by sudden shock (properly defined) or not.

There are cases in which this more liberal conception of aftermath has been adopted, and they can be contrasted with the decisions we have examined so far.

In *Galli-Atkinson* v *Seghal* [2003] Lloyd's Rep Med 285 (CA), the claimant's daughter, aged 16, was killed by a car which mounted the pavement and hit her as she walked to a ballet class. Damages were awarded against the defendant, the driver of the car, for the claimant's trauma suffered as a result of the accident. The claimant had not witnessed the accident. When her daughter failed to return home after her ballet class the claimant went to search for her and came upon a police cordon where officers told her that her daughter had been killed. A police officer described it as the strongest and most distressing reaction that he had ever seen. Her daughter's body had been removed by the time the claimant came upon the scene of the accident. The court agreed that the claimant had suffered an 'extreme reaction' above and beyond the normal grief process. She had fallen to the ground at the scene of the accident, weeping uncontrollably and banging her hands on the pavement. She had then gone to the mortuary, where she had fallen to her knees and hugged her daughter's body apparently trying to bring it back to life. Objectively, it is difficult to distinguish this case from cases such as *Taylor*, *Taylor*, and *Sion*. The subjectively extreme reaction of the claimant is not relevant, so the only conclusion is that a different test was being applied.

Walters v *North Glamorgan NHS Trust* [2003] Lloyd's Rep Med 49, is another case in which the Court of Appeal was willing to add together a number of seemingly separate incidents to form an *Alcock* 'whole' incident. The claimant was the mother of a baby who contracted acute hepatitis, but his condition was negligently misdiagnosed and treated. As a result he suffered a major epileptic seizure which was witnessed by the claimant who was sleeping in the same room at the hospital; she saw him coughing blood and choking. The claimant was later told that no brain damage had occurred but that her baby would have to be transferred to a hospital in London for a liver transplant. She followed the ambulance to London and learnt that severe brain damage had in fact occurred and as a consequence her son was on a life support machine. Later, she agreed to terminate the life support and her son died in her arms. The claimant suffered psychiatric injury caused by the shock of witnessing the last distressing thirty-six hours of her son's life and was awarded damages against the defendant. The Court found that all these events could be added together to form an *Alcock* 'event', in contrast to a situation in which there was a gradual development of psychiatric trauma.

It is a little early to conclude definitely that the requirement of 'sudden shock' has been abandoned, but the most recent cases suggest that this is indeed at least in the course of becoming accepted.

4.3.11 Causation

In *Vernon* v *Bosley (No. 1)* [1997] 1 All ER 577 (CA), the claimant saw his two daughters and their friend drowned when their nanny, the defendant, accidentally drove the family car into a river. The defendant admitted liability but disputed the claim for damages. At first instance, the claimant was awarded a record £1,178,000 (reduced on appeal to £622,000: 30 March 1996) for having been left by the accident, as Sedley J put it, 'a helpless and dependent shadow of his former self'. The claimant and his wife 'watched helplessly' from the riverbank while the emergency services tried to save the children 'not knowing whether they were alive or dead'.

The claimant had, before the accident, been a successful businessman, but his business collapsed and his marriage 'fell apart' after the accident. The effect of seeing the accident had been 'to destabilize for good a previously insecure but manageable personality, provoking chronic reactive anxiety and depression which have now become permanent features of his mental state'. This included features of post-traumatic stress disorder and of pathological grief but 'was not a textbook example of either'. His Lordship said that witnessing the accident was not the sole cause, but it was the initiating cause of an uneven but perceptible sequence of mental deterioration and personality collapse in an already vulnerable individual.

The Court of Appeal dismissed the defendant's appeal, by a majority. Evans LJ, with whom Thorpe LJ agreed, confirmed that damages for 'mere' grief and suffering alone were not recoverable. The question for the court to decide was whether such heads of claim had to be 'discounted', that is, subtracted from the psychiatric damage for which damages were recoverable.

Damages are recoverable in the tort of negligence even where that negligence is only a cause, although it must be a substantial cause, of the claimant's damage. On the present facts, even though the claimant had suffered grief and sorrow because of bereavement the claimant could recover for this provided he could show recognized psychiatric damage caused wholly or partly by the defendant.

The court said it would be 'unrealistic and artificial' to engage in an exercise to dissect the claimant's state of mind into those bits which had been influenced by psychological harm and those bits which had been influenced by ordinary grief and sorrow. In the judgment of Evans LJ the claimant had satisfied the court that he had in substance sustained recognized mental injury as a result of the defendant's negligence and he should recover in full.

It is significant, however, that his Lordship made much of the fact that there were no policy reasons for limiting the damages recoverable by the claimant. To put it another way, there was nothing in the present circumstances to justify the court in denying to the claimant the benefit of the all-or-nothing principle which lies behind the law of tort: where there was no damage, there would be no recovery of compensation, whereas there would be full recovery even though there was only some damage.

Stuart-Smith LJ, in his dissenting judgment, said that the claimant had failed to discharge the legal burden placed upon him to prove that his mental illness was caused by his witnessing the aftermath of the accident.

4.3.12 Self-injury

Policy problems are to the fore where the defendant is his own victim. In other words, 'Does X owe a duty of care to Y not to cause psychiatric damage to Y by injuring himself or placing himself in danger of injury?' The problem may be more acute where there is a clear *Alcock* relationship between X and Y.

In *Bourhill* v *Young* the defendant was his own 'victim', but the point was not dealt with as the case proceeded on another basis. There are, however, dicta of Lord Robertson in the Scottish Court of Session in that case (1941 CS 395, at 399) denying liability on the argument that the line of liability for negligence must be drawn somewhere.

Similar dicta of Deane J in *Jaensch* v *Coffey* were referred to, with apparent approval, by Lord Oliver in *Alcock*. The Law Commission, in its Consultation Paper No. 137 (para. 5.47) came to the same conclusion, though its reasoning was based on the argument that to impose a duty of care in such cases would place an unreasonable restriction on a person's right of self-determination. (This might be of particular importance where a person actually committed suicide or attempted to do so: suicide or attempted suicide being legally acceptable under the terms of the Suicide Act 1961.)

The Law Commission, in its Report No. 249, recommends that a right of action be available against a defendant who imperils himself: see *Cases and Materials* (4.2.4). The Commission proposes a duty of care only for negligent self-harm; it is suggested that intentional self-harm would not be embraced by the duty.

At first instance, on a preliminary issue, however, it has been held that a close relative of a claimant did not owe him a duty of care.

In *Greatorex v Greatorex* [2000] 1 WLR 1970, the defendant carelessly injured himself in a road accident and the claimant, who was a fire officer and the claimant's father, was called to the scene. As a result of what he saw the claimant suffered post-traumatic stress disorder. It was held by Cazalet J that even as a direct witness of the defendant's injuries, the claimant, who had a recognized relationship of love and affection with the defendant, was not owed a duty of care: to hold otherwise would restrict the defendant's right of self-determination. A finding in favour of the claimant would undermine family relationships. It was also found that the defendant did not owe the claimant a duty of care as a rescuer, because the claimant had not been exposed to danger; nor had he reasonably believed himself to be so exposed. (You might like to know that the defendant was uninsured and that the Motor Insurers' Bureau had been joined in this action as a second defendant.)

4.3.13 Statements

It may be that shock suffered as a result of reliance upon a negligent misstatement is recoverable from the misrepresentor, but there is a lack of English authority on the point.

In *Furniss v Fitchett* [1958] NZLR 396, a New Zealand court found the defendant, who was medical adviser to both the claimant and the claimant's husband, liable when he gave the husband a certificate alleging, negligently, that the claimant was a paranoiac; the husband used this certificate in evidence in proceedings brought by the claimant against him for maintenance. The claimant suffered shock on disclosure of the certificate's contents and recovered damages from the defendant. The parties in *Furniss* were in very close proximity indeed, and presumably, a very 'special relationship' will have to be established by a claimant who hopes to succeed for shock caused by a misstatement.

In *Guay v Sun Publishing Co.* [1953] 2 SCR 216, a Canadian case, the defendants published negligently in their newspaper an untrue report that members of the claimant's family had been killed. The court denied recovery for shock caused to the claimant by this report, holding that the defendants owed only a duty to publish in good faith.

A claimant who can establish an assumption of responsibility by the defendant, by analogy with developments in *Hedley Byrne* liability, may succeed in recovering damages for shock caused by a negligent misstatement. *T v Surrey CC* is authority for the proposition that *Hedley Byrne* extends to cases of physical loss (see 3.5.10).

An even more problematic case would be one where the 'story' was true, but the claimant alleged that the defendant was negligent in the way that news was relayed. In other words, is there a duty to break bad news gently? The matter awaits resolution.

In *Allin v City and Hackney Health Authority* [1996] 7 Med LR 167, the defendant admitted a duty of care, but on this occasion the 'shocking' information was incorrect: after a difficult labour the claimant was informed incorrectly that her baby was dead. This information, later corrected, had been communicated in a proper way, but the defendant was found liable on the facts.

In *A and Others* v *Tameside and Glossop Health Authority and Another* (1996), *The Times*, 27 November (CA), the Health Authority found that one of its employees, a health worker, was HIV positive and decided to inform a number of patients that there was a very remote risk that they had been infected by the AIDS virus. It did so by sending them letters containing this warning.

It had to be decided whether the Authority was in breach of its duty of care to these patients because it employed this way of communicating the worrying information. At first instance, it had been found that the Authority was in breach of its duty, because the best method of avoiding the risk of causing psychiatric injury to patients was for an appropriately qualified person (for example, a GP) to communicate this sensitive information to the patients face-to-face.

The Court of Appeal found that the judge had applied the wrong standard; the Authority was not bound to employ the best available method of informing the patients and had acted with reasonable care in the circumstances: it had not breached its duty of care on the facts of the case.

The defendant Health Authority conceded that it owed a duty to take care in the circumstances; the case is not a strong authority on the existence of a duty in the context of liability for causing psychiatric injury by means of careless words.

In *Powell* v *Boladey, West Glamorgan Health Authority and Others* (1997), *The Times*, 26 November (CA), Mr and Mrs Powell developed post-traumatic stress disorder and panic disorder respectively after allegedly discovering that documents had been removed from their son's medical file after his death and different documents substituted. They sued their GP's practice for making a false statement which they could have foreseen would cause psychological harm.

It was held, however, that doctors did not owe, in the words of Stuart-Smith LJ, any 'free standing duty of candour' which, if breached, could lay them open to damages claims for personal injury by relatives of patients. His Lordship said that doctors owe a duty of care to their patients, but explaining about a death does not put them into a doctor–patient relationship with relatives.

This decision supports the view that doctors have no legal duty to tell parents the truth about the death of their child. (It was also successfully alleged that the doctors, including a consultant paediatrician employed by the defendant Health Authority, had negligently failed to diagnose the claimants' son's illness.)

In *AB and Others* v *Leeds Teaching Hospital NHS Trust and Another* [2004] EWHC 644, Gage J held that hospitals had illegally removed the organs of dead children in post-mortem examinations without the parents' consent and families could claim damages if they suffered damage of a psychiatric nature as a result. Doctors had been negligent by not seeking parents' specific permission to remove and retain organs when getting consent to carry out the post-mortem. Three test cases were heard, representing 2,140 claimants. His Lordship ruled in favour of one claim, representing 1,350 families, but the other two claims, representing the others, were rejected because in those cases the organs were retained after coroners' post-mortems which do not require parental consent. As far as the claims based on negligence were concerned it was held that doctors could owe a duty of care to a mother after the death of her baby on a doctor–patient basis, and once the doctor–patient relationship was established, the clinician owed a duty of care when seeking consent for a post-mortem examination. This duty of care extended to giving the parents an explanation of the purpose of the post-mortem and what it involved, including alerting the parents to the fact that organs might be retained. The claimant, said his Lordship, was a primary victim.

At first instance, in *Farrell* v *Avon Health Authority* [2001] Lloyd's Rep Med 458, the claimant was negligently misinformed that his newborn baby was dead and given the body of a dead baby to hold for some twenty minutes. It was then realized that a mistake had occurred. The judge classified the claimant as a 'primary victim' because he was involved physically in the actual incident; he was the only victim.

4.3.14 'Primary' and 'secondary' victims revisited

Page v *Smith* formally introduced the vexed vocabulary of 'primary' and 'secondary' victims into the context of liability for psychiatric damage inflicted negligently. Lord Oliver in *Alcock*, whose speech is often referred to by judges who use these labels, including, in *Page*, Lord Lloyd, the progenitor of the distinction, did not actually employ the words, although he did identify different categories of claimant.

In the words of the Law Commission Report No. 249, *Liability for Psychiatric Illness*, at para. 5.45: 'We have seen that in recent cases the courts have thought it important to distinguish between primary and secondary victims; and that there is confusing inconsistency as to where and why that distinction is being drawn.'

These words, 'primary' and 'secondary', often seem to mean different things to different judges, but the Commission identified at least two different classifications of 'primary' victim, viz. the 'narrow' and the 'broad' classifications. Although not entirely free from doubt, there seems to be more agreement about the meaning of 'secondary' victims: they are those persons who only witness others being injured or exposed to injury. It is these claimants who will have most difficulty in establishing the special proximity requirements laid down in *Alcock*.

The 'narrow' classification was based on Lord Lloyd's classification in *Page* v *Smith* and would embrace as primary victims only those persons within risk of reasonably foreseeable physical injury.

However, the Commission was not convinced that these claimants should receive special consideration in law for three reasons: (i) medical opinion was against it; (ii) psychiatric injury can often be suffered, for example, stress at work, although no one is seen being put at risk of physical injury; and (iii) earlier authority has rejected any distinction between claimants who have suffered fear for their own safety and those who have feared only for the safety of others.

The 'broad' classification of 'primary' victim, which Lord Oliver had in mind in *Alcock*, though he did not actually use the label 'primary', would be based on persons who had participated in the accident. This would be more flexible than the narrow approach, and would include those claimants who could show proximity either via actual participation in the event as primary victims or in terms of their relationships to the immediate victim(s) and their perception of the accident or its immediate aftermath as secondary victims.

In the Commission's view, though, while a 'broad' approach would be preferable to the 'narrow' one because the latter is too exclusive of deserving cases, it is not without its ambiguities and uncertainties because it offers 'little guidance as to where the line between primary and secondary should be drawn'. Difficulties can be encountered with definitions of 'direct involvement' and 'event', for example; there is also the question of deciding upon the requisite degree of participation.

What of the claimant in *Attia* or the claimant who complains of negligent communication of bad news? As the Commission says, these are cases in which the claimants could well be described as 'primary' victims, yet theirs would be 'prime' examples of claims upon which the courts would probably seek to impose 'special restrictions'.

On the whole, the Commission saw the distinction between 'primary' and 'secondary' victims as being 'more of a hindrance than a help' and recommended that the courts should 'abandon attaching practical significance' to the distinction, though its use might well be helpful for descriptive purposes. Certainly, in the Commission's opinion 'the distinction is being given a policy importance which it does not merit.' (Report paras 5.45–5.54; see also paras 2.52–2.60.)

N and Others v *UK Medical Research Council and Dept of Health* [1996] Lloyd's Rep Med 309, illustrates the problems inherent in categorizing claimants as either 'primary' or 'secondary' victims. The claimants had been treated with human growth hormone which might have been contaminated with the prion which causes the brain disease CJD. They established that the authorities had been negligent in treating them with the hormone and that as a matter of law they were entitled to damages for psychiatric injury. The claimants said they were 'primary' victims: they were unwilling participants in the negligence and not mere observers. They likened their claims to that of the claimant in *Page* v *Smith*.

Morland J held that the claimants were not primary victims in the 'usual' sense, that is, the psychiatric harm was not triggered by the physical event (the injection of the hormone), though that event was a 'potent causative factor' in the development of the psychiatric injury, the actual 'trigger' being the claimants' awareness of the risk and nature of CJD because the brain degenerates slowly. However, his Lordship took into account the following facts: (i) the claimants were all children when they were treated, and did not themselves choose the treatment; (ii) there was a limited class of claimants; and on that basis he concluded that the claims should succeed. He rejected the 'floodgates' argument and held that any claimant, whether of normal phlegm and fortitude or having a 'vulnerable personality', who can prove that his/her psychiatric illness was caused by becoming aware of the risk of CJD can recover compensation. See also *CJD Litigation: Group B Plaintiffs* v *Medical Research Council* [2000] Lloyd's Rep Med 161, and *W* v *Essex CC* (below).

Cooper v *Reed* (2001), *The Guardian*, 16 February (CA), is another decision which poses some difficulty in terms of classifying the claimant according to whether he or she was a 'primary' or a 'secondary' victim.

The defendant, a minicab driver, was escorting a deaf girl aged 4 back home after school, and parked her car by the kerb outside the girl's home. Due to the defendant's negligence the girl ran out into the road and into the path of the claimant's car as he was driving along the road. He had no chance of avoiding hitting the girl. He was not personally at fault and suffered post-traumatic stress disorder as a result. The child eventually made a full recovery, but the claimant thought he had killed her at the time of the accident. His claim for damages from the defendant, and her employers, was successful.

You will also find it interesting to look back to *W* v *Essex CC* (1.5.2). The House of Lords thought that it was possible at the trial stage that the claimants could establish a duty of care on the basis that they were 'primary victims'. The category could not be regarded as closed and was still capable of being developed to meet new factual situations.

The claimant in *Farrell* v *Merton, Sutton and Wandsworth Health Authority* (2000) 57 BMLR 158, had a Caesarian section and gave birth to a badly disabled baby because of the defendant's negligence. Although she did not see the child until the following day it was held that the trauma of birth included what happened in the operating theatre and the events leading up to, as well as, her first sight of the baby and her recognition of the baby's disablement. She was a 'primary victim'. (She had also sustained separate physical injury.)

Classifying claimants as to whether they are primary or secondary victims has caused a problem in the context of statutory liability, and the courts have not always arrived at a satisfactory resolution of the issue. The decision in *Hegarty* should be compared with the decisions in *Hunter* and *Glen*, *Hegarty* being more consistent with principle than the two later cases.

In *Hegarty* v *EE Caledonia Ltd* [1997] 2 Lloyd's Rep 259 (CA), the claimant was employed as a painter on the 'Piper Alpha' oil rig and claimed damages for psychiatric injury suffered through witnessing a series of explosions on the rig which killed 167 persons and seriously injured others. At the time of the incident he was on board a support ship which went to help those on the rig. He was present during the rescue operations and claimed to be in danger himself from the fire and explosions, though he claimed only for psychiatric damage.

His claim was brought under two heads: (i) for common law negligence; and (ii) for breach of statutory duty under regs 3, 5, and 32 of the Offshore Installations (Operational Safety Health and Welfare) Regulations 1976 (SI 1976/1019), Mineral Workings (Offshore Installations) Act 1971.

On a preliminary issue it was held that he was not a primary victim of the disaster, although he suffered a genuine fear of death. While the law will recognize the claim of someone such as the pregnant barmaid in *Dulieu* v *White* who sees somebody nearly—but not quite—hitting her, because her fear was a reasonable one in the circumstances, it will not accommodate persons who are not directly threatened but genuinely and irrationally believe that they are so threatened. The court followed the reasoning in *McFarlane* v *EE Caledonia Ltd* and *Page* v *Smith* and the claim under (i) was dismissed.

With regard to claim (ii), the Regulations provided that it was the duty of every person, while on or near an offshore installation, not to do anything likely to endanger the safety or health of himself or other persons on or near the installation. On this point, it was said that if the claimant came within the Regulations, **strict** liability would be imposed and he would not be subject to the control mechanisms imposed on those who merely witnessed disasters. (The action for breach of statutory duty, if a good one, would, said Brooke LJ, '. . . with one bound free [the claimant] from the control mechanisms imposed on the claims of secondary victims by the House of Lords in *Alcock*'.) Their Lordships rejected the claim, however, on the ground that the claimant did not fall within the class of persons the legislation was intended to protect. Under reg. 32 persons who were near the oil rig would only qualify for protection if the breach was likely to endanger their health or safety. It must be likely, not merely foreseeable, that a person in a rescue vessel 100 metres from the rig would suffer impaired mental health. This decision is also relevant in 7.2.

In *Hunter* v *British Coal Corporation and Cementation Mining Co.* [1998] 2 All ER 97 (CA), the claimant, an employee of Cementation, was driving a vehicle in the Coal Corporation's mine when he hit a hydrant causing it to leak. He, and a fellow employee of Cementation, X, could not turn off the hydrant; he went in search of a hose to divert the water and while he was away the hydrant exploded, killing X.

The claimant, who was 30 metres distant at the time of the accident, heard a message over the loudspeaker system to the effect that someone had been injured and, on his way back, he was told by a colleague that it seemed X had been killed. He went into shock on hearing this news and was prevented from returning to the scene. Thinking he was responsible for X's death, the claimant developed a depressive illness and sued the two defendants for psychiatric damage, in negligence and for breach of statutory duty (s. 83 of the Mines and Quarries Act 1954).

At first instance, the judge found both defendants negligent and in breach of statutory duty because at the time of the accident clearances in the roadway were below the prescribed minimum. However, since the claimant was neither a 'primary' nor a 'secondary' victim, as defined by Lord Oliver in *Alcock*, liability was not established.

Brooke LJ, with whom Sir John Vinelott concurred, agreed with this finding and the claimant's appeal was dismissed. The *Alcock* control mechanisms were applied.

Hobhouse LJ dissented:

> . . . But it appears that there is another recognized category which applies to employees and which potentially covers the plaintiff. This category is recognized and discussed in the speech of Lord Oliver in *Alcock's* case, the judgment of Lord Hope in *Robertson* v *Forth Road Bridge Joint Board*, *Rough* v *Forth Road Bridge Joint Board* 1996 SLT 263 and the judgment of Henry LJ in *Frost* v *Chief Constable of South Yorkshire* [1997] 1 All ER 540 . . . In *Alcock's* case [1991] 4 All ER 907 at 923–924, [1992] 1 AC 310 at 408 Lord Oliver formulated the category as:
>
>> where the negligent act of the defendant has put the plaintiff in the position of being, or of thinking that he is about to be or has been, the involuntary cause of another's death or injury and the illness complained of stems from the shock to the plaintiff of the consciousness of this supposed fact.

In other words, it is a *Dooley* case, and the fact that it is breach of statutory duty should make no difference.

On the matter of statutory duty, the Law Commission (paras 2.41–2.44), Brooke LJ himself in *Hegarty* (4.3.14), and Rose J in *Francis Aston* v *Imperial Chemical Industries Group* (unreported, 21 May 1992—cited in the Law Commission's Report at p. 27, n. 124) were of the opinion that this cause of action contained its own control mechanisms regarding proximity. The decision in *Hunter* appears to be at odds with principle on this issue. *Hunter* is also relevant in 7.4, where you will find an explanation of the control mechanisms applicable to the action for breach of statutory duty.

In *Glen* v *Korean Airlines* (4.2.2), in which the claimants had witnessed an air crash and its following events, Simon J applied the *Alcock/White* control mechanisms, that is he ruled that the claimants had to qualify as primary or secondary victims, in a case involving breach of statutory duty. To put it another way, he took the same approach to this issue as had the court in *Hunter*. Liability under the Civil Aviation Act 1982, at issue in *Glen*, is strict: '. . . the control mechanisms [from *Alcock/White*] are appropriate when the defendant is being sued for negligent breach of duty at common law, whereas in the statutory torts there is no room for any such notion' (Weir, p. 111).

Read the extract from Jones, *Textbook on Torts*, 8th edn in *Cases and Materials* (4.2.4).

4.3.15 **Pre-death trauma**

In *Hicks* v *Wright* [1992] 2 All ER 65, the House of Lords unanimously rejected a claim of damages for trauma suffered by two sisters, aged 19 and 15, before they were crushed to death at the Hillsborough disaster. Lord Bridge said:

> No one can feel anything but the greatest sympathy for the relatives of those who died. The anguish of parents caused by the death in such a horrifying event of sons and daughters on the very threshold of life must indeed have been almost unbearable. However, the medical evidence indicated that someone unable to breathe through crushing of the chest, as the girls were, would lose consciousness within seconds and die within five minutes.

The parents had argued that there was a gradual build-up of pressure, causing increasing breathlessness, discomfort, and pain for twenty minutes. His Lordship said:

> both the High Court and Court of Appeal had concluded that the evidence did not establish any injury before the fatal crushing injury, and it was impossible to say they were wrong. Fear itself, of whatever degree, was a normal human emotion for which no damages could be awarded. Those trapped in the crush who escaped injury had no claim for the distress suffered in what must have been a truly terrifying experience.

It followed that the families acting on behalf of the estates of those who died, could not claim damages in relation to fear of impending death. The parents of the deceased received only £3,500 bereavement damages for the daughter aged 15, and nothing for the elder daughter because she was over 18 years of age. (The fixed sum is now £10,000.)

4.3.16 Settlements

It was reported in *The Guardian*, 28 November 1996, that 21 parents had received out-of-court settlements of compensation claims brought against Lincolnshire NHS Trust for post-traumatic stress disorder suffered as a result of their children having been either killed or injured by a homicidal nurse whilst they were patients in the Trust's hospitals. This is noteworthy because the Trust decided to settle with claimants to whom it probably owed no legal obligations. *Alcock* and *White* suggests that the parents would fall outside the range of legal proximity because none of them actually witnessed either the actual infliction of harm upon their children or experienced the immediate aftermath of the relevant incidents.

4.3.17 Reform

You will find extracts from the Law Commission Report No. 249 in *Cases and Materials* (4.2.5).

■ SUMMARY

- A claimant must be classifiable as either a 'primary' victim or a 'secondary' victim.

- Someone who is injured physically and is shocked as a result may recover damages.

- Someone who suffers recognized psychiatric damage because of fear for their own physical safety may recover damages.

- A claimant may recover for shock suffered through fear for the safety of others (it is not necessary that the victims be actually injured) but:

  - the claimant must establish a recognized psychiatric illness;

  - the claimant must experience the event or its 'immediate' aftermath, and suffer shock, by means of his or her own unaided senses: it is not enough to be simply told of an event;

  - a gradual development of psychiatric illness is not acceptable, there must be a sudden shock to the psyche, though in *W* v *Essex CC*, the House of Lords left open the question of whether shock caused by later reflection on some event was an unarguable form of damage.

- The claimant must exhibit appropriate 'phlegm and fortitude'.

- It is necessary for the claimant to show that he or she had close ties of love and affection with the victim(s); in some instances this is presumed, but in others the claimant must establish the tie.

- Claimants who are rescuers or workmates of victims need not establish the tie of love and affection, but they will have to qualify as 'primary' victims.

- Watching an event on television is not acceptable because it is not sufficiently 'instantaneous' unless, perhaps, either a special transmission is involved (see the example given by Nolan LJ in *Alcock*) or the Broadcasting Code of Ethics has been broken and the victims are recognizable as individuals, in which case any action would be against the broadcaster, rather than the person responsible for the event.

- A 'mere' bystander might recover if the event is sufficiently horrific, though authority for this proposition is scanty.

- A person may be entitled to recover for shock suffered in connection with their property, though the authority for that proposition is not confirmed.

- The 'egg-shell skull' rule applies to psychiatric damage.

■ FURTHER READING

Deakin, S.F., Johnston, A., and Markesinis, B.S., *Tort Law*, 5th edn, Oxford: Oxford University Press, 2003, pp. 118–29, 204–8.

Elliott, C. and Quinn, F., *Tort Law*, 5th edn, London: Longman, 2005, pp. 38–55.

Giliker, P. and Beckwith, S., *Tort*, 2nd edn, London: Sweet & Maxwell, 2004, Chapter 4.

Harlow, C., *Understanding Tort Law*, 3rd edn, London: Sweet & Maxwell, 2005, pp. 68–70.

Hepple, Howarth, and Matthews, *Tort: Cases and Materials*, 5th edn, London: Butterworths, 2000, pp. 118–31.

Jones, M., *Textbook on Torts*, 8th edn, Oxford: Oxford University Press, 2002, pp. 100–13.

Kidner, R., *Casebook on Torts*, 9th edn, Oxford: Oxford University Press, 2006, Chapter 9.

Lunney, M. and Oliphant, K., *Tort Law Text and Materials*, 2nd edn, Oxford: Oxford University Press, 2003, Chapter 7.

McBride, N.J. and Bagshaw, R., *Tort Law*, 2nd edn, London: Longman, 2005, pp. 86–110.

Mullis, A. and Oliphant, K., *Torts*, 3rd edn, London: Palgrave MacMillan, 2003, Chapter 4.

Murphy, J., *Street on Torts*, 11th edn, London: Butterworths, 2003, pp. 180–1, 197–203.

Napier, M. and Wheat, K., *Recovering Damages for Psychiatric Injury*, 2nd edn, Oxford: Oxford University Press, 2002.

Nasir, K.J., 'Nervous Shock and *Alcock*: The Judicial Buck Stops Here' (1992) 55 *MLR* 705.

Salmond and Heuston, *Law of Torts*, 21st edn, London: Sweet & Maxwell, 1996, pp. 219–23.

Stanton, K.M., *The Modern Law of Tort*, London: Sweet & Maxwell, 1994, pp. 203–10.

Teff, H., 'Liability for Psychiatric Illness: Advancing Cautiously' (1992) 12 *Oxford Journal of Legal Studies* 280.

Teff, H., 'Liability for Psychiatric Illness after Hillsborough' (1992) 12 *Oxford Journal of Legal Studies* 440.

Weir, T., *A Casebook on Tort*, 10th edn, London: Sweet & Maxwell, 2004, pp. 105–24.

Weller, M., 'Post-traumatic Stress Disorder' (1993) 143 *NLJ* 878.

Winfield and Jolowicz on Tort, 16th edn, London: Sweet & Maxwell, 2002, pp. 49–124.

ANSWER TO EXERCISE 4.1

The following definitions of 'nervous' and 'shock' are taken from *Chambers English Dictionary*, 7th edn, 1988:

- **nervous** *adj* having nerve; sinewy: strong, vigorous, showing strength and vigour; pertaining to the nerves: having the nerves easily excited or weak, agitated and apprehensive (often with *of*): shy: timid: in a jumpy state.
- **shock** *n*. a violent impact, orig. of charging warriors: a dashing together: a shaking or jarring as if by a blow: a blow to the emotions or its cause: outrage at something regarded as improper: a convulsive excitation of nerves, as by electricity: the prostration of voluntary and involuntary functions caused by trauma, a surgical operation, or excessive sudden emotional disturbance: a stroke of paralysis *(coll.)*.— *v.t.* to meet or assail with a shock: to shake or impair by a shock: to give a shock: to shake or impair by a shock: to give a shock to: to harrow or outrage the feelings of: to affect with abashed and horrified indignation.—*v.i.* to outrage feelings: to collide with violence.

You may care to compare these definitions with those you have looked up, where they come from different sources.

If we take 'nervous' as simply referring to the senses, 'shock' does seem to convey the meaning of damage as recognized by the judges; it emphasizes the sudden assault or attack upon the claimant's 'nerves' that judges say is necessary. Could it be, however, that by adopting the expression '**psychiatric** damage', which suggests a somewhat broader approach, the law will eventually recognize **progressive** illness in this context?

To adopt another dictionary approach (see *Chambers*, above), **psychiatry** is concerned with the medical treatment of diseases of the mind.

 CHAPTER 4 ASSESSMENT EXERCISE

Dahlia takes her daughter, Primrose, to a funfair owned and operated by Nigel. Primrose wants a ride on the big dipper so Dahlia, who does not like high speeds, leaves her in the queue and goes for a ride on the big wheel which is about 80 yards away. While Dahlia is watching from the big wheel, the carriage in which Primrose is riding flies off the rails of the big dipper, owing to a loose bolt in the frame-work, and plummets 60 feet to the ground. Primrose is badly injured, and Dahlia is at first hysterical, and later suffers from recurrent feelings of anxiety, and from insomnia.

Sage, who is also on the big wheel at the time of the accident, is so shocked at what he sees that he later suffers from catastrophic neurosis, and is unable to work for 15 months. Some ten years earlier Sage had been a voluntary patient at a mental hospital, where he had been treated for a neurotic condition.

Primrose's father, Chrys, sees pictures of the accident on the television news that evening, and is so shocked that he suffers a heart attack.

Discuss any potential liability in tort on the part of Nigel towards Dahlia, Sage, and Chrys.

See *Cases and Materials* (4.4) for a specimen answer.

5 Negligence V: an employer's liability at common law

5.1 OBJECTIVES

By the end of this chapter you should be able to:

1 Explain the rationale for the employer's common law duty to his employees
2 Describe the three principal elements of the duty
3 Account for current developments in this area

5.2 Introduction

In traditional terms, this is the 'master's common law duty to his servant'. Judges still sometimes use the old-fashioned expression 'master', but in modern usage the word 'employer' is usual. At the outset, you would do well to remember that in actions brought by employees against their employers, claimants often sue for breach of this duty, as well as for breach of statutory duty and vicarious liability (where appropriate). An employer owes a personal duty of care in common law negligence to his employees. According to Lord Herschell in *Smith* v *Baker and Sons* [1891] AC 325:

> [T]he contract between employer and employed involves on the part of the former the duty of taking reasonable care to provide proper appliances, and to maintain them in a proper condition, and so to carry on his operations as not to subject those employed by him to unnecessary risk.

The duty of care in tort is based on the consensual relationship between employer and employee, it is a corollary of the contractual obligation and is influenced by the terms of the contract. It is a duty owed only to employees and independent contractors are not included.

Although it might be said to be a *Donoghue* type of duty, it developed independently of the 'neighbour' principle; after all, the relationship of employer and employee clearly creates proximity. It follows, that:

(a) it is an obligation arising in both contract and tort, but generally litigated in tort;

(b) this is an issue quite separate from that of vicarious liability (see **Chapter 8**).

One of the leading cases is *Wilsons and Clyde Coal Co.* v *English* [1938] AC 57 (HL), in which it was held that the 'master' must use reasonable care and skill for the safety of the 'servant'. This is simply one facet of a single duty of care, but that duty may be divided into an obligation to:

(a) provide reasonably competent supervisors and workmates;

(b) provide premises, plant, and materials;

(c) furnish a safe system of work.

It is a single duty, but of a manifold nature. You will have noticed by now that the three aspects overlap. Indeed some judges and commentators refer to a different set of sub-divisions.

 The duty is personal and 'non-delegable' by the employer. As Lord Wright put it in *Wilsons*: 'It is the obligation which is personal to [the employer] and not the performance.' So if the employer does delegate the duty, he himself remains responsible. If you turn to *Cases and Materials* (5.1), you will find a more recent illustration of the duty in *McDermid* v *Nash Dredging and Reclamation Co. Ltd* [1987] 2 All ER 878.

5.3 General nature of the duty

Before we examine the three aspects of the duty, we will look at the duty's general characteristics. This duty is a branch of the law of negligence; a duty of care developed to fit the relationship between 'master' and 'servant'.

The claimant's task in proving his case may be easier where the employer is also in breach of some statutory duty, and the ambit of each duty coincides with the other. Note that s. 11 of the Civil Evidence Act 1968 provides that a conviction for a criminal offence is admissible in civil proceedings as evidence that the person so convicted committed the offence. (This provision may, of course, also assist a claimant who is suing in tort for breach of a statutory duty.)

We will note later the effect on this duty of the Employers' Liability (Defective Equipment) Act 1969, which is dealt with at 5.6, but in general terms the employer's duty is one of reasonable care. This is not a liability imposed regardless of fault. The obligation is fulfilled by the exercise of due care and skill:

(a) a mere omission may be enough;

(b) actual knowledge on the employer's part of a danger is not necessary if he ought to have known of it;

(c) evidence of conformity to the common practice of those engaged in the activity in question is important in showing due care, as it is in any area of negligence;

(d) whether there has been a breach of the duty is a question of fact, as in all cases of negligence.

In *Harris* v *Bright's Asphalt Contractors Ltd* [1953] 1 All ER 395, Slade J said that this was:

> a duty not to subject an employee to any risk which the employer can reasonably foresee and which he can guard against by any measure, the convenience and expense of which are not entirely disproportionate to the risk involved.

For example, in *Richardson* v *Stephenson Clarke Ltd* [1969] 1 WLR 1695, the claimant was left to choose his own equipment. He was careless in his choice, and suffered injury as a result. The defendant was not negligent in the circumstances, because the claimant was an experienced worker, who could safely be left to select his equipment from that offered by his employer. The equipment itself was safe.

In *Smith* v *Scott Bowyers Ltd* [1986] IRLR 315, the claimant, an employee of the defendant, was aged twenty and had been employed for nineteen months. He was injured through slipping on a greasy factory floor. The defendant knew of this risk and had issued its employees, including the claimant, with wellington boots which had diamond ridge soles. These boots could be replaced on request. The claimant had not asked for new boots to replace his current ones, which were worn out and dangerous. At first instance it was found that the defendant was liable for breach of duty because it had not emphasized the danger nor conducted safety checks of the boots. Damages were reduced by one-third for contributory negligence. However, the Court of Appeal allowed the defendant's appeal. There was no obligation on the employer in this instance to instruct its employees how to wear the boots, or to inspect the condition of the soles from time to time. The claimant's own lack of care, in failing to renew the wellingtons, was the sole cause of his injury.

In *Doherty and Others* v *Rugby Joinery (UK) Ltd* (2004), *The Times*, 3 March (CA), it was found that since knowledge of the dangers of orbital sander use in the woodworking industry took time to disseminate, it was an issue of fact in each case whether an employer ought to have known of the danger at the relevant time so as to trigger its duty of care to its employees.

 QUESTION 5.1

What are the *three* elements of the employer's special common law duty?

These elements are an obligation to provide:

(a) reasonably competent supervisors and colleagues;

(b) proper premises, plant, and materials;

(c) a safe system of work.

We will now consider the three aspects of the employer's common law duty, but always remember that it is a single duty, of a manifold nature, and that its three 'aspects' overlap with each other.

5.3.1 Reasonably competent supervisors and colleagues

This facet of the duty is of less importance since the abolition, by the Law Reform (Personal Injuries) Act 1948, of the doctrine of 'common employment'. According to this common law doctrine, an employee was understood to have agreed to bear the risk arising from the negligence of fellow employees for the purpose of vicarious liability. As a result of this reform many actions that are today brought on the basis of vicarious liability would previously have been pursued under the employer's personal liability. The employer's special duty may still be useful, where employees are given to bullying, practical jokes, and similar behaviour.

> ? **QUESTION** 5.2
>
> Why should this duty be more useful in such situations than vicarious liability?

In vicarious liability such behaviour must come within the employee's 'course of employment'.

In *Hudson* v *Ridge Manufacturing* [1957] 2 QB 348, an employee, described as 'not over-intelligent', had a four-year record of practical joking at work. The claimant, a fellow employee, was injured by one of the joker's pranks, and was held entitled to damages from the employer for breach of the special duty of care. The employer had been negligent in not controlling the activities of the joker, who could have been disciplined or dismissed for misconduct.

However, in *Smith* v *Crossley Bros* (1951) 95 SJ 655, there was no liability on the employer for severe injuries to a 16-year-old employee, caused when two fellow employees played a cruel and highly dangerous prank on him, because this was not a reasonably foreseeable event in the circumstances. There was no record of misdeeds, as in *Hudson*, so the employer was not negligent. The incident was an isolated one.

Actions based on vicarious liability were unsuccessful in both cases, because the acts in question were not within the employee's course of employment.

'Bullying in the workplace' is, today, a high-profile issue and should be considered as a future source of litigation. You should also consider the applicability of vicarious liability of an employer in this context, though difficulties may be encountered in satisfying the requirements of 'course of employment', bearing in mind that bullying will invariably involve intentional behaviour on the part of the offending colleague. Bullying, by whatever means, is essentially harassment and is discriminatory in terms of employment law. Employers who fail to curtail it may find themselves liable with the perpetrator(s). In *Harrison* v *Lawrence Murphy & Co., The Chartered Secretary*, 1 March 1998, a female employee was subjected to several months of bullying and sexual harassment by a senior legal executive, whose actions were witnessed by the senior partner who did nothing. The firm settled the case for £50,000. In July 2006 a successful High Court claim by an employee of a bank was widely reported; the damages, including future loss of earnings, were some £800,000.

The courts are increasingly willing to extend the scope of the course of employment, so as to engage vicarious liability: *Majrowski* v *Guy's and St Thomas's NHS Trust* (2006), *The Times*, 13 July (HL) (see further 8.2.2.4).

> ? **QUESTION** 5.3
>
> Can you think of any *other* circumstances in which an employer might be liable for this aspect of his duty?

Where there is no fault on the part of the other employee, but an injury is caused by negligent staffing, that is, the employer hires an insufficiently qualified person, the employer may be liable. In *Black (or Butler)* v *Fife Coal Co. Ltd* [1912] AC 149, a colliery manager was employed who had no experience of carbon monoxide in a pit where its presence was a possible danger. The employer was found liable to the claimant, who was injured as a result, for negligent choice of supervisor.

The obligation at this point also requires the employer to instruct the employee on the operation of any tools or equipment used in the work involved.

5.3.2 The provision of adequate plant, materials, and premises

This aspect of the employer's duty covers the provision of appropriate equipment, including safety devices and protective clothing, as well as the maintenance of existing equipment.

At common law the ordinary principles of negligence apply. In *Davie* v *New Merton Board Mills* [1959] AC 604, it was held by the House of Lords that where the claimant had been injured by a defective metal 'drift' (a type of tool) which splintered in use, his employer was not liable in negligence if all reasonable care had been taken in:

(a) buying a reputable make of tool;

(b) from a reputable source; and

(c) the defect was of a latent nature, that is was not discoverable upon reasonable inspection.

The court took the view that the employer had not delegated performance of his obligation to the manufacturer, because the latter is not someone for whom the employer is responsible.

Later cases limited *Davie* to its own facts, but the general position was felt to be unsatisfactory in that an employee could in some cases be without a remedy merely for the fact that he could not identify the manufacturer. Today, however, s. 1(1) of the Employers' Liability (Defective Equipment) Act 1969, provides that:

> where . . . an employee suffers personal injury in the course of his employment in consequence of a defect in equipment provided by his employer for the purposes of the employer's business; and the defect is attributable wholly or partly to the fault of a third party (whether identified or not), the injury shall be deemed to be also attributable to negligence on the part of the employer.

? QUESTION 5.4

Draw up a list of the important features of section 1(1) (above).

You might have included the following:

- the Act applies to employees
- who suffer personal injury
- in the course of their employment
- because of a defect in equipment

- provided by the employer
- for the employer's business
- the defect must be due to the fault of a third party
- who need not be identified
- the injury is deemed to be also due to the employer's negligence.

It follows that: 'employee' does not include a self-employed person, that is, an independent contractor; liability on the part of the employer is strict.

The employer may recover from the manufacturer, where appropriate, by suing in contract; by claiming on an indemnity (where he has been indemnified by the manufacturer); by seeking a contribution under the Civil Liability (Contribution) Act 1978. The employee is not prevented from proceeding directly against the manufacturer.

> **?** **QUESTION** 5.5
>
> Can you identify the basis of such a claim?

The employee can sue for breach of the manufacturer's duty (the so-called 'narrow' rule) in *Donoghue* v *Stevenson*; or breach of obligation under Part II of the Consumer Protection Act 1987. The former requires proof of negligence and the latter involves strict liability. Both causes of action are dealt with in **Chapter 9**.

The advantage to the employee of suing under the 1969 Act is that if he can show, on the balance of probabilities, there must have been fault on the part of some third party (say, the manufacturer) because of the nature of the defect in the equipment provided by the employer, the employer is liable whether or not he was at fault. The injury must have been caused by the defect.

In *Coltman* v *Bibby Tankers Ltd ('The Derbyshire')* [1987] 3 All ER 1068 (HL), the claimant claimed her husband had died as a result of the sinking of the defendant's unseaworthy ship. The House of Lords held that the 91,000 ton ship came within the definition of 'equipment' in the Employer's Liability (Defective Equipment) Act 1969. Their Lordships said that it would not be sensible to find that machinery attached to the ship came within the terms of the Act whilst the vessel's hull did not.

In *Knowles* v *Liverpool City Council* [1993] 4 All ER 321 the House of Lords had to deal with a claim by a workman engaged in laying flagstones, who was injured when a flagstone broke and one of the pieces struck him. The employer argued that the Act did not apply, because the flagstone was not 'equipment', but was the actual material being worked on; the job rather than the tools needed to do the job. The House however decided to interpret the Act in a very broad, purposive way. Lord Jauncey said:

> My Lords, I have no hesitation in concluding that the word 'equipment' in section 1(1)(a) is [apt] to cover the flagstone in this appeal. In the first place, the requirement of the subsection is that the equipment is provided 'for the purposes of the employer's business' and not merely for the use of the employee . . . Whatever the meaning of 'equipment' this would go further than the

circumstances in *Davie* v *New Merton Board Mills Ltd* [1959] AC 604, where the defective tool had been provided to the workman for the purposes of his job. In this case, the flagstone had undoubtedly been provided by the appellants for the purposes of their business of repairing and relaying the pavement. In the second place, there can be no logical reason why Parliament having recognized the difficulties facing workmen, as demonstrated by *Davie* v *New Merton Board Mills Ltd*, should have removed those difficulties in part rather than in whole. Indeed, partial removal, as contended for by the appellants, could produce bizarre results. To give one example which I put in argument to counsel, a pump manufacturer buys in tools required for assembling the pumps as well as some components including the bolts for holding together the two parts of the housing. Workman A is tightening a bolt which sheers and injures his eye. Workman B is tightening a similar bolt but his spanner snaps causing him a similar injury. If the appellants are right, workman B could proceed under s. 1 (1) of the 1969 Act, but workman A would have no remedy thereunder. My Lords, I cannot believe that Parliament can have intended the Act to produce results such as these. In my view, the only reasonable conclusion is that Parliament intended the 1969 Act to provide a remedy in the situations where an employer had provided for the purpose of his business an article which was defective and caused injury to a workman but where he was for the reasons set out in *Davie* v *New Merton Board Mills Ltd* not in breach of a common law duty of care owed to that workman.

Note, however, that in *Hammond* v *Metropolitan Police Commissioner* [2004] EWCA Civ 830 the Court of Appeal stated that similar statutory regulations applying to 'work equipment' would not extend to a vehicle on which the workman was working. It was a police dog van and the claimant was a police vehicle fitter. It might have been the 'work equipment' of the dog handler. The court was impressed by arguments that to impose liability would also extend to fitters working on customers' vehicles in commercial garages, but that seems to be a different situation. *Knowles* is not referred to in the judgments.

5.3.3 Plant and premises

The duty at common law is to provide and maintain safe plant and safe premises. In *Toronto Power Co.* v *Paskwan* [1915] AC 734, Channell J said:

> It is true that the [employer] does not warrant the plant, and if there is no defect on reasonable examination, or if, in the course of working, plant becomes defective and the defect is not brought to the [employer's] knowledge and could not by reasonable diligence have been discovered by him, the [employer] is not liable, and further, [an employer] is not bound at once to adopt the latest improvements and appliances.

In the case of plant, mere temporary failure of maintenance might not be enough to breach the duty although regular inspection is probably necessary in the case of complex or dangerous machinery.

The duty includes a failure to provide necessary equipment, or that which a reasonable employer ought to regard as needed. It covers necessary safety devices on dangerous machinery, and the provision of protective equipment where necessary.

Remember that the employer's obligation is one of reasonable care in the circumstances; it is not a warranty of the safety of plant and equipment. In some cases it may be sufficient to rely on the employee himself rectifying simple defects in the equipment used by him. Note also that in many cases there will be statutory duties (see **Chapter 7**) which may well impose rather higher standards.

> **?** **QUESTION** 5.6
>
> Is there any qualification to be made to the requirement of reasonable care in relation to plant and equipment?

The Employers' Liability (Defective Equipment) Act 1969, as we have already seen, imposes strict liability upon an employer in certain circumstances, where equipment is supplied by the employer for use in his business. As far as 'premises, or 'place of work' is concerned, the employer is expected to make the place, and the access to that place, as safe as reasonable care and skill will allow.

In *Latimer* v *AEC Ltd* [1953] AC 643, the claimant was one of 4,000 employees at the defendant's factory; he slipped, at night, on the factory floor, the surface of which was oily. The floor had been flooded as the result of a very heavy thunderstorm, and when the flood subsided it left an oily film on the surface. The House of Lords held that it was not unreasonable for the defendants to put on the night-shift rather than close the factory until the oily surface had been rendered safe. In the circumstances there was insufficient evidence of want of reasonable care. It follows from this reasoning that danger caused by some fleeting, or temporary, or exceptional condition might not invoke liability; but each case must always be considered on its facts.

5.3.3.1 **Premises of a third party**

Liability may extend, in effect, to the premises of some third party; it may also cover a third party's plant and equipment. It all depends on the circumstances of each case; it is an issue of a pragmatic nature. In *Wilson* v *Tyneside Window Cleaning Co.* [1958] 2 QB 110, Pearce LJ said:

> Whether the servant [employee] is working on the premises of the [employer] or on those of a stranger, that duty is still the same; but as a matter of common sense its performance and discharge will probably be vastly different in the two cases. The [employer]'s own premises are under his control: if they are dangerously in need of repair he can and must rectify the fault at once if he is to escape the censure of negligence. But if a [employer] sends his plumber to mend a leak in a private house, no one could hold him negligent for not visiting the house himself to see if the carpet in the hall creates a trap. Between these extremes are countless possible examples in which the court may have to decide the question of fact. Did the [employer] take reasonable care so to carry out his operations as not to subject those employed by him to unnecessary risk? . . . So viewed, the question whether the [employer] was in control of the premises ceases to be a matter of technicality and becomes merely one of the ingredients, albeit a very important one, in a consideration of the question of fact whether, in all the circumstances, the [employer] took reasonable care.

The employee is entitled to be protected against sources of danger created by anyone who should reasonably have him in contemplation, including another contractor working on the premises.

Whether a warning of danger is sufficient in any of the above cases is a matter to be decided in the light of the facts. The question to be answered in this context is: 'Was reasonable care taken to protect this employee in the particular circumstances?'

In some situations the employer may have to take positive action to protect the employee, while in others the fact that the employee knowingly incurs the risk may be evidence of his contributory negligence. You will find in 14.3.1 that *volenti non fit injuria*—the complete voluntary assumption of a risk by the claimant is a difficult defence to establish in employment cases.

? QUESTION 5.7

Is another cause of action available to an employee injured on the premises of a third party?

The employee is a lawful visitor of the occupier, who owes him the common duty of care under the Occupiers' Liability Act 1957 (see **Chapter 6**). In *Square D Ltd* v *Cook* [1992] IRLR 34, the claimant, who was employed by the defendant on a site in Saudi Arabia, was removing a floor tile in a narrow corridor so that wiring work could be carried out. The removal of the tile resulted in four triangular holes being left in the floor. In attempting to avoid the holes, the claimant slipped. This, in turn, resulted in the claimant's foot becoming jammed in one of the holes. It was found that the judge at first instance was wrong in holding that the claimant's employers were liable for injuries he received whilst he was working in Saudi Arabia at premises occupied by another organization. There was no negligence on the part of the defendants, who were satisfied that the site occupiers and the general contractors working on the site were both reliable companies aware of their obligations with regard to the safety of workers on site. Accordingly, the claimant's employers, the defendants, were under no duty to advise the site occupiers to guard against danger in the present case.

5.3.4 The provision of a proper system of working and effective supervision

This is of a twofold nature, namely the putting in place of a system and ensuring its continuing operation.

In *Wilsons and Clyde Coal Co.* Lord Justice Clerk Aitchison (a Scottish judge) said that there is no responsibility on the employer for 'isolated or day-to-day acts of the servant of which the [employer] is not presumed to be aware and which he cannot guard against'. He is responsible for 'the practice and method adopted in carrying on the [employer's] business of which the [employer] is presumed to be aware and the insufficiency of which he can guard against'.

In *Wilsons* the employer had placed dangerous cutting machinery in a narrow mine passage, and employees used this opening on a frequent basis. It was held that this amounted to an unsafe system of work.

This case was considered in *Speed* v *Thomas Swift and Co. Ltd* [1943] KB 557, in which the claimant was engaged in loading a boat from a barge. He was injured when a hook on a winch caught in the boat's rail. The procedure of loading the boat in this way had not occurred on any previous occasion. Lord Greene, agreeing with Lord Justice Clerk Aitchison's description of 'system of work' in *Wilsons*, said:

> It may include the physical layout of the job—the setting of the stage, so to speak—the sequence in which the work is to be carried out, the provision in proper cases of warnings and notices, and the issue of special instructions.

A system may be adequate for the whole course of the job or it may have to be modified or improved to meet circumstances which arise. Such modifications or improvements appear to me equally to fall under the head of systems.

? QUESTION 5.8

Write a short statement, setting out what you think was the outcome of this case.

You might have said that the system of work, used on previous occasions, should be modified for this one operation. Any required modification would be part of the system. The employer was found liable in negligence because the failure to modify meant there was no safe system of work on this one occasion. A normally safe system may be made dangerous in a particular situation, which never recurs, yet there can be an obligation on the part of the employer to see that appropriate modifications are made to the original scheme.

In many instances employees do not follow approved schemes of work, ignoring measures established for their own safety. The reasons for this cover a wide spectrum, ranging from wilful disregard, through inexperience, mere inattention, annoyance, to the system 'getting in the way of the work'.

The employer is always under a duty to take reasonable precautions for his employee's safety, but he is not an insurer of safety, nor is his relationship to his employee similar to that of a school-teacher to his pupil. In appropriate circumstances, no doubt, an employer can rely on the good sense of a skilled worker to avoid danger of which he has been warned. In general, however, an employer cannot expect his employees to establish and operate a system for themselves.

In *General Cleaning Contractors* v *Christmas* [1953] AC 180, the claimant was cleaning outside windows. He opened a window slightly, and held on to the ledge to balance. As he did so, the bottom sash moved; he fell and was injured. It was held by the House of Lords that it is not up to workmen to devise and take safety precautions. It is the duty of the employer to consider the situation, devise a suitable system, instruct the men what they must do, and supply any necessary equipment, for example, window wedges in this case. Lord Oaksey said:

> An employer must take into account that workmen may have disregard for their own safety. This means they must minimize the danger of a workman's own carelessness and take reasonable care to ensure that employees comply with necessary safety precautions.

? QUESTION 5.9

Summarize the employer's duty in general terms.

The duty of care is that of an ordinary, prudent employer. It will normally suffice for the defendant to show that he has provided the protection which accords with the standard practice in the enterprise or undertaking concerned; or that he has complied with the terms of any relevant statutory provisions.

In *Clifford* v *Charles H Challen & Son Ltd* [1951] 1 KB 495, protective cream was provided in the defendant's factory to protect workmen against dermatitis. But the foreman, a 'superior servant', of supervisory status, made known to workmen his dislike of the cream and encouraged slackness regarding its use. It was held that the employer was liable to the claimant who contracted dermatitis. It had not taken reasonable care for the safety of workmen.

In *Woods* v *Durable Suites Ltd* [1953] 1 WLR 857, the facts were similar to *Clifford* but in this case the employers not only provided cream, they also posted warnings in the factory about the consequences of not using it and generally encouraged its use. It was held that the employers had taken reasonable care, and were not liable.

It must always be borne in mind, however, that the duty is of a personal nature, that is, personal to the employer and personal to the employee. The duty is personal to the employer in that it is non-delegable, which means that though practical performance of the duty can be delegated to another, legal responsibility for its performance cannot. As far as the employee is concerned, the employer's obligation is of a personal nature in that it is owed to him, or her, as an individual. There may be circumstances of which the employer is aware, or ought to be aware, making an individual employee a more likely victim of injury than another worker in the same situation.

In *Paris* v *Stepney Borough Council* [1951] AC 367, the House of Lords said that in considering whether employers are negligent, regard must be had to their knowledge of the physical characteristics of a particular employee. In this case the employer had not taken reasonable care to protect the particular employee by providing him with safety goggles when they knew he was one-eyed. A two-eyed employee doing the same job would not have needed the same protection, because the risks in general were not too high.

You will know by now that each case turns on its facts, and we can contrast with this decision *Withers* v *Perry Chain Co.* [1961] 1 WLR 1314. The claimant contracted dermatitis at work, and she was offered 'safer' alternative employment. This she willingly accepted, yet dermatitis recurred. She sued for damages, contending that since her weakness was known to her employer, she should not have been involved in any work which exposed her to the risk of dermatitis. The Court of Appeal held that her employer had acted reasonably in the circumstances, the only alternative was to dismiss her.

Bux v *Slough Metals*, a case referred to at 7.4.1.1, is an example of a finding of an unsafe system because of the individual characteristics of the employee in question. The employer had not taken any steps to persuade the employee to use the safety equipment.

The following cases provide further illustrations of this aspect of the employer's duty of care:

In *Charlton* v *Forrest Printing Ink Co. Ltd* [1980] IRLR 331, the claimant was employed by the defendant to collect wages money. He was instructed to vary his collecting arrangements in order to avoid theft but did not do this and was injured in the course of a robbery. The Court of Appeal held that the defendant was not in breach of its employer's duty because it had taken all reasonable steps to minimize the risk of injury involved in the job. Apparently, it was the usual practice of firms of that size in that area to effect their own payroll collection rather than use a security organization.

In *White* v *Holbrook Precision Castings* [1985] IRLR 215 (CA), the claimant was employed as a labourer for three months, then offered a job as a grinder. Grinders almost always suffer from 'white finger' as a result of vibration. The claimant suffered from white finger and had to go back to a less well-paid job. He sued his employers for negligence in not providing a safe system of work. In fact there was nothing the employer could do to guard against this problem. It was held that if a job has risks to health and safety which are not common knowledge but which the employer knows, or ought to know about and against which he cannot guard, he should tell a prospective employee about the risk if it might affect his decision to accept the offer.

In *Pape* v *Cumbria County Council* [1991] IRLR 493, the claimant, a cleaner, had to give up work because of acute dermatitis caused by contact with chemical cleansing agents. Finding for the claimant, Waite J held that the defendants were in breach of their duty at common law to provide a safe system of work. The defendants had argued that they had discharged their duty by providing gloves and that an employer was not obliged to explain the obvious. However, his Lordship said,

> The dangers of dermatitis or acute eczema from the sustained exposure of unprotected skin to chemical cleansing agents are well known, well enough known to make it the duty of a reasonable employer to appreciate the risks it presents to members of his cleaning staff but at the same time not so well known as to make it obvious to his staff without any necessity for warning or instruction . . . there was a duty on the defendants to warn their cleaners of the dangers of handling chemical cleaning materials with unprotected hands and to instruct them as to the need to wear gloves at all times.

Turner J, in *Williams and Others* v *British Coal Corporation* (1998), *The Times*, 2 January, awarded damages to six out of eight former coal miners who had contracted 'crippling' bronchitis and emphysema through contact with coal dust. It was found that the defendant (and the National Coal Board before it) had been negligent in failing to take reasonable measures to minimize the dust which had been found to trigger bronchitis and emphysema. The compensation was reduced to take account of the parallel effects of smoking.

His Lordship said these cases were only the 'tip of the iceberg' since it was expected that more than 100,000 former miners were expected to submit claims for compensation in the wake of these test cases. Subsequently the state set up a statutory compensation scheme to deal with these claims. By the time entry to the scheme, known as the 'British Coal Respiratory Disease Litigation Scheme', closed on 31 March 2004, some 770,000 claims had been registered.

Finally, in *Tarrant* v *Ramage and Others* [1998] 1 Lloyd's Rep 185, Clark J held that the owners of a tug which was operating in the 'Gulf' War zone in 1987 were liable in damages for personal injury suffered by the claimant when the tug was struck by a missile. The owners owed a duty of care to the crew to exercise reasonable care for their safety. Accordingly, they ought to have given written instructions to the master of the tug detailing what they knew of the missiles in use in the area and how best to minimize the risk of the tug being struck.

5.3.4.1 Safe system on premises of a third party

The employer's duty of care extends, where appropriate, to the provision of a safe system of work on the premises of third parties.

In *General Cleaning Contractors Ltd* (above) the defendants were found liable for failing to provide a safe system of window-cleaning on a customer's premises.

In *Morris* v *Breaveglen Ltd* [1993] IRLR 350, it was held that where an employer sent an employee to work on a site under the direction and control of the main contractor, he remained liable to that employee if the system of work was unsafe. (The employee was sent under a labour only subcontract.) If, in the past, he had allowed his employee to operate plant for which he had no proper training, the employer would be liable for his employee's injuries caused by the lack of training when the employee was using the main contractor's plant. *Wilsons and Clyde Coal Co.* and *McDermid* were applied. The court also found that the employer was liable in tort for breach of statutory duty: the relevant plant had been used in breach of reg. 3 of the Construction (General Provisions) Regulations (SI 1961/1580).

? **QUESTION** 5.10

There is a 'hidden' point to note in *Morris* v *Breaveglen*. Can you spot it?

The employee was found to be under the 'direction and control' of the main contractor, that is, the latter could, where appropriate, be vicariously liable for that employee's torts committed in the course of his employment with the main contractor. Yet the defendant was still under an obligation to the employee to see that a safe system of work was in operation.

In *Multiple Claimants* v *Ministry of Defence* (2003), *The Times*, 29 May, Owen J held that the Ministry of Defence was not under a duty to maintain a safe system of work for service personnel engaged with an enemy in the course of combat. A similar decision had earlier been reached in *Mulcahy* v *Ministry of Defence* [1996] 2 All ER 758 (CA).

5.4 **Contract and tort**

In *Johnstone* v *Bloomsbury Health Authority* [1991] 2 All ER 293 (see also 1.4), it was held by the Court of Appeal that a doctor who is required by his employers to work so much overtime that injury to his health is reasonably foreseeable, may sue his employers in tort. The claimant claimed damages for clinical depression.

The Health Authority, the doctor's employer, contended that the doctor's contractual commitment to work for up to an average of 88 hours per week, as required, either qualified or negated the employer's duty to take reasonable care for the doctor's health. While two judges saw merit in this argument, the Court found, on balance, that the employer could only require the employee to work in line with the employer's duty to take reasonable care for the physical integrity of his employee.

This case provides a good illustration of how the terms of the contract underpinning the relationship of employer and employee impinge on the tortious aspects of that relationship.

5.5 **New types of damage**

Johnstone raises the possibility that the employer's duty may extend beyond care for the employee's mere physical safety. In the past only physical safety seems to have been in issue, but this case was concerned with illness of a 'physical' and 'mental' nature, that is, stress and sleep deprivation.

In *Walker* v *Northumberland County Council* [1995] 1 All ER 737, it was held that the employer's duty of care to provide a safe system of work extended to a case where it was reasonably foreseeable that the employee might suffer psychiatric damage, due to stress brought on by the amount or nature of the work expected from the employee. At this point you may care to look back at the discussion in 4.3.8.

More recently, in *Hatton* v *Sir Thomas Beckett RC High School, Barber* v *Somerset CC, Bishop* v *Baker Refractones Ltd*, and *Jones* v *Sandwell Borough Council* [2002] EWCA Civ 76 (four test cases, heard together), the Court of Appeal redefined the guidelines under which employees can claim damages for stress sustained in the course of their employment. The court made it clear that employees who feel under stress at work should inform their employers and give them a chance to remedy the situation. If they 'suffer in silence' a compensation claim may not succeed. Signs of stress must be plain enough for any reasonable employer to realize that something should be done.

The judges made the following points:

- There are no occupations which should be regarded as intrinsically dangerous to mental health.

- Employers are usually entitled to assume that the employee can withstand the normal pressure of the job unless they know or ought to have known of some particular problem or vulnerability.

- Any employer who offers a confidential counselling advice service with access to treatment is unlikely to be found in breach of duty.

- If the only reasonable and effective step would be to dismiss or demote the employee, the employer is not in breach of duty in allowing a willing employee to continue in his or her job.

In *Bonsor* v *UK Coal Mining Ltd* [2003] IRLR 164 (CA), it was held that an employee could only recover damages for psychiatric injury caused by stress at work where it was shown that the employee had exhibited sufficient signs for it to be reasonable foreseeable by the employer that injury to health would result from that stress.

Ward LJ said there had to be some indication 'plain enough for any employer to realize, to trigger a duty for the employer to do something about it'. The claimant had not manifested by her conduct or by complaints anything sufficient to put the employer on notice of the claimant's vulnerability: the only visible sign being an occasion where she was tearful and upset. The threshold set in *Hatton* was a high one.

The House of Lords in *Barber* v *Somerset County Council* [2004] 1 WLR 1089, one of the conjoined cases to which reference has been made above, approved in principle the Court of Appeal's restrictive interpretation of the law relating to stress at work in *Hatton*.

In *Simmons* v *British Steel Plc* (2004), *The Times*, 4 May, the House of Lords considered an appeal from Scotland. The pursuer (claimant) became angry at the happening of an accident about which he had warned his employers. The accident caused him physical injury resulting in the development of a skin condition, his pre-existing psoriasis was aggravated, which led to a prolonged period off work. He became more preoccupied with the accident and his anger led to his depressive illness. It was held that his employers, whose breach of duty had caused the accident, were liable for the mental illness even though it was only the physical injury which could have been foreseen. The Court, in applying *Page* v *Smith* (4.3.7), held that the defendant must take its victim as it found him. This was an application of the 'egg-shell skull' principle (2.6).

In *Donachie* v *Chief Constable of Greater Manchester Police* [2004] EWCA Civ 405 (CA), the claimant, a police officer, was required to attach a tagging device to a criminal's car while the criminal was in a pub. It was held that the claimant was entitled to damages for a stroke brought on by the stress of having repeatedly to change faulty batteries in the device.

The Court said that the judge at first instance had not considered whether the claimant was a 'primary' or 'secondary' victim. The judge had found that there was an unbroken chain of causation between the Chief Constable's breach of duty and the claimant's stroke, but he had ruled that the claimant had not suffered physical injury of the sort he had feared and his psychiatric injury was not reasonably foreseeable because the Chief Constable was not aware that he was vulnerable to stress.

Auld LJ, with whom the rest of the court agreed, said there was no doubt that the judge on the evidence was satisfied there was a reasonable foreseeability of physical injury. His Lordship said: 'If A puts B in a position where A could reasonably foresee that B would fear physical injury and B, as a result, suffers psychiatric injury and/or physical injury, B is a primary victim'. This decision is relevant to the issues raised in 4.3.14.

The Court of Appeal returned to the issue of stress at work in the conjoined cases of *Hartman* v *South Essex Mental Health and Community Care NHS Trust; Best* v *Staffordshire University; Wheeldon* v *HSBC Bank Plc; Green* v *Grimsby and Scunthorpe Newspapers Ltd; Moore* v *Welwyn Components Ltd; Melville* v *Home Office* (2005), *The Times*, 21 January. The Court emphasized that liability for psychiatric injury caused by stress in the workplace was, in general terms, similar in principle to liability for physical injury. It was pointed out that the 'practical propositions' set out in *Hatton* were 'helpful signposts', but they were not intended to cover all 'the infinitely variable facts that were likely to arise' in stress at work cases.

Liability for psychiatric injury in this context should follow general principles: only reasonably foreseeable injury flowing from an employer's breach of duty gives rise to liability. It did not follow, therefore, that a claimant, who suffered stress at work in circumstances where an employer was in some way in breach of his duty of care in allowing that stress to occur, was able to establish a claim in negligence merely by proving that to be the case.

For example, where a conscientious employer found there was a potential risk of psychiatric injury, it was still open to him to argue that it was a mere possibility or so small that it was reasonable for him to neglect it in accordance with the principles laid down in *The Wagon Mound*. Nor did it follow that if one employer had foreseen a particular risk all others in the same area of work should have done so as well. Again, the mere fact that an employer offered an occupational health service should not lead to the conclusion that the employer had foreseen a risk of psychiatric injury due to stress at work. Essentially, each case must be assessed on its own facts.

The Court of Appeal, in *Validi* v *Fairstead House School Trust Ltd* (2005), *The Times*, 24 June suggested litigants should adopt mediation in stress at work cases to avoid soaring costs because the legal principles applicable in such cases are now settled, as in *Hatton* (above).

However, the injury in question must be of a recognized kind, and fall within the established terms of the employer's duty of care. In *Mughal* v *Reuters Ltd* (1993), *The Times*, 10 November, the claimant, an employee of the defendant, claimed damages for injury suffered as a result of repetitive work, that is 'repetitive strain injury'. It was alleged that the employer had failed to provide a safe system of work in relation to the use of a visual display unit (VDU).

It was held that repetitive strain injury is not in itself a condition known to medical science and, in any event, there was no known safe method of sitting or posture for individual employees. It was not reasonable to expect an employer to provide a safe system of work in such circumstances, because the knowledge required for setting one up was simply not available.

This may prove to be a myopic view, however; recent research indicates that repetitive strain injury (RSI) may well 'exist' as a recognized medical condition. The condition is now more widely accepted. A scientific study conducted for the charity Action Research, which focused not on muscles and joints but on the sensory nerves in the hand, found reduced sensitivity to vibration not only among RSI sufferers but also among office workers who had not developed the condition. The study is published in the International Archives of Occupational and Environmental Health (*The Guardian*, 12 February 1998).

In the *Cumberland 'Times and Star'*, 24 January 1997, it was reported that 'Lilliput Lane', a manufacturer of hand-painted model buildings, had agreed to a settlement of £29,568 damages plus costs in an action brought by an employee for failing to advise her about the risks of RSI. The claimant had been employed by the defendants as a model painter and had to work with very thin brushes; this meant repetitive wrist movements over long periods. She had been medically retired in 1992 because of the condition of her hands and elbows.

The House of Lords has now implicitly recognized RSI. In *Pickford* v *Imperial Chemical Industries plc* [1998] 3 All ER 462, the claimant alleged that she had suffered RSI as a result of her employment as a typist with the defendant. Her claim failed for the following reasons:

(a) she could not prove that her cramp was caused by her typing work, as opposed to being merely associated with it;

(b) RSI was not reasonably foreseeable in her case;

(c) the defendant was not negligent in failing to warn of the risk of such a condition arising in her case.

 EXERCISE 5.1

Look back to *Reid* v *Rush and Tomkins* [1989] 3 All ER 228 (3.2) and state the result.

It was held that the employer's duty of care in tort does not embrace an obligation either to provide, or advise the employee himself to obtain, insurance cover for special risks when working abroad, where the contract of employment is silent on the point.

Reid is a 'pure economic loss' case.

The House of Lords in *Spring* (3.5.10.2), like the court in *Reid*, also had to decide whether an employee could recover damages for pure economic loss, but on this occasion the issue before the court was whether an employer owed a duty of care in negligence with regard to the giving of a character reference for a past or present employee.

In finding that an employer did owe such a duty, some of their Lordships said that the duty rested on an implied term in the contract of employment to that effect. This decision provides an interesting contrast with *Reid*, in which the Court of Appeal refused to follow that line of reasoning for insurance cover.

 EXERCISE 5.2

Consider the following facts: an employee, on medical advice, writes a letter of resignation the effect of which was that he was no longer entitled to benefits under his employer's insurance scheme as of right; he becomes entitled only to discretionary benefits. The insurer pays benefits only for a year. The employee complains that the employer had asked him to submit his letter knowing that he was applying for benefits under the scheme and that resignation would seriously prejudice his entitlement to the benefits. He contends that the court should imply a term into his contract of employment that his employer would take reasonable care for his economic well-being, on the argument that such a term is implied in all contracts of employment, that is that it is a standardized term implied by law in the absence of any contrary intention appearing in the contract. What would be your conclusion?

In *Crossley* v *Faithful and Gould Holdings Ltd* (2004), *The Times*, 29 March, the Court of Appeal, on these facts, refused to imply such a term because it would impose an unfair and unreasonable burden on employers. The court said that although the court would imply such a term in certain restricted circumstances (see *Spring* v *Guardian Insurance plc*) there was no general duty on an employer to take reasonable care for the economic well-being of an employee.

Litigation in relation to 'passive' smoking of tobacco allegedly causing injury to employees at work is almost certainly another issue facing employers. In *Bland* v *Stockport Borough Council, New Law Journal*, 12 February 1993, the claimant claimed damages from the defendant, her employer, for injury to her health caused by exposure to cigarette smoke at work. Without accepting liability, the defendant settled the action for £15,000. Section 7 of the Offices, Shops and Railway Premises Act 1963 requires the effective and suitable provision for securing and maintaining the ventilation of every work room by the circulation of adequate supplies of fresh or artificially purified air. An action for breach of statutory duty may also be possible in this context.

In *Connelly* v *RTZ Corporation* [1997] 4 All ER 335, the House of Lords ruled that the claimant, who had developed throat cancer after working in the defendant's uranium mine in Namibia and who claimed that due to the defendant's negligence he had been exposed to high levels of radioactive uranium and silica dust, could sue his former employers in England. Their Lordships said that legal aid was not available in Namibia; nor was highly professional representation from legal and scientific experts available in that country. These were cogent reasons for finding that the case could be tried in England. This decision may open the door for other multinational companies with headquarters in England to be sued in the United Kingdom for the negligence of their overseas subsidiaries.

Grieves v *Everard and Sons* (2006), *The Times*, 31 January, concerned the effect of pleural plaques (lung scarring) resulting from the penetration of asbestos fibres in the lung caused by the negligence of employers. The defendants admitted that the claimants were negligently exposed to asbestos in the course of their employment so that there could be liability to each claimant. However, they denied, with respect to nine of the cases, that the exposure caused any injury recognized for the purposes of damages. The plaques cause neither pain nor disability. Nevertheless the trial judge found that the quality of life for sufferers was affected. They worried greatly that it might lead to a more serious illness related to asbestos, such as mesothelioma. It was this anxiety and fear for which the claimants should be compensated.

The Court of Appeal, however, reversed this ruling. Lord Phillips LCJ, delivering the majority judgment, said that the exposure to asbestos dust had three foreseeable consequences, viz. the claimant developed pleural plaques; he was at risk of developing one or more long-term asbestos-related disease; he suffered anxiety at the prospect that he might suffer such a disease.

The development of pleural plaques was insufficiently significant of itself to constitute 'damage' for the purposes of an action in negligence; on policy grounds no claim could be made with regard to the chance of contracting a future disease where that disease was not consequent on some physical injury; English law had 'never entertained a claim for fear of future illness, incapacity, or death where [these] were not the potential consequences of physical injury'. He pointed out that there was no legal precedent, apart from three unreported decisions at first instance, for aggregating three heads of claim which, taken individually, could not constitute sufficient 'damage' for the purpose of a claim in negligence. Their Lordships appreciated that they were holding erroneous a practice that courts of first instance had been following for over twenty years.

In the case of Mr Grieves it was argued that he had a free-standing claim for psychiatric injury, because either that injury, or physical injury, was a foreseeable consequence of the defendant's breach of duty under *Page* v *Smith* (4.3.7). Lord Phillips said that the judge at first instance in the present case had not found that the claimant's psychiatric injury was a reasonably foreseeable consequence of the defendant's breach of duty. Moreover, English courts had never applied a simple test of foreseeability as 'determinative of the circumstances in which liability arose in the case of psychiatric harm' inflicted negligently. The *Page* v *Smith* test could not properly be extended to the case of a claimant who, having been negligently exposed to the risk of contracting a disease, then suffered psychiatric harm caused by fear of contracting the disease.

Smith LJ, dissenting, said that the question of whether a claimant had sufficient actionable injury was a question of fact to be determined in the context of each individual case. Her Ladyship considered that the claimant's cause of action was complete at the time when the plaques formed. 'The sum of the very minor physical damage and the much more serious damage comprising the risks [of developing an asbestos-related malignant disease about which a claimant was anxious] amounts to material, actionable damage.'

5.6 Compulsory insurance

The Employers' Liability (Compulsory Insurance) Act 1969 places an obligation on employers to take out insurance against liability, under the common law duty and in respect of breach of statutory duty, to their employees for personal injury sustained in the course of their employment. You will find the Act in *Cases and Materials* (7.2.2).

5.7 **Defences** (see also 14.3)

5.7.1 **Contributory negligence**

An employer may plead the contributory negligence of the employee, under the provisions of the Law Reform (Contributory Negligence) Act 1945, where appropriate. The defence is accepted more readily than it would be in actions, say, under the Factories Act 1961, but where the conduct of the employee, alleged to be negligent, is the result of an effort to get on with his job for the benefit of the employer, the courts will be slow to find contributory negligence. 'Nonetheless, in practice, contributory negligence is often successfully invoked as a defence' (Jones, p. 183).

5.7.2 *Volenti non fit injuria*

Volenti is an extremely difficult defence to establish in employer's liability cases. In principle, however, the defence ought to be available. The objection that it would be contrary to public policy to allow it, as in the case of actions for breach of statutory duty, would not apply here. To succeed, the defendant would have to establish the following:

(a) a genuine full agreement, which was

(b) given in the absence of any pressure, and that there was

(c) a clear assumption by the claimant of the very risk which was the subject of the agreement.

As *Winfield* (p. 220) puts it: '. . . the courts are unwilling to infer an agreement by the worker to run the risk of his employer's negligence merely because he remains in unsafe employment'. The learned author does suggest, however, that the defence might be available where, as the result of a clear agreement to that effect, an employee accepted special remuneration ('danger money') for taking on some specific and dangerous task.

> **?**   **QUESTION** 5.11
>
> Does an *employee* have any obligations to his employer?

Your list of likely obligations might look like this:

(a) an employee owes an implied contractual duty to exercise reasonable care in the performance of his or her duties generally;

(b) as a corollary of this duty, where the employee is solely to blame for damage caused by his or her tort committed in the course of his or her employment and the employer is found vicariously liable for that tort, the employer may seek an indemnity from the employee. The amount of indemnity payable would depend on what the court considered just in the circumstances;

(c) an employee owes an implied contractual duty to take reasonable care of his employer's property which has been entrusted to him;

(d) the Civil Liability (Contribution) Act 1978 provides that where an employer is vicariously liable for an employee's tort, but the employer is also partly responsible for the damage, i.e. he committed a tort himself against the injured person, the employer may seek a contribution from the employee for such amount as the court regards just.

The leading case is *Lister* v *Romford Ice Co.* [1957] AC 555, in which the appellant and his father were employed by the respondent as lorry-driver and mate. The appellant injured his father through negligent driving. The respondent employer was found vicariously liable for this tort. In contribution proceedings, the House of Lords held that the employer could claim an indemnity from the son, for breach of his contractual duty to his employer. The case caused much concern and the insurance industry was obliged to announce that it would not seek to invoke this rule unless there were exceptional circumstances.

■ SUMMARY

- Employers owe their employees a special, personal, non-delegable duty of care at common law. This duty, traditionally known as the master's duty to his servant is a corollary of the contractual relationship between the parties. It requires proof of negligence for its breach.

- The standard of care is a matter for the common law. It is likely, however, that the standards underpinning the general framework of the health and safety regime set up by the Health and Safety at Work Act 1974, will influence standards of care at common law.

- The general duty imposed on employers, by s. 2 of the 1974 Act, '. . . to ensure, so far as is reasonably practicable, the health, safety, and welfare at work of all his employees', is a prime example of potential statutory influence on the common law. In fact, it complements and could be said to strengthen the common law duty.

- Individual regulations will also influence the common law obligation. For example, the Manual Handling Operations Regulations 1992, and the Provision and Use of Work Equipment Regulations 1992, require that where handling cannot be eliminated a detailed assessment must be made regarding the task in question, and employers must make 'suitable and sufficient' assessment of all risks to the health and safety of employees.

- The common law duty of care is still capable of expansion as *Walker* v *Northumberland CC* shows and, although employer's liability depends on proof of negligence, it is also a stringent duty in the sense that whoever actually performs the obligation (it could, for example, be an independent contractor engaged by the employer), the legal responsibility remains with the employer. In *Winfield's* words (p. 221) '. . . the employer's duty is not so much a duty to take care but a duty that care be taken . . .'

■ FURTHER READING

Atiyah, P.S., *Accidents, Compensation and the Law*, 5th edn (Peter Cane), London: Butterworths, 1993.

Hepple, Howarth, and Matthews, *Tort: Cases and Materials*, 5th edn, London: Butterworths, 2000, Chapter 12.

Jones, M., *Textbook on Torts*, 8th edn, Oxford: Oxford University Press, 2002, Chapters 5 and 9.

Markesinis, B.S. and Deakin, S.F., *Tort Law*, 5th edn, Oxford: Oxford University Press, 2003, pp. 307–25 and 485–96.

Murphy, J., *Street on Torts*, 11th edn, London: Butterworths, 2003, Chapters 17 and 22.

Salmond and Heuston, *Law of Torts*, 21st edn, London: Sweet & Maxwell, 1996, Chapter 10 and pp. 464–74.

Weir, T., *Casebook on Tort*, 10th edn, London: Sweet & Maxwell, 2004, Chapter 3 and pp. 117–22.

Winfield and Jolowicz on Tort, 16th edn, London: Sweet & Maxwell, 2002, Chapters 7 and 8.

 CHAPTER 5 ASSESSMENT EXERCISE

See **Chapter 7**, for a specimen question; and *Cases and Materials* (7.4) for a specimen answer.

6 Liability for dangerous premises and land

6.1 OBJECTIVES

By the end of this chapter you should be able to:

1 Describe the different ways in which liability may arise for injury sustained on premises

2 Account for and explain the provisions of the Defective Premises Act 1972, the liability of builders, developers, architects (and others in a similar position), and local authorities at common law

3 Account for and explain the law governing the liability of an occupier to his or her lawful 'visitors' under the Occupiers' Liability Act 1957

4 Account for and explain the law governing the liability of an occupier to his or her 'non-visitor' entrants (e.g. trespassers) under the Occupiers' Liability Act 1984

6.2 Introduction

This chapter deals with the liability of persons who are concerned in some way with premises, but only with regard to damage suffered, in the main, on those premises. Nuisance, and other forms of tortious liability which are also concerned with responsibility for premises, but involve claims for damage sustained off premises, are dealt with elsewhere in this text (see **Chapter 10**).

You will find that:

(a) 'premises' includes 'structures';

(b) the range of persons who may be responsible is wide;

(c) people can be responsible in different capacities;

(d) we are concerned mainly with the question of liability arising under three statutes, that is, the Occupiers' Liability Acts of 1957 and 1984, the Defective Premises Act 1972, and the relevant case law.

We will examine first liability in negligence arising in connection with premises, before proceeding to liability arising under the Defective Premises Act 1972 and occupiers' liability under the 1957 and 1984 Acts. You will find all three Acts set out in *Cases and Materials* (6.2, 6.3, and 6.4).

6.3 Liability arising in various capacities in negligence

6.3.1 Sellers and lessors

A buyer or tenant, or visitor of the tenant, who suffers personal injury or injury to separate property as a result of the defect, may seek to sue in tort a seller or lessor with regard to defects pre-existing the sale or lease.

In *Cavalier* v *Pope* [1906] AC 428, the House of Lords held that a 'bare' landlord (that is, a person with no other interest in the premises but that of a landlord) could not be sued in the tort of negligence for such defects; the rule in *Cavalier* does not apply to furnished lettings. In *Bottomley* v *Bannister* [1932] 1 KB 458, sellers were also given immunity from suit in such circumstances. The defendant in this case had built premises on his land and then sold the premises. Curiously, even at that time, he would have owed a duty of care in negligence had he constructed the building on someone else's land. *Bottomley* is now of historical interest only because, as we will see in *Rimmer* v *Liverpool City Council* [1984] 1 All ER 930, a seller or lessor who is also a builder can be liable in negligence. In this case the local authority was both architect and builder as well as landlord. The claimant, a tenant of the defendants, was injured when he fell through some 'dangerously thin' glass in a wall panel on the premises. Complaints from the claimant and other tenants about the potential danger had been ignored. The defendants were found by the Court of Appeal to owe a duty of care under the *Donoghue* v *Stevenson* neighbour principle.

Defects must usually be latent (and, as you will see in *Murphy* v *Brentwood District Council* [1990] 2 All ER 908, at 6.3.2 cause injury to separate property or to the person) or it must be unreasonable to expect the claimant to abate the danger and reasonable for the claimant to have exposed himself to the risk of damage (that 'damage' must, again, be damage to separate property or injury to the person). This is similar to the position regarding defective goods under the 'narrow' rule in *Donoghue* v *Stevenson* (1932) which you will read about in **Chapter 9**.

The Court of Appeal, in *McNerny* v *Lambeth LBC* (1988) 21 HLR 188, held that the rule in *Cavalier* v *Pope* was still binding authority. A local authority was found not liable (as 'bare' landlord) in negligence for damage caused by condensation in premises which were not in a state of disrepair.

You may care to note, briefly because it is not the concern of this text to look closely at such matters, that statute and common law may imply certain terms into the contract of tenancy between landlord and tenant.

In *Barrett* v *Lounova (1982) Ltd* [1989] 1 All ER 1, for example, it was held that where a tenancy agreement imposed an express obligation on the tenant to repair the inside of the premises, but said nothing about repairs to the outside, and the tenant's obligation was enforceable throughout the tenancy and could not be performed properly unless the outside was kept in repair, the common law could imply an obligation by the landlord to repair the outside to give business efficacy to the agreement.

Sellers will also be open to liability in contract, including defendants in such cases as *Bottomley*, that is builders who are also sellers. The same is true of builders who are also lessors.

There may also be liability in the tort of deceit. Third parties will not be able to sue on the contract, nor will they be able to sue in deceit, because they will not have relied on the fraudulent misstatement.

> **? QUESTION** 6.1
>
> Why do 'bare' landlords and sellers enjoy a special privilege in relation to claims made against them in negligence?

It is because of the old common law policy of 'let the buyer (or lessee) beware', *caveat emptor*: fraud apart, the property is to be taken with all its faults. Sellers or lessors of real property, that is land, have been traditionally placed in a privileged position, compared with sellers of personal property, that is 'goods'. In recent years, inroads have been made into the immunity of builders who are also sellers or lessors, notably by the Defective Premises Act 1972, which is examined at 6.4. You will have already read about the decision in *Rimmer* (above) which also makes this point.

In *Stevens* v *Blaenau Gwent County Council* (2004), *The Times*, 29 June, the Court of Appeal held that the defendant, as landlord, was not liable for injury to its tenant's child when the child fell from an unlocked window. The defendant had adopted a policy to refuse to supply or authorize the fitting of window locks because of fire regulations. After the accident the council fitted a safety catch which apparently would have prevented the accident to the child, aged just over 2. The court said that the defendant, who had been sued in common law negligence, was not liable even though the child's mother had asked for a lock to be fitted. There was no emergency or external threat imposing a duty to act on the council, and there was no evidence that there was any hidden, special, or exceptional danger to the family's safety justifying an exception to the 'no locks' policy. The defendant, who was not in breach of the tenancy agreement or any statute or regulation, could expect 'appropriate vigilance' from the parents with regard to their children's safety by keeping them away from the window sill.

6.3.2 **Architects and others**

Liability may be imposed on persons such as architects, designers, building inspectors, and local authorities, as well as builders, under the *Donoghue* v *Stevenson* 'neighbour' principle.

There is a line of cases which imposed a wide duty of care upon such parties, particularly local authorities. All the cases have been overruled, but their legacy of a basic duty of care remains; they are no longer of specific authority because they imposed liability for 'pure' economic loss. The first case, *Dutton* v *Bognor Regis UDC* [1992] 1 QB 373 (CA), was concerned with facts similar to those encountered in *Anns* (below), the last case in the line.

In *Anns* v *Merton LBC* [1978] AC 728, the House of Lords held that failure by a local authority to inspect building foundations properly or not to inspect at all, in breach of the Building Regulations, could result in liability at common law if done otherwise than in the bona fide exercise of its discretion and negligently. *Dutton* was followed.

Accordingly, Merton LBC was under a duty of care at common law for a block of flats for which it had approved plans and which later came to have serious structural faults. It was found that no actual physical damage need be shown by the claimant, that is it was enough that the defect in the building was such as to create, according to Lord Wilberforce, 'present or imminent danger to the health and safety of persons occupying it'. Health and safety are relevant factors here because of the background legislation, that is, the 1936 Act.

> **?** **QUESTION** 6.2
>
> Is there a special feature to the decision in *Anns*?

In *Anns* there was no actual physical damage to person or property. Damages for 'pure' economic loss, that is, the cost of repair, to make good the defect, which need not have caused actual physical damage, were recoverable. The decision was explained away in some later cases as being concerned with physical damage, that is damage **to** the relevant building caused by the defects(s), but it remained as something of an anomaly until it was re-examined by the House of Lords in *D & F Estates* and *Murphy*.

In *D & F Estates* v *Church Commissioners for England* [1988] 2 All ER 992, the claimants occupied a flat, and had to pay out extra money to repair defective plastering work which had been carried out by subcontractors of Wates, the builders of the flats. As there was no contract between the claimants and the defendants, the claim had to be brought in tort. The House of Lords had to decide two issues:

(a) Were Wates Ltd, the main building contractors, liable for the negligence of their sub-contractor who carried out the defective plastering work?

(b) If so, was the cost of replacing the plaster work recoverable?

It was found, confirming the general position, that a main contractor is not normally liable for the negligence of his subcontractor. He has a duty to appoint a competent subcontractor and, exceptionally, there could be circumstances in which it would be obvious that a subcontractor was doing his work negligently, imposing on the main contractor a duty to intervene.

As Lord Bridge put it: 'A main contractor is not under a general non-delegable duty to ensure that a building [is] free from dangerous defects . . .' This conclusion is relevant to 'vicarious liability', which is dealt with in **Chapter 8** and specifically at 8.2.

Their Lordships also held, more importantly in the present context, that the cost of repairing a defect in a building is recoverable in negligence only if the defect has actually caused personal injury or physical damage to other property.

Anns was interpreted as imposing a duty on local authorities but not on others, such as builders, in respect of the harm or threat of harm, due to non-observance of Building Regulations, to occupiers of the buildings in question.

Lord Bridge suggested that in the case of 'complex structures', a house as opposed to a simple wall, for instance, one part of the structure might be regarded as distinct from another, so that damage to one part caused by a defect in another part might arguably be regarded as damage to 'other property'. For example, defective foundations of a building might cause damage to other parts of the building. *Anns* was said to be a case of that kind, and *D & F Estates* was not. He did not confine his discussion to buildings; his Lordship made a number of references to defective products in general.

In contrast, Lord Oliver thought that *Anns* turned on the issue of a statutory duty, and *D & F Estates* did not; there was no duty of care in the present case.

Murphy v *Brentwood District Council* [1990] 2 All ER 908

The defendant local authority had a statutory power, under s. 64 of the Public Health Act 1936, to approve or reject building plans. Acting on the negligent advice of an independent contractor, a firm of consulting engineers, the defendants approved plans for the foundations of a house; these plans contravened Building Regulations.

The Court of Appeal held that the authority was in breach of its duty of care in so acting, and when the house became imminently dangerous to the health or safety of the occupier they were liable to pay damages either to avert that danger or, if repairs were impracticable, to meet the fall in the value of the house on resale (though for an amount not exceeding the cost of the repairs). *Anns*, as interpreted in *D & F Estates*, was applied.

As a result of the Court of Appeal's decision *Anns* and *D & F Estates* were now difficult to reconcile because local authorities were placed in an anomalous position in comparison with defendants such as builders. *D & F Estates* said a builder could not be sued for the cost of repair of a defective house, while *Anns* said a local authority could be liable in those circumstances.

On appeal, the House of Lords adopted the *D & F Estates* approach to the question of liability in tort for present or imminent danger to the safety and health of owners/occupiers, resulting from damage to buildings. The decision of the Court of Appeal in *Murphy* was reversed; *Anns* and *Dutton* were overruled. It was found that the local authority did **not** owe a duty of care to prevent damage to buildings in these circumstances; the loss was of a 'pure' economic kind, which was irrecoverable in these circumstances. See *Cases and Materials* (6.1).

A local authority, when performing its statutory function of controlling building work, was not liable in negligence to the occupier or owner of a building for the cost of rectifying a defect in the building caused by the negligent failure to see that the building was built, or designed, according to the statutory standards. This would be the case where the defect was discovered before it caused physical injury, to the person or to 'other property', that is it was a patent rather than a latent defect.

Murphy is authority only for the proposition that a local authority is not responsible for 'pure' economic loss, as the cost of repairing the defective building was loss of that kind. The decision leaves open the question of whether a local authority might owe a duty of care with regard to physical damage.

> **? QUESTION** 6.3
>
> Have you noticed an important general feature of *D & F Estates* and *Murphy*?

In both cases the claimants could not succeed in contract, which is the traditionally appropriate means of obtaining damages for the cost of repairing defective items, and so they tried the law of tort. The courts, however, would not allow this. (We have already discussed the reasoning behind such decisions in **Chapter 3**).

In *Murphy*, Lord Bridge showed less enthusiasm for the 'complex structures' theory, imported from the USA. Indeed he said he had used it in *D & F* Estates only to try to make sense of *Anns*. His Lordship now thought it might be useful only in situations where separate items were supplied to a building, for example, a central heating boiler, which exploded, damaging the building. The supplier of the boiler could be liable, where the accident was due to his negligence, or liability might be imposed on him by the Consumer Protection Act 1987, discussed in **Chapter 9** specifically at 9.5.

It was found in *Richardson* v *West Lindsay DC* [1990] 1 All ER 296, that it would not normally be either just or reasonable to impose upon a local authority a duty to the owner of a building to see that he complied with appropriate Building Regulations; this was 'regardless of whether the loss suffered by the building owner as a result of failing to comply with the regulations was physical or economic'. The claimant, the owner, had a statutory duty to comply with the regulations in question. He was in breach of them and suffered loss as a result of faulty construction work. The local authority had an obligation to ensure that a building owner complied with the regulations, but could reasonably expect the owner to obtain competent advice and assistance to discharge his duty and carry out the work in a satisfactory manner.

Stovin v *Wise* (see 1.5.2) and the notion of 'reliance' introduced in that case may have potential for development in the *Murphy* and other public authority contexts. As enunciated by Lord Hoffmann it is, however, a somewhat vague notion, although it may only be in its embryonic stage at the present time.

In *Department of the Environment* v *Thomas Bates and Sons Ltd* [1990] 2 All ER 943 (HL), the court had to consider the liability, in negligence, of a builder with regard to building repairs and economic loss. *Murphy* was applied.

In *Targett* v *Torfaen Borough* Council [1992] 3 All ER 27 (CA), it was held that a landlord who is responsible for the design and construction of a house let by him is under a duty of reasonable care to see that the house is free from defects likely to cause injury to any person whom he ought reasonably to have in contemplation as likely to be affected by such defects. The claimant's knowledge of a defect does not, by itself, always negate the duty of care or break the chain of causation. Here the defect was the absence of lighting in the immediate vicinity of two flights of stone steps which gave access to the claimant's house. The claimant was the council's tenant. There was also no handrail for the lower steps and, before he moved into the house, he complained of the lack of lighting, but nothing had been done. One night the claimant fell down the steps and was injured. At first instance the defendants were found liable, but the claimant's damages were reduced by 25% for contributory negligence.

The defendants' appeal was dismissed. Russell LJ in applying *Rimmer* v *Liverpool City Council*, found that it was still an authority binding on the court and had not been overruled by *Murphy* v *Brentwood DC* 'by implication or otherwise'. Sir Donald Nicholls VC and Leggatt LJ concurred.

In *Nítrigin Éireann Teoranta* v *Inco Alloys Ltd* [1992] 1 All ER 854, physical damage was suffered by reason of an explosion as a result of the defendant supplying a defective product; the claimant had been properly diligent and knew of the defect, which had manifested itself in a cracked pipe, which they had repaired, but they had not been able to discover the cause of the defect. *Murphy* suggests that where a defect is revealed, one cannot wait until damage occurs and then make a claim. The court said, however, that here the claimant's knowledge was not 'knowledge' in *Murphy* terms, because there was no knowledge of the root cause of the defect. May J said even if the claimant had been negligent in not knowing the cause of the defect it could still claim for physical damage caused to other property by the defective product, though it could then be met with the defence of contributory negligence.

It was held that a cause of action in negligence does not accrue when a defect in a chattel (in this case a furnace pipe) occurs if the loss sustained is the pure economic loss in repairing the chattel. However, if the defect subsequently causes physical damage to other property, the loss is not economic loss and a cause of action in negligence then accrues.

In *Invercargill City Council* v *Hamlin* [1996] 1 All ER 756, the Privy Council approved a departure by the New Zealand courts from the reasoning in *Murphy*. The New Zealand Court of Appeal, following a line of authority developed in that country in preference to *Murphy*, found a local council liable for the negligence of their building inspector (this was not vicarious liability) who had failed to discover that the foundations of the claimant's house did not comply with local by-laws.

The house had been built without adequate foundations and as a result it eventually developed cracks and a number of small defects. Since the builder had by now gone out of business the claimant sued the council, and it was found that their building inspector should have known that the foundations were inadequate. A reasonably prudent homeowner would not have discovered the cause of the cracks and defects before they appeared.

The council, relying on *D & F Estates* and *Murphy*, appealed to the Privy Council on the basis that the claimant's loss was of a purely economic nature, in respect of which the council owed no duty of care.

The Privy Council found that the New Zealand courts were entitled to follow New Zealand authority in preference to *D & F Estates* and *Murphy*, because the policy behind the law in that country was different. Local councils were regarded as being in control of building work via their by-laws, and purchasers of properties generally relied on that control. The council therefore owed a duty of care in negligence to the claimant; *D & F Estates* and *Murphy* should not be followed.

It was also held that where latent defects existed in buildings, damage caused by those defects to the buildings was economic, and not physical in nature. The claimant's cause of action did not arise until a reasonably prudent houseowner would have discovered the defect, that is time did not start to run against the claimant when the negligence took place or when cracks in the building first appeared. Nevertheless, in a case where the damage became so obvious that a reasonably prudent homeowner would call in an expert the economic loss occurred at that point, that is that was when the fall in market value of the building took place; in such a case the limitation period would not be postponed. (*Pirelli General Cable Works Ltd* v *Oscar Faber and Partners (a firm)* [1983] 1 All ER 65 (HL) was not followed.)

You can read details of the Latent Damage Act 1986, in *Cases and Materials* (6.1).

In *Storey* v *Charles Church Developments Ltd* (1997) 13 Const LJ 206, it was held that the designer of a building owes a duty to the person whom employs him to take care in both contract and tort, subject to the terms of the contract. This duty extends to 'pure' economic loss. Church, the design and build contractor had, under the contract between the parties, assumed a responsibility to the claimant to exercise reasonable care and skill in designing the house and the claimant had relied on this. A builder, as well as a 'professional', could owe this duty.

However, in *Samuel Payne* v *John Setchell Ltd* [2002] BLR 489, the claimants were the subsequent owners of the house in question. They claimed that the original owners had a claim in tort against the structural engineer, that is there was concurrent liability in tort and contract. This liability arose because the engineers had designed the foundations and certified their suitability. The subsequent purchasers would acquire an identical cause of action under s. 3 of the Latent Damage Act 1986.

The judge, relying on *Murphy* and *DOE* v *Bates*, held that as a matter of policy any person undertaking or providing work and/or services in the construction industry is ordinarily not liable for 'pure' economic loss unless they provided evidence or made statements which were relied upon by their 'Employer' in circumstances under which a *Hedley Byrne* relationship arose. It was found, though, that the engineers owed the subsequent purchasers a *Hedley Byrne* duty in relation to the 'certificates of suitability' which were used by the seller to satisfy prospective purchasers (and those likely to lend money on the property) that the foundations had been built to a satisfactory design. The 'complex structure' theory was rejected as 'no longer tenable'.

The Court of Appeal in *Bellefield Computer Services Ltd* v *E Turner & Sons Ltd* [2000] BLR 97, took the same approach to this matter although there was no express reference to the present legal status of the theory. The court simply thought it was 'unrealistic' to consider two parts of a dairy as 'separate' property just because they were put to different uses. The court followed *Murphy*, and found that the common law imposes no liability where the damage complained of is damage to a building which has been negligently constructed.

6.3.3 Independent contractors

Independent contractors working on premises may be liable under the *Donoghue* v *Stevenson* 'neighbour' principle.

In *Billings* v *Riden* [1958] AC 240, the House of Lords allowed a claim for damages by an elderly lady who was injured while following a 'safe route' advised by contractors working at the house she was visiting. In the words of Lord Reid: '[There was] a duty to take such care as . . . was reasonable . . .'

In *Buckland* v *Guildford Gas Light and Coke Co.* [1944] 1 KB 410, contractors were found liable in negligence to a trespasser: the claimant was electrocuted when she came into contact with an electricity cable passed through the branches of a tree she had just climbed. The trespasser's presence must be foreseeable in such circumstances. Presumably this liability would also extend to activities on premises.

If contractors possess enough 'control' over the premises, they will presumably be 'occupiers', and their liability will depend on the terms of the 1957 Act or those of the 1984 Act, as the case may be. Occupiers' liability is dealt with at 6.5.

6.3.4 Generally

An occupier may be liable generally in negligence under the *Donoghue* v *Stevenson* neighbour principle.

In *Cunard* v *Antifyre* [1933] 1 KB 551, the claimant was a sub-tenant in the defendant's block of flats. Guttering fell from the roof, a part of the building retained by the defendant, through the glass roof of the claimant's kitchen, damaging his goods and injuring his wife. The roof was not covered by the lease, so no claim was possible for repairing covenants. The claimant's wife could not sue in the tort of nuisance because she had insufficient interest in the property.

Talbot J said:

> The [claimant's] true cause of action is for negligence, for failure by an occupier to take reasonable care to see that his property does not get into such a state as to be dangerous to adjoining property or persons lawfully thereon.

There would be liability if the guttering fell on a passer-by in the street, provided the negligence were proved; indeed, it would probably be a case of *res ipsa loquitur*. It was held that there was an equivalent liability in negligence to the tenant and his lawful visitors, therefore the claimant and his wife could sue in negligence.

It is important for you to note that this liability is separate from the obligation placed upon an occupier by the 1957 and 1984 Acts, and that encountered in s. 4 of the Defective Premises Act 1972.

6.3.5 Injuries to firefighters

In *Ogwo* v *Taylor* [1987] 3 All ER 961, the claimant was a firefighter and he was injured while attending a fire at the defendant's house. The fire had been started by the defendant using a blowlamp to burn off the paint on the fascia board under the guttering of the roof, thereby causing the roof timber to catch fire. The claimant went into the roof space to tackle the fire and was seriously injured by steam generated by water poured on to the fire. It was not suggested that the contents of the roof space were unusually combustible or that there was any special danger from a hidden cause. The claimant brought an action in ordinary negligence (the 'neighbour principle') claiming that because the fire was started negligently, and he had been injured as a result, he was entitled to damages.

The Court of Appeal, reversing the judge at first instance, found for the claimant and this decision was confirmed by the House of Lords. It was said that someone, whether occupier, contractor, licensee, or trespasser, who started a fire negligently may in the absence of special circumstances not known to the firefighter be liable to him when he was injured in fighting that fire. Foreseeability of injury was regarded as the crux of the matter.

Approval was given to the decision in *Salmon* v *Seafarer Restaurants Ltd* [1983] 3 All ER 729, where Woolf J held that the defendants were liable to a firefighter, who was called out to attend a fire started negligently by the defendants, and injured fighting the blaze. His Lordship considered whether there was any basis for limiting the duty owed to firefighters, since they are specially trained to deal with the dangers inherent in any outbreak of fire.

> Where it can be foreseen that the fire which is negligently started is of the type which could, first of all, require firemen to attend to extinguish that fire, and where, because of the very nature of the fire, when they attend they will be at risk even though they exercise all the skill of their calling, there seems no reason why a fireman should be at any disadvantage, when the question of compensation for his injuries arises.

The 'rescue' principle was also applied in these cases.

6.3.6 **Landlords**

A landlord might be liable, in negligence, where he is in breach of an obligation to repair or maintain: the contract itself may provide for this obligation, or statute or common law may imply it into the contract.

This form of liability differs from that discussed at 6.3.1 in that it concerns landlords only, not sellers; it applies only where there is an obligation to repair or maintain; and it includes cases where the defect appears after the start of the lease.

Section 4 of the Defective Premises Act 1972 provides that a landlord who is under an obligation to repair:

> owes to all persons who might reasonably be expected to be affected by defects in the state of the premises a duty to take such care as is reasonable in all the circumstances to see that they are reasonably safe from personal injury or from damage to their property caused by a relevant defect. [The] said duty is owed if the landlord knows (whether as a result of being notified by the tenant or otherwise) or he ought in all the circumstances to have known of the relevant defect.

In *Clarke* v *Taff Ely Borough Council* (1983) 10 HLR 44, the claimant who was a visitor of the tenant in a council house, was injured when she fell through rotten floorboards. The house, built before the Second World War, was of a type known to have a potentially dangerous floor construction. The defendants, who were held liable, admitted that rot was foreseeable in the circumstances, and it was said that notice is unnecessary where a defect is obvious on a reasonable inspection. (It is, however, advisable to put the landlord on notice wherever possible.)

The duty under s. 4 is owed to all persons within the 'area of risk', and not merely to tenants and visitors. It could be owed to a trespasser in appropriate circumstances. By s. 4(4) the same duty is owed where the landlord, rather than being under an obligation to repair or maintain, reserves expressly or impliedly, a right or power to enter and repair; but he will not be liable to the tenant if the defect is due to a failure to repair something which the tenant himself has expressly agreed to maintain.

In *Smith* v *Bradford Metropolitan Council* (1982), *The Times*, 22 June, the tenant of a house was injured as a result of a defective patio installed by an earlier tenant. The defendant landlords knew of the defect, and it was held by the Court of Appeal that their power to enter the premises was the equivalent, for present purposes, of an obligation to repair.

An alternative claim was put forward by the tenant in *Barrett* v *Lounova* (see 6.3.1) for breach of the terms of s. 4. It was alleged that as a result of the disrepair there had been extensive water penetration causing damage to the interior of the house. In the circumstances this claim was not pursued, but Kerr LJ thought that in principle there was no reason why an injunction to enforce the statutory obligation could not issue in a proper case.

In *McAuley* v *Bristol City Council* [1992] 1 All ER 749 (CA), the claimant was a joint tenant of the defendants who were obliged by the terms of the contract to maintain the structure and exterior of the property, the tenants undertaking to keep the premises (including the garden) 'in a clean and orderly condition'. Condition 6 (c) of the tenancy agreement gave the council's agents and employees access to the premises 'for any purpose which may from time to time be required by the council'. The claimant was injured due to the movement of a loose concrete step in the garden and sued the defendants, claiming breach of s. 4 (1) of the Defective Premises Act 1972, which imposes a duty of care in negligence upon landlords. Section 4 (4) says that the duty applies [inter alia] where a landlord has 'an express or implied right to enter the premises to carry out any description of maintenance or repair of the premises'.

At first instance the court found in favour of the claimant. However, the defendants appealed, claiming that Condition 6 (c) (above) only conferred the right to enter the house to do repairs; there was no right to carry out repairs to the garden for the purposes of the 1972 Act.

The Court of Appeal dismissed the appeal, applying *Mint* v *Good* [1950] 2 All ER 1159. Condition 6 (c) gave the defendants a right of entry which was not limited to their obligations of repair and maintenance, it conferred a right 'to enter for any purpose for which from time to time entry might be required by the defendants', only limited to the achievement of lawful purposes. Thus the provision included the exercise by the defendants of any express or implied right to repair. An implied right to repair did not, said their Lordships, depend on whether permission to enter could be obtained from the tenant or whether such permission had in the past been given, but depended on whether, in the case of an unwilling tenant, the landlord could insist on entry and obtain an injunction to enter and effect repairs if necessary. In order to give 'business efficacy' to this tenancy it might be implied that the landlords had a right to enter and repair any defect in the premises, including the garden, which might expose the tenants or visitors to the risk of injury.

6.4 Liability arising under the Defective Premises Act 1972

Under s. 1 a seller or lessor is subject to strict liability if he is in the business of, or in the exercise of any statutory power makes arrangements for, the provision of dwellings or installations in dwellings. The duty is

> to see that the work which he takes on is done in a workmanlike or, as the case may be, professional manner, with proper materials and so that as regards that work the dwelling be fit for habitation when completed.

The duty is owed by:

(a) those engaged in erection, conversion, or enlargement of dwellings, as well as by

(b) those who in the course of business or in the exercise of statutory power, engage others in the work.

The duty is owed to:

(1) anyone ordering the work and

(2) anyone who acquires a legal or equitable interest in the dwelling.

 EXERCISE 6.1

List the most important features of section 1, as you see them.

You might have noted the following:

(a) liability is strict, that is negligence need not be proved;

(b) s. 1 contains language relating to 'quality', redolent of contract language;

(c) damages may be claimed for the cost of repair, though the defect(s) in quality must make the property unfit for human habitation on completion;

(d) dwellings only are covered by the Act;

(e) it is not only builders who may incur liability here; people such as architects are also included.

As a result of the decisions in *D & F Estates* and *Murphy* the potential importance of the 1972 Act has been increased because the role of the common law in these building cases has been diminished. Indeed, in *Murphy* some of their Lordships said the very existence of the Act, and the absence of any discussion of it in *Anns*, were reasons for overruling that decision.

Strength is given to s. 1 by s. 3 of the Act, which provides for the survival of a duty of care after disposal of the premises in question. It says:

> where work of construction, repair, maintenance or demolition or any other work is done on or in relation to premises, any duty of care owed, because of the doing of the work, to persons who might reasonably be expected to be affected by defects in the state of the premises created by the doing of the work shall not be abated by the subsequent disposal of the premises by the person who owed the duty.

The section does not, however, impose liability for negligent omissions to effect repairs (though s. 4 may be effective in this respect).

This provision applies to any duty of care coming into effect before disposal and 'disposal' includes leasing as well as selling. Much the same result was achieved in *Dutton* (see 6.3.2) where there was an attempt to abolish the builder/seller's or builder/lessor's immunity from negligence.

? **QUESTION** 6.4

The 1972 Act may not be quite as radical a piece of legislation as it seems. Can you think why this might be?

There is a 'let-out' in the Act. This is to be found in s. 2:

> No action for a breach of duty under section 1 may be brought if there is in existence a scheme or document approved by the Secretary of State conferring rights in respect of defects in the dwelling.

The 'scheme' or 'document' referred to is some arrangement between the defendant and the claimant, like the 'guarantee' that is often given with new houses, which confers on the latter certain rights against the former. For example, the Buildmark Scheme (operated by the National House Building Council) whereby the builder warrants the proper construction of the dwelling and takes out insurance which will cover any claim against the builder. You will, no doubt, have noted that the Secretary of State must approve the scheme in question. However, after changes made to the scheme by the NHBC, the Secretary of State has agreed with the NHBC that the Approved Scheme Order of 1979 is not to be effective. This means that currently no Approved Scheme exists and effectively s. 1 is not excluded by s. 2 (except in relation to properties erected while the Approved Scheme was in effect) (see I. N. Wallace QC (1991) LQR 228 at 242–3). The Buildmark Scheme thus supplements, but does not supplant the statutory arrangements.

6.5 Occupiers' liability to lawful visitors

We will now consider liability arising under the Occupiers' Liability Act 1957. This will be done by examining each of the major provisions of the Act (*Cases and Materials* (6.2)).

6.5.1 Activities

At common law, before 1957, the duty owed by an occupier of premises to his lawful entrants, with respect to the static condition of those premises, for example a hole in a floor, varied according to whether the visitor entered by contract, or as invitee or licensee. It was based on a special line of cases, not on the *Donoghue* neighbour principle. This duty was certainly abolished by the Occupiers' Liability Act 1957, which replaced it with the 'common duty of care'. But there was another duty at common law owed by occupiers and non-occupiers, covering current activities carried out on premises, and it is arguable that this old, separate line of authority based on *Donoghue*, that is, the 'activity duty', remains at common law despite the Act.

A distinction was made in the law between different types of activity. Activities which rendered the premises unsafe, that is, created some danger of a continuing nature, would come within the terms of the occupancy duty; whereas activities which did not affect the condition of the premises as such would be determined by reference to the duty arising in ordinary common law negligence. It is the latter type of activity, sometimes called current activities, which is the concern of our discussion here and in 6.6.4.2.

The activity duty may be unaffected by the restriction in s. 1(3)(b) of the Unfair Contract Terms Act 1977, which applies only to occupation of premises used for business purposes. We will return to the 1977 Act at 6.5.7.

The problem arises because of the apparent conflict between two parts of the 1957 Act:

(a) s. 1(1), which says the Act only applies 'in respect of dangers due to the state of the premises **or to things done or omitted to be done on them**' (*emphasis added*). The part emphasized would seem to be clear on the point that activities are covered by the Act;

(b) s. 1(2) which says that the Act shall 'regulate the nature of the duty imposed by law in consequence of a person's **occupation or control** of premises' (*emphasis added*).

You may think that the spirit of the Act is to include current activities but there have been arguments going both ways in the past. According to *Winfield*, 15th edn, at pp. 291–2, the Act covers only the 'occupancy' duty. A further point is made (at p. 292): 'Defects in the premises which were not created by the occupier but which he has failed to remedy must be within the Act and the Act alone if there is no other relationship between him and the claimant . . .' An 'intermediate' case is identified: '[this] is where the defendant by some positive act creates a danger affecting the condition of the premises and here the matter is probably covered both by the Act and by the law of negligence'.

Salmond at p. 267 identifies both arguments, but says the weight of academic opinion follows the *Winfield* line that '. . . activities wholly unrelated to the particular land in question, but which just happen to be carried on there, are governed by ordinary Atkinian negligence as far as non-trespassers are concerned'.

Lord Keith in *Ferguson* v *Welsh* [1987] 3 All ER 777, took the view that the distinction between the occupancy duty and the activity duty had disappeared as a result of the passing of the 1957 Act, relying on the words emphasized in s. 1(1) above. (See also the robust agreement of D. Howarth, *Textbook on Tort*, London: Butterworths, 1995 at p. 369). In the same case, Lord Goff came to the opposite conclusion, relying on the words '. . . the premises for the purposes for which he is invited or permitted by the occupier to be there' in s. 2(2) of the 1957 Act (see 6.5.5).

Whichever view is correct, this matter can only be one of academic interest. In practice, whether the ordinary duty of care in negligence or the 'common duty of care' under the 1957 Act is applied to 'current activities', the result will be much the same. As you will see, the standard of care applied under the Act is very similar to that applied at common law.

Winfield's argument has some support in the case law. In *Jauffur* v *Akhbar* (1984), *The Times*, 10 February, a boy aged 14 negligently handled a lighted candle, which caused a fire. The claimant, a visitor, was badly burned as a result of the boy's behaviour and she sued the boy together with his father, in negligence. It was alleged that the father owed a duty to instruct his son, a minor, in the handling of lighted candles and to supervise his activities in the house. The boy admitted negligence, and the father was found liable because he had failed to give his son any instructions or warning about the use of candles, knowing that they were in the house. The claimant also alleged breach of the common duty of care, imposed by the 1957 Act, on the father's part, but the judge doubted whether the Act applied to such a case as this and gave judgment in negligence only.

There is also some opinion in the Court of Appeal in *Ogwo* (6.3.5) that the fire in that case did not come within the terms of the 1957 Act. See also 6.6.4.2 where the matter is discussed further, with particular reference to the duty owed by occupiers to trespassers.

Clearly, apart from the question of the 'activity' duty, where an occupier owes a duty (whether at common law or under statute) which is independent of his duty as occupier, he may be sued either under the independent duty or under the 1957 Act, or both. For example, an employee injured on his employer's premises may rely either on the 1957 Act, or on the common law duty owed by an employer to his employee, or on an action for breach of statutory duty (where appropriate).

6.5.2 **Premises**

Under s. 1(3) they include land and buildings and 'any fixed or moveable structure, including any vessel, vehicle or aircraft'. In *Bunker* v *Brand* [1969] QB 480, it was said that this definition included pylons, grandstands, lifts and even tunnels. According to *Wheeler* v *Copas* [1981] 2 All ER 405, even a ladder may be 'premises' for present purposes.

6.5.3 **Occupier**

It is provided by s. 1(2) that:

> The rules so enacted shall regulate the nature of the duty imposed by law in consequence of a person's occupation or control of premises and of any invitation or permission he gives (or is to be treated as giving) to another to enter or use the premises, but they shall not alter the rules of the common law as to the persons on whom a duty is so imposed or to whom it is owed; and accordingly for the purpose of the rules so enacted the persons who are to be treated as an occupier and as his visitors are the same (subject to subsection (4) of this section) as the persons who would at common law be treated as an occupier and as his invitees or licensees.

Section 1(3) extends the liability to the property of visitors, as well as extending premises to include structures (see 6.5.2), while s. 1(4) excludes from the definition of visitor 'a person entering any premises in exercise of rights conferred by virtue of an access agreement or order under the National Parks and Access to the Countryside Act 1949'.

We must therefore turn to the common law for guidance on the question of who is the occupier. An 'occupier' is a person with control of the premises; sometimes this may even include an independent contractor. There may also be more than one occupier of the same premises at the same time.

In *Harris* v *Birkenhead Corporation* [1976] 1 All ER 341 (CA), the defendant corporation acquired X's house by means of a compulsory purchase order. This statutory procedure gave the corporation an immediate right to enter the premises and the court said this made the corporation occupier of the house though it had never actually physically utilized the property. The right to control was enough.

X had let the house to Y, who became the corporation's tenant when the property was compulsorily acquired. Y vacated the premises without informing the corporation and the property became derelict. Children played on the premises and the claimant, who was 4 years old, entered and was injured. The corporation was found liable at first instance and the Court of Appeal confirmed this finding.

The occupier is responsible, because he normally supervises and controls the premises, and decides who shall and who shall not enter.

In *Bunker* (6.5.2) the defendants, who were engineers, were found to be still in control of a machine roller, even though a specialist contractor had been called in to modify the machine.

The House of Lords in *Wheat* v *Lacon* [1966] AC 552, approved the following observation of Lord Denning in the Court of Appeal: 'If a person has any degree of control over the state of the premises it is enough [to make him an occupier]'.

There may be more than one 'occupier', and *Wheat* v *Lacon* is an example of this. The defendants, who were brewers, owned a public house in which they employed a manager. Part of the private accommodation upstairs was used with their consent as a boarding house. The manager and his wife occupied this part of the premises, though there was no tenancy agreement with the brewers. The claimant and his wife, who were paying lodgers of the manager, one night used outside stairs on the premises and the claimant fell down the unlit stairs. This staircase was the only way up to the first floor; the staircase was in darkness because someone had stolen the bulb from the electric light fitting. The claimant died, and it was alleged that his death was the result of a breach of the common duty of care under the 1957 Act.

The House of Lords held that both the brewers and the manager were occupiers. It was not essential, said the court, that an occupier should have exclusive control as long as he retained

some responsibility. As it happened, the claim failed because there was insufficient evidence of negligence on the facts. The defendants were not responsible for the act of the unknown person who had taken the bulb, and the stairs were safe in normal circumstances.

In *Fisher* v *CHT Ltd* [1966] 2 QB 475, Crockfords arranged for independent contractors to run the restaurant in their gaming club. The independent contractors employed a third party to redecorate the restaurant. An employee of the third party was injured when an electrician employed by the independent contractors switched on the electricity without warning.

The Court of Appeal found both Crockfords and the independent contractors liable as occupiers, though the contractors were three times as culpable as Crockfords and liable in that proportion. The claimant's employers (the 'third party') were found most responsible because as employers they had not provided a safe system of working. They were sued as employers, not occupiers, under their special common law duty owed to their employees. All three parties were held responsible in different proportions: Crockfords 10%, the independent contractors 30% and the third party 60%. The independent contractors were insolvent and Crockfords were liable finally for 25% and the third party 75%. This is an example of the apportionment of damages under what is now the Civil Liability (Contribution) Act 1978. You can see from this case that there may be several parties owing different duties of care in relation to premises.

In *AMF International Ltd* v *Magnet Bowling Ltd* [1968] 2 All ER 789, an independent contractor and the owner were found to be occupiers of a building, although part of it was separated by a screen and the contractor only went to the other side of it to see to the heating and lighting.

? **QUESTION** 6.5

Does 'control' have to be exclusive? Is it a matter of 'law' or of 'fact'?

At one time it was the case that a person could only be regarded as an 'occupier' if he or she possessed the actual power to control entry to the premises, but since *Wheat* v *Lacon* this has not been necessary. As Lord Denning said, in the Court of Appeal:

> Wherever a person has a sufficient degree of control over premises that he ought to realize that any failure on his part to use care may result in injury to a person coming lawfully there, then he is an 'occupier' and the person coming lawfully there is his 'visitor'.

Presumably, the same test, but with 'non-visitor'/'trespasser' substituted for 'visitor', would be used to determine occupation for purposes of the 1984 Act (see 6.6.4).

It is also clear from *Wheat* v *Lacon*, the leading case, that control does not have to be exclusive and the question, in any case, of whether control is sufficient is one of fact to be determined on the evidence presented. Each case will turn on its facts, but as a general guide:

(a) even if an occupier engages an independent contractor to do work on his premises, the occupier will usually still retain sufficient control, although the contractor may also be an occupier;

(b) if the owner of land licenses someone to be on his land, but retains a right to enter for purposes of repair, the owner will have enough control to be an 'occupier'; and a landlord (that is where land is leased by him to others) may let part of premises, but keep other part(s) (an obvious example is common parts of blocks of flats, such as staircases) and then he will be an occupier of those other part(s);

(c) in the case of leased premises, the landlord will normally have given up control and the occupier will be the tenant.

6.5.4 'Lawful visitor'

Who exactly is a 'lawful visitor'? Again, reference should be made to ss. 1(2), (3), and (4) which have been examined in 6.5.3 in relation to the issue of 'occupation'. This is one of the trickier problems encountered in occupiers' liability. Again, we must turn to the common law to find the answer to our question.

In brief terms, 'visitors' for the purposes of the 1957 Act are those persons who would have been lawful entrants at common law before the Act came into operation. Such persons used to be classified as invitees, licensees, and entrants under contract. To these must be added those who enter as of right. In other words they are lawful entrants by force of law, it does not matter whether they have the occupier's permission to be on the premises or not (see s. 2(6) of the 1957 Act). Those entrants 'as of right' obtain their authority to be present from various statutes, for example policemen, meter-readers and postmen.

Where an entrant claims to have the express authority of the occupier to be present, any dispute will turn merely on the entrant's ability to prove the fact of permission. Much more in the way of a problem is likely to be encountered where implied permission is in issue, and it is to that form of permission that we now turn our attention.

6.5.4.1 Implied permission

It is for the person who claims the existence of the implied permission to prove on the facts that it exists. The burden is not a light one, because it is not enough to show mere tolerance.

To quote Lord Dunedin, in *Addie (Robert) and Sons (Collieries) Ltd* v *Dumbreck* [1929] AC 358:

> Permission must be proved, not tolerance, though tolerance in some circumstances may be so pronounced as to lead to a conclusion that it was really tantamount to permission; a mere putting up of a notice 'No Trespassers Allowed' or 'Strictly Private', followed, when people often come, by no further steps, would, I think, leave it open for a judge or jury to hold implied permission. There is no duty on a proprietor to fence his land against the world under sanction that, if he does not, those who come over it become licensees.

In *Lowery* v *Walker* [1911] AC 10, members of the public had used a short cut across the defendant's land, to get to a railway station, for nearly 35 years, but he had never instituted legal proceedings against them, because many of the people concerned were his customers. On these facts, it was held that the entrants were licensees, and when one of them was injured by a wild horse, which the defendant had put into the field without warning, he was able to recover damages as a licensee from the defendant.

In *Edwards* v *Railway Executive* [1952] AC 737, the House of Lords warned against finding in favour of claimants for sympathetic reasons, and said that it is not enough to show that the occupier knows of the entrant's presence or has failed to take the necessary steps to prevent his entry. In Lord Goddard's words: '. . . repeated trespass of itself confers no licence. There must be evidence either of express permission or that the landowner has so conducted himself that he cannot be heard to say that he did not give it'.

> **?** **QUESTION** 6.6
>
> Why might it be helpful to an entrant to establish *implied* permission? Also, why should the House of Lords in *Edwards* (above) refer to 'sympathy' in decision-making?

If an entrant can establish that he or she is an implied licensee, then today that would make the entrant a 'visitor' for the purposes of the 1957 Act. Before 1957, the entrant would have been a member of a class of entrants for which a special line of authority had been developed at common law, to confer on them a right to a fairly stringent duty of care from the occupier.

The alternative would be to be classed as a 'trespasser'; trespassers were, as we will see later, entitled at common law under the rule in *Addie* (above) only to a **minimal** degree of protection from an occupier. Today, the 1984 Act applies to such relationships and, when we examine its provisions later, it will be seen to offer considerable protection to a trespasser.

There is the clue to the second question: since trespassers were entitled to much less protection at common law in the old days, courts on occasion were inclined, especially in the case of trespassing children, to find implied licences rather than brand the claimant a trespasser.

Canvassers and similar entrants

It is said that 'common usage' can confer an implied licence on such people as canvassers, deliverers of 'free' news-sheets, those who have lost their way and are seeking directions, and entrants of similar ilk. That is so unless the entry of such persons is expressly forbidden. A notice seen recently on the gate to a private residence read: 'No hawkers, pedlars, or evangelists'. The purport behind the notice seems reasonably clear.

In *Dunster* v *Abbot* [1953] 2 All ER 1572, a canvasser was, on this basis, considered to be a licensee and not a trespasser. The court said he could become an **invitee** if the occupier did business with him. The canvasser left the defendant's premises in the dark, and was injured. The claimant claimed that the occupier had switched off the outside light too soon; he had insufficient time to leave the premises safely. The court found no negligence on the part of the occupier.

In *Robson* v *Hallett* [1967] 2 QB 939, Diplock LJ said:

> when a householder lives in a dwelling house to which there is a garden in front and does not lock the gate of the garden, it gives an implied licence to any member of the public who has lawful reason for doing so to proceed from the gate to the front door and back door and to inquire whether he may be admitted and to conduct his lawful business.

His Lordship went on to say that if the licence was withdrawn the entrant would not be a trespasser during a reasonable period of time which he needed to leave the premises.

Overstepping the mark

Even though there may be permission or authority to enter, it will on occasion be necessary to consider whether the entrant has abused it. As Scrutton LJ put it in *The Carlgarth* [1927] P 93: 'When you invite a person in your house to use the staircase you do not invite him to slide down the banisters.'

An occupier may not be liable to an entrant who goes to a part of the premises where the occupier has expressly or impliedly told him not to go, by notice or otherwise. Again, an entrant may be injured on a part of the premises where he could not reasonably be expected to go.

The 1957 Act itself makes it clear that an occupier will not be liable where an entrant uses the premises for some purpose(s) unconnected with the invitation or permission. If a meter-reader, for example, who enters by right should steal contents from the premises he will have abused his permission.

? **QUESTION** 6.7

How does the legal status of the entrant change when he makes a wrongful use of the premises?

He becomes a trespasser on those premises, although there is authority for two propositions.

(a) Permission to enter one piece of land may by implication be extended to another adjoining piece.

In *Pearson* v *Coleman Bros* [1948] 2 KB 359 a child wandered from a circus to an adjoining menagerie in the process of looking for a lavatory. At the menagerie she was injured; the court found that she was a licensee at the menagerie and said that an occupier must indicate clearly that the visitor (the girl was an invitee at the circus) is limited in terms of time and place.

Your attention is drawn to the point made earlier, about sympathy for the plight of entrants who might be regarded as trespassers, at a time when the law governing the liability of occupiers to unlawful entrants was much harsher than it is today. Even *Pearson* should, perhaps, be read in that light.

(b) A person who is a lawful entrant to begin with will probably not lose that status where it is the fault of the occupier that causes him to 'step out of line'.

In *Braithwaite* v *South Durham Steel Co.* [1958] 1 WLR 986, due to the occupier's negligence a lawful entrant was forced to move out of the area where he had permission to be, into an area outside the remit of that permission. It was held that he was still a lawful entrant.

It is possible for a person to become a trespasser, although that person was a lawful entrant initially, because he goes on to some part(s) of the premises the occupier did not intend him to enter or because he uses his permission for some wrongful purpose. It may also be the case that time is the enemy of the lawful entrant.

 EXERCISE 6.2

X attends a party held by the manager of a public house, after licensing hours, and falls down some stairs outside the pub on emerging from the building. He dies and his widow sues the local brewery, which owns the pub. The defendants say he was a trespasser at *that* time, but he was not aware of the fact that the manager was only allowed to have a private party outside the pub hours if he first obtained permission from the defendants (the brewery company) *and* informed the police. The manager had not satisfied either of these two conditions.

Would you find the deceased a trespasser at the relevant time?

These are the facts of *Stone* v *Taffe* [1974] 3 All ER 1016, in which the Court of Appeal decided that the dead man was not a trespasser, as alleged by the defendant, because an occupier who wants to impose a time limit on the permission given to an entrant must make this condition clear to the entrant. Here, this had not been done and the deceased was a lawful entrant at the relevant time.

Persons who enter premises in pursuance of a public or private right of way

The law is in something of a confused state with regard to public rights of way. Entrants in this case are disowned specifically by the Occupiers' Liability Act 1984, in s. 1(7).

According to the Court of Appeal in *Greenhalgh* v *British Railways Board* [1969] 2 QB 286, neither are they 'visitors' for the purposes of the 1957 Act. It may be that the *Herrington* doctrine of 'common humanity' would apply in such cases. We will see later that the ruling in this case, which was replaced for 'mainstream' trespassing by the 1984 Act, may still be valid for cases falling outside the Act.

There is also an old common law form of liability applicable to public rights of way, but it only covers negligent misfeasance (positive acts) and not negligent nonfeasance (failure to act). If, however, the public right of way is maintained at public expense the highway authority may be liable, under the Highways Act 1980, for both forms of negligence.

In *McGeown* v *Northern Ireland Housing Executive* [1994] 3 All ER 53, the House of Lords confirmed that the owner of land over which a public right of way passes is not liable for negligent nonfeasance towards members of the public using it. A person exercising a public right of way is, as such, neither the licensee nor the invitee of the occupier of the soil over which the right of way runs. Furthermore, said their Lordships, if a licence to use the pathway was granted by the landowner before it became a public right of way, that licence becomes merged in that right of way and is thereby extinguished.

The position regarding private rights of way is more straightforward. By virtue of section 1(1)(a) of the Occupiers' Liability Act 1984, persons using such a right of way are owed a duty of care under that Act. This is also the case for those exercising rights of access under the National Parks and Access to the Countryside Act 1949. See also s. 13 of the Countryside and Rights of Way Act 2000.

In *Ferguson* v *Welsh* [1987] 3 All ER 777 (HL), the claimant, injured because his employers used an unsafe system for demolishing a building, could not establish liability either under the 1957 Act or under any other branch of law against the owners of the building who had engaged independent contractors to do the demolition work, even where it could be established that the contractor had subcontracted the job to the claimant's employers in disobedience of a prohibition in his contract with the owners. The owners of the building, a local authority, accepted that they were occupiers (with the contractor) but disputed the claimant's status as a visitor.

Lord Keith thought there was sufficient evidence to support the argument that notwithstanding the wrongful subcontracting of the work, the contractor had ostensible authority from the council to invite the subcontractors and their employees on to the site. The contractor was put in control of the site for demolition purposes 'and to one who had no knowledge of the council's policy of prohibiting sub-contractors that would indicate that he was entitled to invite whomsoever he pleased on to the site for the purpose of carrying out demolition'. His Lordship said s. 2(4)(b) did not specifically refer to demolition

> but a broad and purposive interpretation might properly lead to the conclusion that demolition was embraced by the word 'construction'. In certain circumstances it could be inferred that an occupier might be liable 'for something done or omitted to be done on his premises by an independent contractor if he did not take reasonable steps to satisfy himself that the contractor was competent and that the work was being properly done.

Furthermore, there might be 'special circumstances where the occupier knew or had reason to suspect that the contractor was using an unsafe system of work' and the occupier might be expected to take reasonable steps to see that the system was made safe. In the present case there was insufficient evidence to suggest that the council knew or ought to have known that the contractor would ignore the prohibition in his contract or that an unsafe system of work would be adopted.

Lords Brandon and Griffiths agreed.

Lord Oliver agreed, but said if an occupier were to be found liable in such a case he would be liable as a joint tortfeasor.

Lord Goff concurred but said, on the assumption that the claimant was a visitor, there was no question

> of the claimant's injury arising from a failure by the council to take reasonable care to see that persons in the claimant's position would be reasonably safe 'in using the premises' for the relevant purposes; for it arose not from his use of the premises but from the manner in which he carried out his work on the premises.

Thus, the 1957 Act did not have anything to do with the present case.

6.5.5 The 'common duty of care'

This is defined in s. 2(2) of the Occupiers' Liability Act 1957 as follows:

> The common duty of care is a duty to take such care as in all the circumstances of the case is reasonable to see that the visitor will be reasonably safe in using the premises for the purposes for which he is invited or permitted by the occupier to be there.

At common law, before the 1957 Act came into operation, there were, as we have already seen, several different levels of duty owed to different kinds of entrant; today that number has been much reduced. As far as lawful entrants were concerned the different duties each had their own standard of care so that, for example, a licensee might be owed a different standard of care from an invitee.

The 1957 Act, by providing a single duty of care owed to all lawful visitors, has reduced the various standards of care to one, that is the common duty of care. This is, in essence, a duty to act without negligence with regard to the safety of the visitor, and the same considerations that are relevant in an action for common law negligence will be relevant here.

Initially, two points may be made concerning this statutory obligation:

(a) as Mocatta J put it in *AMF* v *Magnet Bowling* (see 6.5.3) an occupier is not an insurer against all the risks; he is expected in general to take only reasonable care;

(b) the Act refers to the safety of the visitor, not necessarily the safety of the premises. Thus a visitor may be 'safe' on 'unsafe' premises, provided the occupier has taken adequate precautions in the circumstances: for example, by providing adequate warning of some danger on the premises. It is a question of evidence, on the facts of the case, whether the common duty of care has been observed which means, of course, that it may be necessary in some situations for the occupier actually to make the premises safe in order to ensure the safety of the visitor.

It would be useful if you were at this point to refer back to **Chapter 1** to look at the factors taken into account when considering what the 'reasonable man' would or would not have done for the purposes of determining the standard of care at common law.

> **? QUESTION** 6.8
>
> Write down a list of factors which a court might consider when deciding whether an occupier has discharged his or her obligation(s) under the common duty of care.

In your list you may well have included the following factors:

(a) if there is more than one occupier, it could be that each one will be expected to observe a different standard of care;

(b) the likelihood of the injury occurring in the circumstances;

(c) the nature of the danger itself;

(d) the steps necessary to avert the danger: here the practicalities of taking precautions will come into account, for example, cost, extent and for how long the state of affairs has existed;

(e) was a warning necessary in the circumstances of the case?

6.5.5.1 Hotel guests

In *Lewis* v *Six Continents plc* (2006), *The Times*, 20 January, it was held by the Court of Appeal that s. 2 of the 1957 Act did not impose a duty on the owners of hotels to install blocks, bars, or limiters on sash windows in bedrooms. Ward LJ said it was not reasonably foreseeable that an adult occupying the room leaning out of the window would fall. (See, however, s. 2(3)(a) of the Act, discussed in 6.5.5.3.)

6.5.5.2 General observations

The Act itself makes specific provision for some special cases, but before we look at them there are two cases worthy of note; they help to explain further the general nature of the common duty of care.

In s. 2(2) there is reference to the visitor being 'reasonably safe in using the premises for the purposes for which he is invited or permitted by the occupier to be there'.

Lord Goff, in *Ferguson* v *Welsh* (see 6.5.4.1) claimed that the claimant's injuries did not come within the wording of s. 2(2) because he had been injured as a result of the way in which he did his work on the premises. Lords Keith, Brandon, and Griffiths were of the opinion that the subsection applied to dangers due to the state of the premises (Lord Goff's point) and known dangers arising from things done or allowed by the occupier to be done on the premises. According to this, majority, view the claimant did come within the terms of the Act; his claim failed simply because there was no breach by the occupier of his 'common duty of care'.

In *Cunningham* v *Reading Football Club Ltd* [1992] PIQR 141, the club, which was the occupier of a football ground, was found responsible for the injuries sustained by policemen on duty at the ground when supporters broke off pieces of concrete steps and started throwing them. The concrete was in a poor state due to lack of maintenance, and the club knew that pieces of it had been used by fans for this wrongful conduct on previous occasions.

You may care to contrast this decision with the earlier case of *Simms* v *Leigh Rugby Football Club* [1969] 2 All ER 923. The claimant was playing, as a member of a visiting team, in a match at the defendants' ground. A concrete wall ran alongside the touchline and its position complied with by-laws of the Rugby Football League governing body. The claimant was tackled near the wall, thrown towards it and injured. The evidence was uncertain on the point whether he had come into contact with the wall. There being no evidence of a similar incident in the past, it was held on the balance of probabilities that the claimant's injury was not caused by contact with the wall. This injury (a broken leg) sustained in a tackle was an accepted risk in playing rugby. On the facts, the defendants were found not liable. In any event, said the judge, the risk of injury in the circumstances though foreseeable was so improbable that the defendants could not be expected to take steps to prevent it.

In *Cunningham*, it was found that the defendants knew that it was 'very probable' that lumps of concrete would be thrown.

The claimant in *Brannan* v *Airtours plc* (1999), *The Times*, 1 February (CA), was on a holiday organized by the defendant. He was injured at a party when he stood on a table and came into contact with an electric fan. Guests had been told not to stand on this table. The court took into account the fact that the event was a 'disco', with dinner and free wine; and the people organizing the party had not tried to stop other guests from climbing on to the tables in the room. The defendant was found liable under the 1957 Act, but the claimaint's damages were reduced by 50% for contributory negligence.

Res ipsa loquitur will apply in appropriate circumstances. It was used successfully by the claimant in *Ward* v *Tesco Stores Ltd* [1976] 1 WLR 810, where she slipped in a pool of yoghurt on a supermarket floor. In *Fryer* v *Pearson* (2000) 18 LSGR 37 (CA), the claimant, while installing a gas fire at the defendant's home, knelt on a sewing needle embedded in the carpet. The defendants said the carpet had been laid before they bought the house and that Mrs Pearson, the second defendant, did not do her sewing at that place. She vacuumed the carpet every day and they had no knowledge of the needle. It was found, inferentially, that there was no breach of duty under the 1957 Act.

6.5.5.3 Special cases

We now come to the special cases provided for in the Act itself.

? **QUESTION** 6.9

Can you guess what these special provisions are?

There are two 'special cases'.

In s. 2(3) the Act says:

> The circumstances relevant for the present purposes include the degree of care, and of want of care, which would ordinarily be looked for in such a visitor, so that (for example) in proper cases—
>
> (a) an occupier must be prepared for children to be less careful than adults; and
>
> (b) an occupier may expect that a person, in the exercise of his calling, will appreciate and guard against any special risks ordinarily incident to it, so far as the occupier leaves him free to do so.

Children

Let us deal first with children. Evidently, each case will turn on its own facts; the question must always be: 'has the occupier discharged his common duty of care in the circumstances?' The age of the entrant and the nature of the danger are the two crucial factors to consider in such cases.

In *Titchener* v *British Railways Board* [1983] 3 All ER 770, it was held that older children (a 15-year-old in this case) should be regarded as adults in the present context; but in other cases it is, in broad terms, a matter of special care.

As Hamilton LJ put it in *Latham* v *R Johnson and Nephew Ltd* [1913] 1 KB 398: 'In the case of an infant, there are moral as well as physical traps. There may accordingly be a duty towards infants not merely not to dig pitfalls for them, but not to lead them into temptation.'

The courts have developed a doctrine of 'traps' and 'allurements' with regard to children. Occupiers must be aware that young entrants are likely to 'go where the attraction is', as it were.

In *Glasgow Corporation* v *Taylor* [1922] 1 AC 44, a child, aged 7, picked some berries off a bush in a public park. He died after eating what were in fact poisonous berries. The defendants were found liable because this bush, with its attractive fruit resembling blackberries, was an 'allurement' to a young child who could not be expected to be as aware of the danger as an adult. There was no warning of the danger and the bush had not been cordoned off.

A boy of 7 was also involved as claimant in another leading case, *Liddle* v *Yorkshire (North Riding) County Council* [1934] 2 KB 101. The defendant council had left a pile of soil next to a wall and it was possible, by climbing up the pile to reach the top of the wall. The claimant, while playing with his friends, got on to the wall in this way and fell off, injuring himself. He lost his case against the council because the danger here was obvious, there was no 'trap' or 'allurement', even to the claimant. However, he had been warned off on previous occasions and was regarded as a trespasser.

This case says the idea of an 'allurement' is applicable only where the child is a lawful visitor in the first place, but moves to a part of the premises where he or she should not go. The notion of allurement, in other words, cannot turn a child trespasser into a lawful entrant. In the past, children have successfully used 'allurement' to persuade the courts to create implied licences.

We have seen that the courts were willing to do this to mitigate, by avoiding, the rule in *Addie* v *Dumbreck*. Now that the 1984 Act has introduced a much more flexible formula for the resolution of disputes between occupiers and trespassers it is debatable whether allurement will be as important in this context in the future.

As far as minors are concerned, most people would agree that there are few situations which would not pose some degree of danger to very young children. They may be so young that they cannot appreciate even the most obvious of dangers. In such cases the courts will consider all the circumstances, to decide whether occupiers could have reasonably expected adults to be accompanying the children.

Devlin J in *Phipps* v *Rochester Corporation* [1965] 1 QB 450, considered the nature of an occupier's obligation towards a child who has not yet reached the age of 'reason'. The claimant was aged 5, and engaged on a blackberrying expedition with his sister, aged 7, on the defendant's building site. He fell into a ditch, which was an obvious danger, because he was too young to get across it safely. The court found that the defendant had acquiesced in the presence of members of the public and the children were licensees, but he was entitled to expect very young children to be accompanied by an adult and was not liable for such an obvious danger. The accident would not have happened to an older child, or to the claimant if he had been in the care of an adult, as the defendant could have reasonably expected in the circumstances.

The Court of Appeal gave its approval to this line of reasoning in *Simkiss* v *Rhondda Borough Council* [1983] 81 LGR 460. On the defendant's land there was a slag heap, near to flats and houses, and local children often used blankets and trays as makeshift sleds to slide down this heap. The claimant, a girl of 7, was injured when doing this and sued the council. Since there was no hidden danger, and no duty to fence in those circumstances, the only danger here was the slag heap itself. It was found that the defendants could rely on parents to exercise some control over their children, and to tell them not to play in dangerous places, or even prevent very young ones from doing so. In the circumstances, the defendant was expected to exercise only the care of a careful and prudent parent. It seems that the child's father thought the place in question was not dangerous.

In *Jolley* v *London Borough of Sutton* [2000] 1 WLR 1082, the defendant occupied land on which an abandoned boat had lain for at least two years. While the occupier accepted the argument that the boat was both an allurement and a trap to children, it claimed that it was only liable for reasonably foreseeable injuries, that is those suffered by children who played on the boat and which were caused by the attractiveness of the boat to children, and by its dangerous condition. The claimant was injured when he jacked up the boat to repair it, and the boat fell on him. He was aged 14 at the time. The Court of Appeal, while agreeing with the trial judge that the defendant had been negligent, found against the claimant on remoteness of damage, that is it was not **reasonably foreseeable** that children would jack up the boat to repair it. Lord Woolf, delivering the judgment of the court, said the case was **distinguishable** from *Hughes* v *Lord Advocate* [1963] 1 All ER 705 (see 2.5.1.2) because the accident was of a different type and kind from anything which the defendant could have reasonably foreseen in the circumstances.

The House of Lords, however, reversed this decision and restored the original judgment against the council. *Hughes* was applied. It seems that the simple truth was that the council, having recognized that the boat represented a danger, should have moved it from the grounds of its flats. Lord Hoffmann talked of the ingenuity of children in finding ways of doing mischief to themselves and others. *Jolley* is also relevant in 2.5.1.2.

In *Simonds* v *Isle of Wight Council* [2003] EWHC 2303, the claimant, aged 5, had been attending his primary school sports day at playing fields under the control of the defendant. After the morning's events he had a picnic lunch with his mother. After lunch she had sent her son to rejoin his teachers while she left the field to go shopping. However, instead of returning to school, the claimant went to play on swings which were situated in the playing fields, near to the spot where he and his mother had had lunch. He jumped off the swings and broke an arm.

It was agreed by the parties that the relevant standard of care was to take such care of the children as reasonable, prudent parents would take care of their own children in the circumstances.

The defendants argued that the accident was not due to too few supervising staff, that any reasonable level of supervision would not have prevented the accident, and that in any event the claimant had not been under the school's supervision at the time of the accident because the staff believed that the claimant was still with his mother.

Gross J, finding for the defendant, said the school had not been responsible for the claimant all day. It was arguable that the mother's acts or omissions had broken the chain of causation: this was simply an accident which had not disclosed any causative fault on the school's part. The school's responsibility had been discharged when it delivered the claimant to his mother for lunch and while he remained with her it was 'plain' that the school would not have been in breach of any duty of care owed to him. (Normally, a school remained responsible over a whole school day.) The claimant's mother had not taken him back to the school at any time before the accident.

His Lordship said the event had been properly supervised; the school had had a good plan for dealing with the swings. Only the claimant had played on them. Playing fields could not be made 'free of all hazards'. A prudent parent organizing a sporting event on such a field could not be expected to have immobilized the swings. Rather than the swings being fenced off, 'it was far more likely that sports days and other simply pleasurable sporting events would not be held if word got round that a school could be held liable in such cases'. Such events would become uninsurable or insurable only at prohibitive cost, and his Lordship pointed out that a warning against imposing liability in such circumstances had been given by the House of Lords in *Tomlinson* v *Congleton Borough Council* (see 6.6.4.2).

Special calling or skill

We can now consider the position of those entrants with a special calling or skill. An occupier is, under the Act, quite justified in expecting those entrants to exercise their special skill and to take care to guard themselves against any risks or danger of which they ought reasonably to be aware.

Lord Goddard said in *Bates* v *Parker* [1953] 2 QB 231:

> Where a householder employs an independent contractor to do work, be it of cleaning or repairing, on his premises, the contractor must satisfy himself as to the safety or condition of that part of the premises on which he is to work.

In *Roles* v *Nathan* [1963] 1 WLR 1117, Lord Denning said: 'When a householder calls in a specialist to deal with a defective installation on his premises, he can reasonably expect the specialist to appreciate the need to guard against the dangers arising from the defect.' In this case, two chimney-sweeps were killed by inhaling carbon monoxide fumes, while attempting to seal up a 'sweep hole' in the chimney of a coke-fired boiler which was alight at the time, and which was a special risk ordinarily incidental to the calling of a sweep.

It was held that the occupier could expect the deceased to take special care to guard against danger from flues; there was no liability on his part on these facts. Warnings about the danger had also been given to the sweeps and this was taken into account by the court in arriving at its decision.

We have already seen (at 6.3.5) in *Salmon* and *Ogwo*, the cases involving firemen injured on premises, that it is not enough for an occupier to plead simply that an entrant is skilled and that liability lies only in respect of exceptional risks or dangers. The two cases decide that there is no difference in such circumstances between 'ordinary' and 'exceptional' risks because the issue is simply whether or not the injury is reasonably foreseeable. *Ogwo* tells us, however, that an occupier can reasonably expect a firefighter not to take unnecessary risks by being foolhardy, and to follow standard practice in doing his job. However, *Ogwo* was decided without reference to the Act, let alone s 2(3)(b).

6.5.5.4 Warning notices

An occupier may seek to discharge his or her common duty of care by exhibiting a warning notice. In s. 2(4) we find the following provision:

> In determining whether the occupier of premises had discharged the common duty of care to a visitor, regard is to be had to all the circumstances, so that (for example)—
>
> (a) where damage is caused to a visitor by a danger of which he had been warned by the occupier, the warning is not to be treated without more as absolving the occupier from liability, unless in all the circumstances it was enough to enable the visitor to be reasonably safe; and
>
> (b) where damage is caused to a visitor by a danger due to the faulty execution of any work of construction, maintenance or repair by an independent contractor employed by the occupier, the occupier is not to be treated without more as answerable for the danger if in all the circumstances he had acted reasonably in entrusting the work to an independent contractor and had taken such steps (if any) as he reasonably ought in order to satisfy himself that the contractor was competent and that the work had been properly done.

Section 2(4)(b) is considered separately at 6.5.5.5. It is included here only for purposes of continuity.

'Without more' means without more evidence of other circumstances, or measures taken, for example, such as roping off a source of danger. The notice must be exceptionally clear and unambiguous if the occupier is to rely on it alone. Each visitor must be given the opportunity to avoid the danger in question. Of course, a notice can be used in conjunction with other methods of protecting a visitor, for example roping off an area of danger; in such a case the precise wording of the notice might not be quite so crucial.

? **QUESTION** 6.10

Can you think of an example of a suitably worded warning notice?

All cases will depend on their own facts, but an appropriate notice might read as follows:

WARNING TO ALL ENTRANTS ON THESE PREMISES. TAKE CARE. ENTRY TO THIS ROOM IS EXPRESSLY FORBIDDEN. THE FLOOR IS LIABLE TO GIVE WAY WITHOUT ANY WARNING.

Another notice might read: 'DANGER. CLEANING IN PROGRESS. THIS FLOOR IS SLIPPERY WHEN WET'.

A visitor is thereby assisted in coping safely with the danger.

It seems that the Act approaches the matter in a subjective way; in other words it is the effect of the notice on the individual visitor that matters. It is necessary that the particular visitor should fully understand the warning; it may be useless to rely on a written or visual warning where a blind entrant is concerned. As the Act says, the notice must be enough to make the visitor reasonably safe in the circumstances of the case.

You may have realized by now that an occupier, by referring to a danger in his warning is making it perfectly clear that he is fully aware of its existence, therefore the burden on him to show that his warning alone is sufficient is an onerous one.

The occupier in *Roles* v *Nathan* (see 6.5.5.3) convinced the majority of the Court of Appeal that his unwritten warning was adequate. The deceased were told on several occasions not to stay too long in the flue and that the boiler should not be lit until the access-opening ('sweep hole') had been closed. Actually, agents of the occupier themselves turned the boiler on in contravention of the warnings; for this reason Pearson LJ regarded the warnings as inadequate. We have seen, however, that the sweeps were regarded as persons with a special calling, who ought to have appreciated and guarded against the danger.

In some situations a notice is not necessary. This will be the case where the danger is an obvious one to the visitor in question, and one which he can easily avoid. No warning or other action by the occupier is, in this case, needed to enable the visitor to be safe.

In *Darby* v *National Trust* [2001] PIQR P27 (CA), the widow of a man who had drowned in a pond on the defendant's land sued for damages (under the Fatal Accidents Act 1976), alleging that there was liability under the 1957 Act. It was claimed that the Trust, as occupier, owed the man, as a visitor, a duty under the Act and was in breach of that duty: the absence of any warning referring to the danger of drowning was evidence of a breach of that duty, that is the Trust had failed to take reasonable care in the circumstances. It was held, however, that drowning was an obvious risk, so it was unnecessary to warn visitors about its existence.

Finally, warning notices as such must be distinguished from exclusion or restriction of liability notices and 'risk' notices, whereby a visitor's attention is drawn generally to the risk of danger. This is an attempt to raise the defence of voluntary assumption of risk.

> **?** **QUESTION** 6.11
>
> Can you think of appropriate forms of wording for these notices?

As far as exclusion of liability is concerned, a common expression is: 'The management accept no liability for any accident howsoever caused.'

In the case of risk, a notice might read: 'All patrons enter entirely at their own risk.'

6.5.5.5 Independent contractors

In effect this provision provides a defence to occupiers; it offers a means of establishing that the common duty of care has been discharged on the facts. The burden of proof is on the occupier as to whether he has acted reasonably in the circumstances. He will have to show that he has done all that reasonable care requires in the circumstances. Section 2(4)(b) is relevant here. It is set out in 6.5.5.3.

The obligation can be split up into its component parts as follows.

(a) The occupier must take reasonable steps to ensure that the contractor is competent. As far as the 'man in the street' is concerned, this begs the question as to the means of checking on technical competence. Each case must turn on its facts, but enquiring of trades or professional or technical organizations or local authorities etc., may suffice.

(b) Where the nature of the work involved allows it, the occupier is expected to see that the work has been properly done.

It was said in *AMF International Ltd* v *Magnet Bowling* (see 6.5.3) that in the case of the re-wiring of a building, for example, an occupier could trust a contractor, but much depends on the circumstances of the case. In some cases it might be necessary to see that the contractor's work is supervised by an architect or other professional person where the work is especially complex or potentially dangerous, for example, the construction of a large building. Mocatta J said that the negligence of the architect or other person would not itself involve the occupier in liability; otherwise, in technical cases, the common duty of care would become equivalent to the obligation of an insurer.

Much will depend on the occupier's own knowledge and, presumably, resources. The 'man in the street' would not normally be expected to know of defective technical work.

(c) It must be reasonable in the circumstances for the occupier to give the work to an independent contractor. In general terms this is probably the case where the job needs specialist knowledge and/or equipment (indeed in such cases it may be wrong for an occupier not to employ a contractor and to attempt the work himself) or where it is usual commercial practice to do so.

A few illustrations from the case law will help to make these points clearer. As you will be aware by now, pre-1957 cases can be used for this purpose.

In *Haseldine* v *Daw* [1941] 2 KB 343, the claimant was injured when the defendant's lift failed as a result of the negligence of a firm of contractors employed by the defendant to repair the lift. The defendant had employed competent contractors to maintain the lift so he was not liable. Scott LJ said:

> [T]he landlord of a block of flats, as occupier of the lifts, does not profess as such to be either an electrical or, as in this case, a hydraulic engineer. Having no technical skill he cannot rely on his own judgment, and the duty of care . . . requires him to obtain and follow good technical advice. If he did not do so, he would, indeed, be guilty of negligence. To hold him responsible for the misdeeds of his independent contractor would be to make him insure the safety of his lift. That duty can only arise out of contract.

By way of contrast, in *Woodward* v *Mayor of Hastings* [1954] KB 74, the claimant slipped on an icy step at the defendant's school. The step had been left wet in frosty conditions by a negligent cleaning contractor. The defendant was found liable. The Court of Appeal distinguished *Haseldine*, which involved the maintenance of a lift, requiring technical knowledge. This was not the case in *Woodward*, which merely concerned the cleaning of a snow-covered step. As Du Parcq LJ put it: '[The] craft of the charwoman may have its mysteries, but there is no esoteric quality in the nature of the work which the cleaning of a snow covered step demands.'

In *Wells* v *Cooper* [1958] 2 QB 265, it was held that a householder may undertake an ordinary domestic repair, for example, the fixing of a new door handle. He will have discharged his duty if he does the work with the care and skill of a reasonably competent carpenter. The court said this was not a case where the technical nature of the work required the occupier to employ an independent contractor.

It was held in *Cook* v *Broderip* (1968), *The Times*, 15 March, that the occupier of a flat was not liable to his domestic help who was injured because a contractor had negligently installed a new switch fuse in the flat. The occupier was entitled to trust the contractor.

In *Bottomley* v *Todmorden Cricket Club* [2003] EWCA Civ 1575, the defendant had engaged uninsured independent contractors to organize a firework display on its land. The claimant, who had been hired by the contractors to help them in the display, was injured by the display.

Brooke LJ, delivering the judgment of the court, said there were occasions when an occupier could be legally liable in negligence in respect of activities which he permitted or encouraged on his land. That liability stemmed from his 'activity' duty. The defendant in the present case was liable for the claimant's injuries because it ought to have taken reasonable care in selecting a suitable contractor to run the firework display on its land. It had failed to do so because it allowed a dangerous event to take place on its premises with no public liability insurance and no written safety plans. It made no difference that the contractors had not charged a fee.

We have not yet finished with the problem of independent contractors in relation to s. 2(4)(b) of the 1957 Act. In fact, we need to consider three issues:

(a) the expression 'without more' which appears in the subsection;

(b) the issue of 'demolition'; is work of demolition included?

(c) in s. 2(4)(b), the phrase 'any work of construction, maintenance, or repair' may cause difficulty apart from the issue of whether it can embrace 'demolition'.

First, the words 'without more'. They seem to mean that there may be evidence of the occupier's complicity in events which will not allow him to hide behind the contractor. In *Coupland* v *Eagle Bros Ltd* (1969) 210 *Estates Gazette* 581, the claimant was electrocuted by a live wire because the contractor had not switched off the current while carrying out electrical work. The occupier knew that the wire was dangerous and had not warned anyone. It was held that the 'without more' provision did not absolve him from liability; he was concurrently negligent with the contractor.

Next, we have to consider the word 'demolition'. Section 2(4)(b) refers to 'work of **construction**, **maintenance**, or **repair**' (*emphasis added*). On the face of it, 'demolition' does not easily fit into this formula. Lord Keith, however, in *Ferguson* v *Welsh* (see 6.5.1) expressed the opinion that a 'purposive' approach to the interpretation of the 1957 Act might suggest work of demolition would be included.

? QUESTION 6.12

Do you favour such a broad approach to the interpretation of s. 2(4)(b)? What result would a more literal, 'technical' approach produce?

A 'narrower' view suggests that a simple demolition job is not included within this wording. You may care to consider the view of E. McKendrick, *Tort Textbook*, 6th edn, London: HLT Publications, 1992, p. 209:

> With the greatest respect to his Lordship [Lord Keith] it is difficult to see how construction can encompass demolition; demolition is the very opposite of construction. Where a contractor is employed to demolish a building prior to constructing a new one it is conceded that such demolition work should be caught by section 2(4)(b) but the same reasoning should not apply where, as in *Ferguson*, the contractors were employed only for the purpose of demolition.

What other sort of work comes within the subsection? For example, in *Gaffney* v *Aviation and Shipping Co. Ltd* [1966] 1 Lloyd's Rep 249, it was held not to cover careless stowage by stevedores. As with the word 'demolition', much will depend on whether a 'broad' or a 'narrow' interpretation is given to the wording. According to the 'purposive' view, the purpose behind the Act must be considered and the legislation has to work in practice.

In *AMF International* v *Magnet Bowling* (see 6.5.3) the claimant company had a contract with the defendant company to supply and install bowling equipment in the defendant's bowling alley while it was being built. The building contractors, at a certain stage in the construction, negligently said the claimant could go ahead with its work. As a result of heavy rain the site was flooded and the claimant's equipment was damaged. The defendant should have checked the work of the contractors before allowing the claimant to enter the premises, but the defendant argued that the contractor's failure to prevent flooding was not 'faulty work'. It was held that to give sensible meaning to s. 2(4)(b) incidental work came within it; in the present case this consisted of a failure by the contractors to ensure that flooding did not take place while the building was being constructed. On the facts, the contractors had sufficient control of the premises to make them occupiers too.

6.5.6 Entry by contract

We must here deal with two sections of the 1957 Act.

Section 5(1) of the Act provides that persons entering or bringing goods onto premises under a contract are owed the common duty of care 'insofar as the duty depends on a term to be implied in the contract by reason of its conferring' the right concerned. In the case of contractual visitors or licensees there is an implied common duty of care.

An express provision of the contract will negative the duty. The contract itself is the final determinant of the duty (subject to the provisions of the Unfair Contract Terms Act 1977, which we examine at 6.5.7.1) but in the absence of provision to the contrary the common duty of care applies. The contract can provide that a higher duty than the common duty of care is to apply. Liability here lies in contract and/or tort (under s. 2 of the Act).

In *Sole* v *WJ Hallt Ltd* [1973] 1 QB 574, the claimant was engaged by the defendants, who were building contractors, to carry out work at a house. Whilst working on a staircase without a handrail, he stepped back whilst looking at the ceiling he was installing and was injured when he fell into the staircase well. He claimed damages alleging breach of contract and negligence on the part of the defendants.

It was held as follows:

(a) The defendants were in breach of their common duty of care under s. 2(1) of the Occupiers' Liability Act 1957.

(b) Since the claimant entered the house as a result of a contract with the defendants, s. 5 of the Act imposed on the defendants an implied term of owing the common duty of care to the claimant.

(c) The claimant was not confined to claiming under the implied term; he had the option of claiming under s. 2 as a visitor.

(d) Had his claim only been in contract, his contributory negligence constituting a break in the chain of causation would have been a defence to the claim. But since he had a claim in tort, he was entitled to receive damages reduced in proportion to the extent of his own contributory negligence.

Section 3 deals with the position of persons who enter premises in pursuance of a contract to which they are not parties. Section 3(1) provides that where an occupier is bound by contract to permit strangers to the contract to enter or use the premises, the occupier cannot by that contract exclude or restrict the common duty of care owed to them. This is an exception to the general rule that rights and duties may be modified by contract and the reason is that the stranger should not be adversely affected by the provisions of a contract to which he is not a party. The stranger is entitled to the benefit of any obligations undertaken by the occupier in the contract, in so far as they go beyond the common duty of care, subject to any provision of the contract to the contrary.

> ### ❓ QUESTION 6.13
>
> Write down, in one short paragraph, the general effect of this provision.

Where the occupier is bound by contract to permit third parties, who are strangers to the contract, to enter or use the premises, the duty owed to them cannot be restricted or excluded by the contract, but (unless the contract states otherwise) the third party can take advantage of any term of the contract which confers protection in excess of the common duty of care. For example, if an occupier permits his tenant and a friend of the tenant to use his premises by a contract that provides that the premises are to be lit at night (not specifically required under the common duty of care), the tenant's friend may sue the occupier for injury caused by his failure to light the premises.

A third party is in a specially protected position if he enters as a result of a right conferred by contract. This provision frequently protects the employees of contractors working on the premises. You should note further provisions of s. 3:

By s. 3(2) an occupier who has taken all reasonable care is not responsible for the defaults of an independent contractor unless the contract expressly provides otherwise.

Section 3(4) provides that:

> where by terms or conditions governing any tenancy (including a statutory tenancy which does not in law amount to a tenancy) either the landlord or tenant is bound, though not by contract, to permit persons to enter or use premises of which he is the occupier, this section shall apply as if the tenancy were a contract between the landlord and the tenant.

6.5.7 Exclusion of an occupier's liability under the 1957 Act

Exclusion or modification of the duty must be distinguished carefully from warning and risk notices. Warning notices have already been dealt with, and voluntary assumption of risk is examined at 6.5.8.

Section 2(1) provides that the common duty of care is owed by the occupier to all his visitors, 'except in so far as he is free to and does extend, restrict, modify or exclude his duty . . . by agreement or otherwise'. Evidently, the Act acknowledges that the occupier's freedom in this respect may be limited.

> **?** **QUESTION** 6.14
>
> Write down a brief list of restrictions on the occupier's ability to limit his liability.

You might have written down the following:

(a) liability to those persons who enter as of right under s. 2(6);

(b) liability to third parties cannot be excluded or restricted by contract with someone else, by virtue of s. 3;

(c) there may be some special statutory provision prohibiting exclusion or modification of liability, for example the Public Passenger Vehicles Act 1981 and the Road Traffic Act 1988;

(d) the Unfair Contract Terms Act 1977 may apply.

We will now proceed to examine the effect of the 1977 Act on occupier's liability under the 1957 Act. You may have studied the 1977 Act in detail within the context of the law of contract; in that case you will be acquainted with the Act's terms and general effect. In addition, reference has been made in **Chapter 3** to the Act's effect on exclusion clauses with regard to liability arising under *Hedley Byrne*. Only a basic, and necessarily brief, treatment of the 1977 Act can be given here. You will find the Act set out in *Cases and Materials* (14.1.1.2).

6.5.7.1 'Business liability'

The Unfair Contract Terms Act 1977 applies in both contract and tort, but only in relation to things done or to be done, in the course of a business. 'Business liability' includes liability arising from the occupation of business premises.

This provision is found in s. 1(3) of the 1977 Act. Section 2 of the Occupiers' Liability Act 1984 extends the meaning of 'business liability'. It says that the following words are to be added at the end of s. 1(3) of the 1977 Act:

> but liability of an occupier of premises for breach of an obligation or duty towards a person obtaining access to the premises for recreational or educational purposes, being liability for loss or damage suffered by reason of the dangerous state of the premises, is not a business liability of the occupier unless granting that person such access for the purposes concerned fall within the business purposes of the occupier.

This covers, for instance, situations in which fees are charged for entry to premises but the money goes to charity.

'Business' is defined, in broad terms, in s. 14: it includes, of course, what one would expect in terms of ordinary business or commercial activities; but it goes beyond that to cover the activities of the professions, central and local government, and other public authorities. It does not include contracts of a casual and occasional nature, say where A agrees to dig B's garden for reward during A's Easter vacation. Beyond this, the 1977 Act gives us no better definition of business.

The 1977 Act applies only to exemption clauses in contracts, that is, those which:

(a) attempt to exclude or restrict liability; or

(b) impose onerous conditions on enforcement of liability; or

(c) restrict the right to a remedy; or

(d) restrict or exclude rules of evidence or procedure; or

(e) attempt to modify the contractual obligation.

6.5.7.2 Negligence

Section 2(1) of the 1977 Act provides as follows:

> A person cannot by reference to any contract terms or to a notice given to persons generally or to particular persons exclude or restrict his liability for death or personal injury resulting from negligence.

 QUESTION 6.15

List the features of this provision that relate most strongly to the present discussion.

You might have listed the following:

(a) not only contract terms are covered; 'notices' are included too, so the Act must also extend to **tort**;

(b) only liability in relation to death and bodily injury are mentioned;

(c) it is restricted to damage caused by negligence.

Whether it is contract or tort that is involved, the relevant behaviour of the defendant must be 'negligence'. Not all torts are based on negligence, and many contracts involve strict liability, so s. 2 does not apply in such cases. Where contracts do not contain obligations to take reasonable care or to exercise reasonable skill, the 1977 Act only applies to exemption clauses where one party is a 'consumer' or the contract is based on 'written standard terms of business'.

Having established that s. 2 is not restricted to exemption clauses in contracts, but applies also in tort, we now need to know what 'negligence' means in the present context. This is defined in s. 1 to mean breach of an obligation to take reasonable care or to exercise reasonable skill arising out of the express or implied terms of a contract, or existing at common law in tort, or arising out of the Occupiers' Liability Act 1957.

The absolute ban on exemption of liability for negligence is restricted to cases of death or bodily injury. In the case of liability for other loss or damage, s. 2(2) says that exclusion is possible where the term or notice passes the 'reasonableness' tests set out in s. 11. The burden of proving 'reasonableness' is on the person who wants to rely on the exemption clause or notice.

6.5.7.3 Notice

In those cases of tort where liability may be excluded the task can be achieved by a non-contractual 'notice', because s. 2(1) of the 1957 Act uses the expression 'by agreement or otherwise'. By this means the Act gave effect to the decision of the Court of Appeal in *Ashdown* v *Samuel Williams and Son Ltd* [1957] 1 QB 409.

The defendants had put up a number of notices on their land to the effect that all entrants were present at their own risk, and that they would have no claim against the defendants for any injury whatsoever. It was held that the defendants had taken all reasonable steps to bring the conditions contained in the notices to the claimant's attention. The claimant could not recover when she was injured as a result of the negligent shunting of railway trucks by the defendants.

Today, the 1977 Act would outlaw such an exemption notice on its facts (it was business liability), but the case remains as authority for 'notice' where the defendant is free to 'restrict, modify, or exclude' his liability under the 1957 Act. It is authority for the proposition that actual notice of the condition is not necessary, provided reasonable steps have been taken to bring it to the attention of the claimant. In other words, constructive notice will do. This may lead to difficulty in the case of children and the illiterate.

Ashdown v *Samuel Williams* was applied in *White* v *Blackmore* [1972] 2 QB 651. The claimant was the widow of White and sued the defendants for negligently causing his death. White was a competitor in 'jalopy' races of which the defendants were the organizers. He took his wife and child to the races. At the entrance to the field in which the races were being held, and around the track, were exhibited notices which stated:

> Warning to the public. Motor racing is dangerous. It is a condition of admission that all persons having any connection with the promotion and/or organization and/or conduct of the meeting . . . are absolved from all liabilities arising out of accidents causing damage or personal injury . . . however caused to spectators or ticket-holders.

Since White was a competitor in the races he entered free; his wife and child paid for admission. (It was accepted by both sides in the case that White was not a 'ticket-holder' within the meaning of the notice.) The organizers of the events had arranged the layout of the safety-ropes, so that all the ropes, that is, the rope around the spectators' enclosure, the pit boundary-rope, and the double safety-rope around the track were attached to a single master stake. White left his wife and child in the spectators' enclosure and took part in one race. Afterwards, he joined his family in order to watch the following races, intending to compete again later. He ought to have got under the spectators' rope, but instead he stayed on the track side of the rope, standing next to the master stake. Whilst he was watching a race, the wheel of a competing car caught in the double safety-rope some distance away and all the stakes, including the master stake, were pulled out. He was thrown into the air by the master stake and ropes and later died from his injuries. The trial judge found that the defendants were negligent in tying all the ropes to one stake and were therefore in breach of the common duty of care under s. 2(4)(a) of the 1957 Act. White, however, was one-third to blame for the accident. Further, since he had clearly seen and understood the notices excluding liability, the complete defence of *volenti* applied.

On appeal by the wife the Court of Appeal held that *volenti* did not apply where the risk of injury arose not from participation in the dangerous sport but from the organizers' failure to take reasonable precautions for the safety of visitors to the meeting. Since White did not have full knowledge of the risk involved from the faulty layout of the ropes, he had not willingly accepted that risk. Nevertheless, their liability was excluded under the 1957 Act, s. 2(1), and this they had done by posting the warning notices, the heading of which . . . 'Warning to the Public'. . . was not to be construed restrictively to exclude competitors.

There was a variance of opinion in the Court of Appeal on the question of exclusion of liability where there is no contractual relationship. Lord Denning dissented from the above verdict and said '. . . in the absence of contract, the organizers of a sports meeting cannot get out of their responsibilities by putting up warning notices'. The warning notices were not part of a contract, but only warned the visitor of his position at common law. 'Otherwise' in s. 2(1) did not absolve the defendants from liability, as under s. 2(4)(a) of the Act the warning must be sufficient in all the circumstances to enable the visitor to be safe, which was not so in this case. Buckley LJ held, however, that s. 2(4)(a) did not apply here; the notices of exemption, which White must have seen, effectively excluded liability even though no contract had been made between the defendant and White. This decision, like *Ashdown*, must be read in the light of the 1977 Act.

6.5.7.4 **A minimum standard of care**

Winfield (at pp. 240–1) argues that the original duty owed by occupiers to trespassers, representing as it does a minimum obligation, should be owed to lawful entrants in all cases. In other words, no occupier should be able to exclude this duty of care. The old duty, not to injure the entrant deliberately or recklessly cannot be excluded 'for A cannot lawfully license B to inflict a wilful injury upon him'.

> If it be objected that a lawful visitor [who enters premises subject to the occupier's terms] may therefore be worse off than a trespasser entering without notice of the occupier's terms [the 1984 Act imposes a considerably higher standard of care than the original duty] it may be replied that at least the visitor is, or ought to be, aware of these terms.

Jones (at p. 195) argues that it is the duty laid down in the 1984 Act which applies to lawful visitors in these circumstances.

The present duty of care owed to trespassers is examined at 6.6.4.

6.5.8 *Volenti non fit injuria*

This is one of the general defences in the law of tort (see **Chapter 14**). It applies to liability arising under the 1957 Act, by virtue of s. 2(5), which says there is no liability for 'risks willingly accepted as his by the visitor'. The Unfair Contract Terms Act 1977 preserves the defence, but does say in s. 2(3) that someone's agreement to or awareness of an exemption condition or notice does not 'itself' indicate that person's voluntary acceptance of the risk. Apart from this, the usual conditions for the defence will apply. For example, there must be full, free, and unfettered consent. Although there is some apparent element of overlap between them, it is important to distinguish between '*volenti*', 'warning', and 'exemption of liability'. Your attention has already been drawn to this.

In *Simms* (see 6.5.5.2) it was found that the claimant had willingly accepted the risk, by virtue of s. 2(5), of playing on a football field which, as far as the distance of the wall from the touchline was concerned, complied with the Rugby Football League's by-laws.

? **QUESTION** 6.16

Summarize the main differences between these three concepts.

The main differences between the three ideas are as follows:

(a) A warning merely informs a visitor of a danger which he can guard against if he wishes. It will be a question of fact in each case whether the warning is enough on its own to make the visitor reasonably safe, so discharging the occupier's duty of care.

(b) Knowledge of a risk, while not enough on its own, may be evidence that a visitor has willingly accepted the risk, so absolving the occupier from liability.

(c) An exemption clause or notice, provided it has been adequately brought to the visitor's attention, is a condition of entry; it simply says 'you can come in, on condition that I am not liable for any damage you suffer whilst you are on the premises'.

The end result will be the same, in all three cases, that is, an absence of liability on the part of the occupier.

6.5.9 **Contributory negligence**

Knowledge may also be evidence of contributory negligence on the part of the visitor. This, again, is a general defence in tort (see **Chapter 14**). The provisions of the Law Reform (Contributory Negligence) Act 1945 apply to liability arising under the 1957 Act. For example, in *Stone* v *Taffe* (see Exercise 6.2) the visitor's damages were reduced because of his contributory negligence.

In *Sayers* v *Harlow UDC* [1958] 1 WLR 623 (CA), due to a defective lock the claimant found herself trapped in a cubicle at the defendant's public lavatories. She called for help for about 15 minutes and then tried to climb out by using the toilet-roll holder as a step. Her attempt at escape resulted in injury. The defendant, as occupier, was found liable for the claimant's injury, but her damages were reduced by 25% for contributory negligence.

6.5.10 **Damage**

Under s. 1(3) of the 1957 Act this covers personal injury (presumably this would include nervous shock), damage to the visitor's goods and consequential financial loss. The subsection goes on to say that damage to 'property' includes 'the property of persons who are not themselves his visitors'. *Winfield* says (at p. 242) that would '. . . seem to allow an action by an owner who is not a visitor'. Unfortunately, the 1957 Act imposes its duty of care in favour of the visitor and much would depend on how a court would see the purpose, if a purposive interpretation were taken, of the Act. North, in *'Occupiers' Liability'* (1957) argues that a third party cannot sue directly under the 1957 Act for damage to his property in the possession of a visitor. The visitor would technically be a bailee of the third party's goods and, whether the bailment was for reward or was of a gratuitous nature, the visitor would be liable to account over to the third party with regard to any damages received for damaged goods. In any case, the third party could sue the occupier directly under the Torts (Interference with Goods) Act 1977: under s. 1 of that Act 'negligence' is a form of interference with goods.

In *Smith* v *Vange Scaffolding and Another* [1970] 1 All ER 249, the claimant was employed by the first defendants, who were independent contractors working on a building site which was occupied by the main contractors, the second defendant. At dusk, the claimant was finishing work, and walking to the workmen's hut, when he tripped over a cable which had been left suspended 9 inches above the ground by an employee of the second defendant. The claimant was injured. The first defendant had known that the site was excessively untidy but had not complained. Apparently the second defendant had made no effort to keep the site tidy, or to provide safe routes for the workmen.

The claimant succeeded in an action against his employers. Their failure to complain was a breach of the duty of care owed by an employer to his employee and was a cause of the accident. He was also successful against the second defendant on two grounds:

(i) they were vicariously liable for the negligence of their employee in leaving the cable as, in effect, a trip wire; and

(ii) they were occupiers, and were in breach of their duty under the 1957 Act.

This finding, against the second defendant, is interesting in that, although there was liability both in negligence and under the Occupiers' Liability Act, this dual liability was said to arise only where there is, as here, vicarious liability for the former. The 'neighbour' principle cannot be used to create a primary duty when the duty is already fully covered by the Act. (There was also liability for breach of certain statutory regulations.)

6.6 Occupiers' liability to entrants other than visitors coming within the terms of the 1957 Act

In practice this means liability towards 'trespassers', though we have seen it is not only these entrants who fall outside the protection of the 1957 Act. The Occupiers' Liability Act 1984 (*Cases and Materials* (6.3)) is the main focus of our attention at this stage, though it will be helpful generally to trace briefly the history of liability to trespassers and, indeed, essential in particular to understand the duty which the 1984 Act replaced, because that earlier duty will apply to cases not included within the terms of the 1984 Act.

A special case

Liability for the condition of premises may arise through the rules of a club. In *Robertson* v *Ridley* [1989] 2 All ER 474, the claimant, a member of a club (an unincorporated association) was injured on club premises. He fell off his motor cycle when leaving the premises as a result of failing to see a pothole in the driveway. He sued the chairman and secretary (the club officers), arguing that since the club's rules provided that they had legal responsibility for the conduct of the club a duty was owed to him to keep the premises in a reasonable state of repair and safety. It was found that there was no express provision in the rules concerning the condition of the premises, so no duty of care was owed to the claimant in the terms claimed. The common law rule that no liability existed between an unincorporated association (or its members) and individual members applied in the present circumstances.

6.6.1 Trespassers

We will first refresh our memories as to the definition of a 'trespasser'. What is important is not what is in the mind of the entrant, because one can trespass quite innocently. Honest mistake is no defence and liability for the tort of trespass to land on the part of the entrant in that sense is 'strict'. Voluntary movement is all that is required; there is no necessity for the entrant to intend to trespass. It is the intention of the occupier of the land in question that is important.

In *Addie* v *Dumbreck* [1929] AC 358, Lord Dunedin defined a trespasser as a person 'who goes to the land without invitation of any sort and whose presence is either unknown to the proprietor, or, if known, is practically objected to'.

The term 'trespasser' includes the 'guilty' as well as the 'innocent'. Someone who enters without permission is a trespasser; in this sense, there is no difference between a burglar or a person out for a walk in a field.

The nature of the duty owed by the occupier may differ according to the nature of the trespasser. In any case, although all trespassers are guilty of illegal acts, i.e. the wrongful entry, trespassers such as burglars are likely to be met with the plea of illegality or *ex turpi causa non oritur actio* (see 14.3.2).

Curiously, illegality is not pleaded against all trespassers; probably because modern law will not countenance a departure from an irreducible minimum of protection even for illegal entrants. Even burglars may be protected against the infliction of intentional harm, the setting of traps or the creation of retributive dangers such as electrified fences. The application of force to illegal entrants can only in some cases be justified on grounds of self-defence or defence of others. It is long-settled law that only 'reasonable' force can be used to eject trespassers. Indeed, occupiers may well find themselves facing criminal charges where unlawful force is used. See also 6.6.4.2.

6.6.2 **The original duty to trespassers**

Intentional harm inflicted on a trespasser was actionable unless it was reasonably necessary to protect the property from trespassers.

In *Bird* v *Holbrook* (1828) 4 Bing 628, an occupier of land set a trap for trespassers, namely a spring-gun, on his land. The claimant, a trespasser on the land, was injured by the device and the occupier, the defendant, was found liable under a principle of the common law to the effect that it was unlawful to inflict harm upon the person of another in an intentional and indirect way.

This cause of action was not restricted to the context of occupation of land; it was not a form of trespass to the person because it was not actionable per se. The decision in *Wilkinson* v *Downton* (see 10.4.2) illustrates the application of a similar principle. It is therefore arguable that there still exists at common law a separate, general, head of liability in relation to the intentional infliction of harm on another person.

It became accepted that deterrent measures could reasonably be adopted by occupiers to discourage trespassers, but they were distinguished from measures which could be classed as retributive dangers. These measures of retribution gave rise to liability at common law. It was a question of fact in each case whether a measure would be classified as 'deterrent' or 'retributive'. In general, dangers likely to do serious harm would be 'retributive'. An occupier could also be liable for injury inflicted recklessly on a trespasser. In both cases, the occupier had to know of the trespasser's presence although it might be enough if a trespasser's presence was extremely likely. The leading case was *Addie* v *Dumbreck* [1929] AC 358.

6.6.3 **The duty of common humanity**

In *British Railways Board* v *Herrington* [1972] AC 877, the House of Lords rejected *Addie*. Their Lordships said a new duty was needed in the light of modern society: not only were there more children, but their parents had less control over them and they had fewer places in which to play. Modern technology had produced greater dangers for them.

The claimant, a 6-year-old boy, was playing with his friends on land bounded by an electrified railway line. He got through a fence in poor repair and fell on to a live line. The stationmaster had been warned of the condition of the fence and, despite his knowledge that children frequented the area, the fence had not been repaired.

The Court of Appeal found the defendants liable. The decision was based on the old test of reckless disregard for the safety of the trespasser.

The House of Lords held that, although the general rule remained that a person trespassed at his own risk, an occupier's duty was not limited to not harming the trespasser intentionally or recklessly. Where an occupier knew that there were, or were likely to be, trespassers on his land and that the condition of his land or an activity on it was likely to injure the trespasser, he must take reasonable steps to enable the trespasser to avoid that danger. This duty arose only where the probability of the danger was such that the occupier ought to act in 'common humanity'.

It was held that the Board was in breach of this duty. It had brought on to their land a danger, i.e. an electrified rail, and had not taken reasonable steps to prevent harm to the claimant.

Herrington introduced a duty of a very flexible nature; nowhere was 'common humanity' closely defined, their Lordships preferring a pragmatic approach which would enable the court to fashion the duty to fit the circumstances. Lords Reid and Wilberforce said that the duty would vary 'according to [the] knowledge, ability, and resources' of the occupier. It was a question of whether a conscientious, humane man with **this** occupier's knowledge, skill, and resources, could reasonably have been expected to do something which would have avoided the accident. Their Lordships appeared to have a subjective test in mind. Lord Reid also said:

> [the occupier] might often reasonably think, weighing the seriousness of the damages and the degree of likelihood of trespassers coming against the burden he would have to incur in preventing their entry, or making his premises safe, or curtailing his own activities on his land, that he could not fairly be expected to do anything. But if he could at small trouble and expense take some effective action, again I think that most people would think it inhumane and culpable not to do that.

Lord Diplock said the 'kind of trespasser' (for example a burglar, vandal, or child) could be an important factor, as was 'the degree of expectation that a trespasser will come . . .' Lord Wilberforce mentioned 'the nature and degree of the danger'.

In *Pannett* v *McGuinness & Co. Ltd* [1972] 3 All ER 137, which was decided after *Herrington*, the Court of Appeal appears to have rejected the distinction between the tests of 'common humanity' and reasonable care. Lord Denning's judgment refers to the necessity of taking such reasonable care as the circumstances of the case demand. Certainly, in the case of trespassing children where there are dangerous circumstances, it seems that the duty of an occupier is to take reasonable care. The facts of this case are as follows. The defendants were contractors working on the demolition of a warehouse which adjoined a park used by children. The work entailed lighting fires in the warehouse to burn rubbish, and three men were appointed to warn children to keep away. The claimant, aged 5, having previously been warned off before any fires were lit, returned when the men were absent from the site and was injured when he fell into a fire.

It was held that because of the great likelihood of children entering the warehouse and the extra hazard of the fires, common sense and common humanity imposed on the defendants the duty to take all reasonable steps for the safety of children who might trespass on the site. This they had not done and they were liable to the claimant.

According to Neill LJ in *Revill* v *Newbery* [1996] 1 All ER 291 (CA), *Herrington* enabled a trespasser to recover damages in negligence. (See 6.6.4.2.)

The *Herrington* cases may today be used not only in those circumstances where the 1984 Act does not apply; they may also be helpful for illustrative purposes (only) in connection with arguments concerning liability imposed by the 1984 Act.

The 1984 Act replaces the common law, that is, it replaces *Herrington*.

6.6.4 Liability arising under the Occupiers' Liability Act 1984

6.6.4.1 Entrants to whom a duty is owed

Section 1 of the 1984 Act says it replaces the rules of the common law governing the duty of an occupier of premises to 'persons other than his visitors'. These persons are trespassers, those who enter under private rights of way, or by virtue of s. 60 of the National Parks and Access to the Countryside Act 1949 and s. 13 of the Countryside and Rights of Way Act 2000.

6.6.4.2 The duty arising under the Act

The Act says, in s. 1(1) that its objective is to determine:

(a) whether any duty is owed by a person as occupier of premises to persons other than his visitors in respect of any risk of their suffering injury on the premises by reason of any danger due to the state of the premises or to things done or omitted to be done on them; and

(b) if so, what that duty is.

It can be seen from the language used that so-called current activities may not be covered by this Act (see 6.5.1). There, are, however, obiter opinions in the House of Lords in *Herrington* (above) that there was no distinction in the doctrine of common humanity between the occupancy duty and activities, but this case could only be used as a persuasive authority in the context of liability arising under the 1984 Act.

In an earlier case, *Videan* v *British Transport Commission* [1963] 2 All ER 860, which was concerned with the *Addie* v *Dumbreck* duty (see 6.6.1), Pearson LJ expressed the opinion that current activities came within the terms of the then occupiers' duty.

The Law Commission in its 1976 Report (see below) agreed with the view that the 1957 Act (see above) did not extend to activities, which came within the terms of common law negligence. It was also the Commission's view that the 1984 Act should not embrace activities. It was said that the liability of an occupier under statute should relate only to something which made the premises unsafe, because not all activities or omissions occurring on premises were concerned with the safety of premises as such. In that sense the occupier in relation to activities would be in the same position as a non-occupier who had injured someone on premises: 'Thus, if a person (whether an occupier or not) while shooting rabbits injures another person (whether a trespasser or not), whether he is liable will depend on the ordinary principles of negligence at common law' (para. 26).

In *Revill* v *Newbery* (see below) Neill LJ agreed with this line of reasoning. As his Lordship acknowledged, however:

> This solution [that an occupiers' liability for current activities should be determined by reference to the ordinary principles of common law negligence] may give rise to difficulties. Thus, it would seem that if an occupier of land arranges for a party to shoot on his land and one of the party negligently injures a trespasser, the occupier might be liable under section 1 of the 1984 Act if the conditions set out in section 1(3) are fulfilled. On the other hand, if he goes out shooting alone his liability, if any, would be determined under the common law of negligence.

We will return to this matter of current activities when we examine the decision in *Revill*.

The duty imposed by the 1984 Act is set out in s. 1(4) as follows:

> Where, by virtue of this section, an occupier of premises owes a duty to another in respect of such a risk, the duty is to take such care as is reasonable in all the circumstances of the case to see that he does not suffer injury on the premises by reason of the danger concerned.

This is a duty of a flexible nature, adaptable to widely varying circumstances. It has to be of this nature, to cope with the range of entrants it covers. Not only trespassers are protected by this legislation, as we have seen; but trespassers themselves are a mixed bunch, ranging from the wandering child to the rampaging burglar and beyond. A negligent act, as well as an intentional one could come within the terms of this duty.

? **QUESTION** 6.17

Look at the wording carefully. Can you spot the difficulty?

The point to be made is this: there is no 'automatic' duty. Section 1(4) says 'where, by virtue of this section [a duty is owed] in respect of such a risk . . .' There is no doubt that there is a reference here to some pre-conditions. These are to be found in s. 1(3) which provides as follows:

> An occupier of premises owes a duty to another (not being his visitor) in respect of any such risk as is referred to in subsection (1) above if—
>
> (a) he is aware of the danger or has reasonable grounds to believe that it exists;
>
> (b) he knows or has reasonable grounds to believe that the other is in the vicinity of the danger concerned or that he may come into the vicinity of the danger (in either case, whether the other has lawful authority for being in that vicinity or not); and
>
> (c) the risk is one against which, in all the circumstances of the case, he may reasonably be expected to offer the other some protection.

You must be aware that the duty imposed by the Act arises only if these three conditions are satisfied.

This provision is potentially confusing, because it seems to consist of a mixture of subjective and objective tests. We have seen that *Herrington* imposed an arguably subjective test: 'What could reasonably be expected of this occupier in the circumstances?'

The Law Commission, on whose Report entitled 'Liability for Damage or Injury to Trespassers and Related Questions of Occupiers' Liability' (Report No. 75, Cmnd 6428), 1976, the 1984 Act was based intended that the replacement duty for *Herrington* should be of an objective nature: 'What could be expected of a reasonable person in those circumstances?' It is debatable whether that purpose has been achieved.

As E. McKendrick, *Tort Textbook*, London: HLT Publications, 1992 (p. 214) puts it: 'The words "he knows" suggest a subjective test, but the words "has reasonable grounds to believe" suggest an objective test.' He further points out that it is perhaps intended

> that the Act shall apply to the situation where the occupier knows or is aware of the primary facts but fails to draw the reasonable inference from the known facts . . . It is difficult to see how the Act could apply to the situation where the occupier is unaware of the primary facts in circumstances where the reasonable occupier would have been so aware.

According to *Winfield* (p. 244):

> In some respects this approach [in the 1984 Act] is very close to that of the common duty of care and the ordinary negligence duty: in particular, the occupier incurs liability where he does not know but ought to know the facts which would signal to a reasonable man the presence of a trespasser or of the danger to him; and the standard appears to be objective and not conditional by the occupier's own resources.

It cannot be denied, however, that there appears to be a conflict in the wording between s. 1(3) and s. 1(4). While it is clear that the standard of duty laid down in s. 1(4) is of an objective nature, the same cannot be said of the standard laid down in s. 1(3) which must be satisfied before that duty arises.

Application of the Act

In *White* v *St Albans City and District Council* (1990), *The Times*, 12 March (CA), the claimant easily got through a fence, which was inadequate but not in disrepair, on the defendant's land in order to take a short cut. He was injured when he fell into a trench which he could not have been expected to see. This was a danger of which the defendant was actually aware, so there was no argument on that point. What was in issue was knowledge of someone's presence in the vicinity of the danger (s. 1(3)(b)). It was found that there was no evidence that the land was used as a short cut, and there was no reason for the defendant to believe that there would be anyone in the vicinity of the danger. This was said to be a matter of fact in each case. The claimant's argument, that it was sufficient to satisfy s. 1(3)(b) on the present facts to show that the occupier had fenced his land, thereby establishing that there was reason to believe that someone was likely to come into the vicinity of the danger, was not accepted by the court: each case had to be looked at according to the actual state of affairs on the land at the time of the injury.

In *Swain* v *Puri* [1996] PIQR P442 (CA), a boy aged 9 fell from the roof of a disused factory and claimed damages for his injuries from the occupier. It was argued for the claimant that he was owed a duty of care under the Act, that is that at the time of the trespass there had been reasonable grounds for believing that children would trespass for the purposes of s. 1(3)(b) of the Act.

The court found against a duty of care on the facts. Although the fences round the premises were by no means 'intruder proof', they were of a substantial nature and there was no evidence of earlier trespass. The occupiers had no 'reason to believe' that children would climb on to the roof. 'Reasonable grounds to believe' in the context of s. 1(3)(b) meant that the occupier must have either actual knowledge of the relevant facts or know of facts which would provide evidence of 'grounds to believe' that a certain state of affairs existed. Constructive knowledge, based on an argument that the occupier 'ought to have known', was insufficient for the purposes of s. 1(3)(b).

In *Ratcliff* v *McConnell* [1999] 1 WLR 670 (CA), the claimant was a student who, one winter's evening after a night's drinking, decided to go for a swim in the college's swimming pool, which was closed for the winter. There were high walls round the pool, the gate was locked, and the college had erected signs warning of the depth of the water at the shallow end and prohibiting use of the pool at night. The water level in the pool as a whole was low.

The claimant climbed over the gate and dived into the pool, hitting his head on the bottom of the pool, more likely than not at the shallow end although the evidence was not clear on this point. It was held that the defendant college was not in breach of its duty under the 1984 Act, because it was obvious to any adult that diving into the shallow end of any pool might result in a head injury: the risk involved in this case was not of a hidden nature and no warning was necessary.

In *Donoghue* v *Folkestone Properties Ltd* [2003] QB 1008 (CA), it was held that the defendant, the owner of a harbour, was not liable to the claimant, a trespasser on the defendant's premises. The court unanimously agreed that no duty was owed under the 1984 Act where the claimant had injured himself by hitting a submerged grid bed while swimming in the harbour. The defendant, as occupier, had no reasonable grounds to believe that a trespasser would come into the vicinity of the danger by diving into a tidal harbour after midnight in midwinter.

Lord Phillips MR said the circumstances material to the existence of a duty might change with the seasons or the time of day. That was the position in this case: the test of whether a duty of care existed under the 1984 Act had to be determined by reference to the circumstances prevailing at the time the alleged breach of duty caused injury to the claimant. 'At the time of the claimant's injury in the present case the defendant had no reason to believe that he or anyone else would be swimming from the slipway.'

Another swimming incident is to be found in *Tomlinson* v *Congleton Borough Council* [2004] 1 AC 46 (HL). The claimant went swimming in a lake in a public park owned and occupied by the defendant council. Ignoring warning signs, he went into the lake and was seriously injured as the result of making a shallow dive. The council was well aware that the lake and its sandy beach was, in hot weather, an attraction to members of the public intent on swimming. The council knew of the dangers to swimmers, and that its warnings were ignored. It planned to landscape and plant the beach area as a deterrent, but that work was not completed at the time of the accident to the claimant.

Allowing the claimant's appeal from the first instance ruling against him, the Court of Appeal ruled that under s. 1 of the 1984 Act the defendant local authority owed a duty of care to provide effective protection against 'the grave risk of injury' to those persons who, to the defendant's knowledge habitually, over many years, flouted its 'no swimming' policy. The defendant's placing of warning notices and use of park rangers did not establish reasonable care on its part to prevent injury.

The claimant had accepted that he was a trespasser. It was agreed by the court that a finding of two-thirds contributory negligence on the part of the claimant should stand.

Ward LJ said that the circumstances were such that a duty was imposed on the council to execute the planned landscaping as an effective deterrent to swimmers. Sedley LJ concurred. Longmore LJ dissented, because there were obvious dangers in swimming in places other than a swimming pool. The council was not required to prevent swimming, even though it promoted the site for leisure purposes, unless it knew of a particular hazard. In that case a warning of the hazard 'should probably suffice'.

The House of Lords allowed the defendant's appeal. Their Lordships held that the claimant had no claim under s. 1 of the 1984 Act.

Lord Hoffmann said the claimant was a person of full capacity, who had voluntarily engaged in an activity that carried the inherent risk that he might not execute his dive properly and so suffer injury. The only risk present in these circumstances had arisen out of what the claimant had chosen to do, not out of the state of the premises.

There was no risk of a kind that gave rise to a duty under the Act but, even if there had been, it was still necessary to determine whether the defendant might reasonably have been expected to offer the claimant some protection.

The court had to take into account the cost of precautionary measures (the landscaping and planting of the beach which was completed after the accident was not required under the legal duty owed by the defendant) as well as the social value of the activities that would have to be prohibited to reduce or eliminate the risk. It was necessary to consider whether persons of full capacity should be allowed to decide for themselves whether to take the risk.

Local authorities and other occupiers of land were ordinarily under no duty to incur such social and financial costs to protect a minority, or even a majority, against obvious dangers.

Protection for the outlaw

Revill v *Newbery* [1996] 1 All ER 291, raises a number of important issues. The claimant and another person trespassed on the defendant's premises by attempting to break into a shed on his allotment. At the time, the defendant, aged 76, was sleeping in the shed to guard his belongings from the depredations of thieves and vandals. He was wakened by the sounds of the attempted entry and picked up his shotgun, firing it through a small hole in the door of the shed. His shot hit the claimant, wounding him in the arm and the chest.

At first instance, the defendant was found liable to the claimant in common law negligence which, in the circumstances of the case, was coterminous with the terms of s. 1 of the Occupiers' Liability Act 1984. The defences of self-defence and illegality were rejected, but the claimant was found to be two-thirds contributorily negligent under the terms of the Law Reform (Contributory Negligence) Act 1945.

Neill LJ delivered the main judgment in the Court of Appeal. It was his Lordship's opinion that the defendant's conduct in the present case fell within the terms of a current activity, and that if he were to be liable to the claimant it would have to be on the basis of an application of the principles of common law negligence; the defendant could not be liable as occupier under s. 1 of the 1984 Act.

His Lordship quoted from the Law Commission's 1976 Report (see below):

It seems clear that the wording [of the Occupiers' Liability Act 1957—see 6.5.7] is apt to cover conduct on the premises which causes a continuing source of danger, thereby rendering it unsafe. It is less clear whether the words have the effect of bringing within the scope of the 1957 Act all claims for injuries on the occupiers' premises arising from every kind of activity or omission on them irrespective of whether they are connected with the safety of those premises as such.

He agreed with the view expressed by the Commission that so-called activities were not caught by either the 1957 Act or the 1984 Act (both Acts use much the same wording as we have already seen above and at 6.5.1) and concluded that section 1 of the 1984 Act applied only to an **occupier**:

Section 1 is concerned with the safety of the premises **and** [emphasis added] with the dangers due to things done or omitted to be done on the premises. [It will be noted that his Lordship uses the connecting word 'and' rather than 'or' which is the word in the relevant legislation; 'or' being a word which introduces alternatives. Presumably this is an error in transcription.] In concluding whether Mr Newbery is liable on the facts of this case, the fact that he was the occupier is irrelevant. Accordingly . . . [the liability of the defendant is to be considered] in the same way as one would have examined the liability of a third person, for example a friend of Mr Newbery who was staying in the hut, if that third person had fired the shot.

It was his Lordship's opinion, however, that although the 1984 Act did not apply to current activities it was necessary to look at the duty laid down by the Act to determine the content of the common law duty of care in negligence which did apply to current activities.

On the facts of the present case, since the defendant was engaged in an activity rather than playing the role of occupier as such, his liability would be determined at common law and the parameters of that liability would be set by reference to the provisions of the 1984 Act.

The conditions set out in s. 1(3) were to be satisfied and s. 1(4) defined the relevant standard of care. For example, the 'danger' referred to in s. 1(3)(b) was the gun which was about to be discharged. This was not a mere warning shot, said his Lordship, it was a shot likely to hit anyone in the vicinity of the door to the shed. Neill LJ agreed with the finding at first instance, and found that the defendant was liable by applying principles of law similar to those set out in s. 1 of the 1984 Act.

Evans LJ said:

I agree . . . with Neill LJ that it is not necessary to decide in the present case whether the statutory duty owed by an occupier under s. 1 of the 1984 Act includes activities which he engages in personally on the premises. I therefore express no concluded view in that issue. With the sole reservation, I entirely agree with his judgment.

This is an interesting observation, because Neill LJ appeared to agree with the view that activities did *not* come within the ambit of the 1984 Act and proceeded accordingly. His Lordship found that the defendant was liable under the terms of the activity duty, determined by reference to the 1984 Act. It is not clear, which source of liability Evans LJ has in mind.

Millett LJ, like Evans LJ, agreed with Neill LJ in dismissing the appeal: 'For the defendant's conduct was clearly dangerous and bordered on reckless . . .'

If the reasoning of Neill LJ is correct it has two important effects on the law. First, it means that the 1984 Act is *in effect* extended to cover current activities and, second, it has the effect of extending that Act to cover the liability of non-occupiers in relation to activities. It may be that his Lordship intended only occupiers' activities to be determined by reference to the provisions of the 1984 Act, though this point is not explicit in the judgment.

With regard to the defendant's plea of illegality (see 14.3.2), Neill LJ considered whether the claimant's criminal conduct made it impossible for the court to set a standard of care in the circumstances of the case. He said that the existence of s. 1 of the 1984 Act makes it clear that Parliament is of the opinion a burglar cannot be treated as an outlaw, and the Law Commission in its 1976 Report was in favour of some duty being owed, even to a trespasser 'engaged in a serious criminal enterprise'. In his Lordship's opinion the liability of a person in the defendant's position was to be decided according to a test 'similar to that set out in s. 1(4) of the 1984 Act'.

> There is in my view no room for a two-stage determination whereby the court considers first whether there has been a breach of duty and then considers whether notwithstanding a breach the claimant is barred from recovering by reason of the fact that he has engaged in crime.

Evans LJ agreed that a trespasser/criminal is not an outlaw, and is owed a minimal duty. In the present case there was no illegal transaction or criminal joint enterprise involved.

On self-defence, pleaded by the defendant, his Lordship concluded that the defendant had used unjustified violence towards the claimant, which exceeded that permitted for self-defence. Millett LJ said:

> The assailant or intruder may be met with reasonable force but no more; the use of excessive violence against him is an actionable wrong. It follows . . . that there is no place for the doctrine *ex turpi causa non oritur actio* in this context. If the doctrine applied, any claim by the assailant or trespasser would be barred no matter how excessive or unreasonable the force used against him.

The Court of Appeal upheld the decision at first instance, in which the defendant was found liable in common law negligence, although the claimant's damages were reduced by two-thirds for his contributory negligence (under the terms of the Law Reform (Contributory Negligence) Act 1945).

A final point concerning this case can be made; Rougier J at first instance ((1994), *The Times*, 1 December), said:

> [Illegality applied only where] . . . the injury complained of was so closely interwoven in the illegal or criminal act as to be virtually a part of it or if it was a direct uninterrupted consequence of that illegal act.
>
> The discharge of a shotgun towards burglars who are not displaying any intention of resorting to violence to the person is, in my judgment, out of all proportion to the threat involved, even making all due allowance for the agony of the moment, and therefore any injury, sustained by such discharge cannot be said to be an integral part nor a necessarily direct consequence of the burglary.

See also 14.2.4.

Volenti non fit injuria

Section 1(6) embodies this defence. It says:

> No duty is owed by virtue of this section to any person in respect of risks willingly accepted as his by that person (the question whether a risk was so accepted to be decided on the same principles as in other cases in which one person owes a duty of care to another).

The usual conditions pertaining to the defence will apply (see **Chapter 14**).

In the present context, the issue of whether *volenti* applies may be even more problematic than it is in general. We have already seen that the 1984 Act embraces both unlawful non-visitors (trespassers) as well as lawful non-visitors (those entering under private rights of way, as well as those entering by authority of the National Parks and Access to the Countryside

Act 1949). That is not the only problem because not even all trespassers are the same, and so it is evident that the factual interpretation of the duty of care laid down in the 1984 Act is likely to vary enormously between different entrants, not least between different 'types' of trespasser. It would not be unreasonable to suggest that this will also be the case with the application of *volenti*.

Jones (p. 204) argues, for example, that where trespassers are concerned (and by this he seems to mean adult trespassers, though he does not make the point explicit) the courts take an objective approach to the question of 'agreement' (necessary for all *volenti* cases) 'so that it is possible to argue that knowledge of a risk plus entry on to the land renders a trespasser *volenti*'. He says it would be more difficult to sustain this argument in the case of a lawful non-visitor.

Warnings and other measures bringing dangers to the attention of the entrant

According to s. 1(5):

> Any duty owed by virtue of this section in respect of a risk may, in an appropriate case, be discharged by taking such steps as are reasonable in all the circumstances of the case to give warning of the danger concerned or to discourage persons from incurring the risk.

Clearly, warning notices and other measures are envisaged in this context.

 EXERCISE 6.3

Read s. 1(5) of the 1984 Act and compare it with the provision concerning 'warning' in s. 2(4)(a) of the 1957 Act.

There are two differences to note here:

(a) in the 1957 Act a warning is not sufficient 'without more', unless

(b) it is enough in all the circumstances to make the visitor reasonably safe.

These conditions are absent from the 1984 Act provision, suggesting that it may be easier for an occupier to discharge his duty under s. 1(5) than would be the case under s. 2(4)(a) of the 1957 Act. A warning may have much more 'bite' under the 1984 Act.

It is true that more than a mere notice may be required in the case of children, especially perhaps where 'allurements' are concerned. The notion of allurement was an important factor in *Herrington* (see 6.6.3). Other measures may be needed in such cases. In this context, 'deterrent' and 'retributive' measures may be of importance.

Section 1(5) does refer to 'the danger' and 'the risk' and it is arguable that any warning ought to make it reasonably clear that there is some particular danger or risk for the entrant to avoid. A simply worded notice, for example, saying 'Keep Out. Private' might not be enough, because it would do no more than inform the entrant that he would be a trespasser if he entered. Of course, some dangers are pretty obvious, even behind closed doors, and such a notice might be sufficient in an appropriate case with regard to **those** dangers.

It is quite common today for building sites to have, in addition to such measures as fencing and hoarding, notices displayed at strategic points warning of general danger. A notice observed recently stated:

NOTICE
WARNING TO PUBLIC. This building site is private property. No unauthorized persons allowed.
Liability will not be accepted by the builder for any injury sustained by trespassers.
NOTICE TO PARENTS. Parents are especially requested to warn children of the dangers and
consequences of trespassing on this site.

This is an obvious attempt to activate s. 1(5), although the notice is couched in general terms
and it may be thought that it would not be sufficient to warn of specific dangers.

 QUESTION 6.18

Can you think of any good reason why someone might not be too specific in their warnings about danger on their premises?

You might have thought that a warning which was specific in this sense could, in some situations, make it easier for an entrant to establish liability because it could trigger s. 1(3) of the 1984 Act.

Such a notice raises another issue: 'Can an occupier expect very young trespassers to be accompanied by an adult?' In other words, 'Does the principle of *Phipps* v *Rochester Corporation* (see 6.5.5.3) apply also to trespassing children?' There seems to be no good legal reason why *Phipps* should not also apply in the context of trespass.

Exclusion of liability

We have to deal here with two points, the second of which awaits resolution.

First, the Unfair Contract Terms Act 1977 does not apply to the duty laid down in the 1984 Act: the 1977 Act refers only to common law duties, and the common duty of care under the 1957 Act. (There is doubt, however, whether the doctrine of 'common humanity' formulated in *Herrington* comes within the terms of the 1977 Act.)

Second, the 1984 Act makes no reference at all to the question of exclusion of liability, although the Law Commission (Cmnd 6428) did recommend that occupiers should be able to exclude their liability. It seems to be the general opinion amongst writers that occupiers cannot, as a matter of public policy, avoid their statutory obligations in the absence of clear words allowing them to do so. In any event, it is also argued, the standard of care laid down to trespassers (whether it is the original common law standard, or that of common humanity, or that laid down in the 1984 Act) consists of an irreducible minimum which public policy dictates cannot be excluded.

Jones, however, argues that Parliament cannot have intended that occupiers should be in a worse position *vis-à-vis* non-visitors than they are in relation to their lawful visitors. It may be that the duty laid down in the 1984 Act can be excluded. (It will be recalled that the 1957 Act allows liability to be excluded, in certain circumstances.) If this argument is correct, he continues, occupiers should be free to exclude their liability under the 1984 Act but not liability for an irreducible minimum, which would be liability for intentional or reckless conduct, i.e. the 'original' common law duty. He would draw a distinction, however, between trespassers and those who enter under a private right of way or the 1949 Act (see 6.6.4.1): liability towards these entrants should not be excludable at all.

Finally, Jones argues that if there is a minimum standard which cannot be excluded in the case of trespassers the argument must apply with even more force to lawful visitors in those cases where the 1957 Act duty can be excluded.

6.6.4.3 Damage

Liability under the 1984 Act is limited to personal injury, although that is defined quite widely. The Act says, in s. 1(8):

> (8) Where a person owes a duty by virtue of this section, he does not, by reason of any breach of the duty, incur any liability in respect of any loss of or damage to property.

It seems that an injured entrant could not also claim for loss even of his clothes under the 1984 Act. Any claim for loss of or damage to 'property' must be brought under some appropriate common law principle.

 QUESTION 6.19

Can you think of any appropriate common law action?

You might have listed the following:

(a) presumably, the doctrine of 'common humanity' might apply, but this was developed principally for personal injury;

(b) the ruling in *Addie* v *Dumbreck* (see 6.5.4.1);

(c) if *Tutton* v *AD Walter* [1986] QB 61 is good authority the ordinary law of negligence may be used in such circumstances. Liability in negligence towards 'trespassing' bees was imposed on an occupier in that case.

6.7 Other means of redress

The Acts of 1957 and 1984, and special liability relating to premises deriving from the common law, are not the only sources of redress applicable in the context of premises. Regulation 4 of the Control of Asbestos at Work Regulations 2002 came into force on 21 March 2004. A duty is placed on anyone with responsibility for the repair and maintenance of non-domestic premises to manage any asbestos in the building. It covers all non-domestic premises, regardless of the business carried on there, as well as common areas of residential rented properties, such as entrance halls, stairwells, life shafts, and roof spaces. The duties will fall on anyone with responsibility for the repair and/or maintenance of non-domestic premises or common areas of residential rented properties. Failure to comply with the regulation could raise the possibility of future actions from employees, contractors, or other users of the premises who contract asbestos-related diseases.

■ SUMMARY

- Liability for dangerous premises and land comes in many guises and is of a labyrinthine nature. We are concerned with its tortious aspects, but it is impossible to ignore the contractual and statutory aspects of the subject.

- On many occasions an aggrieved person will find it more advantageous to sue in contract, or bring proceedings under some special statutory provision relating to housing conditions, rather than sue in tort. Often, statutes imply into contracts of letting terms favourable to tenants, so strengthening the cause of action in contract.

- In many instances, there will be no contractual relations between the parties and in others there may be some obstacle in the way of an action in contract; it is here where tortious liability has to be considered.

- We started this chapter by looking at liability arising under the general law of negligence, and it is here where we find such a potentially wide range of persons who might be liable to a fairly restricted range of claimants.

- At this point we are concerned principally with the line of cases beginning with *Dutton* and ending with *Murphy*.

- *D & F Estates* and *Murphy* have severely restricted liability for premises in the general tort of negligence, in fact *Murphy* finally overruled *Anns* itself. In broad terms, since very few rules are completely watertight, liability is limited to cases where defective premises produce latent defects which cause actual physical damage to the person and/or separate property.

- The Defective Premises Act 1972, however, imposes liability of a wider nature, and in s. 1 it imposes strict liability. This Act contains features of both tortious and contractual liability, though the cause of action lies in tort.

- Section 4 of the 1972 Act imposes a wide duty of reasonable care, towards his tenants and others, upon a landlord of premises.

- The Occupiers' Liability Act 1957 imposes a duty upon 'occupiers' of 'premises' to take reasonable care for the safety of their 'lawful visitors'; in other words the Act imposes a 'negligence duty'.

- All these expressions, and others including the 'common duty of care', can and do raise problems of interpretation which have to be resolved where possible by reference to case law.

- The Unfair Contract Terms Act 1977 is concerned with the liability of 'business' occupiers.

- Traditionally, the law has offered more protection to occupiers where entrants have been trespassers. Today, the main body of law on this topic is contained in the Occupiers' Liability Act 1984.

- The 1984 Act duty is of a very flexible nature; it can even include an act of negligence on the part of an occupier.

- The 1984 Act is a very different creature from the 1957 Act. In the case of the former Act, certain difficult conditions, three in number, have to be satisfied before the duty can be activated.

- The 1957 Act deals with a fairly homogeneous class of entrant, that is, the lawful visitor. Under the 1984 Act, not only does the problem of a wide range of trespassers have to be faced, ranging from the 'deprived' to the 'depraved', there is also the fact that some lawful entrants get protection only under the Act, that is, those entering under a private right of way and under the National Parks and Access to the Countryside Act 1949 and the Countryside and Rights of Way Act 2000.

- Both the 1957 and 1984 Acts deal with the safety of the premises in question, so even 'activities' (if they are caught by the legislation) must relate to that issue. It is arguable that where the occupier is engaged in some pursuit which is not directly connected with this sort of safety, for example, injury is sustained as a result of the negligent shooting of pigeons by the occupier on his land, liability would lie in ordinary negligence.

- The 1957 Act covers damage to goods as well as personal injury, the 1984 Act imposes liability only for personal injury. The latter Act, however, offers a wide definition of 'personal injury', to include 'disease' or 'impairment of a mental condition'. This might include 'nervous shock'. It would be surprising if the 1957 Act could not be interpreted in similar fashion.

■ **FURTHER READING**

Hepple, Howarth, and Matthews, *Tort: Cases and Materials*, 5th edn, London: Butterworths, 2000, Chapter 9.

Jones, M., *Textbook on Torts*, 8th edn, Oxford: Oxford University Press, 2002, Chapter 6.

Kidner, R., *Casebook on Torts*, 9th edn, Oxford: Oxford University Press, 2006, Chapters 13 and 20.

McKendrick, E., *Tort Textbook*, 6th edn, London: HLT Publications, 1992, Chapter 17.

Markesinis, B.S. and Deakin, S.F., *Tort Law*, 5th edn, Oxford: Oxford University Press, 2003, pp. 329–58.

Murphy, J., *Street on Torts*, 11th edn, London: Butterworths, 2003, Chapter 16.

North, P.M., *Occupiers' Liability*, London: Butterworths, 1971, generally.

Salmond and Heuston, *Law of Torts*, 21st edn, London: Sweet & Maxwell, 1996, Chapter 11.

Spencer, J.R., 'The Defective Premises Act 1972—Defective Law and Defective Law Reform' (1974) 33 *CLJ* 307.

Stanton, K., *Modern Law of Tort*, London: Sweet & Maxwell, 1994, pp. 193–203.

Weir, T., *Casebook on Tort*, 10th edn, London: Sweet & Maxwell, 2004, Chapter 1 (s. 2).

Winfield and Jolowicz on Tort, 16th edn, London: Sweet & Maxwell, 2002, Chapter 9.

CHAPTER 6 ASSESSMENT EXERCISE

Lax, a students' law society, has organized a dance for its members only at Isadora's, a local nightspot. At the time of the dance the management of Isadora's are in the process of having a new lighting system installed by Flashers Ltd, electrical contractors, and a notice at the entrance to the club reads, 'Beware. Electrical Work in Progress'. Art and Bart, two members of Lax, and Catherine, Bart's 15-year-old girlfriend, turn up for the dance and are admitted on producing tickets which state, 'Valid to Lax members only'. Art is injured when he trips over a trestle left by Flashers in the foyer, which is dimly lit. Bart is injured when a revolving light falls on his head as he is dancing. Catherine goes in search of a toilet through a door marked 'private' and is electrocuted when she feels for a light switch and touches some bare electric wires left by Flashers Ltd.

Discuss the tortious issues, if any, arising in these circumstances.

See *Cases and Materials* (6.5) for a specimen answer.

7 The common law cause of action for breach of statutory duty

7.1 OBJECTIVES

By the end of this chapter you should be able to:

1 Explain the principles governing the common law action for breach of statutory duty
2 Describe, in particular, the conditions that a claimant must establish to succeed in an action for breach of statutory duty

7.2 Introduction

Some statutes have been passed specifically to provide a remedy in tort: for example the Nuclear Installations Act 1965 and the Occupiers' Liability Act 1984. New torts may be created by statute, such as the tort of illegal eviction, provided for in the Housing Act 1988.

Many statutes, such as the Occupiers' Liability Act 1957, consolidate the previous common law, or provide special schemes of compensation, for example, the Vaccine Damage Payments Act 1979.

Other statutes contain sections specifically preventing action in tort, when their provisions are breached. See, for example, the Safety of Sports Grounds Act 1975.

> **? QUESTION** 7.1
>
> Can you guess what the next point is going to be?

It is a different matter, however, where statutes are silent on the question of civil liability in tort. The problem we face here is one concerned with legislation which says nothing about claims for compensation in tort. As *Winfield* (p. 189) puts it:

> What it [the chapter] is concerned with is when a court will conclude that a statute which is primarily regulatory or criminal in its purpose should be treated as giving rise to a civil action at the suit of a person who is injured as a result of non-compliance with it. Fundamentally, the question is one of interpretation of the particular statute but enough case law has accumulated around the subject to require treatment in a book on torts.

It is this type of statute on which we focus our attention in this chapter, although we also speak of an 'action for breach of statutory duty' when referring to an action brought under, for example, the Occupiers' Liability Act 1957.

7.3 How is it done?

Many claimants have been successful in their claims for damages for breaches of statutory duty, although the statutes themselves have made no apparent provision for this. There are many cases where such claims have failed miserably. Why should some claims be regarded as meritorious, whilst others are dismissed?

The answer depends on the interpretation placed upon the statute(s) in question by the court, in the particular case. Since 'statutory interpretation' is involved, the 'Mischief Rule' and other guides to statutory interpretation will be important, and you should refer to your earlier studies on this topic.

An action may be brought in tort for damage sustained as a result of the breach of a statutory duty, if the true construction of the statute establishes that it was the intention of the legislature that such a remedy should be available. It is the express or presumed intention of the legislature that determines whether there is a civil action for breach of statutory duty. Put in these terms the issue looks deceptively simple, but in truth the litigant who decides to bring such an action is often entering a legal minefield.

Salmond puts the matter into perspective: 'It is doubtful . . . if any general principle can be found to explain all the cases on the subject'. Again, at p. 252, '. . . much depends in each case upon the context of the statute and the court's perception of the policy considerations involved'.

Lord Denning in *Ex parte Island Records Ltd* [1978] 1 Ch 122, went so far as to say that the court might as well 'toss a coin' to decide the issue. He was referring to certain 'presumptions' which have become established guides for the courts, in helping them to determine whether or not a civil action in tort is available in a difficult case. In his Lordship's opinion, there was so much conflict between the presumptions that he found them singularly unhelpful. However, while Lord Denning would simply reject them and decide each case on its 'facts' or 'merits', these presumptions, through the force of precedent, seem to be firmly established in the law and we must examine them in some detail to see 'how it is done'. Before we do, it will be helpful to take a brief look at the historical development of the action for breach of statutory duty.

7.3.1 Background to the action

Actions for breach of statutory duty are as old as the Statute of Westminster II of 1285, but the modern history of the action dates from *Ashby* v *White* (1703) 2 Ld Raym 938, in which a cause of action in tort was held to apply in respect of an interference with the claimant's statutory right to vote.

There are some old cases which assert that wherever a statutory duty exists, the common law should allow a claim in tort to a person who can show he has suffered damage as a result of a breach of that duty. This is not the modern approach. As Salmond says (p. 251): 'The modern approach is to limit the extent of liability by treating the question in each case as one relating to the intention of the legislature in creating the duty'.

As Lord Simonds said, in *Cutler* v *Wandsworth Stadium Ltd* [1949] AC 398: 'The answer must depend on a consideration of the whole Act and the circumstances, including the pre-existing law, in which it was enacted.'

Each statute tends to contain its own rules and peculiarities. The golden rule in this context is that whether the claimant has a remedy in tort depends upon a construction of the particular statute. As Lord Diplock said, in *Boyle* v *Kodak Ltd* [1969] 2 All ER 439: 'The statutes say nothing about civil remedies for breaches of their provisions. The judgments of the courts say all.' (His Lordship was, of course, referring to the 'silent' statutes to which reference has been made.)

We can now examine the 'presumptions' that Lord Denning found so difficult to apply in *Ex parte Island Records* (see 7.3), in the context of the confusing and conflicting case law on the subject.

7.3.2 **The presumptions**

The following statement by Lord Tenterden in *Doe d. Murray, Lord Bishop of Rochester* v *Bridges* (1854) 1 B & AD 847 is a useful starting point:

> where an Act creates an obligation, and enforces the performance in a specified manner, we take it as a general rule that performance cannot be enforced in any other manner . . . but [if] no mode of enforcing its performance is ordained, the common law may, in general, find a mode suited to the particular nature of the case.

The relevant legislation must place some basic obligation upon the defendant. *Harrison* v *National Coal Board* [1951] AC 639 provides a good illustration of this point. It was held, by the House of Lords, that where statutory duties relating to safety in mines were imposed on the mine owner, and duties relating to shotfiring were imposed on the shotfirer, the mine owner was not liable for breach of statutory duty regarding injuries caused by the shotfiring.

We will now examine each of the presumptions outlined in Lord Tenterden's speech (above).

7.3.3 **A special remedy**

Where a special remedy is provided in a statute, it is presumed in the absence of indications to the contrary to be the sole remedy, and to exclude a right of action in tort.

> **? QUESTION** 7.2
>
> Consider the set of facts given below, and then write down your opinion on the likely interpretation that would be given to them by a court.
>
> The Waterworks Clauses Act 1847 required the defendants to maintain a certain pressure of water for the purpose of extinguishing fires. The statute provided that a failure to perform this duty should be an offence punishable by a fine of £10; it said nothing about any civil remedy. The defendants failed to maintain the pressure and the claimant's house caught fire and was burned down. He sued for damages for breach of statutory duty.

7.3.3.1 The answer

The facts you have just considered are taken from *Atkinson* v *Gateshead Waterworks Co.* (1877) 2 ExD 441: it was held that although the destruction was caused by the defendant's breach of statutory duty, the statute intended that the fine should be the sole remedy available and no action in tort could be entertained.

7.3.3.2 The special remedy approach qualified

However, Lord Diplock, in *Lonrho Ltd* v *Shell Petroleum Co. Ltd (No. 2)* [1981] 2 All ER 456, identified two exceptions to the case of a criminal penalty where:

(a) on the true construction of the Act it is apparent that the obligation or prohibition was imposed for the benefit of a particular class of individuals;

(b) the statute creates a public right and an individual member of the public suffers particular, direct and substantial damages other and different from that which is common to the rest of the public.

In this case, the British government had prohibited trade with Southern Rhodesia (a former British colony, now Zimbabwe) under certain statutory powers, which provided for penalties of a criminal nature in the event of non-compliance with the prohibition. One oil company, Lonrho, which had complied with the sanctions and incurred heavy financial losses, sued competitors, who had breached the sanctions, for breach of their statutory obligations.

It was held that Lonrho did not come within either exception, because sanctions against Rhodesia were intended to create only public rights for Rhodesian citizens.

7.3.3.3 Benefit of a class

The first exception given by Lord Diplock is not new. It has long been the case that a claimant must usually show he is within the class of persons whom the statute was intended to protect. According to Lord Diplock, in *Lonrho*, if a statute prescribes a duty for the protection of a class of the community, it is deemed, in the absence of evidence of a contrary intention, to confer a corresponding right of action on any member of the class who may suffer damage as a result of a breach of the duty.

It does not, however, follow necessarily that a claimant will be without a civil remedy merely because the statute can be shown to be a measure for protecting only the public. Of course, the burden on the claimant to prove that the statute has created a private right will be lighter where the duty is imposed for the benefit of a particular class of persons, of which he is a member.

In *Phillips* v *Britannia Hygienic Laundry Co.* [1923] 2 KB 832, Atkin LJ said:

> the question is not to be solved by considering whether or not the person aggrieved can bring himself within some special class of the community or whether he is some designated individual. The duty may be of such paramount importance that it is owed to all the public. It would be strange if a less important duty, which is owed to a section of the public, may be enforced by an action, while a more important duty owed to the public at large cannot. The right of action does not depend on whether a statutory commandment or prohibition is pronounced for the benefit of the public or for the benefit of a class. It may be conferred on anyone who can bring himself within the benefit of the Act, including one who cannot be otherwise specified there as a person using the highway.

This dictum has been applied in many subsequent cases, and it indicates clearly that the 'protection of a class' test is not conclusive. The balance of authority, see *Lonrho* for example, suggests, however, that something in the nature of an overwhelming case would have to be shown by a person who could not bring himself within an appropriate 'class'.

In *Phillips* it was held that, although a major purpose of the Motor Cars (Use and Construction) Order 1904 was to prevent damage from unroadworthy vehicles to persons and other property on the highway, a breach of the Order did not give rise to an action in tort at the suit of an individual.

A statutory duty may be so expressed as to limit the classes of persons for whose benefit it was designed, and in such a case it will depend on the construction of the relevant statutory provision whether the claimant is a member of the protected class.

In *Knapp* v *Railway Executive* [1949] 2 All ER 508, a statute provided that gates must be erected at level crossings and supervised and maintained by the railway authorities. A motorist attempted to stop his car at a crossing but, due to faulty brakes, the car hit the gate. The gate had not been maintained, and swung back and injured the train driver. The court held that there was no remedy under the statute available to the train driver, against the railway authorities because the purpose of the statute was to protect **road users** against danger from the railway.

Again, in *Hartley* v *Mayoh & Co.* [1954] 1 QB 383, a fireman was electrocuted while attending to a fire at the defendants' factory. Statutory regulations for the protection of 'persons employed' existed. It was held that since firemen did not come within the description, his widow must fail in her action for breach of statutory duty by the defendants.

In *Keating* v *Elvan Reinforced Concrete Co.* [1968] 1 WLR 722, the court, as one of its reasons for holding that the Public Utilities Street Works Act 1950 gave no right of action to individuals, cited provisions in the Act creating civil liabilities in favour of public authorities.

In *Coote* v *Stone* [1971] 1 WLR 279, the Court of Appeal decided that the defendant's breach of a statutory regulation prohibiting the parking of a car on a 'clearway' did not give rise to a civil action by the claimant, who had collided with the defendant's parked car. The court classified the duty imposed by the regulations as being owed to the public and not to any class or individual.

The court reviewed some of the earlier traffic statutory duty cases, and gave as examples of breaches of public duties not giving rise to civil actions: parking on double yellow lines; failure to show rear lights during the hours of darkness; parking opposite double white lines.

As examples of breaches of such duties which did give rise to civil actions, as being not merely public duties but having also been designed to prevent injury to a class of persons, the court referred to *Monk* v *Warbey* (below); and breach of pedestrian crossing regulations.

Coote emphasizes the important element of 'public' duties.

In general a statute creating public duties, and not affecting the rights of private persons, is enforceable only by criminal prosecution; or the Attorney-General may apply for an injunction; or application may be made for judicial review. As Salmond puts it (p. 251): '[T]here is no civil remedy if a statute merely prohibits or makes conduct criminal without imposing a duty to a specific class.'

We will return to the question of public duties later in this chapter at 7.2.6. The next issue we have to address concerns legislation, and there is much of it, passed to protect employees in the workplace. You will recall that a claim was made at 7.2 to the effect that actions for breach of statutory duty are common in this context; they are also generally more successful than actions brought in other contexts.

Actions against employers

These cases illustrate the argument that whatever the first of Lord Tenterden's presumptions may say about the law in general terms, in practice (at any rate where fines are imposed on employers for breaches of safety legislation passed for the protection of their employees) there seems to be no bias against civil claims.

Salmond (p. 253) argues that this is true wherever the remedy laid down in the Act or Regulation is a fine. It is submitted, with respect, that the only clear and extensive authority for this proposition can be found in the Factories Act cases.

These 'industrial' cases, it is further submitted, are easier 'targets' for the 'class' approach, because the safety legislation can only have been passed for an easily ascertainable class, that is employees. Indeed, Lord Diplock, in arguing for the 'class' approach in *Lonrho*, took his analogy from the '. . . case of the Factories Act and similar legislation'.

'Industrial' cases may be rather special, and it could arguably be potentially misleading to use them to extend the 'class' argument (and to support the point made by Salmond on fines). Employees are clearly a homogeneous group of persons with, in this context, only personal safety as their interest. It will be seen later that the nature of the interest to be protected by the action for breach of statutory duty may well influence the outcome of a case.

The genesis of this cause of action occurred in the late nineteenth century when the courts were plainly reacting somewhat to the earlier raw, *laissez-faire* philosophy governing attitudes to the safety of employees. Since then, a huge body of precedent has been built up on the topic, and account must be taken of that fact. Is 'like' being compared with 'like'? It is submitted that the answer is 'No'.

The courts have long been inclined to the view that statutes passed for the protection of employees give rise to rights of action for breaches of statutory duty. There is a wealth of precedent on the matter.

The 'class' test was applied in *Groves* v *Lord Wimborne* [1892] 2 QB 402, which is an early example of this approach. The defendant's servant was injured as a result of the failure of the defendant to fence dangerous machinery as required by statute, the Factory and Workshop Act 1891 (see now the Factories Act 1961). It was held that the statute, which imposed only a fine on the defendant for the breach, created a duty for the benefit of a specified class of persons, that is employees, and must be presumed to give a remedy to a member of that class injured in consequence of a breach of the duty. The fine of £100 was regarded as inadequate.

Many other examples can be found in the 'industrial' case law, but only one further instance is given here. In *Westwood* v *Post Office* [1974] AC 1, Westwood was a Post Office employee who, while trespassing in a part of the telephone exchange at which he worked, fell to his death through a defective floor over a lift shaft. The claimant, his widow, suing on behalf of his estate, under the Offices, Shops, and Railway Premises Act 1963, succeeded, in spite of the fact that Westwood had been outside the course of his employment at the time. The House of Lords said that the Act covered the safety of all those 'employed' at the premises, regardless of whether they were actually doing their job at the time.

Care should be taken in using decisions from the 'industrial' cases as authority in **other** statutory contexts.

Other classes

The courts do not generally favour construing penal statutes to create torts. For example, in *Badham* v *Lambs Ltd* [1946] KB 45, it was held that a vendor of a vehicle who contravened a provision of the Road Traffic Act then in force as to the condition in which the car sold could legally be put on the road, and which imposed a fine for any contravention, was found not liable to a third party injured in an accident caused by the condition of the car.

This decision is more typical of the general position concerning penal legislation, although occasionally exceptional cases such as *Monk* v *Warbey* [1935] 1 KB 75, have to be considered. In *Monk* the statute concerned, the Road Traffic Act 1930 (see now the Road Traffic Act 1988), which provided a penalty for breach of the provision concerned, was held also to give a right of action in tort to a person injured as a result of a breach of duty. The defendant lent his car to a friend, although he was not insured against third-party risks unless he was driving himself. This was a breach of s. 35 of the Act. The friend injured the claimant, who was unable to recover against the insurance company, which did not cover such an accident. It was held that this was the very kind of case which the Act was passed to discourage, and that the statutory penalty should not be deemed to exclude an action in tort by a party aggrieved. The claimant recovered damages from the defendant.

Monk was followed in *Martin* v *Dean* [1971] 3 All ER 279. The claimant was injured by a vehicle being driven by X, who had borrowed it from the owner, the defendant. The owner's insurance did not cover the vehicle while it was being driven by X. The claimant successfully claimed damages against X on the ground of his negligence.

The claimant also claimed against the owner, who was in breach of his duty under the replacement for s. 35 of the 1930 Act, section 201 of the Road Traffic Act 1960 (see now the Road Traffic Act 1988). It was held that the owner was in breach, and that such breach did give rise to a civil action, but in such circumstances as these the damage caused by the owner's breach was dependent upon the driver's ability to satisfy the judgment made against him. If the driver was well able to satisfy the judgment, the owner's breach caused no damage but where, as here, the driver was unable, because of his limited means, to make prompt payment, judgment could be made against the owner for the full loss.

Cases such as these are now dealt with under an agreement (which has the force of law) between the Motor Insurers' Bureau and the Department of the Environment, whereby the Bureau (which is maintained by the insurance companies) will pay out in the event of damage caused by uninsured drivers of vehicles on the public highway, provided there is, in the circumstances, a legal obligation to take out insurance. *Monk* and *Martin* are now relevant only for purposes of illustration.

? QUESTION 7.3

Can you identify the policy reasoning behind *Monk* (and *Martin*)?

It is one of the universal features of the action for breach of statutory duty that, unless there are clear words to the contrary in the Act in question, the courts will not favour a claim for damages in tort where to do so would subvert or supplant the existing common law. If, to allow the claim would supplement the common law, that objection would have no relevance and the court might more readily find in the claimant's favour.

On the facts, at that time, *Monk* supplemented the existing action in common law negligence, by allowing a claim for damages directly against a person who was not liable in negligence, but who had the funds available to pay compensation. This argument is advanced by *Winfield* (p. 197) as the real explanation for the decision in *Monk*, and it is an attractive proposition; but the 'class' approach is the stated basis for the decision. It is, perhaps, significant that the decision was given at a time when there was no Motor Insurers' Bureau.

You will recall that in both *Monk* and *Dean* it was the drivers who were liable in the tort of negligence.

Road users have not been generally favoured as a class in the context of the action for breach of statutory duty. *Winfield* (p. 197) says this is due to the fact that 'isolated pockets of strict liability' (many of the statutes concerned impose strict liability, i.e. liability in which the defendant's fault need not be proved) would be introduced into an area of liability which is based on common law negligence.

Another factor is surely the size of the class in this case, and the question of how heavy the burden will be on the defendant if liability is imposed.

It will be found in **Chapter 10** that road users, as a class of persons, may have certain claims in public nuisance. They can also bring claims for personal injury or damage to property, in certain circumstances, concerning the condition of the highway, against the highway authority under the Highways Act 1980.

According to *Wentworth* v *Wiltshire County Council* [1993] QB 654, the action under the 1980 Act is not available to someone who has a business next to the highway, and who suffers pure economic loss due to the fact that access to his premises is denied to vehicular traffic because of the highway's condition. The 1980 Act contains a special method of enforcement in such a case. This legislation, unlike the legislation which is the subject matter of our study here, actually confers a civil remedy upon road users.

Lonrho says little about how a class is to be ascertained in any given situation, though the answer may be pretty obvious in some instances (for example, employees or, as in *Ex parte Island Records Ltd*, musical performers). In fact, this issue can be likened to the duty of care problem in the tort of negligence, where policy invariably plays a pivotal role in 'hard cases'.

? QUESTION 7.4

Does the class protection approach provide the conclusive answer, in all cases?

The answer is 'No'.

Not only is the question 'Is a particular statute passed for the benefit of a "class" of persons?' often a difficult one to answer, influenced as it is by policy considerations; even where a court accepts the claimant's argument that legislation was passed with the intention to confer upon a class of persons some benefit, it does not follow that an action for breach of statutory duty will be recognized.

The House of Lords, in *R* v *Deputy Governor of Parkhurst Prison, ex parte Hague* [1992] 1 AC 58, found that the Prison Rules 1964 did not confer upon prisoners an action in tort for damages, in the event of their breach by the prison authorities. The claim was based on a breach of Rule 43, concerning the segregation of prisoners by the prison authorities.

It was held that a court cannot escape its duty to determine the intention of Parliament. The existence of a clearly defined class of persons cannot be the sole determinant of the issue.

On the facts, the court said, the Prison Act 1952 and the Rules made thereunder were intended **only** for the governance of prisons, including the control of prisoners. It was found that the claimant, as a prisoner, could pursue alternative claims to protect his rights viz. in public law (via judicial review) and in tort (negligence, trespass to the person, and misfeasance in public office). (See, further, 10.4.5.4.)

EXERCISE 7.1

Read this extract from *Calveley* v *Chief Constable of Merseyside* [1989] 1 All ER 1025 and state the reason given by Lord Bridge for the decision.

It has not been, nor could be, seriously argued that the duty imposed by s. 49 of the 1964 Act and reg. 6 of the 1977 Regulations to investigate a complaint by a member of the public against a member of a police force was intended to give a cause of action in damages to the member of the police force who is the subject of the complaint if the duty is not performed. Whether the officer conducting the investigation owes a duty of care at common law to the person under investigation is quite a different question. It was, however, submitted that the duty under reg. 7 to give notice to the member subject to investigation as soon as is practicable of the matters alleged against him was intended to give the member a cause of action in damages if not performed. That the duty is imposed for the benefit of the police officer subject to investigation is plain. But it seems to me equally plain that the legislature cannot have contemplated that the object of the duty was to protect the officer from any injury of a kind attracting compensation and cannot therefore have been intended to give him a right to damages for breach of duty. The duty is imposed as a procedural step to protect the position of the officer subject to investigation in relation to any proceedings which may be brought against him. If he is not prejudiced in any such proceedings by failure to perform the duty, he has no ground of complaint. If, as in the case of the defendants . . . the delay in giving notice under reg. 7 coupled with other factors causes irremediable prejudice to the officer in disciplinary proceedings which result in his conviction of an offence against the discipline code, he has his remedy by way of judicial review to quash that conviction and nullify its consequences . . .

The reason given by his Lordship was that although the legislation certainly gave a benefit to the claimant, a police officer, it was not one for monetary compensation. In fact, the benefit was the protection of fairness in procedural matters where the officer was under investigation, after a complaint had been made against him.

There are other matters of which we must now take note, for example the question of 'public' duties mentioned above, and the position where the remedy provided by the statute is not a criminal sanction. Before we do that, however, we have to direct our attention to the second 'exception' outlined by Lord Diplock in *Lonrho*.

QUESTION 7.5

Can you remember what that 'exception' is?

The second exception is the case where a statute has created a public right and an individual suffers different damage from that sustained by the rest of the public. Please note that this is not the 'public duties' issue referred to above.

7.3.3.4 Public rights and particular damage

Lord Diplock's second exception is remarkably similar to the concept of 'special damage' in public nuisance, which you will learn about in **Chapter 10**.

This exception suffers from even greater vagueness than the 'class exception' given in *Lonrho*.

Both exceptions are open to judicial interpretation, but at least 'class' is rather less opaque than the notion of particular damage coupled to public rights. It is the 'public rights' aspect of this exception which causes the problem of definition.

According to Lord Diplock in *Lonrho*, a public right is some right which is available to the Queen's subjects where they wish to enjoy it. His Lordship drew a distinction between those Acts which create public rights (that is, statutes which create crimes) and those which simply prohibit the public generally from doing something which they could otherwise do legally ('mere prohibitions' do not create any public right in the present context). There is a distinction, for this purpose at least, between 'crimes' and 'prohibitions'. In *Lonrho* itself the sanctions provisions came into the second category.

His Lordship seemed to be at a loss to explain his reasoning much beyond this. Jones (at p. 296) says this is simply asserting that some criminal legislation is actionable in the present case, while some is not.

 You should consider the extract from *Winfield* in *Cases and Materials* (7.1.1.1).

In *Dear* v *Newham LBC* (1988), *The Times*, 24 February (CA), it was found that the defendant had no obligation to remove items of rubbish from a flat if those items did not fit into a dustbin.

The council had made a by-law under the Public Health Act 1936 requiring occupiers to put all house refuse in dustbins, and a weekly refuse collection service was operated by the council. However, refuse collectors would remove only refuse which had been put into dustbins and placed in the street.

The claimant, a child, was injured when she fell from a balcony at her home. The balcony was obstructed by rubbish which the claimant's mother had placed there. This rubbish was found in the roof space by the mother when she moved into the flat, and she had made several unsuccessful requests to the council for the removal of this refuse.

The council claimed that the rubbish was not 'house refuse' within the meaning of s. 72 of the 1936 Act, which imposed a duty to remove 'house refuse'. According to Slade LJ, this phrase was not defined by Parliament in the Act and the court could not 'insert a definition by a process of judicial legislation'. In the circumstances, said his Lordship, the council's claim was correct: their definition of 'house refuse' accorded with the ordinary use of language and this approach was given strong support by s. 72(3) of the 1936 Act which empowered local authorities to provide dustbins and make by-laws requiring their use. Such power would be of limited use if it remained open to a householder to serve a notice requiring the local authority to remove bulky items of rubbish which were not capable of fitting in a dustbin. It was more likely that the legislature intended such items to be dealt with by s. 74 (which empowers a local authority, at an occupier's request, to 'remove any refuse . . . which they are under no obligation to remove'). Since the council were under no obligation to remove the rubbish in this case, they owed no duty of care to the defendant.

EXERCISE 7.2

Consider *Richardson* v *Pitt-Stanley and Others* [1995] 1 All ER 460 in *Cases and Materials* (7.1.1.1), and state the points of significance.

You might have listed the following:

(a) Existing remedies at common law were regarded as adequate.

(b) It was considered to be significant that the claimant's loss was 'economic'.

(c) Also of significance was an alleged distinction between a statute which creates merely a criminal offence, and one which declares that certain conduct is 'unlawful' and then, separately, imposes a criminal sanction. It is claimed that it is easier to infer a civil remedy in the latter case, that is where conduct is made generally unlawful (rather than being classified simply as a criminal offence, as in the former case).

(d) The Act in question imposed 'very substantial' fines for breaches of its provision.

(e) Parliamentary debates were considered and *Hansard* consulted.

(f) Although a clearly definable class was involved (there was considerable reference to Lord Diplock's judgment in *Lonrho*) this was not regarded as conclusive by the majority.

(g) The dissenting judge, referring to the first exception in Lord Diplock's speech (above) regarded the class factor as being overwhelmingly in favour of inferring a civil remedy. The statutory duty imposed was not, he said, an 'entirely general' duty, owed to 'the world at large'; it was a duty owed to a clearly definable class of persons of which the claimant was one.

(h) Sir John Megaw, the dissenting judge, also thought it significant that the duty was not of an 'absolute' nature. On the contrary, it required proof of fault on the part of the defendant.

There are still two issues of general importance to consider; these include the issue of 'public' duties referred to above. Since they are concerns which are germane to the topic as a whole, we will leave discussion of them until after we have dealt with some special matters, i.e.:

(a) where the special remedy provided by the statute is not a criminal sanction;

(b) the second presumption laid down by Lord Tenterden in *Doe d. Murray* (see 7.3.2).

7.3.3.5 **Where the statutory remedy is not a criminal sanction**

Lord Diplock in *Lonrho* said:

> Where the only manner of enforcing performance for which the Act provides is prosecution for the criminal offence of failure to perform the statutory obligation or for contravening the statutory prohibition which the Act creates, there are two classes of exception to this general rule.

He then went on to specify the two exceptions which we have already examined. The words 'this general rule' here is a reference to the first of Lord Tenterden's presumptions.

It is clear, from the cases we have considered in the context of 'class' interests, that it is not always sufficient for a claimant to bring himself within the benefit of a class, even where the statute imposes a criminal sanction. Where the means of enforcement is some other method, the class argument is correspondingly weaker. Lord Tenterden's first presumption has greater force in such circumstances.

Lord Diplock has made it clear that his 'exceptions' to the general rule are applicable to the case of the criminal sanction, but this does not mean that the class argument is never likely to appear elsewhere. The 'general rule' is based only on a presumption after all; this case can be rebutted in appropriate cases by argument, but it will need to be a strong argument.

In *Wyatt* v *Hillingdon London Borough Council* (1978) 76 LGR 727, the Chronically Sick and Disabled Persons Act 1970 (see now the Disability Discrimination Act 1995) had placed a duty on social services authorities to provide for the needs of a class of persons, that is disabled persons; the claimant was clearly a member of this class and there was no doubt on the question of whose benefit the statute had been passed to promote. The 1970 Act, in common with a number of other social services measures, was subject to section 36 of the National Assistance Act 1948, which contained a 'default' procedure, empowering the Secretary of State for Social Security to apply for a court order where social services authorities, including the defendant council, were failing to perform their statutory duties. Despite the fact that this procedure had at that date never been activated, the Court of Appeal found that the existence of the procedure impliedly excluded an action for damages at common law.

Cases involving methods of enforcement other than criminal sanctions are likely to be similar to this one. It is not suggested that the procedure will be the same, but similar, i.e. some administrative form of relief; it might, for instance, be an appeal to some tribunal.

Sometimes provision is made for an appeal to a court. In any event, where decisions of public bodies are concerned judicial review (see 3.5) may be available. In short, where a number of alternatives to the action for breach of statutory duty are available, as a means of enforcing the statute, this factor may militate against a finding of a civil remedy in tort.

? **QUESTION** 7.6

Can you guess what the policy reasons might be behind the decision in *Wyatt*?

There are several policy reasons for this because a public authority was involved:

(a) Jones (pp. 296–7) claims that while there is no 'specific' presumption applying to public authorities, the courts are generally reluctant to find a civil remedy if liability is likely to be extensive. Jones refers to public 'utilities', but we can include public authorities generally here;

(b) where public duties are involved, and this point will be raised again under 'public duties' (see 7.2.6) the obligation is invariably expressed in wide, general terms which give the public body concerned considerable discretion, especially where the expenditure of public money is involved concerning, as it does, issues of policy-making on the part of the public body in question. The issue may be felt to be too 'political' for the court to intervene, and on the facts of *Wyatt* it was felt intervention would be better left to the Secretary of State.

Salmond (at p. 254) speaking generally says '. . . provisions which are highly specific and detailed in laying down the precise content of the duty are more likely than others to lend themselves to enforcement by way of an action for damages.'

(c) The fact that the Secretary of State was given the special power of enforcement may have confirmed the essentially 'public' nature of the local council's obligation under the statute.

7.3.4 Where the statute is silent on the question of enforcement

This is where we have to consider the second of Lord Tenterden's presumptions. According to his Lordship, in such cases '. . . the common law may, in general, find a mode suited to the particular nature of the case'.

The discretion given to the court in such cases may be noted in the wording of Lord Tenterden's speech. It is often said that the courts will more readily read into such a statute a cause of action in tort. As in all cases, it is assumed that Parliament and the parliamentary draftsman know the case law, and the ways of the judges, and so where nothing is said at all about means of enforcement it is assumed that will be no objection to a civil remedy.

In *Thornton* v *Kirklees Borough Council* [1979] QB 626 Megaw LJ said: 'where an Act imposes a duty . . . for the benefit of a specified category of persons but prescribes no special remedy for breach of that duty, it can normally be assumed that a civil action for damages will lie'. While no doubt this is a correct statement of principle, it should in general be regarded only as a strong starting point.

Please remember that in any context of breaches of statutory duty, that is of the type under discussion in this chapter, there are so many considerations to take into account in determining the so-called 'intention of Parliament'. The absence of a specific remedy in the Act in question cannot be regarded as conclusive of whether or not a civil remedy in tort is available.

In *Thornton* the issue involved was the duty owed by local authorities to homeless persons under the then Housing (Homeless Persons) Act 1977 (see now Housing Act 1996).

? QUESTION 7.7

Can you think of any particular legal obstacles there might be in the way of establishing *civil* liability in cases such as *Thornton*?

Among the obstacles facing a litigant in such cases, you might include the following:

(a) While an easily discernible class was involved in *Thornton*, the size of it and the extent of potential liability could be a problem.

(b) The wording of the duty itself could be a problem. How much discretion and policy-making power does it confer on the body involved?

(c) There might well be some alternative method available of enforcing the obligation, such as judicial review.

Where a statute makes no provision at all for enforcement, a court might look favourably on an argument that the only way of enforcing the statute is by way of an action in tort; otherwise the law would never be activated. In general, that is unlikely to be the case, because there will probably be another remedy in existing law. (This point is taken up in 7.3.6.) In practice, the argument is likely to revolve around the adequacy of some already existing remedy or procedure.

Public duties, and alternative methods of enforcement, are taken up below, in more detail. We will deal first with public duties.

7.3.5 Public duties

The observations made here are relevant to the action for breach of statutory duty generally. It has already been noted that it is Jones's contention that public utilities stand in a special position in the present context, that is, that there is a marked reluctance on the part of the courts to infer an action for breach of statutory duty where liability is likely to be extensive. He suggests that *Atkinson* (see 7.3.3.1) can be explained on this basis. Where public bodies have failed to observe duties imposed on them by statute the courts, on the whole, are not in favour of allowing an action in tort.

 **QUESTION** 7.8

Return to the decision in *X and Others* v *Bedfordshire County Council (and Other Appeals)* [1995] 3 All ER 353 in *Cases and Materials* (1.2), and state the basis of the decisions on breach of statutory duty.

The reasoning in these cases, behind the decision that no action in tort for breach of statutory duty was available, is twofold:

(a) the duty flowing from the Children and Young Persons Act 1969, the Child Care Act 1980, and the Children Act 1989, is expressed in very general terms; and

(b) local social services authorities, who owe the duty, are given extensive discretion to act under the terms of the duty.

Furthermore, factors such as 'parliamentary intention', 'class of persons' protected (if any), and the means of redress available where a breach of statutory duty occurred have all to be weighed in the balance. The first two factors were considered to be of particular importance in this case and it was concluded that the Act in question had been passed for the benefit of society as a whole. Not only that, it was regarded as significant that some public law actions were available to the claimants, as alternatives to an action in tort.

Where public bodies are concerned, the distinction between 'public' law and 'private' law may have to be considered. We have looked at this in **Chapter 1** in relation to actions in negligence, but we must also note its importance in the present context.

The House of Lords, in *O'Rourke* v *Camden LBC* [1998] AC 188, which involved a local council's obligation to accommodate homeless persons under the Housing Act 1996, adopted a similar approach to that taken in *X*. As Lord Hoffmann put it:

> Public money is spent on housing the homeless not merely for the private benefit of people who find themselves homeless but on grounds of general public interest: because, for example, proper housing means that people will be less likely to suffer illness, turn to crime, or require the attention of their social services. The expenditure interacts with expenditure on other public services such as education, the National Health Service and even the police. It is not simply a private matter between the claimant and the housing authority . . . the existence of all these [statutory] discretions makes it unlikely that Parliament intended errors of judgment to give rise to an obligation to make financial reparation. Control by public law remedies would appear much more appropriate.

The availability of public law remedies for breach of statutory duty was stated as a deciding factor in the decision given in *Feakins* v *Dover Harbour Board* (1998) 36 LS Gazette R 31. The claimants exported sheep to the continent via Doverport and they were prevented from pursuing their business activities because of delays caused by demonstrations organized by animal rights protestors. The court said the statutory duty owed by the Board was not imposed for the benefit of a particular class of persons, it was imposed for the public benefit.

7.3.5.1 'Public' law and 'private' law proceedings

The common law action, in tort, for breach of statutory duty, is concerned with the question of a claimant seeking damages for breach of duty; it is not concerned with efforts to obtain a declaration or an order of *mandamus* or some other administrative (or public) law remedy. That is a matter of 'public' law, which involves judicial review proceedings, via s. 31, Supreme Court Act 1981 and Order 53 of the Rules of the Supreme Court, in the High Court. An action in tort, a matter of 'private' law, is started via a writ or an originating summons.

In *Cocks* v *Thanet District Council* [1983] 2 AC 286, the claimant sought a declaration that the council were in breach of duty under the Housing (Homeless Persons) Act 1977 but the council, on a preliminary point, claimed that he should have sought judicial review. It was held in the House of Lords, following *O'Reilly* v *Mackman* [1983] 2 AC 237, that a 'dichotomy [now exists] between a housing authority's public and private law functions'. The decision as to whether the claimant satisfied the statutory criteria (to qualify, for example, as a 'homeless person' under the Act) was a 'public' law deliberation by the council. Once it was satisfied on this count, any obligation to provide housing under the Act was a matter of 'private law', via the action of breach of statutory duty.

This makes it clear that a claimant may have no choice but to institute proceedings for judicial review in respect of some decisions. The possibility of an action for breach of statutory duty in tort can only arise at the second stage. It is not only cases arising under housing legislation which are caught by this ruling: *Cocks* only follows *O'Reilly*, which is of general application. The position is further complicated by the fact that it is possible to obtain damages in Order 53 proceedings, as well as other remedies such as an injunction and declaration, where an infringement with a private right can be shown. There might be a tendency in these cases to force claimants to use Order 53 throughout.

It is not suggested that it is impossible in 'public' law cases to establish a cause of action in tort, merely that it may be more difficult to do so than is the case in other contexts.

In *R v Northavon District Council ex parte Palmer* (1994), *The Times*, 22 February, it was held that a housing authority's breach of duty arising out of the Housing Act 1985 [this replaced the 1977 Act, but see now the 1996 Act] to conduct inquiries where applications were made for accommodation by persons who claimed to be homeless or threatened with homelessness, did not give rise to any private law action in tort for damages.

The 1985 Act imposed a duty upon a local authority to conduct inquiries where application was made for help under the Act. A further duty to secure accommodation was imposed on the authority if it was satisfied that the application met the various statutory criteria qualifying the applicant for help under the Act. The judge said:

> Inquiries by a local authority . . . are part of its decision-making and therefore public law functions. The proper conduct of these inquiries is a matter concerning not only the applicant. It affects the public purse and the general community and those people already on the housing list. The duties of a local authority . . . are duties in public law and do not afford any individual a cause of action in private law.

The alternative claim for damages for breach of statutory duty [to secure accommodation] can only arise once a local authority has reached a decision, in the exercise of its public law functions, that the conditions necessary to give rise to a duty to secure accommodation . . . are satisfied. **Once the existence of a duty to provide accommodation has been established, an action for damages for breach will lie.** . . . [*emphasis added*].

7.3.6 **The state of the pre-existing law, including the common law**

We have already seen that the courts tend to look at the possibility of alternative remedies being available to the claimant, that is alternatives to a cause of action for breach of statutory duty. The existence of some remedy in the statute itself is a factor to be considered. In this respect there may be a distinction between criminal penalties and other methods of enforcement.

Traditionally, where a crime is involved there is perhaps more hope of success because the sanction may not be regarded as adequate in the circumstances. An analogy may be made with the common law crime of public nuisance and the special action available in tort in that case. Nuisance is dealt with in **Chapter 10** (10.4 and 10.5).

According to the majority view in *Ex parte Island Records* (see 7.2.1) a civil action would be available to any person whose private rights were infringed as a result of criminal conduct. This very broad approach, however, is now subject to the 'Diplock qualification' imposed in *Lonrho* (see 7.3.3.2). In *Island Records* injunctive relief was sought, not damages.

? **QUESTION** 7.9

Was it significant that the claimant wanted an injunction in *Island Records*?

The injunction is a discretionary remedy, while damages are available as a right once a wrong has been established. It might be thought that *Island Records* would not 'open the floodgates' too much, as the courts would not have to award an injunction. It appears, however, that the *Lonrho* ruling applies whatever the form of relief sought by the claimant.

In *Rickless* v *United Artists Corporation* (1985), *The Times*, 17 June, in an action brought under the Dramatic and Musical Performers Protection Act 1958, it was held that the Act was passed primarily to protect the economic interests of performers, so that to construe the Act as ceasing to apply after the performer was dead would be partly to frustrate and not fulfil its purpose. Unless the Act conferred civil remedies as well as imposing criminal sanctions the performer's protection was inadequate. Civil remedies would include, said Hobhouse J, a right to apply for an injunction to restrain potential criminal actions.

In *Lonrho*, he said, Lord Diplock drew a distinction between language in a statute which created a legal right and language which created a mere prohibition (a distinction criticized often for its vagueness); he recognized that statutory prohibitions could give rise to civil remedies as well. It was a matter of examining the purpose of the legislation. If it was legislating for the protection of a particular class, then prima facie the statute should be construed as giving a right to a civil remedy to the members of that class. The decision was confirmed by the Court of Appeal at [1987] 1 All ER 679.

The law on this specific point was changed by the Copyright, Designs and Patents Act 1988, but *Rickless* can still be used for purposes of illustration and example in the general context of the action for breach of statutory duty.

The existence of some alternative remedy, and its adequacy is, however, a factor taken into account in all cases. It may have more importance where the statute in question does not provide a specific remedy, but the absence of a special remedy is only another factor to be weighed by the courts. As Lord Simonds said, in *Cutler* v *Wandsworth Stadium Ltd* [1949] AC 398:

> The only rule which in all circumstances is valid is that the answer must depend on a consideration of the whole Act and the circumstances, including the pre-existing law, in which it was enacted. The adequacy of the pre-existing common law may be considered.

In *Phillips* v *Britannia Hygiene Laundry Co.* (see 7.3.3.3) a lorry in use on the public highway had a defective axle, which was in breach of certain statutory regulations relating to the construction and use of vehicles on the roads. It was held that there was no right to a civil action in tort for breach of statutory duty available to the owner of another vehicle damaged in consequence of the breach. The existing law of negligence, the court said, was sufficient to provide a remedy.

The authorities are not consistent on this point in the sense that the existence of an adequate common law remedy can sometimes be given as the reason for finding against an action for breach of statutory duty, although it is debatable as to how conclusive this is. The absence of an alternative common law remedy is not necessarily fatal to a claim for redress.

There is also the vexed question of 'adequacy'. How is that to be assessed? *Winfield* argues that policy considerations may well enter the equation at this point. The learned author suggests that all might be well where the statute in question supplements rather than supplants the common law. Does the statute fit into the existing common law basis of liability? Jones (p. 292) suggests that a claimant's task might be easier where the standard of care set in the statute 'more or less corresponds to a common law duty'.

We have seen in **Chapter 1** that English judges are not, on the whole, keen advocates of strict liability, and many statutes impose such a standard. That factor has not prevented judicial willingness to accept actions for breach of statutory duty in industrial safety cases, so it cannot be regarded as a conclusive consideration. The adequacy of the statutory means of enforcement, where one exists, may also be raised by the claimant.

Groves v *Wimborne* (see 7.3.3.3) proceeded on this basis, though it may be unwise to regard this decision as a strong general authority. Indeed, there was an alternative common law remedy available to the claimant, that is, an action for breach of the special duty an employer owes to his employee.

As with 'class', the interpretation of 'adequate remedy' is open to policy considerations and can only be regarded as one factor to be considered in all the circumstances of the case.

In 'public' duties cases, the existence of an appeal procedure laid down in the statute, or the availability of judicial review, may be taken into account in determining the question of an adequate alternative remedy. This factor may be relevant in such cases whether the statute lays down some 'alternative' remedy or makes no provision at all for a remedy.

 EXERCISE 7.3

Read the decision in *West Wiltshire District Council* v *Garland and Others* [1995] 2 All ER 17 (CA) in *Cases and Materials* (7.1.2).

 Write down a list of the findings, and answer the question: 'What exactly were the claimants trying to establish?'

In your list of the findings you should have the following:

(a) The lack of any other effective remedy against the auditors meant that 'Parliament could be taken to have intended an action for breach of statutory duty to be available to the local authority'.

(b) There was no reason why, where a claimant had available an action for breach of statutory duty for a negligent performance of that duty, he could not also have an action for common law negligence in respect of the same act of negligence. In principle there was no reason why the two should not coexist. That cause of action in negligence was, however, only available to the local authority and not its officers.

(c) The purpose of external audit was to protect the local authority and not its officers. Since the proximity between the auditors and the officers only came about because of the operation of the statute, it would be 'unfair, unjust, and unreasonable' to hold that a duty of care in negligence was owed by the auditors to the officers.

The defendants were officers of the local authority and had been criticized by the district auditor in his report on the council's accounts. They were being sued by their employer, the local authority, for breach of contract and breach of fiduciary duty relating to the payment of certain moneys. The defendants were here trying to bring in as third parties the district auditors on the basis that they had advised the defendants as to the legality of the payments in question. Obviously, to do this, they had to establish some tort(s) on the part of the auditors, hence the claims for breach of statutory duty and common law negligence.

The decision in *Ministry of Housing* v *Sharp* [1970] 1 All ER 1009, which is also considered in relation to 'pure' economic loss in **Chapter 3**, is of some interest in the present context. *CBS Songs Ltd* v *Amstrad Consumer Electronics plc* [1988] AC 1013 which is found in *Cases and Materials* (7.1.2) offers a further illustration.

In *Sharp* the Court of Appeal had to consider s. 17 of the then Land Charges Act 1925, the relevant portion of which reads as follows: '(2) The Registrar shall thereupon make the search required and shall issue a certificate setting forth the results thereof. (3) In favour of a purchaser, or an intending purchaser, as against persons interested . . . the certificate . . . shall be conclusive.'

All three judges interpreted the Act after a lengthy detailed consideration of its statutory history. Lord Denning and Salmon LJ considered that a civil action would lie, but Cross LJ thought not. It was said that *if* it is found that a civil action lies it must then be shown that it lies at the instance of the particular plaintiff. The plaintiff succeeds if he can show:

(a) that he was a member of the class of persons the statute was designed to protect (the statute in this case was designed to protect the purchaser and also those who registered their charges, for example, the Ministry);

(b) the injury suffered is the precise injury that the statute was designed to protect, i.e. the financial loss arising from loss of the benefit of their charge;

(c) that the statute imposed a duty upon the defendant, which duty has been broken. It was on this point that the Ministry's action failed in this case. The majority of the court held that, by implication, the defendant's duty was to search 'diligently', but the plaintiff alleged breach of an absolute duty and so had not attempted to prove any lack of care by the defendant;

(d) that breach of the duty caused the injury. (Since no breach had been proved the question of causation did not arise in this case.)

7.4 The elements of the cause of action for breach of statutory duty

The claimant must establish each of these elements:

(a) There must first be an obligation placed by the statute on the defendant.

(b) The statute must 'intend' an action in tort.

(c) The statute must protect the claimant.

(d) Having already examined the first three elements, we must now consider three other factors:

   (i) the defendant must have breached the statute (see 7.4.1);

   (ii) the defendant's breach of duty must have caused the damage (see 7.4.1.1);

   (iii) the harm suffered is within the scope of the general class of risks at which the statute is directed (see 7.4.2).

7.4.1 **The defendant must have breached the statute**

The standard of care is set in the statute itself, so each case must be looked at on its own facts. A body of precedent builds up over the years on commonly used expressions, particularly in industrial injuries cases, where there has been so much litigation. In many instances liability is strict (the word 'absolute' is often used instead of 'strict') as, for example, under the Factories Act 1961 where one comes across the expression '[some part of machinery] shall be securely fenced'.

In *John Summers* v *Frost* [1955] AC 740, s. 14(1) of the Factories Act 1961 required that every dangerous part of a machine be fenced. The claimant won damages for injury to his thumb caused by contact with a grinding wheel, despite the fact that putting a guard over the only unfenced part of the wheel would have rendered it unusable.

Frequently, the duty is to protect workers, operators, and others 'so far as is reasonably practical', or words to that effect.

In *Larner* v *British Steel plc* [1993] 4 All ER 102, the claimant brought an action for a failure on the part of his employer to see that his workplace was 'made and kept safe', 'so far as it was reasonably practicable to do so'. The duty on the employer to do this was imposed by s. 29(1) of the Factories Act 1961.

The claimant gave evidence that reasonable steps could have been taken, but the defendant submitted no evidence. It denied liability, but did not specifically plead that it was not reasonably practicable to make the workplace safe.

The trial judge found for the defendant, and the claimant appealed. His point of appeal was that the defendant could only claim, within the terms of s. 29(1), that it was not reasonably practicable to do something if the matter was actually pleaded and proved by the defendant.

It was contended by the defendant, however, that 'safe' in the present context meant 'safe from a reasonably foreseeable danger'. To prove that the workplace was unsafe, the claimant had to show that the danger in question was reasonably foreseeable by the defendant.

The Court of Appeal agreed with the claimant that s. 29(1) made no reference to foreseeability, so foreseeability was not relevant to liability here. To imply such a test, said the court, would limit a claim for breach of statutory duty to a situation where negligence would also succeed.

This decision shows that while a 'reasonably practicable' standard is not as strict as a 'shall do' standard, it is still stricter than a negligence standard. Where a duty is qualified, whether or not it has been complied with will depend on all the circumstances. If the regulation requires 'reasonably practicable' (or similar) precautions, then the risk has to be measured against the availability and practicability of those precautions, and the general practice must be considered, as in common law negligence.

In *Adsett* v *K & L Steelfounders* [1953] 1 WLR 773, Singleton LJ declared: 'In deciding whether all the practicable measures were taken one must have regard to the state of knowledge at the material time, particularly, to the knowledge of scientific experts.'

7.4.1.1 **Statute and negligence**

Each statute must be carefully construed to see whether it was the intention that the duty should be strict or that it is dependent on wrongful intent or negligence. The term 'statutory negligence' has been used in some cases to refer to statutory standards based on negligence. However, although in some cases the common law action for negligence may resemble the tort of breach of statutory duty, the modern tendency is to keep the two causes of action separate. As Lord Wright said, in *London Passenger Transport Board* v *Upson* [1949] AC 155:

> a claim for damages for breach of a statutory duty intended to protect a person in the position of the particular plaintiff is a specific common law right which is not to be confused in essence with a claim for negligence. The statutory right has its origin in the statute, but the particular remedy of an action for damages is given by the common law in order to make effective, for the benefit of the injured plaintiff, his right to the performance by the defendant of the defendant's statutory duty. It is an effective sanction. It is not a claim in negligence in the strict ordinary sense . . . whatever the resemblances, it is essential to keep in mind the fundamental differences of the two classes of claim.

The decision in *Bux* v *Slough Metals* [1973] 1 WLR 1358, shows that the torts of breach of statutory duty and negligence are separate and distinct. In actions for breach of statutory duty the existence and nature of the duties depend on a proper interpretation of the relevant statutes; in claims for negligence the matters are determined by reference to the well-established principles of the common law. Where both statutory and common law duties exist, an action for negligence may succeed where an action for breach of statutory duty may fail, since the nature of the statutory duty may be very different from the reasonable care required by the common law.

In this case, the claimant, who worked in a foundry, was splashed with molten metal and as a result lost the sight of an eye. To protect such workers, certain statutory regulations provided that: 'There shall be provided . . . suitable goggles or other suitable eye protection.' The claimant sued the defendants, his employers, for breach of that duty and of the common law duty of care owed by a master to his servant. (We deal with the common law duty of care at 5.3.2.)

After working for the defendants for a year the claimant, along with his fellow workers, had been provided with goggles. He found that, when used, they soon misted over and he had constantly to wipe them clean. This interfered with the speed of his working and, because he was paid on a piecework basis, limited his earnings. In common with the other workers, he stopped using the goggles after a few days.

The defendants had issued this type of goggles only after testing various other types and obtaining the advice of the British Safety Council. It seems, however, that they simply acquiesced in their employees' practice of not using the goggles.

The Court of Appeal held that the defendants had 'provided suitable goggles' and the claim for breach of statutory duty failed. There was no duty laid down in the regulations to see that the goggles were used.

The defendants then argued that the regulations provided a complete safety code, and compliance with that code made it impossible to say that there had been any failure to show reasonable care. The claim for common law negligence must also fail.

The court rejected this argument. The statutory duty was the limited one of 'providing'. The defendants had failed to take reasonable care for the safety of their employees; it was not enough to provide the goggles and then stand by while the men did dangerous work with their eyes wholly unprotected. While the claimant succeeded in his claim for negligence, he was held to be 40% to blame and apportionment was made under the Law Reform (Contributory Negligence) Act 1945.

While failure to conform to a standard imposed by statute may be a breach of statutory duty, it is not in itself conclusive evidence of negligence; it may, however, sometimes be prima facie evidence of negligence. There is an element of overlap between the two torts, where a claimant makes a claim in both causes of action.

Differences between the action for breach of statutory duty and an action in negligence

(a) A defence of *volenti non fit injuria* may be available in the common law action for negligence but not for breach of statutory duty. This point is taken up at 8.2.2.3.

(b) Moreover, in most cases arising under statutes the statute defines the standard of care and the defendant is liable if he fails to show that standard of care. In negligence at common law, however, the standard of care is determined by the court, not by the legislature.

Where there is a criminal prosecution for breach of some statutory provision the standard of proof, which is 'beyond all reasonable doubt', differs from the tortious standard, which is proof on the 'balance of probabilities'.

The illustrations given so far concern industrial relationships, but actions for breach of statutory duty and actions for negligence occur in other contexts. It is regarded as axiomatic that the two actions go hand-in-hand, and whenever a statutory duty arises it follows that there will be a possibility of liability in negligence. The statutory duty creates 'proximity' for the purposes of negligence.

 Your attention is drawn to *West Wiltshire DC* v *Garland* (see Exercise 7.3) which illustrates this point. Refer also to *M* v *Newham LBC*, and *E* v *Dorset CC*, both of which appear in *Cases and Materials* (1.1, 1.2) for guidance on the relationship between these two causes of action.

Bux illustrates the action for breach of statutory duty and the special duty of care in negligence owed by an employer to his employee.

It is for the claimant to prove legal causal connection between the breach and his injury. In Lord Reid's words, in *Bonnington Castings* v *Wardlaw* [1956] AC 613: 'at least on a balance of probabilities [that] the breach of duty caused or materially contributed to his injury'. This case involved liability for inhalation of silica dust, due to inadequate ventilation in breach of the Factories Act.

In *McWilliams* v *Arrol* [1962] 1 All ER 623, a steel erector fell to his death because he was not wearing a safety harness. The defendants had failed in their statutory duty to provide a safety harness, but the evidence did not establish that the deceased would have worn the harness even if one had been provided. Indeed the reverse seemed likely, because the defendants were able to show that the deceased, and his workmates, rarely ever used safety harnesses, which was common practice in the construction industry.

The House of Lords held that the claimant had not discharged the burden of proving that the death was caused by the breach of statutory duty, so the defendants were entitled to succeed, as it was 'probable' that the deceased would not have used the safety equipment. There was no duty on the defendant to see that the harness was worn. It is now over 40 years since the decision in *McWilliams* and, in that time, a much more rigorous safety regime has been developed under the Health and Safety at Work Act 1974. It is unlikely, therefore, that the facts of this case will be repeated.

7.4.1.2 Who owes the duty?

The statute must impose the duty on the defendant himself. It is a question of interpreting the Act, or regulation, to see on whom the burden is imposed. In some cases the duty may be imposed, in effect, on the claimant. This issue has arisen most frequently in actions by employees against their employers. Once the statute has been interpreted to impose a duty on the defendant, the general principle is clear: the obligation is personal to the defendant and he cannot escape liability by delegating its performance to someone else. As Lord Warrington said in *Lochgelly Iron Co.* v *M'Mullan* [1934] AC 1, a case involving an action by an employee against his employer: '. . . the owner cannot relieve himself of his obligation by saying that he has appointed reasonably competent persons and that the breach is due to negligence on their part . . .' This rule applies whether the 'reasonably competent person' is an employee or an independent contractor.

> **?** **QUESTION** 7.10
>
> Can a *claimant* put a defendant in breach of statutory duty?

In some cases, the act or omission of the claimant himself has the legal result that both claimant and defendant are in breach of the same duty.

In *Ginty* v *Belmont Building Supplies* [1959] 1 All ER 414, the claimant was an experienced employee employed by the defendants, who were roofing contractors. Statutory regulations, binding on both parties, required that crawling boards should be used for work done on fragile roofs. Although the defendants provided such boards, the claimant did not use them and consequently fell through a roof, sustaining serious personal injury. Both parties were, in law, in breach of their statutory duties, but the judge held that the only wrongful act was that of the claimant. Pearson J said:

> it would be absurd if, notwithstanding the employer having done all he could reasonably be expected to do to ensure compliance, a workman, who deliberately disobeyed his employer's orders and thereby put the employer in breach of a regulation, could claim damages for injury caused to him solely by his own wrongdoing.

If, however, the claimant establishes the defendant's breach of duty, and that he suffered injury as a result, he establishes a prima facie case against the defendant, who will escape liability only if he can rebut this by proving that the only act or default which caused the breach was that of the claimant himself. Where some fault can be attributed to the defendant, for example an employer fails to provide adequate instructions or supervision, the claimant will recover some damages though these will be substantially reduced for any contributory negligence by the claimant.

In *Ross* v *Associated Portland Cement Manufacturers Ltd* [1964] 2 All ER 452, the deceased, a charge-hand steel erector, and two colleagues had to repair a safety net which was situated some 22 feet above ground level in the employer's factory. He was simply left to get on with the work as he thought best and without any proper equipment. The evidence showed that the deceased could use any equipment he could find, and could also ask the chief engineer for advice or equipment, though no encouragement was given with regard to the latter possibility, in spite of the fact that he was a newcomer to the job and the task was of an unusual nature for a steel erector. While using a ladder (the evidence indicated that a moveable platform should have been used) the deceased met his death.

His widow sued (under what is now the Fatal Accidents Act 1976) and it was first held that the employer was in breach of its statutory duty, under s. 29(1) of the Factories Act 1961, but the sole cause of the accident was the deceased's own negligence in using the ladder.

The House of Lords, however, found that the employer was partly responsible (66%) because it had not provided proper equipment to keep the place of work as safe as was reasonably practicable; in particular, it was important that the deceased's decision to use the ladder was forced upon him because of the absence of appropriate equipment for the job.

Lord Reid referred to the judgment of Pearson J in *Ginty* v *Belmont Building Supplies* [1959] 1 All ER 414 (in which the test of causation was said to be, 'Whose fault was it?') and said:

> If the question is put in that way one must remember that fault is not necessarily equivalent in this context to blameworthiness The question really is whose conduct caused the accident . . . That approach appears to me to avoid the difficulty which has sometimes been felt in explaining why an employer, put in breach of a statute by the disobedience of his servant, can escape liability to that servant for injuries caused by the breach. If the employer exercised all due diligence, and the breach and resultant injuries were solely caused by the servant's conduct, the employer is liable vicariously for injuries sustained by a third party just as he would be for injuries caused solely by his servant's common law negligence: but he can say to the disobedient servant that his conduct in no way caused or contributed to that servant's injuries.

According to Lord Donovan there was no evidence that Ross (the deceased) was an expert or specialist at repairing safety nets suspended between aerial ropeways; there was no evidence that he had done this kind of work before. '[In] *Ginty* . . . suitable appliances **were** provided by the employer but the man refused or neglected to use them.'

7.4.2 The harm suffered is within the scope of the general class of risks at which the statute is directed

In *Gorris* v *Scott* (1874) LR 9 Ex 125, a statute required animals on board ship to be penned in. In breach of the statute sheep were not penned in and were washed overboard. The court held that an action for breach of statutory duty would fail because the statute was intended to prevent the spread of disease, not to prevent animals from drowning.

Evidently, the claimant's damage must come within the terms of the statute concerned; and it is likely that the stricter the duty imposed by the legislation, the stricter the court will be in requiring the claimant to keep within the letter of the law.

In *Chipchase* v *British Titan Products Co.* [1956] 1 QB 545, a workman fell off a platform 9 inches wide and 6 feet above the ground. Certain statutory regulations, which applied to all platforms 6 feet 6 inches or more above the ground, required that platforms should be 34 inches wide. The claimant tried to argue that as his case was so nearly within the regulations they ought to be taken into account by the court. The court would not accept this argument, and there was no liability for breach of statute.

In *Close* v *Steel Co. of Wales* [1962] AC 367, the House of Lords had to consider s. 14 of the Factories Act 1961, which imposes a duty to see that dangerous parts of machinery 'shall be securely fenced'. The claimant, an employee of the defendants, was injured when a dangerous fragment flew out of a machine and hit him. It was held that he could not recover by basing his claim on s. 14. An employee can only rely on a breach of s. 14 where he comes into contact with the dangerous part of the machine; an injury caused in a different way is not covered.

Again, in *Hands* v *Rolls-Royce* (1972) 69 LSG 504, the claimant, who was injured when a defective lavatory seat came adrift from the pan, was found to have no remedy under s. 7 of the Factories Act 1961, because that section related only to the spread of infection.

It must be said, however, that the general approach to the application of *Gorris* is somewhat less strict.

In *Grant v National Coal Board* [1958] AC 649, the House of Lords approved that decision, although in this case the statute was held to cover the damage suffered. The claimant was employed in the defendants' mine. The Coal Mines Act 1911 provided that 'the roof and sides of every travelling road . . . shall be made secure'. The accident occurred because a bogie on which the claimant was travelling was derailed as a result of a fall of stone from the roof. It was held that the protection of the statute was not limited to direct falls from the roof but covered accidents caused indirectly by such falls. This case illustrates the modern tendency not to apply the decision in *Gorris* too strictly.

In *Donaghey v Boulton and Paul Ltd* [1968] AC 1, a statutory regulation was designed to prevent employees from falling off roofs on which they were working. The House of Lords held that it made no difference that the claimant fell through a hole in the roof rather than through fragile roofing material.

Lord Reid said that provided the claimant's damage is of the kind that the statute was designed to prevent, it is irrelevant that it occurred in a way not contemplated by the statute. The problem with risk in the present context is the same as in the tort of negligence. In both torts the risk, or danger, must be foreseeable (or within the Act(s) in the case of statutory duties) but the exact way in which the accident occurs need not be so.

Young v Charles Church (Southern) Ltd (1997), *The Times*, 1 May (CA) illustrates the point that damages for psychiatric injury may be obtained in a cause of action other than that of negligence. In *Young* the claimant suffered psychiatric illness through seeing a colleague electrocuted in very close physical proximity to himself: indeed, the claimant was most fortunate in the circumstances to escape electrocution himself. It was held, in an action for breach of statutory duty, that reg. 44(2) of the Construction (General Provisions) Regulations (SI 1961 No. 1580) which embraces 'electrically charged overhead cables or apparatus' provides a cause of action in tort where an employee suffers mental illness.

The House of Lords, in *Cullen v Chief Constable of the Royal Ulster Constabulary* [2004] 2 All ER 237, said that breach of a statutory duty should usually cause damage of a kind recognized in tort, that is, damage to property, personal injury, or economic loss. It was also of significance in this case that the court considered that the alternative remedy of judicial review, a 'public law' remedy, was available to the claimant. (However, two of their Lordships had strong reservations on the adequacy of this remedy in the circumstances of the case.) The claimant, who had been unable to obtain reasons from the police for their refusal to allow him access to a solicitor, lost his case.

7.4.2.1 **Common law duty**

You should always remember that there may be a right of action for the general common law tort of negligence, or the employer's special duty of care where relevant, where there is no breach of a statutory duty or the breach of such a duty does not give a right of action in tort.

No statute will be construed to exclude an existing common law duty unless it says so, expressly or by necessary implication.

 EXERCISE 7.4

Consider *Pickering v Liverpool Daily Post and Echo Newspapers plc* [1991] 2 AC 370 in *Cases and Materials* (7.2.1), and state the outcome of this case.

You might have expressed yourself in terms similar to the following: even a member of a class of persons for whose benefit a statute has been passed will not succeed unless the injury suffered is of a kind or type recognized by the law as sounding in damages.

The claimant was, in effect, complaining of an invasion of privacy. This is not yet recognized entirely as a tort in its own right.

General observations

Ultimately, the answer to the question of whether or not an action lies in tort for the breach of some statutory provision where the statute is silent on the matter is determined by policy factors, a state of affairs redolent of the duty of care issue in the tort of negligence.

As Jones puts it at p. 290:

> In the vast majority of legislation, however, there is no express provision to indicate whether contravention will be actionable or not. Where the statute is silent the courts purport to 'discover' the intention of Parliament, but the truth is that, Parliament having pointedly omitted to express an intention, the construction of the statute, aided by certain 'presumptions', amounts to little more than judicial legislation. This in itself would not necessarily be a major ground of criticism, if it were possible to discern any coherent guiding principles employed by the courts to determine this question. However, there are so many conflicting 'presumptions' and contradictory statements as to the value of particular presumptions, that it is virtually impossible to predict how the courts will respond to a particular statute.

Again, as *Street* says at p. 299:

> the existence of a cause of action for violations of a statute thus becomes primarily a matter of construction of the relevant statute. But in the vast majority of statutes to which the tort has been held to extend Parliament has imposed a duty on the defendant, expressly made breach of that duty a crime, and given no indication of whether a cause of action in tort is intended. On occasion, judges will readily imply such an intention. Yet in other circumstances, they equally adamantly deny the existence of any such parliamentary intent. Many of the decided cases can for the most part be regarded as decisions of policy whether breach of particular statutory provisions should be compensated for by way of damages awarded to the victim.

The Law Commission has expressed views on this issue: *The Interpretation of Statutes* (Law Com. No. 21 of 1969); see *Cases and Materials* (7.2.2).

7.5 Defences

Two of the **general** defences discussed in **Chapter 14** require special consideration in the present context.

7.5.1 *Volenti non fit injuria*

It may be that public policy does not allow this defence to be used by an employer who is in breach of his statutory duty, at least where the duty is of a strict (or 'absolute') nature. The reasoning for this argument rests on the claim that Parliament cannot have intended defendants to 'contract out' of their statutory responsibilities.

In *Imperial Chemical Industries Ltd* v *Shatwell* [1965] AC 656, two employees were injured in an explosion caused by their own failure to observe safety precautions required by statutory regulations in the interests of their own safety. One of them sued the employer, alleging that the employer was vicariously liable for the other employee's share of the responsibility for the accident. The House of Lords found as follows:

(a) Where employees are themselves under a statutory duty, and jointly do something in breach of that duty, the employer is not vicariously liable.

(b) Each employee in this case could plead *volenti* against the other, thus the defence was available to the employer when sued as being vicariously liable for their torts.

(c) It would be otherwise if the duty concerned had been a statutory duty placed on the employer or if the wrong had been that of a superior (employee) whose orders the claimant had been bound to obey.

7.5.1.1 Other cases

The *ICI* decision is clear authority for the proposition that in actions by employees against their employer for breach of statutory duty it is only where the employer is sued vicariously for the breach of a statutory obligation on the part of an employee that the employer can plead *volenti*.

It is not clear whether the defence is available in other cases of breach of statutory duty; that is, in cases not involving claims by employees against their employers.

Winfield (p. 203) argues that the defence does apply in other contexts, subject to contrary provision in the legislation itself. *Street* (p. 411) suggests that it might be contrary to public policy generally to allow someone to avoid their statutory duty.

You may be surprised to learn that such an important point awaits resolution by the courts. It is submitted that it cannot be the case that Parliament intended the defence to apply generally to statutory obligations.

7.5.2 Contributory negligence

In general, the rules provided by the Law Reform (Contributory Negligence) Act 1945 apply. The only qualification is that since the object of statutes such as the Factories Act 1961 is to protect workers from acts of inattention, slight inadvertence tends to be ignored, even though such a slip by the servant might be enough to make the master vicariously liable to an injured third party. As Stable J put it in *Carr* v *Mercantile Produce Ltd* [1949] 2 KB 601:

> The Factories Act [the predecessor of the 1961 Act] is there not merely to protect the careful, the vigilant and the conscientious workman but, human nature being what it is, also the careless, the indolent, the inadvertent, the weary and even, perhaps, in some cases, the disobedient.

In *Mullard* v *Ben Line* [1970] 1 WLR 1414, the claimant, an experienced ship repairer, fell through a hatch left open by the defendant in breach of statutory duty. The Court of Appeal, reducing the assessment of the claimant's share of the blame from 50% to 33%, held that an employee should not be blamed too severely for a momentary error.

In *Ryan* v *Manbre Sugar Ltd* (1970) 114 SJ 492, Lord Denning MR found that pure inadvertence (slipping down factory steps known to be slippery) did not amount to contributory negligence.

The standard of care is that of the ordinary prudent worker (or other person protected by the statute) assessed in all the circumstances of the case.

There are a number of decisions in which claimants have failed owing to their contributory negligence, but that has been where the claimant was 'fantastically wrong' or where 'it was a crazy thing to do'. The courts favour the employee where he is injured as a result of his employer's breach of statutory duty, at least where that duty was imposed for the protection of the employee. The courts, it seems, will find an employee guilty of contributory negligence only in cases where that negligence is very clearly established as the part cause of the injury.

In the context of statutory duties (at any rate in the industrial sphere) a more subjective approach is taken to the issue of contributory negligence.

 EXERCISE 7.5

Consider *Westwood* v *Post Office* [1974] 3 All ER 184. What was the outcome in relation to the defence of contributory negligence? There was a divergence of views in the House of Lords as to whether Westwood had been contributorily negligent in ignoring the 'keep out' sign on the motor room door, but Lord Kilbrandon, delivering the majority decision, said '. . . the sole act of negligence giving rise to this accident was the respondent's breach of statutory duty. Any fault on the part of the deceased was a fault of disobedience, not a fault of negligence, because he had no reason to foresee that disregard of the order to keep out of the lift motor room would expose him to danger. It would indeed not have done so, had it not been that, unknown to him, the respondents were in breach of their duty to take care for the safety of those employed in the premises'.

It appears from the decision of the majority of the Law Lords in *Westwood* that no reduction in damages for contributory negligence will be made where the claimant's 'conducive folly' has taken the form of disobedience (the claimant was suing his employer for breach of statutory duty) rather than of negligence.

7.5.2.1 Experience

As we have seen, an employer who is put in breach of a statute solely by an employee's default can claim, where the circumstances allow, that the injury and breach of duty have been caused by the employee.

It may be, although this is on the whole more likely where the common law duty of care is involved (see **Chapter 5**), that in some circumstances a competent and experienced person can be expected to look after himself. Much depends on the circumstances of the case. In *Norris* v *Moss* [1954] 1 WLR 346, the claimant began to repair some scaffolding in a way described as 'fantastically wrong' and was held solely responsible for his consequent injuries.

In *Boyle* v *Kodak Ltd* [1969] 2 All ER 439, the House of Lords held that once the claimant has established that there was a breach of statute imposing strict liability on the employer, and that the breach caused the accident, he need do no more. The employer has a good defence if he can prove that it was only the act or default of the claimant himself which caused or contributed to the non-compliance.

In this case, the relevant statutory obligation was imposed on **both** the employer and the employee. It was held that the employers had not proved that they had instructed the claimant, who was inexperienced, on how to comply with the regulations; their breach of statutory duty was a cause of the damage. The claimant's damages were reduced by one-half, as he was also in breach of the statutory duty.

Their Lordships said that if the duty had been imposed solely on the employer the claimant's damages would not have been reduced although performance of the duty was delegated to him, unless the employer proved that he had been contributorily negligent in accordance with the terms of the 1945 Act.

7.5.3 **General observations on defences**

We have seen that there is uncertainty about the application of *volenti* to breach of statutory duty in cases other than those involving employers and employees.

You will also have noticed that the cases discussed in relation to contributory negligence are all employment cases, but the defence applies to the action for breach of statutory duty generally.

It has been suggested that the courts tend to take a more subjective approach to the question of contributory negligence where employees are concerned, and this factor should be taken into account when considering the use of these authorities for purposes of argument by analogy.

 QUESTION 7.11

Review the action for breach of statutory duty. What does the claimant have to establish?

The claimant must prove that:

(a) there was an obligation on the defendant;

(b) the statute intends to allow an action in tort;

(c) he was one of the class of persons protected by the statute;

(d) the harm suffered by him is within the scope of the general class of risks at which the statute is directed;

(e) the defendant has breached the statute;

(f) the breach caused the damage.

The learner must always bear in mind, of course, that all of this relates only to those statutes which do not prima facie confer a civil cause of action in tort for their breach, because they are silent on the point. Statutes such as the Occupiers' Liability Act 1957 exist only to give such an action, while others state expressly that no action in tort is available. See, for example, the Safety of Sports Grounds Act 1975. Some statutes, however, while not created solely for this purpose, do state that an action in tort is available for their breach.

The Consumer Protection Act 1987 provides an example of this type of legislation. Section 41 of that Act provides that breaches of consumer safety regulations (a matter for criminal sanctions) made under Part II of the Act are enforceable by actions in tort for breach of statutory duty. This provision must not be confused with Part I of the Act, which imposes strict liability in tort for defective products and which is discussed in **Chapter 9**.

The Health and Safety at Work Act 1974, is a further example of this more modern approach. This is mainly concerned with the imposition of criminal offences and does not provide for compensation in the civil law.

Section 47 of the 1974 Act provides that a breach of the general duties arising under the Act, which is a criminal offence, is not actionable in civil law. A breach of regulations, made under the Act, will be actionable in tort unless the regulations themselves provide otherwise.

An example of regulations made under the 1974 Act are the Construction (Design and Management) Regulations 1994 (SI 1994/3140), which came into force on 31 March 1995. In s. 22 of the Act, 'Enforcement', it is provided as follows:

> Breach of a duty imposed by those Regulations, other than those imposed by regulation 10 and regulation 16(1)(c), shall not confer a right of action in any civil proceedings. The Act will eventually replace legislation such as the Mines and Quarries Act 1954, the Factories Act 1961, and the Offices, Shops and Railway Premises Act 1963, with an appropriate safety regime. Central to the scheme are the Management of Health and Safety at Work Regulations 1992.

In broad terms, the 1974 Act provides for general duties, laid down in the Act; for regulations, to be made under the Act; and for codes of practice, to be made under the Act.

This statutory scheme is administered by the Health and Safety Executive, and is now substantially complete, having been given fresh impetus in recent years by a spate of European Community Directives.

The House of Lords, in *Fytche* v *Wincanton Logistics Plc* (2004), *The Times*, 2 August, had to consider a claim for breach of Regulation 7 of the Personal Protective Equipment at Work Regulations (SI 1992 No. 2966).

This regulation imposes a duty on an employer to ensure that any protective personal equipment provided to his employees is maintained in an efficient state, is in efficient working order, and in good repair. (Regulation 4(1) imposes an obligation to supply employees who might be exposed to a risk to their health or safety while at work with suitable protective personal equipment.)

The claimant had been provided with steel toecaps on his boots because his employers considered that there was a sufficient risk of heavy objects falling on his feet during the performance of his duties. The boots were not meant to be waterproof or to be used in extreme weather conditions.

In freezing conditions water penetrated into one of the boots through a tiny hole next to one of the claimant's little toes. He suffered frostbite and permanent sensitivity to cold. His claim against his employers alleged negligence in failing to supply him with boots which were adequate to protect his feet in freezing conditions.

The claimant drove a milk tanker and it got stuck on an icy country road in December 1999. The company's standard instructions were for the driver to use the telephone in his cab to call for help and then wait to be rescued. The claimant decided, however, to dig himself out of the ice and snow. It was during this exercise that the boot leaked. The employer said that the claimant's duties did not require him to walk about for long periods in snow and ice and the boots were adequate for his ordinary conditions of work.

The basis of the claimant's argument was that even though the boots complied with Regulation 4 ('suitability'), indeed because of that compliance, they were 'protective personal equipment'; therefore the employer had a duty to maintain them in good repair and a boot which developed a hole, however small, was not in good repair.

Lord Hoffmann, delivering the majority judgment in favour of the employer (there were two dissenting speeches) said 'efficient state, in efficient working order, and in good repair' was not an absolutely concept but had to be construed in relation to what made the equipment 'protective equipment'. What counted as being in an efficient state? Efficient for what purpose? It was for the purpose of protecting against the relevant risk. Under Regulation 7 it was not enough just to provide appropriate protective equipment and then leave the employee to 'his own devices'. The employer had a duty to maintain it so that it continued to be 'suitable protective equipment'. But, said his Lordship, he did not have a duty to do repairs and maintenance which had nothing to do with the protective function; the defect in question, the hole, had no effect on the boots in relation to their function of providing impact protection.

The Court rejected the argument of the claimant that there ought to be a general duty to keep protective equipment in repair in every respect because the employee was obliged by law to wear it. He could not say that he would rather wear better quality boots of his own. As Lord Justice Waller said in the Court of Appeal, the compulsory element was taken into account in the standard of care which the employer has to observe to comply with his duty of care to his employees. But, even taking that into account, the claimant failed to prove a breach of the duty of care.

 EXERCISE 7.6

Consider the decision in *Hewett v Alf Brown's Transport Ltd* [1991] ICR 471. State the result in one paragraph.

In this case the claimant's husband was a lorry driver employed by the defendants and his job entailed contact with lead waste. The claimant always banged his overalls against the garden wall or in the sink before washing them. She also banged or wiped his boots. As a result, 'she either inhaled, or came into contact with, lead oxide powder' and was diagnosed as suffering from lead poisoning. The claimant claimed damages for negligence and breach of statutory duty (Control of Lead at Work Regulations 1980) alleging that she was exposed to lead in relation to the conduct of demolition work. Otton J said that there was a foreseeable risk to families 'from clothing worn by employees exposed to a significant risk of lead poisoning', but that the husband had not been exposed to any risk while removing the waste from the site. Accordingly, the defendants were not in breach of their statutory duty to their employee, the claimant's husband, under the 1980 Regulations. Neither were the defendants in breach of their common law duty of care to their employee. It followed that the defendants could not be liable for the claimant's injury: '. . . even assuming a duty of care to Mrs Hewitt . . . she had failed to establish any negligence. [T]he degree of exposure of her husband was minimal. So, in a sense, it was to her'.

It was found that there existed a foreseeable risk of injury to families of the defendant's employees but, on the facts, the claimant's husband had not actually been exposed to the risk of lead contamination while removing waste from the site. The defendant was not liable for breach of statutory duty to the husband, nor was it liable for breach of its common law duty (see 6.6.4.2) to him. There could be no liability to the claimant because the degree of exposure to contamination of her husband was minimal and not culpable.

7.6 European law

In those instances where European Community law has a direct effect on English (or UK) law, and this applies whether it is a treaty provision or a secondary legislation provision, any claims arising will come within the tort of breach of statutory duty. See, for example, *Garden Cottage Foods Ltd* v *Milk Marketing Board* [1984] AC 130, which involved a breach of what is now Art. 82 of the Treaty of Rome.

7.7 Employment cases

In actions in tort brought by employees against their employers in respect of accidents at work you will often find that actions for breach of statutory duty, vicarious liability, and breach of the employer's duty of care to his employees at common law are brought together. The action for breach of statutory duty and vicarious liability are not limited to claims by employees against their employers.

■ SUMMARY

The action for breach of statutory duty:

- Liability under statute is usually strict; in all cases, the relevant standard is contained within the statute in question.

- The word 'absolute' is often used, in the context of statutory standards. 'Absolute' liability carries the implication that there are no defences available and, in the sense that the word is often used as a synonym for 'strict', confusion may often arise. It is probably better to talk of degrees of strictness, at least as far as the law of tort is concerned.

- The action for breach of statutory duty is of great practical importance in the context of industrial injuries, but it is not confined to such cases; it is of general application. In non-employment cases, an action for common law negligence is often combined with an action for breach of statutory duty.

- The action for breach of statutory, in the sense that we understand it in the present context, must be distinguished from those causes of action in tort which have been specifically created by statute. An obvious example of this latter type of action can be found in the legislation on occupiers' liability.

- This chapter is concerned with statutes which say nothing about any remedy in tort. Indeed, many of these statutes are concerned with the imposition of criminal penalties. The action for breach of statutory duty at common law is therefore implied and its basis and rationale is the subject of much confusion.

• Few examinations in tort require detailed knowledge of particular legislation outside those statutes which regulate tortious activity itself. It is the general principles, such as they are, which are important in respect of any question on the action for breach of statutory duty. Fictitious statutes are often given in such contexts, the idea here being to work out a solution based on first principles.

• If reference is made to real legislation, it is common practice to set out the actual provision(s) which require attention. Again, unless the particular context dictates otherwise, it is a matter of applying principle to the given situation.

■ FURTHER READING

Atiyah, P.S., *Accidents, Compensation and the Law*, 5th edn (Peter Cane), London: Butterworths, 1993.

Buckley, R.A., 'Liability in Tort for Breach of Statutory Duty' (1984) 100 *LQR* 204.

Hepple, Howarth, and Matthews, *Tort: Cases and Materials*, 5th edn, London: Butterworths, 2000, Chapter 12.

Jones, M., *Textbook on Torts*, 8th edn, Oxford: Oxford University Press, 2002, Chapters 5 and 9.

Markesinis, B.S. and Deakin, S.F., *Tort Law*, 5th edn, Oxford: Oxford University Press, 2003, pp. 307–25 and 485–96.

Murphy, J., *Street on Torts*, 11th edn, London: Butterworths, 2003, Chapters 17 and 22.

Salmond and Heuston on the Law of Torts, 21st edn, London: Sweet & Maxwell, 1996, Chapter 10 and pp. 464–74.

Stanton, K.M., *Breach of Statutory Duty in Tort*, London: Sweet & Maxwell, 1986.

Stanton, K. et al, *Statutory Torts*, London: Sweet & Maxwell, 2003.

Weir, T., *Casebook on Tort*, 10th edn, London: Sweet & Maxwell, 2004, Chapter 3 and pp. 117–22.

Winfield and Jolowicz on Tort, 16th edn, London: Sweet & Maxwell, 2002, Chapters 7 and 8.

 CHAPTER 7 ASSESSMENT EXERCISE

Chill Hall is a hall of residence at the University of Radical Thinking. Under the Halls of Residence Act 1995, a fictitious statute, it is provided that all premises coming within the terms of the Act shall be heated from 1 October to 30 April to a temperature of at least 68°F, except between 11.00 p.m. and 6.00 a.m.

During icy winter weather the hall's boiler stops working. The temperature falls gradually during the evening until it is below freezing point. Paul, a student, suffers from frostbite and pneumonia as a result of exposure to the cold. Wally, the University handyman, is called in by the Warden of Chill Hall to attempt to repair the boiler. He is unable to do so and, in an attempt to heat the building, he drags a heavy oil heater out of a storeroom, injuring his back in the process.

Advise Paul and Wally on any rights of action they may have in the law of tort.

See *Cases and Materials* (7.4) for a specimen answer.

8 | Vicarious liability

8.1 OBJECTIVES

By the end of this chapter you should be able to:

1 Define the difference between 'primary liability' and 'vicarious liability'

2 Explain the difference between an 'employee' (or 'servant') and an 'independent contractor'

3 Describe the circumstances in which the torts of an independent contractor may lead to liability on the part of the person who engaged him (his 'employer')

4 Account for the vicarious liability of an employer (or 'master') for the torts of his employee (or 'servant'), committed in the course of the latter's employment

5 Demonstrate awareness of the fact that vicarious liability may apply in situations outside the employer and employee relationship

8.2 Introduction

'Vicarious liability' means liability which falls on one person because of the behaviour of another person, that is, it is not personal, primary liability. It is the liability of someone for the act(s) or omission(s) of someone else. In terms of the law of tort, it means that one person is made to account for the damage caused by another person's tort.

Tort liability is generally primary, that is, defendants are responsible only for damage caused by their own tortious behaviour. However, in some legal relationships where a tort is committed by one party to the relationship, and that act is specifically referable to the relationship, it is possible that the law of tort will impose vicarious liability on another party to the relationship.

There are, as you will find later, many relationships in tort where one party is found liable for the behaviour of another, but that liability is personal liability. For example, in the tort of negligence there may be a breach of a personal duty to control the behaviour of someone else, as in *Home Office* v *Dorset Yacht Co.* [1970] AC 1004 which is discussed in **Chapter 1**. It may also be the case that X employs Y to commit a tort, or authorizes him to do so: again, X's liability is of a personal nature. We are not dealing with personal liability in this chapter; it is our exclusive concern here to explore the principles of vicarious liability.

Often, someone may be vicariously liable, as well as personally liable. This commonly applies in actions by employees against their employers for (i) breach of the employer's personal common law duty to take reasonable care for the safety of his employees which includes an obligation to his employees to engage competent fellow employees; and (ii) vicarious liability for the tort of that incompetent employee. This special, personal duty of the employer is discussed in **Chapter 5**.

The important point to grasp at this stage is that although it might be difficult to separate personal liability from vicarious liability in many factual situations, it is imperative that they are kept distinct. Primary liability is, in the law of tort, largely based on some notion of fault on the part of the actor; vicarious liability is strict liability, that is, it does not rest on the proof of any fault on the part of the person who is found vicariously liable.

Vicarious liability may occur in different tortious contexts, for example in relation to principal and agent, and partnership. We concentrate, however, on only one instance of vicarious liability: the vicarious liability of an employer for his employee (by far the most common instance of this form of liability).

We are concerned only with vicarious liability at common law, and not with any special responsibility which statute may impose on one person for the acts of another. For example, the Town Police Clauses Act 1847 imposes liability on the owners of taxicabs or 'hackney carriages' (not 'minicabs' or private hire cars) for their drivers' torts, although the drivers are not employees of the owners; and business partners are jointly and severally liable for each others' torts committed in the course of the partnership business: ss 10–12 Partnership Act 1890. Under the Police Act 1996, Chief Constables (the Metropolitan Commissioner in London) are responsible for the torts of police officers (who are office holders not employees) committed in the course of their duties, with the police fund meeting the costs and damages.

8.2.1 An employer's vicarious liability for the torts of his employee

This form of liability is based on the satisfaction of the following **three** conditions:

- there must exist a relationship of 'employer' and 'employee' (in older, traditional, language there must be a relationship of 'master' and 'servant') and
- that employee must have committed a tort (for which he is always personally liable) and
- that tort must have been committed 'in the course of the employment' of the employee.

> **?** **QUESTION** 8.1
>
> Can you think of two reasons for employers' vicarious liability?

It is commonly said that the reasons behind the doctrine of vicarious liability are first, that the employer is in a better position to absorb the legal costs either by purchasing insurance or increasing his prices. Secondly, that the imposition of liability should encourage the employer to ensure the highest possible safety standards in running his business. In *Bartonshill Coal Co.* v *McGuire* (1853) 3 Macq 300, Lord Chelmsford LC said: 'every act which is done by a servant in the course of his duty is regarded as done by his master's orders, and consequently is the same as if it were his master's own act'. Indeed, there was a theory that the employer was vicariously liable for any 'act' committed by the employee in the course of his employment. The modern view, however, is that that 'act' must be a tort.

E. McKendrick, *Tort Textbook*, 6th edn (London: HLT Publications, 1992) points out, however, that the doctrine has, on the whole, no clear rationale.

> It is probably true to say that there is no one justification for the imposition of vicarious liability. The best conclusion may be that of Professor Williams when he said in his article Vicarious Liability and the Master's Indemnity ((1957) 20 MLR 220, 232):
>
> . . . that vicarious liability owes its explanation, if not its justification, to the search for a solvent defendant. It is commonly felt that when a person is injured . . . he ought to be able to obtain recompense from someone; and if the immediate tortfeasor cannot afford to pay, then he is justified in looking around for the nearest person of substance who can plausibly be identified with the disaster. Where there is no immediate tortfeasor at all, the same sentiment works itself out through rules of strict liability.
>
> . . . This lack of a coherent rationale for the doctrine does not appear to have troubled the judiciary. Lord Pearce in *Imperial Chemical Industries Ltd* v *Shatwell* [1965] AC 656, 685 said: 'The doctrine of vicarious liability has not grown from any very clear, logical, or legal principle but from social convenience and rough justice'. Despite this apparent lack of concern on the part of the judiciary . . . the issue is an important one and . . . its resolution would help to stabilize the law and give it greater coherence.

? QUESTION 8.2

Are all persons 'employed' by any particular 'employer' of one, homogeneous group?

They are not, and the law draws a distinction, for various purposes, between ordinary 'full-blown' employees ('servants') and 'independent contractors'. The distinction, broadly, is between employed persons who are paid a wage or salary, and self-employed persons working under a contract. It is important to know if someone is an independent contractor for example, for the purposes of taxation, social security, and some statutory duties imposing safety regulations.

You have seen, in **Chapter 5**, that employers owe a special duty of care to their employees, but not to their independent contractors.

8.2.1.1 Independent contractors and employees

Employers of independent contractors are not generally liable for their contractors' torts, whereas employers are generally vicariously liable for their employees' torts.

Employers are under a personal common law obligation, in the tort of negligence, to take reasonable care in the selection of contractors; the contractors must be reasonably competent.

In *Payline* v *Naylor* [2004] EWCA Civ 560 (CA), it was held that while there was a duty on a night club to see that an independent contractor engaged to provide security services was competent, only exceptionally would there be a duty imposed on the owner to ensure that the contractor possessed public liability insurance cover.

Neuberger LJ said an employer of an independent contractor might owe a duty to check the latter's insurance credentials where, for example, the employer was himself under a duty to insure; or where he accepted special responsibility to insure himself for the protection of the public, as in *Gwilliam* v *West Hertfordshire NHS Trust* [2003] QB 443.

The court expressed the view that where a scheme was operated by a local authority, and a local police authority, for licensing persons to perform security work, it would require special circumstances to find an employer negligent in selecting a licensed person to carry out this task where he was satisfied that the contractor and employees were properly accredited.

The case law has also generated a number of special situations in which employers might be liable where their independent contractors commit torts, although it an arguable point whether these are instances of employers being liable for their contractors' torts. It is more likely that both parties are personally liable, as joint tortfeasors: see *Winfield* (p. 615).

These special situations are as follows:

• where the contract is to perform an illegal act like a nuisance and the employer in effect authorizes or ratifies the act

• where the employer 'takes over', and directs, the work of the independent contractor.

In *Winfield*'s words, however (p. 615): 'The true question in every case in which an employer is sued for damage caused by his independent contractor is whether the employer himself was in breach of some duty which he himself owed to the claimant.'

This is also the explanation for the so-called 'non-delegable duty', which an employer may owe to a claimant injured solely by the wrong of an independent contractor. There is no exhaustive list of such duties; all that can be said in general terms is that where common law or statute imposes some special onerous duty to achieve a particular result or to see that all care is taken (rather than to take reasonable care) it may be classed as of a non-delegable kind, and it will be no excuse for the person upon whom it has been placed to plead simply that he took all reasonable care by entrusting its performance to a competent independent contractor. He will, in effect, be expected to ensure that the result is achieved, or that all care has been taken, without the commission of a tort by the person to whom the performance of the obligation has been delegated.

Where the contractor tortiously injures the claimant in performing the obligation, not only will the contractor be personally liable, say for negligence, but his employer will remain also personally liable.

Other examples of this non-delegable duty are:

(a) where the employer is under a common law obligation involving strict liability. You can read about strict liability at common law, including liability arising under the rule in *Rylands* v *Fletcher* (1868) LR 3 HL 330 in **Chapter 10**;

(b) where the employer is under a statutory obligation involving strict liability, for example industrial legislation. You can read about this legislation in **Chapter 7**;

(c) where the work entrusted to the contractor inherently contains the risk of the contractor committing a public or private nuisance. You can read about the law of nuisance in **Chapter 10**;

(d) the special common law duty owed by an employer to his employees;

(e) where the contractor has been employed to carry out a task which is 'extra hazardous'. *Alcock* v *Wraith* [1991] *The Times* LR 600 (CA) involved such a task.

The claimant was the neighbour of the Swinhoes, in terraced houses, and the Swinhoes had employed Wraith, subsequently declared bankrupt, to carry out roofing work on their house. The Swinhoes had concrete interlocking roof tiles installed to replace slates. Before this work was carried out, each house in the terrace was roofed with slates extending as a continuous roof, uninterrupted by the party walls between neighbouring properties. The interlocking tiles had encroached onto the claimant's premises, and newspaper, which had been stuffed in the joint between the new tiles and his slates, had become saturated allowing damp to penetrate into the upper floors of his house.

At first instance the Swinhoes were found liable to the claimant in trespass, nuisance, and negligence, and their appeal against this judgment was dismissed. According to Neill LJ:

> Mr and Mrs Swinhoe had the right to interfere with the joint between the two roofs but if they exercised that right, they were under a duty to see that reasonable skill and care was used in the operation. That duty could not be delegated to an independent contractor.

The Court applied the decision in *Honeywill and Stein Ltd* v *Larkin Bros Ltd* [1934] 1 KB 191.

The Court of Appeal, in *Rowe* v *Herman* (1997), *The Times*, 9 June, followed *Salsbury* v *Woodland* [1969] 3 All ER 863. Occupiers of land engaged independent contractors who, after leaving the site, left some metal plates on the public footpath adjacent to the land. The claimant tripped over these plates and was injured. It was held that the principle that an employer is not liable for the negligence of an independent contractor is subject to two exceptions: (i) where the work involves extra-hazardous activities and (ii) where danger is created by work on the highway. Since neither exception applied on the facts, the defendant occupiers were not liable. They were not to be treated as if they were occupiers of the highway.

The performance of a duty of care in negligence, owed by the employer, can be delegated, and it may be a defence for the employer to plead that he has taken all reasonable care in the circumstances to employ a competent contractor to do the work. You will find an example of such a delegable duty in the occupiers' duty, arising under the Occupiers' Liability Act 1957, in **Chapter 6**.

? **QUESTION** 8.3

What is the legal meaning of 'delegable' and 'non-delegable' duties?

In strict legal terms, if a duty is 'non-delegable', it cannot be delegated to another person. A distinction is drawn in the law, however, between legal responsibility for the performance of such a duty and delegation in practical terms. It is evidently the case that some tasks require expertise not possessed by the employer, so a contractor must be called in to do the job. Indeed, unless this is done the employer will not, in such cases, be able to perform the obligation imposed on him by law.

The fact, however, that performance is delegated in these cases does not relieve the employer from legal responsibility if the contractor commits a tort while he is undertaking the work in question.

There is no closed list of non-delegable duties; new duties are being developed all the time.

In *Rogers* v *Nightriders* [1983] RTR 324, the defendant ran minicabs and contracted to hire one to the claimant, using an independent contractor to drive the vehicle. At first instance, the defendant was found not liable on the ground that an employer of a contractor was not vicariously liable for the torts of that contractor. The Court of Appeal, however, held that since the defendant had contracted with the claimant to provide a vehicle, and injury to the claimant was foreseeable if the vehicle was defective, the defendant owed a personal, non-delegable duty of care to the claimant to see that the vehicle was in a reasonable state of repair. It was a legal obligation which could not be delegated to a contractor, though its performance could be. If, however, the contractor neglected to fulfil his part of the bargain, the employer remained personally liable where that negligence caused injury to a third party. The contractor in such a case will, of course, also be liable to the injured claimant in negligence.

We now have to consider how the law distinguishes between 'independent contractors' and 'employees' (or 'servants'); the employer is only vicariously liable for the tortious behaviour of the latter.

8.2.1.2 Who is an employee (or servant)?

It is very important to be able to identify an employee, but you may be surprised to learn that the law is rather uncertain on the definition of 'employee' (or 'servant').

An independent contractor is said to have a contract for his **services** with his employer, while an employee (or servant) works under a contract of **service**. A convenient starting point for our inquiry is the terms of the contract between the parties: how does the contract classify the person in question—as an employee or as an independent contractor?

The terms of the contract are not conclusive where liability to third parties is concerned and, in any case, the contract may be silent or ambiguous on the matter. As we will see, the court considers all the facts of the case before it, and does not necessarily regard any one factor as conclusive.

In *WHPT Housing Association Ltd* v *Secretary of State for Social Services* [1981] ICR 737, Webster J said:

> . . . the difference between a contract of service [employee] and one for services [independent contractor] must reside, essentially, in the terms of the principal obligation agreed to be undertaken by the employee—a word which I use without begging the question. In a contract of service, it seems to me, the principal obligation . . . is to provide himself to serve: whereas in a contract for services the principal obligation . . . [is to provide] his services for the use of the employer.

Cases are drawn not just from the context of general vicarious liability; some of the authorities are concerned with matters of social security, taxation, and employment legislation. The policy factors underlying decisions from different contexts are **not**, however, identical and you should always bear this factor in mind; but all the decisions can at least be used for the purpose of constructing an argument by way of analogy.

In *Airfix Footwear Ltd* v *Cope* [1978] ICR 1210, for example, a worker who was classified as self-employed by the Inland Revenue was nevertheless found to be an employee for the purposes of employment protection legislation. Again, in *O'Kelly* v *Trusthouse Forte plc* [1983] ICR 728, bar staff, who were called 'regular' casual workers, and who worked only when called in to work as required by their employers, were held not to be employees for purposes of claiming unfair dismissal. The workers could refuse any work that was offered to them, and the Court of Appeal emphasized the lack of mutuality of obligation in the relationship.

The classification of a worker, i.e. the label that is attached to him, in cases of doubt must depend on the legal issue before the court. As McKendrick puts it in 53 *MLR* 770 ('Vicarious Liability and Independent Contractors—A Re-Examination'):

> the test for the existence of an employment relationship should depend upon the legal question which is being asked and on the fact that there is nothing irrational in classifying a worker as an employee for the purposes of vicarious liability but not for the purposes of employment law, social security law and taxation.

8.2.1.3 **The tests**

No single test for determining this issue is available, but tests have been formulated in the cases. The oldest of these is the 'control' test.

As *Salmond, The Law of Torts* (21st edn), puts it at p. 449:

> The test [for determining who is an employee] is the existence of a right of control over the agent in respect of the manner in which his work is to be done. A servant is an agent who works under the supervision and direction of his employer; an independent contractor is one who is his own master. A servant is a person engaged to obey his employer's orders from time to time; an independent contractor is a person engaged to do certain work, but to exercise his own discretion as to the mode and time of doing it—he is bound by his contract, but not by his employer's orders.

In *Honeywill & Stein Ltd* v *Larkin Bros Ltd* [1934] 1 KB 1991, for example, it was held that a person is a servant where the employer retains the control of the actual performance of the work.

The weakness of this traditional approach is that in the case of modern, highly specialized tasks it is difficult for the employer to exercise control over the method of doing the work, for example, in the case of lawyers and surgeons. (Since 1991, National Health Service (NHS) hospital authorities have funded the defence of medical negligence cases through the system of Crown Indemnity and hospital doctors are no longer contractually bound to insure themselves against claims in negligence. Previously, when a health authority was found vicariously liable for a doctor's negligence it would seek an indemnity from him or her via this insurance.)

In *Watkins* v *Birmingham City Council* (1976) 126 NLJ 442, a schoolboy, aged 10, was given the task of taking milk round his school by his teacher. He left his cycle outside a classroom door, and a teacher fell over it and was injured. It was held by the Court of Appeal that the boy was not an employee of the education authority, because it was part of his education to do the job. It was also decided that he was not an agent of the defendant authority.

In *Stevenson Jordan and Harrison Ltd* v *Macdonald and Evans* [1952] 1 TLR 101, Denning LJ suggested the 'organization or integration test':

> under a contract of service a man is employed as part of the business, and his work is done as an integral part of the business; whereas under a contract for services, his work, although done for the business, is not integrated into it but is only accessory to it.

On this reasoning a chauffeur would be an employee, whereas a taxi driver would be an independent contractor. This test has been little used as a discrete formula; it is regarded by *Street on Torts* (9th edn) at pp. 486–7 as just another, wider, way of looking at 'control'.

The same can be said for the 'economic reality' test suggested by MacKenna J in *Ready Mixed Concrete (South East) Ltd* v *Minister of Pensions and National Insurance* [1965] 2 QB 497. This would take into account such factors as the method and frequency of payment, and the power of selection, suspension, and dismissal, and the intention of the parties.

? **QUESTION** 8.4

Think of three other factors that might have to be considered by a court in the present context.

You might have included in your list: holiday entitlement; pension rights; whose tools, equipment, and premises are to be used? It is still probably the case that 'control' is the main criterion considered by the courts. *Salmond* says (at p. 449) that the right to control is 'a necessary, but not a sufficient, mark of a contract of service'. It is not, however, as we have seen, the only criterion.

You should read about the decisions in the following cases:

1 *Sime* v *Sutcliffe Catering (Scotland) Ltd* [1990] IRLR 228, a Scottish case, which of course is of persuasive authority only in this country, in which 'control' was the determining factor.

2 *Lane* v *Shire Roofing Co. (Oxford) Ltd* (1995) *The Times*, 17 February, in which 'control' was considered as only one of the factors to be taken into account in deciding whether the claimant was an employee, for purposes of health and safety at work. [In *Cases and Materials* (8.1.1.1).]

8.2.1.4 **Borrowed employees**

This issue raises the problem of who employs the loaned person.

On the authority of *Mersey Docks and Harbour Board* v *Coggins and Griffiths (Liverpool) Ltd* [1946] 2 All ER 345, where an employer lends an employee to someone else, the 'lender' will usually still be responsible for the torts of that employee. In this case the Board hired out a crane and its skilled operator to Coggins. Although the power of dismissal remained with the Board, the contract provided that the operator was to be the servant of the hirers. The operator was negligent in handling the crane while under the immediate control of Coggins in unloading a ship, although the hirers could not instruct him in the working of the machine, and the court had to decide who would be vicariously liable.

The House of Lords held that the Board still had ultimate control over the operator and the crane and were therefore vicariously liable. Their Lordships emphasized that there was a heavy burden of proof on the lending employer if he wished to establish that the hirer should be vicariously liable in such circumstances.

In fact, there is a rebuttable presumption in such a case that the employee is still in the employment of the lender, and the lender will only shift the presumption in exceptional circumstances.

It seems that the lender in *Mersey Docks* was still in sufficient possession and control of the machinery and operator to be vicariously liable, so the lender must show that he no longer has sufficient control in this sense.

Again, each case must turn on its own facts, and the familiar questions of power of dismissal etc., will no doubt be raised. It may be easier to show complete transfer of control where a contract, or agreement, provides for the loan of 'labour only', particularly in the case of unskilled labour. In such a case, there will be no equipment to operate, so the borrower may have more control over how the work is actually done. Even where equipment is involved, it may make a difference that the machinery is of a simple nature, such as an ordinary motor van: see *Winfield* at p. 599 and Jones, *Textbook on Torts* (4th edn.) at p. 274.

In *Sime* (above) a borrower of labour only was found vicariously liable on the basis of 'control'.

You may be interested to learn that many 'lenders' in these situations put a clause into the contract of loan, providing that the 'borrower' is to indemnify the 'lender', where the lender pays damages for the loaned employee's tort.

One further point to note: the borrower can, in any event be liable vicariously, as principal for his agent's wrongs, with regard to a tort committed by the loaned employee while carrying out a specific instruction issued by the borrower; see Jones at p. 274.

If the lender passes on defective equipment or an incompetent operator, he will be in breach of his personal, primary duty in such matters, where damage is caused thereby: *McConkey* v *Amec plc* (1990) 27 Construction LR 88. We should always remember to distinguish carefully between a person's primary liability and their vicarious liability. In one of the 'hospital cases', *Cassidy* v *Ministry of Health* [1951] 2 KB 343, Denning LJ suggested that the hospital authorities could be liable personally to an injured patient for their own negligence in providing adequate hospital facilities, as an alternative to being liable vicariously for the negligence of, say, an employed doctor or nurse.

Support for this view can be found in the judgments of Browne-Wilkinson V-C in the Court of Appeal in *Wilsher* v *Essex Area Health Authority* [1986] 3 All ER 801, and of Slade LJ in *Bull* v *Devon Area Health Authority* [1993] 4 Med LR 117 (CA). In *Bull*, Slade LJ said that the Authority owed a personal duty of care to their patients. On the facts, this was a duty to provide for the safe delivery of a baby and for the health of both mother and baby.

In some cases, of course, a claimant may have a contractual relationship with the doctor who is treating his private patient on the hospital premises; or there may be a contract with both hospital and doctor. The tortious duty owed by a hospital would seem to be of the non-delegable kind, therefore the hospital would not escape liability by merely employing a doctor or nurse, for example, who were independent contractors: *Street* (pp. 493–4).

A further illustration of the distinction between primary and vicarious liability can be found in *Nahhas* v *Pier House (Cheyne Walk) Management* (1984) 270 EG 329. The landlords of a block of flats operated a system whereby absent tenants left their keys with a porter, who was employed by the landlord. During a stay in hospital the claimant duly left his key with the porter, who used it to gain entry to the claimant's flat and steal some jewellery. The landlords, the defendants, were not aware that the porter had a lengthy criminal record. It was held that the defendants were liable (a) personally, in the tort of negligence, because they should have checked thoroughly the porter's background (the deposit of keys was not a negligent system); and (b) vicariously for the act of the porter in the course of his employment.

The Court of Appeal, in *A* v *Ministry of Defence and Another* (2004), *The Times*, 17 May, had to consider the case of a child of a serving soldier stationed in Germany who had suffered brain damage at birth because of the negligence of a German doctor at a German hospital. The defendant, the Ministry of Defence, had arranged, under a contract with an English NHS trust, for hospital treatment to be provided for the dependants of service personnel in a German hospital rather than itself providing the treatment directly.

It was held that there was no justification in imposing upon the Ministry a duty of care to see that the German hospital exercised appropriate care and skill.

Lord Phillips MR, delivering the judgment of the court, said the claimant was arguing that the court should extend the boundaries of the law concerning non-delegable duties. Hitherto, in English and Australian law, a non-delegable duty had only been imposed 'where the claimant suffered an injury while in an environment over which the defendant was in control'. The claimant was inviting the court to expand this area of tortious liability on policy grounds. His Lordship said that Germany was the appropriate forum and the German hospital the appropriate defendant in the present circumstances because the Ministry had, from 1996, decided that it would no longer directly provide secondary health care in Germany. It had a contractual relationship with an English NHS trust under which that trust provided for secondary health care in Germany. The Ministry had 'no direct contractual nexus with the German providers'.

Reference was made to the 'organizational duty' (see, for example, *Cassidy*) owed by hospitals to use reasonable care to see that the staff, facilities, and organization were appropriate to provide a safe and satisfactory medical service for the patient. It was accepted by the claimant, however, that there was no question of any breach of this duty in the present case.

? **QUESTION** 8.5

List the other conditions required to establish liability on the part of an employer for his employee.

The remaining conditions are the commission of a tort by the employee; and proof that this tort was committed in the course of the employee's employment.

Proving that an employee has committed a tort is no different from establishing proof in any other case, so we do not have to consider this point any further. We do, however, have to examine the issue of whether the tort was committed in the course of the employee's employment.

In *Crédit Lyonnais Bank Nederland NV* v *Export Credit Guarantee Department* [1999] 2 WLR 540 [HL], the tort in question was deceit: the employee had committed some of the constituent elements of the tort within the course of his employment and the remainder outside the ambit of his duties. It was held that an employee can only be held vicariously liable for the fraud of an employee if **all** the elements of the tort have occurred within the course of his employment.

8.2.2 Course of employment

The claimant must establish that the employee was acting in the course of his employment at the time of the accident.

This is often difficult to resolve in practice because the issue is essentially one of fact in each case. Although the decided cases are useful for purposes of analogy and illustration, they must be treated with caution, and not regarded as binding authority other than in relation to the particular issue(s) before the court.

Most of the cases cannot be reconciled with each other. The decisions often turn on fine distinctions, and are influenced by policy factors.

Smith offers some general guidance on this issue.

***Smith* v *Stages* [1989] 1 All ER 833 (HL)**

X was employed by the defendant (appellant) to install insulation in power stations. Together with the claimant, a colleague, X was on an urgent job in Wales. The claimant and X were paid for eight hours' travelling time from the Midlands to Wales and the same amount of time for the return journey. They were also paid the appropriate rail fare.

X used his car for the trip and on the way back the claimant was badly injured in an accident caused by X's negligence. The claimant sued X, who was uninsured, and the defendant, alleging vicarious liability on their part for X's negligence committed in the course of his employment.

At first instance the judge found for the defendant on the ground that X was not acting in the course of his employment at the time of the accident.

The Court of Appeal, however, found for the claimant on the issue of vicarious liability and the House of Lords confirmed this decision unanimously.

Read the extracts from the speeches in this case in *Cases and Materials* (8.1.2).

Course of employment is very much an issue in which the facts are paramount. As *Winfield* (p. 601) puts it: '. . . it contains no criteria to decide when or why an act is within or outside the scope of employment and no single test is appropriate to cover all cases'.

It is evident that the courts in general take a broad view of what is and is not within the course of a particular employee's employment. We have seen that the cases have laid down some very general lines of guidance, but these provide only a sense of direction; they do not give us any firm guidance on the solution that the court is likely to arrive at in any given case.

8.2.2.1 **Authorized acts**

The courts have evolved a general rule that if an employee is performing an act that he is not expressly or impliedly authorized to perform, he will not be acting in the course of his employment, and the employer is not liable. If, he is still doing his job, but performs it in an unauthorized manner, this factor alone will not take him outside the course of his employment.

The actual terms of employment must always be considered, but they are not binding on third parties, and are not necessarily conclusive of the issue.

In *Limpus* v *London General Omnibus Co.* [1862] 1 H & C 526, a bus driver, employed by the defendant, injured the claimant when he negligently drew his bus across the road, contrary to orders, to obstruct a rival driver. The defendant was found vicariously liable for the driver's negligence, which was committed within the course of his employment because he was doing his job at the time, albeit in an unauthorized way.

Again, in *Century Insurance Co. Ltd* v *Northern Ireland Road Transport Board* [1942] AC 509, the driver of a petrol tanker, while transferring petrol from the vehicle to the tank at the garage, struck a match to light a cigarette, causing an explosion and subsequent fire. His employers were found vicariously liable because the driver was doing what he was authorized to do, in an unauthorized way, i.e. delivering petrol while smoking.

In *Harrison* v *Michelin Tyre Co. Ltd* [1985] 1 All ER 918, employers were held liable when their employee, as a joke, deliberately steered his vehicle at the claimant, who was at his place of work in a factory at the time. The claimant was injured as a result of this tomfoolery. The truck was driven a few centimetres from an officially designated passageway in the factory to 'catch' the claimant, but the act was found to be within the prankster's course of employment, because he was still driving at the relevant time, although he was momentarily motivated by the 'joke'. In *Beard* v *London General Omnibus Co.* [1900] 2 QB 530, the employer was not vicariously liable when the conductor, instead of the driver, turned the bus round at the terminus, injuring the claimant. This decision was followed by the Court of Appeal in *Iqbal* v *London Transport Executive* [1973] KIR 329, on very similar facts.

8.2.2.2 Spatial factors

The question of authorized limits of time and place have often to be considered in the present context. As a general proposition, if the employee can still be said to be substantially pursuing his employment he will be regarded as acting in the course of his employment during, or within a reasonable time outside, his normal working hours.

In *Ruddiman & Co.* v *Smith* (1889) 60 LT 708, a clerk was held to be still within the course of his employment when, shortly after finishing work, he used the company washroom and left a tap running, with the result that the claimant's premises were flooded.

In some cases, drivers of vehicles have deviated from their 'official' routes. The courts have taken a 'common sense' approach to this problem, looking at the degree of the detour or deviation in each case.

In *Whatman* v *Pearson* [1868] LR 3 CP 422, an employee, in charge of a horse and cart drove a quarter of a mile out of his way, without permission, to have lunch at home. The horse, left to its own devices outside the employee's house during the lunch break, bolted and injured the claimant. It was held that this incident occurred during the employee's course of employment.

In *Hilton* v *Burton (Rhodes) Ltd* [1961] 1 WLR 705, four workmen, permitted by their employer, the defendant, to use the defendant's van to travel to work to a demolition site, decided to stop work and drive to a café. While on this 'frolic', one of them drove negligently, injuring another, who failed to win damages from the defendant because there was no vicarious liability on his part; the negligent employee was acting outside the course of his employment at the time of the accident.

This colourful expression ('frolic of his own') first appeared in an early nineteenth-century case, and is nothing more than a **label** used to describe behaviour that falls outside the course of employment.

Decisions in this field turn often on fine distinctions. In *Storey* v *Ashton* [1869] LR 4 QB 476, the employee delivered wine. After making a delivery, he was returning to his employer's premises with some empty flagons, when he made a detour to collect the belongings of a fellow employee, who was with him on the job, and take them elsewhere. His negligent handling of his horse and cart during this unofficial journey (no purpose of his employers was being furthered by it) resulted in injuries to the claimant. On the facts, his employers were found not to be vicariously liable for his negligence because the detour was too substantial to be within the course of his employment.

In broad terms, the determination of the issue must depend on whether or not it can be said that the employee was still engaged substantially enough on what he was expressly or impliedly employed to do.

In *Harvey* v *O'Dell* [1958] 1 All ER 657, the employee who had agreed to put his motor-cycle and sidecar into the service of his employer, was driving from a place he had been sent to by his employer, to perform a task, to a café some miles away for a meal, when he caused an accident due to his negligent driving. The claimant was injured in this accident. The employee's temporary workplace did not have a canteen, and his journey in search of food was found to be within the course of his employment. *Jones* says (p. 277): 'Mealbreaks seem to produce particular problems'. Much seems to depend on what is authorized, and what can be impliedly authorized.

In line with the general position concerning travelling to and from work, there being a duty upon the employee to get to work which is independent of his course of employment, authorized meal breaks themselves may be outside the course of employment on the authority of *Crook* v *Derbyshire Stone Ltd* [1956] 1 WLR 432. Presumably, the same must be true of implied meal breaks. It could be said that the employee in *Harvey* was on his way to a meal break, and not actually engaged in the meal break itself at the time of the accident. No doubt, the same reasoning could be true of other types of rest breaks.

The courts usually take as broad a view as possible of this matter, and if some benefit or advantage to the employer can be found in any of these situations, it may be enough to bring the event into the employee's course of employment.

In *A & W Hemphill Ltd* v *Williams* [1966] 2 Lloyd's Rep 101 (HL), the claimant was a member of the Boy's Brigade which had been camping in Argyllshire. At the conclusion of the camp the boys were to be taken back to Glasgow in the defendant's coach. The boys persuaded the defendants' driver to leave the more direct route and drive through Stirling, though the driver had been refused permission to do this. Later, the driver was persuaded to make another detour and on the way an accident occurred due to the negligence of the driver, and the claimant was injured.

The House of Lords held that the defendants were liable because the driver remained in the course of his employment as he was primarily employed to drive the boys to Glasgow, and this he was still doing at the time of the accident.

Taking an unauthorized 'route' on an authorized journey is within the employment, but an unauthorized journey takes the employee outside his employment. This suggests that the journey, rather than the route, which is merely a means to an end, must be completely independent of the job if it is to be outside the course of employment. The objective of the employee in pursuing the journey is going to be an important factor in determining whether the employee is still acting within the course of his employment.

Performance of his fundamental obligation under his contract of employment was again the employee's main objective in *Kay* v *ITW Ltd* [1967] 3 All ER 22. An employee employed by the defendants to drive a fork-lift truck, was unable to get into the warehouse which was obstructed by a lorry. The driver of the lorry could easily have been asked to move it, but the employee got into the lorry to move it himself. In doing so he negligently injured the claimant. The act was foolhardy and unnecessary but it was still held to be within the course of the employee's employment, as it was his job to move certain obstacles, for example a packing case obstructing the path of his fork-lift truck. To do what he did, therefore, was a wrong mode of doing what he was employed to do, rather than something which he was not employed to do.

8.2.2.3 Expressly forbidden acts

It is a question of fact in each case whether the prohibition relates to the scope of his employment, or the method of performance. In *Limpus* v *London General Omnibus Co.* [1862] 1 H & C 526, a bus driver, contrary to express instructions, raced a rival bus to collect passengers at a bus stop. This was held to be within the course of his employment because he was simply doing what he was authorized to do, but in a wrongful and unauthorized manner.

Similarly, in *LCC* v *Cattermoles (Garages) Ltd* [1953] 2 All ER 582, a garage assistant was employed to move vehicles inside a garage by pushing them; he was forbidden to drive the vehicles. His employer was found vicariously liable when he drove a van on to the nearby road to make a space in the garage, and damaged the claimant's vehicle on the road.

In *Twine* v *Bean's Express Ltd* (1946) 175 LT 131, the driver of a vehicle, contrary to express orders from his employer, gave the claimant a lift and, due to the driver's negligence in relation to his driving, the passenger was injured. Not only was the claimant passenger a person who fell outside the group of persons that the driver had been told he was authorized to carry, there was also a notice in the cab of the vehicle which limited the people who could travel in the vehicle. The Court of Appeal held that this prohibition limited the very scope of the employee's employment, not just the way of performing his job so the defendant employer was not vicariously liable for the driver's negligence.

It was also suggested that the passenger was a 'trespasser' on the vehicle, in relation to the defendant as 'occupier' of it, therefore no liability arose on the part of the defendant. This decision was followed by the Court of Appeal in *Conway* v *George Wimpey and Co. Ltd* [1951] 2 KB 266, on the same grounds.

The 'trespasser approach', however, is not now favoured; it was said in *Rose* v *Plenty* (below) that there was little point today in taking this approach, since an occupier's duty to his trespassers is of a substantial nature. You can read about this 'occupier's duty' in 6.6.

In any event, as Denning LJ pointed out in *Young* v *Edward Box and Co. Ltd* [1951] 1 TLR 789, a passenger's injury in such a case arises not because of the state of the vehicle, but because of the driver's negligence in handling his vehicle in the course of his employment, therefore the ordinary rules of negligence would apply. It might be otherwise if the injury was caused by a defective vehicle.

Young v *Edward Box* suggests that where the claimant passenger is also an employee of the defendant employer he may have a better chance of success when the question of authorization for the lift falls for determination. In the event of an express order from the employer against the giving of lifts being effective in limiting the actual scope of the employee's course of employment, i.e. not merely determining the mode of performance, a superior servant, such as a supervisor, may have sufficient 'ostensible', i.e. apparent, authority to sanction the otherwise unauthorized lift, so making the employer vicariously liable for the driver's negligence.

In *Rose* v *Plenty* [1976] 1 WLR 141, the employee was a milk roundsman employed by the defendant. Despite a prohibition against such conduct, the employee engaged the claimant, a boy aged 13, to help with the round. The claimant fell off the milk float while assisting the employee, and was injured by the employee's negligent driving. It was held, by a majority decision, that the defendant was vicariously liable, subject to a reduction of 25% for the claimant's contributory negligence.

Lord Denning MR said the boy had benefited the defendant by helping with the milk round, whereas Scarman LJ, while assenting to the idea of 'benefit' to the employer, generally contented himself with the argument that the court should take a broad approach to the definition of course of employment. The prohibition limited only the **way** in which the employee did his job, it did not affect the course of his employment.

In an earlier case, *Ilkiw* v *Samuels* [1963] 2 All ER 879 (CA), a lorry driver, employed by the defendants, was loading up on a third party's premises and allowed an employee of that third party to assist him in his work by driving the vehicle. The lorry driver's employers, the defendants, had given him strict instructions not to allow anyone else to drive the lorry. The lorry driver knew nothing about his 'assistant's' driving ability; in fact, the latter had never driven a lorry before that occasion and did not possess a driving licence. The claimant was injured as a result of the 'assistant's' incompetent handling of the vehicle.

At first instance the defendants were found liable for the negligence of their lorry driver in allowing this person to drive his vehicle, and the Court of Appeal affirmed this decision. It was found that the lorry driver was negligent either:

• in allowing the person to drive without first checking his ability to handle the vehicle;

or

• because the lorry was driven negligently while it was in his control;

and in either case

• that this negligence arose in the course of his employment.

His employer's prohibition against unauthorized persons driving the vehicle affected only the mode of doing his job. Thus, his disobedience did not take his behaviour outside the course of his employment.

In **Chapter 6** we discussed *Stone* v *Taffe* [1974] 3 All ER 1016, which is concerned principally with the question of 'occupiers' liability'; but an argument on vicarious liability is also involved in the decision. The licensee of the pub, its manager, who was an employee of the owners of the pub, had been told quite clearly not to entertain customers after drinking hours. He ignored this instruction and, in so doing, was acting illegally when he continued his nocturnal activities. Due to this disobedient employee's negligence in failing to light some steps, the claimant (a visitor to the premises) fell to his death one night after leaving one of the illicit drinking sessions. (The action in tort for damages was brought by representatives of the deceased's estate.)

It was held by the court that the employers' prohibition did not in the circumstances limit the scope of the employee's employment; it only limited the mode of performance of his work, and the employers were vicariously liable for the death. The court took into account the following factors:

(a) the claimant was not aware of the employer's order;

(b) the claimant could not have avoided the danger created by the employee (although his damages were reduced by 50% for contributory negligence: see **Chapter 14**));

(c) there was no evidence that the claimant was likely to have known of the order.

Under the Road Traffic Act 1988, insurance for passengers in vehicles used on the public highway is compulsory, and the question of whether an 'unauthorized' passenger can claim against the insurance policy of the owner of a vehicle, where the passenger is injured as the result of the negligent driving of an employee of that owner, will depend on the determination of the 'course of employment' issue. This is a matter separate from that of the effect of s. 149 of the 1988 Act on the defence of *volenti non fit injuria*. You will find this issue discussed in **Chapter 14**.

The drivers in these cases are always personally liable to their passengers, and the fact that the 'lift' falls outside the course of employment does not necessarily affect any vicarious liability to other claimants, for example pedestrians, i.e. the driver can still be acting within the course of his employment to some claimants, though he is acting outside his employment regarding the passenger.

8.2.2.4 Connection with employer's business

Winfield (p. 608) says that an act may come within the 'course of employment if it is necessarily incidental to something which the servant is employed to do'.

In *Elleanor* v *Cavendish Woodhouse* [1973] 1 Lloyd's Rep 313, it was in the employer's interest, and ancillary, though not central, to the employee's employment, that he should give a lift home to the claimant, who was a fellow employee. Due to the driver's negligence the claimant was injured; it was held that the driver was acting in the course of his employment while giving the lift.

However, in *R* v *National Insurance Commissioner, ex parte Michael* [1977] 1 WLR 109, a policeman who was injured while playing football for his force could not claim industrial injury benefit under s. 5(1) of the National Insurance (Industrial Injuries) Act 1965, which provided that such benefit could only be claimed for injuries suffered in an 'accident arising out of and in the course of employment'.

In *Racz* v *Home Office* [1994] 1 All ER 97, the House of Lords held that the Home Office could be vicariously liable for the (alleged) deliberate mistreatment of a prisoner by prison officers. The issue before the House was an argument on the pleadings, i.e. whether the claimant's statement of claim disclosed an arguable legal point for resolution by the court. Their Lordships decided that the alleged mistreatment of the claimant by the officers, the result of the commission of the tort of misfeasance in public office, could be an unauthorized mode of performing their authorized duties, provided there was a sufficient nexus between the unauthorized acts and the officers' official duties. This was a matter which could only be resolved by hearing the evidence at a trial, therefore the House remitted the case back to the court of first instance for determination. (The tort of misfeasance in public office is committed where a public official in effect abuses his official position, by maliciously misusing his office in such a way as to cause loss to the claimant.)

In *Costello* v *Chief Constable of the Northumbria Police* [1999] 1 All ER 550 (CA), the claimant, a police officer, was injured by a prisoner at the police station. It was found that a senior colleague, who was standing nearby at the time and, who, in breach of his common law duty of care failed to help the claimant when she was attacked, was acting in the course of his employment at the time and vicarious liability applied.

Much depends on the nature of the tort which the employee has committed. In the case of intentional, deliberate wrongs, rather than casual acts of negligence, it may be more difficult to satisfy the requirement of 'course of employment'.

Warren v *Henlys Ltd* [1948] 2 All ER 935, was concerned with an attendant at a petrol station who thought that the claimant was trying to avoid paying for his petrol; after an argument, the attendant punched the claimant. The employee was held to be acting outside the course of his employment at the time.

Again, in *Daniels* v *Whetstone Entertainments Ltd* [1962] 2 Lloyd's Rep 1, a doorman at a dance hall assaulted the claimant whilst evicting him from the premises. This was outside the doorman's course of employment, because it was said to be an act of personal revenge.

An employee in *Irving* v *The Post Office* [1987] IRLR 289 (CA), who was authorized to write on letters for the purpose of ensuring that the mail was properly despatched, wrote racial abuse on a letter addressed to the claimants, his neighbours, with whom he was not on speaking terms. It was held that writing the abuse was not an authorized act, therefore the employee was not acting in the course of his employment at the time he uttered the abuse, and his employer was therefore not vicariously liable for his actions.

Firemen in *General Engineering Services Ltd* v *Kingston and St Andrew Corporation* [1988] 3 All ER 867 (PC), were involved in a 'work to rule' in support of a pay claim. They took 17 minutes rather than the usual three-and-a-half minutes to reach a fire at the claimant's premises which were destroyed as a result of the delay. If the firemen had been 'on time' the premises might not have been destroyed completely. It was held that the firemen were not employed to proceed to a fire as slowly as possible: their conduct amounted to an unauthorized act and not an authorized act performed in an unauthorized way. It is, of course, hardly surprising that the court should find industrial action to be outside the course of employment.

> **? QUESTION** 8.6
>
> Do you think that deliberate conduct could ever amount to an 'authorized' act?

The answer to this question, as you might have guessed is: 'It all depends on the circumstances of the case'!

Deliberate acts, committed by the employee in the reasonable belief that they are necessary for the protection of his employer's property, may come within the course of his employment.

An employee of the defendant in *Pollard* v *John Parr & Sons* [1927] 1 KB 236, mistakenly, but on reasonable grounds, suspected that the claimant, a young boy, was stealing sugar from his employer's truck. He hit the claimant, a young boy, who fell, and was injured. The employer was found vicariously liable because the act was committed in defence of the employer's property, and was not sufficiently excessive to be outside the scope of the employee's employment.

In *Fennelly* v *Connex South Eastern Ltd* [2001] IRLR 390 (CA), the claimant was buttonholed by a ticket inspector employed by the defendant about his purchase of a ticket. He had in fact bought a ticket and a dispute ensued; offensive language passed between them. Eventually the claimant was 'headlocked' and evicted from the railway station. The ticket inspector was found to be in the course of his employment throughout: this was not a case of separate acts on the part of the employee—the whole affair was a single incident during which the inspector regarded himself as doing the job for which he was employed by the defendant.

Indeed, it is possible for criminal acts to come within the terms of an employee's employment. In the leading case of *Lloyd* v *Grace, Smith & Co.* [1912] AC 716, a firm of solicitors employed a senior managing clerk to handle conveyancing transactions on his own. He dishonestly conveyed the claimant's property for his own benefit. The House of Lords held that the solicitors were vicariously liable, because it was the position in which they had placed the clerk which enabled him to carry out the fraud.

It was said that the clerk represented the firm of solicitors, so the circumstances were rather special. The clerk was regarded as the agent for the solicitors rather than a mere employee. As Lord Loreburn put it:

> If the agent commits the fraud purporting to act in the course of business such as he was authorized, or held out as authorized, to transact on account of his principal, then the latter may be held liable for it.

In *Generale Bank Nederland NV* v *Export Credits Guarantee Dept.* (1997) *The Times*, 4 August (CA), the employee was liable to X as a joint tortfeasor with Y in deceit (Y and the employee having acted together, in concert). It was held that Z, the employer, could only be vicariously liable if the deceit was within the employee's actual or ostensible authority. The employee's authority ran to the underwriting of guarantees and it was this act which the court had to examine, i.e. did it fall within the course of employment? It was found that deceit did not come within the employee's course of employment.

 EXERCISE 8.1

Consider *Morris* v *C W Martin and Sons Ltd* [1965] 2 All ER 725.

The claimant sent her fur coat to be cleaned. The work was entrusted to the defendant (a subcontractor) and the defendant's employee stole the coat. Was he acting in the course of his employment?

(1) What was the outcome of the case?

(2) Were the reasons given for the unanimous decision on similar lines?

Lord Denning MR observed that *Lloyd* v *Grace Smith* recognized that dishonesty might be in the course of employment, and regarded the key question to be the nature of the duty owed by the employer to the owner of the goods:

> If the master is under a duty to use due care to keep goods safely and protect them from theft and depredation, he cannot get rid of his responsibility by delegating his duty to another. If he entrusts that duty to his servant, he is answerable for the way in which the servant conducts himself therein. No matter whether the servant be negligent, fraudulent, or dishonest, the master is liable. But not when he is under no such duty.

Diplock LJ treated the relevant relationship as being the bailment:

> the defendant bailees are a corporate person. They could not perform their duties to the [claimant] to take reasonable care of the fur and not to convert it otherwise than vicariously by natural persons acting as their servants or agents. It was one of their servants to whom they had entrusted the care and custody of the fur for the purpose of doing work upon it who converted it by stealing it. Why should they not be vicariously liable for this breach of their duty by the [agent] whom they had chosen to perform it?

Salmon LJ regarded *Lloyd* v *Grace Smith* as decisive.

The defendants were found liable on two grounds: (a) the goods had been entrusted to him, therefore the theft was committed in the course of his employment; (b) the defendants, as bailees of the coat, owed the claimant a duty to take reasonable care of it. The theft by the employee, to whom they had delegated responsibility, was a breach of that duty.

You should have answered as follows:

1. The employers were found vicariously liable for their employee's theft of the claimant's mink stole.

2. Their Lordships gave different reasons for their decisions:
   • Diplock LJ found against the employers on the ground that their non-delegable duty as bailees for reward to take care of the stole had been broken;
   • Lord Denning and Salmon LJ regarded the employee as having committed the theft in the course of his employment, thus making his employers, the defendants, vicariously liable for his dishonesty.

It was pointed out in *Morris*, however, that it is not enough that an employee is given an opportunity by his job to steal or otherwise act dishonestly. The act must have been committed 'in the course of doing that class of acts which the company had put the servant in its place to do': per Diplock LJ. The company would not have been liable if the garment had been stolen by an employee who was not employed to clean it or have care and custody of it.

The decision in *Morris* was said in *ST* (below) to apply only in cases of bailment (i.e. cases where goods are handed over by the owner to a third party for some temporary purpose—here, cleaning or repair, but it could be storage or transportation).

In *Heasmans* v *Clarity Cleaning Co. Ltd* [1987] ICR 949 (CA), the defendants provided cleaning services to the claimants, and one of the defendants' employees, while on the claimants' premises, made illegal use of the claimants' telephones. It was found that before an employer could be liable vicariously for the wrongful acts of an employee, there must be some 'nexus' between the employee's tortious or criminal act and the circumstances of his employment. Here, from the obligation to dust and disinfect the telephone, nothing more existed than the provision of the opportunity to commit the tort or crime. As Purchas LJ said, that factor was insufficient to establish a nexus in the present case and the defendants' appeal was allowed: they were not vicariously liable for their employee's illegal act.

This decision was followed in *ST* v *North Yorkshire C.C.* [1999] 1 RLR 98 (CA), which concerned an opportunity to commit a sexual assault. The claimant, a school pupil on a school outing, had to sleep in the same room as his assailant, a teacher, because he, the claimant, had to be supervised at night due to his epilepsy. The employer was found not to be vicariously liable in these circumstances.

In *Lister* v *Hesley Hall Ltd* [2001] 2 All ER 769 (HL), the Court of Appeal found, following *ST*, that sexual abuse by a house-father at a children's home was outside his course of employment, so his failure to report the risk or fact of harm caused to the abused children by his own acts did not attract vicarious liability. It was unrealistic, said the court, to distinguish the act itself, which was of a secret nature, from the fact that the abuser had kept it a secret from his employer.

It was held by the House of Lords, however, that a broad approach should be taken in deciding whether a particular tort had a close enough connection with the nature of the employment in question. The court should ask the question: 'What was the job on which the employee was engaged at the time?' It would not then be necessary to inquire whether the abuse was a way of performing authorized acts; it was better to consider vicarious liability in the light of whether the employer had taken on the care of the boys through the employee (the abuser) and if there was sufficient connection between his employment and his torts.

On the facts, the torts had been committed on the premises of the employer and in the employer's time: the employee was caring for the boys, on behalf of his employer, in discharge of his duties at the relevant time. The torts were sufficiently connected to the employer's duties, and his employer was vicariously liable. The decision of the Court of Appeal was reversed and *ST* was overruled.

> **? QUESTION 8.7**
>
> Can an employer escape vicarious liability by use of an exclusion clause?

Lister was applied by the Court of Appeal in *Mattis v Pollock (t/a Flaming's Nightclub)* (2003), *The Times*, 16 July (CA). A doorman at a nightclub stabbed the claimant in the vicinity of the club in revenge for an earlier violent attack on him in the club. It was held that the doorman had committed this act in the course of his employment, making the club owner vicariously liable for his actions.

The doorman had been involved in a fight in the club, and was pursued outside. He went to his flat, some 500 yards away, and returned with a knife. The claimant was stabbed in the back about 100 yards from the club.

Judge LJ said it was clear that where an employee was expected to use violence while carrying out his duties, the likelihood of establishing that an act of violence fell within the broad scope of his employment was greater than it would otherwise be. It was essential to concentrate on the closeness of the connection between the act of the employee and his duties, broadly defined.

The doorman was employed by the defendant to keep order and discipline, and was encouraged and expected to perform his duties in 'an aggressive and intimidating manner', which included manhandling customers. The defendant should not have been employing this particular doorman at all (he was unlicensed) and should certainly not have been encouraging him to perform his duties as he did. On the facts, there was 'little doubt' that the doorman would have been as violent within the premises as he was outside them. The words he used when he stabbed the claimant showed his actions were directly linked to the earlier incident. Approaching the matter 'broadly', at the time of the stabbing the defendant's responsibility for his employee was not extinguished. 'If the court had to decide the point, the defendant's *personal* (emphasis added) liability was also established.'

In *Majrowski v Guy's and St Thomas's NHS Trust* (2006), *The Times*, 13 July, the Court of Appeal held an employer potentially vicariously liable for breach of a statutory duty, that is, harassment under ss 1 and 3 of the Protection from Harassment Act 1997 committed by an employee in the course of her employment. The statutory duty was imposed on the employee, not the employer.

Auld LJ said there was no English authority on this point but, in the light of *Lister*, and *Dubai Aluminium v Salaam* [2003] 2 AC 407, it was not clear, in general, that an employer could be vicariously liable for breach of a statutory duty imposed on his employee although not on him. What mattered was the closeness of the connection between the offending conduct of the employee and the nature and circumstances of the employment in question.

His Lordship said that the imposition of vicarious liability had to be just and reasonable in the circumstances. He pointed out that this form of strict liability was 'a loss distribution device used on grounds of social and economic policy'.

The claimant was employed by the defendant Trust as a clinical audit coordinator. He alleged that he was bullied, intimidated, and harassed by his departmental manager, acting in the course of her employment.

Scott Baker dissented in part. You should also know that this was an appeal against a 'striking out' of the claim at first instance; the court had therefore not reached a decision on the actual merits of the claim.

The House of Lords unanimously confirmed the majority decision. Lord Nicholls said the rationale for vicarious liability was to be found in a combination of policy factors: all forms of economic activity created a risk of harm to other persons; in fairness those persons carrying on the activity should be liable in law to someone who suffered harm as a result of wrongs committed 'in the conduct of the enterprise' because financial recompense would come from 'a source better placed financially that individual wrongdoing employees . . .'; financial loss could be spread more widely via vicarious liability insurance and higher prices; and employers would be encouraged to see that their employees observed standards of good practice. Furthermore, subject to any statutory provisions to the contrary, his Lordship said he could see no 'coherent basis' for confining vicarious liability to common law wrongs. This decision is discussed further in **Chapter 11**.

In *Banks* v *Ablex Ltd* (CA) (2005), *The Times*, 21 March, it was held that an employer was neither in breach of his contractual duty to provide a safe system of work nor vicariously liable for abusive an aggressive behaviour of a male employee towards a female employee at their place of work unless the tort of harassment was proved, that is the tort was 'complete'. The conduct complained of must have been intentional and directed at another person on more than one occasion, knowing it would cause harassment to that person.

8.2.2.5 Exclusion clauses

In *Photo Production Ltd* v *Securicor Transport Ltd* [1980] AC 827, the defendant's employee, employed to guard the claimant's factory, had burnt it down in the course of his employment, but the House of Lords found that the defendant had effectively excluded its liability by a term in the contract with the claimant, notwithstanding the fundamental breach of the contract.

? **QUESTION** 8.8

Does an exclusion clause extend to the employee?

If an exclusion clause in a contract made between a client (or customer) and an employer states categorically that it applies also to employees, those employees can claim exemption from liability as a result of the Contracts (Rights of Third Parties) Act 1999. In other cases it is generally assumed that employees cannot claim the benefit of the exclusion clause.

There is, however, persuasive argument that such exclusion clauses should be implicitly extended to employees, and this is to be found in the Canadian case of *London Drugs* v *Kuehne and Nagel International* (1993) 97 DLR 4th 261.

8.2.3 **Vehicle drivers**

The decisions here have been especially influenced by policy considerations; the courts try to see that road accident victims may recover from the insurers. Frequently the driver of the defendant's car is described as the defendant's 'agent' rather than his 'servant' or 'employee', but 'the word "agency" in contexts such as these is merely a concept, the meaning and purpose of which is to say "is vicariously liable" . . . ' in the words of Lord Wilberforce in *Morgans* v *Launchbury* (below).

It is best to regard this form of vicarious liability not as resting on any general conception of agency, but as a form of liability *sui generis* ('of its own kind'; 'the only one of its kind') developed by the courts to meet the exigency of the moment.

The rule was described by du Parcq LJ in *Hewitt* v *Bonvin* [1940] 1 KB 188, in the following words:

> The driver of a car may not be the owner's servant and the owner will nevertheless be liable for his negligent driving if it be proved that at the material time he had authority, express or implied, to drive on the owner's behalf. Such liability depends not on ownership, but on the delegation of a task or duty.

In this case a son borrowed his father's car to take home two girlfriends who were injured as a result of the son's negligent driving. The father was held not vicariously liable for the negligent driving, for no purpose of his was being served at the time.

In *Ormrod* v *Crosville Motors* [1953] 1 WLR 409, however, an uninsured driver was taking the defendant's car from Birkenhead to Monte Carlo so that the defendant could use it there on holiday. On the journey the claimant was injured by the driver's negligent driving. The defendant was found to be vicariously liable.

Morgans v *Launchbury* [1972] 2 All ER 606, is the leading authority. It places great emphasis on the owner's 'purposes' or 'interests'.

The defendant owned and insured the family car, which her husband used often for work and pleasure. With her consent he took the car on a journey round some pubs (a 'pub crawl') having entrusted the driving to a friend. The claimant was injured when the friend, who was not insured, drove negligently and crashed the car.

The claimant sued the wife in her capacity as principal of her husband who was alleged to have been acting as her agent at the time of the crash. The House of Lords held the defendant not liable. Lord Wilberforce said:

> if the husband was, as he clearly was, using the car for his own purposes, I am unable to understand how his undertaking to delegate his right to drive to another can turn the driver into the wife's agent in any sense of the word.

In many cases, drivers are themselves insured and *Monk* v *Warbey* [1935] 1 KB 75 suggests that the owner of the vehicle may be liable for breach of statutory duty where he allows an uninsured person to drive his vehicle (see **Chapter 7**). *Morgans* is not the only route for a claimant to follow in search of compensation. This form of vicarious liability is, in practice, now of much less importance than used to be the case.

8.2.4 **Contribution and indemnity**

The provisions of the Civil Liability (Contribution) Act 1978 may enable the employer or principal, as the case may be, to recover some, or all, of the damages from his employee or agent. Also, at common law, a servant will be liable to compensate the master for the amount of damages paid by him: *Lister* v *Romford Ice Cold Storage Co. Ltd* [1957] AC 555.

■ SUMMARY

- In this chapter we have been concerned with vicarious liability at common law, and not with any form of special liability that might be imposed by statute. When someone is found to be vicariously liable, he is being made responsible for the act(s) of another person and, though that other person will remain personally liable for whatever form of liability he is guilty of (usually the tort of negligence), the one who is vicariously liable will be strictly liable, i.e. his liability is not personal fault of any kind.

- Vicarious liability is commonly associated with the liability of an employer for the tort(s) of his employee, committed in the course of the latter's employment. Indeed, we focus on that form of liability; but it is very important to appreciate that this form of liability is not limited to such relationships; or for that matter to the law of torts: it can be found, for example, in the law of partnership and agency.

- The law of agency is an aspect of commercial or business law, and can only be touched upon in the present context. In the commercial world agents are commonly appointed by contract to negotiate deals for their principals; the agent's authority may be 'actual', 'implied', or 'ostensible' (i.e. 'apparent') and many legal disputes turn on the question of whether the agent's authority extended to the particular transaction in question and whether, as a consequence his principal is liable for his acts. In the law of tort the idea of agency is often used, as *Winfield* (p. 613) puts it, on an ad hoc (i.e. 'for this purpose') basis; in other words, not as part of a consistent application of the 'commercial' concept of agency. In any case, there will not often be a contract of agency in existence between the parties, thus it is usually a matter of implying an agency relationship in the circumstances of the case.

- This concept of ad hoc agency, if we may borrow that expression, can be used to extend vicarious liability wherever it is thought by the courts to be appropriate. It seems, in some cases at least, to be based on the idea of 'control' and 'direction'. The hirer of another's employee could, for example, be vicariously liable on this basis.

- In any context, it is always important to distinguish between a person's primary liability and his vicarious liability, and nowhere is this point made more clearly than in the relationship of employer and employee.

    The vicarious liability of an employer ('master') for the tort(s) of his employee ('servant') is the classic instance of this form of liability. In general, the relationship of employee and employer is a contractual one, based on financial reward for service, and in practice this is the type of relationship we encounter in the cases.

- An 'employee', for the purposes of vicarious liability in tort, need not be the one who is paid for his service, particularly in view of the use made in the cases of the concept of implied agency.

- In connection with an employer's vicarious liability for the torts of his employee, we have seen that there are essentially two potential areas of difficulty:
    (a) is the person in question an 'employee' (or 'servant') or an 'independent contractor'?
    (b) was the tort(s) committed in the course of the employee's employment?

You will have gathered by now that neither of these issues is amenable, in the present context, to any 'scientific' or systematic analysis. We can only sum up the situation in the phrases, beloved of lawyers: 'each case turns on its own facts'; and 'it all depends on the circumstances of the case'.

- There is no closed list of non-delegable duties; new ones are being developed all the time.

- 'Course of employment' is very much an issue in which the facts are paramount. As *Winfield* (p. 601) puts it: '. . . it contains no criteria to decide when or why an act is within or outside the scope of employment and no single test is appropriate to cover all cases'.

- It is evident that the courts in general take a broad view of what is and is not within the course of a particular employee's employment. We have seen that the cases have laid down some very general lines of guidance, but these provide only a sense of direction; they do not give us any firm guidance on the solution that the court is likely to arrive at in any given case.

- An express prohibition issued by the employer against certain acts is not conclusive of the issue; the prohibition must restrict the scope of employment, not merely the way of performing the job.

- The main problem in determining the course of employment issue is the plain fact that there is such a wide diversity of jobs, occupations, pursuits, callings, professions, etc., that it is virtually impossible to do anything more than decide each case essentially on its own facts.

- You will have seen that the factors of time and place are often of importance in these cases. Yet 'time' in the present context may mean something different; it might be less crucial for a salaried employee than for an employee paid on a piece-rate or bonus-rate basis. The same is true of the factor, 'place'.

- You have read about some of the so-called 'driving' cases in which these factors have played their part. Yet not all drivers' terms of employment are the same; the 'course of employment' of a long-haulage truck driver, for example, for the purpose of determining whether a detour is an entirely new and independent journey from his authorized route, or only a 'momentary' deviation which can be overlooked, may not be the same as that, say, of a van driver who is engaged only on local deliveries. The range of employed drivers alone is immense, including, for example, coach and bus drivers, and travelling salespersons.

■ **FURTHER READING**

Giliker, P. and Beckwith, S., *Tort*, 2nd edn, London: Sweet & Maxwell, 2004, Chapter 7.

Hepple, Howarth, and Matthews, *Tort: Cases and Materials*, 5th edn, London: Butterworths, 2000, Chapters 17 and 18.

Jones, M., *Textbook on Torts*, 8th edn, Oxford: Oxford University Press, 2002, pp. 268–89.

Kidner, R., *Casebook on Torts*, 9th edn, Oxford: Oxford University Press, 2006, Chapter 17.

Markesinis, B.S. and Deakin, S.F., *Tort Law*, 5th edn, Oxford: Oxford University Press, 2003, pp. 571–603.

Murphy, J., *Street on Torts*, 11th edn, London: Butterworths, 2003, Chapters 15, 27, and 31.

Rose, F.D., 'Liability for Employee's Assaults' (1977) 40 *MLR* 420.

Salmond and Heuston on the Law of Torts, 21st edn, London: Sweet & Maxwell, 1996, Chapters 20 and 21.

Weir, T., *Casebook on Tort*, 10th edn, London: Sweet & Maxwell, 2004, Chapters 6 and 7.

Winfield and Jolowicz on Tort, 16th edn, London: Sweet & Maxwell, 2002, Chapters 21, 22, and 25.

CHAPTER 8 ASSESSMENT EXERCISE

Chris lends to his friend, Ray, a van driver, Geoff, as a temporary replacement for Ray's own driver who is ill. While making deliveries in Ray's van one day, Geoff decides to pull in for lunch at a café, and in so doing negligently knocks down and injures Liz. He is so upset by this that he drives to a pub some miles away and proceeds to get drunk. At the pub he meets Michelle and offers to drive her home, but on the way he negligently collides with another vehicle and Michelle is injured.

Advise Liz and Michelle on any claims they may have for damages in the law of tort.

See *Cases and Materials* (8.3) for a specimen answer.

9 Product liability

9.1 OBJECTIVES

By the end of this chapter you should be able to:

1 Explain what is meant by product liability

2 Describe the scope of common law manufacturer's liability

3 Explain the development of strict tortious liability

4 Compare the Consumer Protection Act and the Consumer Protection Directive

5 Explain the operation of the Act and the principal difficulties of interpretation which it presents

9.2 Introduction

 EXERCISE 9.1

Write down what you understand by 'product' and 'product liability'.

A developed economy such as the United Kingdom manufactures an enormously diverse range of products, either directly from raw materials (e.g. smokeless fuel), from partly processed materials (e.g. cutlery, typically produced by the cutler from block or strip steel), or from previously manufactured components which are assembled to form a larger whole (e.g. a motor vehicle).

These processes may be carried out by a single manufacturer, but typically, part-processed materials and components are purchased from other manufacturers and further processed or assembled.

The finished product may be intended for consumption (e.g. food, cleaning products), for long-term use by consumers (e.g. washing machines), for consumption or long-term use in commerce and industry (e.g. copier toner, machine tools respectively) or may be used equally readily by consumers as by commercial organizations (e.g. electricity and gas supplies, products such as stand-by generators and many types of motor vehicle).

In any case, the product may be made available to the end user directly by the producer or via one or more middlemen.

The end user may have bought, hired, or otherwise acquired the product contractually. However, he may be a family member or employee of the acquirer, or the recipient of a gift. The contractual relationship may only relate indirectly to the product, e.g. the hotel guest scalded by a defective shower unit.

A product which is unsatisfactory may cause damage to person or property, or simply be inadequate or unsuitable. For instance a washing machine might cause injury if the drum continues to revolve with the door open, trapping the user. It may cause property damage if it catches fire following an electrical fault, or it may simply fail to wash very well, or break down altogether. The problem may lie with the instructions rather than the product. If the manual does not explain that the filter must be cleaned regularly, a blockage may occur, leading to flooding.

In the case of a durable product, the harm may only occur well into the product's design life. In the meantime it may or may not have been well looked after; it may even have been modified, or used for purposes other than those it was designed for. It may have passed through the hands of several users.

Some forms of harm may not have been anticipated (e.g. teratogenic (causing deformities) or toxic effects of new drugs not revealed by testing).

The law of product liability is, in principle, concerned with all the legal ramifications arising from the above, although emphasis is placed on the position with regard to consumers, and on physical damage to person or property. The primary liability is seen as that of the producer, but there are other potential defendants.

In civil terms all these claims will involve a breach of an obligation, although it may be largely accidental whether that breach is of a duty arising under, or affected by, a contract, or a tortious one amounting to common law negligence or breach of statutory duty. It must be noted that some liabilities are strict, while others depend on the proof of fault.

There may be criminal liability, and in such cases, as with other areas of statute, there may or may not be a parallel liability for breach of statutory duty. For example, it is an offence under s. 75 of the Road Traffic Act 1988 to supply a motor vehicle in an unroadworthy condition. There is no liability in civil proceedings for breach of this statutory duty. It is also an offence to supply goods which contravene the general safety requirement contained in s. 10 of the Consumer Protection Act 1987, or to supply goods which contravene safety regulations made under the Act: s. 12. However the latter is also normally actionable civilly while the former is not: s. 41.

? QUESTION 9.1

At various times this almost random association of the factual harms arising from products and their legal categorization has led to fairly bizarre results. What was the decision in the following cases? (They are all real ones!)

P purchased a hot water bottle from L. It was used to warm the bed where P and his wife slept. It burst, owing to a manufacturing defect. P and his wife were scalded. Both sued, relying on a breach of implied terms as to fitness.

A mouse crawled into an opaque lemonade bottle to die. The consumer of the lemonade became ill, and sued the manufacturer, alleging negligence.

A purchaser of long johns contracted dermatitis. This was due to an excess of sulphites left over from the manufacturing process. It was the only case known to the manufacturers, who produced millions of items.

D purchased a bottle of W's lemonade from T, asking for it by name. He received a properly sealed bottle. He took it home and drank some, as did his wife. Both became ill, and analysis showed that the lemonade was heavily contaminated with carbolic acid. The manufacturers operated a very up-to-date and 'foolproof' system.

In the first case P could recover both for his own injuries and for the loss of his wife's services. The wife could not recover as there was no contract: *Preist* v *Last* [1903] 2 KB 148.

In the second case it was held that the producer of a product does not, in general owe a duty of care to his ultimate customer: *Mullen* v *Barr & Co.* (1929) 45 SC 245. This may seem like a trick question, since it goes the other way to *Donoghue* v *Stevenson* (but look at the date!).

In the third case it was held that the presence of the sulphites amounted to negligence. The product was within the rule in *Donoghue* v *Stevenson*: *Grant* v *Australian Knitting Mills* [1936] AC 85. The rarity of the occurrence was not fatal to a finding of negligence.

In the final case Lewis J accepted that these facts raised a prima facie case of negligence (i.e. D could rely on *res ipsa loquitur* as lemonade should not emerge from the defendant's plant contaminated). W gave evidence of their washing and bottling process, which the judge accepted was 'foolproof'. The judge held that W had satisfied him that there was in fact no negligence. The obligation was not an absolute one. D, but not his wife, could recover against T on the basis of the implied terms in his contract with her. The judge noted, acidly, that she was certainly not at fault: *Daniels* v *R White and Sons* [1938] 4 All ER 258.

This is an unscientific, and indeed unfair, sample of cases, but you should now have a rather better idea of the difficulties involved.

9.3 **Contractual remedies**

This section is mainly intended for those who have not (yet) studied contract law. If you have studied or are studying it, all you need to do is skim read this section.

9.3.1 **Basic expectations**

When you buy goods, you expect them to be of good quality and safe. This expectation is reflected in the law. Supply of defective goods under a contract of sale, hire, hire purchase, etc. is, prima facie, a breach of the obligations of the seller.

The law merchant recognized this as an incident of merchants' and industrialists' contracts from a relatively early date. Terms as to compliance with description, fitness for purpose, and adequate quality were implied unless the contrary was expressed. These implied terms were incorporated into the Sale of Goods Act 1893 when this codification of the law merchant and common law took effect.

This was a powerful weapon for the claimant: liability was strict, not fault related, and the measure of damages was the expectation one, which included consequential loss arising from damage to person or property, loss of profit and diminution of value of the goods affected or the cost of repairs.

9.3.2 Limitations on contractual remedies

Only the buyer of the goods could sue. Other users/victims were not in privity of contract with the seller.

The implied terms did not cover all aspects of the goods, e.g. durability. The term as to merchantability was particularly complex, and unhelpful to the consumer in that goods were merchantable if suitable for one of the purposes for which they were commonly traded, which might not be the purpose of the consumer.

The implied terms could be excluded without any restriction and only applied to sales and not to other transfers of possession. Sales otherwise than in the course of trade were excluded.

 EXERCISE 9.2

How far do you consider this set of rules protected consumer rights?

Generally speaking the law worked effectively in business transactions. The parties dealt on a basis of equality. If implied terms were excluded, this was on a basis of genuine negotiation. Losses were typically financial. Where appropriate they could be passed down a chain of transactions until they fell either on the person to blame or on someone who had specifically contracted to take the risk.

The position in consumer transactions was very different. Problems arose from the abuse of power by the business party to the transaction, in terms of selecting transaction types where there were no implied terms, excluding implied terms, and otherwise imposing unfair terms and conditions.

There was, however, a further problem. Goods in consumer use, if defective, were as likely to harm a third party as they were the buyer. Traded goods were less likely to cause physical harm, otherwise than to the employees of the buyer. These often in turn had a remedy against their employer (although there were many anomalies).

Some of these problems were addressed either by development of the common law or by statutory intervention. The following developments were amongst those which helped, to some degree, to alleviate the problems:

(a) restrictive construction of exclusion and limitation clauses by the courts;

(b) extension of implied terms to all forms of transfer of possession: Supply of Goods (Implied Terms) Act 1973, Supply of Goods and Services Act 1982;

(c) non-excludability of implied terms: Unfair Contract Terms Act 1977;

(d) non-excludability of certain liabilities: Unfair Contract Terms Act/Unfair Terms in Consumer Contract Regulations 1999;

(e) extension of employers' common law duty in relation to equipment: Employers' Liability (Defective Equipment) Act 1969;

(f) replacement of 'merchantable quality' by 'satisfactory quality': Sale and Supply of Goods Act 1994.

The rules on privity of contract restricted these developments to the party to the contract only. Such a restriction is not essential. It had largely been abandoned in the USA by 1916 (*MacPherson* v *Buick Motor Co.* (1916) 217 NY 382). The process of allowing third parties to rely on the terms of a warranty had started much earlier: *Thomas* v *Winchester* (1852) 6 NY 397. As a result, consumer claims have been brought against manufacturers and by non-buyers with considerable success.

The Law Revision Committee proposed in 1937 that there should be a general recognition of the rights of third-party beneficiaries, but this was not acted upon. The Contracts (Rights of Third Parties) Act 1999 may assist some non-contracting parties, but it must be clear that the contract is intended to give them rights. This is unlikely to be the case in ordinary consumer transactions.

The net position is that the rights of the consumer purchaser are in principle fully protected. His only risk is the insufficient means of his seller to meet his claim. Subject to this he can claim on a strict liability, non-excludable, basis in relation to shoddy goods and for damage caused by dangerous goods. The only surviving grey area is the interpretation of the term as to 'satisfactory' quality.

The non-purchaser is left in limbo by the rules of privity, and must seek a remedy in tort. He is joined by the purchaser when the latter seeks a remedy against the manufacturer.

A contractual claim, where available, will in principle cover consequential and pure economic loss, but not injury to feelings or loss of enjoyment. It thus follows the usual contract rules.

9.4 Tortious remedies: common law

9.4.1 Introduction

Initially the common law did not recognize a general duty of a manufacturer or repairer to anyone other than his customer. In a series of cases a range of victims went without remedy: victims of road accidents caused by defective vehicles, workmen damaged by defective plant acquired by their employer, users of defective consumer goods. In all these cases the defect was latent, in the sense that the manufacturer had failed to use proper care, but had not appreciated that the product was defective as a result. The position was different if:

(a) there was 'fraud' in the sense that the manufacturer was aware of the defect and covered it up, either by lying about it or otherwise;

(b) the product was inherently dangerous.

In such cases a remedy could be granted. The cases are not set out here, because they are all now obsolete, but they are discussed in full in *Donoghue* v *Stevenson*, if you are interested in them.

> **? QUESTION** 9.2
>
> When, and why, did this rule change? You will need to read *Donoghue* v *Stevenson* in *Cases and Materials* (9.1).

> ***Donoghue* v *Stevenson* [1932] AC 562**
>
> You are well aware of the broader significance of *Donoghue* (see *Cases and Materials* (9.1)) as the source of the neighbour principle. It is also more specifically the leading case on the common law of manufacturer's liability. Lord Atkin said (at p. 599):
>
> [A] manufacturer of products, which he sells in such a form as to show that he intends them to reach the ultimate consumer in the form in which they left him with no reasonable possibility of intermediate examination and with the knowledge that the absence of reasonable care in preparation or putting up of the products will result in an injury to the consumer's life or property, owes a duty to the consumer to take that reasonable care.

The rather antiquated expression 'putting up' covers packaging, instructions etc. It is perhaps wrong to read too much into the references to knowledge that absence of care will lead to harm. This suggests *Wagon Mound* foreseeability, but is probably more directed to the issue of want of care, in the sense that there can be no liability without fault.

The scope of liability has been extended by case law and it is necessary to consider the various aspects one by one.

9.4.2 Manufacturers

This includes those who assemble items. In *Malfroot* v *Noxall* (1935) 51 TLR 551, the defendant had fitted a sidecar to a motorcycle. It was successfully argued that the process was akin to manufacturing. Similarly in cases where water undertakers have been held liable for supplying unwholesome water, while they did not 'make' the water, they were in a position analogous to the manufacturer: *Read* v *Croydon Corp* [1938] 4 All ER 631. A further extension by analogy is to the intermediate distributor who ought to be alert to the potential risks of the product, or is specifically instructed to carry out some test or examination, but fails to do so. In *Kubach* v *Hollands* (1937) 53 TLR 1024, the distributor was liable on the latter basis, but the original manufacturer was not. In *Watson* v *Buckley, Osborne Garrett & Co. Ltd* [1940] 1 All ER 174 it was the former aspect. The defendants were wholesalers of a hair dye of 'dubious provenance' and were held to be negligent in not carrying out their own tests to establish its safety and efficacy.

The liability of repairers and suppliers is perhaps more difficult to classify, if classification be needed. Works of repair are analogous to original manufacture. In *Stennett* v *Hancock & Peters*

[1939] 2 All ER 578, the claimant was injured when a wheel flange came off a lorry which the defendant had just repaired and mounted the pavement, striking him. This was held to be within *Donoghue* v *Stevenson*.

Generally, dealers are not responsible in tort, but there are exceptions. In *Andrews* v *Hopkinson* [1957] 1 QB 229, a second-hand car dealer was held liable for supplying a car with dangerously defective steering, about which there was not even a warning. However, there was a problem in that the car had been sold to a finance company who let it on hire purchase to the claimant. At that time it was easy for the finance company to exclude liability, and the only possibilities of redress were a collateral contract with the garage and tortious liability.

In the more recent case of *Hurley* v *Dyke* [1979] RTR 265, a disclaimer by the seller of a car at auction that it was sold 'As seen and with all its faults' was sufficient to avoid liability to a passenger injured in a crash caused some days later by the defective state of the vehicle. Such a disclaimer would today need to be considered in the light of the Unfair Contract Terms Act 1977 if the seller were acting in the course of a business. Does it amount to an exclusion of liability for negligence, or does it fulfil the duty of care by giving an adequate warning, such that it is unforeseeable that the vehicle will be used until it has at least been checked?

In *Stennett*, liability was for misfeasance, and in the other two cases it was for nonfeasance. The statutory duty under s. 75 of the Road Traffic Act does not carry a civil action.

 EXERCISE 9.3

Is the dealer's liability the point at which the incremental progression should stop?

A cursory inspection of the cases just referred to shows that most were decided in the 25 years immediately after *Donoghue* v *Stevenson*, i.e. at a time before the neighbour principle had reached general acceptance, and when the categories of negligence exercised a decisive influence. It is now easier to see that repairers owe a duty of care on ordinary principles of proximity and foreseeability, and that it is just and reasonable for them to be liable, at least for personal injury and property damage.

A striking recent example of liability claimed under the 'narrow rule' is the Scottish case of *McTear* v *Imperial Tobacco Ltd* (Court of Session) (2005), *The Times*, 14 June, in which it was held that a manufacturer of cigarettes whose products were smoked by a person who was aware of the health risks associated with smoking did not owe that person a common law duty of care in negligence to see that he was not injured by its products. One crucial factor in the case was that the claimant, according to Lord Nimmo Smith, had failed to prove that but for the deceased (the claimant's late husband) having smoked cigarettes he would probably not have contracted lung cancer. See 2.3 for a discussion of the 'but for' test in causation.

9.4.3 Goods

The rules on manufacturers' liability only apply to dangerous goods, i.e. things which go beyond being shoddy and needing repair or replacement. They have never been applied to buildings. All the cases on buildings concern economic loss, and are outside this rule for that reason.

?　**QUESTION** 9.3

How far can disputes over building work be seen as equivalent to product liability? What should the boundary of the law of tort be in this area?

Such protection as there is, is under statute: s. 1 of the Defective Premises Act 1972. *Junior Books* v *Veitchi* [1983] 1 AC 520 may provide an exception where there is a special relationship, despite the rather dismissive treatment by Lord Goff in *Henderson* v *Merrett* [1994] 3 All ER 506.

In general terms there is no tortious liability of a manufacturer for pure economic loss. This certainly seems to follow from *Simaan* v *Pilkington* [1988] QB 758, and comes as no surprise when the general reluctance to allow such claims in tort is considered. This sort of harm is covered by a warranty of quality which can only arise in a principal or collateral contract (and in some cases the only function of the collateral contract appears to be a peg to hang this warranty on, as in *Shanklin Pier* v *Detel Products* [1951] 2 KB 854 and *Wells (Merstham) Ltd* v *Buckland Sand & Silica* [1965] 2 QB 170). In these cases the manufacturer personally made efforts to get the user to use the product, but the user actually bought from a middleman. The same conclusion was reached in *Muirhead* v *Industrial Tank Specialities* [1986] QB 507. Even if the item is potentially dangerous, provided this is recognized in time the costs of scrapping or repair are pure economic loss: *Murphy* v *Brentwood District Council* [1991] 1 AC 398.

While it is no doubt the case that the average commercial utilizer of products has only a distant relationship with the manufacturer, there will be exceptions. In most of these there will of course be privity of contract, as the goods will be being produced to an agreed specification. Cases such as *Junior Books* are not that rare, although the more normal situation may be that typified by *Simaan* v *Pilkington*. This is the situation addressed by Lord Goff in *Henderson* where he denies liability on the ground that there is no assumption of responsibility. He does accept that *Junior Books* has caused 'some difficulty' in this area. It will probably continue to do so, since the general thrust of the decision in *Henderson* is to promote the *Hedley Byrne* special relationship where it exists, even where there is a co-existing contract.

Some difficulty has been caused where the item supplied is itself two separate components, one of which damages the other. This happened in *Aswan Engineering* v *Lupdine* [1987] 1 All ER 135. Waterproofing compound was sent to Kuwait in plastic buckets which could not stand the heat. As a result the compound leaked away and was lost. One view is that this is a single entity so it is economic loss, namely money wasted on the compound. An alternative view is that the buckets were separate, and their failure led to physical damage to the compound. The actual decision was that the harm which had occurred was too remote. The buckets were reasonably fit for their purpose and it was not reasonably foreseeable that they would be left out in the desert sun for long periods. The defendants were not in breach of their duty of care. Nicholls LJ acknowledged that there was force in the argument that the buckets were a separate item, but he thought the argument unattractive as it would lead to any number of disputes as to who was responsible for ensuring that packaging was suitable for intended use, especially when the packaging and contents were separately sourced by a middleman.

The rationale of the rule is that the defect is latent, i.e. one against which a victim cannot protect himself. If the defect is not only patent, but has been noticed, if the claimant then chooses to carry on and run the risk, this is a break in the chain of causation, as in *Farr* v *Butters Bros* [1932] 2 KB 606, where the claimant's late husband was responsible for erecting a crane manufactured by the defendants. The crane was defective, and the deceased realized this. He nevertheless decided to carry on with the erection and was killed when the defective part failed. This victim fully appreciated the precise defect. A mere general feeling of hazard may not be enough, particularly if there is no safe alternative: *Denny* v *Supplies & Transport* [1950] 2 KB 374. This case may be an example of the general rule in negligence, which is broader than the product liability rule and requires a consideration of the total responsibilities of all concerned, as in *Clay* v *A J Crump & Sons* [1964] 1 QB 533, where an architect remained (at least partly) liable for negligently advising the retention of a wall during demolition and rebuilding operations. The wall fell on one of the builders and the fact that the demolition contractors and the builders were on site and in a position to inspect did not absolve the architect.

9.4.4 **Proving negligence**

Very often the claimant will rely on *res ipsa loquitur*. In effect the burden will then be on the defendant to negative negligence. In the case of a construction defect it is common ground that something has gone wrong. The claimant is often in no position to say exactly what, but the inference is that there was some casual or other negligence somewhere in the defendant's operation.

> **? QUESTION** 9.4
>
> Is it reasonable to expect the claimant to prove negligence positively before he can recover damages for a dangerously defective product or should *res ipsa loquitur* be available?

In some cases reliance on this procedure is entirely justified, as in *Mason*.

> *Mason* v *Williams & Williams and Thomas Turton* [1955] 1 All ER 808
>
> The claimant lost an eye when a chisel supplied to his employers by the manufacturers shattered because it was too hard (and therefore brittle). This was a case where the source of supply could be traced, and where the manufacturer had, prima facie, produced a dangerously defective chisel as a result of some misapplication of the manufacturing process or casual negligence (*Cases and Materials* (9.1)).

In other cases the burden on the defendant appears to be a heavy one, as in *Grant* v *Australian Knitting Mills* [1935] All ER Rep 209. It can be rebutted as in *Daniels* v *White and Sons* [1938] 4 All ER 258, although there has been criticism of the judge for failing to address the possibility of casual negligence as opposed to a deficient system. The claimant's task is harder if the product has been incorporated into a larger whole as in *Evans* v *Triplex Safety Glass* [1936] 1 All ER 283. This was a rather optimistic claim against the manufacturers of a windscreen which shattered after about 12 months use. As the judge pointed out, a lot of time had passed and there was every possibility of impact damage, the screen had been fitted into an aperture and screwed in place, which might have created stress, the car manufacturer had the opportunity of a visual inspection at least. There was in short no finger of suspicion pointing straight at the manufacturer.

The claimant gets some help from the maxim *res ipsa loquitur* for manufacturing defects, but is on his own in relation to design defects. These are notoriously problematic. It is very difficult to infer negligence for a design defect. The claimant has to prove that the manufacturer ought to have been aware of the problem and ought to have taken action to avoid the defect. The classic example is thalidomide. The defence was that the tests which were done at the time the drug was developed were the necessary and proper ones in the light of scientific knowledge at the time. This is a powerful argument in relation to 'state of the art' products. A similar process of reasoning was at work in *Roe* v *Minister of Health* [1954] 2 QB 66. This is not strictly a case of product liability, as the complaint was not against the manufacturer of the anaesthetic, but it does show the difficulties in proving a system error as opposed to an operational one.

The duty is, however, a continuing one. If a manufacturer becomes aware of defects affecting a product already in use, it may be necessary to issue a recall or a warning. The principle was accepted in relation to cars in *Walton* v *British Leyland* (1978) (unreported). The discussion was on the question of how many reports of problems are needed to constitute a cluster rather than a coincidence. The defect may be a manufacturing defect affecting a specific batch or a design defect affecting the whole production. The proof of the pudding is in the eating, and if the experience of the product is that there is a problem, action will be required. The most celebrated such case is the Ford Pinto, immortalized in Ralph Nader's book, *Unsafe at any Speed*. In this case the problem was compounded by the apparent callousness of management in refusing to issue an alert to the public so as not to damage the company's reputation.

9.4.5 Current relevance of the common law

Common law claims are still the only redress where the Consumer Protection Act (CPA) 1987 does not apply. The CPA does not protect businesses, so a common law claim will still be necessary in respect of the allowable heads of damage in cases like *Muirhead*. The same will be true if and to the extent that *Junior Books* makes a comeback.

In particular it may be necessary to rely on this tort action when contribution or indemnity is being sought for complex multiparty actions. These are regulated by the Civil Liability (Contribution) Act 1978, which makes it plain that it is immaterial whether the liability to pay the original victim or to contribute arose in contract or tort (or otherwise). This resolved some earlier complexities.

The limitation period may be more favourable, although this will require quite abnormal circumstances. The CPA has a blanket limit of ten years from the date of supply: s. 11A of the Limitation Act 1980. In tort the limit is six years from the date of harm, with an overriding limit of fifteen years: s. 2 and 12A–B of the Limitation Act 1980, unless there are personal injuries, when it is prima facie three years subject to discretionary and theoretically open-ended extension: ss 11 and 33 of the Limitation Act 1980.

However, except in these limited cases, it will be better to rely on CPA so it is always best to look at the Act first.

 QUESTION 9.5

What problems still remained outstanding? How could these best be addressed?

9.5 **Statutory liability**

9.5.1 **Pressure for reform**

The US strict product liability, albeit founded on contract rather than tort, was a magnet for consumer groups anxious to secure a similarly broad and transparent basis without the uncertainties and inconsistencies of the narrow rule. This was reinforced by news of legislative implementation of strict product liability by statute in various parts of the common law and civil law world. The Pearson Committee and a joint report of the English and Scottish Law Commissions all recommended a form of strict liability at the end of the 1970s. By this time a product liability Directive was also on the agenda of the EU, although it fell victim to the Eurosclerosis of the 1970s. The UK authorities took no action on the domestic recommendations pending a revival of the EU initiative. This was probably sensible, as it is unlikely that a domestic scheme would have been wholly compatible with the EU one, leading either to early amendment or to the sort of complex interrelationship which has occurred in relation to the Unfair Contract Terms Directive and the pre-existing Unfair Contract Terms Act.

The EU proposal, which became Directive 85/374 (*Cases and Materials* (9.2)), had two aims, namely levelling the competitive playing field and consumer protection.

The first is clearly an EU objective, as recognized by the first recital to the Directive:

> Whereas approximation of the laws of the Member States concerning the liability of the producer for damage caused by the defectiveness of his products is necessary because the existing divergences may distort competition and affect the movement of goods within the common market.

This obviously involves both Art 81 (competition) and Art 28 (free movement) of the EU Treaty and establishes a legitimate EU interest in creating a level playing field. It is a bit forced, as the existence of fault based rather than strict liability for faulty products is not a massive advantage competitively or a massive barrier to trade.

The second is more social than economic at first glance. There are clear arguments for imposing strict liability on the basis that employers can in effect insure the risk. As the second recital puts it:

> liability without fault on the part of the producer is the sole means of adequately solving the problem, peculiar to our age of increasing technicality, of a fair apportionment of the risks inherent in modern technological production.

Here one finds the converse difficulty that this obvious area of utility is not obviously within an area of EU responsibility. At the time consumer protection was not an explicitly defined EU activity, except so far as it came within the general category of 'approximation of the laws of the Member States to the extent required for the proper functioning of the common market'. The Directive is expressly made under Art 94 of the EU Treaty which is the provision governing approximation. Following Maastricht there is a specific reference to consumer protection as an activity of the EU. This may seem to be a mere quibble, but objection has successfully been taken in other cases to EU legislation on the grounds of want of legal foundation. No such objection was taken to this Directive, perhaps because the combination of the firm legal basis and marginal factual one and the firm factual basis and marginal legal one was enough to dissuade potential dissentients.

The UK government enacted the Directive into domestic law as it was obliged to do, combining it with other related measures in the Consumer Protection Act 1987. This Act was somewhat rushed through its final stages so as not to fall at the Dissolution preceding the 1987 general election. It may have suffered in the process. It certainly contains a number of departures from the wording, and possibly the sense, of the Directive. These were the subject of Art. 226 proceedings against the UK government (see below 9.5.4) although they do not yet seem to have caused serious problems in practice. There have been few reported cases on the Act as yet, although this is perhaps understandable, given the time it takes litigation to reach the appellate courts.

Leaving aside technical arguments on the scope of EU competence in the field, there has been little complaint as there was a consensus that such a measure was necessary.

? **QUESTION** 9.6

Explain why there was a consensus that a strict product liability rule was required.

The Law Commission had suggested that the main reasons for imposing strict liability were:

(a) that it is economically sound to promote loss sharing, where the producer can insure;

(b) that the producer is in the best position to influence design and safety and strict liability provides an incentive to strive proactively for the best standards (this can be challenged on the basis that it is only the highest cost effective level of safety that is so promoted, rather than the best available);

(c) distributors are not usually responsible for quality, although they may be in the sense of inspecting or modifying the product;

(d) there should be a minimum of technical bars to litigation, and multiplicity of actions should be discouraged.

These are all reflected in the Directive and are supplemented by a more detailed rationale for the precise scheme created under the Directive. The CPA was introduced to give effect to the Directive (see s. 1), and although they do not use the same language or follow the same structure, it is possible to place the provisions in parallel.

EXERCISE 9.4

List the provisions of the Directive and, beside them, the equivalent provisions of the CPA. There is no need to set out the words in full, merely the article/paragraph and section/sub-section numbers at this stage. (See *Cases and Materials* (9.2).)

9.5.2 **The general scheme of the Consumer Protection Act 1987/Directive 85/374**

When considering the Act and the Directive it is important to have them to hand (*Cases and Materials* (9.2)). This discussion will not make proper sense otherwise. You should turn to the sections and articles being discussed and read them carefully as you consider the text below.

The producer of dangerously defective products will be liable to a consumer/user of those goods for death, personal injury, and damage to other property (excluding the defective property itself) on proof of the identity of the producer and causation only. Fault is not required, although there are limited defences which must be proved by the defendant. A supplier may be liable if he cannot or will not identify the source of the product.

9.5.2.1 **Products**

The Directive defines these (Art. 2) as all movables, even if incorporated into another movable or an immovable. In English terms this means all chattels, even though incorporated into land as fixtures (e.g. a central heating system) and also crops. Electricity is specifically included.

The only initial exclusion was primary agricultural products and game. These are the produce of the soil, stock farming, and fisheries until they have undergone 'initial processing'. It can be argued that these are particularly susceptible to natural defects which are more 'Act of God' than manufacturer's liability. By virtue of Directive 99/34, the exclusion from the Product Liability Directive of primary agricultural products was removed from December 2000.

The Act defines product as any goods or electricity, including items incorporated into other items (s. 1(2)). By s. 45(1) goods includes substances, growing crops, and things comprised in land by virtue of being attached to it, together with ships, vehicles, and aircraft. This appears to be the same in substance if not in language. Blood prepared for transfusion was found to be a product in *A* v *National Blood Authority* [2001] 3 All ER 289.

9.5.2.2 **Defective**

The Directive defines this concept in Art. 6 as follows:

A product is defective when it does not provide the safety which a person is entitled to expect, taking all circumstances into account, including:

(a) the presentation of the product;

(b) the use to which it could reasonably be expected that the product would be put;

(c) the time when the product was put into circulation.

There is a proviso to the effect that a product is not defective merely because a better one is later put into circulation. The main definition does of course make some allowance for developments in knowledge and techniques.

The Act is somewhat more specific (s. 3):

> There is a defect in a product . . . if the safety of the product is not such as persons generally are entitled to expect; and . . . 'safety', in relation to a product, shall include safety with respect to products comprised within that product and safety in the context of risks of damage to property as well as in the context of risks of death or personal injury.
>
> In determining . . . what persons generally are entitled to expect in relation to a product all the circumstances shall be taken into account, including:
>
> (a) the manner in which, and purposes for which, the product has been marketed, its get-up, the use of any mark in relation to the product and any instructions for, or warnings with respect to, doing or refraining from doing anything with or in relation to the product;
>
> (b) what might reasonably be expected to be done with or in relation to the product; and
>
> (c) the time when the product was supplied by its producer to another.

There is a similar proviso as to subsequent improvements. The effect of the Act and the Directive appear to be the same.

? QUESTION 9.7

Consider the wording of Art. 6 and s. 3. How far must a manufacturer go with packaging and labelling to comply with his obligations?

The burden is a heavy one, especially in relation to warnings and instructions. Perhaps some of the American horror stories will not be repeated here, but if hot air paint strippers carry, as they do, a warning that 'This is not a hair dryer', then warnings about not microwaving pets, or mooning out of windows, or swallowing open safety pins, let alone health warnings on beer, may become essential. In a case before the Act, *Heil* v *Hedges* [1951] 1 TLR 512, a butcher was held not liable for selling a pork chop which contained parasites. These parasites were common in pork, but were killed by proper cooking. The butcher was entitled to assume that the meat would be properly cooked. This may give some indication of the approach under the Act. Consider in this context the decision in *Bogle* v *McDonalds Restaurants* [2002] EWHC 490 (QB) where it was held that McDonalds hot beverages were not defective, even though they could and did scald customers when spilled. Customers expected hot drinks to be hot, the packaging was appropriate and overall safety was in line with expectations.

One of the few cases under the Act is *Abouzaid* v *Mothercare* (2000) LTL, 21 December. In this case the claimant was injured while attaching a 'Cosytoes' sleeping bag to a push chair when an elastic strap slipped and the buckle hit him in the eye. It was held that the product was defective because there were no warnings and it could not be secured safely. It was expressly held that there was no liability in negligence because the relevant danger, while present, was not one which a reasonable manufacturer should have appreciated.

In *A* v *National Blood Authority* [2001] 3 All ER 289, the blood was held to be defective once a specific risk of contamination was recognized, but available steps to screen for this risk were not taken. By contrast, in *XYZ* v *Schering Health Care & ors* (2002) LTL, 29 July, the evidence did not show that certain contraceptive pills carried a higher risk than their 'safe' predecessors, so there was no defect.

9.5.3 **Producers and suppliers**

The Act and Directive are agreed on defining as the producer the person who manufactures it, and the winner or abstracter or alternatively producer of any raw material. The Directive refers specifically to the manufacturer of a component part. The Act by contrast has a negative definition (s. 1(3)):

> A person who supplies any product in which products are comprised, whether by virtue of being component parts or raw materials or otherwise, shall not be treated by virtue only of his supply of that product as supplying any of the products so comprised.

The Directive appears to impose cumulative liability in relation to a complex product such as a car. Even if the defect can be traced to a specific component supplied by a third party, the car manufacturer remains liable. The Act appears to have the opposite effect, transferring liability onto the component manufacturer. The *intention* appears to have been otherwise. 'Product' is defined in the Act as including a product comprised in another product. This is a remarkably convoluted way of achieving the objective.

The first importer into the European Union (EU) and anyone who holds himself out as producer by applying his own name or trademark to the product (an 'own brander') are assimilated to the producer.

? | **QUESTION** 9.8

Who will actually bear liability under the Act (interpreted in the light of the Directive) when there is uncertainty as to the identity of the producer?

Primary liability is on the producer or importer. Suppliers are liable only when they are requested by the potential claimant to supply details of the producer within a reasonable time, and where the proposed claimant cannot already identify them by other means, and fails either to identify the producer or their own supplier. It is really in this context that s. 1(3) should operate. It is unreasonable for the seller of a TV to identify the source of every transistor, etc. in it.

Liability is joint and several.

9.5.4 **Scope of liability**

The Directive provides that:

(a) the producer shall be liable for damage caused by a defect in his product (Art. 1);

(b) the injured person shall be required to prove the damage, the defect, and the causal relationship between damage and defect (Art. 4).

The Act provides that: 'Where any damage is caused wholly or partly by a defect in a product [the producer] shall be liable for the damage (s. 2(1)).'

Damage is death, personal injury, and property damage (Art. 9, s. 5(1)). Contributory negligence will apply (Art. 8.2, s. 6(4)). There are three qualifications for property damage:

(a) a threshold of €500 (£275);

(b) exclusion of property not ordinarily intended for private use or consumption and used by the injured party for his private use or consumption;

(c) the defective product itself. The Act specifies that this includes any product in which the defective product is comprised. This appears to go beyond the Directive, and thus to be invalid. It reflects the traditional distinction between liability in contract for reducing the value of the thing and liability in tort where the thing damages something else, and the inclusion of the whole commodity appears to reflect the decision in *Aswan* v *Lupdine* [1987] 1 All ER 135 that items supplied together are within the economic loss category. The result appears to be that if a car crashes as a result of a defective tyre, the Act applies to the car if the tyre is a replacement, but not if it was original equipment, but this is subject to the overriding effect of the Directive.

? QUESTION 9.9

Gordon decides to purchase a sports car from Heritage, a small specialist manufacturer. Twelve months later Gordon takes delivery of his car. He goes out for a drive and after a few minutes loses control and crashes into a shed at the side of the road.

The car and the shed and its contents, which belong to Karamjit, are badly damaged. The main items damaged are a generator (value £400) which Karamjit uses as a backup to mains power for his home, and a collection of sound equipment, discs, and tapes (value £3,000) which Karamjit uses in his part-time work as a disc jockey.

The cause of the accident is traced to a fault in the electronic car management system.

Advise Gordon and Karamjit.

Gordon will almost certainly claim in contract. The car is not of satisfactory quality. Karamjit may be able to claim under the Act. The shed is almost certainly covered but:

• Is the generator (although actually used for domestic purposes) of a kind ordinarily so intended?

• Are the items of sound equipment, and records (although of a kind ordinarily intended for domestic use) actually being so used? or,

• Are both to be classed as commercial property and excluded?

If Karamjit cannot claim under the Act he may have a common law claim in negligence.

9.5.5 **Defences**

There are strict limitation periods. A claim must be brought within three years of becoming manifest, and within ten years of the supply of the product: s. 11A of the Limitation Act 1980 inserted by the Consumer Protection Act 1987. Contrast the periods at common law discussed at 9.4.5.

There is no liability if the defect arises from compliance with mandatory public requirements as to the product, e.g. recipe laws. This does not apply simply to licensing procedures if these do not prescribe the composition and processes.

The Directive and the Act apply only to business liability, so production and supply otherwise than in the course of business is excluded.

There will be no liability if:

(a) a product is distributed without the producer's consent, e.g. where something is stolen;

(b) the defect did not exist at the time the product was supplied by the defendant, e.g. if it has been modified by a later supplier, sabotaged, or allowed to deteriorate in an unforeseeable way;

(c) the product is not itself defective but when incorporated as a component in a larger product produces a defect attributable to the design of the larger product or the specifications given for the component.

These are all relatively uncontroversial, representing acceptable areas of non-liability.

The final defence is far more controversial. It is the so-called 'development risks defence'. The Act and the Directive exclude retrospective liability on the basis of hindsight and improvements in practice, but this defence concerns issues related to the state of the art. In essence the question is whether the developer of an innovative product bears the costs of design or testing defects (in practice spreading them by insurance) or whether these fall on the victim as part of the price of progress. It is somewhat surprising that the Directive allows Member States to opt in or out of this defence. Some have done so, some have not, while some have applied it to high risk products like pharmaceuticals. There is a serious risk of distortion because drugs will always be tested in areas where the defence applies, and the competitive position of a manufacturer operating in a 'state of the art protected' market is different from that of one in an unprotected market.

The Directive provides for a defence as follows: 'That the state of scientific and technical knowledge at the time when he put the product into circulation was not such as to enable the existence of the defect to be discovered.'

The wording in the Act is distinctly different:

> That the state of scientific and technical knowledge at the [time when he supplied the relevant product to another] was not such that a producer of products of the same description as the product in question might be expected to have discovered the defect if it had existed in his products while they were under his control.

The Directive test is both clearly objective and absolute. The test under the Act is certainly not absolute, since it appears to envisage different standards for different industries. It was meant to be objective. Lord Lucas of Chilworth said at *Hansard* HL Vol. 483, no. 25 col. 841:

> Only if the producer can prove to the court that he took all the steps that a producer of products of that kind might reasonably have been expected to take, and that the state of scientific and technical knowledge would have allowed him to take, will this defence be of any value.

It is not entirely clear that the wording achieves this. In any event the understanding of scientific and technical issues in a given industry may fall short of the knowledge actually extant. The Directive catches this situation, but the Act clearly does not.

The Commission took the view that this was defective implementation. Originally it had other complaints but these were resolved during the discussions prior to the commencement of Art. 226 proceedings.

 EXERCISE 9.5

Consider how the court might resolve this dispute.

The ECJ in *Commission* v *UK* (Case C-300/95) [1997] All ER (EC) 481 stated:

> The Commission takes the view that inasmuch as section 4(1)(e) of the Act refers to what may be expected of a producer of products of the same description as the product in question, its wording clearly conflicts with Article 7(e) of the Directive in that it permits account to be taken of the subjective knowledge of a producer taking reasonable care, having regard to the standard precautions taken in the industrial sector in question.
>
> That argument must be rejected in so far as it selectively stresses particular terms used in section 4(1)(e) without demonstrating that the general legal context of the provision at issue fails effectively to secure full application of the Directive. Taking that context into account, the Commission has failed to make out its claim that the result intended by Article 7(e) of the Directive would clearly not be achieved in the domestic legal order.
>
> The Court has consistently held that the scope of national laws, regulations or administrative provisions must be assessed in the light of the interpretation given to them by national courts. Yet in this case the Commission has not referred in support of its application to any national judicial decision which, in its view, interprets the domestic provision at issue inconsistently with the Directive.
>
> There is nothing in the material produced to the Court to suggest that the courts in the United Kingdom, if called upon to interpret section 4(1)(e), would not do so in the light of the wording and the purpose of the Directive so as to achieve the result which it has in view and thereby comply with the third paragraph of Art. [249] of the Treaty.
>
> Moreover, section 1(1) of the Act expressly imposes such an obligation on the national courts.

In essence, the ECJ did not accept that, as a matter of pure textual analysis, the Directive necessarily meant what the Commission said it meant, or that the national court was bound to interpret s. 4(1)(e) contrary to the Directive. Although a submission that the proceedings were premature was rejected, the ECJ appears to be saying that it cannot rule on the issue unless and until there is a disputed interpretation of s. 4(1)(e) by the English courts. It is, all in all, a rather unsatisfactory and inconclusive decision.

> **? QUESTION** 9.10
>
> Return to Question 9.7. The following additional facts emerge:
>
> The electronic car management system was supplied to Heritage by Leiden Autoelektronik of the Netherlands. This is the first production model of this system. Research on equivalent systems in aviation has revealed problems of 'system interference' and this is the probable cause of this accident. Four similar failures (not resulting in accidents) have been reported to Heritage in the six months since the system was introduced. During this time they have sold 500 cars.
>
> How does this affect the position?

The development risks defence may be pleaded. Information about the problem does exist, but in a wholly different field. Is this the concrete case the ECJ are awaiting, i.e. is this covered by the Act but not the Directive? In principle the Directive should prevail, and this is a 'known' defect in the sense of known to science. The Act/Directive do not deal with recalls, but there may be liability at common law (see *Walton* v *British Leyland*).

In *A* v *National Blood Authority* [2001] 3 All ER 289 it was held that the development risks defence applied initially to the contamination of blood with a virus, but once this possibility was clearly established, the defence ceased to apply.

9.5.6 **Continuing problem areas**

There are two significant areas of possible discrepancy between the Act and the Directive: namely damage to a complex product and the scope of development risks. There are three possible approaches:

(a) benevolent or purposive construction of the Act as implementing legislation following *Pickstone* v *Freemans* [1988] 2 All ER 803 and *Litster* v *Forth Dry Dock Engineering Co. Ltd* [1989] 1 All ER 1134. It is not clear how far ministerial statements asserting a non-congruent intention will be considered;

(b) overriding construction under the *Marleasing* Case (106/89) [1992] 1 CMLR 305;

(c) a claim against the government under *Francovich* v *Italian State* (Cases C–6 and 9/90) [1992] IRLR 84).

Causation may be an issue, especially if the consumer has used the product over a period and two or more producers are involved. This has usually saved alcohol and tobacco companies, although in the USA pharmaceutical companies have been held jointly liable in such cases.

It is still much more difficult to prove that a design fault amounts to a defect than a construction or operational fault. This is partly the state of the art and hindsight rule, but it also has a cost benefit aspect. How far is a producer to go to seek out a potential design problem?

The scope of responsibility for products which are used unconventionally is also a grey area. Is unconventional use to absolve the producer on the grounds that the product was safe for its intended and expected uses? Will it be contributory negligence etc.?

■ SUMMARY

Product liability is one key area (professional liability is another which you have already met) where causes of action in tort and in contract, and the various rules regulating them can be used in conjunction to provide remedies for a range of claims. You should now understand:

- the nature and extent of contractual liability for goods which are either defective or dangerous, and the limitations imposed by the doctrine of privity of contract;

- the development of the common law of negligence in cases where goods are actually dangerous;

- the theoretical basis of the UK and EU statutory protection, including the difficulties of reconciling the texts.

For the first time, it is probably true to say that there is a comprehensive and effective network of causes of action which should ensure that anyone injured, or suffering property damage, as a result of dangerously defective goods will receive adequate compensation.

■ FURTHER READING

Cooke, P.J. and Oughton, D.W., *The Common Law of Obligations*, 3rd edn, London: Butterworths, 2000, Chapter 24 (especially recommended because it brings the various causes of action and rules together and compares them).

Howarth, D., *Textbook on Tort*, 2nd edn, London: Butterworths 2004, Chapter 8. (Caution! There is a lot of theoretical and advanced discussion of economics and policy. It is good stuff, but quite difficult.)

Jones, M.A., *Textbook on Torts*, 8th edn, London: Blackstone Press, 2002, Chapter 10.

Markesinis, B.S. and Deakin, S.F., *Tort Law*, 5th edn, Oxford: Oxford University Press, 2003, Chapter 6.

Murphy, J., *Street on Torts*, 11th edn, London: Butterworths, 2003, Chapter 17.

Winfield and Jolowicz on Tort, 17th edn, London: Sweet & Maxwell, 2006, Chapter 10.

CHAPTER 9 ASSESSMENT EXERCISE

(1) Latifa buys a fish tank from Allpets Pet Stores. It is fitted with a heater, which came separately packed and labelled as the Allpets Allstar Tankkosy. In fact it was manufactured in China and imported to Finland (in January 1995) by Finchin Impex A/S. Latifa is impressed with the heater and buys a second one for another tank which she has owned for some time. The English instructions simply refer to the need to use a 3 amp fused plug. There are additional instructions, in Finnish and Chinese only, which state that the heater has a dual level transformer which should be set to H for connection to a 230v supply as in the UK and to L for connection to a 110v supply.

After the heaters have been in use for a month there is an explosion because they have been set at L. The two tanks, the valuable fish in them and an antique oriental carpet are destroyed and Latifa's cleaner sustains serious personal injury.

Advise on liability.

Would it affect your advice if Latifa's main source of income was selling fish she had bred?

(2) Norman recently bought a 'Flamegrill' barbecue set from his local branch of Wyoming Homecare. It incorporated an accessory described as 'The latest miracle of Japanese electronic wizardry: a fully automated, foolproof infrared temperature sensor'. The instructions state that if the sensor is touched against any item of food, a light will flash if the food is fully cooked through. The sensor is pre-programmed to recognize most common barbecued foods, including beef, chicken, and pork.

Norman organizes a barbecue to raise funds for the village church steeple appeal. The ticket price includes refreshments. Many of the guests, and Norman himself, suffer food poisoning which is diagnosed as resulting from the consumption of marinaded pork spare-ribs, which Norman purchased from Bob, the local butcher. These were affected by trichinella. This is commonly present in raw pork, but is killed by adequate heating. The sensor was used on all the ribs and indicated that they were fully cooked.

Most of the guests bought their own tickets. The exceptions were Cynthia, the vicar, who was admitted free, and Ann and Ben who turned up without tickets. Just before leaving, Ann wrote out a cheque for the cost of two tickets.

Considerable development work has been done on this form of sensor. This indicates that it does perform as indicated above. Some three months before this particular barbecue was manufactured, a research paper was delivered to a seminar at Hamburger University, in which it was demonstrated that inaccurate readings could be obtained in respect of 'bone-in' meat, especially pork.

Consider the liability of:

(a) Norman;

(b) Any other potential defendant.

See *Cases and Materials* (9.4) for a specimen answer.

10 Trespass torts

10.1 OBJECTIVES

By the end of this chapter you should be able to:

1 Explain the historical development of the trespass torts

2 Explain how the trespass torts are commonly used to resolve apparently unrelated issues such as disputes over the ownership of goods and the protection of civil liberties

3 Explain the characteristics of the different trespass torts

4 Apply the rules relating to trespass torts in practice

10.2 Introduction

 EXERCISE 10.1

Make a list of the behaviour which you consider to be trespass on a separate piece of paper. Put this to one side.

10.3 General historical background to the trespass torts

> The protection of the person from deliberately inflicted physical harm and restriction on freedom of movement, and the protection of interests in tangible property, especially the right to non-interference with land and goods, were originally the most important concerns of the law of torts. (*Street on Torts* at p. 9.)

These are very old established torts. They are based on the Writ of Trespass which is one of the original writs (kinds of action) developed in medieval times. Strictly speaking this writ only covered direct and intentional harm to the interests referred to above. The action of trespass on the case covered indirect harm, and as the law developed this evolved into the separate action for negligence. Although we say the harm is 'intentional', that word is used in a rather specialized sense, as we will see later in relation to the individual torts.

> **?** | **QUESTION** 10.1
>
> Fred is driving down the street. He intends to cross over a junction even though the lights are turning to red against him. He collides with, and injures, Ben, who is in the car in front, and who braked to stop at the lights.
>   Is this:
>
> - a trespass
> - actionable negligence
> - both
> - neither?

10.3.1 The meaning of intention

For the moment keep in mind that 'intentional' is not the same as 'deliberate'. In general, it is more a question of the act being voluntary than that you are seeking to achieve a particular result. In areas covered by trespass you act at your peril, in the sense that if the result of your act is a direct interference with the defendant's interests, you will be liable for the consequences whether you meant to interfere or not. You might therefore think that this is a trespass, as Fred clearly meant to drive over the piece of road in question, irrespective of Ben's presence.

Modern law has, however, moved away from absolute liability. In nineteenth-century America a man struck out at a dog with his walking stick; he caught a bystander with his 'back-lift' and this was held to be trespass, as the defendant acted at his peril. This absolute test where you 'act at your peril' still applies in relation to some trespasses (e.g. conversion), but not trespass to the person. Where harm is a side effect, as it appears to be here, it is not a trespass. The driving, rather than the collision, is intentional. After all Fred may well have expected Ben to go through the lights, so it is to that extent 'accidental' that he is a careful driver and does not run the risk. Fred may be liable in negligence if his driving fell below a proper standard. However, if Ben had annoyed Fred and Fred was retaliating by driving his car at Ben's it would be trespass as the contact is intended (and as it happens it is also deliberate).

10.3.2 How the trespass torts are handled

As these are old torts, their rules are often well defined, and can be set out very concisely. There is surprisingly little to say about them in a strictly legal sense. As we go through you will see that the ingredients of each separate tort have been briefly set out. The definitions are usually from *Street on Torts*, 12th edn, edited by John Murphy, but this is a personal preference and does not suggest that *Street* is more definitive than other books. Indeed, an alternative definition will be used if it is more complete, or accurate, or better expressed.

10.3.3 **Legal inventiveness**

The trespass torts are in fact more interesting from the point of view of legal inventiveness, actions devised for one purpose being adapted to serve others. It is also notable that the various trespass actions are often utilized as the legal mechanism for litigating disputes which are essentially concerned with other areas of the law, such as civil liberties, contract, and personal property.

10.3.4 **Human rights**

This is particularly relevant today in the light of the Human Rights Act 1998 (*Cases and Materials* (10.1)). This Act incorporates into English law the substantive provisions of the European Convention on Human Rights and Fundamental Freedoms (ECHR). In turn this was drafted just after the Second World War, largely by English legal draftsmen. The civil and human rights which it protected were therefore often modelled on existing English concepts. These in turn often rested on the trespass torts. Two examples will illustrate this:

1. As long ago as 1765 the case of *Entick* v *Carrington* (1765) 2 Wils 275 used trespass to goods to determine the scope of the government's powers to search for and seize allegedly seditious documents. The judges held that there must be a specific statutory or common law entitlement to justify search and seizure, and none could be found in the circumstances of the case. As a result the officials concerned were liable in trespass, as they could not justify their actions. Article 8 ECHR now guarantees respect for everyone's 'home and his correspondence. There is to be no interference with the exercise of this right except such as in accordance with the law and is necessary in a democratic society' on a number of clearly defined grounds, including national security, prevention of disorder and crime, and the protection of health and morals. While the modern criteria for legal searches are different from the eighteenth-century ones, the modern law is clearly founded on trespass principles.

2. A claim for false imprisonment is the usual means of testing whether detention, by the police or otherwise, is lawful. In effect, if someone is detained, it is for the person detaining to demonstrate that they have a legal justification to do so. Article 5 ECHR provides that 'everyone has the right to liberty and security of the person'. Any deprivation of liberty must be according to law, under judicial control, and for a specified purpose of which imprisonment for crime and detention of the mentally disordered are the principal instances. In *L* v *Bournewood NHS Trust* [1998] 3 All ER 289 the House of Lords ruled that an autistic patient, who was in hospital, was not detained when it was the case that he was not physically prevented from leaving, although had he attempted to leave he would have been prevented. The statutory procedure formally to detain under the Mental Health Act had not been applied. The House also ruled that if he were regarded as being detained, the detention would be lawful pursuant to the doctrine of necessity. The European Court of Human Rights subsequently concluded in *HL* v *United Kingdom* (2005) 40 EHRR 32 that there was in effect a detention, that the operation of the doctrine of necessity was too unpredictable and there was therefore no proper legal control over the clinical judgment of the doctors. Accordingly the detention was unlawful.

In many cases the judges will be able to conclude that English law adequately reflects the ECHR standards, if necessary by applying a purposive approach to interpretation to give effect to the underlying intention, rather than the precise terms of the legal rule in question: *Ghaidin* v *Ghodin-Mendoza* [2004] UKHL 30. The developing case law under the Human Rights Act is likely to lead to developments in the law of trespass, of which the *Bournewood* case is an early example.

10.3.5 A list of trespasses

There are a number of separate torts comprised within the general heading of trespass. These include:

(a) trespass to the person (assault and battery);

(b) false imprisonment (including wrongful arrest);

(c) trespass to land. This is technically known as trespass *quare clausum fregit* (i.e. in the narrow modern popular sense, by going on to someone's land, literally 'by breaking a boundary');

(d) trespass to goods;

(e) interference with goods (conversion).

How does this compare with the list you made for **Exercise 10.1**?

Although related, each of these torts derived from a different form of writ and represented a different form of action, each with its own detailed procedural rules. There are therefore distinctions between them which can be explained only on a historical basis. You will, however, be relieved to learn that we do not need to carry out any substantial historical investigation. It is enough to know the present scope of each tort.

10.3.6 Allegations of force: fictions and the royal courts

When instituting an action for trespass there was always an allegation that the defendant had acted *vi et armis, et contra pacem domini regis* (with force of arms and contrary to the King's Peace). This allegation (which might be, and often was, wholly fictitious) was originally inserted in medieval times to give a royal interest in the subject matter of the action (represented by the breach of the King's Peace) so as to confer jurisdiction on the Royal Court, rather than the competing local courts. It also harks back to the original reasons for giving a civil remedy for such matters at all, which were: first, a desire to avoid remedies by way of self-help, which in violent medieval times could readily lead to an unacceptable level of feuding; and secondly, a wish to reinforce the enforcement of the criminal law.

10.3.7 Trespass: tort and crime

Most trespasses are also crimes; various forms of assault, rape, theft, and robbery. The cases in which women have sued in trespass to the person for rape, adult victims have sued for child abuse, and the civil action against Michael and Fitzroy Brookes for killing Lynn Siddons: *Halford* v *Brookes* [1991] 1 WLR 428, were very obvious examples of trespass, since it is hard to imagine more obvious examples of the intentional and direct infliction of physical force. They sometimes raise interesting issues as to procedure and evidence (e.g. the adoption of the higher criminal standard of proof in the 'murder' case, which has been adopted in the most recent abuse cases).

They were also unusual as the first modern examples of such actions which were not preceded by a criminal conviction. If such cases are rare, it is because the defendant is usually not 'worth powder and shot'. In *Stubbings* v *Webb* [1993] 1 All ER 322, where a woman was complaining of physical and sexual abuse by two relatives, the judges pointed out that neither defendant appeared to be in a position to satisfy an award of damages. This seems to be an implied criticism of the use of civil proceedings for cathartic purposes (to 'see justice done' and 'work out' the grief and anxiety).

It is sometimes possible to pursue a claim and recover large damages. In *W* v *Meah* [1986] 1 All ER 935, a minicab driver underwent a personality change as a result of head injuries sustained in a road traffic accident. He then sexually assaulted two women. It was worthwhile to sue him because he had received damages for his personal injuries. Indeed the issue of liability of the original tortfeasor to pay additional damages by reason of this further damage flowing ultimately from his negligence has also engaged the court: *Meah* v *McCreamer* [1985] 1 All ER 367 and *Meah* v *McCreamer (No. 2)* [1986] 1 All ER 943.

In earlier days, the availability of damages was an incentive for the claimant to bring the defendant to justice, so doing the job of the police and magistrates. The criminal law and civil law of trespass remain closely allied in relation to offences against the person, and cases in one field are generally regarded as authorities in the other, but the criminal law of offences against property has developed along very different lines.

The main difference in relation to offences and trespasses against the person is that the criminal law is more concerned with the degree of moral responsibility of the defendant, to ensure that punishment is justified by that moral responsibility. In civil proceedings, the level of compensation is based on the claimant's loss. The defendant, in this respect, 'acts at his peril' and this may result in heavy damages arising from a trivial interference with the claimant.

It should also be noted that, while the substantive law may be the same, procedural aspects, such as the burden and standard of proof, may be different. In a case where self defence is an issue, in a criminal trial it is for the prosecution to satisfy the court so that it is sure beyond reasonable doubt that the defendant was not acting in self defence, while in a civil trial it is up to the defendant to establish on the balance of probabilities that he was acting in self defence: *Ashley* v *Chief Constable of Sussex* [2006] EWCA Civ 1085. This is an example of the general proposition that it is for the defendant in a tort claim in trespass to establish lawful justification for what is on the face of it a wrongful act; see 10.4.3.6 and also 10.4.5.4 for a discussion in relation to justification for false imprisonment.

10.3.8 **The place of trespass**

The interests protected by the trespass torts are also the most important recognized by society, although there is perhaps an excess of conservatism in the continuing primacy accorded to tangible belongings over intangible wealth. The state of the law reflects the condition of society at the time it developed, a period when wealth was largely tangible. It is, however, difficult to criticize the survival of this anomaly in trespass when a similar distinction is jealously guarded in negligence and other 'modern' torts in relation to economic loss as opposed to physical injury or damage.

> **? QUESTION** 10.2
>
> Compare the trespass torts with negligence.

The trespass torts are closely based on a notion of rights, and the action relates to the infringement of the right, rather than the harm caused. Only specific areas of activity are within the specific kinds of trespass. In negligence, the emphasis is on compensation and so actual, tangible harm must be shown. Against this, there is considerable room for development; 'the categories of negligence are never closed'. It is not necessary to fall within a strictly defined category, provided the claim is analogous to an existing category it can be entertained.

10.4 Trespass to the person and false imprisonment

10.4.1 Objectives

By the end of this section you should be able to:

- define both assault and battery in tort;
- describe and apply the justifications for and defences to assault and battery in tort;
- distinguish between criminal and civil assaults and batteries;
- state what is meant by imprisonment;
- describe and apply the justifications for imprisonment;
- explain the relationship between trespass to the person and civil liberties.

10.4.2 Trespass to the person

There are two forms of trespass to the person, assault, and battery, and there is the related *Wilkinson* v *Downton* tort. There is some doubt as to the exact classification of this tort. In this text it is discussed in conjunction with harassment in the chapter on nuisance (i.e. **Chapter 11**). In this area criminal and civil rules as to the substance of the offence/tort (i.e. in criminal terms the *actus reus*) are largely the same, so the criminal law case law on offences under the Offences Against the Person Act 1861 is directly relevant. The crucial distinction is that in tort there is not the same detailed consideration of the mental element, i.e. *mens rea*, and there is no subdivision of the various categories of assault for purposes of sentencing. As assault is defined by reference to battery, it is logical to consider the latter first.

10.4.3 Battery

Battery: any act of the defendant which directly and either intentionally (or possibly negligently) causes some physical contact with the person of the claimant without the claimant's consent. (*Street on Torts* at p. 32.)

We need to consider all the components of the definition.

10.4.3.1 **Directly**

There must be force, and the contact with the claimant must be the immediate result of the force. This will be a question of fact. If the harm is delayed there may be an action in negligence. The distinction is often illustrated by the example of a log being thrown from a window. If it hits a passer-by as it falls to the ground, that may be battery (it must of course have the necessary element of intention in relation to a victim). If it falls harmlessly, but a pedestrian later trips over it, that is, at most, negligence. This is one of the distinctions between negligence and trespass.

10.4.3.2 **Intentionally or negligently**

It is now clear that a mere and innocent accident will not do. There must be a victim in view.

> *Fowler* v *Lanning* [1959] 1 All ER 290 (*Cases and Materials* (10.2.1.1))
>
> The defendant discharged a shotgun while out shooting birds. The claimant was in the vicinity and sustained pellet wounds. In consequence the claimant started proceedings and served a statement of claim alleging that at a stated time and place 'the defendant shot the claimant'. There was no suggestion of a deliberate act, and the claimant did not allege negligence.
>
>   Diplock J ruled that in the absence of an allegation of negligence the pleading was inadequate. In other words, even if the claimant proved what was in the statement of claim, this did not amount to a battery. It might have been otherwise if the defendant ought to have appreciated the presence of and risk to the claimant. The claimant was then allowed to amend the statement of claim to allege negligence and the action proceeded to trial. Unfortunately for the claimant there were several people in the shooting party and it was impossible to prove from which gun the pellets which had wounded the claimant came. She could not prove that, on balance, the defendant was responsible.

In *Letang* v *Cooper* [1964] 2 All ER 929 the claimant was sunbathing in a grassy area forming part of the grounds of a hotel. The defendant drove his car over the claimant. It was not suggested that this was deliberate, although it was arguably negligent. The claimant for some reason did not sue within the negligence limitation period of three years, and tried to sue in battery, relying on the six-year limitation period applicable. The Court of Appeal refused to allow her to do so, relying on the fact that the three-year limitation period was intended to apply to all cases involving negligence. While suggesting that negligent trespass fulfilled no useful purpose, the Court did not actually declare that it did not exist.

> **?** **QUESTION** 10.3
>
> In the light of the judgments in *Fowler* v *Lanning* and *Letang* v *Cooper* how strong is the case for retaining 'negligently' in the definition of battery?

It is now probably the case that negligence will not be enough. In the USA battery is now restricted to intentional acts, in the sense that contact with the claimant was intended, and not merely a negligent side effect. This would mean that, in the example given earlier of the log, it would now be necessary to show that the log was being thrown at someone. It does not matter if it hits someone other than the intended victim: *Livingston* v *Ministry of Defence* [1984] NI 356. English law is still somewhat unclear on the point. No case requiring the point to be decided has come before the courts, but most commentators regard 'negligent trespass' as redundant and ripe for abolition.

It has been suggested that battery is now confined to intentional acts. In *Letang* v *Cooper* when the defendant directly harmed the claimant it was not intentional, although it was at least arguably negligent. The Court of Appeal held that the absence of intention was fatal to a claim in battery. However, the issue before the court was really one of limitation of actions, and the decision could be justified on other grounds. The court concentrated on whether the limitation period differed for trespass and negligence and found that it did not. The claimant was therefore too late anyway. While in their comments about the case (obiter) the judges were clearly encouraging claimants to bring allegations based on negligence under the tort of negligence, it is not clear that they meant to reach a final and binding decision on the scope of battery.

> **?** **QUESTION** 10.4
>
> Should trespass to the person exclude negligent acts?

In *Stubbings* v *Webb* [1993] 1 All ER 322, the House of Lords considered the limitation period applicable to intentional trespass, and concluded, following an analysis of the parliamentary history of the relevant provisions of the Limitation Act, that the intention had been to separate out 'accident' cases from trespass cases generally. The usual limitation for tort, including trespass, is six years, while for accident cases it is three years, with a discretion to extend it. As a result, although *Letang*, which was clearly an accident case, was rightly decided, it was wrong to apply the shorter limitation period to other trespass cases. In *Stubbings* v *Webb* itself this worked against the claimant, who was outside the six-year period (she was claiming in relation to childhood sexual abuse which she had allegedly 'suppressed' for a number of years since reaching adulthood, so was seeking unsuccessfully to rely on the various extensions permitted in accident cases where the claim cannot be brought within the three-year period).

The House did not feel it necessary to consider the passages in *Letang* v *Cooper* as to whether there could be a negligent trespass. It would seem, however, in view of the way in which the procedural rules have been assimilated, that there is no meaningful difference between the two causes of action in an accident type case. What, after all, is to be gained from suing in trespass rather than negligence if the object of the exercise is to obtain compensation for harm suffered? Virtually any harm amounting to trespass to the person will amount to negligence, and the procedural rules are similar.

It is clear that criminal batteries can be committed recklessly (although the court must be satisfied that the defendant was conscious of taking an unjustified risk): *R* v *Savage; DPP* v *Parmenter* [1991] 4 All ER 698. See also the Law Commission Paper 122 *Legislating the Criminal*

Code: Offences against the Person and General Principles (1992), where the same definition (i.e. intentional or reckless) is used. It may accordingly be the case that something short of direct intention will suffice for a civil claim.

10.4.3.3 **Physical contact**

Injury is not required. As a trespass, battery is actionable *per se* (i.e. with no need to prove substantial harm). It is not necessary to prove injury or tangible loss, merely that the claimant's rights have been infringed. An action can be brought to establish a principle, e.g. in relation to unlawful fingerprinting. It can also be brought where there is indignity but no physical injury. Negligence is of less assistance here as it will provide compensation only for actual tangible loss. It is worth noting, however, that where a technical touching is intended, but what actually transpires is something substantial (as in *Savage*, where the defendant meant to throw beer over the victim, but lost control of the glass and struck the victim with it), there is both criminal and civil liability for what actually occurs.

There are a number of cases in which it is accepted that the contact can be less than entirely direct. So it is battery to strike the horse on which the claimant is riding: *Dodwell* v *Burford* (1669) 1 Mod Rep 24, or to touch the claimant's clothing: *Piggly Wiggly Alabama Corp.* v *Rickles* (1925) 103 So 860 (USA). In *Haystead* v *Chief Constable of Derbyshire* [2000] 3 All ER 890 the defendant punched a woman, causing her to drop the child she was holding. This amounted to the criminal offence of 'assaulting by beating' the child, which requires a battery.

The defendant must be an active, not a passive, party: *Innes* v *Wylie* (1844) 1 Car & Kir 257. The claimant had been expelled from a society. It was known that he intended to attend a dinner of the society and a policeman, acting on the orders of the defendant, was stationed to prevent him doing so. There was a dispute on the facts as to whether the policeman had merely stood in the way or had taken active steps to move the claimant back. It was held that it would be battery only if the latter were proved.

10.4.3.4 **Without consent**

This raises a number of quite complex issues, which go beyond the trespass torts. See the discussion in 14.3.1.

Express consent

If you have ever undergone elective surgery you will know that you are required to sign a consent form. This consent must be genuine, but where the claimant is really complaining that, although they signed the form, they only did so because they were not properly informed about the implications of treatment, they are regarded as consenting. Any claim must be brought in negligence on the basis that advice on these matters is part of the doctor's professional responsibility.

Chatterton v *Gerson* [1981] 1 All ER 257 (*Cases and Materials* (10.2.1.2))

The claimant was suffering from chronic and serious pain. Having exhausted a large number of orthodox treatments she consulted the defendant, who had undertaken study in the USA and was prepared to use techniques he had observed and practised there, including the application of intrathecal phenol (acid into the spinal cord!) which is what he recommended for the claimant. At the time this was still experimental in the UK and there was little evidence of what was the general practice in terms of warnings and advice to patients. The treatment did not prove effective and the claimant framed a claim in battery on the footing that she had not given true or informed consent to the treatment in the absence of proper explanation of the possible complications. This argument was rejected. Bristow J ruled:

> [W]hat the court has to do in each case is to look at all the circumstances and say: 'Was there a real consent?' I think justice requires that in order to vitiate the reality of consent there must be a greater failure of communication between doctor and patient than that involved in a breach of duty if the claim is based on negligence. When the claim is based on negligence the claimant must prove not only the breach of duty to inform, but that had the duty not been broken she would not have chosen to have the operation. When the claim is based on trespass to the person, then what the claimant would have decided if she had been given the information . . . is irrelevant.
>
> [O]nce the claimant is informed in broad terms of the nature of the procedure which is intended, and gives her consent, that consent is real, and the cause of action on which to base a claim for failure to go into risks and implications is negligence not trespass.

? QUESTION 10.5

Is it reasonable for doctors to operate on you without your full, free, and informed consent? If so, why? If not, why not?

There is a very serious issue here; should the *Bolam* test which you have already met as the standard test for medical negligence cases (see 1.7.1.3), apply to advice given as to the risks and benefits of proposed treatment, or is some other test applicable? In the USA there must be informed consent. The doctor must tell the patient everything that a prudent patient would want to know about the risks and benefits of the treatment being offered. If not, the patient can sue in battery. In Canada and Australia a similar result is reached in a different way. Such cases are treated as being part of the doctor's professional responsibility, but in deciding whether the doctor has fulfilled that duty, a similar prudent patient test is applied.

Chatterton v *Gerson* was followed in *Hills* v *Potter* [1983] 3 All ER 716 where the trial judge, Hirst J, considered the American case of *Canterbury* v *Spence* (1972) 464 F 2nd 772 (which established the American doctrine of informed consent) and the Canadian cases of *Hopp* v *Lepp* (1980) 112 DLR (3rd) 67 and *Reibl* v *Hughes* (1980) 114 DLR (3rd) 1 (which established that the Canadian test for negligence was the prudent patient). He used these only to support his conclusion that negligence rather than trespass was the appropriate action. Although both English cases were at first instance only, they have been accepted as representing the law.

Although it was now clear that the claim lay in negligence, it could still be argued that the prudent patient test should apply, rather than the *Bolam* test. The position was finally resolved by the House of Lords in the case of *Sidaway* v *Bethlem Royal & Maudsley Hospital Governors* [1985] 1 All ER 643. The case concerned an alleged failure to warn of the risks associated with a particular operation. The risk that eventuated was one which was significantly less than a 1% chance! There were difficulties because the claimant's evidence that no warning had been given was not accepted, but the surgeon had died before the trial so could not give evidence as to the scope of the warning. Unfortunately, the House was divided as to the proper test to be applied. The minority view was that one or other version of informed consent should apply, but the majority considered that the *Bolam* test was of universal application. Lord Diplock said:

> In English jurisprudence the doctor's relationship with his patient which gives rise to the normal duty of care to exercise his skill and judgment to improve the patient's health in any particular respect in which the patient has sought his aid has hitherto been treated as a single comprehensive duty covering all the ways in which a doctor is called upon to exercise his skill or judgment in the improvement of the physical or mental condition of the patient . . . This general duty is not subject to dissection into a number of component parts to which different criteria of what satisfy the duty of care apply, such as diagnosis, treatment, and advice (including warning of any risks of something going wrong however skilfully the treatment itself is carried out).

His Lordship pointed out that *Bolam* itself concerned an allegation of failure to warn, which had been dealt with in the same terms as the allegation about inappropriate treatment. The US version of informed consent, which created an action based on trespass was again expressly rejected. Reliance was placed on the old case of *Slater* v *Baker* (1767) 95 ER 860, where the patient's action was said to lie in case (in modern terms negligence), not trespass. The Canadian attempt to incorporate 'informed consent' into a negligence context was disapproved.

? **QUESTION** 10.6

Is English law right to reject both the US and Canadian concepts of informed consent and continue to apply the *Bolam* test to cases involving the assessment of risks and benefits of alternative treatment strategies.

You may think that applying the *Bolam* test is an abdication of responsibility by the law, allowing expert medical evidence to determine the outcome. Two of their Lordships (Lord Bridge and Lord Keith) asserted that medical evidence was not conclusive:

> [E]ven in a case where . . . no expert witness in the relevant medical field condemns the nondisclosure as being in conflict with accepted and responsible medical practice, I am of opinion that the judge might in certain circumstances come to the conclusion that disclosure of a particular risk was so necessary to an informed choice on the part of the patient that no reasonably prudent medical man would fail to make it.

Hirst J said much the same in *Hills* v *Potter*:

> I do not accept that, by adopting the *Bolam* principle, the court in effect abandons its power of decision to the doctors. In every case the court must be satisfied that the standard contended for on [the defendant's] behalf accords with that upheld by a substantial body of medical opinion, and that this body of medical opinion is both respectable and responsible, and experienced in this particular field of medicine.

These fine words have not generally been backed up by action, and it remains the case that medical negligence is one of the hardest things to prove, unless there has been an obvious mistake, such as the amputation of the wrong leg. Of course there may be cases where the advice given by the doctor is inadequate, as in *Chester* v *Afshar* [2004] UKHL 41.

 EXERCISE 10.2

List the advantages and disadvantages of the three approaches to consent to treatment discussed below.

Patient autonomy

In general, a patient with full mental capacity has the right to consent or not to treatment. Enforced treatment will be a battery: *In re B (Consent to Treatment: Capacity)* (2002), *The Times*, 26 March; *St Georges NHS Trust* v *S* [1999] Fam 26. Even where a patient lacks capacity, treatment not in his best interests is unlawful: *Airedale NHS Trust* v *Bland* [1993] AC 789.

Consent and duress

Consent extorted by fear is void; there is no modern authority, but the proposition is self-evident. There are old cases to the contrary, but no one considers they will be followed today. These include *Latter* v *Braddell* (1881) 50 LJQB 448, where a maidservant's claim that a medical examination on which her mistress insisted, and to which she had submitted in an obviously tearful and distressed condition, amounted to battery was dismissed.

Consent and fraud

Consent given by reason of fraud or abuse of power may be void: *Hegarty* v *Shine* (1878) 12 Cox CC 125. It will, however, depend on the nature of the fraudulent representation. English law takes a narrow view. If the deception goes to the essence of the transaction it will negative consent, but if it goes only to the surrounding circumstances it will not. Many of the cases are of seduction. If a man seduces a naive girl by pretending that what he is doing is a surgical operation there is no consent. Seducing a woman by a promise of marriage, or an assurance of infertility is a different matter; the woman does consent to intercourse, although fraud has been used. However, in Canada it has been held that the consent of the 'wife' of a bigamist is no defence to an action for deceit: *Graham* v *Saville* [1945] 2 DLR 489.

 EXERCISE 10.3

Which approach to consent by deception do you prefer?

10.4.3.5 **Burden of proof**

It is for the claimant to negative consent, as in a case where a prisoner objected to medical treatment which he had been given: *Freeman* v *Home Office (No. 2)* [1984] 1 All ER 1036 (CA). See also *L* v *Bournewood NHS Trust* [1998] 3 All ER 289 (*Cases and Materials* (10.2.3.2)).

In the context of bona fide medical treatment it may be reasonable to put this onus on the claimant; is it always? We are really only considering contexts in which consent can normally be inferred. Given the scope of the defendant's liability, it may be only fair to place this onus on the claimant.

10.4.3.6 **Implied consent: general social contact**

In a crowded society, some unpermitted contact is inevitable. Apart from casual contact in the street or public transport, friends and acquaintances may accept more intrusive behaviour. However, there are limits, especially if the person causing the contact is part of the machinery of government.

?   **QUESTION** 10.7

Which of the following are and are not batteries (paying particular regard to issues of implied consent)?

(a) Hanif collapses in the street. Jane gives him mouth-to-mouth resuscitation and also tries to administer cardiac compression treatment.

(b) Brooklyn and Jordan are 'playfighting' at school. Jordan knocks Brooklyn down. Brooklyn trips over his sarong and breaks his collar-bone.

(c) PC Plod puts his hand on Noddy's shoulder because he wants to tell Noddy that his car is causing an obstruction.

(d) Sam has just scored the first century for England at Lord's for seven years. As he goes into the pavilion, well-wishers slap him on the back and grab his arms. The following morning his shoulders are red and sore.

Necessity may justify intervention. This is the basis on which doctors may treat a patient who is unconscious or too ill to consent. It would also justify pushing someone out of the path of an approaching car. However, this intervention is only justified if it is in the best interests of the person concerned. In *Airedale NHS Trust* v *Bland* [1993] AC 789 Tony Bland was a victim of the Hillsborough disaster. He was rescued alive and treated in the hope that he would recover. That initial treatment was clearly justified by necessity. Unfortunately it was not successful, and it became clear that he was suffering from complete destruction of the higher brain functions and was in a persistent vegetative state. At this point continued invasive treatment, such as nutrition tubes, could not be justified as being in his best interests, as he effectively had none. Technically, to continue these treatments was a battery, and it was accordingly lawful for them to be withdrawn.

> *Wilson* v *Pringle* [1986] 2 All ER 440 (*Cases and Materials* (10.2.1.3))
>
> The defendant and the claimant were both schoolboys. The defendant, from behind, pulled at a bag on the claimant's shoulder. The claimant fell and hurt himself. The claimant sought summary judgment, on the basis that this was a clear battery.
>
> It was held, having regard to the age of the parties, the general habits of schoolboys and the absence of malice (in the sense of actual malevolence), this was not so clearly a battery that summary judgment should be given. This case can be contrasted with *Williams* v *Humphreys* (1975), *The Times*, 20 February, where the defendant, a 15-year-old, pushed the claimant into a swimming pool by way of a prank. The court held this amounted to battery. It went beyond any activity which could be described as permitted child's play.

In *Collins* v *Wilcock* [1984] 3 All ER 374, which is a criminal case, the prosecutrix, a WPC, tried to question the defendant. The defendant walked off; the prosecutrix tried (without arresting her) to restrain her. The defendant tried to break free, and in doing so, scratched the prosecutrix. She was prosecuted for assaulting a police officer in the execution of her duty. The crucial question was whether the prosecutrix had stepped outside the line of duty. The court held that the prosecutrix's action in restraining the defendant amounted to a battery, and as such the prosecutrix ceased to be acting in the execution of her duty. A distinction was drawn between a touch to attract attention and a restraint. A police officer is not on duty to break the law, and doing so cannot be an exercise of duty. It is clear that no physical harm was either intended or caused by the prosecutrix.

In *Mepstead* v *DPP* [1996] Crim LR 111 the defendant parked illegally. He was asked to move but declined. An officer started to write out a parking ticket and the defendant became seriously annoyed and abusive. Another PC took hold of the defendant's arm to attract his attention to explain what was going on. The defendant hit him and was charged with assault on a police officer in the execution of his duty. He was convicted and appealed. The conviction was upheld. Taking hold of someone to attract or hold their attention, or to give an explanation would be lawful (and within the lawful duties of a constable) if it was 'acceptable by the ordinary standards of everyday life'. This was a question of fact for the justices and there was no suggestion that their decision was perverse.

While this decision certainly suggests greater leeway than *Collins* v *Wilcock*, it is possible to distinguish them, if only on the basis that the defendant in *Collins* had turned away and did not want to talk, while the defendant in *Mepstead* was agitated and not, apparently, addressing his mind to the actions of the policeman. It may be better to see the later case as an indication of a less restrictive approach.

Where the police are exercising statutory powers, they are protected from actions for trespass to the person, but it may be necessary to explain what those powers are: *O'Loughlin* v *Chief Constable of Essex* (1997), *The Times*, 11 December, where the claimant succeeded in a claim against the police when he was assaulted and battered during an incident where the police acted without explaining the statutory basis for their actions. See, also, the wrongful arrest cases discussed under false imprisonment (10.4.5.4), where the same issue arises.

? **QUESTION** 10.8

What is the linking factor explaining why these cases were decided as they were?

The distinction is sometimes put on the basis of a hostile touching or touching in anger, as distinct from incidental contact. This is based on a comment by Hale CJ in *Cole* v *Turner* (1704) 6 Mod 149. While this may be a useful test it is not universal. Does it explain why the acts of a surgeon who operates on an unconscious accident victim will not amount to battery, but the lightest restraint by a PC who is not exercising a power of arrest will do so? Lord Goff suggested both in *Collins* v *Wilcock* and in *Re F* [1990] 2 AC 1 that the real point is that any contact must be justified. This may be as a result of the acceptance of incidental contact as part of 'life's give and take', but considered acts, like surgery, need to be positively justified as being in the recipient's 'best interests'. This emphasis on justification rightly focuses on the defendant. He must account satisfactorily for his behaviour. He has chosen to act and does so at his peril.

10.4.3.7 **Sports**

What do you think the law says about harm caused by participating in sports and games? There will often be contact authorized by the rules of the game, and also contact which results from a clumsy or ineffective failure to abide by the rules. Generally this sort of contact is deemed to be with the consent of the victim. It is part of the risk accepted when agreeing to play. Deliberate foul play is outside that consent: *Condon* v *Basi* [1985] 2 All ER 453. This case involves soccer, but there have also been cases involving cynical foul play in both codes of rugby, e.g. *R* v *Billinghurst* [1978] Crim LR 553. *Condon* is in fact a case in negligence, but it was not suggested that this made any difference so far as this point is concerned. (See also 1.7.1.2.)

10.4.3.8 **Other deliberate acts**

The limits of consent in areas other than 'manly sports' are now set by *R* v *Brown* [1993] 2 All ER 75. A number of men were prosecuted and convicted for causing actual or grievous bodily harm to adult sado-masochists. The victims had in fact consented. The trial judge ruled that this consent was not legally valid. The House of Lords, dismissing appeals against conviction, held that while consent might be an effective defence in relation to 'manly sports' and other harm of a trivial and transient nature, it could not in law be a defence where there was more serious harm, as there was in this case. The House considered that violence had always to be justified: sport could be justified positively in a way that prizefighting (*R* v *Coney* (1882) 8 QBD 534) and general scuffling and fighting (*A-G's Reference (No. 6 of 1980)* [1981] 2 All ER 1057) could not be. In each case it was the element of disorder or breach of the peace which made the difference. It has always been accepted that consent is not ordinarily a defence in relation to serious and permanent harm, a fortiori death. Do you think that this decision cuts down the area for consent too far?

You should bear in mind that many, although not all, of the injuries in this case were quite serious, and it is a matter of some surprise that none of the 'victims' required medical treatment or suffered complications or permanent damage. If a 'victim' were to bring civil proceedings claiming damages, defences would be available that are irrelevant in the criminal context, namely *volenti non fit injuria, ex turpi causa non oritur actio,* and contributory negligence (which, despite its name, is available in trespass as well). There was a very forceful dissent from Lords Mustill and Slynn, who took the view that these were really sexual offences and should be dealt with as such. The Court of Appeal has held that where a husband branded his initials on his wife's buttocks 'at her express request', this was within the scope of legitimate consent: *Wilson* [1996] Crim LR 573; [1996] 3 WLR 125. This appears to be rather different in tone from *Brown.* See also **Chapter 14** on defences generally. The Law Commission, in the criminal context, propose that it should only be an offence to inflict minor harm (love bites, minor bumps, etc.) if this is without consent. Consent would only be a defence to the infliction of more serious harm where it is consent to a risk of reckless infliction (e.g. contact sports) or there is specific justification (e.g. medical treatment). This principled approach should avoid the inconsistencies of a case law approach. This specific proposal is however, likely to drive a wedge between civil and criminal trespass to the person as the Theft Act has done in relation to trespass to goods. Consultation Paper 119, November 1995. *Cf.* the draft Offences Against the Person Bill, clause 4.

10.4.3.9 **Other defences**

A person is entitled to use reasonable force to defend himself against an actual attack or one which he perceives to be being launched against him. The force must be proportional to the threat as perceived. Standards of reasonableness differ, according to the values and practices of society at the relevant time. In *Fraser* v *Berkeley* (1836) 7 C & P 621, Lord Abinger said: 'If an author is to go and give a beating to a publisher who has offended him, two or three blows with a horse-whip ought to be enough to satisfy his irritated feelings.' His Lordship may have had his tongue in his cheek when he said that, but it would certainly not reflect modern views on the matter.

Any response by a defendant must be proportionate to the threat, or damage inflicted upon the defendant. This requirement is evident even in earlier authority. In *Cockroft* v *Smith* (1705) 2 Salk 642, for example, during an altercation in court, an attorney moved his hand towards the eyes of a clerk attending the court; it was held that the clerk could not justify biting off one of the attorney's fingers.

 EXERCISE 10.4

Think of a typical situation in which self-defence might apply.

You might have had in mind a fight between two or more people (not a regulated boxing match, in which the question of consent might arise).

According to Lord Oaksey in *Turner* v *MGM* [1950] 1 All ER 449:

> If you are attacked by a prize fighter you are not bound to adhere to the Queensberry Rules. It is clear, however, that even in the lowest of brawls any force used in self-defence must be both reasonable and proportionate to the threat of, or actual, force offered by the plaintiff.

In *Lane* v *Holloway* [1968] 1 QB 379, the Court of Appeal found that in a fight between a man aged 64, who was drunk at the time, and a man aged 27, a 'savage' blow struck by the latter upon the former was out of all proportion to the more feeble attempt of violence on the part of the older man. In other words, a light blow struck by the older man did not justify a savage blow in response by the younger man.

In *Barnes* v *Nayer* (1986), *The Times*, 19 December, the Court of Appeal weighed the defendant's response against the behaviour of his victim and her family. The defendant had attacked a woman with a machete, killing her in a most hideous way. He was convicted of manslaughter, but a civil claim for damages in trespass to the person was brought against him by her estate. Although he claimed that the dead woman and her family had made life a misery for him and his family, and had encouraged the sons of both families to fight each other, and had made violent threats to one of his sons, it was found that his deadly attack was out of all proportion to anything offered by the deceased.

This case was not directly concerned with self-defence; in fact it was concerned with a plea by the defendant that the defences of *volenti*, *ex turpi causa*, and contributory negligence applied. The court found that these defences, which are examined below, could not be sustained in the light of the defendant's response with the machete. Although it is not concerned with self-defence, *Barnes* can be used by way of analogy in this connection on the issue of 'reasonableness' and 'proportion'.

In *criminal* law a defendant may rely on the defence even where he makes an unreasonable mistake of fact, provided he has acted honestly in the circumstances: see, e.g., *Beckford* v *R* [1987] 3 All ER 425. In tort the mistake must be both honest and reasonable: *Bici & Bici* v *Ministry of Defence* [2004] EWHC 786 (QB); *Ashley* v *Chief Constable of Sussex* [2006] EWCA Civ 1085. The latter case contains a lengthy review of the authorities, and concludes that the discrepancy between the position in criminal and civil law is intentional.

In *Cross* v *Kirkby* (2000), *The Times*, 5 April, C attacked K with a baseball bat. K succeeded in wresting the bat from C and struck him once, causing serious injuries. The Court of Appeal considered that, on the facts as K (and independent witnesses) perceived them, this was self-defence.

In addition, the same case confirmed that the defence of illegality or *ex turpi causa* will apply in battery where the claimant is himself guilty of criminal behaviour to such an extent that it is offensive to justice that he be allowed to bring a claim: *Holman* v *Johnson* (1775) 1 Cowp R 341. This was the assumed position in the earlier case of *Murphy* v *Culhane* [1977] QB 94, although where the illegality of the claimant was trivial (*Lane* v *Holloway* [1968] 1 QB 379) or of a different category (*Revill* v *Newbery* [1995] 2 WLR 239) this would not be the case.

Contributory negligence may apply in a 'two-way' situation. At first instance in *Cross* v *Kirkby* the judge had rejected the two complete defences which the Court of Appeal accepted, but held the claimant, as the initial aggressor, to be 60% contributorily negligent.

EXERCISE 10.5

On St Valentine's Day Liz approaches John from behind and kisses him passionately on the neck, leaving a love bite which is visible for several days.

Consider Liz's potential liability in tort on the basis that John:

(a) objected from the start to Liz's attentions;

(b) initially welcomed those attentions, but is now upset because of ribald remarks about the love bite from his friends.

10.4.4 Assault

> Assault: Any act of the defendant which directly and intentionally (or possibly negligently) causes the claimant immediately to apprehend the imminent infliction of a battery. (*Street on Torts* at p. 36.)

You should note that in tort the expression 'assault' is reserved for this threat of contact (or battery). In common parlance, and in the criminal law (assault occasioning actual bodily harm, indecent assault) the word has absorbed the significance of battery as well: see *R* v *Savage*; *DPP* v *Parmenter* [1991] 4 All ER 698. The Law Commission (Paper 122 *Legislating the Criminal Code: Offences against the Person and General Principles* (1992)) recognizes the way the two expressions are now being used interchangeably.

While it is possible to have a battery without an assault, as in the case of an attack from behind, or on an unconscious victim, all assaults are at least potential batteries, although in some cases the battery is prevented or not proceeded with. As a result much of the law is the same and this section only considers the aspects of assault which are distinctive.

10.4.4.1 Act

This used to be regarded as indicating something more than mere words, and indeed it was said that words are no assault (Holroyd J in *Meade & Belt's Case* (1823) 1 Lewin 184). If the words are clear and threatening enough, very little more by way of gesture was required, however: *Wilson* [1955] 1 All ER 744. The context of the cases was different. The earlier one was that of an unruly crowd, singing and chanting. This was no doubt intimidatory, but could be said to lack specific and direct threat. The latter concerned a gang of men confronting a single gamekeeper in an isolated place at night. In the criminal law the Public Order Act distinguishes between serious offences involving the use or show of force (ss 1–3), and lesser offences involving insult and abuse alone (ss 4, 5). The position has now changed. Lord Steyn (in a speech with which the rest of the House of Lords agreed) said in *Burstow &* *Ireland* (*Cases and Materials* (10.2.2.1)):

> The proposition that a gesture may amount to an assault, but that words can never suffice, is unrealistic and indefensible. A thing said is also a thing done. There is no reason why something said should be incapable of causing an apprehension of unlawful physical violence, e.g. a man accosting a woman in a dark alley saying 'come with me or I will stab you'. I would, therefore, reject the proposition that an assault can never be committed by words.

EXERCISE 10.6

Consider where the line should be drawn between words which do, and words which do not, constitute an assault.

A silent telephone call (or at least a campaign of such calls) had been held capable of amounting to an assault in the same case in the Court of Appeal: *Ireland* [1997] QB 114. The court indicated that it was immaterial whether words or silence followed the making of the connection, and approved of the ruling in the Australian case *Barton* v *Armstrong* [1969] 2 NSWR 451 that a threat made over the telephone was capable of amounting to an assault. The key issue is said to be whether the victim acquired an apprehension of immediate harm, usually physical, but possibly purely psychological, as a result of the behaviour of the defendant. The House of Lords endorsed this, although accepting that there would need to be proof of a sufficient degree of immediacy of harm, which would not always be present. (Lord Steyn and Lord Hope, with both Lord Slynn and Lord Hutton expressing specific reservations on the issue of immediacy.) This behaviour could include, or even be limited to, words. Some commentators (e.g. Allen, 'Look Who'stalking: Seeking a Solution to the Problem of Stalking' [1996] 4 *Web JCLI*; Herring, 'Assault by Telephone' [1997] *CLJ* 11, both discussing the CA decision in *Ireland*) argue that this is an illegitimate extension of the tort/crime of assault to meet the social need for a device to restrain and punish stalkers. However, they are mainly concerned with the issues of immediacy and the question whether the defendant has caused harm rather than fear. These issues are discussed further in the context of harassment in **Chapter 11.**

? **QUESTION** 10.9

Why may words alone constitute an assault? Do you agree that they should?

Where the words are spoken face to face, there is immediacy and the only question is one of degree. In other cases the main issue will be immediacy. If the threat is known to come from far away, precautions can be taken. If the phone call may be from the street outside, then there is immediacy. The cases appear to suggest that, at least in criminal law, it is enough that what you say produces a psychic shock, quite distinct from the apprehension of subsequent physical attack.

10.4.4.2 **Immediately**

Words used may negative the threat of a gesture. In *Tuberville* v *Savage* (1669) 1 Mod Rep 3, the claimant during an argument with the defendant put his hand on his sword-hilt and said 'An 'twere not assize time, I would not take such language from you'. The defendant drew his own sword and stabbed the claimant in the eye. The claimant claimed battery and the defendant pleaded self-defence. The court held that this was a battery by the defendant and not self-defence. The claimant's conduct did not constitute an assault, because the words counteracted the gesture.

What about a future threat, or a present threat which the defendant manifestly cannot carry out? Generally this will not be an assault. In the first case there is no threat to the peace, the claimant can take precautions; in the second, there can be no apprehension. The example usually given is of the threat shouted from one river bank to the other, there being no bridge, boat, ford etc. available. This is illustrated in *Thomas* v *NUM* [1985] 2 All ER 1. The action was brought on behalf of working miners during the 1984 strike. They were seeking an injunction to restrain aggressive mass picketing by strikers. They claimed, among other things, that the various threats shouted by the strikers as the workers were driven into the pit in buses at some speed and with a substantial police guard, were assaults. There were gestures as well as words. It was held that these threats did not amount to assaults, because there was no basis to fear that they could be carried out then and there. As Scott J said:

> Assault is defined in *Clarke and Lindsell on Torts* (15th edn, 1982) para. 14/10 as 'an overt act indicating an immediate intention to commit a battery, coupled with the capacity to carry that intention into effect'. The tort of assault is not, in my view, committed, unless the capacity in question is present at the time the overt act is committed. Since the working miners are in vehicles and the pickets are held back from the vehicles, I do not understand how the most violent of threats or gestures could be said to constitute an assault . . .

So we can conclude that the test is whether the defendant is clearly in a position to carry out the threat. If there is a serious risk, it will be an assault even though the attack is frustrated. In *Stephens* v *Myers* (1830) 4 C & P 349 the defendant was at a public meeting. He became annoyed at the conduct of the chairman and started to threaten him and move towards him shouting that he would drag him out of the chair. His progress was halted by other members of the audience. Do you think that this was an assault, bearing in mind all that you have read so far?

It was held to be one. It was not a case where the defendant manifestly could not carry out his intention.

10.4.4.3 **Apprehend**

You must consider this aspect from the claimant's viewpoint. What construction should he reasonably place on the defendant's conduct? An apparent threat which the defendant knows to be an empty one can be an assault, because the claimant reasonably perceives it as one. The obvious example is a threat with an unloaded gun. In the USA and in Australia there is no doubt that such a threat is an assault. The same probably applies in England: *R* v *St George* (1840) 9 C & P 483. Unfortunately there are comments in another case in the same year to the contrary: *Blake* v *Barnard* (1840) 9 C & P 626. The problem is that the precise effect of these early cases remains disputed. Oddly the issue never seems to have arisen for decision since.

? **QUESTION** 10.10

What torts, if any, have been committed in the following situations:

(a) Just as Alice is sitting down in a chair, but before she has touched it, Beryl, who has crept up from behind, whips the chair from under her. Alice falls to the ground and sustains a fractured coccyx.

(b) Charles is asleep in his seat in a cinema. His feet are stretched out, blocking the passage along the row of seats. Duncan, who wishes to pass, shakes Charles vigorously by the shoulder. Charles awakes with a start and falls from the seat, sustaining serious injury to his clavicle.

(c) While driving his car Edgar is carved up by Freda, who is driving a large lorry. Edgar shakes his fist at Freda, and leans out of the window of his car to shout that he will swing for her. Freda laughs and drives away.

(d) Grace is having an affair with Horace. Horace has falsely told Grace that he has had a vasectomy. Grace becomes pregnant and Horace arranges for Igor, a surgeon, to carry out a surgical abortion. The formalities prescribed by the Abortion Act have not been complied with. Although Igor was careful, the operation leaves Grace sterile. This is a recognized but accepted side effect in a small minority of cases where the method selected by Igor is employed. Grace is particularly distressed because it was her dearest wish to have children in due course.

(e) Jeremy points a toy gun at Kate as a practical joke. Kate, who is short-sighted, thinks that the gun is real, and faints, hitting her head on the edge of a table.

(f) Louise telephones Michael. On the first two occasions she tells Michael to meet her under the clock at Waterloo station in two days' time. If he does not, she says, she will 'Get him'. The tune 'Misty' is playing in the background. In later calls over a four-week period nothing is said when the phone is picked up, but 'Misty' is playing. Michael develops a traumatic neurosis.

10.4.5 Interference with liberty

Here we are concerned with two torts which overlap, namely false imprisonment and wrongful arrest. In many cases the latter is accompanied by an action for malicious prosecution, but that is outside the scope of this book.

10.4.5.1 False imprisonment

An act of the defendant which directly and intentionally (or possibly negligently) causes the confinement of the claimant within an area delimited by the defendant. (*Street on Torts* at p. 40.)

10.4.5.2 False

The word is not used in the sense of 'not true'. The imprisonment is real enough! It is used in the sense of bear 'false witness'; something which is improper or unjustified.

10.4.5.3 Imprisonment

This means any confinement or total restriction of freedom of movement. Incarceration in the narrow sense (i.e. locking up in a cell) is a form of imprisonment, but is not necessary. There may, but need not, be an assault or battery associated with a false imprisonment. It depends on whether force or threats were used to restrain the claimant. What is the position if the claimant voluntarily enters a room and the defendant then locks him in? There is imprisonment but no assault or battery.

What is being protected? It is the claimant's freedom of movement; because you 'act at your peril' in relation to trespass, a deliberate act leading inadvertently to imprisonment will be covered. If the defendant locks the claimant in a room, the claimant's freedom of movement is just as effectively curtailed if the defendant acts deliberately with regard to the claimant as where he fails to realize that the claimant is in the room. The locking of the door is the direct cause of the restraint in each case. The concept of trespass is that of a class of acts which may not be done unless they are positively justified; this is the concept of acting at one's peril, and certainly mere inadvertence is not a positive justification. However, if the person 'accidentally' imprisoned is acting wrongfully, e.g. by trespassing, or carelessly, e.g. by getting drunk and falling asleep in a corner, there may well be a defence available. In the USA there is no liability in false imprisonment for negligently imprisoning, although there will be for negligently failing to release, e.g. at the end of a period of lawful custody. What is clear is that mistake as to the circumstances is no answer. How far do you think the law should go in protecting claimants and penalizing defendants?

? QUESTION 10.11

Henrietta falls asleep in the loo at a club. She wakes up at nine a.m. and the club is deserted. No one comes to release her until noon. Advise her as to her claim for false imprisonment.

If Henrietta cannot prove that the staff deliberately left her asleep and locked in, we must consider whether negligence will suffice. Clearly the loos should have been checked (for 'break-out' thieves if not comatose revellers). She may only recover for her waking period, but in principle those who control premises and invite the public in act at their peril in failing to secure that they are out before the place is locked.

How complete must the confinement be? It is not false imprisonment to block off one route but not others, provided these are not unduly hazardous. The claimant may not be able to go where he wants, but he still is free to go elsewhere.

Bird v *Jones* (1845) 7 QB 742 (*Cases and Materials* (10.2.3.1))

The defendant improperly erected a temporary grandstand in the highway. The claimant entered it. The defendant's servants refused to allow him to go forward as he wished, but did not prevent him from returning, or going in other directions.

The court held that such a partial restraint was not an imprisonment. It might amount to a public nuisance. (See 11.6.)

Being locked in a third-floor room would, however, be imprisonment, albeit that the window is open.

Imprisonment may be static or dynamic. Confinement within a room or other space will count, but it is equally an imprisonment to force someone to travel to a particular place. Wrongful arrests often result in an imprisonment of this kind.

10.4.5.4 **Justification**

 EXERCISE 10.7

Read *Robinson* v *Balmain New Ferry* and *Herd* v *Weardale* in *Cases and Materials* (10.2.3.2). Who do you think was in the right?

As with the other trespass torts most of the legal interest centres on the various forms of justification. Consent is a defence to any tort unless excluded by public policy. It is no imprisonment to rely on the terms of an agreement regulating the claimant's access to the defendant's premises.

Robinson v *Balmain New Ferry Co. Ltd* [1910] AC 295 (*Cases and Materials* (10.2.3.2))

The claimant entered the ferry terminal, paying one penny before travelling, and then changed his mind. The defendant would only allow him to leave on payment of a further penny. The claimant tried to climb over the turnstile but was restrained. It was held that there was no false imprisonment.

(a) First, the claimant entered the defendant's premises on the understanding that one penny was payable for passing the turnstile in either direction.

(b) Second, there was nothing to stop the claimant leaving on the ferry.

(c) Third, it was suggested that the defendant was entitled to impose such conditions as he saw fit, whether the claimant was told of these or not. An analogy was drawn with a railway passenger, who was only entitled to be set down at a station. Was this a condition in this sense, or was the defendant really detaining the claimant in order to compel payment of a civil debt, namely the penny payable on leaving?

Similar issues arose in *Herd*.

> **Herd v Weardale Steel, Coal and Coke Co.** [1915] AC 67 HL (*Cases and Materials* (10.2.3.2))
>
> The claimant was, as you have read, a miner in the defendant's mine. While working underground during a shift, the claimant stopped work. He demanded to be taken up to the surface. The defendant refused until the end of the shift. It was held that there was no false imprisonment. The claimant had agreed to go down the mine for a particular length of shift. The defendant's obligation was to wind the claimant up at the end of the shift, and not before.

Necessity

In *Austin & Saxby v Metropolitan Police Commissioner* [2005] EWHC 480 (QB) the claimants were among a large number of people who were detained in Oxford Circus as a response to a demonstration called at short notice on May Day 2001. One was a demonstrator, the other a bystander. It was held that although there was a detention, it was lawful because the police were minded to arrest those present who were guilty of breaches of the peace, and in any event, the defence of necessity applied because of the need to ensure that the demonstration was effectively managed. Tugendhat J suggested that the position of the bystander was analogous to that of a motorist caught up in the tailback after a road accident on a motorway.

? **QUESTION** 10.12

Richman attended a match at Fulchester Rovers FC as a guest of Dives plc in their hospitality suite.

The chief constable had entered into an agreement with Fulchester Rovers FC to police matches; the agreement provided inter alia that the senior police officer present was to control egress from the ground after matches. Notices were posted around the ground in the following terms: 'Admission to and exit from the ground are subject to police control. Departure from the ground after matches may be delayed in the interests of public safety'. A similar term appeared in the lease of the hospitality suite.

When Richman set out to leave the ground after the match, his way was blocked at the exit from the hospitality suite by Inspector Morse, who told him that he could not leave for twenty minutes while an adjoining area was cleared of visiting fans.

Does Richman have any claim in tort against Inspector Morse?

Is there consent or other justification for the detention? Consent in *Herd* was clearly contractual. That in *Robinson* only arguably so. Some of the judges suggested that it was immaterial whether the regulations were incorporated into the contract. Richman is (exceptionally) not a party to a contract.

Richman is a licensee on the premises and the licence is conditional. Is this the true ratio of *Robinson*? If so it will apply whether or not the licence is contractual and whether or not the restrictions have actually come to Richman's notice. It may be necessary to show that reasonable steps have been taken to notify them but the notices appear to comply.

The inspector may be able to justify his actions as a proper exercise of police powers in relation to public order. This would be an independent justification based on necessity, where consent/notice is immaterial.

Custody

Imprisonment pursuant to a lawful order of a court is justified. There has been no successful modern attempt to demonstrate that imprisonment of this kind has become false as a result of the conditions in which the claimant is being detained. There have been several unsuccessful attempts, culminating in *R v Deputy Governor of Parkhurst Prison, ex parte Hague, Weldon v Home Office* [1992] 1 AC 58. These cases raise a number of issues but we concentrate on false imprisonment. (See *Cases and Materials* (10.2.3.2).)

Each case concerned a serving prisoner who alleged that his detention in prison was improper, in that the circumstances and conditions of detention were in breach of the Prison Act and Prison Rules. In each case it was alleged that a serving prisoner retained a residual liberty, in that the order of the court which sentenced him allowed detention only according to law, and that detention in other circumstances amounted to a deprivation of that liberty which amounted to false imprisonment. This contention had met with some success in the lower courts in *Weldon* but not in *Hague*. The House of Lords unanimously held the following.

(a) The relevant statutory provisions authorize detention and that necessarily involves a complete loss of liberty. There is no concept of residual liberty, and false imprisonment is therefore not available to challenge the circumstances of detention. (It may of course be available to challenge a detention which is itself wrongful, e.g. a failure to release a prisoner on the due date on completion of a sentence. See later in this section.)

(b) The appropriate remedy for a prisoner who alleges that the Prison Rules have not been applied properly to him, e.g. that he has been placed in solitary confinement without justification, is a public law remedy, i.e. an action for judicial review or for a declaration.

(c) The prison authorities owe a duty of care to detainees. An action for negligence can be maintained on the usual principles if a breach of this duty results in physical harm. This will certainly cover illness or disease resulting from detention in dangerous or insalubrious conditions. Suggestions in *Middleweek* v *Chief Constable of Merseyside* [1990] 3 All ER 662 that such detention could amount to false imprisonment were firmly disapproved of. In theory this would also include psychiatric illness attributable to the improper detention, but it will be interesting to see how a court approaches any such case which is brought. There have been several cases brought in negligence, some with success, where the prison authorities or police as gaolers have not taken proper care of prisoners who were suicide risks, or at risk from other prisoners, or known to be ill.

In *H v Home Office* (1992), *The Independent*, 6 May, *Weldon* was applied. The claimant prisoner alleged that the prison authorities had negligently revealed his background of sexual offences (although his current sentence was for burglary). As a result he had to go on rule 43 (self-chosen segregation) for his own protection. The claimant's claim was rejected by the Court of Appeal. *Weldon* had decided that there was no cause of action in trespass in respect of unlawful conditions of detention, and this covered the claim here. H was not, so far as can be seen from the brief report, alleging any physical injury.

Detention must actually be justified in law. In *R v Governor of HMP Brockhill, ex parte Evans* [2000] 4 All ER 15, the governor calculated Evans' release date according to the officially prescribed formula, which had been judicially considered and approved of. Evans herself successfully challenged the use of the formula and on the proper basis of calculation she had been detained beyond her true release date. The House of Lords, while accepting that the governor had done nothing wrong (he would have been disobeying orders and going against court rulings if he had released Evans on what later proved to be the correct date) nevertheless ruled that Evans had been falsely imprisoned. This is a very strong affirmation of the primacy of the right to liberty, particularly as against the state.

Arrest and detention

Statute, in the form of the general powers in ss 24 and 24A of the Police and Criminal Evidence Act 1984 (see *Cases and Materials* 10.2.3.2) (and many specific powers in other statutes), and the common law give powers of arrest to constables and to ordinary citizens. How far will the claim of arrest by a constable (or a citizen) acting within a statutory or common law power of arrest be a sufficient answer to an allegation of false imprisonment? In principle it is such an answer, but the defendant must be able to satisfy all the conditions of the power, and, where he cannot, absence of malice is irrelevant. Similar considerations apply also to detention by immigration officers: *ID* v *Home Office* [2005] EWCA 1554.

For the arrest to be lawful the officer must have a reasonable suspicion that an offence has been, is being or is about to be committed, as the case may be, and also that the person arrested is guilty. This is an objective test, and it is not enough for the claimant to show that he was in fact not a wrong-doer, e.g. *Al Fayed* v *Metropolitan Police Commissioner* (2002) LTL, 12 August. Note that under Art. 5 of the European Convention the State must provide for compensation for improper deprivation of liberty, but this will not apply to cases where the arrest and detention were objectively justified. In other cases damages for false imprisonment represent that compensation.

This is a significant area in practice. Actions are relatively common, frequently successful, and attract substantial damages. Damages for humiliation and distress may themselves exceed £400 per hour of detention, and exemplary damages may be awarded. The Metropolitan Police alone pay out over £1,000,000 each year. The use of the law of trespass to control the function of the police force is a prime example of the revision of the scope of an action already mentioned. The key aspect of these cases is that, for an arrest to be lawful, all the requirements of the provisions giving the power of arrest must be met. So far as police powers are concerned, these are best considered in relation to other aspects of civil rights and liberties.

We need to consider here how the rules apply to citizen's arrests. The citizen has a limited power of arrest under s. 24A of the Police and Criminal Evidence Act 1984 (*Cases and Materials* (10.2.3.2)). It has always been the case that, where the arrest is in relation to a past offence, that there must have been an actual offence. In *Walters* v *W H Smith* [1911–13] All ER Rep 170, W.H. Smith suspected that the claimant, the manager of a station bookstall, was stealing books, so they arranged for marked goods to be supplied. The claimant's wife's shop was then searched. Some of the marked goods were found. He was tried but was subsequently acquitted. It is a condition precedent of the right to make a citizen's arrest that an offence has been committed, and as the acquittal of the only possible defendant demonstrated that there was no offence, it followed that the arrest was unlawful. A similar result followed in *R* v *Self* [1992] 3 All ER 476. The defendant was apprehended in a citizen's arrest at the instance of a shopkeeper who believed he had been shoplifting. The defendant resisted the arrest but was finally subdued. He was ultimately acquitted of the theft. His conviction for assault while resisting arrest was quashed; the conditions for a lawful citizen's arrest were not met and the defendant was entitled to use reasonable force in self-defence to prevent a false imprisonment. The same rules would apply to any civil claim.

However, recent amendments to the power of citizen's arrest (introduced on 1 January 2006) create another very significant restriction. The power can now only be exercised where it is necessary to prevent the suspect inflicting or sustaining injury, damaging or destroying property, or making off before he can be apprehended by a constable, and where it is not practicable for a constable to effect the arrest. This really restricts the use of the power to 'the heat of the moment', so a planned operation such as that in *Walters* will no longer be possible, even if an offence has been committed.

In *Davidson* v *Chief Constable of North Wales* [1994] 2 All ER 597 the claimant and her friend were arrested by the police after a store detective wrongly suspected they had stolen a cassette. The action against the police failed because of their reasonable suspicion based on the initial statement of the store detective. Could the detective, however, be said to have 'instigated, promoted and actively incited' the arrest, rendering herself and her employer liable for false imprisonment? No, according to the Court of Appeal. The police had exercised their own judgment, even though the detective said in evidence that she was accustomed to the police acting on her information, and clearly expected them to.

 EXERCISE 10.8

Read s. 24A of the Police and Criminal Evidence Act 1984.

Do you consider that the activities of the person arresting in *Walters* and *Self* are or are not legitimate citizen's arrests?

In *Walters* the 'offence' was clearly complete, and there was no basis for saying that the police could not have been informed and invited to make the arrest, as occurred in *Davidson*—but in *Self*, should the court have proceeded on the basis that, in practical terms, the offence was still in process? If so, then there may well have been a need to act in order to prevent the suspect escaping: s. 24A(4)(d).

? **QUESTION** 10.13

Elvis is behaving strangely. He is going from shop to shop, taking an item from each but leaving it in the next shop. Irene, a law student, thinks this is wrong and tells Elvis to go with her to the police station. Elvis does so. Irene tells PC Rex that Elvis has been stealing. PC Rex arrests Elvis. The custody sergeant arranges for Elvis to be seen by Dr Watson, the police medical officer, who considers that Elvis is mentally ill. Dr Watson takes Elvis to the local psychiatric unit without making any formal decision under the Mental Health Act.

Has Elvis been falsely imprisoned at any stage?

NOTE: To be guilty of theft, you have to dishonestly assume the rights of the owner of property intending to treat the property as your own to dispose of. If Elvis is mentally disturbed, he may lack the capacity to form a dishonest intention.

> *L v Bournewood Community and Mental Health NHS Trust* [1998] 3 All ER 289
> (*Cases and Materials* (10.2.3.2))
>
> The House of Lords determined that detention of an incompetent person in a mental hospital
> was not false imprisonment, even though Mental Health Act powers were not used and the
> patient did not positively consent. The justification was that it was necessary in the best inter-
> ests of the patient. This patient was too disturbed to indicate an objection.
>
> The Court of Appeal had held that this was false imprisonment on the ground that the
> Mental Health Act machinery replaced the common law of necessity; s. 131 of the Mental
> Health Act 1983 allows informal admission and treatment with a patient's consent. Since L
> lacked the capacity to consent it followed that his detention amounted to false imprisonment
> and the common law defence of necessity could not be used to justify this. The House appeared
> more impressed with arguments that using the formal machinery would be very costly than
> with the civil liberties arguments. Subsequently the European Court of Human Rights
> concluded that there was a detention, and that the use of necessity was not sufficiently legally
> established to be justified, particularly since there were no established procedures for formal
> review or for judicial control of his detention. The lack of procedural safeguards to protect
> an applicant against arbitrary deprivation of liberty on the ground of necessity after he had
> been compulsorily detained breached his right to liberty guaranteed by Art. 51 of the European
> Convention on Human Rights. It was also held, unanimously, that Art. 5.4 had been breached
> in that the applicant's right to have the legality of his detention reviewed by a court had not
> been ensured: *HL* v *United Kingdom* (2005) 40 EHRR 32.

10.4.5.5 Knowledge

Can you be imprisoned without realizing it? There are conflicting authorities as to whether
there can be a false imprisonment where the claimant is in fact under restraint but he does not
know this. In *Herring* v *Boyle* (1834) 1 Cr M & R 377 the defendant, a schoolmaster, in effect
exercised a lien over a pupil for unpaid fees; in other words he refused to allow him to go home
until the fees were paid. The claimant (the pupil) was unaware of this, and was not in any
obvious way restrained. The claimant's mother knew the full story, and brought an action in
respect of the claimant. This action failed, with the court holding that there could be no false
imprisonment in the absence of overt restraint and knowledge. In *Meering* v *Graham-White
Aviation* (1919) 122 LT 44 the defendant suspected the claimant of theft. The claimant was not
told of the suspicion. He was asked to wait in an office, and did so voluntarily. In fact, but unbe-
known to him, guards were posted who would have prevented him leaving the room if he had
tried to, which he did not. The question of whether there had been an imprisonment was left
to the jury.

 QUESTION 10.14

What decision would you have come to if you had been a member of the jury?

The verdict was that this was imprisonment. This was upheld on appeal as a proper verdict. The claimant's freedom of movement had in fact been curtailed; the state of his knowledge went only to the amount of damages. This view has been supported by comments made obiter in *Murray* v *Ministry of Defence* [1988] 2 All ER 521, where *Herring* was strongly disapproved. (See *Cases and Materials* (10.2.3.3).) In this case, too, Lord Griffiths pointed out that damages should be minimal. The position is again clearer in the USA, where it is laid down that the claimant must either be conscious of his confinement or actually harmed by it.

10.5 **Interference with goods**

10.5.1 **Conversion and trespass to goods**

This general heading includes two separate torts, namely conversion and trespass to goods. The whole law relating to interference with goods is complex and difficult. It was described by a judge as long ago as 1903 as being particularly technical, and although there has been intervention by Parliament, in the form of the Torts (Interference with Goods) Act 1977, this has affected the rules relating to remedies and procedures, but not the main substantive rules. (See *Cases and Materials* (10.3.1) for this Act and the relevant provisions of the Limitation Act 1980.)

10.5.2 **Legal inventiveness**

You have already seen that the torts of trespass to the person may be relied on where there is an underlying dispute that is, in substance, a matter of civil liberty. The torts relating to interference with goods may, similarly, be the legal format for a dispute which really raises issues in the law of contract or personal property: *Ingram* v *Little* [1961] QB 31 and *Lewis* v *Averay* [1973] 2 All ER 229 are both cases you may recall from contract where this was the case. You should bear in mind that in many cases conversion and trespass to goods cover the same ground (in rather the same way as common law negligence and breach of statutory duty). In practice the claimant will normally claim in conversion where he can.

10.5.3 **Conversion**

Conversion is an intentional dealing with goods that is seriously inconsistent with the possession or right to immediate possession of another. (*Street on Torts* at p. 49.)

 EXERCISE 10.9

List the sort of behaviour you consider might fall within this definition of conversion.

10.5.3.1 Intentional

The act constituting the dealing must be deliberate, as opposed to negligent or accidental. However, the consequence of the act is irrelevant. As Cleasby B said in *Fowler* v *Hollins* (1878) LR 7 QB 616: 'The liability . . . is founded upon what has been regarded as a salutary rule for the protection of property, namely, that persons deal with the property in chattels or exercise rights of ownership over them at their peril.' There are many cases where the defendant has dealt with goods in entire good faith, with no suggestion of any want of care in all the circumstances, e.g. an auctioneer who sold goods which did not in fact belong to his client. The contract mistake cases (such as *Ingram* v *Little* and *Lewis* v *Averay*) also provide many instances of morally innocent converters. You must simply ignore any temptation to bring in any element of 'morality'. To this extent the rules in conversion are even more restrictive than in relation to trespass to the person, where innocent accidents are now excluded and negligence is progressively being excluded from the trespass rules. The only real protection against the true owner's claim in most cases is the passage of time. The limitation period for claims in conversion is normally six years from the date of losing possession. However the rules are fairly complex.

There is one statutory exception to the general rule that conversion requires a positive act. This is constituted by s. 2(2) of the Torts (Interference with Goods) Act 1977. This provides that where a bailee of goods (i.e. someone to whom goods have been entrusted by the true owner for safe-keeping, delivery, or repair, or for some other limited purpose) who is under a duty of care in relation to the goods fails to prevent their loss or destruction, this will be treated as conversion. Before the Act, such failure did not amount to conversion, although it did amount to the separate tort of detinue. When detinue was abolished by the Act, it was necessary to provide for this situation, and this was done by a statutory extension of the definition of conversion. This form of conversion can occur without any act, intentional or otherwise, and is a form of negligence liability.

As with trespass to the person, the emphasis is on positive justification. It is a little harder to get to grips with here. We can all see that threatening people, sticking knives in them, or locking them up requires to be justified. It is a little more difficult in the context of dealing with goods, which we have to do every day as part of ordinary life.

10.5.3.2 Forms of conversion

Dealing with goods covers a number of types of behaviour. The following list aims to cover and explain the main cases, but is not intended to be exhaustive.

Taking goods or dispossessing the claimant

Theft, or an unjustified seizure under legal process, will amount to conversion, but merely moving goods (e.g. to get at other goods stored behind) is not necessarily conversion, although it might become conversion if the goods were exposed to risk as a result of the removal. You should also note that the limitation rules are different for theft cases than for other forms of conversion. Time under the Limitation Act can never run against a thief, so the owner can always recover the goods. It will only start to run once the thief has sold to a buyer in good faith. See s. 4 of the Limitation Act 1980.

Destroying or altering goods

Damaging goods is not in itself conversion (although it may amount to trespass to those goods). There is no assertion of ownership in such cases. If the damage is the unintended result of an action, then the appropriate cause of action will be negligence. Destruction of goods will be conversion where this was advertent, and the distinction between damage and destruction is one of fact. Alteration which alters the nature of the goods, e.g. making wine from grapes, or reformatting and using a floppy disk, will amount to conversion. Only the owner has the right to make such irrevocable decisions about the way in which his property is to be exploited. Such dealings are normally advertent in the sense that the defendant means to subject this item to this process, and doing so is clearly asserting the rights of the owner.

Using goods
This assumes that the user has come by the goods legitimately. A bailee who misuses goods does not necessarily convert them. It depends whether his misuse is inconsistent with the bailment. Thus a hirer of a car who crashes it is not converting it, but if he transforms it into a stock car he is doing so. In other circumstances (e.g. finding) use of the goods represents an assumption of the rights of the owner, and thus conversion. There will of course be an action only if the owner finds out where the goods have got to!

Receiving or taking delivery of goods
If the reception of the goods is intentional and represents the completion of a transaction, e.g., a purchase, which is designed to give the defendant rights over the goods, then this will amount to conversion. However, what about someone who receives goods merely as agent for another (e.g. a warehouseman or carrier)? He will not be liable to the original owner merely by taking delivery, since the purpose of the transaction is not to give him rights over the goods. It may be otherwise if he refuses to hand them over to the person entitled to them.

There are a number of exceptions to the rule that receipt of goods is conversion:

(a) market overt (abolished as from 3 January 1995, but still relevant for earlier transactions);

(b) estoppel, including the Factors Act 1889;

(c) actions of a seller or buyer in possession;

(d) voidable title.

Although a mixed bag, these exceptions reflect the collision at this point of two fundamental principles, namely the primacy of rights of ownership and the need to foster trade by promoting free disposability of goods. See 10.6 for further discussion.

Disposal of goods
The mere agreement to dispose of goods is not a conversion, but a delivery in pursuance of the disposal will be, at all events where the defendant is instrumental in the disposition. In *Hollins* v *Fowler* [1874–80] All ER Rep 118 (HL), on appeal from *Fowler* v *Hollins* (1878) LR 7 QB 616 (see 10.5.3.1) the defendant was a cotton broker who held cotton actually belonging to the claimant, in the belief that it belonged to X. He disposed of it for the benefit of X and was held liable in conversion despite the fact that he was acting in entire good faith and had no ready means of knowing that the goods did not belong to X. Likewise in *Hiort* v *Bott* (1874) LR 9 Exch 86 the claimant's agent G fraudulently represented to the claimant that the defendant had bought a quantity of oats to the value of £180. The claimant sent the goods to a warehouse and an invoice and delivery order to the defendant. G visited the defendant and said that a mistake had been made. He induced the defendant to endorse the delivery order to him by saying that this was the easiest way of returning the goods and cancelling the invoice. G then produced the order to the warehouseman, obtained the goods, sold them and absconded with the

proceeds. The defendant was held liable to the claimant on the basis that he had, albeit as a result of G's fraud, interfered with the title to the goods by endorsing the delivery order, enabling G to obtain them.

Just in case you thought that this sort of case only belongs in the pages of a Dickens novel, here is a rather more up-to-date example.

R H Willis and Son v British Car Auctions [1978] 3 All ER 392

X obtained a car on hire purchase from the claimant. In breach of the hire purchase agreement he sold the car to Y, using the defendant as auctioneer. X went bankrupt and Y disappeared with the car. The claimant sued the defendant for his net loss.

The Court of Appeal held that the defendant had been instrumental in the sale, and was liable. Lord Denning departed from tradition in explicitly taking note of the fact that the defendant actually insured itself against the possibility of having to meet conversion claims arising from defective titles by taking a £2 premium from each buyer. The benefit of the insurance went to the defendant and the net result was that the original owner got damages, the defendant was indemnified and the buyer got to keep the car. To refuse a remedy to the claimant would have given the defendant's insurers a windfall. See *Cases and Materials* (10.3.2.1) for *Fowler* and *Willis*.

? **QUESTION** 10.15

How do you think the case was decided, and why?

However, if the auctioneer merely receives the goods with a view to sale, but does not actually sell them, this does not amount to conversion: *Marcq* v *Christie Manson & Woods Ltd* [2003] 3 All ER 561. This may be an agreement to dispose, but that, as we have seen, is not itself a conversion.

Refusal to surrender on demand

The motive for the refusal is irrelevant. In *Howard E Perry & Co. Ltd* v *British Rail* [1979] 2 All ER 579 the defendant held steel belonging to the claimant but refused to hand it over because this might inflame their own workers at a time of industrial unrest. This was not a valid excuse. Nothing was allowed to interfere with the claimant's property rights. It may be reasonable for someone who is storing or otherwise holding goods to seek advice in the face of a demand for them where there is doubt as to the true entitlement, and a delayed response of this kind will not amount to a conversion. After all, the warehouseman is caught between the devil and the deep blue sea, since he often cannot be sure which of two or more claimants is truly entitled. In such cases there is a legal procedure called interpleader, whereby the person in actual possession notifies the court that he has no claim of his own (other than a possible lien for his charges) and asks the court to resolve the issue between the competing parties.

EXERCISE 10.10

Compare your list from Exercise 10.9 with the list you have just read.

10.5.3.3 **Goods**

This will include all types of chattel, including crops once severed from the land, with the single exception of cash (although coins as collectors' items or bullion are included). In the case of valuable paper (cheques, bonds, etc.) the subject matter of the conversion is the paper, but the value for purposes of damages is the commercial value.

10.5.3.4 **Possession or the immediate right to possession**

The primary concern of conversion is not with ultimate ownership where this does not coincide with possession. *Roberts* v *Wyatt* (1810) 2 Taunt 268 arose out of a conveyancing transaction. The defendant as vendor delivered an abstract of his title to land to the claimant. The claimant returned it with requisitions endorsed. The defendant could or would not answer these, and retained the abstract (which in strictness he owned since it was written on his paper). The claimant successfully sued in conversion, as he was entitled to possession for the purposes of the conveyancing transaction.

 EXERCISE 10.11

List the arguments for and against the imposition of liability without reference to fault and moral blame in conversion.

10.5.3.5 **Separation of possession and ownership**

In most cases possession and ownership will in fact coincide. The following are the commoner special cases.

Bailment

A bailment arises whenever the owner of goods (the bailor) parts with possession, otherwise than by way of security for a loan or debt, to a bailee. This sounds highly technical, but is in fact an everyday occurrence. Can you think of situations where you get involved in bailments? Common examples are borrowing, lending or hiring out (including hire purchase), or consigning goods for carriage, storage, or repair.

While most bailments are contractual in nature there are legal consequences which flow from the bailment as such, and vary with the precise nature of the transaction. The bailee, being in actual possession, will always be able to maintain an action for conversion against someone who has dispossessed him. The bailor will be able to do so only where he has an immediate right to possession. He will have this where the bailment is at will, i.e. terminable forthwith, or if it has already been terminated. The bailor may sue the bailee in conversion if the bailee departs from the terms of the bailment, e.g. a repairer who sells the goods.

Lien and pledge

These are security interests (i.e. goods are handed over to secure payment of a debt or loan (pledge), or are retained pending payment of outstanding charges (lien)), but otherwise similar to bailment.

Sale

A party to the sale in actual possession of the goods, whether the seller or the buyer, can maintain conversion against a third party. Whether the other party to the sale has an immediate right to possession will ordinarily depend on whether he has the property in the goods. The situation must be viewed in the light of the general law of personal property.

Finders

The finder's possessory title is good against anyone other than the true owner. This is demonstrated in *Armory*.

Armory v *Delamirie* [1558–1774] All ER Rep 121 (*Cases and Materials* (10.3.2.2))

The claimant, a chimney sweep's boy, found a jewel. He took it to the defendant, a goldsmith, for valuation. The claimant refused the defendant's offer to buy the jewel; the defendant's servant refused to return the jewel. Did the claimant's action succeed?

Although he was only a finder, his title dated back to the time of finding. He had a better title than the goldsmith, who also had a possessory title, but a newer one. So the claimant won. There are, however, exceptions to this rule:

(a) an employee who finds in the course of employment has no title as against his employer (but the employer has finder's rights);

(b) where goods are physically within or attached to land or the structure of a building the property owner has a better right than the finder: *South Staffs Water Co.* v *Sharman* [1896] 2 QB 44 (rings in the mud at the bottom of a pond); *Elwes* v *Brigg Gas Co.* (1886) 33 Ch D 562 (prehistoric canoe six feet underground);

(c) goods found on or in premises will belong to the owner of the premises rather than the finder if (but only if) the owner has, previously to the finding, manifested an intention to exercise control over the premises and anything found therein or thereon. How does this work in practice?

? QUESTION 10.16

A passenger at an airport found a valuable gold bracelet in a lounge. He handed it to the airport operator's employee, with a note of his own name and address. He intended to claim it if the owner did not come forward. The airport operator sold the bracelet when the owner did not come forward after several months. The passenger claimed its value. Did he succeed?

In *Parker* v *British Airways Board* [1982] 1 All ER 834 on the facts above it was held that he did. There was insufficient intention to control access to and use of the lounge. It was a public place and therefore the finder's rights prevailed. There is of course no precedent of fact and other cases must be considered on their merits. In *R* v *Rostron & Collinson* (2003) LTL, 16 July, golf balls lost in water hazards were held to belong to the golf club as that was the general custom of the golfing fraternity, and so divers who recovered the balls without the approval of the club in order to sell them were guilty of theft and by extension would have been liable in conversion. In any case, the finder must take reasonable steps to trace the true owner.

10.5.3.6 Complex disputes

It is easy to see that complex situations may arise, with several claimants. In some cases several of them will have rights. Take, for instance, a car owned by A, leased to B Motor Hire, hired by them to C, stolen from C by D, sold by D to E, an innocent buyer, who has resprayed it and replaced the engine and gearbox, which were worn out. Such cases are not uncommon. Can you work out who has rights against whom and why? It is fairly obvious that D has converted the car, but did you spot that E's acts amount to conversion as against C, and possibly A and B depending on the terms of the bailments?

The Torts (Interference with Goods) Act 1977 seeks to deal efficiently and justly with *jus tertii* (or third-party rights) which arise in these cases. Section 8 of the Act makes provision for the defendant to bring into the action anyone who has, or may have, a better title than the claimant. This is designed to achieve three objectives namely to:

(a) avoid double liability, i.e. to the claimant and the third party;

(b) avoid multiplicity of actions;

(c) limit the claimant's claim to his actual loss.

10.5.3.7 Remedies

The rules relating to remedies for conversion are a detailed subject of study in themselves. What follows is a brief overview.

Damages

The claimant can recover the value of his interest in the goods. If the interest is a limited one then the claimant will recover only that. Where there are several interested parties, the damages may be apportioned. Prima facie the value will be market value, ascertained as may be appropriate. Consequential loss (e.g. hire of a replacement) is recoverable. The calculation will be done on the basis most favourable to the claimant. This may involve an element of restitutionary damages based on the advantage secured by the defendant rather than the loss suffered by the claimant. In *Strand Electric* v *Brisford* [1952] 1 All ER 796 the claimant hired electrical equipment to the defendant, who failed to return it. The claimant's loss would have been nominal if he had had items of that kind still in stock to hire out to others. His loss would have been substantial only if he had had to turn other hirers away. Otherwise all he lost was wear and tear on the items detained. The defendant, on the other hand, got a substantial advantage. He did not have to pay the market rate for hiring the items from elsewhere. As a result the full hire fee for the electrical equipment was recoverable, whether or not the claimant could prove he had lost an alternative hiring. Similarly in *Hillesdon Securities* v *Ryjack Ltd* [1983] 2 All ER 184, the contractual hiring charge for a car was due for the period of detention, even though it far exceeded the market value. Is this a fair way of approaching the problem?

Delivery up

See s. 3 of the Torts (Interference with Goods) Act 1977. This is a remedy peculiar to interference with goods, primarily conversion. It is a specific remedy, in the sense that the claimant gets back the thing itself rather than compensation for losing it. Such an order may be made whenever the defendant retains the subject matter of the claim. The defendant may be given the option of delivering up the goods or paying their value by way of damages, and the order will in any event carry with it any consequential damages.

Improvement

Quite frequently someone who acquires goods will repair or upgrade them, enhancing their value. How should he be dealt with if the goods have been converted? Equity demands that he be reimbursed for this work, provided he acted in good faith. If he is ordered to pay damages, this will be on the basis of the value at the time of the conversion. If an order for delivery up is made, compensation for the improvement can be ordered: s. 6 of the Torts (Interference with Goods) Act 1977.

? **QUESTION** 10.17

Del hires out a sound system to Ingrid for two days for Ingrid's 21st birthday party. At the party Tom asks Ingrid if he can borrow the system for use at his own party, a week later. Ingrid agrees. At Tom's party one of the speakers is ruined when a bottle of champagne is spilled over it. The sound desk disappears from the party and is traced to Khaled. Khaled bought the sound desk from a reputable dealer and has subsequently upgraded the electronic system.

What claims does Del have in conversion?

Del clearly has some rights. He is entitled to possession as Ingrid's bailment has expired. Ingrid has wrongfully disposed of the goods and Tom has wrongfully received them. Both will be fully liable for the value of what has been destroyed or misappropriated. Tom will also be liable for a hire fee (*Strand Electrical*). In theory the thief is also liable in conversion, if traceable and worth suing. Khaled and the dealer are also liable for the sound desk; they cannot acquire title through the thief, except possibly after six years under the Limitation Act. Khaled should be entitled to an allowance for the improvement under s. 6 of the 1977 Act. Del cannot recover more than once.

10.5.4 Trespass to goods

Trespass to goods is an intentional or possibly negligent direct interference with goods in the possession of the claimant.

10.5.4.1 Intentional or negligent

The same observations apply here as in the case of trespass to the person. Accidental damage is no trespass, and if goods are negligently damaged the claim will probably be brought in negligence.

10.5.4.2 **Direct**

This means immediate in the sense of occasioned by the operation of a physical force set in motion by the defendant.

10.5.4.3 **Interference**

The tort protects three separate interests of the claimant.

(a) Retention of possession. In this aspect there is a substantial overlap with conversion and in practice it is the latter which is more usually employed;

(b) Physical damage. Appreciable damage to goods is clearly a trespass. It is a moot point whether any alteration of goods is actionable. There are three possible positions, none of which is excluded by the authorities:

   (i) the tort is actionable per se on the analogy of the other trespass torts;

   (ii) there must be some element of hostility present to render a nominal interference actionable;

   (iii) substantial harm is a requisite.

   Which do you think is correct? Why?

(c) Inviolability. This prevents intermeddling by moving goods and carrying them away even though there may be no damage. The claimant is entitled to have his goods where he wants them. The same argument arises in relation to a nominal moving and there is some authority that this is actionable as in *Kirk* v *Gregory* (1876) 1 Ex D 55 where moving rings from room to room in a house was held to be a trespass.

10.5.4.4 **Possession**

As in conversion the emphasis is on actual possession and not ownership. An immediate legal right to possess (e.g. that of a bailor at will or a trustee) will suffice. An owner who is out of possession cannot maintain an action in trespass, but can maintain an analogous action in relation to the destruction or damage of the goods to his prejudice: *Mears* v *LSWR* (1862) 11 CBNS 850. There will be no claim if the goods are repaired before they were due for return.

10.6 **Title conflicts**

[A] person who has neither title nor authority to sell may sometimes confer a good title on a third party. He lacks the right to dispose, for his action is unauthorized, yet has the power of disposal in that in given conditions the law will treat his disposition as effective, binding the true owner even though he did not consent to it. (Goode, *Commercial Law* at p. 392.)

10.6.1 **The general position**

As you may already have realized, there are two aspects to a sale of goods transaction, the aspect of obligation (i.e. that there is a contract, performance of which can be enforced, and breaches of which can be compensated) and the aspect of property, or conveyance (i.e. that the end result is intended to be that the goods pass from the ownership of the seller to that of the buyer). Most of the cases concern outright disposals, usually sales in the strict sense, but some concern disposals for limited purposes, pledges, hirings-out, etc. The legal analysis is similar, and cases of one kind are often regarded as authority in relation to another. You should bear in mind that any reference to buyer (B) and seller (S) will also refer, with the necessary changes of name, to pledges, hirings-out, etc. However, the position of the original true owner will be slightly different. In the case of a sale, where the power of a non-owner to give a good title to the goods is recognized, the true owner's rights in the goods are extinguished, although he may have rights against the seller or proceeds of sale. Where the unauthorized disposal is of a limited interest only, the rights of the true owner in the goods are not extinguished, but are postponed to the rights of the owner of the limited interest created by the disposal. So in the case of a pledge the true owner can recover the goods by redeeming the pledge, i.e. by paying the pledgee what is due.

10.6.2 The basic principle: *nemo dat quod non habet* (no one can transfer a better right than he has)

What do you suppose this principle means? Rights of ownership are sacred and paramount; in principle an owner can be divested of his rights only by his own voluntary (in the sense of deliberate rather than gratuitous) act in a private law context (the state may possess rights of expropriation or compulsory purchase). Anyone (e.g. a thief) who wrongfully purports to exercise those rights acts without effect; the original rights remain in full vigour and can be enforced at any time and against any person in wrongful possession, even when that person is personally morally blameless and unaware of the earlier depredation (subject only to rights acquired by passage of time under the Limitation Act 1980, which is quite complex in this area!). This is an example of the general preference of the common law for the preservation of rights of property. The owner can maintain an action in conversion for his property, in so far as another has interfered with it, except to the extent that the other is protected under the rules set out below, or by the Limitation Act. Any defence to the claim in conversion will be by asserting the rights the defendant believes he has under these rules. See ss 21 and 23–26 of the Sale of Goods Act 1979 in *Cases and Materials* (10.4.1).

10.6.3 The counter principle: *pacta sunt servanda* (effect should be given to agreements)

This is another fundamental consideration. It is a commercial rather than a legal principle. It is connected with the equitable concept of the bona fide purchaser for value without notice. Put in another way, there are contexts in which it is expedient that the rights of the original true owner be postponed to those of one who has acquired goods, or an interest in goods, in good faith, and in the ordinary course of commerce. Otherwise the risks of buying goods without good title would be too great.

10.6.4 Proof of title

In practical terms much of the difficulty stems from the fact that there is no way of establishing in a convenient way title to tangible personal property (goods or chattels). It is by no means easy to establish title to real property (land), and the system of conveyancing, registered or unregistered, although developed over centuries with an immense application of intellect and ingenuity, is by no means foolproof (it suffers from boundary disputes, overriding interests, and documentary fraud, to name but three bugbears). No such system could by any stretch of the imagination be extended to the vastly greater number of inherently mobile and largely perishable items of tangible personal property which are the subject of commercial and consumer transactions in a modern economy. This in part explains why the law accepts liability without fault in this area. However, since the buyer must in effect take the seller's title on trust, commerce depends on that trust being protected by the law. This will not of course apply where the buyer has acted in an unbusinesslike manner, or carelessly, let alone where he is party to any species of fraud.

10.6.5 Priority of claims

At their simplest these cases involve three parties. The true owner (TO), the 'seller' (S), and the buyer (B). In practice, things are often not that simple, as we will see. A common case is theft. If a thief steals goods from TO and, as S, purports to sell them to B, and then disappears with the price that B has paid, the net result is that TO and B are competing for the goods. Whoever is awarded the goods is satisfied. The other is left to an action against S either for the value of the goods (TO) or for the return of the price (B).

?   **QUESTION** 10.18

Will this be an acceptable remedy? If not, why not?

S will probably be untraceable, and even if he is traceable, he will probably be penniless. The question is which of the claimants should be given the better remedy and which the worse.

Other common cases are those where S is a bailee who sells without authority, e.g. the hirer under a hire purchase agreement who sells the goods to a third party, or is a wholesaler who sells goods for which he has not yet paid. While problems here are infrequent, since S can usually satisfy the money claim, there is a precisely similar problem whenever S absconds or becomes insolvent before doing so. In each such case you can see that to award the goods to TO is to prefer rights of property, and to award them to B is to accord primacy to the free movement of goods.

10.6.6 Apportionment

It would in theory be possible to apportion the value of the goods (and the net value of any damages claims) among the legitimate claimants, spreading the loss. It would also be possible to incorporate in this system differentials to reflect the degree of responsibility of each party for the débâcle that has occurred, by analogy with contributory negligence. Would this be a good idea? This proposal was in fact put forward by Devlin LJ in *Ingram* v *Little* (1960), but was rejected by the Law Reform Committee in their *Twelfth Report on the Transfer of Title to Chattels* (Cmnd 2958: 1966).

10.6.7 **An alternative view**

'*En fait de meubles la possession vaut titre*': Code Civil (France), Art. 2279. This has nothing to do with furniture, but is a statement that, under French law, the person in possession of personal property ('moveables') can transfer a good title, i.e. a full recognition of the primacy of commercial considerations over property. In England, the main principle is still *nemo dat*, although there are exceptions.

> In the development of our law, two principles have striven for mastery. The first is for the protection of property: no one can give a better title than he himself possesses. The second is the protection of commercial transactions: the person who takes in good faith and for value without notice could get a good title. The first principle has held sway for a long time, but it has been modified by the common law itself and by statute so as to meet the needs of our own times. (*Bishopsgate Motor Finance* v *Transport Brakes Ltd* [1949] 1 KB 322 *per* Denning LJ.)

? **QUESTION** 10.19

What are the arguments for and against the *nemo dat* principle? What priority would you give to owners' rights and buyers' rights?

10.6.8 **Problem areas**

10.6.8.1 **Sale under a voidable title**

Where a contract is entered into in circumstances such that it can be avoided by one party, e.g. where there has been a misrepresentation, but TO has delivered goods in pursuance of his prima facie obligations, the rule is that, if the contract is avoided, the rights so created determine and TO resumes his status as such. Until then his buyer has title and can pass this to any third party. Is this really an exception to the *nemo dat* rule? It is often described as one. Although in economic, or practical terms, the dispute will still usually be whether TO or B is entitled to the goods, and therefore which of them is left to his action against S, the legal analysis is different. The essence of a voidable title is that it is good unless and until avoided. If B acquires in good faith before TO avoids, he gets good title, and will not be liable to TO in conversion.

 Car and Universal Finance v *Caldwell* [1964] 1 All ER 290 is a standard case of a contract procured by (fraudulent) misrepresentation, and therefore voidable. TO could not trace S to give orthodox notice of rescission, but took all practical steps open to him before the sale to B. This was held to be an effective rescission; the contract was avoided and S's title annulled before B acquired it. Ordinarily the position will be governed by s. 23 of the Sale of Goods Act 1979 (see *Cases and Materials* (10.4.1)). Can you see why these rules give rise to an argument as to whether or not certain categories of fraud constitute a mistake as to identity or a misrepresentation? If there is a mistake as to identity and as a result the contract is void s. 23 does not apply and the *nemo dat* rule does.

10.6.8.2 **Estoppel: apparent authority and apparent ownership**

In an estoppel, the court is effectively penalizing TO by declining to allow him to rely on his usual legal rights because he has in some way, by word or deed, induced B to act to his prejudice, and it is equitable to grant B the better remedy, and therefore deprive TO of his action in conversion. Let us look at the two expressions more closely.

Apparent authority

This is an aspect of agency. An authorized agent can of course sell goods, and his act is regarded in law as the act of the principal (i.e. the person for whom the agent acts). The same result should, in equity, follow where the authority is illusory, but the principal is responsible for creating the illusion.

Apparent ownership

While this may arise in an agency context, it need not. Neither doctrine will operate where TO has merely failed to take care of his property. There is no duty of care to prevent a third party acting to his prejudice. In *Moorgate Mercantile* v *Twitchings* [1976] 2 All ER 641 TO let a car on hire purchase to S. Usually TO registered all hire purchase agreements with a central registry, HPI, who would be consulted by any trade buyer, and would disclose to them any registered transaction. The intention was not to prevent further dealings but to ensure that existing commitments were cleared. In practice, if an agreement were revealed the dealer would obtain a settlement figure and pay this amount to TO. He would pay the balance to the hirer or credit it against another transaction. This agreement was one which 'slipped through the net'; TO simply forgot to register it. When B bought the car he did an HPI search, which came back blank. The House of Lords held:

(a) the blank search did not create an estoppel; it simply stated that there was no registration, and could not be construed as a representation that the car was free of hire purchase altogether;

(b) TO was not negligent; he owed B no duty of care.

TO's claim in conversion against B succeeded.

The crucial question is: what steps will suffice for the court to hold that TO had constituted S the apparent owner, given that mere carelessness will not do?

In *Central Newbury Car Auctions* v *Unity Finance* [1956] 3 All ER 905 TO parted with possession of a car and its log book to S. S sold to B. Held, this was carelessness on the part of TO, but they owed no duty of care and there was no holding out or estoppel. It might have been different if the log book were a document of title, but the vehicle licensing system does not provide a guarantee of ownership. It is the keeper who is registered, and keeping and owning are not at all the same thing. Not many people know that!

In *Eastern Distributors* v *Goldring* [1957] 2 All ER 525 TO gave S certain documents to use as part of a scheme to evade hire purchase controls. The details of the scheme are too complex to set out here. The documents, which included a receipt, showed S to be the owner of TO's vehicle. S used them, not to carry out the proposed fraud, but to sell the vehicle to B. Held: TO was estopped from asserting a claim against B because the effect of the documents was to hold S out as owner. The result was in theory reached without relying on TO's own involvement in the original fraud, but this could quite properly be a consideration when deciding equitable priorities.

> **?** **QUESTION** 10.20
>
> Let us see how well you have grasped how these rules operate. How should the following case be decided?
>
> TO, who knew S reasonably well, and believed him to be honest and respectable (despite the fact that she knew him to be a second-hand car dealer!), enlisted his help to raise a loan on the security of her car. At S's request she signed, without reading in full, what she thought was a loan application, but which in fact was a document which enabled S to represent himself to B as the owner of the car and sell it to B.

These were the facts of *Mercantile Credit* v *Hamblin* [1964] 3 All ER 592. It was held that TO did owe a duty of care to B for the document (*not* for the car itself!) and if she had been negligent would have been estopped, but on the facts was not negligent since there was no reason to be suspicious of S. Most people would say TO was a rather lucky lady:

> The defendant only authorized Mr Phelan to make inquiries as to the amount obtainable and to report back to the defendant. Mr Phelan never had actual authority from the defendant to complete the forms or to present them to the [claimants] . . . The crucial question is whether as against the [claimants] the defendant is estopped from denying Mr Phelan's authority to complete the forms and present them on her behalf. Did she give him ostensible authority? Did she hold him out to the plaintiffs as having authority?
>
> . . . Whether the presentation of the documents be regarded as the making of an offer or the making of a representation, the fact remains that there was no actual authority, and the plaintiffs to succeed most show an ostensible authority based on negligence. In order to establish an estoppel by negligence the plaintiffs have to show (i) that the defendant owed to them a duty to be careful, (ii) that in breach of that duty she was negligent, (iii) that her negligence was the proximate or real cause of the plaintiffs being induced to part with the £800 to Mr Phelan . . .
>
> [When] the defendant signed the documents in blank, she was not then making a contract but she was contemplating and contingently intending that she would eventually enter into a contract with some persons who would provide her with money on the security of the car . . .
>
> She was arming the dealer with the means to make a contract ostensibly on her behalf. In my judgment there was a sufficient relationship or proximity between the defendant and any persons who might contract to provide her with the money that she was seeking, to impose on her a duty of care with regard to the preparation and custody of the contractual documents. The duty was owing to these persons, whoever they might eventually be found to be. . . .
>
> The next question is whether the defendant committed any breach of duty, that is to say whether she was negligent. On the peculiar facts of this case I think there should not be a finding of negligence against her. She was well acquainted with Mr Phelan, and he was apparently respectable and solvent and prosperous, and the blank cheque which he gave her would naturally give her confidence that she could rely on his due performance of the arrangement which they had made.
>
> Suppose, however, that she was negligent. There is then the question whether her negligence was the proximate or real cause of the [claimants] being induced to part with the money. In my judgment the proximate or real cause was the fraud of Mr Phelan. She gave him the means to commit his fraud, but his fraud was not, in the situation as it reasonably appeared to her, a natural or foreseeable consequence of what she did, and she should not be held responsible for it.

10.6.8.3 Section 2(1) of the Factors Act 1889

This section is to be found in *Cases and Materials* (10.4.2.2) and deals with the position of 'mercantile agents' (defined in s. 1(1) of the Act) who may give good title to buyers of goods in their possession, even though they neither own them nor have actual authority from the owner to sell.

This does not only mean a person habitually carrying on such a business. It can include a one-off transaction, and also such arrangements as 'sale or return'.

Ordinary course of business

This could be construed as:

(a) the way in which a mercantile agent could in general be expected to act;

(b) the precise manner in which someone in the trade in question can be expected to act.

Which interpretation is correct?

In *Oppenheimer* v *Attenborough and Sons* [1908] 1 KB 221 a mercantile agent who was a diamond broker pledged some diamonds belonging to his principal. Diamond brokers do not customarily do this. However s. 2(1) applied because the pledge was not suspiciously carried out, and was the sort of thing which a mercantile agent in general might be expected to do, even though it was not usual for this particular subspecies of agent.

General considerations

Although providing a considerable measure of protection, the Factors Act 1889 is not without technicalities and complexities, which are capable of working injustice. It is also fair to say that the majority of the judges who have applied it have done so from a standpoint that, as an exception to the principle of *nemo dat*, it should be construed narrowly. What is the position of the buyer from a non-mercantile agent?

In *Jerome* v *Bentley & Co.* [1952] 2 All ER 112 TO entrusted a ring to S with a view to S selling it on TO's behalf. S was simply an acquaintance, not in business at all, and thus not a mercantile agent. TO's instructions were to sell at not less than £550, and to return the ring to him after seven days if it was still unsold. S actually sold the ring eleven days later to B at £175, representing himself as the owner. There was no holding out of S as an agent by TO (i.e. TO had not assisted S to masquerade as the owner by anything other than actually giving him possession of the ring, e.g. by giving him documents relating to the ring), and the Factors Act did not apply. The transaction was of course outside S's actual authority, which had in any event come to an end. B had to return the ring to TO in pursuance of a judgment in conversion.

10.6.8.4 Sellers and buyers in possession

The position here is governed by ss 8 and 9 of the Factors Act 1889 and parallel, but slightly narrower and essentially redundant, provisions in ss 24 and 25 of the Sale of Goods Act 1979.

Section 24

This section may be found in *Cases and Materials* (10.4.1). There is a link with apparent ownership. The seller retaining possession, and probably able to document his original title to the goods as well as anyone, may appear to be the owner, but where s. 8 applies there is no necessity for the first buyer (B1) to have done anything to create this state of affairs. Indeed in the typical case he will at most have given S the opportunity by not taking delivery himself. This may be remiss of him, but would not, under the principles already explained, create a duty of care to possible later buyers. It should be noted that by definition B1 has property (i.e. he already has ownership) but not possession, while the second buyer (B2) must have possession; a sale to B2 will not invoke the section, only delivery of the goods or documents of title in pursuance of that sale. The primacy of possession, i.e. of a conveyance (albeit flawed) over a merely contractual right, reflects a number of equitable principles.

Continues or is in possession

A good example is *Pacific Motor Auctions* v *Motor Credits (Hire Finance)* [1965] 2 All ER 105. S sold a car to B1, but remained in possession as the hirer under a hire purchase agreement with B1. The section was applied to a sale to B2; the character of the continued possession was immaterial. In this case the continued possession (in the character of hirer) was with the consent of B1, but this is not a requirement.

Certain goods may be represented by documents of title, such as bills of lading, warehouse receipts etc. In such cases by usage the documents represent the goods, and transfer of the documents is equivalent to delivery of the goods.

Section 9 and section 25

These sections may be found in *Cases and Materials* (10.4.1).

Bought or agreed to buy This does not include the hirer under a hire purchase agreement. Although there is an option to buy at the end of the hire period, and the normal expectation is that that option will be exercised, the hirer is not obliged to do so. This is indeed the vital attribute of hire purchase. It was finally established in the House of Lords decision in *Helby* v *Matthews* [1895] AC 471. It is from this decision that the attractiveness of hire purchase to finance companies derives. Whatever the legal categorization of hire purchase, in economic terms it is the provision of finance to enable the hirer (H) to have the beneficial use of goods, paying by instalments and with the TO/lender retaining rights over the goods by way of security. This last consideration is an essential part of the deal, and if the rights of TO could routinely be overridden by H selling to B and giving a good title under s. 9 it would become worthless. Today statutory protection under the Consumer Credit Act 1974 and the low resale value of many second-hand items make hire purchase less important. It is still significant in commercial financing of plant and machinery. The protective rules do not apply, and the products in question hold their value better than household items.

Other forms of deferred purchase Section 9 does in principle cover such forms of deferred purchase as conditional or credit sale. In practice most such transactions are excluded because any consumer transaction within the Consumer Credit Act 1974 is expressly removed from the scope of section 9 as the buyer is deemed not to be a person who has bought or agreed to buy goods. Commercial agreements, e.g. where the buyer is a company, will be covered by s. 9.

Consent of the seller This may have been obtained by fraud. It may have been revoked, e.g. where S under a conditional sale agreement rescinds the agreement because of B's default. This does not matter.

? **QUESTION** 10.21

On balance do you consider the title conflict rules to be (a) consistent and (b) just?

10.6.9 **Summary**

When two major principles are brought into opposition the result is often unsatisfactory. This is particularly so when the conflict resolution has to be achieved within the common law case-by-case procedure, with a series of narrow precedents established by judges of differing opinion at times of varying social and economic priorities. Should the rules for bearing loss in the event of merchants' insolvency and dishonesty be the same as those for priority in secured consumer credit? That is what, in essence, we still have. The latter problem could indeed be addressed by the creation of a system of protection of security interests, by registration or otherwise. The former problem may require one solution for consumer cases and others for purely commercial ones.

10.7 **Trespass to land**

This brief section defines the behaviour which constitutes trespass to land and indicates what remedies are appropriate.

10.7.1 **A definition**

> Intentionally or negligently entering or remaining on, or directly causing any physical matter to come into contact with, land in the possession of another. (*Street on Torts*, at p. 73.)

10.7.1.1 **Intentionally or negligently**

It is clear that intentional movement of oneself or one's goods which does put you or them on someone else's land is trespass whether or not you are aware that you have crossed the boundary: *Baseley* v *Clarkson* (1681) 3 Lev 37. There is the same debate as in the other trespass torts over liability for 'pure' negligence. If I park my car, but fail to set the handbrake with the result that it rolls down a hill and into someone's garden, is that trespass?

10.7.1.2 **Entering on**

This will cover undermining, or entry into that part of the airspace actually in use. So an advertising sign fixed to the side wall of a tall building and projecting into the airspace above the lower neighbouring building is a trespass. That airspace is at least potentially in use, as the building could be extended: *Kelsen* v *Imperial Tobacco* [1957] 2 All ER 343. Similarly a site crane swinging over the claimant's land will be trespass: *Anchor Brewhouse Developments* v *Berkeley House* (1987) 2 EGLR 187. Where redevelopment is only possible if airspace is encroached on, this can provide a lucrative windfall for adjoining owners, who can demand substantial sums in return for their consent. Is this fair and reasonable?

There is a line to be drawn. Overflying and photographing a house from a safe height is not trespass: *Bernstein* v *Skyview and General* [1977] 2 All ER 902. Why is this? The area entered is not actually or potentially being utilized; to give the owner such extensive control would interfere with the public interest in commercial aviation. There is statutory provision for civil aviation to be conducted in a normal and proper way. There is no liability for overflying at a reasonable height, and strict liability for actual harm done to person or property on the ground by an aircraft or anything falling from one: s. 76 of the Civil Aviation Act 1982.

10.7.1.3 Remaining on

This simply makes it clear that there is a continuing liability.

10.7.1.4 Land

This includes some rights over land (e.g. a right of way). It is also a trespass against the owner of the subsoil to commit an abuse of a highway: *Hickman* v *Maisey* [1900] 1 QB 752. This means use other than for passing and repassing and other incidental use which does not interfere with, or obstruct, the highway. In *Hickman* the defendant was loitering on a path to spy on racehorses in training nearby. Reasonable use may include political and other demonstrations of a peaceful kind as a result of the House of Lords decision in *DPP* v *Jones* [1999] 2 All ER 257. This decision marks a relaxation of the previous rule and appears to take into account the importance of European Convention rights of free assembly and expression.

10.7.1.5 Possession

A legal estate or equitable interest and exclusive possession (as understood by land law) are required, i.e. the appropriate claimant is the freeholder, tenant for years in possession, or the equitable owner. There is some argument that a licensee with exclusive possession or a spouse with rights of occupation under the Matrimonial Homes Act 1983 can claim. A squatter acquires no right as against the true owner (although, like the finder of a chattel, he has a right against others), but a tenant in possession has an action against a landlord who wrongfully dispossesses him. A reversioner (i.e. someone to whom the land will revert at the end of a lease, etc.) may have a remedy, provided that the defendant's activities have injured his interest by permanent or long-term damage to the land, but this will not technically be in trespass. Merely walking over the land does not harm the reversion, but extracting minerals, or making tracks with large vehicles may well do.

10.7.2 Basis of actionability

It is well-settled that trespass to land is actionable per se. This means without proof of any damage resulting.

10.7.3 Remedies

10.7.3.1 Damages

If an action is brought for damages, nominal damages at least will be awarded to a successful claimant. Substantial damages are available where recompensable damage has occurred. In some cases an action in trespass to land is brought primarily to establish ownership. In a boundary dispute one disputant will allege that the other has trespassed on 'his' land. The judge will need to determine the question of ownership and if the claimant succeeds, the defendant has indeed trespassed. A judgment for nominal damages forms the basis of the claimant's title to the disputed land.

10.7.3.2 **Injunctions**

The remedy of choice is often the injunction (see 13.5), which prevents a continuance or repetition of the trespass.

10.7.3.3 **Possession orders**

These are in practice used against squatters, whose presence is continuous and threatens to be permanent, rather than against the casual user of a short cut or private path. In those cases an injunction is more appropriate. An expedited procedure is available in the case of pure trespassers (i.e. those who have simply entered without any arrangement with the landowner, as opposed to those who have outstayed their welcome in legal terms).

The police have powers under s. 61 of the Criminal Justice and Public Order Act 1994 to remove squatters on land who have refused to leave on request and who have caused damage, been aggressive, or are present in numbers. The Act also strengthens the powers under the Criminal Law Act 1977 which provide enforcement mechanisms for civil procedures against squatters in houses.

10.7.3.4 **Self-help**

Self-help is available in the sense that the landowner or those he authorizes may use reasonable force to repel or expel trespassers. This remedy is not available when the trespasser has effectively obtained full possession of the property. Why is the use of self-help not encouraged? It may lead to breaches of the peace. Prevention of these was one of the original reasons for developing tort remedies for trespass through the courts as we have seen. The landowner acts at his peril in relation to the degree of force: *R* v *Chief Constable of Devon & Cornwall, ex parte CEGB* [1982] QB 458.

It is possible to use self-help in cases of a minor, continuing trespass (e.g. by branches or tree roots) or where there is urgency. The law also leans against this form of self-help, for much the same reasons. It will cease to be available (at the latest) once an application for a mandatory injunction has been refused: *Burton* v *Winters* [1993] 3 All ER 847.

10.7.3.5 **Distress damage feasant**

A chattel which has 'trespassed' and caused damage may be detained under the ancient remedy of distress damage feasant as security for compensation. This has been applied to a railway engine trespassing on the wrong tracks: *Ambergate Rly* v *Midland Rly* (1853) 2 E & B 793. Most of the case law relates to cattle trespass, which is now regulated by statute (ss 7 and 9 of the Animals Act 1971).

10.7.4 **A case study: wheel clamping**

There has for some time been concern over the activities of vehicle clampers. It is very much a question of two wrongs not making one right. Both the wrongs are, as it happens, within the trespass categories. The vehicle owner (VO) commits a trespass to land by parking his car on private land without consent. Sometimes it is clear that parking will seriously inconvenience the landowner or his visitors. Sometimes the land is generally vacant or derelict. In many cases there are clear warning signs. In some cases these are inadequate or absent. It has been suggested that decoy cars are sometimes parked to encourage others to believe that parking is tolerated. None of these complaints factors affects the illegality of the VO's action. The land owner (LO) or his agent immobilizes the vehicle. If this were done by a blockade there would be no trespass. If a clamp is physically attached to the vehicle there is a trespass to it. It is probably not a conversion. It is argued that VO is *volens* or consents to the clamping by parking in defiance of the warnings. Large sums are sometimes demanded for release of the vehicle, sometimes where there has been unconscionable behaviour (clamping the car of a VO who is succouring an accident victim, clamping a car with the engine running which has not actually parked). In Scotland this has been held to amount to the criminal offences of theft and extortion: *Black* v *Carmichael* (1992), *The Times*, 25 June. If VO uses self-help to release the vehicle, this will amount to criminal damage to the clamp: *Lloyd* v *DPP* [1992] 1 All ER 982. The Queen's Bench Division in that case declined to investigate the civil rights and wrongs. It is understood that VOs who have paid release fees under protest and pursued actions for trespass and money had and received under duress of goods have found LOs settling out of court to avoid a possibly adverse precedent. The Court of Appeal in *Arthur* v *Anker* [1996] 3 All ER 783, expressly ruled that clamping was in principle lawful, subject to certain conditions:

(a) that there is notice of the operation of the clampers;

(b) that the release fee is reasonable;

(c) that the vehicle is released promptly;

(d) that there is an available means of contacting the clamper.

In *Vine* v *Waltham Forest LBC* [2000] 4 All ER 169 the Court of Appeal held, to general surprise, that whether there was effective notice depended, not on whether objectively adequate notice was given, but whether the car owner was subjectively aware of the notice.

The police clamp cars parked illegally on the street under statutory powers. While unpopular, this activity is tolerated as lawful. There is no doubt that unauthorized parking can be a nuisance or worse, and that some form of self-help is appropriate. There has been partial regulation of clampers under the Private Security Industry Act 2001, but this only requires the clamping operatives to be licensed under the Act and does not extend in any way to substantive questions of what is lawful or not. It may be that a restricted right to clamp is appropriate, but, as in *Arthur* v *Anker*, subject to conditions. There should also be criminal sanctions for improper clamping.

 EXERCISE 10.12

On a separate sheet of paper, draft a short Bill to regulate wheel clamping.

■ SUMMARY

There are clearly common threads running through this chapter.

- The notion of acting at one's peril in relation to the infringement of rights.

- The emphasis on vindication of the right infringed rather than recompense for harm. If compensation is the desired remedy most trespasses will also be actionable as negligent breach of duty. This has of course led to assertions that merely negligent behaviour is not trespassory.

- The use of a tortious cause of action as a vehicle for resolving disputes arising out of a wide range of legal areas, such as civil liberties, and ownership of both personal and real property.

■ FURTHER READING

Cooke, P.J. and Oughton, D.W., *The Common Law of Obligations*, 3rd edn, London: Butterworths, 2000, Chapter 1.

Herring, J., 'Assault by Telephone' [1997] *CLJ* 11.

Howarth, D., *Textbook on Tort*, 2nd edn, London: Butterworths, 2004, Chapters 9 and 10.

Jones, M.A., *Textbook on Torts*, 8th edn, London: Blackstone Press, 2002, Chapters 11 and 12.

Markesinis, B.S. and Deakin, S.F., *Tort Law*, 5th edn, Oxford: Oxford University Press, 2003, Chapters 4 and 5 (ss 1 and 2 only).

Murphy, J., *Street on Torts*, 11th edn, London: Butterworths, 2003, Part II, Chapters 2–6.

Winfield and Jolowicz on Tort, 17th edn, London: Sweet & Maxwell, 2006, Chapters 4, 11, and 17.

 CHAPTER 10 ASSESSMENT EXERCISE

Yuri, an official of the St Petersburg Heritage Museum, is in a transit lounge at Heathrow airport when he observes in a corner, behind a counter, an icon which he believes to be one missing from his museum. Although there is a notice on the counter stating 'Authorized Personnel Only Beyond This Point', Yuri goes behind the counter to inspect the icon. Close inspection reinforces his belief that the icon is the missing one. He takes possession of it. He is observed by Susan, a security officer, who suspects him of theft and apprehends him. While she is doing so, there is a scuffle, Susan suffers a dislocated finger and the icon is seriously damaged. Yuri is prosecuted for theft and acquitted.

The Airport Authority retains possession of the icon. The icon is claimed by Carlos, who left it in the lounge. Carlos can prove that he bought the icon at a respectable auction two years ago.

The icon is also claimed by Yuri on behalf of the museum. Yuri can prove that the icon was in the museum collection in 1939, and that it has never been officially disposed by the museum authorities.

Advise Yuri as to his rights and liabilities in tort arising out of this incident.

See *Cases and Materials* (10.6) for a specimen answer.

11 Nuisance and related torts

11.1 OBJECTIVES

By the end of this chapter you should be able to:

1 Describe the elements of the nuisance torts

2 Analyse the factors which lead to particular fact situations being defined as nuisances in law

3 Explain the relationship between nuisance and the law relating to hazardous activities

4 Explain the law relating to harassment and its relationship to nuisance

5 Outline the relationship between the nuisance torts and other environmental and planning legislation

6 Explain the remedies available and the principles on which they are awarded

11.2 Introduction

> Few words in the legal vocabulary are bedevilled with so much obscurity and confusion as 'nuisance'. . . Much of the difficulty and complexity surrounding the subject stems from the fact that the term 'nuisance' is today applied as a label for an exceedingly wide range of legal situations, many of which have little in common with each other. (Fleming, *Law of Torts*, 8th edn, p. 409.)

While offputting, this statement is true. One distinct side of nuisance is the regulation of the way land is used, usually to protect neighbouring landowners from adverse impact on the value or amenity of their land or the cost of making good harm. In this respect there is a link with wider environmental issues such as pollution, planning control, and water management. However, in those areas, while a particular activity may affect the private interests of a great number of individual landowners, there is a clear distinction, and often tension, between those private rights and interests and a wider public interest. Another very different side of nuisance is those activities which affect people rather than property, and which today might well be called 'antisocial behaviour'. Again there is a public as well as a private dimension.

It has always been the case that a public remedy is available through prosecution and injunctions obtained in the public interest. Now there is also the Antisocial Behaviour Order (ASBO), which is also a public law remedy. Private actions for damages and injunctions do however remain available. Ideally, one would deal with these two aspects, which may be summarized as indirect injury to land and antisocial behaviour respectively, in separate sections, but unfortunately they overlap considerably.

 EXERCISE 11.1

Find the dictionary definition of the word 'nuisance'. Which parts of this meaning appear to be legally significant?

11.3 Definitions

The first thing to keep firmly in mind is that there are two distinct torts with names incorporating the word nuisance, i.e. private nuisance and public nuisance. Some commentators deny that there is anything other than the name in common, and that this similarity of names produces only confusion and an illegitimate tendency to apply rules relating to the one in the context of the other. The two torts certainly do not share a common history; although both deal with activities which are unacceptable as between neighbours, public nuisance is considerably broader. In effect it is an interference with rights enjoyed by the public, for example the right to use the highway. However, it may also cover something which affects everyone within a large area—a neighbourhood rather than individual neighbours. It is not tied to the use of land, so is used for many kinds of antisocial behaviour.

The word 'nuisance' is, of course, well established in everyday English as being an activity, state of affairs, or person which or who is upsetting, annoying, or discommoding, in virtually any context from vexatious litigation (a 'nuisance value offer' is a small sum paid to avoid the hassle, even when you are confident of winning) to sexual harassment ('making a nuisance of himself' is often used as a mild euphemism).

In law the word is restricted to:

(a) a harmful or noxious continuing activity or state of affairs;

(b) the harm resulting from (a).

The nuisance must be 'actionable' which means the sub-class of (a) which is within the scope of legal liability.

11.4 Private nuisance

This occurs where the defendant culpably creates or permits a state of affairs which (a) causes or permits physical damage to the claimant's property or (b) appreciably interferes with the claimant's enjoyment of his property. This is not taken from the textbooks, but has been drafted specially for this text. This is because recent House of Lords' decisions have significantly affected this area of the law. Note that this tort is very much focused on property interests, harm to the owner and others is the province primarily of negligence, although in the past, confusion has arisen where the same event gave rise to both a claim for damage to property interests and for personal injury.

The judges have tended to reduce the principle of private nuisance to a Latin tag: *sic utere tuo ut alienum non laedas* (you must use your own property so as not to damage the property of others). This does not sufficiently emphasize the balancing of interests. Some word such as 'culpably' is required to qualify 'damage'. This word is used as it is more precise than 'improperly' in suggesting the notion of legal liability.

'Culpably' needs to be handled with care. It is used as a synonym for 'actionably', in the sense that it is bringing into the equation the fact that not all nuisances in fact are recognized and penalized by the law, and can be analysed into three quite separate elements. The first relates to the mental element of intention or negligence, the second to the foreseeability of the damage complained of and the third to the extent or quality of the interference, which goes to reasonableness.

There is scope here, rather surprisingly at first sight, for use of the Human Rights Act. In *Marcic* v *Thames Water* [2002] 2 All ER 55 the Court of Appeal held that flooding of the claimant's land by sewage overflowing from the defendant's sewers was a nuisance and also agreed with the trial judge that it was an actionable infringement of his Art. 8 rights to enjoyment of his home. As we shall see, the House of Lords disagreed on both counts (see 11.4.9.4 and 11.5), but did recognize that in principle Art. 8 could be relied on. Indeed it has been relied on in the context of environmental pollution in other European countries: *López Ostra* v *Spain* (1995) 20 EHRR 99.

11.4.1 **Who can sue?**

Before we address these issues, it is important to grasp firmly a significant limitation to the scope of private nuisance. It is an action only available to an owner or occupier with a recognized legal or equitable interest (which excludes family of the occupier, visitors etc.), and is in respect of damage to his interest in the land. Although in some cases this damage takes the form of interference through noise or smells, which are actually perceived by the occupier, the claim in nuisance is for the diminution in value or utility of the land which this produces.

In *Malone* v *Laskey* [1907] 2 KB 141 the wife of the occupier was injured when a defective cistern fell on her while she was using the lavatory. Her claim fell between two alternatives. At that time a claim in 'pure' negligence did not lie for defective premises in these circumstances. The position here has now changed (see *AC Billings & Sons Ltd* v *Riden* [1958] AC 240). Although it was found as a fact that the reason for the fall of the cistern was that the supporting bracket had been loosened by vibrations from the working of machinery on the defendants' adjoining property, which is an entirely typical form of nuisance, the claimant could not recover in nuisance for her personal injuries as she was regarded as a mere licensee (i.e. having no interest of her own in the land).

This case was disapproved of in the Canadian case of *Motherwell* v *Motherwell* (1977) 73 DLR (3rd) 62 where no distinction was made, in granting a remedy for harassment by nuisance phone calls, etc. between those family members who owned or leased property and those who occupied by virtue of marital status. The majority of the Court of Appeal took the same view in a similar case in *Khorasandjian* v *Bush* [1993] 3 All ER 669, where the occupation in question was by an adult child of the family. It should, however, be noted that the activity complained of was not really related to the land, but was a species of personal harassment. It is now clear that this is not really private nuisance. The inconvenience complained of is essentially personal, and it is coincidental that the phone calls are received at home rather than at work, or on a mobile phone or car phone. It is now clear that private nuisance is not available in this class of case. The majority of the House of Lords in *Hunter* v *Canary Wharf* [1997] 2 All ER 426 expressly approved *Malone* v *Laskey*. Lord Goff cited with approval passages from an article by Professor Newark asserting a very traditional view of the scope and purpose of nuisance ('The Boundaries of Nuisance' (1949) 65 LQR 480):

> *Disseisina, transgressio* and *nocumentum* [nuisance] covered the three ways in which a man might be interfered with in his rights over land. Wholly to deprive a man of the opportunity of exercising his rights over land was to disseise him, for which he might have recourse to the assize of novel disseisin. But to trouble a man in the exercise of his rights over land without going so far as to dispossess him was a trespass or a nuisance according to whether the act was done on or off the claimant's land . . . In true cases of nuisance the interest of the claimant which is invaded is not the interest of bodily security but the interest of liberty to exercise rights over land in the amplest manner. A sulphurous chimney in a residential area is not a nuisance because it makes householders cough and splutter but because it prevents them taking their ease in their gardens. It is for this reason that the claimant in an action for nuisance must show some title to realty . . . The term 'nuisance' is properly applied only to such actionable user of land as interferes with the enjoyment by the claimant of rights in land.

Hunter v *Canary Wharf* [1997] 2 All ER 426

Hunter concerned claims in nuisance made by residents of neighbouring properties arising from the construction of the Canary Wharf Tower. Some of the residents were owners or tenants, some were not. There were two main types of claim, interference with terrestrial television signals because the tower was between the properties and the transmitter, and injury resulting from dust created by the construction works. Two issues were considered by the House of Lords:

(1) whether television interference arising from the presence of a building as such was capable of being a nuisance in law;

(2) whether it was essential that claimants had an interest in land.

In relation to the first issue, the House concluded that the reception of television signals was the equivalent of enjoying a particular view. The basic proposition is that one may at common law build anything on one's land and, as Lord Hoffmann puts it:

> The general principle is that at common law anyone may build whatever he likes upon his land. If the effect is to interfere with the light, air or view of his neighbour, that is his misfortune . . . That such has until now been the law of England seems to me indisputable. A right to an uninterrupted prospect cannot be acquired even by prescription: *Aldred's Case* (1610) 9 Co.Rep 57b. The same is true of a right to the uninterrupted flow of undefined air to a chimney: *Bryant* v *Lefever* (1879) 4 C.P.D. 172.

In relation to the second issue, the majority decided that nuisance related solely to injury to property, and that where this resulted in damages these reflected the cost of reinstatement or the loss of amenity value. *Malone* v *Laskey* was correctly decided, and it would distort the function of private nuisance to detach it from its roots as a property related tort. As Lord Goff puts it:

> In truth, what the Court of Appeal [in *Khorasandjian*] appears to have been doing was to exploit the law of private nuisance in order to create by the back door a tort of harassment which was only partially effective in that it was artificially limited to harassment which takes place in her home. I myself do not consider that this is a satisfactory manner in which to develop the law, especially when, as in the case in question, the step so taken was inconsistent with another decision of the Court of Appeal, viz. *Malone* v *Laskey*, by which the court was bound. In any event, a tort of harassment has now received statutory recognition: see the Protection from Harassment Act 1997. We are therefore no longer troubled with the question whether the common law should be developed to provide such a remedy. For these reasons, I do not consider that any assistance can be derived from *Khorasandjian* v *Bush* by the plaintiffs in the present appeals. It follows that, on the authorities as they stand, an action in private nuisance will only lie at the suit of a person who has a right to the land affected. Ordinarily, such a person can only sue if he has the right to exclusive possession of the land, such as a freeholder or tenant in possession, or even a licensee with exclusive possession.

Lord Cooke of Thorndon, in a vigorous dissent, argued that the extension to non-owners in the 'harassment'-type cases should be confirmed, but the effect of the majority decision is to exclude such claims from the scope of private nuisance altogether.

? QUESTION 11.1

To what extent do you regard the conservative restatement of the law of private nuisance in *Hunter* as being justified by strict regard for authority and to what extent does it contribute to the development of the law to assist individuals threatened with unacceptable invasions of their 'personal space'?

In the last decade there were many actions similar to *Khorasandjian* v *Bush*. Antisocial behaviour of this kind, often referred to as stalking, was either becoming commoner or attracting more forceful legal action. Assimilating it to private nuisance was clearly an extension of the existing law, but one which could, in principle, be justified by the application of the incremental approach advocated in *Caparo* v *Dickman* [1990] 1 All ER 568. Indeed Lord Cooke endorsed this approach in his very forceful dissent in *Hunter*. However the majority overruled *Khorasandjian* and made it clear that harassment was not a sub-species of private nuisance. The reasoning of Lord Goff is formidable, and certainly draws on and develops in a coherent way the old case law. The existence of the new statutory tort of harassment under the Protection from Harassment Act 1997 does remove some of the necessity for the common law to fill this gap. It can, however, be seen as a victory for historical analysis over a developmental one. We will look at this area in more detail when we consider harassment generally (11.7).

However it should be noted that the action for breach of Art. 8 of the European Convention is not restricted to landowners. A person's entitlement to enjoyment of his home does not depend on him owning or renting the home: *McKenna* v *British Aluminium* [2002] Env LR 30.

11.4.2 Culpability I: The mental element

11.4.2.1 Liability for acts

Nuisance is essentially a tort of strict liability, in the sense that it will be no defence to show that the nuisance was not created intentionally, or even that the defendant used all reasonable care. Of course in many cases the behaviour complained of is either deliberate or careless. This is, however, largely irrelevant to liability in private nuisance. The emphasis, in other words, is on the impact of the defendant's actions, rather than whether the defendant was subjectively doing wrong, or objectively falling below a reasonable standard. However, not all behaviour is caught, since there must normally be an element of continuity or repetition to engage liability in nuisance.

? QUESTION 11.2

Fred drops a tin of paint stripper as he is trying to open it while standing on his front porch. The stripper splashes. Some goes on Bert's car, which is parked in the street. Some goes on to a planter in the next door garden. The pansies and petunias in the planter are poisoned. They belong to Fred's neighbour, Gladys.

What cause of action do Bert and Gladys have against Fred?

This could easily be seen as negligence—Fred should be careful handling this product. The harm is foreseeable. It is unlikely to be nuisance. Although Bert is a road user whose use of the highway is affected (which could be public nuisance) and Gladys is a neighbour whose property is harmed, this does not arise from a state of affairs but from a single action. It is thus not likely to be nuisance even though it is one neighbour harming another neighbour's property. Although there is a separate rule regulating harm caused by the escape of dangerous things from property, this must be in the course of a 'non-natural user' of the property, which is not the case here (see 11.4.7).

Most nuisances do arise from a positive act of the defendant, and are therefore covered by the general rule. There are, however, three exceptional cases.

11.4.2.2 Positive duty to act and liability for omissions

There are a limited number of circumstances where the defendant is under a positive duty, either by a specific assumption of responsibility or by a general rule of law, such as the liability of the owner of premises fronting the highway to keep them in repair: *Tarry* v *Ashton* (1876) 1 QBD 314. This is of course not actually *private* nuisance, but it is treated as equivalent by the courts. The defendant bought a property with a gas lamp suspended from a wall bracket overhanging the pavement. As a prudent man he had this inspected by a competent gas fitter, who negligently reported that it was in good condition. In fact it was old and decayed, and a few months later after it had been weakened when a workman rested a ladder against it, climbed up the ladder, slipped and fell, the lamp itself fell on a passer-by. Although the defendant was not negligent, he owed a non-delegable duty in relation to the lamp, and remained liable for the non-performance of that duty, notwithstanding the employment of an apparently competent contractor.

A similar duty can arise in a private nuisance context, where, for example, one property owner has assumed a liability to repair, as in *Wringe* v *Cohen* [1939] 4 All ER 241, where the Court of Appeal relied on *Tarry* v *Ashton* to hold an owner liable when a wall for which he was responsible collapsed on to his neighbour's shop. Where premises were a nuisance as a result of want of repair, rather than the act of a trespasser or concealed natural forces, liability was strict. The defendant had the right and responsibility to inspect and repair, and would be liable for default. The rule is expressed as relating to harm on the highway or to neighbours where the property fronts the highway. It is thus not universally applicable in nuisance. The defendant was not actually aware of any defects, but he had been fairly lackadaisical in inspecting the property, and could therefore be said to be at fault, but the court considered that immaterial. A similar conclusion was reached in *Spicer* v *Smee* [1946] 1 All ER 489 (defective electrical system causing a fire).

Professor Fleming (*The Law of Torts*, 8th edn, p. 430) suggests that the relevant dicta in *Wringe* v *Cohen* are too wide. There was no evidence of recent inspection and this might amount to culpability in the sense of omission to act. The House of Lords has subsequently regarded liability for trees as dependent on the usual standard of good estate management, not as a strict rule. However, the standard required will be high where the tree overhangs a highway because of the high degree of risk of harm: *Caminer* v *Northern and London Investment Trust* [1951] AC 88. A tree on the defendants' premises was internally diseased; a branch fell on a car parked on the adjacent street. The defendants argued that they had employed expert and competent technical experts to advise. It was held that they were not under an absolute liability, but an obligation to act reasonably, albeit up to a very high standard of performance, given the impact of any default on the public. However, this may be regarded as an example of the natural causes category discussed below, rather than a true *Tarry* v *Ashton* type case.

 EXERCISE 11.2

What are the reasons for and against imposing strict liability?

There is a possible further category of extended strict liability. In *Cambridge Water* v *Eastern Counties Leather* [1994] 2 AC 264 the Court of Appeal treated a claim in respect of harm to groundwater percolating under the claimant's land as being an interference with the claimant's 'natural rights'. This was held to be a nuisance on the authority of *Ballard* v *Tomlinson* (1885) 29 Ch D 115. In this case the defendant had used a well on his land as a cess pit, thus polluting the claimant's nearby well and preventing the claimant using the water for brewing. This meant that the claimant was deprived of his natural right to abstract unpolluted water. The Court of Appeal in *Cambridge Water* was faced with an unchallenged decision at first instance that the defendant had not been negligent in causing the pollution, which was an unintended side effect of the perfectly proper, and as the judge below held, natural user of his land for industrial purposes. The Court was therefore imposing strict liability in nuisance in natural rights cases.

> **?** **QUESTION** 11.3
>
> Was the Court of Appeal right to treat the two cases as being equivalent?

In *Ballard* there was a quite deliberate course of antisocial conduct, and the issue was one of the definition of the right and proof of causation; it is certainly far from clear that a Victorian judge would impose liability for an inadvertent side effect of a proper use. Indeed in three earlier cases of diversion of water referred to by the court in *Ballard* the defendant was exonerated in two cases where his proper activities caused damage to the claimant: *Smith* v *Kenrick* (1849) 7 CB 515 and *Wilson* v *Waddell* (1876) 2 App Cas 95, but held liable in a third where he imported water which then escaped and caused harm: *Baird* v *Williamson* (1863) 15 CB (NS) 376. In view of these criticisms, and the fact that the House of Lords certainly did not endorse the approach of the Court of Appeal, the status of this category must be regarded as extremely dubious.

11.4.2.3 Nuisance arising from natural causes

In this situation, the defendant has not brought the nuisance about himself, he is simply the unwilling host to a natural phenomenon. In such cases liability is dependent on fault in a sense equivalent to the position in negligence. The defendant must act reasonably in the position in which he finds himself placed. The following cases illustrate the scope of this principle:

Goldman v *Hargrave* [1967] 1 AC 645: A tree on the defendant's land was struck by lightning. The defendant felled the tree and took steps to extinguish the fire which were inadequate; as a result the fire spread. The defendant was liable in nuisance.

Leakey v *National Trust* [1980] 1 All ER 17 (*Cases and Materials* (11.1.1.1)): The claimant's property was damaged as a result of natural subsidence of land forming part of the defendant's property. The defendant knew of the situation, had failed to take measures which were reasonable, proportionate, and affordable and was liable in nuisance.

Bybrook Barn Garden Centre v *Kent CC* [2001] Env LR 543: This principle was applied to a case where a culvert in a stream was adequate when installed, but became inadequate after a change in the nature of the catchment area. The Council knew, or ought to have known, of this, and were held liable on the *Leakey* principle for flood damage (which resulted from natural rainfall).

Wandsworth LBC v *Railtrack plc* [2002] Env LR 218 where the nuisance was from pigeon droppings from a roost in a railway overbridge. The criteria for liability are a nuisance in fact, arising on premises for which the defendant is responsible and which it is reasonable to expect the defendant to take action to abate.

However, this rule does not apply where a landowner is faced with the threat of flooding. He is entitled to protect his own property against the 'common enemy' of the river or sea, even if this results in his neighbour's property flooding: *R v Commissioners of Sewers for the Levels of Pagham* (1828) 8 BC 356; *Nield v LNWR* (1874–75) LR 10 Exch 4. Here, of course, the water does not arise on the defendant's land. There is a *Leakey* duty in relation to water actually on one's land which runs off onto your neighbour's land: *Green v Lord Somerleyton* (2003) 11 EG 152 (CS), or which you divert onto your neighbour's land: *Whalley v Lancs & Yorks Rly* (1884) LR 13 QBD 131. In other words the common enemy rule only applies to precautions taken in respect of the possibility of future flooding, not action taken to deal with the impact of a current flood: *Arscott v The Coal Authority* [2004] EWCA Civ 892.

> **? QUESTION** 11.4
>
> How do you account for defendants being held responsible for the consequences of the operation of natural forces?

In the above cases it was recognized that the duty owed by the defendant was not absolute; it was conditioned by reference to the defendant's resources. It is also a duty of care, in the sense that, where what is relied on is non-feasance following an extraneous incident, there must be an appreciation (assessed objectively) of the foreseeability of harm. This obviously introduces concepts and terminology familiar from the law of negligence. It has been suggested as a result that nuisance, rather like occupiers' liability, is merely a special case of negligence. This goes too far. It is pointless to deny similarities which do exist, but in nuisance liability for malfeasance depends on the result produced, not on the mental attitude thereto of the producer. In relation to physical harm one acts at one's peril, and in discomfort cases it is not carelessness but the character of the locality and the degree of disturbance which will decide. Consider, however, the observations of Lord Goff in the *Cambridge Water* case (*Cases and Materials* 11.1.2) which adopt the above analysis of *Leakey* and *Goldman*. Since lack of foreseeability is, in practice, very much a long-stop to deny liability where proper activities, carried out without consciousness of risk creating potential, turn out to have adverse effects, and since those consciously doing things which have a potential to disrupt are well aware of this, foreseeability is not generally a live issue. Markesinis argues that cases like *Leakey* are really cases of negligence arising between neighbours, rather than nuisance, but he does tend to see much of what is generally regarded as nuisance as being something else. A claim against Scarborough council over the collapse of the Holbeck Hall Hotel because of lack of support from the council's adjoining land was framed in nuisance by analogy with *Leakey*, although the court regarded negligence as being a necessary ingredient of the cause of action: *Holbeck Hall Hotel Ltd and Another v Scarborough Borough Council* [2000] 2 All ER 705. Does this reasoning account satisfactorily for the flood prevention cases?

11.4.2.4 **Acts of third parties**

In *Sedleigh-Denfield v O'Callaghan* [1940] 3 All ER 349 the local authority put a culvert into a stream on the defendant's land. The culvert was inefficient, and flooded the claimant's land when it became clogged with leaves. The defendant knew of the problem (although he had not granted permission for the construction of the culvert), but did nothing either to get those responsible to improve the position or to clear the blockage. This was sufficient to found liability. It was, however, essential to the decision that the defendant was aware of the position and had not acted reasonably in the light of the position in which he was placed, i.e. that there was negligence. It was also the case that the defendant had adopted the nuisance in the sense that he took advantage of the improved drainage of his land which the culvert normally provided.

11.4.3 **Culpability II: Foreseeability**

The principle applied here is exactly the same as that in negligence. The type of harm complained of must be reasonably foreseeable.

> *Cambridge Water* v *Eastern Counties Leather* [1994] 1 All ER 53 (*Cases and Materials* (11.1.2))
>
> This case concerned pollution to a borehole. Eastern Counties Leather (ECL) had for many years operated a tannery. One of their operations was the degreasing of hides which took place in machines resembling industrial dry cleaning machines. The solvent used was known as PCE. Originally it was stored in drums and poured into the machines as required. Later a piped delivery system was used. PCE is extremely volatile, and evaporates very rapidly. As a result, it was generally believed that the only hazard from spillages was to the workforce, who might be intoxicated by the fumes. It was assumed that no PCE persisted on the site. When PCE contamination was detected in the water from the borehole, rendering it unfit for use for drinking, it took an unprecedented scientific investigation by the British Geological Survey to establish the cause. Some of the PCE which had been spilled had not evaporated but percolated through the floor and then into the subsoil. It had then collected in a sort of natural saucer of clay, and had then very slowly leaked through the clay and into lower strata which formed the aquifer from which the borehole was fed.
>
> It was found by the courts that supervisors at ECL at the time when the PCE was being poured from drums could not have anticipated this accumulation of PCE in the subsoil.
>
> Lord Goff gave the only speech. In his Lordship's view, there was no strict (in the sense of absolute: note the apparent verbal inconsistency) liability in nuisance. It was an essential prerequisite that there should be foreseeability of the relevant kind of harm. In this respect he relied on the decision in *The Wagon Mound (No. 2)* [1967] 1 AC 617.

Ballard v *Tomlinson* is dealt with rather obliquely. Lord Goff clearly considers that the case is not authority for any proposition that the defendant is liable for unforeseeable harm. It is either an orthodox *Rylands* v *Fletcher* case, or it is a case of private nuisance, subject to the ordinary rules. The harm in *Ballard* was certainly foreseeable, at least in the modern sense. A layman might not appreciate the potential for the spread of pollution, but a reasonable operator of the business would. In *Cambridge Water*, on the other hand, this was not the case, and so the claimant's claim failed. The case is discussed in more detail later (11.4.7.1; 11.4.7.2).

> **?** **QUESTION** 11.5
>
> Does Lord Goff's approach mean that we can forget about the first meaning of 'culpable'?

It is clear that there is now much more emphasis on the effects of the defendant's behaviour. Where action is deliberate you will not need to enquire what the reasonable man ought to have foreseen. The requirement of foresight where the behaviour is not designed to produce the results the claimant complains of, does retain some element of fault. A defendant who sees a risk, and runs it, believing that he has the situation under control, is 'culpable' even if only to a very limited extent. At the least he has put his interests ahead of others. The defendant who acts with the best intentions, but who has not weighed up the risks properly, is more clearly 'culpable'. He has not had proper regard for the interests of others.

> **?** **QUESTION** 11.6
>
> Why does the law impose liability for omissions and treat acts as culpable by reference to the results and not to the culpability of the defendant in nuisance, but not in negligence?

Negligence is not a relationship. The only necessary link between the claimant and the defendant is the incident. The key is that the defendant must have been at fault in handling the circumstances surrounding the incident. In nuisance the two occupiers each have rights, and it is the infringement of the rights, not the fault involved, which is crucial.

11.4.4 Culpability III: Unreasonableness

What would be a nuisance in Belgrave Square would not necessarily be so in Bermondsey: *Sturges* v *Bridgman* (1879) 11 Ch D 852 at p. 865 *per* Thesiger LJ.

11.4.4.1 Striking the balance

Most of our activities impinge on our neighbours. Theirs in turn impinge on us. To a great extent we accept this on a basis of live and let live, or even tit for tat. However, when there is a claim that someone has gone outside this region of civilized coexistence, a balance must be struck. The law generally seeks to hold a fair balance between the gravity, persistence, and motive of the defendant's conduct and the nature and quality (but not duration) of the claimant's occupation of his land, in the light of the character of the locality. Judges have tried down the years to sum up this process in a single sentence:

> Those acts necessary for the common and ordinary use and occupation of land and houses may be done, if conveniently done, without subjecting those who do them to an action: *Bamford* v *Turnley* (1862) 3 B & S 62 at p. 83 *per* Bramwell B.

A balance has to be maintained between the right of the occupier to do what he likes with his own and the right of his neighbour not to be interfered with: *Sedleigh-Denfield* v *O'Callaghan* [1940] AC 880 at p. 903 *per* Lord Wright.

[A] useful test is perhaps what is reasonable according to the ordinary usages of mankind living in society, or, more correctly, in a particular society: *Ibid.*

There is here no dispute that there has been and is likely to be in the future an interference with the claimant's enjoyment of [his property]. The only question is whether this is unreasonable. It is a truism to say that this is a matter of degree: *Miller* v *Jackson* [1977] 3 All ER 338 *per* Geoffrey Lane LJ (*Cases and Materials* (11.1.3.1)).

The judge in concluding that the noise did not constitute an actionable nuisance had applied the correct test, namely whether according to the standards of the average person and taking into account the character of the neighbourhood, the noise was sufficiently serious to constitute a nuisance: *Murdoch* v *Glacier Metal Ltd* (1998), *The Times*, 21 January, *per* Pill LJ.

It is equally a truism that the resolution of this question is going to involve a balancing exercise which will in the end be categorized as a question of fact. This is to be assessed pragmatically, case by case, and not by reference to abstract criteria. In the *Glacier Metal* case the judge was held to have rightly refused to accept that the fact that the noise was marginally above a World Health Organization approved level for disturbance of sleep was itself conclusive that there was an actionable nuisance. On the other hand there are certain recurrent factors which the courts have recognized as having weight where they are relevant. There will inevitably be a degree of overlap, in the sense that certain facts will fit into two or more categories.

 EXERCISE 11.3

What factors do you consider relevant for the balancing exercise described above? See *Sedleigh-Denfield* and *Miller* in *Cases and Materials* (11.1.3.1).

11.4.4.2 Material considerations

The defendant's unworthy motive

Some activities are either lacking in social utility (e.g. storing unsightly refuse) or are motivated by spite or malice. This will be taken into account when deciding whether they are unreasonable.

In *Christie* v *Davey* [1893] 1 Ch 316 the claimant was a music teacher. The defendant took exception to what he perceived as a noise nuisance arising from lessons and other musical activities, and retaliated by creating a cacophony of his own to distract the claimant. How should these conflicting interests be reconciled? The judge accepted that the claimant's actions were in good faith, but the defendant's were not, and appears to have assumed that the claimant's actions were not sufficiently disruptive to be unreasonable. The defendant was enjoined from creating a further nuisance because he was not acting in good faith. It was not legitimate to use his property for the purpose of annoying his neighbours.

In *Hollywood Silver Fox Farm* v *Emmett* [1936] 1 All ER 825 following a difference of opinion over a right of way, the defendant arranged for his son to go shooting near the boundary of the claimant's fur farm. There were rooks and other vermin there to be shot, but the defendant also knew that loud noise deterred mating, impeded whelping and provoked infanticide among silver vixens. How do you think the balancing act came out this time? Again the malicious intent was enough to constitute a nuisance. There is no absolute right to make a noise, and motive is relevant.

Utility of the defendant's activity

It is easy to condemn those who are acting out of spite or malice. Should particularly beneficial activities be given special privileges? This is not what happens in practice, although they are not treated with undue rigour. There is also a need to distinguish between the activity as such and an unreasonable approach to carrying it out.

In *Southwark LBC* v *Mills*; *Baxter* v *Camden LBC* [1999] 4 All ER 449 it was held that the activities of neighbouring occupiers in a block of flats would not amount to a nuisance unless there was something excessive or unusual about them, even where the sound insulation was poor. This is an example of things being 'conveniently done'. In *Sampson* v *Hodson-Pressinger* [1981] 3 All ER 710 the claimant recovered damages in nuisance against the occupant of an uninsulated terrace above his sitting room in respect of noise and vibration. This was explained in *Southwark* as an example of an excessive or inconvenient use.

In *Andreae* v *Selfridge* [1937] 3 All ER 255 the defendant was rebuilding his shop which adjoined the claimant's hotel. In order to reduce the period of closure to a minimum, work went on unabated round the clock, rendering sleep impossible. To what extent was this a nuisance? The court acknowledged that a certain amount of disruption during normal working hours was inevitable, and would not be a nuisance, on a basis of mutuality or 'live and let live'. The defendant conceded that he had not in fact had proper regard to the effect of his operations on the claimant, with the result that there was an actionable component to the disruption which the claimant had suffered.

In *Bellew* v *Irish Cement* [1948] IR 61 an injunction was granted in respect of nuisance from a cement factory, which had the effect of closing the factory down although it was the only domestic source of supply at a time of shortages. What message do we get from this decision? Powerful interests must be at stake if one of the main engines of the economy is being turned off to protect them. On a smaller scale, in *Adams* v *Ursell* [1913] Ch 269 the local fish and chip shop was closed down because it caused unreasonable interference, although it too was, in its way, a valuable local resource.

 EXERCISE 11.4

Read *Miller* v *Jackson* [1977] 3 All ER 338 in *Cases and Materials* (11.1.3.1). What was the basis of the complaint, and what was the reaction of the judges?

The defendant was a cricket club, the claimants the owners of a house recently built on land adjoining the club, and in easy range of the wicket. It was generally agreed that cricket was a good thing on health and cultural grounds. A majority of the Court of Appeal (Lord Denning dissenting!) held that the regular hitting of balls into the claimants' property, with an appreciable risk of injury or damage, constituted a nuisance. The decision was reached reluctantly, but the reluctance was largely on the basis of the claimants coming to the nuisance (and taking the benefit of a quiet open area beyond their boundary on all but twenty or thirty days in the year). The utility of cricket as a healthy pastime or essential part of English culture cut little ice with the majority.

Coming to the nuisance

Is it fair for a newcomer to complain? He can see what the defendant is up to, and if he does not like it, he should settle down elsewhere. Indeed, if the law had not been laid down in the last century, when there was much greater stress on rights of property and less respect for activities, this point might have been accepted. However, the position is otherwise.

In *Sturges* v *Bridgman* (1879) 11 Ch D 852 the defendant was a manufacturing confectioner, whose operations were long established, and provoked no complaint until the claimant, a physician, erected a consulting room on his property immediately adjacent to the workroom. Noise and vibration in the consulting room were intolerable. The claimant's action succeeded. His property right to use his premises as he wished had been interfered with. It was an area where the preponderance of activity was professional rather than industrial. The claimant was thus appropriate to the area, the defendant was not. The fact that the claimant had 'come to the nuisance' was regarded as subsidiary. There was some reluctance to accept this argument in *Miller* v *Jackson*, but the matter was regarded as being concluded by authority. If you had the chance to do so, would you change the law to protect established occupiers from complaints by newcomers?

Character of the locality

How is this relevant? Is everyone not entitled to the same level of amenity? It has sometimes been argued that the law of private nuisance operated as a primitive form of town and country planning control. How effective do you think it was to allow the pattern of development to be controlled by those who complained about their neighbours? There may have been some impetus given to the concentration of noxious trades in particular places, on the ground that they would not complain of each other, but this seems to be largely accidental. The factories were certainly well away from their owners' houses, but the owners could afford to move away from the nuisance!

There has, however, traditionally been a distinction drawn between nuisances involving 'material injury to [the claimant's] property' and those 'productive of sensible personal discomfort', and we need to consider what this is.

This distinction was made in those terms in *St Helen's Smelting Co.* v *Tipping* (1865) 11 HL Cas 642. In the former category of case, the claimant's rights are absolute while in the latter there is an element of relativity. This must of course all be read subject to the question of 'natural rights', which according to *Ballard* v *Tomlinson* are of an unconditional nature. This rediscovery appears to be unaffected by the House of Lords decision in the *Cambridge Water* case, provided that the harm is of a foreseeable kind.

> **?** **QUESTION** 11.7
>
> Karl operates a chemical plant in Coketown, one of the last centres of heavy industry in England. Fumes from the plant create nasty smells and smuts which make life very messy for Vladimir and Joe. Vladimir is Karl's immediate neighbour, and the operator of a smelting plant. Joe lives half a mile away, across the river on the edge of Squire's Chase, an exclusive residential area. In addition, chemicals in the fumes are eroding the stone mullions of Nikita's boardroom windows. Nikita is Karl's neighbour on the other side, and runs an oil refinery.
>
> Advise Karl as to his liability in nuisance.

Nikita appears to have an action: he has suffered physical damage. Joe also appears to have an action: he is relying on discomfort, but is entitled to the environmental quality appropriate to an exclusive residential area. Only Vladimir is likely to miss out: his claim is based on discomfort, but he is only entitled to the environmental quality appropriate to a heavy industrial zone.

Sensitive users

The concept of reasonableness cuts both ways. If the defendant can cause only a reasonable amount of disturbance, the claimant is entitled only to a reasonable quality of amenity. As I hope you can see, this category is confined to the interference type of nuisance.

In *Bridlington Relay* v *Yorkshire Electricity* [1965] 1 All ER 264 the claimant claimed that the defendant's main power cable would interfere with TV reception by its relay station. Is such interference a nuisance? The judge was 'prepared to take judicial notice of the fact that the reception of television has become a very common feature of domestic life', but as it was recreational rather than occupational, and there was no (perceived) element of noxious or dangerous interference, it was held no nuisance to interfere with TV reception as such. The claimant required a greater freedom from interference than a domestic viewer to justify charging for a relay service. Bridlington at the time had poor reception from domestic aerials because the transmitters were hidden behind hills. The Bridlingtonians, being Yorkshiremen, would only pay for the relay if it gave a much better picture. This need for an ultra-high quality of reception was an undue sensitivity which itself disentitled the claimant from a remedy.

Is TV really so unimportant? Couch potatoes will be relieved to learn that the low value placed on TV as such has been rejected in the later Canadian case *Nor-Video* v *Ontario Hydro* (1978) 84 DLR (3rd) 221, and in *Hunter* v *Canary Wharf* the House of Lords accepted that TV is a significant aspect of modern life. The more serious point is that it is settled law that the claimant is not entitled to protection for an ultra-sensitive use of his property, and that what is ultra-sensitive will be a question of fact.

11.4.5 **Who is liable?**

The definition refers to 'cause or permit'. The person actually physically responsible will be liable, as will anyone who actually employed or requested him to do so.

11.4.5.1 **The actual perpetrator**

The actual perpetrator can be liable whether or not he is in control of premises: *Hubbard* v *Pitt* [1975] 3 All ER 1.

11.4.5.2 **Landlords**

The test of liability is whether the letting (and the same rule applies to a licensee) necessarily involves the commission of a nuisance: *Tetley* v *Chitty* [1986] 1 All ER 663 where the premises were let specifically as a go-kart track. McNeill J said:

> [The claimants' case] was that a landlord, as the council were here, or licensor prior to the granting of the lease, is liable if he authorizes a nuisance on his land or grants a lease of his land with a nuisance on it or knowing that a nuisance is going to be caused on it, or for any operation which inevitably will cause a nuisance. Counsel for the council did not dissent from this as a formulation of the appropriate test.
>
> It is not enough that the nuisance may be foreseeable. In *Smith* v *Scott* [1973] 1 Ch 314 the claimant lived in a house in an area which the local authority wished to redevelop. The claimant did not want to sell. A family known to be liable to cause a nuisance were put into the house next door, though on terms expressly prohibiting the committing of a nuisance. Pennycuick V-C held that the council were not liable, as landlords, for a nuisance committed by their tenants for they had neither expressly nor impliedly authorized the nuisance.
>
> It is established beyond question that the person to be sued in nuisance is the occupier of the property from which the nuisance emanates. In general, a landlord is not liable for nuisance committed by his tenant, but to this rule there is, so far as now in point, one recognized exception, namely, that the landlord is liable if he has authorized his tenant to commit the nuisance: see *Harris* v *James* (1876) 45 LJQB 545. But this exception has, in the reported cases, been rigidly confined to circumstances in which the nuisance has either been expressly authorized or is certain to result from the purposes for which the property is let . . .
>
> Whatever the precise test may be, it would, I think, be impossible to apply the exception to the present case. The exception is squarely based in the reported cases on express or implied authority—see in particular the judgment of Blackburn J in *Harris* v *James*. The exception is not based on cause and probable result, apart from express or implied authority. In the present case, the [council let the house] to the Scotts as a dwelling-house on conditions of tenancy which expressly prohibited the committing of a nuisance, and, notwithstanding that the corporation knew the Scotts were likely to cause a nuisance, I do not think it is legitimate to say that the corporation impliedly authorized the nuisance.

? QUESTION 11.8

Jeremy lets a shop to Ken. Ken undertakes to operate the shop as a fried fish shop and for no other purpose. Jeremy's object is to provide a service to the 5,000 residents of a nearby housing estate with no other fast food outlets. Jeremy lets the house next door to Lout. Lout, as Jeremy knows full well, is a 'neighbour from Hell'. He plays loud music at all hours, his twelve children are totally out of control, and he always has three or four cars semi-dismantled in the garden. This fits in well with Jeremy's plans to upset Minnie, who lives next door, and who once rebuked Jeremy for smoking when he was 11. Minnie also complains that the smell and fumes from the fish shop are adversely affecting her bedroom.

Advise Jeremy as to his potential liability in nuisance.

The landlord will be liable where premises are let solely as a fast food outlet where this is bound to create a nuisance (see *Adams* v *Ursell* [1913] Ch 269 and 11.4.4.2). The position is different where the nuisance is collateral. In *Smith* v *Scott* [1973] Ch 314 a local authority which put a problem family into a house as tenants was not liable to the next door neighbour in nuisance for their depredations. This was so even though it seemed fairly clear that the local authority wanted to get the claimant to move, as he was holding up their development plans, and the tenants had been carefully chosen to cause mayhem. Having answered the question, and considered the response, do you think the law is fair?

In two recent decisions the Court of Appeal:

- refused to hold a local authority liable for the actions of tenants who racially harassed a local shopkeeper. This was a collateral nuisance, like that in *Smith* v *Scott*: *Hussain* v *Lancaster City Council* [1999] 4 All ER 449;
- held a local authority liable for the activities of travellers encamped (as long-term trespassers) in a council-owned lay-by. The council was held to be in occupation of the lay-by and were responsible for their failure to evict or control the trespassers: *Lippiatt* v *South Gloucestershire Council* [1999] 4 All ER 149.

Again, does the law as stated in these two cases seem to be either consistent or fair?

In *Fowler* v *Jones* [2002] LTL, 27 June, the claimants complained of a series of activities, some of which were actually perpetrated by visitors to the defendant's home. The judge held at first instance that the acts of the visitors could be counted as part of the nuisance for which the defendant was liable if she acquiesced in them; it was not necessary to show that she actively aided and abetted them. This was of course a case in which the defendant was in actual control of the situation, not one where she had handed over control of the premises altogether to tenants.

There seems to be a separate rule for nuisances arising from want of repair. The landlord remains liable for those parts of the building over which he retains control, but will also be liable for the part which is let, provided that the tenant cannot be shown to be exclusively responsible: *Wringe* v *Cohen* [1940] 1 KB 229, *Mint* v *Good* [1951] 1 KB 517.

11.4.6 Physical damage or appreciable interference

The interference must be to an interest recognized in law. One of the claims in *Hunter* v *Canary Wharf* [1997] 2 All ER 426 was for interference with TV reception because of the 'shadow' cast by the Canary Wharf tower. This was considered to be analogous to interference with a view. This has been consistently held in a series of cases from the sixteenth century onwards not to be actionable as a nuisance or otherwise. TV reception is an important amenity of life, but it cannot outweigh the right to develop one's land in an otherwise reasonable manner. There is, of course, no reason why interference to TV reception caused by the operation of machinery which is not 'suppressed' should not be a nuisance, by analogy with vibrations etc. perceived by the occupier directly.

Interference may be moral. In *Thompson-Schwab* v *Costaki* [1956] 1 All ER 652 the claimant's complaint was of the activities of the staff and clients of a brothel operated in a disorderly fashion by the defendant across the road from the claimant's property. This was held to be a sufficient potential threat both to current convenience and to property values to be a nuisance. See also *Hubbard* v *Pitt* [1975] 3 All ER 1, where the claimant was an estate agent whose activities in relation to tenanted property attracted adverse attention, taking the form of a picket of its premises. Although this was business disturbance it related to preventing the use of premises.

Are these the only categories of harm, or will others do? What if the defendant damages the claimant's economic interests by broadcasting racing commentaries of races on the claimant's track from a convenient vantage point, thus devaluing the 'exclusive' broadcasting rights the claimant had sold to someone else? It has been held in Australia that this does not constitute nuisance: *Victoria Park Racing* v *Taylor* (1938) 58 CLR 479.

? **QUESTION** 11.9

Where do you draw the boundary between those activities which are, and those which are not nuisances, where what is complained of is not the result of physical processes?

The distinction between the cases above is that in the successful claims, occupation of premises became less beneficial in a direct sense; it was less pleasant. In the unsuccessful case, the real problem was loss of money, not loss of amenity.

11.4.7 **Hazardous activities**

Although the regulation of hazardous activities at common law is an aspect the law of nuisance, according to Lord Goff in the *Cambridge Water* case, the rules are a little different. In general these are activities which have been made possible only by the scientific and technical advances of the nineteenth and twentieth centuries: rock blasting, chemical plants, oil refineries, nuclear power stations, aircraft, etc. In some cases, such as reservoirs, it is not so much new technology as the increased scale of operation required by modern society which creates the extra risk.

There is one exception, namely 'playing with fire'. Fire has always been a hazard. Although in principle it is on a par with the other risky activities, it is regarded differently in law because it was recognized much earlier.

  EXERCISE 11.5

On a separate piece of paper, make a list of activities you consider would merit special treatment on the grounds set out above. Put it to one side for the present and read on.

It is impossible to prohibit these hazardous activities. Some are essential to modern life, such as oil refineries and chemical plants. Others are at least arguably beneficial, such as nuclear power stations. A balance has to be struck, as in cases of 'ordinary' nuisance, between the rights and responsibilities of those concerned.

11.4.7.1 **How the 'hazardous activities' rule developed**

The starting point in examining how the law strikes this balance is the leading nineteenth-century case, *Rylands* v *Fletcher*.

This case has in the past usually been regarded as stating the elements of a discrete tort. In a recent major case in the field, *Cambridge Water Co.* v *Eastern Counties Leather* [1994] 1 All ER 53 (see 11.4.3 above), Lord Goff prefers to regard it as a species of nuisance. This is also the view of the House of Lords in *Transco* v *Stockport MBC* [2003] 3 WLR 1267.

Rylands v *Fletcher* **(1866) LR 1 Ex 265, Court of Exchequer Chamber (1868) LR 3 HL 330, House of Lords (***Cases and Materials***(11.1.4.1))**

The defendant was a mill owner, who employed contractors to construct a reservoir on land which he owned. It was accepted that the contractors used all proper care and skill in the design and construction of the reservoir. Although there were known to be old mine workings on the site, these were properly capped off. After the reservoir was filled, water leaked into some active mine workings, the property of the claimant, who was obliged to abandon them. It was clear that the building and operation of the reservoir caused the claimant's loss. It also seems clear that the defendant was not at fault. He had done his best, as had the contractors. Could he nevertheless be liable?

There seems to be a difference between the reasoning of Blackburn J in the Court of Exchequer Chamber and that of Lord Cairns in the House of Lords. Blackburn J stresses that the defendant brought the water on to his land, 'The person who, for his own purposes, brings on his land and collects and keeps there anything likely to do mischief if it escapes, must keep it in at his peril.'

According to Lord Cairns, had the flooding been by the operation of natural forces, albeit altered by works done by the defendant on his land, it was for the claimant to take precautions, but if defendants,

> not stopping at the natural use of their close, had desired to use it for any purpose which I may term a non-natural use . . . and if in consequence of their doing so, or in consequence of any imperfection in the mode of their doing so, the water came to escape . . . [t]hat which the defendants were doing they were doing at their own peril.

Blackburn J gives a number of examples of analogous situations. These fall into two groups:

(a) cattle trespass, which is an old common law tort of strict liability (see today s. 4 of the Animals Act 1971, which gives statutory form to the tort, but retains the strict liability);

(b) situations which appear to be orthodox nuisance, e.g. sewage from a privy flooding a cellar, fumes from an alkali works. There is clearly a state of affairs brought about by the accumulation.

On a narrow view, all that Blackburn J is deciding is that in those circumstances a single escape will create liability. There does not have to be a persistent infliction of damage or inconvenience. This at least is a firm basis for distinguishing the 'Rule in *Rylands* v *Fletcher*' from 'ordinary' private nuisance.

> **?** **QUESTION** 11.10
>
> Lord Cairns, after the passage cited above, went on to cite with approval the above passage of Blackburn J's judgment, the principles of which he said led to the same result. Are the two judges indeed saying the same thing, and if not, what is the difference?

There is no doubt that dangerous escapes arising from the non-natural user of land are a distinct category: it is not entirely clear what sort. It is unlikely that Blackburn J was conscious of creating a new tort, as opposed to developing the law of private nuisance by declaring that it applied to isolated escapes rather than a state of affairs. Lord Goff in *Cambridge Water* confirms this view. Until 1946 there was often a confusion of this special rule and 'ordinary' nuisance, to such an extent that these earlier cases must often be treated as being of doubtful authority. The confusion was resolved by the decision of the House of Lords in *Read* v *J Lyons* [1946] 2 All ER 471.

11.4.7.2 **The current rules**

For the special rule to apply, a number of ingredients must be present:

- a deliberate accumulation
- of things which are hazardous in the event of an escape
- in the course of a non-natural user of the land
- an actual escape
- causing harm which is reasonably foreseeable.

We now need to examine each of these points.

Accumulation

The rule does not apply to things which arrive or occur naturally, e.g. rainfall or groundwater: *Wilson* v *Waddell* (1876) 2 App Cas 95, wild vegetation: *Giles* v *Walker* (1890) 24 QBD 656, soil and rock: *Pontardawe RDC* v *Moore-Gwyn* [1929] 1 Ch 656, but will apply to, e.g. planted vegetation, reservoirs, chemicals, etc. Where rocks were scattered by blasting the rule can apply, on the basis that the blasting powder had been accumulated: see *AG* v *Cory Bros* [1921] AC 521, and the US case, *Caporale* v *C W Blakeslee Inc* (1961) 149 Conn 79, 175 A 2d 561.

Hazardous things

The cases give a long catalogue of hazardous things: water, electricity, gas, petrol, fumes, etc., chair-o-planes and explosives. They do not need to be dangerous in themselves (although many of them will be), merely liable to cause harm if they do escape.

Where the claimant's user of his land is abnormally sensitive, it cannot be said that any escape is dangerous if it adversely affects only the sensitive use.

There have been decisions which suggest that a defendant may be liable for the actions of people he brings together on his land. In *AG* v *Corke* [1933] Ch 89 the defendant allowed caravan-dwellers on his land; they caused annoyance and damage in the neighbourhood. It was held that the rule could extend to people. However, this has been doubted in New Zealand: *Matheson* v

Northcote College [1975] 2 NZLR 106 (on the footing that people operate under free will) and an extension to the case of undesirable tenants or licensees (even where put in by way of harassment of the neighbours) has been refused on the ground that the landlord had insufficient control of the tenants: *Smith* v *Scott* [1973] Ch 314 (see 11.4.5.2). It is unlikely that people will in future fall within the rule. Is this a good thing?

It is suggested that there is no need to go beyond the questions 'did the defendant bring this on to the scene?' and 'is it likely to cause harm if it escapes from his control?'

Non-natural user

This requirement is of course based on Lord Cairns' speech in *Rylands* v *Fletcher*. The formulation by Lord Moulton in *Rickards* v *Lothian* (*Cases and Materials* 11.1.4.2) has always been considered to be the best: 'It must be some special use, bringing with it increased danger to others, and must not merely be the ordinary use of the land or such a use as is proper for the general benefit of the community.'

The question of whether or not a user is non-natural is one of fact and degree, which, being interpreted, means, a question of discretion for the court. In 1919 garaging a car with a full petrol tank was non-natural: *Musgrove* v *Pandelis* [1919] 2 KB 43. In 1964 storage of strips of metal foil was natural: *British Celanese Ltd* v *A H Hunt (Capacitors) Ltd* [1969] 1 WLR 959. During the First World War a munitions factory was non-natural: *Rainham Chemical Works* v *Belvedere Fish Guano* [1921] 2 AC 465; during the Second World War probably natural: *Read* v *J Lyons* [1947] AC 15 (*Cases and Materials* (11.1.4.2)).

The tendency until the early 1990s was to take a narrow approach in order not to stifle proper economic activity. Indeed, the reluctance of courts to declare that user was non-natural was the main limiting factor on the rule, and there were suggestions that the rule was being marginalized by the strict requirements for a user to be non-natural. The high-water mark was probably the decision of Ian Kennedy J at first instance in *Cambridge Water Co.* v *Eastern Counties Leather* (unreported, 31 July 1991).

He decided that, as a matter of policy and balance, industrial activities of the kind carried on by Eastern Counties Leather were not non-natural, at least in this geographical context:

> In reaching this decision I reflect on the innumerable small works that one sees up and down the country with drums stored in their yards. I cannot imagine that all those drums contain milk and water or some other like innocuous substance. Inevitably that storage presents some hazard, but in a manufacturing and outside a primitive and pastoral society such hazards are a part of the life of every citizen.

 EXERCISE 11.6

Consider the following observations and make a note of your conclusions.

Is there a valid distinction between the metal foil, which was harmful only to immediate neighbours, and was a disruption rather than a toxin, and the PCE, which poisoned a whole aquifer? Can we establish a criterion of the state of the neighbourhood? Is it relevant that at the time when the PCE was being handled without restraint (up to 1976), the hazards which occurred (i.e. pollution of groundwater) were not foreseeable?

Lord Goff rejected the narrow view and preferred a wider concept of what is non-natural:

> I cannot think that it would be right [if the risk of harm were foreseeable] to exempt ECL from liability under the rule in *Rylands* v *Fletcher* on the ground that the use was natural or ordinary. The mere fact that the use is common in the tanning industry cannot, in my opinion, be enough to bring the use within the exception, nor the fact that Sawston contains a small industrial community which is worthy of encouragement or support. Indeed I feel bound to say that the storage of substantial quantities of chemicals on industrial premises should be regarded as an almost classic case of non-natural use.

 QUESTION 11.11

Can you reconcile Lord Moulton's concept of non-natural user with Lord Goff's? If not, which seems best adapted to ensuring just results?

Escape

 EXERCISE 11.7

Read *Read v J Lyons* [1947] AC 156 in *Cases and Materials* (11.1.4.2). Why did the claimant's claim fail?

You should have seen that this case clearly spells out that there must be an escape from the defendant's land or hereditament. As Viscount Simon said: 'Escape from a place where the defendant has occupation of or control over land to a place which is outside his occupation or control.' This was fatal to the claimant's claim under the rule, as she was employed on the premises.

What is the 'place' from or to which there is an escape? In either case it need not be premises in the ordinary sense, but may be a conduit under the highway, or a part of a building: *Midwood* v *Manchester* [1905] 2 KB 597. Indeed Taylor J accepted in *Rigby* v *Chief Constable of Northants* [1985] 1 WLR 1242 that the rule might apply in the case of things brought on to the highway and allowed to escape on to other property.

There is no requirement that the defendant have any interest in the property from which the thing escapes, merely that he be in control of the thing: *Benning* v *Wong* (1969) 122 CLR 249.

Reasonable foreseeability

It is clear that this now applies exactly as in negligence and private nuisance. Liability may not extend to acts of third parties because these are unforeseeable. An example of this is *Rickards* v *Lothian*. The claim failed not only because the user was natural, but because the harm was caused by a third party for whom the defendant was not liable. But if vandalism was foreseeable, failure to take precautions may result in liability; see *Environment Agency (formerly National Rivers Authority)* v *Empress Car Co.* [1998] 2 WLR 350 (HL).

? **QUESTION** 11.12

How has the operation of the rule in *Rylands* v *Fletcher* been affected by the decision in *Cambridge Water*? (See *Cases and Materials* (11.1.4.1).)

The position is now regulated by *Cambridge Water*. The test is whether harm of the kind which transpired was foreseeable. This is the same test, derived from the *Wagon Mound (No. 1)* [1961] 1 All ER 404, which you have already met in relation to nuisance and to negligence generally. Lord Goff's speech is clear support for those who have regarded *Rylands* v *Fletcher* as a species of nuisance rather than an independent entity largely because the *Wagon Mound* test of foreseeability is applied. In the *Cambridge Water* case, his Lordship accepted that, at the time of the escapes, it was not foreseeable that the relevant type of harm would occur because the solvent in question was thought to be so volatile that it presented no risk of contamination of the soil and groundwater.

You should note that the decision in *Cambridge Water* has been criticized on the basis that the judges wrongly treated the standard of knowledge against which foreseeability was judged as being that of a reasonable foreman, rather than the higher standard to be attributed to a qualified technical director, but the principle is not objectionable, unless the tort is expected to operate as a general purpose absolute environmental protection rule. Lord Goff declined to adopt the general purpose absolute rule approach, and pointed out that the Law Commission had expressed reservations about a strict liability rule for hazardous activities: *Civil Liability for Dangerous Things and Activities* (1970, Law Com No. 32).

He did stress that environmental protection was now regarded as important and was the subject of much legislation, national (e.g. the Nuclear Installations Act 1965) and international (without referring to the previous UK government's attempts to dismantle significant elements of the EC legislation in this field) and clearly considered that legislation was preferable to an extension of the common law. This approach was confirmed by the Privy Council in *Hamilton* v *Papakura DC* (2002), *The Times*, 5 May.

11.4.7.3 **Should the rule be abolished?**

Transco **v** *Stockport MBC* **[2003] 3 WLR 1267**

Transco concerned a leak in a substantial water supply pipe serving a block of flats. The pipe was, however, part of the landowner's 'private' system, not the water undertaker's 'public' system, which was regulated by the Water Act 1991. The leak was undetected for some time and caused substantial and expensive damage to a nearby embankment.

The interest of the case lies not so much in the actual case decision—unsurprisingly it was held that the provision of a water supply, even in a large pipe designed to supply a whole tower block, was a natural use of the land, and indeed that water in this form was not a hazardous thing—as in the submission of counsel for the defence that the whole status of the rule should be reviewed. All of their Lordships addressed this issue. Their speeches collectively give a very full account of the genesis, rationale, and development of the rule.

In the event the House rejected the abolition of the rule, either because it should be subsumed into ordinary negligence (as in Australia) or was inconsistent with the rest of the law in the area. However, the opportunity was taken to clarify its scope and application.

Lord Bingham (with whom Lord Scott and Lord Walker expressly agreed) gave four reasons for retaining the rule:

1. there is a small category of cases where liability should be strict, i.e. without fault;

2. the statutory imposition of strict liability in many hazardous situations was predicated on the rule, and its abolition might destabilize these regimes;

3. consistency with the approach in *Cambridge Water;*

4. consistency with civil law jurisdictions. One might also add the United States (although not Australia or Scotland).

The rule is firmly stated as being an aspect of private nuisance (as in the *Cambridge Water* case). This means that there can be no claim for personal injuries and, although this is not said in terms, only an occupier may claim. There must of course be an escape, and the harm must be foreseeable in the event of an escape.

The other requirements, that the item must be hazardous and that the user of the land be non-natural, are confirmed, and it is clear that they will not lightly be satisfied. Lord Bingham talks of 'an exceptionally high risk of danger or mischief if there should be an escape' and 'ordinary user is a preferable test to natural user, making it clear that the rule in *Rylands* v *Fletcher* is engaged only where the defendant's use is shown to be extraordinary and unusual. This is not a test to be inflexibly applied: a use may be extraordinary and unusual at one time or in one place but not so at another time or in another place'. This decision has clarified a number of issues, and makes application of the rule easier, although there will continue to be debate about where to draw the various lines.

11.4.8 Fire

11.4.8.1 Early history

There was an early common law remedy by way of trespass on the case in respect of the escape of fire. Although the authorities are obscure the liability was probably regarded as strict in that a man kept a fire at his peril. The tort is seen as analogous with the rule in *Rylands* v *Fletcher*, although it is not so much the escape of something accumulated as the spread of something hazardous. There is also a separate action which now does require proof of negligence.

11.4.8.2 The negligence-based action

The law was reformed in 1774 to prevent claims where fires started 'accidentally': 'No action . . . shall be prosecuted . . . against any person in whose house . . . or other building or on whose estate any fire shall . . . accidentally begin . . .' Section 86 of the Fires Prevention (Metropolis) Act 1774 (despite its name, this Act applies throughout the country).

The word 'accidentally' does not mean non-deliberately. It means by pure accident or where the cause is not established. The defence given by the Act accordingly does not apply to a fire that is started or continued negligently: *Filliter* v *Phippard* (1847) 11 QB 347.

In *Balfour* v *Barty-King* [1957] 1 All ER 156 a fire resulted from the negligence of contractors and it was held that the owner was liable. Liability for fire is an anomaly in the sense that there is vicarious liability for the acts of a contractor or other lawful visitor. This extends to the unauthorized acts of visitors if these acts are foreseeable, as where demolition contractors are forbidden to burn rubbish, but have done so on previous occasions and have not heeded warnings: *H & N Emanual Ltd* v *GLC* [1971] 2 All ER 835.

In *Johnson* v *BJW Property Developments Ltd* [2002] 3 All ER 574 the fire in question was lit in a fireplace which had been partially renovated by contractors. In the course of the renovation firebricks were removed and not replaced, thus exposing timber fillets which caught fire when the fire was lit. The owner was liable. The rule on vicarious liability in the *Balfour* case was confirmed, and it was held that the 1774 Act did not apply where a fire was negligently controlled and also to the case where other negligence created a fire hazard, as was the case here.

 EXERCISE 11.8

Read *Musgrove v Pandelis* [1919] 2 KB 43 and *Sochacki v Sas* [1947] 1 All ER 344 in *Cases and Materials* (11.1.5.1). What is the basis of the decisions?

In each case the court distinguished between two fires. The initial one was 'accidental' in *Musgrove* and deliberate in *Sochacki*. However, this was not the relevant fire. In *Musgrove* the relevant fire was the major one which was due to the chauffeur's negligence. In *Sochacki* the relevant fire was accidental.

11.4.8.3 **Quasi *Rylands* v *Fletcher***

This form of the liability antedates the decision itself, although it was not relied on to support it.

In *Tubervil* v *Stamp* (1698) 1 Salk 13 which was 'an action on the case upon the custom of the realm' [whereby if the defendant so kept a fire in his close that it escaped and burned the claimant's property on the claimant's own land, it was held that the defendant was liable], 'for the fire in his field was his fire as well as that in his house; he made it, and must see that it did no harm, and must answer the damage if he did. Every man must use his own so as not to hurt another. (*Vaughan* v *Menlove* (1837) 3 Bing NC 468, *per* Park J.)

The language used here is archaic, and the reference to using his own so as not to hurt another should remind you of nuisance. It is, however, clear that there is strict liability, in the sense that fault does not need to be proved.

In *Musgrove* v *Pandelis* it was held that this was the same principle as that in *Rylands* v *Fletcher*, and it was also held, as something almost self-evident, that s. 86 of the Fires Prevention (Metropolis) Act would not apply. Why was this? It would not apply to the facts of *Tubervil* v *Stamp* (1698) 1 Salk 13 because the relevant fire was deliberate, or to those of *Musgrove* v

Pandelis, because the relevant fire was negligent. The latter case was, however, expressly decided on the second ground of *Rylands* v *Fletcher*, it having been decided that the keeping of a motor-car was a non-natural user. How does this help claimants?

> **Mason v Levy Autoparts of England [1967] 2 All ER 62 (*Cases and Materials* (11.4.8.2))**
>
> The defendant stored large quantities of vehicle parts, petrol, acetylene, and paint in rather cramped conditions in a predominantly residential area. A fire started (the cause was never discovered) and spread to the claimant's property. The defendant pleaded the Act. The claimant failed to prove negligence, which meant that for the first time in modern experience, the *Rylands* v *Fletcher* liability was crucial. MacKenna J was not happy with the decision in *Musgrove* v *Pandelis*. Why do you think this was? In the event he decided that he was bound by the earlier decision. He did, however, restate the ingredients of this tort in a rather clearer way.
>
> The defendant is liable if:
>
> (a) he brought on to the land things which were likely to catch fire . . . and the fire to spread;
>
> (b) he did so in the course of some non-natural use; and
>
> (c) the things ignited and the fire spread.
>
> Although fires are common, lawsuits are not. This is because most fire damage is compensated under first party insurance. There will be a need to sue only if the victim is uninsured or under-insured, or the victim's insurer exercises his right of subrogation and pursues the defendant for his own benefit.

11.4.9 **Defences**

11.4.9.1 **Prescription**

> **EXERCISE** 11.9
>
> Do you know what this expression means? If not, look it up in a dictionary (preferably a law dictionary!).

You will now know that it relates to the process whereby a right is acquired by long user. Where the subject matter of the alleged nuisance is capable of being an easement (e.g. a right of eavesdrop—to allow water to run from your eaves on to a neighbouring property) it can be acquired prescriptively (i.e. by twenty years user without action). Many of the nineteenth-century cases leave a rather larger ambit for prescription than would be the case today; there is less emphasis on rights of property now.

11.4.9.2 **General defences**

Most of the general defences discussed in **Chapter 14** will apply, where the facts admit. It is thought that contributory negligence will apply only when the behaviour complained of is other than deliberate, but there is no direct authority.

11.4.9.3 **Statutory authority**

This defence is available to an individual or authority exercising functions or doing works in pursuance of statute. There is a presumption that Parliament intended the defendant to carry out functions without causing a nuisance so far as practicable: *Metropolitan Asylum District Managers* v *Hill* (1881) 6 App Cas 193.

Allen v *Gulf Oil Refining* [1981] 1 All ER 353 (*Cases and Materials* (11.1.6.1))

The defendant was authorized by statute to construct an oil refinery. The claimant complained that the refinery as built and operated constituted a nuisance. The defendant pleaded statutory authority.

It was held that the defence succeeded in relation to those matters of complaint which related to 'the nuisance which inevitably resulted from any refinery on the site' but not to other matters which might arise because of the economic and operational choices of the defendant as to the actual construction and operation of the refinery. It is sometimes said that the statutory powers must be exercised without negligence, but the word is being used in a special sense; the statutory immunity carries with it an obligation to use all care and skill to avoid harm. In *Gulf Oil* it was also said that the approval of development by statutory authority might alter the prevailing environment, thus 'moving the goalposts' in relation to nuisances affecting enjoyment of the property.

In *Gillingham BC* v *Medway (Chatham) Dock Co.* [1992] 3 All ER 923 there was a nuisance in fact (it was treated as a public nuisance but this is immaterial for the present discussion) arising out of the use twenty-four hours a day by commercial traffic of residential streets in the vicinity of the old Chatham dockyard. The local authority sought an injunction (using powers under s. 221 of the Local Government Act 1972 authorizing it to act as the custodian of the local public interest). The claim failed because the council had itself granted planning permission for the use of the dock for this purpose, and this had moved the goalposts in the same way. Note that the grant of permission necessarily involved the use of this access to this extent (pending the creation of a new access at some unspecified future date). This was therefore a foreseeable side effect. If the dock company had a choice of access routes and had selected this one for their own convenience the result might have been different. This basis of the decision would apply to other potential claimants.

? QUESTION 11.13

Is it right that the goalposts can be moved in this way? Are the rights of neighbours adequately protected?

While planning authorities are normally careful to research the environmental and disturbance implications of planning decisions, a grant is not normally a binding assurance that the activities can be lawfully carried on (c.f. restrictive covenants which may be enforceable by individual neighbours).

11.4.9.4 Statutory regulation

This is a linked but distinct area. Many service providers, particularly utility companies, operate under statutory schemes even where they are formally private companies as a result of privatization legislation. Typically there is a regulatory scheme which establishes procedures for prioritizing remedial work if facilities are inadequate. Statutory regulation seeks (not always successfully) to balance the interests of all concerned, while inevitably an action in private nuisance focuses on the interests of the claimant, to the exclusion of others. This is likely to lead to a distortion, as can be seen in an important recent case.

Marcic v *Thames Water Utilities Ltd* [2004] 1 All ER 115

Marcic involved the 'regular and serious' flooding of the complainant's garden and damage to his house by surface water and foul sewerage from the public sewers which had become inadequate as a result of building developments in the vicinity. At first instance this was held to be an infringement of the Art. 8 right to private life and inviolability of the home and the Protocol One Art. 1 right to enjoyment of possessions; the Court of Appeal agreed and also held that this amounted to actionable private nuisance.

In the House of Lords the primary focus was on the statutory regulatory scheme. It should be noted that water and sewerage undertakers are now commercial companies, although subject to regulation, and enjoying certain statutory powers. Section 94 of the Water Industry Act 1991 imposes a duty on the sewerage undertaker to ensure the its area is 'effectually drained'. The claimant's property was not effectually drained. However, the Act provides that the sole means of enforcing the duty is an enforcement order made by the regulator under s. 18 of the Act. Section 18(8) provides:

> Where any act or omission constitutes a contravention of . . . a statutory or other requirement enforceable under this section, the only remedies for that contravention, apart from those available by virtue of this section, shall be those for which express provision is made by or under any enactment and those that are available in respect of that act or omission otherwise than by virtue of its constituting such a contravention.

There is an action for breach of statutory duty where an enforcement order is not complied with: s. 22.

No enforcement order had been made in this case (and the claimant had not asked the regulator to consider making one). The claimant's case was that he was asserting rights not based on s. 94 and these were therefore not barred off by s. 18(8).

Lord Nicholls observed that there was a consistent line of cases in which the courts had rejected claims in nuisance for breach of the equivalent obligation in earlier statutes regulating sewers, holding that the statutory provisions were self-contained and self-sufficient:

[See] *Robinson* v *Workington Corpn* [1897] 1 QB 619, where the facts were strikingly similar to the present case. Mr Robinson's houses were damaged by water overflowing from the council's public sewers. The sewers were adequate for the district until new houses were built. Mr Robinson claimed damages in respect of the council's failure to build a new sewer of sufficient dimensions to carry off the increased volume of sewage. The Court of Appeal dismissed the claim . . . The Public Health Act 1875 expressly provided a mechanism for enforcing performance of the statutory drainage obligation. Thus the question of what remedy was available for breach of the drainage obligation was a question of interpretation of the statute. Section 299 of the 1875 Act provided that in cases of default the Local Government Board should make an appropriate order which, if not complied with, was enforceable by a writ of mandamus. Was this intended by Parliament to be the only remedy for breach of the drainage obligation? Lord Esher MR said, at p. 621:

It has been laid down for many years that, if a duty is imposed by statute which but for the statute would not exist, and a remedy for default or breach of that duty is provided by the statute that creates the duty, that is the only remedy. The remedy in this case is under section 299, which points directly to s. 15, and shews what is to be done for default of the duty imposed by that section. That is not the remedy sought for in this action, which is brought to recover damages.

The existence of this general principle of statutory interpretation, and the correctness of this application of the principle to the Public Health Act 1875, were confirmed by your Lordships' House in *Pasmore* v *Oswaldtwistle Urban District Council* [1898] AC 387. The courts have consistently followed this view of the law in relation to the Public Health Act 1875 and in relation to the Public Health Act 1936: see, for instance, *Hesketh* v *Birmingham Corpn* [1924] 1 KB 260 and *Smeaton* v *Ilford Corpn* [1954] 1 Ch 450. In both these cases the court expressly rejected a claim for nuisance: see Scrutton LJ in the *Birmingham* case, at pp. 271–2, and Upjohn J in the *Ilford* case, at p. 463.

The Court of Appeal felt able to depart from this line of authority by asserting that the sewerage authority should be in the same position as the landowner in cases such as *Goldman* v *Hargrave* [1967] 1 AC 645 and *Leakey* v *National Trust for Places of Historic Interest or Natural Beauty* [1980]. Lord Nicholls disagreed:

I must respectfully part company with the Court of Appeal. The *Goldman* and *Leakey* cases exemplify the standard of conduct expected today of an occupier of land towards his neighbour. But Thames Water is no ordinary occupier of land. The public sewers under Old Church Lane are vested in Thames Water pursuant to the provisions of the 1991 Act, s. 179, as a sewerage undertaker. Thames Water's obligations regarding these sewers cannot sensibly be considered without regard to the elaborate statutory scheme of which section 179 is only one part. The common law of nuisance should not impose on Thames Water obligations inconsistent with the statutory scheme. To do so would run counter to the intention of Parliament as expressed in the Water Industry Act 1991.

His Lordship went on to point out that the statutory regulatory scheme allowed for the regulator to consider overall priorities and also explicitly ensure that the remedial measures were commensurate with the resources of the sewer undertaker, and allowing any aggrieved occupier to intervene through his own claim, where only the merits of his case were considered would sabotage the whole statutory scheme. This disposed of the common law claim.

There is considerable merit in this approach. This is a public rather than a private issue, and the claimant had not even sought to use the prescribed statutory scheme.

11.4.9.5 **Public interest**

The defence of statutory authority is in effect a form of public interest defence. In *Dennis* v *Ministry of Defence* [2003] Env LR 34 the claimants alleged that the operation of flights at RAF Wittering constituted a noise nuisance. Their house was under the flight path, and noise was extreme. Carrying out the ordinary balancing exercise led to the conclusion that there was a nuisance in fact. It was accepted that pilot training was an activity in the public interest, but this was not accepted as a complete defence. Although the court refused to prohibit the flying activity, damages were awarded to reflect the loss of amenity and value of the property. We can therefore conclude that public interest in the wider sense is relevant, but not decisive.

11.4.10 **Remedies**

The remedies of choice will be damages or, more usually, an injunction. The injunction may be *quia timet* (i.e. to restrain a threatened harm) as long as the potential nuisance is established. Harm will be foreseeable if the potential victim can demonstrate that it is liable to occur. An injunction may be granted on terms (i.e. with its full operation suspended) to give the defendant the opportunity to put his house in order. An injunction can only restrain the actionable element of a nuisance, e.g. excessive noise. Damages may be awarded in lieu of an injunction under s. 50 of the Supreme Court Act 1981, but this will not allow the defendant to effect a compulsory purchase of the right to make a nuisance of himself; see *Allen* v *Gulf Oil*. However, an injunction is a discretionary remedy and this may explain the actual decision in *Miller* v *Jackson*.

? **QUESTION** 11.14

Raisa is the proprietress of the 'Tap'n'Tutu Academy of Dance', which is established on the top floor of a three-storey building. The middle floor is used as a lace warehouse until the tenant moves out, and is then let to Shady, the proprietor of the 'Intimate Bliss Massage Parlour'. After three months Shady complains that the noise and vibration of Raisa's tap-dancing classes is disturbing his customers and affecting his trade. A number of parents of Raisa's pupils complain that Shady's customers regularly ogle and occasionally proposition their teenage daughters on the stairs while they are on their way to and from dancing classes.

Advise Raisa as to her rights and liabilities in tort.

The first question is whether the tap dancing is a nuisance; it may be intrusive enough to disturb a normal neighbour, as opposed to a very undemanding one. If so, Raisa will be liable. It is not relevant that she is performing a socially useful function. The harassment of her pupils may be a nuisance. It does directly affect the property. However, it is not clear whether Shady is responsible for the activities of his visitors. This scenario shows up some of the weaknesses of nuisance.

11.5 **Article 8 of the European Convention**

As we have seen, this Article assures respect for one's private and family life, the home and correspondence. It has been accepted by the European Court of Human Rights in *López Ostra* v *Spain* (1994) Case 41/1993/436/515 that environmental issues, which might be seen as nuisances in English law, were within the scope of Art. 8. The case concerned a plant for the treatment of tannery effluent, built with state approval and funding, which, owing to a malfunction emitted fumes, smells, and contamination. Although the plant was partially closed, the public authorities continued to endorse its partial operation, even though there was clear evidence of unacceptable impact on both amenity and health.

In the *Marcic* case, such a claim was advanced, and succeeded before the trial judge and the Court of Appeal. The House of Lords however, while recognizing that such claims were available in principle, adopted a much more restrictive approach to the analysis of whether the claim was made out. The House held that, while Art. 8 and 1 were engaged, the critical question was:

> [I]s the statutory scheme as a whole, of which th[e] enforcement procedure is part, Convention-compliant? Stated more specifically and at the risk of over-simplification, is the statutory scheme unreasonable in its impact on Mr Marcic and other householders whose properties are periodically subjected to sewer flooding?

This question was to be answered in the light of the European Court of Human Rights Grand Chamber decision in *Hatton* v *United Kingdom* (2003) Application No. 36022/97 where the court had in effect ruled that in this type of case, where there were many policy considerations and a diversity of possible approaches in a modern democracy, considerable weight should be given to the domestic policy maker. With reservations the House concluded that the scheme was compliant; it struck a fair balance between the respective competing interests. The claim therefore failed on its merits, and although such claims are open, it will be surprising if many will succeed, since it will be necessary to show that the statutory scheme in question is disproportionate.

The clear implication is that the claimant should have invoked the statutory scheme, and if this was not administered and applied properly, seek judicial review.

11.6 **Public nuisance**

In origin and essence public nuisance was (and is) a crime, although many of the antisocial activities formerly charged as a common law public nuisance are now the subject of specific statutory offences, e.g. offences under the food and drugs legislation, and matters covered by the Environmental Protection Act 1990.

> An act not warranted by law or an omission to discharge a legal duty, which act or omission causes damage or inconvenience to the public in the exercise of rights common to all of Her Majesty's subjects. (Stephen, *Digest of the Criminal Law*, 1883.)

An act or omission which 'materially affects the reasonable comfort and convenience of life of a class of Her Majesty's subjects' (Romer LJ in *AG* v *PYA Quarries Ltd* [1957] 2 QB 169). A nuisance which 'is so widespread in its range or indiscriminate in its effect that it would not be reasonable to expect one person to take proceedings as his own responsibility to stop it' (Lord Denning, ibid).

It is, however, worth noting that there is a conceptual distinction between a nuisance affecting the public as such, such as obstruction of a highway, and what might be called a 'private nuisance writ large'.

11.6.1 Scope

As with private nuisance, the judges have consistently avoided general pronouncements seeking to define the scope of public nuisance. Why is this? There are two principal reasons. In the first place, a definition which will comprise disturbance from quarrying, failure to repair highways, permitting an offensive encampment of transients, and the incompetent operation of public transport services, all of which have been held to be public nuisances, will be so wide as to be valueless. In the second place, the existence of a definition would fetter the discretion of the courts to declare a novel factual situation to be a nuisance, thus rendering the law less flexible.

This was done, in a rare instance of a criminal prosecution, in *Johnson (AT)* (1996), *The Times*, 22 May, where the making of hundreds of obscene phone calls to at least eleven women throughout South Cumbria was held to be not only (self-evidently) a private nuisance in respect of each victim, but also a public nuisance under the above tests (especially Lord Denning's). The decision on private nuisance probably cannot stand after *Hunter* v *Canary Wharf*, but as there is no requirement for an interest in land in public nuisance, this aspect of the decision would seem to be valid. It therefore follows that some matters which are really harassment may qualify as public nuisance, although they would not be private nuisances.

11.6.2 Remedies

The primary remedy in public nuisance is by way of prosecution, or by an action for an injunction on the part of the Attorney General, or by a local council under s. 221 of the Local Government Act 1972.

In theory the Attorney General represents the public interest. In practice he is simply invited to lend his name to an action carried on by and at the expense of a private objector (known because of the original legal terminology as a relator). The Attorney General may refuse his consent to the institution of a relator action, but this is very much a reserve power.

11.6.3 Private actions

 There is a derivative action in tort giving a private remedy in damages where there is special damage, e.g. *Halsey* v *Esso* [1961] 2 All ER 145 (*Cases and Materials* (11.2.1)). This is a case where public and private nuisance were both occasioned by the same acts. It is also a rare modern environment/pollution case not brought under specific legislation. Note that the claim for damages is a by-product, not the main reason for an action.

11.6.4 **Examples of public nuisances**

11.6.4.1 **Highways**

Many of the cases relate to highways. The right to free passage and free access to one's premises is an essentially public one.

Obstruction

A minor obstruction such as a hosepipe across a country lane may not be a nuisance: *Trevett* v *Lee* [1955] 1 All ER 406, but the position will be very different for a busy street: *Farrell* v *John Mowlem & Co.* [1954] 1 Lloyd's Rep 437. Temporary scaffolding for a reasonable purpose may not be a nuisance: *Harper* v *Haden & Sons* [1933] Ch 298. Again it is a question of degree. In many areas there are specific by-laws which regulate building operations. Scaffolding and other disruptions require a licence. Note that a navigable river may also be a highway: *Tate & Lyle* v *GLC* [1983] 1 All ER 1159. The special damage which the claimant must prove will usually be business disruption.

Danger on the highway

There is an overlap with obstruction. Many of these cases are older ones and appear to be nuisance/negligence hybrids. Today there would be a duty of care apparent, and the action would be in negligence, based on this. *Dollman* v *Hillman* [1941] 1 All ER 355 is a good example. A piece of fat was thrown or swept from a butcher's shop on to the pavement, where it was left lying. The claimant slipped and injured himself. This was held to be a nuisance. Today the natural cause of action would be negligence. The special damage is fairly obvious: the injuries resulting from exposure to the danger.

Abuse of right of passage

Although there is normally a public right to pass and repass on the highway, a grossly excessive and disruptive use of this right is capable of amounting to a public nuisance: *Gillingham BC* v *Medway (Chatham) Dock Co.* [1992] 3 All ER 923 (see 11.4.9.3).

11.6.4.2 **Others**

Many types of activity will qualify, e.g. quarrying affecting a whole village: *AG* v *PYA Quarries*; factory operations affecting a neighbourhood: *Halsey* v *Esso*.

11.6.5 **Status of the tort**

A loose parallel can perhaps be drawn with the tort action for breach of statutory duty, although the action derived from public nuisance is of greater antiquity. In each case the primary thrust of the relevant provisions is criminal, with a private remedy as a side effect. Public nuisance may perhaps have influenced the development of the younger tort, but any temptation to draw close parallels should be resisted, as the specific ingredients of the two torts are very disparate.

11.6.6 **Particular damage**

The claimant must suffer 'particular damage' over and above the general inconvenience which the defendant's activities cause to the public at large. What does this mean, and why is it necessary? This is generally accepted as a control measure to prevent the opening of the floodgates.

11.6.6.1 Physical harm

As we have seen in relation to *Dollman* v *Hillman* such harm will count. This is as you should expect. This is the form of harm most likely to be compensated. There appears to be a requirement of something akin to negligence in such cases. The situation is confused by the fact that a cause of action in negligence may well coexist.

11.6.6.2 Economic loss

Economic loss is recognized as constituting particular damage. In *Rose* v *Miles* (1815) 4 M & S 101 the defendant obstructed a waterway, as a result whereof the claimant, who was a regular user, was put to the expense of offloading his barges and transporting the cargoes by land round the obstruction. This was held to be particular damage, although no property belonging to the claimant had actually been physically harmed in any way.

> **?** **QUESTION** 11.15
>
> Why is this recognition of pure economic loss surprising? (You should cross-refer to the chapters on negligence.)

In negligence pure economic loss is only recoverable in special situations, e.g. where there is a special *Hedley Byrne* relationship, or where it can be shown to be consequential on physical harm.

11.6.6.3 Loss of trade

This may be seen as economic loss, as in *Tate & Lyle* v *GLC* [1983] 1 All ER 1159. The defendant's construction of a ferry terminal under statutory powers caused unnecessary silting of the approaches to the claimant's jetties. The claimant incurred substantial costs in extra dredging. A claim in negligence was dismissed, but a claim in public nuisance for interference with the public right of navigation on the Thames succeeded.

11.6.6.4 Inconvenience

Mere inconvenience will not suffice, but extreme and exceptional inconvenience may. There are a number of cases dealing with disruption to the trade of shops by crowds, queues, or parked vehicles attracted by neighbouring activities. If the disruption is, on the facts, extreme, a remedy will be given. Is this just the floodgates argument at work? It could be said that some inconvenience is part of give and take. I have a builder's lorry parked outside my house this week, you have your brother's minibus parked there next week. We each inconvenience the other, but not to such an extent that the law should intervene.

11.7 **Harassment**

11.7.1 **What is harassment?**

 EXERCISE 11.10

Write down a definition of what you understand by harassment, in the legal sense.

There are many examples of unacceptable behaviour by one person to another. The motive may be personal, when a relationship breaks down, or when one person does not reciprocate the feelings of another, or as a consequence of some other dispute. The modern name for this form of harassment is 'stalking'. Harassment may also be ideological or political, where picketing or protests go too far. The position is complicated by the fact that, especially in 'personal' cases, the defendant may be obsessive or actually mentally ill. In the ideological/political cases, there is a need to balance the human rights of the protesters with those of the subjects of the protests.

Some activities comprised within harassment amount to existing recognized torts. Physical attacks will amount to assault and/or battery. Entry on to land will be trespass. Verbal attacks may amount to defamation if they are published to others. We have seen how the House of Lords in *Burstow & Ireland* (*Cases and Materials* (10.2.2)) were prepared, against the consensus of academic opinion, to extend the ambit of assault to some verbal threats: 'psychological warfare'. Other activities either do not amount to such torts or only arguably do so. Sending unwanted messages or presents or loitering in public places to observe or speak to the victim are two common examples.

There has thus been a need for an apparent lacuna in the law, which is effectively a gap between trespass and nuisance in the legal sense, to be filled. The key question is whether the common law is still flexible and lively enough to do so, or whether statute is the appropriate method.

11.7.2 **Remedies for harassment**

11.7.2.1 **Matrimonial and family harassment**

In the area of marital breakdown, statutory provision has long been in place to restrain harassment and molestation. This protection has been gradually extended to cover cohabitees. The current statute is the Family Law Act 1996, which we will look at shortly. This was, until recently, an exception, although in the last year or two there has been an explosion of statutory protection. Some of this is tortious in nature, but in some cases the matter is treated as being either criminal in nature or a matter of public law, so that a public authority, rather than the victim, takes action.

11.7.2.2 *Wilkinson* v *Downton*

There is one established relevant common law head of liability, the tort in *Wilkinson* v *Downton:* 'A wilful act (or statement) calculated to cause physical harm to the claimant and in fact causing physical harm to him.' (*Street on Torts* slightly modified.) This is a tort which is in many respects unique; it is not strictly a trespass, since the harm is not direct. It is arguable whether it is actionable per se. There is very little authority in England, although the tort has been taken up in the USA, and today the effective overlap with negligence is almost total, although the conceptual basis is very different.

> **Wilkinson v Downton (1897) 66 LJQB 493 (*Cases and Materials* (11.3.1.1))**
>
> The defendant told the claimant by way of practical joke that the claimant's husband had been seriously injured in an accident. The claimant suffered nervous shock amounting to illness. The case was treated as one of first impression. (There are some old cases imposing liability for injuries caused by spring-guns (a kind of man-trap) which are now regarded as representing the same principle.)
>
> Wright J was clearly impressed by the fact that this was conduct which was wholly deliberate, unjustified, and mischievous. As the law then stood, damages were not readily recoverable for negligently inflicted nervous shock, but a remedy was granted on the basis that this went beyond negligence.

One of the few English cases to apply *Wilkinson* is *Janvier* v *Sweeney* [1919] 2 KB 316 (CA). The defendant, a private detective, in order to induce the claimant to hand over some private letters, threatened to inform the authorities falsely that the claimant's fiancé was a traitor. The claimant suffered nervous shock amounting to illness.

The modern law would probably allow recovery in negligence on these facts on the usual basis. The special tort is perhaps redundant, but:

- it is odd to sue in negligence in respect of intentional conduct; there are dicta in *Letang* v *Cooper* which segregate intentional harm (trespass) and negligence, and the limitation period is different;

- it may be that imputed intention and direct harm cover a different field than foreseeability;

- in *Khorasandjian* v *Bush* [1993] 3 All ER 669 the defendant was quite deliberately harassing the claimant by unwanted telephone calls and in other ways. The claimant said in an affidavit that she was under great stress. The court did not regard that as being self-evidently nervous shock amounting to illness, but considered that *Janvier* would apply to such a case if there were the relevant evidence. It was noted that injunctions had been granted in several unreported cases where acute harassment appeared to be causing actual illness. The court granted an injunction in private nuisance. Lord Hoffmann in *Hunter* v *Canary Wharf* suggested that the decision in *Khorasandjian* was too restrictive, and that distress was sufficient damage. He would therefore have been prepared to support the decision, but not the reasoning, as Ms Khorasandjian was not an appropriate nuisance claimant.

'Harassment' was recognized as a cause of action in *Burris* v *Azadani* (1995), *The Times*, 8 August. It is, however, questionable whether it was seen as an independent tort or a sub-species of trespass to the person or nuisance. The actual use of the phrase appears to have been almost as a piece of shorthand. In the criminal sphere the Court of Appeal held in two decisions by the same court on the same day that harassment by nuisance telephone calls could amount to an assault (and if the victims sustained appropriate psychological trauma, an assault occasioning actual bodily harm): *Ireland*, or alternatively a nuisance, and if widespread a public nuisance: *Johnson (AT)* (1996), *The Times*, 22 May. As we have seen, the former decision has been upheld by the House of Lords, thus extending some protection to victims of harassment. So far as private nuisance is concerned, the decision in *Hunter* has effectively denied the applicability of this tort to personal harassment. Lord Cooke delivered a very powerful dissent, deprecating the wish of the majority to return to the roots of nuisance rather than adapt it to the social circumstances of today.

The net position is that the common law has shown flexibility in relation to expansion of assault to cover harassment and public nuisance may be available (but in practice most stalkers target a single victim) as may *Wilkinson* v *Downton*. Only private nuisance can be excluded.

? **QUESTION** 11.16

Return to Question 10.10, and consider whether *Wilkinson* v *Downton* is relevant to any of these scenarios.

If (a) is not a battery (although it seems to be directly inflicted harm) it will clearly fall within *Wilkinson* v *Downton*. Scenario (e) is fairly clearly *Wilkinson* v *Downton*; it is a classic practical joke gone wrong, but with sufficient serious intent to qualify as malice, at least if Jeremy realized Kate was vulnerable.

11.7.3 Statutory harassment

11.7.3.1 Protection from Harassment Act 1997

One reason why the House of Lords excluded private nuisance as a remedy for harassment was that, by the time they decided *Hunter*, the Protection from Harassment Act 1997 (see *Cases and Materials* (11.3.2.1)) was on the statute book. This gives both civil and criminal remedies, and the civil remedy is by a specific statutory tort.

⋀ **EXERCISE** 11.11

Read the extracts from the Protection from Harassment Act 1997, Family Law Act 1996, Housing Act 1996, and Crime and Disorder Act 1998 in *Cases and Materials* (11.3.2.1). What activities do they cover?

Harassment is not fully defined in the Protection from Harassment Act 1997, although there was considerable debate about this. Indeed a previous private member's Bill introduced by Janet Anderson MP failed to attract government support largely over this issue of definition. There is obviously concern that unwanted but justifiable attention, e.g. of investigative journalists pursuing allegations of financial misconduct, might be the subject of action, although this would probably qualify as reasonable. The Act must also be seen in the context of the Human Rights Act and the European Convention on Human Rights, especially Arts 8, 10, and 11 which concern the right to privacy, the right to freedom of expression, and the right of free assembly respectively. One particular concern was over the extent that the actions of demonstrators could be classed as harassment. The position has been clarified by *Huntingdon Life Sciences Ltd* v *Curtin and Others* (1997), *The Times*, 11 December.

The claimants, a company which undertook research on animals, had been granted an injunction against the defendants, among others, restraining them from any course of conduct amounting to harassment. The claimants had complained of a sustained and menacing anti-vivisection campaign directed at itself and its employees, which included many breaches of s. 1 of the 1997 Act. In the light of evidence adduced by the defendants for the first time at a further hearing, the claimants' allegations could not be sustained and the defendants' application was granted.

Eadie J added that the legislators of the Act would no doubt be surprised to see how widely its terms were perceived to extend by some people. The 1997 Act was clearly not intended by Parliament to be used to clamp down on the discussion of matters of public interest or upon the rights of political protest and public demonstration which was so much a part of our democratic tradition. He had little doubt that the courts would resist any wide interpretation of the Act as and when the occasion arose. It must be remembered that these cases are fact-sensitive. In *Silverton* v *Gravett* (2001) LTL, 31 October a judge held that the activities of protesters in relation to a furrier's shop were excessive. Although the protesters were no doubt exercising rights of expression under Art. 10 of the ECHR, their activities went beyond what was acceptable. See also *University of Oxford* v *Broughton* [2004] EWHC 2543 (QB) where animal rights protests were restricted on an interim basis to avoid harassment while attempting to respect the defendants' rights to assembly and expression.

The primary focus of the Protection from Harassment Act, as Douglas Brown J said in *Tuppen* v *Microsoft Corp.* [2002] EMLR 4, after referring to the speeches of the then Home Secretary and Lord Chancellor in the debates on the Bill, is directed at 'stalking, anti-social behaviour by neighbours and racial harassment'. It is not clear if this list was intended to be exhaustive, or just to give an indication. Allegations of the oppressive use of litigation against the claimant were held to fall clearly outside the Act.

In *Thomas* v *News Group Newspapers* (2001), *The Times*, 25 July the Court of Appeal declined to strike out a claim against the *Sun* for harassment allegedly arising from three articles and a number of readers' letters which contained extreme and intemperately worded criticism of the claimant's role in reporting racist comments by police officers which led to disciplinary proceedings against them. The court held that the claim was arguable. There had been a course of conduct constituted by publication of the initial article and the subsequent letter and articles, and that this could amount to causing the claimant alarm or distress. The claimant had apparently received 'race hate mail' at work. The court was not expressing a concluded opinion on whether the *Sun* could justify its activities as legitimate expression under Art. 10 ECHR.

In *Majrowski* v *Guy's and St Thomas's NHS Trust* (2006), *The Times*, 13 July, the House of Lords accepted that, in principle, persistent bullying and belittling by a manager at work could constitute harassment. A substantial award (*c.* £800,000, largely comprising loss of earnings) was made in *Green* v *DB Group Services Ltd* [2006] EWHC 1898. In this case the harassment was committed by a defined group, was very much public knowledge and had been brought to the knowledge of management. However, it is important to note that there must be a 'course of conduct', and general complaints about the attitude of work colleagues generally may not qualify: *Daniels* v *Metropolitan Police Commissioner* [2006] EWHC 1622 (QB).

In *Singh* v *Bhakar* [2006] LTL, 11 August, it was held in Nottingham County Court that the Act could apply in a domestic context and that in this case the cumulative effect of various acts of maltreatment of a daughter-in-law by a mother-in-law did amount to harassment.

 EXERCISE 10.12

Draft a definition of harassment, either for an Act amending the Protection from Harassment Act, or as part of a speech in the House of Lords giving judgment in a case under the Act.

11.7.3.2 **Family Law Act 1996**

The current provision in family disputes is s. 42 of the 1996 Act. Although this covers many categories, it does not cover boy/girlfriends (other than fiancés) or someone who stalks a stranger or who has fantasized a relationship. There is no jurisdiction to award damages (although if the molestation does amount to assault, etc., a separate action could be brought). Very often the defendant is of modest means, so damages are not a practical remedy. Orders may be made by any court with domestic jurisdiction (magistrates, and county courts and High Court), although there are some limitations in particular on the powers of magistrates.

Molestation is a word which judges consider has an established and common meaning. It has no legal definition. There must be some element of interference with physical or psychological well-being, although this need not be conduct amounting to a recognized tort. These limits were restated in *C* v *C* *(Non-molestation Order: Jurisdiction)* (1997), *The Times*, 16 December.

The parties had been married but had obtained a divorce in September 1997. In October two articles detailing the former wife's complaints about her husband appeared in the press and the husband attempted to restrain the wife from providing further information to the newspapers by applying for a non-molestation order under s. 42. While there had been no direct threat or molestation in the physical sense, nor any indirect interference by telephone or letter, he contended that her conduct in supplying newspaper reporters with revelations which resulted in the publication of the offending articles justified the making of a non-molestation order. The claim failed. Although there was no legal definition of molestation, the word implied some quite deliberate conduct aimed at a high degree of harassment of the other party sufficient to call for the intervention of the court. Section 42 is in a part of the Act concerned with domestic violence, not breaches of privacy. The behaviour complained of could not be construed as harassment and therefore was not molestation within the Act.

It might amount to an improper interference with the husband's right to respect for his private life, and thus now fall within Art. 8 of the European Convention.

11.7.3.3 **Housing Act 1996**

A new, specific power to control harassment by injunction is contained in the Housing Act 1996. There has for some time been a power to evict a tenant for antisocial behaviour (Housing Act 1985 for public sector tenants and Housing Act 1988 for private sector tenants) and these powers are strengthened by the 1996 Act.

11.7.3.4 **Crime and Disorder Act 1998**

More far-reaching powers are contained in the Crime and Disorder Act 1998.

Section 1 provides for 'Antisocial Behaviour Orders' now universally known as ASBOs. The protections afforded to the potential subject of the order are significantly less stringent than those afforded at common law or under the statutes considered above. The application is to the magistrates, not to the county or High Court, and is civil in nature, so the civil standard of proof applies. There is no need to prove violence and, as several speakers in the Second Reading debate in the House of Lords observed, no requirement that those suffering alarm or distress should be of 'reasonable firmness'. There is also provision (in s. 11) for 'Child Safety Orders' which apply to children under 10. One of the conditions for the making of such an order is causing the kind of alarm and distress referred to in s. 1(1). Parenting orders may be made against the parents of children and young persons made the subject of either of the above two orders. However, in all these cases the initiative must come from the public authorities. The victims will no doubt seek to persuade them to act, but these are public law remedies. They are, however, seen as an essential addition to the armoury of the law, particularly to aid those who are too inarticulate, too intimidated, or too impecunious to take action themselves:

> Many, many people are afraid to be complainants in court when they have to make public allegations against their neighbours and against people who have made their lives an absolute misery. We are saying that prosecutions under the public order legislation and the Protection from Harassment Act have their place. But this is prior to that. I repeat that it is to endeavour to safeguard the vulnerable in our society, those who have their lives made a daily misery. I regret to say that at the moment our law does not protect them. Therefore, this is a much more considered remedy for a real social evil. (Lord Williams of Mostyn, HL, 3 February 1998, Committee Stage.)

11.7.4 **The overall position on harassment**

In summary then, the remedies available are:

- common law: action for damages/injunction in trespass to the person or to land; *Wilkinson* v *Downton* or public nuisance;

- statutory private action: damages/injunction, Protection from Harassment Act 1997; non-molestation order, Family Law Act 1996;

- public law: injunction, Housing Act 1996; Antisocial Behaviour/Child Safety Orders, Crime and Disorder Act 1998.

11.8 Relationship of public and private nuisance

The same factual situation may constitute both public and private nuisance. The claimant in public nuisance does not need to be an occupier of property. Although the same facts may give rise to an action in both public and private nuisance, the theoretical basis is different; see *Halsey* v *Esso Petroleum* [1961] 2 All ER 145. In this case Esso's depot was in a mixed area; there were complaints of traffic noise at unsocial hours and smuts from a boiler contaminated washing in gardens and cars parked on the street. The first and last of these constituted public nuisances and the middle one a private nuisance.

11.8.1 Examples of the overlap

(a) A tumble-down house may fall into the street or on to a neighbouring property.

(b) Pollution from a factory may poison passers-by or neighbours.

11.8.2 Relationship between public nuisance, private nuisance, and negligence

11.8.2.1 Test of remoteness of damage

All three share a common test of remoteness of damage: *The Wagon Mound (No. 2)* [1967] 1 AC 617; *Cambridge Water Co.* v *Eastern Counties Leather* [1994] 1 All ER 53.

11.8.2.2 The place of fault

Is fault always required in private nuisance, and if so what degree of fault? What, in any case, is meant by fault? Many commentators suggest that this is one of the instances where there has been an unjustified transfer of rules from negligence to private nuisance via public nuisance, by means of an equation of the two senses of the word nuisance.

Fault is generally required in public nuisance and the category of fault is generally to be equated with the negligence standard.

There are cases in public nuisance where fault has been held not necessary: *Farrell* v *Mowlem* (see 11.6.4.1). In *Dymond* v *Pearce* [1972] 1 QB 496 it was held that parking a lorry on the road overnight, albeit under a street light and with its own lights lit, was a nuisance. It is hard to see that the defendant was at fault. The claimant failed because, on the facts, the nuisance did not cause his loss, but it was said that if there had been fog etc., then as between the creator of the nuisance and the innocent victim, the former would be liable, even though the harm was not foreseeable.

In these residual cases you can see a distinction between negligence and nuisance, at all events public nuisance.

11.8.2.3 Economic loss

Certainly in public nuisance pure economic loss is recoverable. It is not normally recoverable in negligence or private nuisance, but see *Hubbard* v *Pitt* at 11.4.6.

11.8.3 **Status of private nuisance**

On one view private nuisance would simply become a special case of negligence, rather like occupiers' liability. Now that there is a renewed stress on the proper categorization of torts, and a retreat from the high-water mark of Lord Wilberforce's doctrine of proximity and foreseeability, there appears to be a greater emphasis on the nature of the relationship of the parties, the nature of the interest invaded, and the description of harm sustained.

There is also sometimes apparent a confusion between the question: 'did the defendant unreasonably interfere with the claimant's enjoyment' and the question: 'did the defendant cause unreasonable interference with the claimant's enjoyment?' The first of these is a 'negligence' question, the second a 'nuisance' one.

■ SUMMARY

We have now seen how the law of tort can protect one's entitlement to enjoyment of land without disturbance or pollution. This is of course only part of the story and much of the protection comes through the powers of local authorities and other statutory bodies (such as the Environment Agency) to restrain and punish unacceptable behaviour under statutory powers. The key areas are (always assuming that the defendant is creating a risk of foreseeable harm):

(a) Private nuisance:

  (i) absolute protection against damage arising from a continuing source of harm;

  (ii) conditional protection from interference with enjoyment. The level of amenity depends on the nature of the area, and it is far from clear how far the law will deal with injury affecting the emotions rather than the senses;

  (iii) enhanced protection in the case of hazardous activities.

(b) Public nuisance:

  (i) absolute protection against interference with public rights;

  (ii) protection in respect of special harm arising from conduct affecting a large number of people.

(c) Harassment:

  (i) limited common law remedy (although facts may support other torts);

  (ii) active development of statutory remedies, both generic and specific. Almost a crusade against antisocial behaviour;

  (iii) need to balance rights of the parties, and not produce excessive interference with the right to free expression in particular.

Always remember that public nuisance is primarily a crime, and that civil liability is secondary, rather like civil liability for breach of statutory duty. It is also vital to recognize that much activity which impacts on the environment of a property is regulated by statute, and where this is the case it is primarily by the methods provided in the statutory scheme that disputes are to be resolved. In addition there are public remedies under environmental legislation which may be more effective than a private action. While nuisance is more than a mere footnote, it is certainly only part of the legal armoury available.

■ FURTHER READING

Conaghan, J. and Mansell, W., *The Wrongs of Tort*, London: Pluto Press, 1993, Chapter 6.

Cook, K, 'Environmental Rights as Human Rights' [2002] 2 *EHRLR* 196.

Cooke, P.J. and Oughton, D.W., *The Common Law of Obligations*, 3rd edn, London: Butterworths, 2000, Chapter 29.

Gearty, C., 'The Place of Private Nuisance in a Modern Law of Torts' [1989] *CLJ* 212.

Howarth, D., *Textbook on Tort*, 2nd edn, London: Butterworths, 2004, Chapters 7, 11.

Jones, M.A., *Textbook on Torts*, 8th edn, London: Blackstone Press, 2002, Chapter 7.

Markesinis, B.S. and Deakin, S.F., *Tort Law*, 5th edn, Oxford: Oxford University Press, 2004, Chapter 5 (section 3 only).

Murphy, J., *Street on Torts*, 11th edn, London: Butterworths, 2003, Chapter 18.

Newark, 'The Boundaries of Nuisance' (1949) 65 *LQR* 480.

Winfield and Jolowicz on Tort, 17th edn, London: Sweet & Maxwell, 2006, Chapter 12.

CHAPTER 11 ASSESSMENT EXERCISE

(1) Harvey is the owner of a smallholding on which he has established a riding school. He has two immediate neighbours, Oenone, an elocution teacher and Sonya, a taxi-driver.

Harvey has a contract to provide weekly riding lessons to the 400 pupils of St Trinian's, a local girls' school. Oenone complains that on the days when the junior girls are receiving lessons, there is so much disturbance and disruption from their chattering, screaming, and shouting that she and her own pupils cannot hear themselves think.

Every summer Harvey holds two or three large charity gymkhanas. Sonya complains that on these occasions the approach roads to her house are so congested by parked cars, horseboxes, and other vehicles attracted by the gymkhana that she cannot get her taxi out, and she has lost business as a result.

Advise Harvey as to his liability to Oenone and Sonya.

(2) What torts, if any, have been committed in the following cases:

(a) Damian has bought an old rubbish tip to use as a lorry park. Methane from the tip builds up in the basement of Enid's bungalow, which explodes, injuring Enid and her mother, Gertrude, who is visiting her.

(b) Hamlet establishes a hostel for wayward children. In early November the children scour the neighbourhood for timber and remove gates and fences belonging to various neighbours. On Guy Fawkes Night the resultant bonfire causes such dense smoke that the nearby motorway is closed for an hour. Two days later the fire, which has been left to burn itself out, is revived by a strong wind and burns down the neighbouring bus shelter.

See *Cases and Materials* (11.5) for a specimen answer.

12 Defamation and protection of privacy

12.1 OBJECTIVES

At the end of this chapter you should be able to:

1 Distinguish between the forms of defamation

2 Explain the elements of libel and slander

3 Account for the respective roles of judge and jury in cases of defamation

4 Explain the terms 'defamatory meaning', 'reference to the claimant', and 'publication'

5 Explain the function and scope of the defences to defamation

6 Analyse the role of the law of defamation and critically account for its present form

7 Explain the relationship between the law of defamation and the law relating to the protection of privacy.

12.2 Introduction

> Good name in man and woman, dear my lord,
> Is the immediate jewel of their souls:
> Who steals my purse steals trash; 'tis something, nothing;
> 'Twas mine, 'tis his, and has been slave to thousands.
> But he that filches from me my good name
> Robs me of that which not enriches him
> And makes me poor indeed.
>
> (Shakespeare, *Othello*, Act III, Scene 3.)

The law of defamation seeks to protect individual reputation. Its central problem is how to reconcile this purpose with the conflicting demands of free speech. Both are highly valued in our society, the one as perhaps the most dearly prized attribute of civilized man, the other the very foundation of a democratic community. (Fleming, *Law of Torts*, p. 500.)

Following the enactment of the Human Rights Act 1998 (*Cases and Materials* (10.1)) the equation has become more complicated. The right to protection of reputation is not, as such, a Convention right. However, the right to protection of private life (Art. 8) and freedom of expression (Art. 10) are, and protection of reputation is one of the specific permitted grounds for restricting freedom of expression. However it only operates so far as is necessary in a democratic society.

Protection of privacy and protection of reputation overlap. However, they are by no means the same thing. Some breaches of privacy do not adversely affect reputation at all (e.g. a revelation that a married celebrity is pregnant, or disclosure of someone's private charitable activities). Some do (e.g. revelations of sexual or financial misconduct) but these are only defamatory if they improperly damage reputation. Some remarks damaging to reputation do not involve an invasion of privacy at all (e.g. remarks about the public activities of politicians, actors, or sportspeople). There is now a much more complex matrix of rights and rules, with the Convention rights rather awkwardly grafted on to the established common law rules.

> **? QUESTION** 12.1
>
> How important do you consider reputation to be, weighed against money, physical health, and freedom of speech?

12.3 General considerations

12.3.1 Freedom of speech versus the protection of reputation

Some legal systems, such as those of the USA, give primacy to freedom of expression, either by constitutional provision or by general law. Distinctions are often drawn between those who put their characters in issue by seeking public office or status, who are protected only against defamation which is malicious (i.e. demonstrably untrue and/or not part of legitimate public debate), and private citizens, who enjoy wider protection. Other systems, such as Germany and Italy, lay greater emphasis on the right to reply, i.e. to publish a prominent and prompt refutation of the defamatory material, than they do on the action for damages. The Human Rights Act 1998 undoubtedly affects the balance by introducing both a positive right to privacy (Art. 8) and a right to freedom of expression (Art. 10); the latter is given special protection, for example in relation to restraining orders before the full hearing. The European Court of Human Rights has given considerable weight to the right of expression especially but not only in relation to political and public affairs, including criticism of those in the public domain. Our existing strong bias to the protection of the claimant's reputation may not adequately protect freedom of speech.

12.3.2 Protection of privacy and protection of reputation

Can you see a link between these two 'moral rights'? There is certainly a link in practice between the right to privacy and the right to reputation, although this is not recognized by the English law in any formal sense. This may be because the two have developed separately so we do not recognize that each protects an aspect of personal integrity and dignity. French law, for example, has general categories of *préjudice matérielle* and *préjudice morale* (to cover those harms which respectively can and cannot be reduced to mere financial loss). Defamation has been controversial because of a number of substantial awards and settlements, which were so obviously disproportionate to damages for serious personal injury as to amount, some have argued, to a scandal: Jeffrey Archer (£500,000), Koo Stark (£300,000), Elton John (£1m, including costs and a lot of 'tree' publicity and a further £350,000 in a later case) and Lord Aldington £1.5m (later held, by the European Court of Human Rights, to be excessive and an abuse of the defendant's human rights). Perhaps the last part of Iago's observation in *Othello* needs rewriting, although in *John* v *MGN* [1997] QB 586 it was stated that damages should not exceed the maximum award of general damages for personal injuries (now £200,000), and the Court of Appeal can reduce an 'excessive' jury award under s. 8 of the Courts and Legal Services Act 1990. See *Kiam* v *MGN* [2002] 2 All ER 219 (*Cases and Materials* (12.1.1)).

 EXERCISE 12.1

List the arguments for and against a strong law of defamation.

12.4 **Defamation in general**

12.4.1 **Defamation defined**

Defamation is where the defendant publishes a statement about the claimant which reflects on the claimant's reputation so as to lower him in the estimation of right-thinking members of society or which tends to cause the claimant to be shunned and avoided. (Jones, *Textbook on Torts*, slightly altered.) (See also, *Cases and Materials* (12.1.2).)

12.4.2 **Forms of defamation**

12.4.2.1 **Historical introduction**

As you are probably aware, there are two major subdivisions of defamation, namely libel and slander. What exactly is the difference? The distinction is purely historical in origin. Libel was in medieval times the preserve of the ecclesiastical courts. These were concerned with the moral or spiritual aspect of the tort. The defamer was committing a sin, and recognizing and punishing that was the main objective. It was a fortunate side effect that the victim would see his reputation vindicated. A common law action on the case for defamatory words which caused temporal loss (i.e. monetary loss recompensable in damages) then developed independently, becoming known as slander. The ecclesiastical jurisdiction then passed at the Reformation to the Court of Star Chamber and then at the end of the Civil War to the Common Law courts. The two forms of action were never assimilated.

12.4.2.2 Libel

Definition

Libel was originally defamation in written form. The word derives etymologically from the Latin *liber*, a book. It refers now primarily to matter which is both permanent and visible to the eye. What does this cover beyond actual writing? It naturally covers pictures and statues. What about the broadcast media, films, recordings, etc.? Although gestures and sign language 'appeal to the eye', they are transient, and are regarded as slander. It seems to be the case that defamation by e-mail is libel. Although the e-mail is apparently transient, in that it can be deleted, in fact it stays in the system and is of course potentially accessible to others: *Multigroup Bulgaria Holdings Ltd* v *Oxford Analytica Ltd* (1997) (unreported).

Statutory extension

Defamatory material in a stage play is libel by statute: s. 4 of the Theatres Act 1968. Defamatory material broadcast by means of wireless telegraphy (radio and television) is also libel by statute: s. 166 of the Broadcasting Act 1990. The definition in the Act covers words (including Morse code) and visual methods of conveying meaning (including gestures). It extends only to broadcasts intended for general reception. This will exclude, e.g. police frequencies. Cable and satellite TV services are included.

Doubtful cases

Audio tapes and records still constitute a grey area. There is no direct authority. Which side of the line should they fall? Some academic authorities suggest that as there is a permanent medium, the defamation is libel, others that as the actual publication of the material is transient and purely aural, that it will be slander.

For films, the authority is *Youssoupoff* v *MGM* (1934) 50 TLR 581. A film about the last years of the Romanovs contained a scene suggesting that Princess Youssoupoff had been raped by Rasputin. The information was primarily conveyed by visual means, although comprehension was aided by the soundtrack. The strict *ratio* of the case is that cinematographic images, being perceived by the eye, and being permanent in the sense that the film stock is retained, will be libel and not slander. The case is normally treated as authority that a defamation in the form of an anecdote in the soundtrack, unaccompanied by any image, is libel, but the point is technically still open.

Effect of libel

Libel is regarded as being a sufficiently serious invasion of the claimant's rights to be actionable per se, that is, the claimant need not prove actual harm expressible in money terms.

Libel and crime

Libel is a crime as well as a tort although prosecutions are rare. In criminal libel, justification, i.e. the truth of what is said, is not a defence. You may have heard the adage 'the greater the truth, the greater the libel'. What does this mean? It is only in this context that the adage is strictly correct. It is something of a paradox. The essence of the crime is that public order is threatened or public decency outraged. A true allegation is more likely to achieve this than an obvious fabrication. However, this approach seems obviously inconsistent with the Convention right to freedom of expression, despite the possible availability of 'public interest' restrictions.

12.4.2.3 **Slander**

 EXERCISE 12.2

Now you know what libel is, try working out your own definition of slander.

Definition

Slander is defamation in a form that does not amount to libel, primarily word of mouth. In principle the key factor is transience and the necessarily limited scope of publication, which render slander less damaging, but the case law is not quite as neat and tidy as that.

Effect of slander

Slander is normally actionable only on proof of special damage, e.g. the loss of a job, a tenancy, business, etc.

Exceptional cases

Let us look at the four exceptional cases (although, as you will see, they cover quite a lot of the ground!) where slander is actionable per se.

(a) Imputation of crime: the crime must be a serious one, i.e. it must carry a possible custodial sentence. Why is this sort of allegation an exception? Some say it is because belief in criminality will lead to ostracism, others that it puts the claimant in jeopardy. Allegations of conduct that is disreputable, but not technically criminal have been held to fall outside the rule, but an allegation that the claimant is a convict to fall within it: *Gray* v *Jones* [1939] 1 All ER 798. Does this help to choose one explanation or the other?

(b) Imputation of venereal disease: it has been suggested that the rule is wider than venereal disease in the strict sense. It seems to be the case that the disease should not simply be contagious, but should carry some moral opprobrium. HIV/AIDS would probably qualify.

(c) Office, profession, trade, calling, or business: in an action for slander in respect of words calculated to disparage the [claimant] in any office [etc], it shall not be necessary to allege or prove special damage, whether or not the words are spoken of the [claimant] in the way of his office [etc]: s. 2 of the Defamation Act 1952 (*Cases and Materials* (12.1.2)).

The rule looks to the effect of the words on the claimant's employment, not to the context in which they were said; so an allegation of immorality against someone who should be moral, such as a headmaster, or of dishonesty in any case, will count, even though they do not directly relate to the performance of the duties. A voluntary office is within the rule, but the rule is modified in such cases so that alleged incompetence will only count if it is of such a degree as to warrant the claimant's removal from the office.

(d) Unchastity of a woman: words spoken and published . . . which impute unchastity or adultery to any woman or girl, shall not require special damage to render them actionable (Slander of Women Act 1891).

Lesbianism is unchastity for this purpose. A male partner cannot rely on the rule. Slang expressions will suffice. Why did women need special protection in 1891? Do they still need it today?

What qualifies as special damage

It must be tangible, pecuniary loss, such as loss of employment or business contracts. Loss of the hospitality of friends will count, but only in so far as this is expressed in tangible form, e.g. food, drink, and accommodation, not loss of companionship.

Nervous shock, or physical illness and financial loss arising therefrom are not relevant special damages (and will not make a slander actionable); if the defamation is otherwise actionable, any such effects may be reflected in the size of the award of general damages. The primary concern of the tort is to protect reputation, not physical integrity.

12.4.2.4 **Procedural oddities**

(a) An action is extinguished by the death of either party before judgment.

(b) There is a right to trial by jury (unless a judge considers the case is too complex): s. 69(1) of the Supreme Court Act 1981. This right may be waived by both parties jointly. It is otherwise absolute, and unless s. 8 of the Defamation Act 1996 applies, a judge cannot give summary judgment if a party objects: *Safeway plc* v *Tate* (2001), *The Times*, 25 January. The Court of Appeal can overturn a jury verdict if it is perverse (although the House of Lords decided that there was a non-perverse explanation of the verdict on the facts of the case): *Grobbelaar* v *News Group Newspapers Ltd* [2002] 4 All ER 732.

(c) Public funding is not available.

(d) The limitation period is twelve months: s. 4A of the Limitation Act 1980 (inserted by the Defamation Act 1996).

(e) Public bodies, such as local authorities: (*Derbyshire CC* v *Times Newspapers Ltd* [1993] AC 534) and political parties (*Goldsmith* v *Bhoyrul* [1997] 4 All ER 268) cannot themselves sue in defamation. Commercial entities may, and of course members and officers may sue in their personal capacity.

(f) Special procedures for injunctions: no relief where the defendant is not at the hearing, except in exceptional cases and no injunction to restrain publication unless the claimant can establish a strong case: s. 12 of the Human Rights Act 1998. These measures are to protect the right to freedom of expression (Art. 10 ECHR).

? **QUESTION** 12.2

Othello suspects his wife, Desdemona, is having an affair with Cassio. He writes the words 'Cassio is a wife stealer' on the beach between low- and high-water mark. He pays Iago to produce an ice sculpture clearly showing Desdemona and Cassio in a compromising position and puts the sculpture on display in the market place.

What type of defamation do we have here? Will Desdemona or Cassio be able to sue Othello if they cannot prove special damage?

12.5 **What is defamatory?**

 EXERCISE 12.3

What does the claimant have to demonstrate to show that he has been defamed?

12.5.1 **Definition**

He must show that a statement has been made about him which reflects on his reputation so as to lower him in the estimation of right-thinking members of society or which tends to cause the claimant to be shunned and avoided. At one time the expression 'Brings the [claimant] into hatred, ridicule, or contempt' was used, but this is a little wide. To win the case he must also prove the defendant published the statement.

12.5.2 **Damage to reputation**

How far does this go? Will a statement which makes the claimant a figure of fun suffice, or must there be a 'moral element'? In *Blennerhasset* v *Novelty Sales Services Ltd* (1933) 175 LT Jo 393 the defendant placed a full-page advertisement headed 'Beware of Yo Yo' which referred to a Mr Blennerhasset who ate lobster at Pim's (a City restaurant) and had to be taken to a quiet place in the country after becoming hooked on Yo Yo. The claimant was a Mr Blennerhasset who lunched at Pim's and was a stockbroker. He was subjected to ribaldry in the Stock Exchange as a result of the advertisement. This was clearly annoying, but was it actionable?

It was held that the words were not capable of being defamatory, as they did not reflect on his moral or social character. In this case the ridicule was transient and transparently unconnected with any moral failing but a satire or lampoon which does attack character may be defamatory, although it uses the medium of humour.

12.5.3 **'Right thinking members of society'**

The expression comes from a dictum of Lord Atkin in *Sim* v *Stretch* [1936] 2 All ER 1237. The aim is to exclude the two extremes: those who will tolerate anything, and those who are excessively censorious. This is best illustrated by a rather tongue-in-cheek decision: *Byrne* v *Dean* [1937] 2 All ER 204. A golf club had an illegal gaming machine. Someone sneaked to the police, and the machine was suppressed. The defendant placed on a club noticeboard a poem expressing the hope that the sneak might 'byrne in Hell, whoever he is'. The claimant became very unpopular at the club. Was it defamatory to suggest he had advised the police of a breach of the law? It was held that those who would believe the claimant to be the sneak and as a result think less of him for doing his duty as a citizen were not 'right-thinking members of society' and so the words were incapable of being defamatory.

12.5.4 **'Shunned and avoided'**

Why does the second limb of the definition exist? What about an allegation that a woman has been raped? This is clearly not prima facie denigratory of her character: *Youssoupoff* v *MGM* (see 12.4.2.2). The particular allegation may not be defamatory even in this sense in today's moral climate, where a rape victim is more likely to be pitied and counselled than shunned and victimized. Or is she?

12.5.5 Mixed views

Problems clearly arise when the allegation is one which, while not absolutely reprehensible, is nevertheless likely to excite strong feelings in a section of the public who are not self evidently wrong thinking, e.g. to call a man a strike breaker, or a Communist. It is probably necessary for such an allegation to carry overtones of hypocrisy. Is it defamatory to say that X is a connoisseur of wine? Would you change your mind if X were a leading temperance campaigner?

12.5.6 Some examples

Accusations of incompetence or dishonesty in the claimant's trade, profession, or calling are defamatory (although in an Australian case it was held not defamatory to call a leading rugby player 'fat and cumbersome'). It has been held that calling an actor, or a beauty therapist, 'ugly' is capable of being defamatory, but this is clearly very near the borderline. Allegations of insolvency are defamatory in the case of a businessperson, although it is not defamatory merely to say that the claimant has ceased to trade.

Mere words of abuse will not be defamatory, but if, properly understood, they indicate specific wrongdoing or immorality, then they are defamatory.

12.5.7 Respective functions of the judge and jury

12.5.7.1 The judge

The judge is the sole judge of law. It is a question of law whether words (or other communications of meaning) are capable of bearing a particular meaning and whether that meaning is capable of being defamatory.

12.5.7.2 The jury

If the words are so capable it is a question of fact for the jury, who are the sole judges of fact, whether those words do bear that meaning and do defame the claimant. In the *Grobbelaar* case (see 12.4.2.4) it was held that it was for the jury to decide whether the words used meant that the claimant had actually 'thrown' football matches or just that he had corruptly agreed to do so and taken the money, but had not actually carried out his side of the bargain.

Some cases are heard without a jury. Is it still important to make these distinctions?

12.6 Reference to the claimant

12.6.1 Explicit reference

There is no problem if the reference is fully explicit: '[the claimant] is a damn rogue who has been swindling his customers and sleeping with their wives for years'. A degree of obliqueness in the reference is not fatal: 'there is a red-headed milkman in this town who . . .' will do just as well.

12.6.2 Indirect reference

There is a division of function (similar to that for defamatory meaning) where the words do not directly refer to the claimant. The judge has to rule on whether the words are capable of applying to the claimant, even where there are witnesses who allegedly understood them in this sense.

> *Knupffer* v *London Express Newspapers* [1944] 1 All ER 495
> (*Cases and Materials* (12.2.1))
>
> The defendant published an article suggesting that the Mlado Russ or Young Russia party were a gang of pro-Nazi quislings to be numbered among the 'despised dregs of society'. The claimant was the leader of the English branch of Mlado Russ, which had some forty members. He was not referred to by name in the article, but witnesses testified that they understood the article as referring to the claimant. How should the case be decided?
>
>   The judge held that the words were an unfounded generalization, applying to a class and not to each and every member and were not capable as a matter of law of referring to the claimant, even though as a matter of fact they were clearly so understood. Why do you think the judge flew in the face of apparent common sense here?

12.6.3 Mistaken identity

12.6.3.1 Accidental confusion

It is not necessary that the defendant meant to refer to the claimant, or even knew of his existence.

> **EXERCISE** 12.4
>
> Read *Hulton & Co.* v *Jones* and *Newstead* v *London Express Newspapers* in *Cases and Materials* (12.2.2.1). Does the later case fulfil the fears of those involved in the earlier case?

Was the defendant in *Hulton & Co.* v *Jones* [1910] AC 20 careless? He could have made it clear that this was a piece of fiction. The denigration of the imaginary character was quite gratuitous, done only to boost sales of the magazine.

  Two of the judges in the Court of Appeal were concerned lest allowing the claimant's action would expose the defendant to liability where he published a story, true of X, but defamatory of a namesake. They thought such a result would be absurd, and one said it was impossible.

12.6.3.2 **Namesakes**

Exactly this situation arose in *Newstead*.

Newstead v *London Express Newspapers* [1940] 1 KB 377
(*Cases and Materials* (12.2.2.1))

The Court of Appeal took the view that the risk should fall on the defendant, and so upheld the decision in favour of the claimant, but indicated that such cases would be rare, because the circumstantial detail of the story would usually prevent it being reasonably possible to consider the story to relate to the namesake. Damages were assessed at one farthing, which indicates that the jury had not entirely taken leave of its senses. Again, it might be said that there was carelessness in not giving adequate circumstantial detail.

12.6.3.3 **Statutory intervention**

 EXERCISE 12.5

Look up sections 2–4 of the Defamation Act 1996 in *Cases and Materials* (12.12). What are they designed to achieve?

These sections apply, among other things, to unintentional defamation of the *Newstead* type. The concept of the offer of amends derives from the Defamation Act 1952, but the procedure under that Act was so complex that it was little used, although many newspapers would publish a correction or disclaimer on request anyway. Although the offer of amends under the 1996 Act includes an offer of compensation as well as a correction/apology, it is likely that in a *Newstead* case this compensation will be nil or nominal.

12.6.3.4 **The current position**

You should now be clear that the question of whether the defendant has defamed the claimant is to be answered objectively in the light of the effect of the publication, rather than subjectively in the light of the defendant's intentions and knowledge.

? **QUESTION** 12.3

Is the present law on unintentional defamation unfair? How could it be further reformed?

As we have just seen, cases do arise where a claimant can show that an article can be read as applying to him, or at least confusing him with someone else. In practice an informal disclaimer or correction is all that is required, but there has been no efficient means of compelling the publisher to make one, or of insisting that the aggrieved party accept one if it is offered. As it is rare for real harm to arise from accidental defamation, it seems unreasonable to involve the publisher in the cost and trouble of a full scale defamation action. The offer of amends is designed to protect the unintentional defamer. If the offer is accepted there will be no trial, and the matter is resolved relatively quickly and cheaply. Even if the offer is rejected it may be pleaded as a defence, and the onus is on the claimant to defeat that defence by showing that the defendant believed that the statement referred to the claimant. Even if the defence fails it may be relied on in mitigation of damages. It will be a bold, or perhaps foolhardy, claimant who launches an action in *Newstead* circumstances in future where there is an offer of amends.

12.7 **Natural meaning and innuendo**

This relates to the sense which is to be attributed to words. Sometimes words are clear on their face, whether in the context of the meaning they convey or the person to whom they refer, but often there are uncertainties or layers of possible meaning, and these need to be elucidated.

12.7.1 **Inferences**

In many cases it is not just the natural meaning of the words which is claimed to be defamatory, but some subsidiary meaning or inference. There are limits to how far this process can be allowed to go.

Lewis v *Daily Telegraph Ltd* [1963] 2 All ER 151 (*Cases and Materials* (12.3.1))

The defendant published articles headlined 'Fraud Squad Probe Firm' and 'Inquiry on firm by City Police'. The reference was clearly to the claimant and his company. Are the words defamatory? The claimant alleged that these words meant not only that there was an investigation but, by implication or inference, that there was ground for suspicion, or even a presumption of guilt. (No smoke without fire.) Was this a legitimate meaning? Not according to the judges. This was a case of an attempt to extend the natural and ordinary meaning which failed. It was to draw an inference, not from the facts, but from a further inference which had itself been drawn from the facts. It worked like this:

- Fact: there was an investigation

- First (legitimate) inference: the police considered there were good reasons to investigate

- Second (illegitimate) inference: these reasons were valid and the claimant was guilty of some offence or other.

12.7.2 **Innuendo**

Do you know what the word means? If not, look it up in the dictionary. Unfortunately this only helps you to a limited extent. The expression 'innuendo' is doubly confusing in the context of defamation. The ordinary meaning of a 'sly' or 'malicious' attack on character is of no help in appreciating the legal meanings, and there are two of these!

12.7.3 **True (or legal) innuendo**

This occurs where the words are harmless in themselves, but become defamatory when considered in the light of other material. Only those with access to the additional evidence will grasp the defamation, but this is immaterial to success in an action.

 EXERCISE 12.6

Read *Morgan* v *Odhams Press* in *Cases and Materials* (12.3.2). Can you connect the claimant to the story? Can you see how his witnesses did?

Morgan v *Odhams Press Ltd* [1971] 2 All ER 1156 (HL)
(*Cases and Materials* (12.3.2))

The defendant seems to have fallen foul of judges' beliefs that people are all too ready to believe the worst and will do so even if a detailed perusal of the document would show such inconsistencies as to render the conclusion unreasonable. This was stressed by several members of the House of Lords in *Lewis* v *Daily Telegraph*. In the present case, the dates did not add up, but the witnesses had not sat down and worked it out.

The Court held that the article should be judged in the light of the standards of accuracy and reader sophistication associated with the newspaper in question, the *Sun*.

Similarly, in *Cassidy* v *Daily Mirror* [1929] 2 KB 331 the defendant published a picture of Mr Cassidy and Miss X, 'celebrating their engagement'. How could this be defamatory? The claimant was Mrs Cassidy, who was legally married to Mr Cassidy. Although they were effectively separated, Mr Cassidy did spend occasional nights with her. What exactly was she alleging? That the effect of the picture was to lead her friends and neighbours to the conclusion that she was not married to Mr Cassidy but was his kept mistress. The additional facts which made the photo defamatory constituted a true innuendo, and she succeeded. Nowadays a more obvious inference to draw would be that she was now divorced, but divorces were harder to come by in the 1920s.

In *Tolley* v *Fry* [1931] AC 333 the defendant published a caricature of the claimant, a well known amateur golfer, as part of its advertising. Can you identify the innuendo? The claimant successfully argued that publication of the caricature implied that he had received reward for the use of the picture. This was strictly taboo for an amateur.

12.7.4 **False innuendo**

This is really only the use of an extended meaning. It will usually be pleaded to avoid any suggestion that it is not part of the natural meaning, but there are no additional facts to be specifically put in issue. In *Allsop* v *Church of England Newspaper* [1972] 2 All ER 26, the defendant described the claimant as 'preoccupied with the bent'. As Lord Denning said, this clearly did not relate to the dictionary meanings (look them up!). It was clearly a slang meaning, and there were several to choose from, involving sexual and financial impropriety as well as merely eccentricity. The claimant had, by way of false innuendo, to specify which of the derogatory meanings of the word he was relying on. This was both to help the defendant formulate his line of defence, and to enable the judge to decide whether the meanings actually relied on were capable of being defamatory.

12.7.5 **The sting**

This is a technical expression; what do you think it means? It has nothing to do with complicated frauds and ragtime melodies. It is used to connote the precise defamatory meaning on which the claimant relies. If you were the defendant you would need to know this, and the Rules of Court ensure that the defendant is entitled to know what meanings the claimant alleges, and what innuendo facts are to be proved. He is entitled to defend each sting independently by the use of any tactic of pleading or defence. Where the claimant complains of a lengthy article or passage the defendant may defend by reference to the whole of it, i.e. the claimant may not convert an innocent message to a defamatory one by malicious editing.

A good indication of the correct approach to the last issue is the decision in *Charleston* v *News Group Newspapers* [1995] 2 All ER 904. The claimants complained of an item in the *Sun* comprising a photomontage of their heads on bodies forming part of a pornographic photo and accompanying an article. The burden of the text was that the claimants, who were soap actors, were the unwitting victims of entrepreneurs who had manipulated their pictures into images for a pornographic computer game. The impression given by the photos and headlines alone might be that the claimants were willing participants. The court ruled that the defendant was able to have the whole item considered as a whole, even though some readers might have done no more than glance at the picture and caption.

Some of the cases appear to go a long way. However, there will be cases where an artful author will 'hide' the identity of his victim, although clues will allow some people to make the connection. There is also the problem of the victim referred to by necessary implication, such as in *Cassidy*. There is a danger of overreacting to extreme cases like *Morgan* v *Odhams Press*.

? QUESTION 12.4

Some people may think that the law has gone too far in holding that the publisher of a defamatory statement which identifies no one is liable if knowledge of special facts which the publisher could not know causes sensible people to think that the statement applies to someone the publisher had never heard of. That may be arguable (*Morgan* v *Odhams Press* per Lord Reid.)

Should defamation be restricted to those cases where the statement on its face refers to the claimant?

12.8 Publication

12.8.1 What is publication?

It is an essential element of defamation that the defamatory material should have been published, i.e. have come to the attention of at least one person other than the claimant (or the defendant's spouse). Why does this requirement exist?

12.8.2 Harm to reputation

The essence of defamation is damage to the claimant's reputation (or at least the possibility of such damage). Insulting the claimant to his face has no effect on his public reputation. The exclusion of spouses can be justified on a variety of grounds; it may be the *de minimis* rule at work (although this would be an anomaly), or it may be a distaste for prying into the realms of matrimonial pillow talk.

12.8.3 Extent of publication

12.8.3.1 Number of readers/hearers

A publication to a single person will be enough, although the extent of publication will affect the likely *quantum* of damage to the claimant's reputation and will influence the damages to be awarded.

12.8.3.2 Incidental publication

If the defendant dictates a letter to his secretary, prior to sending it to the claimant, there is a publication to the secretary. Other incidental publications, e.g. to a filing or copying clerk will count. There may be a defence of qualified privilege in these circumstances (see 12.10.2.2): *Bryanston Finance* v *De Vries* [1975] QB 703. This does not affect the principle that this is publication.

12.8.3.3 Untoward events

A publication which is foreseeable, even though unintended, will count. In *Pullman* v *Hill* [1891] 1 QB 524, the defendant wrote a letter addressed to the claimant, accusing the claimant of obtaining money by false pretences. The letter was not marked as being private and was opened by a clerk employed by the claimant, and read by other clerks. This was publication to all the clerks.

But what if the unintended publication was also unforeseeable? In *Huth* v *Huth* [1915] 3 KB 32 the claimant's butler allegedly opened and read a letter addressed to the claimant in which the defendant (the claimant's estranged husband) suggested that the claimant and the defendant were not lawfully married, and that their children were illegitimate. The defendant was not held responsible for the butler opening and reading the letter in breach of his obligations as a servant. The view of the court may have been coloured by strong suspicions that the butler had been put up to testifying that he had opened and read the letter by his employer.

It is foreseeable, and will be assumed, that a postcard or telegram will be read by employees of the post office: *Sadgrove* v *Hole* [1901] 2 KB 1. In this case the claimant was employed as a quantity surveyor on a building project by the defendant. When the drawings and bills of quantities went out to the builders, the defendant thought they were wrong and sent postcards to some of the builders, saying that the quantities were wrong. There was no overt reference to the claimant. As against the builders, the publication was privileged (see 12.10.2.2). Although it was assumed that the cards would have been read there was no publication *of a libel* to the postal officials, etc. who would have seen the cards, because there was no possibility of their connecting the material with the claimant.

Where a re-publication is not intended or foreseen by the original author, the re-publisher may become liable, but this will depend on the circumstances of the re-publication: *Cunningham* v *Essex CC* (2000) LTL, 3 July; *McManus* v *Beckham* [2002] 1 WLR 2982.

12.8.4 Multiple publishers

Normally each publisher is liable for his own part in the publication process. Who will be the defendants in the case of a book? A newspaper? In the typical case of a book the author, publisher, and printer will all be liable, and in the case of a newspaper the author, editor, publisher and printer. The claimant has a free choice of whom to sue. A printer will normally have a contractual indemnity from the publisher, but this is only as effective as the publisher's assets. The claimant can ignore it. Where it is alleged that a person not obviously the author of a piece is nevertheless a direct source and therefore a publisher by providing the material for the actual author, the claimant must adduce adequate evidence to demonstrate the link between the source and the piece: *Campbell* v *Safra* [2006] EWHC 819 (QB). An Internet service provider who merely provides facilities for others to publish material is not as such a publisher: *Bunt* v *Tilley* [2006] EWHC 407 (QB); again the claimant must prove active involvement in the presentation of the material.

12.8.5 Innocent disseminators

At common law many people other than the author of the piece and the editor and publisher responsible for the publication could be liable in defamation. They included the printer and the wholesale and retail distributors, who were often entirely ignorant of the contents of the material which they were handling. A newsagent cannot read every magazine for libel, and even the printer may be working on material in a foreign language or where he is ignorant of the context of the material.

Such people are now protected by s. 1 of the Defamation Act 1996 (see *Cases and Materials* (12.1.1)). This section creates a statutory defence for anyone who '[is] not the author, editor, or publisher of the statement'. The editor is the person responsible for the decision to publish and the publisher is the person responsible in the commercial sense for the publication in question (not the wider meaning usual in defamation). The printer and distributors are expressly declared not to be the author, editor, or publisher: s. 1(3)(a). The defence only applies where the defendant 'took reasonable care in relation to [the] publication' and 'did not know, and had no reason to believe, that what he did caused or contributed to the publication of a defamatory statement'.

The defence is intended to clarify the earlier law. There is, however, a requirement for diligence, and a potentially exempt innocent disseminator may be deemed to have actual knowledge. The limits of the earlier law, and of the scope of the defence, can be seen in

Vizetelly v *Mudie's Select Library* [1900] 2 QB 170. The defendant operated a circulating library. The claimant complained of a libel in a book the defendant stocked. The publisher had circulated a notice asking for the book to be returned for the libel to be expunged. The defendant did not employ a reader for libel. The court held that the defendant must prove:

(a) that he did not know of the libel;

(b) that he was not put on notice of any libel;

(c) there was no negligence in not knowing of the libel.

It was not negligent not to employ a reader for libel but the circular meant that the defendant was on notice as to this particular libel. This is some indication of the approach that will be taken to the defence in s. 1. The new defence expressly requires that 'regard shall be had to . . . the previous conduct or character of the author, editor, or publisher': s. 1(5)(c). It follows that certain periodicals may be suspect and require a higher degree of caution. In *Goldsmith* v *Sperrings Ltd* [1977] 2 All ER 566, the claimant claimed to have been libelled in *Private Eye*; he was allowed to pursue an action against thirty-seven distributors of the *Eye*, as well as the author, editor, and printer. However, all the distributors had been advised of the alleged libel by a circular from the defendant. The defendant suggested that the general reputation of *Private Eye* was such that the distributors were on notice even without the warning. The court concluded that this was a legitimate means of pursuing the defamation action, not primarily a ploy to close down *Private Eye* by scaring off distributors, as the defendant alleged.

12.8.6 **Mere carelessness**

Intention to defame is unnecessary: *Cassidy* v *Daily Mirror* (see 12.6.4.3). That case could have been decided on the basis that the information was not adequately checked. It is still not clear whether it will be a defence to prove that the material was published in good faith and that all possible measures were taken to establish that the facts were true. This goes beyond mere innocence, as there is a positive duty to use all due diligence. Look at s. 1 of the Defamation Act 1996 (in *Cases and Materials* (12.1.1)).

> | ? | **QUESTION** 12.5 |
>
> Should there be a defence of due diligence? In other words no one will be liable in defamation unless they ought to have realized that the material was defamatory if they had taken reasonable care to check it.

Printers and distributors already have this defence: s. 1 of the Defamation Act 1996. Other publishers may make an offer of amends which is a defence unless it can be shown that they knew or ought to have known that the material referred to the claimant and was false and defamatory of him: ss 2–4 Defamation Act 1996. A defence of due diligence would exonerate the defendant in such cases and also leave the claimant without a means of correcting the false impression. Amends appears to strike a better balance by ensuring that a correction appears.

It will also be necessary to consider whether qualified privilege will apply where there is no doubt about the reference to the claimant; see *Reynolds* v *Times Newspapers Ltd and others* (*Cases and Materials* (12.4.1)).

12.9 **What must the claimant prove?**

 EXERCISE 12.7

List the matters which the claimant must prove. What mental element is involved?

You should have written down something along the following lines. The words (etc.) must be proved to be capable of bearing a defamatory meaning, to refer to the claimant and to have been published by the defendant; the jury must then find 'libel or no libel'. The truth or otherwise of the words is irrelevant at this stage. The claimant is entitled to a verdict in the absence of a relevant defence. Intention and carelessness are not normally relevant.

How easy is it to establish these elements of defamation which the claimant must prove? It seems as though it is fairly simple, at least in principle. As a result defences are of considerably greater significance than in other areas of the law.

12.10 **Defences**

12.10.1 **In general**

It should be remembered that, in accordance with normal practice in civil proceedings, the burden of proof lies upon him who asserts affirmative issues, so in this instance the burden is on the defendant to establish his defence.

12.10.2 **Privilege**

The doctrine of privilege is the expression in English common law of the primacy of free speech as against the protection of private interests in reputation. A privileged statement, that is one made on a privileged occasion and within the limits of the relevant privilege, is not actionable. There are two species of privilege, absolute and qualified.

12.10.2.1 **Absolute privilege**

Absolute privilege, as its name implies, cannot be defeated. Where it exists, the claimant has no action. There are three broad categories.

Parliamentary proceedings

No action may be brought on anything said in either House. To do so would be a contempt of Parliament which is itself a High Court. Hence the invitation often extended to MPs who have said something apparently defamatory under the cloak of parliamentary privilege to repeat the remark outside the House. In *Jennings* v *Buchanan* [2005] AC 115 the Privy Council confirmed that the privilege did not apply even where the statement outside Parliament was no more than a repetition of the earlier one, although qualified privilege (see later) might apply.

Judicial proceedings

This covers statements made in the ordinary course of such proceedings by a party, counsel, witness, or judge. The absolute privilege of an expert witness is at least substantially the same thing as the witness' immunity from suit: *Meadow* v *GMC* [2006] EWHC 146 (Admin); *Tufano* v *Vincenti* [2006] EWHC 1496 (QB). It extends to quasi-judicial proceedings (e.g. solicitors' or doctors' disciplinary proceedings), but not administrative hearings, such as planning enquiries: *Richards* v *Cresswell* (1987), *The Times*, 24 April. Anything not said in the course of the case (such as an interjection from the public gallery, or a gratuitous remark by the judge about something unconnected with the trial) is unprotected. The privilege is extended by statute to fair and accurate contemporaneous newspaper reports of such proceedings. There have been a number of cases on the scope of this head of privilege. In *Daniels* v *Griffiths* (1997) 127 NLJ 1809 it was held that communications to the Parole Board did not attract absolute privilege as the Board was not analogous to a court. In *Waple* v *Surrey CC* [1998] 1 All ER 624 it was held that a solicitor's letter relating to an application for a contribution to child maintenance was too far removed from legal proceedings and in *S* v *Newham LBC* (1998), *The Times*, 5 March, it was held that statements held on the official register of those considered a risk when working with children did not attract absolute privilege.

In all these cases it is accepted that qualified privilege (see below) will apply. There are, however, significant consequences flowing from the denial of absolute privilege. Absolute privilege is a complete defence and all these cases were on the preliminary issue of its existence, since if the defendant won the claimant had no case. Although there may be a heavy burden on the claimant to negate qualified privilege, the case still has to be fought.

Official communications

The scope of this head is much narrower than the title implies. It relates only to communications between ministers and similarly, senior officers of state on official business.

 QUESTION 12.6

Can you explain what links the three heads of absolute privilege? Are they each and all necessary in modern society?

The status of absolute privilege

Is there a common thread between the three types of absolute privilege? Are they all justified? The first two heads are legitimate; while it is not inevitable that the legislature has an absolute right to free speech, any attempt to fetter it would be tendentious. In the case of court proceedings it would similarly be intolerable for the proceedings to be second-guessed by a libel jury. Public affairs must be carried on without fear or favour. This particularly applies to the two public forums for debate and resolution of public affairs, namely Parliament and the courts. Allowing challenges of any kind gives an opportunity to the obsessed and aggrieved to reopen issues which have been decided. There is a technical link as Parliament is also a court. The third category is perhaps misplaced. A qualified privilege may be all that can be justified, but we do have an excessive veneration for official secrecy. It could be said that it is equivalent to the others in the sense that they cover between them the three arms of the State namely: Legislature, Judiciary, and Executive.

12.10.2.2 Qualified privilege

The qualification is that this category may be defeated by proof of malice, i.e. that the defendant disseminated the material for an improper ulterior motive of, e.g., mischief towards the claimant.

Common law qualified privilege

EXERCISE 12.8

Read *Adam* v *Ward* [1917] AC 309; [1916–17] All ER Rep 157 (HL) in *Cases and Materials* (12.5.1.1). What is the common law meaning of qualified privilege?

The key concepts seem to be reciprocity and proportionality. While here the use of *Hansard* to make charges 'made the world the audience', usually the dissemination of the material must be strictly controlled to those who 'need to know'.

Extent of common law qualified privilege

The privilege attaches to the relationship of the parties to the communication and not to the message itself, if it gets into the 'wrong' hands. In *Watt* v *Longsdon* [1930] 1 KB 130, the defendant was director of a company of which the claimant was an overseas director. The defendant received evidence of the claimant's misconduct, financial and sexual, and communicated it to colleagues and to the claimant's wife, who was an old friend. Was this covered by qualified privilege? The communication to the colleagues was privileged. The misconduct affected the claimant's position with the company and there was a clear reciprocity of interest, if not duty. The publication to the wife was, however, excessive and unprivileged. She undoubtedly had an interest in the information, which related in part to the claimant's morals, but the defendant had no sufficient duty to her to pass the information on.

A common interest may suffice, as in *Bryanston Finance* v *De Vries* [1975] QB 703 where the defendant dictated a business letter defamatory of the claimant to his secretary. There was no other publication. It was held that the defendant and the secretary had a sufficient common interest in the business of the company to confer qualified privilege. However, casual publications to members of staff may not be covered: *Cunningham* v *Essex CC* [2000] LTL, 3 July.

The interest may take various forms, including a complaint about a public official addressed to the proper authorities, or a tenant's complaint to his landlord about work done by the landlord's contractor. It will also apply to a legitimate reply to an attack on the defendant (as was the case in *Adam* v *Ward*); see more recently *Vassiliev* v *Frank Cass* [2003] EMLR 761; *Fraser-Armstrong* v *Hadow* [1995] EMLR 140 and *Campbell* v *Safra* [2006] EWHC 819 (QB).

One area where English law has long been held to be deficient is that there has been no proper protection for serious publications of facts giving rise to suspicion about matters of public concern, including the probity and competence of public figures. This applies particularly to 'investigative journalism'. Note that we are not talking about comment here, but about assertions of a factual nature. The position is different in the United States, where respect for freedom of speech as enshrined in the Constitution, is much stronger. A public figure may only pursue an action there for material which has been published maliciously: *Sullivan* v *New York Times* (1964) 376 US 254. The status of the 'public figure' replaces any other need for a 'common interest' in publication. In consequence, the US courts will not enforce English libel judgments because of the lack of protection here for free speech. This will be likely to receive early attention in the courts in the light of the incorporation of the right to freedom of expression in Art. 10 of the European Convention on Human Rights.

 Some progress has been made in this area by the House of Lords decision in *Reynolds* v *Times Newspapers Ltd* [1999] 4 All ER 609 (*Cases and Materials* (12.4.1)).

The case concerned classic 'responsible' investigative journalism and allegations of political misconduct. It is strongly arguable that such matters should be ventilated, but the traditional test of mutuality of interest was not met. The Court of Appeal ([1998] 3 All ER 961) had suggested that journalists would in due time be able to rely on Art. 10 to justify a submission that the courts should redefine qualified privilege to cover such cases of political speech. At present the only protection in respect of facts is justification (see 12.9.3) or qualified privilege. Comment is more adequately protected by the defence of fair comment (see 12.9.4).

EXERCISE 12.9

Read the extracts from the speech of Lord Nicholls in *Cases and Materials* (12.4.1). What did the case decide?

The result is somewhat inconclusive. The House has certainly not expanded qualified privilege as the defendants wished either to cover all public figures, as in the United States, or to cover particular categories of activity or allegations. Lord Nicholls did indicate the ten listed conditions which may enable publications to be brought within qualified privilege on a case by case basis when they would not otherwise have done so. You should note these carefully.

In considering whether allegations made in the press attracted qualified privilege, the matters to be taken into account, depending on the circumstances, included: the seriousness of the allegation; the nature of the information and the extent to which the subject matter was a matter of public concern; the source of the information; the steps taken to verify the information; the status of the information; the urgency of the matter; whether comment had been sought from the claimant; whether the article contained the gist of the claimant's side of the story; the tone of the article; and the circumstances of the publication, including the timing. That list was not exhaustive, and the weight to be given to those and any other relevant factors would vary from case to case.

There is still a balance to be struck. Article 10 is not absolute in its terms, and muckraking journalism is not necessarily a public service. It is also necessary to secure the victims' right to privacy under Art. 8. These rights can of course be abused. Robert Maxwell was notorious for his use of the 'chilling effect' of the libel writ to stifle any investigation of his financial affairs. After his death it became clear that the criticisms were fully justified and that fraud on a massive scale had taken place. Was it in the public interest to allow Maxwell to use the 'chilling effect' in this way? What is easier to argue is that matters of merely salacious interest should result in the balance tipping in favour of privacy and against disclosure.

The Court of Appeal has suggested that 'tabloid' journalism will not qualify. In this case the essential calculation is a financial one, and allowing qualified privilege will merely encourage more lurid and less well checked stories: *Grobbelaar* v *News Group* [2001] 2 All ER 437. This aspect is not affected by the subsequent House of Lords decision. Is this objectively justifiable, or does it reflect merely judicial distaste for the activities of the 'gutter press'.

In *Al-Fagih* v *HH Saudi Research and Marketing* [2002] EMLR 215 Smith J reiterated that there was no special category of political speech, and that the availability of qualified privilege depended on the maintenance of a proper balance between checking of sources, the damage to the victim's reputation and the public interest in the issues being aired. This has now been reaffirmed by the Court of Appeal in *Loutchansky* v *Times Newspapers* [2002] 1 ALL ER 652, a case which concerned very serious allegations of money-laundering and other business misconduct:

> The interest is that of the public in a modern democracy in free expression and, more particularly, in the promotion of a free and vigorous press to keep the public informed. The vital importance of this interest has been identified and emphasized time and again in recent cases and needs no restatement here. The corresponding duty on the journalist (and equally his editor) is to play his proper role in discharging that function. His task is to behave as a responsible journalist. He can have no duty to publish unless he is acting responsibly any more than the public has an interest in reading whatever may be published irresponsibly. That is why in this class of case the question whether the publisher has behaved responsibly is necessarily and intimately bound up with the question whether the defence of qualified privilege arises. Unless the publisher is acting responsibly privilege cannot arise. That is not the case with regard to the more conventional situations in which qualified privilege arises. A person giving a reference or reporting a crime need not act responsibly: his communication will be privileged subject only to relevance and malice.

The court also indicated that *Reynolds* qualified privilege should be regarded as distinct from the traditional type. The court reserved the right to pass judgment on whether the journalist had lived up to the appropriate standards and ensure that Art. 10 rights were not being abused.

Subsequent cases have made it plain that what constitutes responsible journalism will vary from case to case. While usually it will be responsible to put the allegations to the subject and invite comment, with the result that failure to do so was the critical feature for the Court of Appeal in *Jameel* v *Wall Street Journal* [2005] EMLR 17, it was found not to be in *Armstrong* v *Times Newspapers* [2005] EWCA 1007. The House of Lords reversed the decision in *Jameel* on this point ([2006] UKHL 44) and held that all factors should be weighed in each case, with no factor to be regarded as decisive. A 'practical and flexible approach' was required, applying *Bonnick* v *Morris* [2002] UKPC 31 and the dicta in *Reynolds* itself. In *Roberts* v *Gable* [2006]

EWHC 1025 (QB) the disputed article was a report in an anti-fascist periodical of a dispute within the British National Party. The article reported the various allegations without adopting them. Eady J held that reporting of matters directly affecting political parties, their officers and candidates carried a high level of public interest; so long as the actual reportage was objective and disinterested, it was unlikely that the claimant could undermine the privilege by cavilling over the manner in which the information was gathered. By contrast, in *Charman* v *Orion* [2006] EWHC 1756 (QB), the privilege did not attach where the author had adopted some of the allegations and the reportage lacked objectivity and disinterestedness.

Remember that the rule relates only to bona fide communications. If the defendant is being malicious, the claimant will still have an action. While qualified privilege is not concerned with the truth or otherwise of the allegations, it does mitigate for the defendant the harshness of the rule that liability rests on the fact of defamation rather than motive or fault.

Qualified privilege and reports

Fair and accurate reports of parliamentary and judicial proceedings have long attracted qualified privilege, although in the case of Parliament the privilege was hard won. Qualified privilege for court reports is wider than the statutory absolute privilege.

Section 15 of the Defamation Act 1996 extends qualified privilege to a substantial range of reports of proceedings of administrative tribunals, local authorities, foreign legislatures, public enquiries, official registers, trade, professional or sporting regulatory bodies, public meetings, and official public notices.

12.10.2.3 **Malice**

Express malice will defeat qualified privilege (and also the defence of fair comment; see 12.10.4).

Absence of belief in truth

By far the most important way of rebutting the privilege is to show that the defendant did not believe in the truth of his statement or was recklessly careless whether the statement be true or false. (*Street on Torts*, at p. 469.)

The proposition is clear in principle, although it may be difficult to apply in practice. May there be cases where the nature of the matter and the position of the defendant are such as to sanction the transmission of a message which the defendant believes to be false? Take the case of a manager at a nuclear plant who is advised that a colleague is in the pay of a hostile State. The circumstances would appear to justify transmission of the information to a superior for investigation, even if the defendant firmly disbelieved it.

Abuse of purpose

This is commonly referred to as personal spite or ill will. The wrong motive must be dominant.

 EXERCISE 12.10

Read *Horrocks* v *Lowe* in *Cases and Materials* (12.5.1.2). Was the defendant telling the truth and making honest comments as he saw the matter? Where is the boundary where the privilege is lost?

In *Horrocks* v *Lowe* [1975] AC 115 the trial judge found that the claimant's conduct was in fact above reproach, and that the defendant had lost the qualified privilege because, although honestly believing what he had said, he was so blinded by gross prejudice that he had abused the occasion, and lost the privilege. The Court of Appeal and House of Lords disagreed. It was the honesty of the view which was paramount. It follows that honestly expressed opinions enjoy very wide protection.

Excessive publication

The privilege is lost if distribution goes beyond those covered by the rationale of the privilege: see *Watt* v *Longsdon* (at 12.10.2.2). This may be used as evidence of malice, or, under a separate though analogous rule, it may negate the privilege. The relevant distinction is that malice is ultimately a question of fact for the jury, but excess of privilege is a question of law for the judge. Excess of privilege may relate to publishing additional, unnecessary matter, as well as to the people to whom publication is made. This limitation does not apply to the *Reynolds* type of qualified privilege, where the material has by definition been widely distributed.

The test applied in practice is that approved by the court in *Telnikoff* v *Matusevich* [1991] 1 QB 102.

> In order to enable the plaintiff to have the question of malice submitted to the jury, it is necessary that the evidence should raise a probability of malice and 'be more consistent with its existence than with its non-existence'.

Given that qualified privilege covers publication of material that is subsequently admitted to be wrong or unsubstantiated, the claimant may well have suffered distress or even tangible harm. In such cases he may be able to pursue an independent claim for breach of privacy under s. 7 of the Human Rights Act in respect of Art. 8 of the ECHR: *W* v *Westminster CC* [2005] EWHC 102 (QB).

12.10.3 Justification

Normally, the claimant does not have to prove that the defamatory material is false. It is assumed to be so. A defence of justification is where the defendant tries to prove that the matter is substantially true.

12.10.3.1 Justification and meaning

Whether words can be justified does depend very much on the meaning that is to be attached to them, so the cases on justification are intimately associated with the rules which govern the attachment of meaning to words, as we saw in the section on the rules as to true and false innuendo. In *Lewis* v *Daily Telegraph* (see 12.7.1) the defendant was ready and able to justify the primary meaning of the words used, namely that the claimant was under investigation. The case turned on whether the claimant was allowed to allege that the words bore a further meaning, namely that the claimant was guilty, a meaning that the defendant was unable to justify. When it was ruled that he was not, the defendant was home and dry. Most cases of justification will in the end be seen as turning on interpretation: does the justificatory material cover the whole sting of the defamation?

In *Wakley* v *Cooke* (1849) 4 Exch 511, the defendant called the claimant 'a libellous journalist'. He proved that the claimant had once had a verdict for libel given against him. Did this cover the whole of the sting of the libel? It was held that it did not. The sting was the implication that the claimant was a habitual libellist.

Sometimes the boot is on the other foot. In *Clarke* v *Taylor* (1836) 2 Bing NC 654, the defendant accused the claimant of being 'involved in a grand swindling concern' at Manchester, adding that the claimant had also been at Leeds, and was supposed to have made purchases there, but that it was hoped that his detection had prevented further losses. The defendant justified the Manchester allegation, but could not specifically justify the Leeds allegation. Did this matter? It was held that the Leeds allegation did not of itself add any further allegation of criminality, and so the defendant had met the whole sting.

12.10.3.2 Taking a fair view

The claimant cannot select parts of what, on a fair view, is to be seen as a single passage. In other words the defendant is allowed to seek to justify the sting of the passage as a whole, or common sting.

12.10.3.3 Part justification

EXERCISE 12.11

Look up s. 5 of the Defamation Act 1952 in *Cases and Materials* (12.1). Take a case where the defendant describes the claimant as 'a corrupt politician and depraved fornicator who always drives too fast', and justifies the first two counts only. Will he succeed under the section?

On the face of it, there is little left of the claimant's reputation, so s. 5 should apply. However, it might be suggested that there is a separate reputation in relation to driving habits. In such a case, the relative level of harm would be reflected in the level of damages (or at least should be).

In *Cornelius* v *Taranto* [2002] CMLR 6 the defendant justified statements that the claimant had lied about her psychiatric history, and that she lacked insight into her psychiatric state, but failed to justify a statement that she had stolen drugs some considerable time earlier. It was held that s. 5 applied.

12.10.3.4 Failed justification

Persistence in an attempt to justify, which fails, and which will have resulted in a republication of the defamatory material, is likely to cause the damages to be increased (see *Aldington* v *Watts and Tolstoy* (unreported)). It is for this reason that justification is regarded as tactically risky, to the extent that there is a dictum, attributed to the late Viscount Hailsham, current among the libel bar: 'never justify'. Where the persistence is particularly contumacious (gross, obvious, and offensive), a jury may properly award aggravated damages: *Kiam* v *MGN* [2002] 2 All ER 219 (*Cases and Materials* (12.1.1)).

12.10.3.5 Effect of justification

With certain limitations in relation to the publication of spent convictions, justification is a complete defence. Malice is irrelevant and, in principle, although there is no case on the point, if the defendant spreads a story which he believes to be false, but which turns out coincidentally to be true, he may justify.

12.10.4 **Fair comment**

 EXERCISE 12.12

What do you understand by fair comment?

Criticism of matters of public interest, in the form of comment upon true or privileged statements of fact, such comment being made honestly by a person who did not believe the statements to be untrue and who was not otherwise actuated by malice. (*Street on Torts*, at p. 479.)

12.10.4.1 **The public interest**

The public interest does not embrace everything in which the public is interested. What does it cover? It covers the activities of central and local government (including the policies of the opposition parties), and other institutions of a religious or public character. It also covers anything put into the public domain, such as a work of literature, a play or film, the work of an architect, or the qualities of goods which are advertised. It does not, in theory, cover the private morality of public figures except to the extent that this reflects on their fitness to fulfil their public duties.

? **QUESTION** 12.7

Quixote, a Cabinet Minister, is reputed to be a homosexual. He nevertheless always votes against any measure designed to improve the legal position of homosexuals. Snipe, a homosexual rights campaigner, publishes a pamphlet in which he compares Quixote's voting record with that of Oscar, an avowedly homosexual MP and strong supporter of homosexual law reform. Snipe goes on to say 'Honesty is always the best policy. If Quixote won't stand up to be counted on his own sexuality, can he be trusted ever to tell the truth?'
   Advise Snipe how he should defend Quixote's libel action against him.

The main problem is establishing a factual basis. If this can be done, then a defence of fair comment should succeed. The voting record is a matter of fact, and although sexual orientation itself is not a matter of legitimate (as opposed to prurient) public interest, it becomes so where, as here, it impinges on the integrity of a public figure. There is a possibility of malice, but if the facts are correct, strong, even unreasonable, views are protected in the interest of free speech. Note that privilege and justification relate to facts. If these are true, or there is a good reason to publish them, then there may also be good reason for comment, and the comment need only be honest. In one sense fair comment is a secondary defence since it will only arise once the status of the facts has been resolved, if it is in dispute.

12.10.4.2 Comment on true facts

This can cause complications in practice, where there is a single passage of mixed fact and comment: this leads to a defence which is 'rolled-up' so that those statements which are found to be of fact are justified, while those which are comment are alleged to be fair. *Horrocks* v *Lowe* (see 12.5.1.2) will be relevant here, as will *Kemsley*.

Kemsley v *Foot* [1952] AC 345 (*Cases and Materials* (12.5.2.1))

The claimant was a newspaper proprietor. The defendant (Michael Foot) attacked another newspaper by referring to it as 'lower than Kemsley'. The defence was fair comment, but can you see how it was argued?

It was held in the House of Lords that what Michael Foot said amounted to fair comment on facts which were implied (and true), namely that the Kemsley Press had a bad reputation.

12.10.4.3 Partially true facts

Section 6 of the Defamation Act 1952 makes similar provision to s. 5 in the context of fair comment.

12.10.4.4 Honesty

The law gives considerable latitude to the expression of opinion. Strong feelings, strongly expressed are protected. Some of the cases use words rather loosely, since the extremist is unlikely to appeal in his views to the ordinary reasonable man of moderate habits, although the judges seem to think that the test is one of reasonableness. In effect the result is that only the grossest of calumnies will be seen as dishonest, in the absence of express malice.

12.10.5 Amends

This is a new statutory defence under the Defamation Act 1996 (*Cases and Materials* (12.1.2)). Anyone alleged to be guilty of defamation may make an offer of amends, either generally or in respect of a specific defamatory meaning (a 'qualified offer'): s. 2(2). This offer must be in writing, expressed to be an offer of amends under the Act (s. 2(3)), and is an offer to:

- make a suitable correction and apology;
- publish the correction and apology in a reasonable manner;
- pay such compensation (if any) and costs as may be agreed or ordered: s. 2(4).

The offer of amends may not be made after a defence has been served in any proceedings which have been brought: s. 2(5).

12.10.5.1 **How the procedure operates**

If the offer is accepted it is a bar to proceedings for defamation. The only proceedings which may be taken are proceedings to ensure that the offer is carried into effect: s. 3(2)–(6). This may involve the court determining how the apology is to be published and/or fixing compensation.

If the offer is not accepted it will be a defence to proceedings. A qualified offer is a defence only in relation to the defamatory meaning specified: s. 4(2). The defence is disallowed if the person by whom the offer was made knew or had reason to believe that the statement complained of:

(a) referred to the aggrieved party or was likely to be understood as referring to him, and

(b) was both false and defamatory of that party

but it shall be presumed until the contrary is shown that he did not know and had no reason to believe that was the case (s. 4(3)). For the exception to apply it must be shown that the defendant was at least 'recklessly indifferent' to these matters: *Milne* v *Express Newspapers* [2005] 1 All ER 1021.

It is in this context that an offer of amends is a defence for unintentional defamation. It is likely that it would have applied in *Cassidy*, *Newstead*, and *Morgan*. It might also have applied in *Hulton* v *Jones*.

The offer of amends has a double operation.

(a) It protects the inadvertent defamer. In these cases compensation is likely to be very modest (*cf.* the farthing damages in *Newstead*) and the claimant is at risk if he does not accept. The claimant also bears the burden of proof that the defendant had the requisite knowledge.

(b) Even where there is a non-accidental defamation, although the claimant has the option of proceedings, he may accept amends if he considers this adequate. He avoids the cost, hassle, uncertainty, and delay of proceedings. In these cases the compensation is likely to be substantial rather than nominal, although often the retraction and apology is the crucial element.

The parties may deal with an amends case entirely by themselves, but there may be cases where the claimant accepts the offer of amends in principle but the parties cannot agree the terms of the correction, the amount of the compensation, or other issues. In *Cleese* v *Clark* [2003] LTL, 11 February, guidelines for dealing with unresolved issues were given. The parties should be proactive in negotiation, with the judge involved only to break the logjam. Compensation should be assessed in the same way as libel damages.

Where the defendant has made an early and complete retraction and apology by way of amends, he will normally be entitled to a substantial discount on the award which would be made under normal defamation principles: *Nail* v *NGN* [2005] 1 All ER 1040. Where there is delay, or an attempt to argue another defence, there should still be a discount, but it will be reduced to meet the justice of the case: *Campbell-James* v *Guardian Media Group* [2005] EMLR 24.

12.10.6 **Consent**

If the claimant expressly or impliedly authorized publication, this will be a defence.

12.11 **Remedies**

12.11.1 **Damages**

The prime remedy is damages. Where the case is tried with a jury, the assessment of damages is a question for them, and the judge can only give general indications of what will be an appropriate level. This has produced some odd results. In the late 1980s there were a number of scandalous awards. As a result the Court of Appeal has ruled that the judge should give the jury directions on the likely impact of particular awards of damages, so that they understand what any sum they fix on means in terms of purchasing power: *Sutcliffe* v *Pressdram* [1991] 1 QB 153. Where an award is excessive the Court of Appeal may now assess damages itself, rather than order a new trial: s. 8 of the Courts and Legal Services Act 1990 and will do so if the award appears unreasonable, particularly if it appears to be an unreasonable infringement of freedom of expression: *Rantzen* v *Mirror Group Newspapers* [1993] 4 All ER 975. Count Tolstoy successfully argued before the European Court of Human Rights that the award in his case was excessive and an unlawful restriction on his right of freedom of expression: *Tolstoy Miloslavsky* v *UK* Case 1995/520, [1995] 20 EHRR 442. The European Court of Human Rights acknowledged that the rules had already been changed. See also *John* v *MGN* [1996] 2 All ER 35 where an award of £350,000 was reduced to £50,000 and the Court of Appeal indicated that as well as the guidance authorized in *Sutcliffe* the judge could make comparisons with awards for pain, suffering, and loss of amenity in personal injury cases.

There is a new summary procedure under ss 8 and 9 of the Defamation Act 1996. This allows the court to dismiss a hopeless claim at a preliminary hearing or to give judgment where there is no arguable defence and award summary relief. The claimant may elect for summary relief. If he does not the court may impose it but only if the court is satisfied this will provide an adequate remedy. Summary relief may comprise:

(a) a declaration that the statement was false and defamatory;

(b) an order for the publication of a correction and apology;

(c) damages not exceeding £10,000;

(d) an order restraining further publication.

> **? QUESTION** 12.8
>
> What appears to be the rationale of the reforms made by the Defamation Act 1996?

It has been long considered that defamation, even more than other litigation, is a form of casino. The worst excesses of this have been addressed by the reform of the level of awards of damages, but this work is continued by the 1996 Act. The changes are all restrictions on the claimant: reducing the limitation period, excluding innocent disseminators more effectively from the scope of liability, more effective protection in cases of accidental defamation, and the amends and summary relief procedures. There is also a tilting of the balance towards correction and apology and away from damages.

12.11.2 Injunctions

Injunctions are available, but there is a well-established rule that an injunction will not issue where the defendant proposes to rely on a defence which the claimant cannot prove to be wholly spurious: *Bonnard* v *Perryman* [1891] 2 Ch 269. See also s. 12 of the Human Rights Act 1998, which provides that when considering interim relief pre-publication, 'No such relief is to be granted so as to restrain publication before trial unless the court is satisfied that the applicant is likely to establish that publication should not be allowed.' *Greene* v *Associated Newspapers* [2005] 1 All ER 30 confirms that the original rule remains valid. However the judge had doubts whether the rule should be maintained, or whether the test applied in *Cream Holdings Ltd* v *Banerjee* [2005] AC 253 in privacy cases, namely that the burden on the applicant would normally be to show that it was more likely than not, although in some cases 'likely' might mean something less than that, although always more than the general test of a 'real prospect of success': *American Cyanamid Co* v *Ethicon Ltd* [1975] AC 396.

12.12 **Protection of privacy**

In future this topic may require a chapter, not just a section. There is certainly a link between reputation and privacy, but it is not yet clear exactly how this will develop, and indeed, if the protection of privacy will be seen as being tortious in nature. Initially dicta of Sedley LJ in *Douglas and Others* v *Hello!* [2001] QB 967 suggested a tortious solution, but subsequent case law suggests that the judges at present regard the protection of privacy as a function of the law on breach of confidence which is of equitable, not common law origin and is therefore not strictly a tort.

12.12.1 **Historical development**

The common law did not recognize a right to privacy or allow compensation for invasion of privacy as such. This was affirmed as recently as 1991 in *Kaye* v *Robertson* [1991] FSR 62, where tabloid journalists had tricked their way into the hospital room of a celebrity suffering from serious head injuries following an accident and purported to interview him. Equity recognized that those who came into possession of confidential information were under a duty not to make unauthorized disclosure of it. Originally this regulated only a narrow range of confidential or fiduciary relationships, but it is now much broader. In *Earl and Countess Spencer* v *United Kingdom* (1998) 25 EHRR CD 105, the European Commission on Human Rights declined jurisdiction over a claim on the grounds, inter alia that there had been a failure to exhaust domestic remedies by failing to pursue a claim for breach of privacy, so such a claim cannot have been regarded as wholly unarguable. However, the non-existence of a common law right was restated in *Wainwright* v *Home Office* [2003] 4 All ER 969. This case concerned a strip-search of a mother and son during a prison visit to a relative. It was accepted that the prison services procedures had not been followed. Both claimants had suffered embarrassment and stress and the son quite serious psychological trauma.

The major claim was that the strip-searching itself constituted an actionable invasion of privacy. The incident predated the Human Rights Act, so the decision is based on the common law.

It was conceded that a touching of the son's penis, which was not in accordance with the rules regulating the search, amounted to a battery at common law. It could not be justified by reference to the rules and was not acceptable as part of ordinary life.

The trial judge however held that there was an actionable invasion of privacy both because the searches were excessive and because they were irregular. He related this to *Wilkinson* v *Downton* [1897] 2 QB 57. The Court of Appeal rejected this, seeing it as an unacceptable extension of the principle.

The House of Lords approached the case from the standpoint of whether there had been an infringement of a legal right of the claimants. Lord Hoffmann, who gave the main speech, reviewed the US position, starting with Warren and Brandeis's 'The Right to Privacy' ((1890) 4 Harvard LR 193); he accepted that there was a defined right to privacy in the USA, infringement of which was actionable. In England, on the other hand, while it was recognized that several torts served to protect privacy interests, citing Sir Brian Neill's article 'Privacy: a challenge for the next century' in *Protecting Privacy* (ed B. Markesinis, 1999), there was no specific legal right or remedy, apart from breach of confidence which could be seen as founded on privacy.

There is no right to privacy as such, as stated in *Malone* v *MPC* [1979] Ch 344; *Kaye* v *Robertson* [1991] FSR 62. While the judges in the latter case all supported a statutory right to privacy, provided it could be and was suitably defined, all also stated that a judicial creation of such a right was undesirable, because of the scope of the issues involved. Lord Hoffmann agreed:

> There seems to me a great difference between identifying privacy as a value which underlies the existence of a rule of law (and may point the direction in which the law should develop) and privacy as a principle of law in itself. The English common law is familiar with the notion of underlying values—principles only in the broadest sense—which direct its development. A famous example is *Derbyshire County Council* v *Times Newspapers Ltd* [1993] AC 534, in which freedom of speech was the underlying value which supported the decision to lay down the specific rule that a local authority could not sue for libel. But no one has suggested that freedom of speech is in itself a legal principle which is capable of sufficient definition to enable one to deduce specific rules to be applied in concrete cases. That is not the way the common law works.

Nor is there anything in the jurisprudence of the European Court of Human Rights which suggests that the adoption of some high level principle of privacy is necessary to comply with Art. 8 of the Convention. The European Court is concerned only with whether English law provides an adequate remedy in a specific case in which it considers that there has been an invasion of privacy contrary to Art. 8(1) and not justifiable under Art. 8(2). So in *Earl and Countess Spencer* v *United Kingdom* (1998) 25 EHRR CD 105 it was satisfied that the action for breach of confidence provided an adequate remedy for the Spencers' complaint and looked no further into the rest of the armoury of remedies available to the victims of other invasions of privacy. Likewise, in *Peck* v *United Kingdom* (2003) 36 EHRR 41 the court expressed some impatience, at para. 103, at being given a *tour d'horizon* of the remedies provided and to be provided by English law to deal with every imaginable kind of invasion of privacy. It was concerned with whether Mr Peck (who had been filmed in embarrassing circumstances by a CCTV camera) had an adequate remedy when the film was widely published by the media. It came to the conclusion that he did not.

In relation to *Wilkinson v Downton* Lord Hoffmann stated that the tort is unrelated to trespass to the person and does not at present cover the infliction of distress as distinct from psychological or physical harm (although he left open the possibility of this which he mentioned in *Hunter v Canary Wharf*). However, the case was inapplicable in any event because it required there to be an intention to cause harm, and that was not the case here, where the officers had acted outside the rules, but there was no evidence that they had deliberately sought to inflict psychological harm.

Both Lord Scott and Lord Hoffmann left open the question of when there would be a remedy under Art. 8 to be enforced through ss 6 and 7 of the Human Rights Act. Both expected it to apply to intentional acts. This was described as 'misfeasance in public office' by Lord Scott, and as 'intentional invasion of privacy by a public authority, even if no damage is suffered other than distress for which ordinarily no damages can be recovered' Lord Hoffmann. Lord Hoffmann seemed not to favour its application to negligent acts.

 EXERCISE 12.13

Consider whether the common law can successfully reconcile the demands of the media for protection of free speech and of others for privacy in the light of the Human Rights Act 1998. Is further legislation necessary, and if so, what form should it take?

12.12.2 **The impact of the Human Rights Act**

The Human Rights Act 1998 operates to protect the Convention right to the enjoyment of private and family life. Although Article 8 only states that there will be no interference by a public body with this right, it must be remembered that the courts are public bodies, and although in most cases within the scope of our discussion the primary interference is by a private sector media organization, when the courts adjudicate on these cases they must give effect to Convention rights. Since the media organization will be asserting an Art. 10 right to freedom of expression which is subject, inter alia, to restrictions intended to ensure respect for the rights of others, the court must inevitably weigh the Art. 8 and Art. 10 rights together.

In the first major case to require the courts to assess the position under the new dispensation, *Douglas and Others v Hello!* [2001] QB 697, the question was whether Michael Douglas and Catherine Zeta-Jones could restrain the publication of unauthorized photographs of their wedding. In an interim hearing to decide whether to restrain publication the Court of Appeal acknowledged that there was an arguable case in breach of confidence. Sedley LJ went further in saying that 'The law no longer needed to construct an artificial relationship of confidentiality between intruder and victim: it could recognize privacy itself as a legal principle drawn from the fundamental value of personal autonomy.' However, when the action came for trial, the judge found for the claimants on the basis of confidentiality and expressly declined to rule on the question of whether there was a common law right to privacy as such (Lindsay J [2003] 3 All ER 996).

In the meantime two other important cases had established some of the parameters for the interface between freedom of expression and privacy.

A v *B plc* [2002] 2 All ER 504 (*Cases and Materials* (12.6.1))

A professional footballer (Gary Flitcroft) sought to prevent publication of 'kiss and tell' material on the ground that it infringed his privacy. Although he was initially successful, the Court of Appeal allowed publication on the basis that a casual relationship of this kind deserved little protection, and also that the right of the women concerned and the newspaper to freedom of expression should prevail. There were very clear statements that the press, in particular, should be free to publish what the public wanted to read, subject to compliance with the Press Complaints Commission Code. This is clearly reminiscent of the approach taken to professional negligence (see **Chapter 3**). The courts are not, in theory, abdicating responsibility to the press, although in practice they are. In the particular case it was stated that footballers are role models for the young, so it is in the public interest for them to be exposed if they do not live up to expectations. It was also stated that the level of confidentiality to be attached to a sexual relationship varied, with marriage at one end, and a casual encounter at the other, of a quite lengthy continuum.

Lord Woolf made it clear that the requirements of the ECHR were to be included in the action for breach of confidence:

> [A]rticles 8 and 10 of the European Convention of Human Rights ('ECHR'). . . . have provided new parameters within which the court will decide, in an action for breach of confidence, whether a person is entitled to have his privacy protected by the court or whether the restriction of freedom of expression which such protection involves cannot be justified. The court's approach to the issues which the applications raise has been modified because under s. 6 of the 1998 Act, the court, as a public authority, is required not to act 'in a way which is incompatible with a Convention right'. The court is able to achieve this by absorbing the rights which Art. 8 and 10 protect into the long-established action for breach of confidence. This involves giving a new strength and breadth to the action so that it accommodates the requirements of those articles.

His Lordship went on to provide detailed and lengthy guidelines for the courts, specifically for interim applications, but which sought to highlight the key relevant considerations. He noted that the Parliamentary Assembly of the Council of Europe had recognized that there was a tension between media intrusion and the rights of celebrities (Resolution 1165 of 1998—a response to the coverage of the life, and death, of Diana Princess of Wales). However it was not for the courts to act as censors, or to be influenced by whether the material was of 'legitimate' or merely prurient interest.

In *Campbell* v *MGN* [2003] QB 633 the model Naomi Campbell complained that coverage of her drug-related problems was unduly intrusive. She accepted that the content of the story was accurate, so no issue of defamation arose. She also accepted that by making public assertions that she did not take drugs which were untrue, she had put that aspect of her life into the public domain and could not complain if the media sought to put the record straight. She therefore complained about the level of intrusion into her treatment and other aspects of the coverage. The trial judge accepted that this coverage was unduly intrusive, but the Court of Appeal disagreed. They accepted the argument that it was for the media to decide how to present a story and to deal with the news value of a story. This echoes the testimony of Paul Dacre, the editor of the *Daily Mail*, to the Commons Select Committee on Culture, Media and Sport, where he said that a newspaper had to balance hard or serious news, sport, and 'soft' celebrity-related material to produce a commercially viable newspaper. In the House of Lords there was a three to two split in favour of Ms Campbell. The minority considered that, while the additional elements of the story did intrude on her privacy, this intrusion did not exceed what was permissible for journalists. In the majority Lord Hope and Baroness Hale, essentially, regarded photographs in the story as so intrusive that they went beyond the journalistically permissible, while Lord Carswell did not single out the photographs but relied on the overall impact of the 'private' material.

? **QUESTION** 12.9

Jamie is a television personality with a 'wholesome' image. After a drunken night in the West End he finds himself in a brothel, and subsequently learns that the girls in the brothel are trying to sell a story and photographs to the press.

Can Jamie prevent publication?

Clearly the incident happened, so unless the story has been elaborated or the photographs manipulated there is no action in defamation. While there is an invasion of privacy, any relationship is of the most perfunctory kind, and the public interest is strong. Someone in the position of Jamie is even more plausibly a role model than a footballer. These are, broadly, the facts of *Theakston* v *MGN* [2002] EMLR 398. The newspaper was allowed to publish the story, but the photographs were held to be too intrusive. In the light of the decision in *Campbell*, where the principal reason for the decision of the majority was that photographs were an improper intrusion, while the story itself was legitimate, it may well be that the decision on the photographs would be followed in similar future cases.

■ SUMMARY

As we have seen, the world of defamation is a world apart. The jury still prevails and as a result the old arts of pleading to an issue still largely survive. The art of any text on defamation is to get over a coherent narrative without drowning in procedural complexities relevant only to specialist practitioners. The key issues, as you should now be aware are:

(a) the procedural oddities, including the division of labour between the judge and the jury and the attitude of the appellate courts to jury verdicts;

(b) the often unequal struggle between the protection of free speech (at its strongest in the political context) and the protection of reputation;

(c) the relatively light task faced by the claimant, who need only prove publication of defamatory matter referring to him. This must be contrasted with the burden on the defendant who must normally assert a positive defence;

(d) the mismatch of damages for bruised haloes and bruised heads. Not every judge actually gives full guidance about damages as recommended by the Court of Appeal. This criticism was levelled following a £600,000 award in February 1996 to a doctor libelled by allegations of inadequate endeavours to save a patient, and who alleged in turn that he had been scapegoated by the Secretary of State for Health to deflect attention from inadequacies in NHS provision.

■ FURTHER READING

Howarth, D., *Textbook on Tort*, 2nd edn, London: Butterworths, 2004, Chapter 12.

Jones, M.A., *Textbook on Torts*, 8th edn, London: Blackstone Press, 2002, Chapter 13.

Markesinis, B.S., and Deakin, S.F., *Tort Law*, 5th edn, Oxford: Oxford University Press, 2003, Chapter 7.

Murphy, J., *Street on Torts*, 11th edn, London: Butterworths, 2003, Part VI.

Winfield and Jolowicz on Tort, 17th edn, London: Sweet & Maxwell, 2006, Chapter 12.

 CHAPTER 12 ASSESSMENT EXERCISE

(1) *The News of the People* recently carried the following story headlined, 'Wife of Acrobat Sues Other Women':

> Mrs Rita Kyte, ex-trapeze artist wife of world-famous acrobat Jasper Kyte is suing her husband for divorce citing two women as co-respondents. The first is well known; she is a historian of circuses who has been researching into the history of Big Tops, and was to be seen with Mr Kyte both during and outside working hours in the last two months.
>
> The other is Eleanor Rigby, a 38-year-old spinster from Neasden with a passion for fairs and circuses.

Annabelle Lee, famed for studies of popular entertainment in the nineteenth and twentieth centuries, issues a writ alleging libel. She says that she did do research into Big Tops and that she was to be seen in the company of many circus employees, including Kyte, but that there was never any affair between them.

Eleanor Rigby (the 'real' one who alleges she is only a good friend of Kyte) issues a libel writ, as does another lady of the same name.

Advise the paper.

NB: when (if ever) the Family Law Act 1996 is fully in force, adultery will no longer be a component of a divorce petition.

(2) During a debate in the House of Commons on the subject of education, questions were raised, by way of example, about the running of a comprehensive school at Eatanswill by the headmaster, Mr Micawber. The speeches of several members showed considerable bias, and some of the charges against Mr Micawber were clearly defamatory and also (no doubt unintentionally) untrue. Next day the *Eatanswill Chronicle*, a local newspaper, published a detailed précis of this part of the debate and also a 'Parliamentary sketch' giving a reporter's impressions of these speeches and referring to the fuller précis. The reporter honestly believed in the truth of what he wrote, but his personal acquaintance with Mr Micawber led him to show unreasonable prejudice against those speakers who had supported the headmaster.

Advise Mr Micawber as to his prospects of a successful action for damages against Wardle & Co. Ltd, the proprietors of the newspaper.

See *Cases and Materials* (12.8) for a specimen answer.

13 | Remedies

13.1 OBJECTIVES

By the end of this chapter you should be able to:

1 Identify and describe the various types of remedy available in tort

2 Indicate where each will be relevant

3 Distinguish between the different bases of award of damages

4 Describe in outline the procedure for calculating damages in various categories of case, including personal injury and death

5 Distinguish between the various types of injunctive relief and indicate where each is likely to be relevant

13.2 Introduction

Remedies are often, and wrongly, neglected by students of law. Why this should be so is not clear. It is of course vital to the litigant to know what remedy he may expect to receive if he is successful as claimant, and conversely what his liability may be if he is an unsuccessful defendant. One difficulty is that torts are so disparate that it is often easier to discuss remedies in the context of the individual torts, and this has sometimes been done in this book, as you will have noticed. There is, however, a range of more general issues, and it is these that you are about to consider.

There are two distinctions that you must clearly understand at the outset.

13.2.1 Legal remedies and equitable remedies

Some remedies are described as 'legal' (e.g. damages) and others as 'equitable' (e.g. injunctions). Originally the distinction arose from the division of the courts into those which were courts of common law and those which were courts of equity. A court could only grant remedies from its own side of the divide. This is no longer the case and all courts have for many years administered both law and equity, including the relevant remedies.

The distinction is still important because, while legal remedies are available 'as of right', which means that if the claimant proves his case he must obtain the remedy, equitable remedies are discretionary. The court may decline to award them if it would be unreasonable to do so. There are nevertheless well-established areas (such as the grant of injunctions to restrain trespass and nuisances) where there are clear guidelines indicating how the discretion is likely to be exercised.

In theory, equity only intervenes to remedy the deficiencies of the common law, and this means that an equitable remedy will only be granted if damages, or some other legal remedy, are inadequate. In practice, as stated above, there are areas where the equitable remedy has become the norm.

13.2.2 Remedies in tort and remedies in contract

Remedies in tort are intended to compensate for or protect from harm done or, in some cases, threatened. In contrast, remedies in contract are designed to compensate for failure of the other party to fulfil his promise. The distinction has been discussed many times in the courts. Two succinct expressions of the purpose of damages, which point up the contrast between the two approaches are:

> Tort: '[The measure of damages is] that sum of money which will put the party who has been injured, or who has suffered, in the same position as he would have been in if he had not sustained the wrong for which he is now getting his compensation or reparation.' (Lord Blackburn, *Livingstone* v *Rawyards Coal Co.* (1880) 5 App Cas 25.)

> Contract: 'The rule of common law is that where a party sustains a loss by reason of a breach of contract he is, so far as money can do it, to be placed in the same situation with respect to damages as if the contract had been performed.' (Parke B, *Robinson* v *Harman* (1848) 1 Exch 850.)

There is a large area of potential overlap, where a claim can arise in both contract and tort. This includes the area of professional responsibility, arising both out of the specific contract and out of the general tortious obligation resulting from the professional undertaking to engage his professional responsibility. Professional is used in a wide sense to include a trade or service. This does not, however, cause much difficulty in relation to the remedy. The nature of the contractual obligation is to take reasonable care in carrying out the contract, so, in broad terms, the tortious measure will apply.

 EXERCISE 13.1

What do you consider to be appropriate and adequate remedies to deal with the following tortious activities? Do not confine yourself to remedies you know or believe the courts can in fact award. If you consider money damages to be appropriate, think what they are designed to cover and how they should be calculated.

- A prosperous doctor with a young family is rendered quadriplegic in a road accident.
- A police officer wrongly, but without violence or any public humiliation, arrests and detains (a) a fine upstanding pillar of the community, (b) a habitual criminal, against whom the evidence is not quite strong enough this time.

- Your next-door neighbour proposes to hold a four-day rock and reggae festival in his (relatively small) garden.

- Your next-door neighbour deliberately tips a load of hedge trimmings on to your patio.

- A newspaper is held to have libelled an actress by stating that (a) she engaged in a sexual act with her boyfriend in public, (b) she is a talentless and boring person who cannot convey a character convincingly to save her life, (c) she is a hypocrite because, while publicly espousing animal rights she has a large collection of fur coats. (Consider these as three separate cases.)

13.3 **Self-help**

In some situations the law allows the victim of a tort to take action without recourse to the courts to put matters right. There is some overlap with the defence of self-defence here. If you consider the case of *Tuberville* v *Savage* (1669) 1 Mod Rep 3, where the claimant apparently threatened the defendant by putting his hand on his sword as though to draw it, but negated the threat by saying that he would have done something about the insults the defendant had uttered to him if it had not been assize time, the defendant argued that he was exercising his right to self-help by self-defence in drawing his own sword and getting his retaliation in first. This was a perfectly good argument in principle, but failed on the facts as the defendant was not actually under threat.

There is also an overlap with the defence of necessity. A man may trespass on his neighbour's land to prevent major harm, e.g. to extinguish a fire before it spreads: *Cope* v *Sharpe (No. 2)* [1912] 1 KB 496.

The law does not favour self-help, but tolerates it. There is obviously a danger (as happened in *Tuberville*) that matters will get out of hand. The self-help remedies tend to arise in the context of trespass torts:

(a) A landowner may use reasonable force to deter or remove a trespasser. The owner of a chattel may likewise use reasonable force to recover it if he is entitled to immediate possession (but not if it has been hired out for a period which has not expired, or he owes money for repairs, storage, etc.).

(b) Material which is trespassing may be removed and returned. This may apply to overhanging branches, or to a wall built in the wrong place.

(c) Material which is trespassing may be detained as security for compensation for damage it has caused. There is no right to sell things, but in the case of animals, while the assumption is that the owner will wish to recover them on payment of compensation, there is power under s. 7 of the Animals Act 1971 to sell them if they are not claimed within a specified time.

? **QUESTION** 13.1

Does self-help provide a solution to any of the scenarios in Exercise 13.1?

13.4 **Damages**

13.4.1 **Generally**

While damages are normally seen as representing substantial compensation to the victim for harm suffered by him, this is by no means their only function.

Even where damages are compensatory, a distinction must be drawn between those cases where the loss is monetary (loss of earnings following an accident, the cost of repairs to or replacement of a damaged motor car, or loss of profits, etc. where allowable) and those where the harm is either physical (death or personal injury) or 'moral' (loss of reputation or infringement of privacy). In the former case there may be complexities of calculation, but the damages do represent direct and actual compensation. In the latter, the award of a cash sum is not direct amends, but an attempt to provide a monetary equivalent. This is inevitably an imprecise exercise. One of the most notorious examples is the disparity between awards for pain and suffering (where the maximum is around £180,000–£200,000 for a young adult reduced to quadriplegia, in physical pain, and fully aware of his/her plight) and those for defamation (where Lord Aldington was awarded £1.5m for allegations that he was implicated in war crimes).

Historically, the award of damages was a matter for the jury. Now juries only hear some defamation cases, some cases of false imprisonment, and some cases of fraud. There is no provision for other types of case to be heard by jury. An attempt was made in the early 1990s to have damages assessed by a jury where the main injury was a traumatic amputation of the penis. It was argued that only a jury could come to a balanced view of the value to be placed on this claim. It was held that there was no jurisdiction to empanel a jury even in such an extreme case.

Juries are normally expected to assess damages without specific guidance as to comparables. The foreman of a jury which awarded the late Telly (Kojak) Savalas £30,000 for an allegation that, in effect, he was not a very good actor, wrote to the press to complain of the lack of guidance, saying that the jury felt they could have collectively made a fair stab at the proper award for damage to a car, but they 'were not experts in haloes'. Judges do now give some guidance by reminding them what particular awards mean in practice, so £1,500 will buy a reasonable holiday, £10,000 a new car, and £1,000,000 provides an income of £1,000 or more a week for life.

Judges can and do have regard to the awards made in comparable cases. There are textbooks such as Kemp & Kemp, *Quantum of Damages*, which simply collate and compare awards, using multipliers to account for inflation. This material is used both for argument in court and when settlements take place out of court. There is in effect a tariff for various types of injury, e.g. £5,000 for a simple fracture of the leg, £20,000–£25,000 for the loss of an eye. This is adjusted in the case of multiple injuries, but there is a fair measure of certainty. The Judicial Studies Board also produce guidelines, which are similar, although based on hypothetical typical cases rather than collation of all actual cases.

 EXERCISE 13.2

Does this account square with your answers for Exercise 13.1?

In the USA it is still normal for civil cases to be tried by jury and some of the awards they give appear very high by English standards. There are, however, several factors which in part account for this:

(a) Juries know that the claimant's attorney will receive a substantial proportion of the award as a contingency fee, and may inflate the award accordingly.

(b) US awards include a higher element for medical expenses.

(c) Only the highest awards are reported. This gives a distorted picture. Most jury awards are at or about the level of an English award. Often the higher awards are reduced on appeal, or a settlement is negotiated to avoid an appeal.

(d) Some of these awards are made demonstratively, rather than with any expectation of them being satisfied. In one case a jury in New York awarded a woman many millions of dollars for deliberately inflicted facial injuries, although they knew that the defendants were penniless and uninsured. The foreman explained that they were expressing sympathy and indicating what they thought disfigurement was worth in moral terms.

(e) Some awards include specified or unspecified sums by way of punitive damages, especially in categories such as product liability, where the producer is, in effect, being fined as well as ordered to make compensation. This punitive element is not distinguished from the compensatory one in ordinary press reports.

 EXERCISE 13.3

Which procedure, trial by jury or by judge alone, is more likely to produce (a) fair and (b) consistent awards of damages?

13.4.2 **Economic theories**

There is a divergence of views on why victims of torts should be compensated. It is highly probable that there is no one single basis, since torts are so disparate. There are, however, several bases which have been and are influential in the development and operation of the law.

Fault is the traditional basis for imposing liability for negligent breach of duty. The defendant has culpably failed to live up to the expected standard, and 'ought' to compensate his victim. This leads on to the argument that it is not 'fair' to extend this liability to certain forms of harm which are unforeseeable or otherwise problematic. They fall outwith the defendant's moral responsibility.

Another basis is enterprise liability, or loss distribution. Any enterprise carries a risk of harming others. That risk is run to allow the enterprise to operate and accrue benefits for its owners and for those who utilize the goods or services which it produces. If the risks come to pass, compensating the victims is one of the costs of the enterprise, to be absorbed or passed on to the customers. It is immaterial whether the risk arises because of poor organization and management, which is the 'fault' of the enterprise or the casual negligence of a worker, for which the enterprise is vicariously but not morally liable.

The essential link with moral fault is broken in favour of loss distribution. Similar considerations apply to strict liability. Indeed the major cases of this, product liability and hazardous escapes, are typically cases of enterprise liability.

It can of course be argued that this is merely a halfway house. If loss distribution is the prime concern it can be better achieved by comprehensive insurance schemes, coupled with no fault compensation. In New Zealand most accident claims are covered by such a scheme, largely funded by 'insurance' premiums. In Sweden medical accidents are covered by a government funded, no fault scheme. In the UK, until recently, there was National Insurance no fault compensation for industrial injuries in parallel with the fault based tort scheme. Recent changes have modified National Insurance cover significantly. One interesting comparison is the transaction costs of the two schemes. There are no recent definitive figures, but the Pearson Commission established that in the early 1970s annual tort damages amounted to £202 million, while the legal and other costs of the system amounted to £175 million. Industrial injuries benefits at the same period amounted to £259 million, while the cost of administration was £28 million.

 QUESTION 13.2

Can you identify the arguments which support the use of the fault principle? Are they convincing?

The fault principle is often defended on the basis of deterrence. A rational entrepreneur, aware that if he harms others through fault he will be penalized in damages, will take steps to eliminate fault. What if, however, the cost of the precautions to eliminate the risk exceeds the likely cost of a claim? Market economists will argue that this is inefficient. Resources are being squandered in precautions; it is better to bite the bullet and pay the compensation. This is a largely American approach. Judge Posner gave the example of a railroad company considering whether to install crossing gates, on the assumption that they would be liable to compensate those injured in accidents at ungated crossings. If installing and operating the gates costs $10,000 a year, and the average cost of an accident in compensation and legal fees is $60,000, it is rational to install the gates if there is likely to be an accident once every five years, but not if it is once every seven years.

This approach can be extended to other torts. In its pure form, the Coase Theorem (named after the American academic who developed it) states that rational parties will maximize resources. He gives the example of a polluter causing a smoke nuisance. If it is worth $100,000 to him to carry on polluting, but the detriment to his neighbour is only $70,000, it is efficient to let him carry on and pay compensation. If the figures are reversed it is not. The actual price paid to continue or stop is of course negotiable in the $70,000–100,000 range. In practice the picture is complicated by the transaction costs, e.g. of litigation or installing alternative technology. There is a close analogy with the principle of environmental law that the polluter pays for the costs of pollution. He will only meet these costs as long as there is no cheaper alternative.

Economic theories carry little weight in English law. In the first place, they assume that people act only in the manner dictated by economic rationality. This is not true in the real world. Non-economic criteria are interposed, and it is also far from clear in practice where the line of economically rational behaviour is. Secondly, they are based on a particular ideology, of extreme market-oriented, laissez-faire capitalism. This ideology is not necessarily compatible with established common law doctrine. Thirdly, at best, the economic argument only applies to business liability. It is absurd to suggest that a driver decides to drive carefully to avoid the cost of an accident. There is no clear correlation between good driving and cost, and the individual has only occasional episodes of liability. Businesses, on the other hand, can plausibly be said to plan for liability, and their costs, whether in meeting claims or in insuring, are a material consideration.

? **QUESTION** 13.3

What principles should underlie the imposition of liability in tort?

There is no simple, obvious answer. Fault and loss distribution have some merit, but loss distribution only really works where the liability arises from a prolonged activity. It can also be argued that some interests are so important that they should be protected in all cases, even where there is no fault. See the trespass torts in particular.

13.4.3 **Compensatory damages**

13.4.3.1 **Land and buildings**

Where land or (more likely) buildings are damaged by the defendant, the claimant is entitled at least to the diminution in value of this holding, although if it is land being held by way of speculative investment and the destruction of buildings reduces the cost of site clearance, this must be set against the claim: *C R Taylor (Wholesale) Ltd v Hepworths Ltd* [1977] 1 WLR 659. This is not mitigation as such but simply an accurate calculation of the net loss. Where the claimant is occupying the premises he is entitled to the cost of reinstatement: *Ward v Cannock Chase DC* [1986] Ch 546, but may have to settle for a reasonably workmanlike repair rather than meticulous restoration if the latter is disproportionately expensive, as the excess amounts to over-compensation: *Dodd Properties (Kent) Ltd v Canterbury City Council* [1980] 1 WLR 433.

This is one area where the English courts have taken some account of efficient use of resources. In *Lodge Holes Colliery Co. v Wednesbury Corporation* [1908] AC 323, the council insisted on restoring a road damaged by subsidence exactly, including building it up to its original level, when it could have been left at a lower level just as well and far cheaper. Allowing the claimant to insist on exact replacement whatever the cost and whether it benefited him or not 'might lead to a ruinous and wholly unnecessary outlay' (an early instance of '*Wednesbury* unreasonableness'?) This was a case where there was no reason to insist on exact replacement, but if the property is of historical, architectural, or merely sentimental value, this must be weighed in the equation.

Generally, damages are assessed at the time of the tort, but if the cost of repairs is awarded, these will be assessed at the time they were incurred if it was reasonable to defer them until then. In considering what is reasonable, the claimant's financial position will be considered, particularly if liability is being denied: *Dodd Properties; London Congregational Union* v *Harriss & Harriss* [1985] 1 All ER 335.

13.4.3.2 **Chattels**

The basic measure of damage where a chattel is damaged or destroyed is diminution in value. This is usually taken as the cost of repair or replacement, which in turn will normally be market value. Where a unique item is destroyed the compensation, although reflecting the market value will, of course, not allow for replacement.

The cost of repair will not be allowed where it is excessive in relation to the pre-accident value. In *Darbishire* v *Warran* [1963] 1 WLR 1067 a vehicle was repaired at a cost of £192, but could have been replaced for under £100. This was held to be a case where the repair cost was disproportionate and the lower figure was awarded. Compare *O'Grady* v *Westminster Scaffolding* [1962] 2 Lloyd's Rep 238 where repairs costing £450 to a car valued at £150 were allowed because it was a cherished vehicle.

Compensation for loss of use is also recoverable. It is possible to use accountancy and actuarial techniques to calculate this accurately, but the courts have tended not to do this, but to adopt common-sense methods. Where the chattel is not being used to make a profit, damages for loss of use are typically calculated by reference to the notional cost of the capital tied up in the chattel. This approach has been taken in respect of publicly owned ships, such as warships and lightships: *Admiralty Commissioners* v *SS Chekiang* [1926] AC 637. An alternative approach is to consider the actual operating cost; this approach was taken in a case involving a Birmingham Corporation bus, although the court was concerned that this might reward inefficiency if the operating cost were unreasonably high: *Birmingham Corporation* v *Sowsbery* [1970] RTR 84.

Where the chattel is a profit-earning one, it will normally be appropriate to hire a substitute if it is damaged. This should avoid most claims for loss of profits, although any which arise in the period which elapses before the replacement is in place will be recoverable, as will the hire costs. There will of course be cases where no replacement is available and the measure of damages is then the actual or reasonably anticipated loss of profit.

A similar rule applies where a profit-earning chattel is destroyed, but the appropriate response is to replace the chattel as soon as possible. The measure of damages will therefore be the cost of the replacement, including any necessary adaptation and transport to the location of the destroyed item, together with any additional expenses incurred in the intervening period, such as wages for operatives who are kept idle, and compensation payable to third parties for delay.

> *Liesbosch Dredger* v *SS Edison* [1933] AC 449 (*Cases and Materials* (13.1.1.1))
>
> This case is also celebrated for the ruling that the financial position of the claimant must be ignored. In this case the owner of a dredger which was sunk did not have the capital available to buy a replacement, although one was available. Instead he hired a replacement. This was more expensive overall, but could be financed out of income earned while completing the dredging contract. The additional cost was not recoverable.

This rule has been forcefully criticized. It is not followed in contractual cases, was held inappropriate in the *Dodd Properties* case (see 13.4.3.1), and was specifically rejected in a 'consumer' case where the victim of a car accident was held justified in not paying to replace the car until after the litigation was settled, incurring higher hire costs and paying more in money terms for the replacement due to inflation: *Mattocks* v *Mann* [1993] RTR 13. However, the *Liesbosch* rule has been upheld against a haulage company who could not afford to replace an uninsured lorry, but were refused hire costs: *Ramwade Ltd* v *W J Emson & Co. Ltd* [1987] RTR 72.

  EXERCISE 13.4

What is the reason for disallowing claims based on the claimant's impecuniosity? Should the rule be specifically abolished or restricted to particular categories of case?

  QUESTION 13.4

Compare and contrast the damages rules for land and chattels. Are there any significant differences?

13.4.4 **Personal injuries**

Awards must be broken down into non-pecuniary loss (general damages for pain, suffering, and loss of amenities), pecuniary loss (loss of earnings, medical expenses, and other outlays) to date, and future pecuniary loss. The main reason is that interest is paid at different rates on these heads. Non-pecuniary loss is assessed at the date of trial and carries a fairly nominal rate of interest from the date the action was commenced. This reflects the fact that the claimant gets the benefit of an award at the higher figure appropriate to the date of trial. Interest on pecuniary loss to date runs from the date of the accident at half the normal rate. This is a rough and ready way of reflecting that the loss occurred over the period to trial. No interest is payable on future pecuniary loss; this is in fact a payment in advance: *Jefford* v *Gee* [1970] 2 QB 130.

13.4.4.1 **General damages**

Loss of amenity and pain and suffering normally attract a single award, but cover different ground. Loss of amenity is in essence the reduction in the capacity to enjoy life. It will depend in part on the nature of the injury, so that it will be greater where there is permanent loss of mobility, or of an organ or limb. Tetraplegia is regarded as the most serious loss of amenity, and attracted an award of £75,000 in 1986 (equivalent to some £165,000 in 2006): *Housecroft* v *Burnett* [1986] 1 All ER 332 (*Cases and Materials* (13.1.2.1)). The level of these awards has to be 'conventional' as money is not a direct recompense for suffering. The Law Commission in its Report on Damages for Pain Suffering and Loss of Amenity (No. 257) in 1999 considered that values of award had slipped behind legitimate expectations, based on various research exercises, although that was of course disputed by defendants (such as the NHS and insurance companies) who have to foot the bill; the Commission recommended very substantial increases across the board. In consequence the Court of Appeal held what amounted to a general review of a number of cases of varying levels of seriousness. The Court indicated that awards for the most serious injuries did need to be reviewed upwards by about one-third, although small awards were broadly correct and there was a tapering adjustment in between: *Heil* v *Rankin* [2000] 3 All ER 138. It will also depend in part on the characteristics of the claimant, so that there will be a higher award if the injury prevents or curtails continued enjoyment of sport or hobbies: *Moeliker* v *Reyrolle & Co. Ltd* [1977] 1 All ER 9.

One vexed area has been the level of award appropriate to a claimant so seriously injured as to be largely or wholly unaware of the reduction in quality of life. Logically it can be argued that the unconscious patient has not lost any amenity, in the sense of subjective enjoyment of the quality of life, but the practice is to award a reduced figure (it seems to be about 25% of the 'full' figure) on the basis that there is an objective diminution in the quality of life actually enjoyed.

? QUESTION 13.5

How does the fact that the claimant is unaware of his/her condition affect the award? (See *West & Son Ltd* v *Shephard* [1964] AC 326; *Lim Poh Choo* v *Camden & Islington AHA* [1980] AC 174; [1979] 2 All ER 910 (HL) (*Cases and Materials* (13.1.2.1).)

Pain and suffering is essentially subjective, and so no award will be made to a claimant who is wholly unconscious. It may include distress due to a consciousness of reduced life expectancy: section 1(1)(b) of the Administration of Justice Act 1982.

13.4.4.2 Pecuniary loss

Loss of earnings is recoverable, and usually causes little conceptual difficulty. There may be problems establishing exactly what the net loss was, particularly where the employment pattern was irregular, or overall earnings depended on overtime or piecework.

The cost of care is also recoverable. This includes the cost of private medical treatment, and the defendant cannot argue that NHS facilities were available free of charge: s. 2(4) of the Law Reform (Personal Injuries) Act 1948. Problems have arisen in relation to nursing care. If this is provided by a professional, it is clearly recoverable. Where it is provided by a relative out of a sense of moral obligation, it is strictly the case that the claimant has not suffered a loss, in the sense of paying for the care. The law takes the common-sense view that there is a need which is being met and the claimant should be in a position to reward the provider, even though it may, in these family cases, actually amount to compensation to a third party rather than to the accident victim: *Cunningham* v *Harrison* [1973] QB 942. This is the logic behind the refusal to allow the claim where the tortfeasor himself provided the care: *Hunt* v *Severs* [1994] 2 All ER 385 (*Cases and Materials* (13.1.2.2)).

It is clearly relatively easy to assess pecuniary loss to date, although in practice, especially in cases of average or below average complexity, a settlement figure is reached which can take a broad approach rather than analysing each item of the claim in fine detail.

On the other hand, it is extremely difficult to assess future loss. There are three key variables:

(a) the future progress of the injury;

(b) the impact of all the other vagaries of life, such as unrelated illness, on the claimant;

(c) the claimant's future employment prospects.

Until recently it was necessary to assess all these in every case, as the court was obliged to award a final lump sum to cover all heads of claim.

In all cases assumptions were made. In the case of the development of the injury, the main problem in practice is the uncertainty surrounding such complications as late onset post-traumatic epilepsy following head injuries or osteoarthritis following limb and joint injuries. In these cases the impact of the complication if it occurred is assessed and then discounted by the likelihood of it occurring. If osteoarthritis has a 'value' in the particular case of £30,000, and there is a 10% chance of it occurring, the damages are increased by £3,000. This of course has the result that the claimant is in effect gambling. He is hoping that he is getting £3,000 for 'nothing' against the risk of suffering substantial uncompensated additional harm. Clearly the figure for damages must always be the 'wrong' one.

The other factors, together with the necessary allowances for inflation and for the fact that the claimant receives a lump sum now rather than a stream of income over a period, and can invest that lump sum to produce further income, are dealt with by a complex process of discounting. The total loss per annum is calculated, and a multiplier is then used to get the final figure. Calculating such returns, for annuities, life assurance, etc. is a highly skilled task, and there is a profession, that of actuary, devoted to it. Judges have tradition-ally had little time for actuaries. As recently as 1984 Oliver LJ said in *Auty* v *NCB* [1985] 1 All ER 930: 'The predictions of an actuary can be only a little more likely to be accurate (and will almost certainly be less entertaining) than those of an astrologer.' There has been considerable pressure from the Law Commission and elsewhere for a more scientific approach. Shortly after the decision in *Auty* a set of actuarial tables for use in this situation was published by HMSO. In more recent cases there have been suggestions that the judges are prepared to use them, at least as the basis for the decision; e.g. Bingham MR in *Hunt* v *Severs* [1993] 4 All ER 180.

The traditional method has been rough and ready at best. In particular it has led to under-compensation because inflation has not been fully allowed for. Further, the courts have been very ready to accept arguments for reducing the multiplier. A young man on the threshold of his working life is unlikely to receive an award based on a multiplier of more than 18, although his potential working life is more than double that.

In *Wells* v *Wells* [1998] 3 All ER 481, the House of Lords redressed the balance slightly. Traditionally, it was assumed that damages would be invested in a mixture of shares and government securities as a prudent investor would do with his earnings. This provided a better rate of return, so a smaller capital sum was needed to secure a given annual multiplier. There was, however, a risk of loss, particularly with the shares. The House accepted that a recipient of very high damages was wholly reliant on them, and could take no risks. A more cautious investment strategy was indicated, and so the capital sum was to be increased accordingly.

> **?** **QUESTION** 13.6
>
> Does the tort system achieve full compensation in personal injury cases? If not, how could it be improved?

It is impossible to say what the 'right' level is for pain and suffering. Our awards are low compared to the USA, but this may not mean they are wrong. Compensation to the date of trial is fairly accurately assessed. Thereafter, the use of multipliers and the refusal to give proper weight to actuarial evidence tends to depress the value of awards.

13.4.4.3 Social security and other benefits

Awards of damages are tax free, so the calculations, e.g. of loss of earnings, must all be net of tax: *BTC* v *Gourley* [1956] AC 185.

Where the claimant has himself taken out insurance, or is entitled to a pension or other allowance as part of his terms of employment (whether the scheme is contributory or not), benefits received are regarded as independent of the defendant, and will thus not be set against damages. The principle was first established in relation to insurance, being justified on the basis that the claimant had paid for and earned those benefits: *Bradburn* v *GWR* (1874) LR 10 Exch 1. It was extended by analogy to the pension situation by *Parry* v *Cleaver* [1970] AC 1 (see *Cases and Materials* (13.1.2.3)), and applies even where the pension provider is also the tortfeasor: *Smoker* v *London Fire & Civil Defence Authority* [1991] 2 AC 502 (*Cases and Materials* (13.1.2.3)). The defendant is taken to be wearing two separate hats in this situation. *Parry* v *Cleaver* is also authority for stating that voluntary payments from charitable or other benevolent sources will be treated as independent and thus not set off.

Until about ten years ago a similar rule applied to contributory state benefits. One half of these only could be set off against damages for loss of earnings, on the basis that the claimant had in effect insured himself with his own national insurance contribution, so the *Bradburn* principle applied. This rule then applied to small claims up to £2,500 until 1998. There is provision in the latest legislation for its reinstatement, but no regulations have been made to allow this.

The rule for state benefits currently applying to all claims is that all benefits arising during the first five years of the incapacity period may be recouped from damages. The onus is on the defendant to obtain the recoupment figure and account to the Department of Social Security for it. However, recoupment applies only to the amounts awarded for loss of earnings and other specified heads, and applies to benefits which are directly relevant to this head of claim: Social Security (Recovery of Benefits) Act 1997. There is a detailed schedule indicating which benefits are recoupable against loss of earnings, cost of care, and loss of mobility respectively. Damages awarded for pain and suffering cannot be recouped.

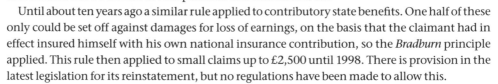
Sick pay received from an employer, or under a scheme administered by the employer will be deducted from the claim. The principle was established in *Hussain* v *New Taplow Paper Mills* [1988] AC 514 (*Cases and Materials* (13.1.2.3)), where the employer was also the tortfeasor, and the sick pay could be seen as in effect a payment on account of damages. The rule also applies to sick pay where the employer is not the tortfeasor unless the contract of employment contains, as it normally will, an obligation to refund sick pay if it is paid in consequence of a tortiously inflicted injury. In essence the law treats the employee as an agent for the purposes of reimbursing his employer who has shouldered a burden which properly falls on the tortfeasor.

EXERCISE 13.5

Consider the various types of payment. What, if any, is the basic rule which determines whether they are or are not deductible from damages?

13.4.4.4 **Provisional damages**

There is now a limited exception to the rule that damages must be awarded as a single lump sum. Where there is a recognized potential complication, there is now provision for an award of damages based on the claimant's condition on the assumption that this complication or deterioration will not arise. This award is of course itself a lump sum, with the imperfections discussed above.

The court records the nature of the anticipated problem, and the claimant is then allowed to apply to the court for a further award if, within the timescale set by the court, the problem does occur.

This provision (s. 32A of the Supreme Court Act 1981) is useful in some cases, where there is a specific and serious potential complication. It can only be used where there is a clearly identifiable problem; it will not assist where the claimant's prognosis cannot be firmly established. The provision has been further restricted by the decision in *Willson* v *Ministry of Defence* [1991] 1 All ER 638 (*Cases and Materials* (13.1.2.4)) that the section applies only to a specific 'clear and severable' event rather than the general risk of deterioration posed by conditions such as osteoarthritis. A further restriction on the use of the provision is the reluctance of insurers to agree to provisional awards. They have to keep their file open and cannot finalize their financial situation, so they put pressure on claimants to accept a conventional lump sum settlement. Such awards have, however, been made in cases where claimants have been affected by asbestos but are not suffering from serious asbestos-related disease and the risk of this is low. The awards have been very modest—£4,000 compared to a final award of £5–6,000: *Grieves and others* v *Everard and others* (2005), *The Times*, 22 March.

13.4.4.5 **Other exceptions to the lump sum rule**

There is power to obtain interim payments of damages on account of the final award. Although there are restrictions these do not apply to the majority of personal injury cases where the defendant will be insured. This power is particularly useful in cases where the claimant is suffering financial hardship, but a final resolution cannot be reached because his medical condition has not stabilized.

A recent development is the so-called 'structured settlement'. In these quite elaborate schemes, which are only suitable for the most serious cases, a lump sum award is made for general damages and pecuniary loss to date in the usual way, but all or part of the award for future pecuniary loss is made in the form of the purchase of annuities for the claimant by the defendant, rather than in a lump sum. This is cheaper than giving the claimant a lump sum to buy his own annuity, as the whole of the receipts under a structured settlement is treated as being capital and is not liable to tax, while part of the proceeds of any annuity which the claimant bought for himself, and any dividends or interest on investments he made would be taxable. While the claimant is guaranteed a certain level of income, this must be properly calculated and inflation-protected in exactly the same way as a conventional lump sum award. Such arrangements may now be ordered by the court irrespective of the consent of the defendant under s. 2 Damages Act 1996 (as amended by the Courts Act 2003), provided there are suitable guarantees of continuity of payment. The default rule is that inflation proofing is by reference to the Retail Price Index, but wage related inflation measures may be substituted where appropriate: *Flora* v *Wakom (Heathrow) Ltd* [2006] EWCA Civ 1103.

13.4.5 **Death**

Where the victim dies, the case cannot be treated just as a serious instance of personal injury. The main difference is the treatment of dependants. An award to an injured claimant is intended to replace his total income, out of which he is expected to maintain his dependants as he would have done out of his earnings. This is not how fatal cases are treated.

Funeral expenses are payable. The deceased person's personal representatives may have a claim for personal injuries on behalf of the estate if there was a significant gap between the infliction of injury and death, and this is assessed on the usual principles as set out above. Where death is essentially immediate there will be no claim under this head, as was established in the case brought on behalf of two victims of the Hillsborough disaster: *Hicks* v *Chief Constable of South Yorkshire* [1992] 2 All ER 65.

Statutory damages for bereavement are recoverable by the parents of a deceased minor, and by a bereaved spouse. This is a fixed, conventional sum under s. 1A of the Fatal Accidents Act 1976, which is currently £10,000. It is designed as recognition of, rather than in any real sense compensation for, the grief and distress of close relatives. There are some calls for higher awards to be made, but these seem to be for punitive rather than compensatory awards.

 EXERCISE 13.6

Consider whether you agree that bereavement should be recognized, as at present, by a modest conventional award.

   If not should there be:

- no compensation because it is indecent to place a monetary value on a life;
- very large compensation to reflect the enormity of the loss the bereaved have sustained.

At common law no action lay for the death of another, but there is now provision for dependants to make a claim for loss of dependence under the Fatal Accidents Acts 1846–1976.

In law, dependants include all ascendant and descendant relatives, close collateral relatives, established cohabitees, and children treated by the deceased as a child of the family. In fact they must prove that they were receiving some support from the deceased.

The usual situation is where the deceased was a breadwinner and supporting the claimant. Such claimants will typically be spouse or children, but if it can be shown that a child is supporting, or would in the future have supported elderly parents, etc., then they may claim: *Kandalla* v *BEA* [1981] QB 158. An alternative situation is where the deceased was providing benefits to the dependants by work as a homemaker. The value of the benefit must be established: *Berry* v *Humm & Co.* [1915] 1 KB 627. It may not be the full commercial cost of the services: *Spittle* v *Bunney* [1988] 3 All ER 1031.

In the typical case of a breadwinner with little surplus savable income, the dependence can virtually be calculated as the net income less the amount actually spent by the deceased on himself. When calculating the period of the dependence, allowance must be made for the vagaries of life as they affect the deceased, e.g. the possibility of unemployment, ill health, etc., and also as they affect the dependant, including the possibility of premature death, the point at which children are likely to achieve independence, and the possibility of divorce between a widow and the deceased (but not the widow's prospects of remarriage: s. 3(3) of the Fatal Accidents Act 1976).

13.4.6 **Aggravated and exemplary damages**

The normal principle for the award of damages in tort is a compensatory one. You have seen this at work in relation to common law negligence, occupiers' liability, breach of statutory duty, and product liability. Although this is the dominant principle, it is not the sole one. It is clearly recognized that in certain circumstances exemplary damages may be awarded. These are 'awarded by reference to the defendant's conduct and are intended to deter similar conduct in the future . . . and to signify condemnation or disapproval'. (Law Commission Consultation Paper No. 132, *Aggravated, Exemplary and Restitutionary Damages*, 1993.) Aggravated damages occupy a debatable middle ground between the exemplary and the compensatory principles. They are intended to cover intangible loss arising from injury to feelings, reputation, and personality as a result of the nature of the defendant's actions. The Law Commission's subsequent final report (No. 247, December 1997), confirmed the original analysis.

13.4.6.1 **The present law**

At present, entitlement to exemplary damages is based on a schematic rather than a principled approach. This derives from Lord Devlin's speech in *Rookes* v *Barnard* [1964] AC 1129 as reinterpreted by the House of Lords in *Broome* v *Cassell* [1972] AC 1027 (*Cases and Materials* (13.1.3.1)). The schematic approach is reinforced by the decision in *AB* v *South West Water Services Ltd* [1993] QB 507 that exemplary damages are only available in relation to causes of action where they had been established as available before the *Rookes* case.

Until recent cases and statutory reforms which gave the judges some control over the level of awards, there was also concern that jury awards could be capricious. In *Thompson* v *MPC* [1997] 3 WLR 403, the Court of Appeal laid down guidelines for the calculation of damages in police assault/malicious prosecution cases, which are an important category. Other guidance has been given for defamation cases. In *Thompson* it was stressed that exemplary damages are only relevant if a significant amount (say £5,000 minimum) would be the appropriate figure, but that they are demonstrative, and should be moderate. The sum of £25,000 is a high figure, and £50,000 the absolute ceiling for cases involving serious personal misconduct by senior officers. There are three categories of case where exemplary damages may be awarded.

Oppressive, arbitrary, or unconstitutional action by the servants of the government

These terms are *disjunctive*, so unconstitutional action which is not oppressive or arbitrary may qualify. This derives from the eighteenth-century civil liberty cases: *Wilkes* v *Wood* (1763) 98 ER 489, *Huckle* v *Money* (1763) 95 ER 768. The category is now a broad one. It extends to policemen, solicitors executing search and seize orders, and EC officials.

Many trespasses to the person fall squarely into this category. The Law Commission points out that it plays 'an important role in the protection of civil liberties' and 'it has been the basis for significant development in the law concerning police misconduct'.

Wrongdoing which is calculated to make a profit

It is not necessary that there be a precise calculation. The concept is a broad one and covers those cases, such as defamation in a tabloid newspaper, where the conduct is designed to be commercially profitable, and also cases of winkling out of tenants to use premises more lucratively. These are of course not typically cases of trespass to the person.

Statutory cases

The main instances are provisions of the Copyright, Designs and Patents Act 1988 which allow additional damages for breach of copyright and design right depending on the flagrancy of the breach and any benefit accruing to the defendant from the breach.

The last two categories of case could in fact be said to be restitutionary in nature. Albeit in a rough and ready way the defendant is being deprived of the fruits of his unjust enrichment, obtained by disregarding the claimant's legitimate interests. See also the use of a restitutionary measure in conversion (see 10.5.3.7 above).

13.4.6.2 **Proposals for reform**

The Law Commission proposed in its Report (No. 247, December 1997) the following reforms:

(a) that exemplary damages be renamed 'punitive damages' and that 'punitive damages would be available for a legal wrong (other than breach of contract) if the defendant has deliberately and outrageously disregarded the claimant's rights'. This will replace the current arbitrary and schematic approach: paras 1.19–1.23;

(b) that aggravated damages be renamed 'damages for mental distress' and be clearly understood to be compensatory in nature: para. 1.9;

(c) that the courts have power to award restitutionary damages in lieu of punitive damages where the justice of the case is best served by depriving the defendant of his improper gains rather than penalizing him, but that the detailed development of restitutionary damages be left to the judiciary: paras 1.10–1.13.

The central proposals for the reform of exemplary/punitive damages (which are incorporated into a draft Bill) are:

(a) The judge will decide on the availability and level of punitive damages;

(b) Punitive damages will only be available if the defendant has 'deliberately and outrageously disregarded the claimant's rights';

(c) Punitive damages may be awarded for any tort (common law or statutory) or equitable wrong. The cause of action test is to be abolished. No punitive damages are to be awarded for breach of contract;

(d) Punitive damages are to be additional to other remedies, but only given if the other remedies do not adequately punish the defendant for his conduct. They will not normally be given where the defendant has been convicted of an offence arising out of the same conduct.

(e) The amount must be sufficient to punish, but proportional to the gravity of the conduct, and take account of the defendant's culpability, the benefit he sought to achieve and other relevant matters.

(f) There are no proposals to include a punitive element in damages for bereavement.

No action has yet been taken to implement these proposals.

 EXERCISE 13.7

Consider whether there is room in the law of tort for damages which are not compensatory. Is it still part of the function of this branch of the law to punish rather than compensate?

13.4.7 Nominal damages

These are awarded when the claimant has established his case, particularly in relation to torts actionable per se, such as trespass, but has not shown that there is any actual loss. The award marks his success. It does not reflect badly on the claimant, who may have been making an important, if not expensive, point about, for instance, the existence of a right of way. There is a conventional figure (currently £10) which is awarded. In a jury trial particularly, if less than this (the traditional figure was a farthing, but it cannot now be less than a penny, being the smallest current coin of the realm) was awarded, this usually indicated that the claimant, though legally in the right, had acted harshly or unreasonably, and such an award is known as contemptuous damages. Such an award does of course reflect on the claimant.

13.4.8 Multiple defendants

As we have seen, many cases involve numerous parties. This can have an impact on liability in damages.

Independent tortfeasors
In this case there are two separate wrongs, and each defendant is responsible for his own actions as in *Performance Cars v Abraham* [1962] 1 QB 33 (2.2).

Joint tortfeasors
This may involve two or more parties acting together in a joint venture, as where two men agree jointly to beat up another, or where in law one person is regarded as legally responsible for another—as in the case of vicarious liability, or liability for breach of a non-delegable duty.

Each is fully liable for the whole of the damages, but because it is a single liability, if the claimant formally releases one defendant from liability, this also releases the others. However merely agreeing not to sue one defendant is not regarded as a release.

Several tortfeasors

This is where two or more tortfeasors separately contribute to the same harm, as in *Fitzgerald* v *Lane* [1989] AC 328 where two motorists collided in quick succession with the claimant.

Contribution

In principle the claimant can sue any one or more joint and several tortfeasors. He can only recover the total amount of his loss. If he does recover it all from one, that one can seek contribution from the others under the Civil Liability (Contribution) Act 1978. The liability must be in respect of the same damage, but it does not matter whether it arises in contract or in tort. Section 2(1) of the Act provides that the contribution shall be 'such as may be found by the court to be just and equitable having regard to the extent of that person's responsibility for the damage in question.' In principle this operates in the same way as contributory negligence does between the claimant and the defendant (see 14.3.4), although there have been cases where other factors, such as responsibility for a cover-up, have been held to be relevant: *Re-source America International* v *Platt Site Services Ltd* [2005] EWCA Civ 665.

13.5 Injunctions

Damages are all very well when harm has occurred and can be calculated, but in many cases prevention is better than cure. Also in many cases it will be difficult to work out what loss has been sustained. It is to deal with these cases that the equitable remedy of the injunction was developed. You saw in the introduction at 13.2 how injunctions are designed to supplement the common law remedy of damages and it is now time to explore this remedy in more depth.

The word injunction simply means 'order'. In this context it is an order of a court addressed to a party to litigation and requiring him to do, or refrain from doing, something on pain of punishment for contempt of court by way of fine, imprisonment, or sequestration of goods. Where the defendant is a public body an application may be made for a declaration that they are acting wrongfully. This will have much the same effect as an injunction.

It is important to recognize that there are different types of injunction. The main subdivisions are between interim and final injunctions and between negative and mandatory injunctions.

The first distinction is as to the stage in the proceedings that the injunction operates. An interim injunction takes effect, during the case, usually to maintain the existing position until the rights and wrongs can be sorted out. A final injunction is normally permanent and represents part of the final disposal of the case. A mandatory injunction positively requires the addressee of the injunction to do something, while a negative injunction requires him not to act. Negative injunctions are much commoner overall, and particularly at the interlocutory stage.

13.5.1 **Principles of the injunction**

The High Court may grant an injunction in any case where it is 'just and convenient' to do so: s. 37(1) of the Supreme Court Act 1981. This may be the only relief sought. In the county court an injunction may only be granted as ancillary to some other relief, but a purely nominal claim for damages will suffice: s. 38 of the County Courts Act 1984.

Although law and equity remain separate, they are administered together and the rules of equity prevail where there is a conflict. This had been recognized in the case of remedies since the *Earl of Oxford's Case* (1615) 21 ER 485, 576.

Equity operates on the conscience, so the judge must consider it to be the right and conscionable thing to do before he will grant an injunction. Injunctions are, in common with all equitable remedies, discretionary. However, this discretion is in the hands of judges, who behave consistently. There are clear guidelines as to when an injunction is likely to be granted, and on what terms.

13.5.2 **Where injunctions are likely to be useful**

There are many areas not involving tort where an injunction will be sought, but in relation to tort the most common areas of application will be those where there is a course of conduct, rather than a single incident. Unless that incident has been foreshadowed, it will not be practicable to seek an injunction, and damages will have to suffice.

If harm to the claimant is being clearly threatened, as where a neighbour is planning a rock festival, then an injunction may well be appropriate on a *quia timet* ('because he fears' (i.e. that there will be a nuisance)) basis.

The victim of a nuisance or repeated trespass, or indeed of harassment falling into the area in between and recognized as a tort by the Protection from Harassment Act 1997, is usually more concerned to prevent or halt the defendant than to claim damages. It is now accepted that where proprietary rights are being interfered with by a defendant who intends to carry on doing so, the claimant is 'entitled' to an injunction unless there is strong evidence that damages are an appropriate remedy: *Pride of Derby & Derbyshire Angling Association* v *British Celanese* [1953] Ch 149 (*Cases and Materials* (13.2.1)), a case concerning pollution of the River Derwent, over which the claimants had rights, which was likely to damage fish in an unpredictable manner.

An injunction can only be granted in respect of a legal wrong. So when a defendant called his house by the same name as the claimant next door, no injunction could be granted. The similarity of names was no doubt annoying, but there is no exclusive right to a house name: *Day* v *Brownrigg* (1878) 10 Ch D 294. The position might have been different if they were both traders or professionals and the similarity amounted to passing off the defendant as the claimant. Similarly, if a claimant complains of a range of activities, but not all are held to be tortious, the injunction can apply only to the tortious activities: *Kennaway* v *Thompson* [1981] 3 All ER 329 (*Cases and Materials* (13.2.1)).

 EXERCISE 13.8

Return to Exercise 13.1. Are injunctions relevant to any of these situations?

13.5.3 **Interim injunctions**

The court has to be careful in granting these. If the status quo is not preserved or restored, one party may be so damaged by what happens in the period before a full trial that he will not enjoy the benefit even if he wins. If, for example, a noise nuisance so affects a music teacher that all his pupils desert him, he may never be able to rebuild his practice. Care must, however, be taken that action is not taken on inadequate evidence, bearing in mind that the full trial is not taking place.

The normal approach is that in *American Cyanamid* v *Ethicon* [1975] AC 396 (*Cases and Materials* (13.2.2)):

(a) The claimant must first establish that there is a serious issue to be tried. This is not a major hurdle; it is really designed to weed out the frivolous and hopeless cases.

(b) The court will then investigate whether damages are an adequate remedy. If they will be then, unless there are special circumstances (e.g. that it is quite clear that the defendant will not be able to pay any damages) no injunction will issue.

(c) The court next considers the effect on the defendant of the grant of an injunction. In other words, assuming he wins at trial, whether damages will be an adequate remedy to him for the restrictions on his freedom of action imposed by the injunction.

If the issue remains balanced the court considers whether the claimant has acted expeditiously, whether the injunction is designed to restore the status quo or to maintain it, and finally, the relative strength of the parties' cases.

13.5.4 **Negative injunctions**

Although these are the most common they require little further discussion. The defendant is ordered not to behave in a particular way. If he does he is in breach. This is easy for the court to control. Provided the prohibited activity is properly defined it will be easy to recognize when there has been a breach.

It is, however, important to note that the injunction must be framed so as to cover only those activities which are actionable. Thus an injunction against noise from a factory may be expressed to apply only at night and at weekends.

13.5.5 **Mandatory injunctions**

These can be problematic for the court, in that they require the defendant to do things. The court is not in a position to police this, and there is considerable reluctance to grant a long-term mandatory injunction. In *AG* v *Staffordshire CC* [1905] 1 Ch 336 this was given as a reason for not granting an injunction to keep a right of way in a specified state of repair. Injunctions requiring one-off actions, such as demolishing a wall or other structure, will be granted more readily, at least where the application has been made before the work was too far advanced. In *Truckell* v *Stock* [1957] 1 WLR 161 an injunction was granted to remove a completed outbuilding which was built in part over the boundary, so was trespassing. It was significant that it was built almost up to an existing wall and this would be very difficult to maintain if the new structure were allowed to remain.

13.5.6 **Damages in lieu of an injunction**

An injunction will not normally be granted where damages is an adequate remedy, so it may seem surprising that there is power to award damages on a claim for an injunction. The power originated in Lord Cairns' Act 1858, which reduced the procedural difficulties then existing by allowing the equity courts to award damages, so avoiding the need for a second action if an injunction was refused. It is now contained in s. 50 of the Supreme Court Act 1981. It is sparingly exercised, since the effect of substituting an award of damages where the proper remedy is an injunction is to allow a wealthy defendant compulsorily to purchase the right to infringe the claimant's rights. You have already met *Miller* v *Jackson* [1977] 3 All ER 338 in relation to nuisance (see **Exercise 11.4**). The court declined to grant an injunction to restrain a continuing nuisance from cricket balls being hit into a garden. One argument was the relative utility of the activities of the parties, but this was rejected in *Kennaway* v *Thompson* [1981] 3 All ER 329 which is a similar case of nuisance by sporting activities. It is possible to support the decision in *Miller* on the grounds that the claimants moved to the nuisance. This line has been adopted in several US cases.

In *Dennis* v *Ministry of Defence* [2003] Env LR 34 (see 11.4.9.5) a declaration requiring the cessation of flying at RAF Wittering was refused on the ground that the activity was in the public interest, although the claimants were entitled to damages to compensate for their loss.

Where the wrong complained of is one which is commonly resolved by money payments, the judges are more willing to decline to grant an injunction or use this power. See, for instance, *Wrotham Park Estate* v *Parkside Homes* [1974] 1 WLR 798, where the complaint was that houses were built in breach of a restrictive covenant. It is well known that such covenants are released for cash. The judge indicated that the demolition of these houses would be a criminal waste of resources in the circumstances, which indicates some element of economic utility in his thinking. Similar considerations may apply to interference with rights of light: *Regan* v *Paul Properties* [2006] EWHC 1941 (Ch).

13.5.7 **Undertakings as to damages**

These are important in relation to interlocutory injunctions. The claimant must normally undertake to pay damages in respect of harm suffered by the defendant if the injunction is granted. Some claimants seek to get round this by applying for a final injunction, without also applying for an interlocutory one and in this case they do not have to give the undertaking. If the defendant carries on in the meantime, and then loses at trial, he may well have to undo all his work. This will be a substantial deterrent if this is, for instance, building work. Normally the claimant will be allowed to act like this, as in *Oxy Electric Ltd*.

Oxy Electric Ltd v *Zainuddin* [1990] 2 All ER 902 (*Cases and Materials* (13.2.3))

The claimants objected to the defendants' plan to erect a mosque on a particular site. The defendants argued that they could not proceed until after the trial, and that if they won, they would have to build the mosque later and at greater cost. This would have been covered by a cross-undertaking in damages. Nonetheless no order was made preventing the claimants from acting as they did.

It might have been otherwise if they had misled the defendants by initially indicating that they had no objection, or were ready to negotiate: *Blue Town Investments* v *Higgs & Hill* [1990] 1 WLR 696. Recently the Court of Appeal has reiterated in *Mortimer* v *Bailey* [2005] BLR 85 that there is no requirement to apply for an interlocutory injunction, at least where the claimant has made his objections clear, and has not suggested that he will settle for financial compensation.

■ SUMMARY

You should by now have some idea of this large, but often little explored aspect of the subject. Some of what you have read will no doubt be familiar from other subjects which you may have studied such as contract, land law, trusts, and equity. Indeed some of the other chapters of this text have touched on particular aspects of remedies. You cannot separate the claim and the remedy, either in real life or in the study of law.

The assessment of damages is a particular issue in tort. In the extracts from the cases in *Cases and Materials*, you will have seen comments from the judges about the imprecision of calculations, the difficulty of accurately predicting the future, and the absence of proper guidance (although the House of Lords has had much more to do with remedies in recent years, not always for the better). Many similar comments ended up on the cutting-room floor.

You should, however, have grasped the basic rule, that the claimant is to be put back as near as possible into the position he was in before the tort occurred, or that the tortfeasor should compensate for the harm he has done, and also recognized the main problems or anomalies:

- As damages for pain, suffering, and loss of amenity are consolation not compensation, the level of awards will always depend on judicial interpretation of the level of consolation society deems proper, which may well be too low.

- Where a claimant is too poor to take the cheapest option to restore his position, he may not be able to land the defendant with the excess costs.

- How far can the defendant bring collateral benefits into account?

In recognition of the nature of the topic there is rather more additional reading than usual. This is of particular relevance if you are thinking of becoming a professional lawyer.

Injunctive relief, which we have only touched on, is a rather better ordered branch of the law. Indeed one could almost say, tongue in cheek, that in the case of damages there is a right to a remedy but a fairly capricious allocation of awards, while with injunctions the grant is discretionary, but the discretion is applied on time-honoured and consistent principles.

■ FURTHER READING

Burrows, A., *Remedies for Torts and Breach of Contract**, 2nd edn, London: Butterworths, 1994.

Cooke, P.J. and Oughton, D.W., *The Common Law of Obligations*, 3rd edn, London: Butterworths, 2000. Section C (especially recommended because it brings the various causes of action and rules together and compares them; it is a long section of nearly 100 pages).

Harris, D., Campbell, D., and Halson, R., *Remedies in Contract and Tort**, 2nd edn, London: Butterworths, 2002.

Howarth, D., *Textbook on Tort*, 2nd edn, London: Butterworths, 2004, Chapters 11 and 13.

Jones, M.A., *Textbook on Torts*, 8th edn, London: Blackstone Press, 2002, Chapter 15.

Law Commission, Consultation Papers and Law Com Papers forming part of the review of damages, especially Nos 125 and 224 *Structured Settlements and Interim and Provisional Damages*; Nos 132 and 247 *Aggravated, Exemplary and Restitutionary Damages*; No. 140 *Damages for Personal Injury: Non-pecuniary loss*, No. 225 *Personal Injury Compensation: How much is enough*, and No. 257 *Damages for Pain, Suffering and Loss of Amenity*. (These papers provide a clear account of the present state of the law, the problems identified, and proposals for reform. They usually also contain an instructive comparison with the position in other common law jurisdictions.)

Markesinis, B.S. and Deakin, S.F., *Tort Law*, 5th edn, Oxford: Oxford University Press, 2003, Chapter 8.

Murphy, J., *Street on Torts*, 11th edn, London: Butterworths, 2003, Chapters 26–27.

Winfield and Jolowicz on Tort, 17th edn, London: Sweet & Maxwell, 2006, Chapter 28.

*These are full treatments, at book length.

 CHAPTER 13 ASSESSMENT EXERCISE

(1) Penny, a sole practitioner solicitor and Alf, her husband, who does not work but looks after their two small children, are injured in a car crash. This is entirely the fault of the other driver, Dan.

Penny is unable to work for twelve months. Her net profits after tax for the last three years averaged £50,000. She has received state benefits totalling £10,000 in that period. She suffered multiple injuries including a fractured pelvis. She will not be able to have any more children, although she and Alf were hoping to have a family of six. One of her arms has suffered very serious soft tissue damage and may have to be amputated at some time in the future.

Alf is in a coma for two weeks. He then recovers consciousness. He is totally paralysed and helpless. After a further six weeks he dies.

Penny's mother looks after Penny and the children until Penny is able to return to work. Penny then employs a nanny and housekeeper at a total cost of £20,000 per annum.

Advise Dan of the basis on which he will be liable in damages.

You have been given some figures to assist you in working out the likely award under some of the heads of damage, but you will only be able to indicate others in outline.

(2) Charon operates a number of speedboats on the River Styx. Pluto, who has lived near the river for thirty years and Persephone, who has just moved to the area, both complain about noise. This is mainly when the boats are starting out and when engines are being tested. There is a large fence on Charon's land to deaden the sound, but this has fallen into disrepair. Charon offers to provide double glazing for both the complainants. Pluto rejects the offer out of hand, Persephone provisionally agrees, but later changes her mind. Both Pluto and Persephone apply for a final injunction preventing Charon operating speedboats at all, or in the alternative requiring him to repair and keep in repair the fence. Charon is in the process of erecting a large boathouse.

Advise Charon.

See *Cases and Materials* (13.4) for a specimen answer.

14 | General defences

14.1 OBJECTIVES

By the end of this chapter you should be able to:

1 Explain the principles governing the defences applicable to the law of tort generally

2 Distinguish them from each other

3 Apply them to factual situations, where relevant

14.2 Introduction

'Defences' is a topic which the learner should have in mind throughout a study of the law of tort, and always have at the ready when attempting to solve a problem.

As a general rule the burden of proving a defence is on the defendant. The defences themselves are as follows:

- *volenti non fit injuria*
- illegality/*ex turpi causa non oritur actio*
- necessity
- contributory negligence
- mistake
- inevitable accident
- duress
- self-defence
- defence of property

In this chapter we shall concentrate on *volenti*, illegality, necessity, and contributory negligence; but first we will examine briefly mistake, inevitable accident, duress, self-defence, and defence of property.

Other general defences—Act of God and, particularly, statutory authority—are of more importance in the context of some of the named, or 'nominate', torts, such as nuisance, and some forms of trespass. Accordingly, you will find discussion of these defences, where relevant, in those chapters.

It is also the case that:

(a) reference will be made in specific contexts to specific defences, for example, fair comment in relation to defamation;

(b) causation and remoteness of damage are in reality forms of defence because issues relating thereto will be raised by the defendant (see **Chapter 2**).

14.2.1 **Mistake**

It is probably more accurate to state that there is no general concept of mistake as a defence per se in tort. Mistake can be pleaded, however, by a defendant in specific circumstances as a means of escaping liability.

Some torts require no intent beyond a voluntary act as in conversion and trespass to land. In *Baseley* v *Clarkson* (1681) 3 Lev 37, it was said that if X walks on to Y's land under the honest mistake that he thinks it is his, or that he has a right to be on it, his mistake will be no defence. It seems to follow, therefore, that mistake is no defence where liability is strict.

As a general proposition it can be stated that in those torts where liability is strict, for example, nuisance, trespass to land, and conversion, a defendant is liable irrespective of any mistake or negligence on his part.

 QUESTION 14.1

Can you guess what the position is in the case of other types of tort?

Where liability depends on intent, or motive, or unreasonable behaviour, mistake is a factor taken into account when determining liability. In the tort of deceit, for example, the claimant must prove the dishonesty, or fraud, of the defendant and obviously, the question of honest mistake will be relevant. The tort of negligence is based on the behaviour of the 'reasonable man' and the question may arise as to whether this hypothetical being would have made the mistake made by the defendant.

Any mistake pleaded by a defendant must be one of fact, because of the principle summed up in the Latin expression '*ignorantia juris neminem excusat*', that is, ignorance of the law is no excuse. This principle is of universal application in law, and applies equally to the law of tort.

14.2.2 **Inevitable accident**

If a defendant pleads 'inevitable accident' he is really saying that a 'reasonable man' in his position at the time of the accident could not have avoided doing what he did in the circumstances, taking into account any precautions that would have been expected from the reasonable man.

According to *Winfield* (pp. 746–7) inevitable accident has no place in the tort of negligence, or any other tort based on fault, because it is the claimant's task to prove that the defendant was at fault, **not** for the defendant to exonerate himself. The learned author contends that it is equally irrelevant in torts of strict liability, simply because the defendant's fault in those cases is not in issue. It may, however, have a role to play in those cases of negligence where *res ipsa loquitur* applies. In these cases some burden of exculpation is placed on a defendant. This topic is dealt with at 1.7.3.

By the same token, 'inevitable accident' may be relevant in any other tortious situation in which the defendant is expected to extricate himself from an inference of liability. *Winfield* suggests this may be the case with highway authorities' liability for injury resulting from the state of the highway (p. 747, n. 84).

14.2.3 Duress

> **? QUESTION** 14.2
>
> Can you think of the forms 'duress' might take?

You might have written that 'duress' can take the following forms:

(a) threats of force, violence, or unlawful acts;

(b) physical compulsion;

(c) 'economic' duress.

The balance of opinion amongst academic writers seem to be that only actual physical compulsion will suffice for the defence of duress.

It seems that duress may also negative the defence of consent. Consent is dealt with later in this chapter, at 14.3.1.1.

14.2.4 Self-defence

It is a well-established defence for a defendant to plead that the damage complained of by the claimant is inflicted by way of self-defence, certainly of the defendant's own person and possibly of the person of a third party. A 'third party' defence would probably be all the stronger if the defendant had a duty to protect that third party. Most cases where self-defence is alleged are cases of trespass, so this topic is dealt with in more depth in connection with those torts in **Chapter 10** (10.4.3.9).

> **? QUESTION** 14.3
>
> Would a defendant be allowed to plead that he had a right of self-defence because he acted under the mistaken, but honest, belief that he could so act?

In *Rigby* v *Chief Constable of Northants* [1985] 2 All ER 985, it was held that the defence cannot be based solely on such a basis. There must be an objective case for self-defence in the circumstances. See also *Bici & Bici* v *Ministry of Defence* [2004] EWHC 786 (QB); *Ashley* v *Chief Constable of Sussex* [2006] EWCA Civ 1085. Note, however, the point made by Street in connection with defence of property; see 14.2.5.

There are three main characteristics of the defence (though each case must be assessed in the light of its factual circumstances):

(a) the response of the defendant must be reasonable in the circumstances; and

(b) the defensive measures must be proportionate to the harm threatened;

(c) the defensive measures may be taken before any physical contact occurs; in other words, the defence can be activated as soon as an attack is threatened.

In *Collins* v *Renison* [1754] Say 138, the claimant, a trespasser, was on a ladder in the defendant's garden and refused to descend when requested to do so by the defendant. The defendant's plea, that he '. . . gently shook the ladder . . . and gently overturned it and gently threw the plaintiff from it upon the ground' was rejected by the court. It was found that the defendant's use of force was disproportionate to the claimant's resistance and he was liable in damages in trespass to the person.

The issue of an occupier's liability to trespassers upon his land, including the question of deterrent and retributive measures taken against such entrants, is discussed in 6.6.

Where the defendant has responded to a threat, as distinct from actual contact, he will have to show that the claimant was likely to carry out the threat. This will include the ability of the claimant to do so.

14.2.5 Defence of property

This defence, though apparently recognized in principle, is not so readily accepted in practice as self-defence, so it is harder to justify. It seems to overlap with necessity; indeed, the same is true of self-defence.

As Street puts it (p. 92): 'One may use reasonable force to defend land or [goods] in one's possession against any person threatening to commit or committing a trespass to the property.'

The author further indicates, however, at p. 93:

> As with defence of the person, if the defendant has a reasonable belief that force is essential to end the trespass, he may use it although he is mistaken in thinking it to be necessary, but if he mistakenly believes that the claimant is a trespasser, he has no defence. What is reasonable force . . . depends on the facts.

In relation to self-defence we saw that the question of whether reasonable force had been used was a matter of fact in each case, and the same is true in the present context. No doubt, violence can be met with proportional force; non-violence will require an equally appropriate response.

There is a defence of defending the property of other persons from one's own household, according to *Street* (p. 90) quoting Blackstone (an eighteenth-century jurist).

14.2.6 Provocation

Provocation does not appear to be a defence in the usual sense, but it may operate as a mitigating factor. In *Gray* v *Barr* [1971] 2 QB 554, Lord Denning said: '. . . [the court] can take into account [in awarding damages] not only circumstances which go to aggravate damages, but also those which go to mitigate them'. This is authority for the proposition that provocation may well affect the amount of damages awarded.

In *Lane* v *Holloway* [1968] 1 QB 379, it was said that provocation could eliminate any exemplary damages but would not affect any general, compensatory award. The claimant's conduct in this case was, however, regarded as trivial in comparison with the defendant's retaliatory action, and the defendant was treated as being solely responsible for the claimant's damage. The retaliatory response of the defendant was the result of the claimant's description of the defendant's wife as 'a monkey-faced tart'.

In *Barnes* v *Nayer* (1986), *The Times*, 19 December, May LJ seemed to agree with the point on mitigation of exemplary, but not compensatory damages; he said that a person who provokes someone else is still entitled to full compensation if the response to the provocation is out of all proportion to what has been offered by the other side.

14.3 **The remaining major defences**

We now have to deal with the general defences: *volenti non fit injuria*; illegality; necessity; contributory negligence.

 EXERCISE 14.1

Read *Murphy* v *Culhane* [1976] 3 All ER 533, in *Cases and Materials* (14.1). Explain the issue before the Court of Appeal and the outcome of the appeal.

The question to be answered by the court was whether the defences of *ex turpi causa*, contributory negligence, and *volenti* applied in a claim for trespass to the person. The question was answered in the affirmative.

14.3.1 *Volenti non fit injuria*

We are concerned here with a defence of general application in the law of tort, which is also a complete defence, that is, a defendant who is successful in his plea of *volenti non fit injuria* ('no injury is done to one who consents') will escape liability completely. It is usually encountered in cases of personal injury, though it could apply to damage to property. This is a defence of considerable antiquity, and it embraces the whole spectrum of 'acceptance', by the claimant, of the defendant's tortious, or potentially tortious conduct. *Volenti* embraces three forms of 'acceptance', which are not always sufficiently articulated:

- consent
- exclusion of liability
- voluntary assumption of risk

Rather than use *volenti* indiscriminately, as is often the case, it is preferable, and avoids confusion, to differentiate between each of the three elements of acceptance.

Jones (p. 387) puts the point well:

> *Volenti non fit injuria*, the plaintiff's voluntary assumption of risk, is a defence that is in a state of some confusion. This is partly due to a considerable overlap with other conceptual techniques employed to limit or reduce a defendant's liability, such as the exclusion of liability, contributory negligence, and the standard of care in negligence. The main problems, however, stem from the indiscriminate use of the word 'consent' in different contexts and for different purposes.

14.3.1.1 **Consent**

This expression is best understood as conveying the defence for intentional torts; the majority of writers seem to be agreed on this point—*Salmond*, *Street*, and *Winfield* hold this view. There is 'consent' to something specific; it is commonly encountered in cases involving trespass to the person, dealt with at 10.4. Consenting to a surgical operation, or other medical procedure, or to a fair rather than foul, tackle in a rugby match, are only some examples of consent to interference with the person in the form of assault and battery. Consent in these contexts, and others, is dealt with as appropriate throughout this book.

In these cases it is said that the effect of the permission, or consent, is to prevent conduct, which would otherwise be actionable, from being tortious. To put it another way, consent prevents a duty in tort arising at all; it legalizes what would otherwise be tortious. An occupier's permission to enter premises, or land, for instance, makes entry legal that would otherwise be a trespass. As *Winfield* (p. 823) says this sort of permission, or consent, is usually described as the claimant's 'leave' or 'licence'; but this is, in essence, only a matter of nomenclature: the legal effect is the same.

In *Gillick v West Norfolk and Wisbech Area Health Authority* [1985] 3 All ER 402 (HL), it was held that a circular issued to Area Health Authorities by the Department of Health and Social Security, advising them that a doctor, consulted by a girl under 16, would be acting lawfully if he prescribed contraceptives for her use, was found by the House of Lords to be lawful. The girl's mother had asked the court for a declaration that the advice was unlawful. Their Lordships said that a person under 16 could consent to such advice and treatment without the need for any parental consent, provided the child had the ability to appreciate the situation.

In *Re T* [1992] 4 All ER 649 (CA), it was held that prima facie every adult has the right and capacity to decide whether or not he/she will accept medical treatment even if such refusal may risk permanent injury to his/her health; or even lead to premature death; and regardless of whether the reasons for the refusal are rational or irrational, unknown or even non-existent. However, if an adult patient did not have the capacity to decide at the time of the purported refusal and still does not have that capacity, or if his/her capacity to make a decision has been overborne by others, it is the duty of the doctors concerned to treat him/her in whatever way they consider (in accordance with their clinical judgment) to be in his/her best interests: *F v West Berkshire Health Authority* [1989] 2 All ER 545(HL); *Frenchay Healthcare NHS Trust v S* [1994] 2 All ER 403 (CA). You will find extracts from these cases in *Cases and Materials* (14.2.1.1).

In *Airedale NHS Trust v Bland* [1993] 1 All ER 821 (HL), it was held that artificial feeding and antibiotic drugs may lawfully be withheld from an insensate patient with no hope of recovery when it is known that the result will be that the patient will shortly thereafter die, if responsible and competent medical opinion is of the view that it would not be in the patient's best interests to prolong his life by continuing that form of medical treatment.

Permission to withdraw treatment must always be sought from the courts before any action is taken, otherwise the person(s) in charge of the treatment may be acting unlawfully. Withholding treatment is regarded as an omission, not a deliberate or positive act.

You may think that the provisions of the European Convention on Human Rights would be relevant in this context, more particularly Art. 2, the right to life, and Art. 3, the right not to suffer degrading treatment.

In *NHS Trust A* v *M* [2001] Fam 348, it was found that an omission was not, in general terms, sufficient to satisfy Art. 2 and *Bland* was approved on this point; nor was there any breach of Art. 3, which was only applicable, in any case, where a patient could feel pain and be aware of the effects of the treatment in question.

See, also, the important decision in *Chester* v *Afshar* (2.4.2.3); and the discussion of *Sidaway* in 10.4.3.4, where you will find reference to the notion of 'informed consent'.

? QUESTION 14.4

Consider whether consent can be implied from a claimant's conduct.

Although consent is commonly said to be 'express', that is the claimant has specifically addressed his mind to the issue, for example, giving written consent to a surgical operation (oral consent would perform the same function, though problems of evidence might then arise), consent may be implied from the circumstances.

Taking part in a sporting activity is one example of this. A participant in such an activity is taken to have consented, within the rules of the game, to bodily contact with other participants that might otherwise amount to trespass to the person. You may wish to refer to the decision in *Condon* v *Basi*, which is discussed in **Chapter 10** (10.4.3.7).

Implied consent can also be used to justify emergency medical treatment, though the defence of necessity probably offers a more plausible rationale for the doctor's, or other medical worker's, immunity from suit in such circumstances. Necessity cannot be used where the defendant knows that the claimant does not wish to have the treatment.

In *Arthur* v *Anker* [1996] 3 All ER 783, the Court of Appeal held that a claimant who had parked his car on private land without permission, but who had seen a notice to the effect that vehicles would be clamped and subject to a release charge, had impliedly consented to the terms of the notice.

Duress or fraud may vitiate consent where it affects the very nature of the interference to which the claimant has consented. In *Hegarty* v *Shine* (1878) 4 LR Ir 288, the claimant contracted venereal disease from her lover. It was held that there was no battery (trespass to the person) on the facts, because the sexual intercourse which had taken place was not obtained by deceit (fraud). The claimant knew full well the nature of the physical interference; she had not been deceived as to the nature of the act itself. The defendant's false statement that he did not have the disease did not affect the nature of the act of intercourse. Had there been fraud she could have sued in the tort of deceit. This Irish authority must be treated with caution on its facts, because the court based its decision partly on the illegality of the claimant's conduct; but it can still be used as authority to illustrate the basic point about the nature of consent.

In *R* v *Tabassum* (2000), *The Times*, 26 May (CA), three women consented to the defendant feeling their breasts because they thought he was medically qualified; the defendant had asked several women to take part in a breast cancer survey he was carrying out in connection with preparing a database software package to sell to doctors. He gave the impression that he was medically qualified. It was held that there was no true consent on the part of the complainants because they were only consenting to contact for medical purposes, by someone with relevant medical qualifications: they were consenting to the nature of the act but not to its quality. The defendant had rightly been convicted of indecent assault.

The question of consent to an illegal act also arises. Although in criminal law consent may be no bar to proceedings, as in *R* v *Brown* [1993] 2 WLR 556, in which the House of Lords held, by a majority, that participants in certain sado-masochistic practices could be criminally liable for their mutual infliction of harm, in spite of each person's willingness to undergo the physical abuse, it was held in *Murphy* v *Culhane* (see 14.3.4) that consent can block a claim for damages in the civil law. Illegality is examined at 14.3.2.

14.3.1.2 Exclusion of liability/agreements not to sue

This is sometimes referred to as 'express' *volenti* but it is submitted that this is a misnomer. Exclusion of liability is better understood as a distinct defence, separate from consent (discussed above) and voluntary assumption of risk (discussed below).

At common law a defendant, could, by means of contract or other agreement or notice, either exclude or restrict any duty in tort which he would otherwise owe the claimant. Issues may arise in these cases involving the incorporation of terms, and the bringing of conditions to the notice of the claimant. **Chapter 6** deals with occupiers' liability, which illustrates the general point now being made.

The essential point to grasp here is that the terms of the agreement will govern whether the defendant is able to escape liability. Certain limitations may exclude or restrict a party's liability.

In the case of business contracts, the Unfair Contract Terms Act 1977 imposes some important limitations on a party's power to exclude or restrict liability. There is a more detailed discussion on this matter in **Chapter 6**. Although the matter is discussed in relation to occupiers' liability, what is said is also illustrative of the position in tort generally. It may be noted that the 1977 Act applies not only to attempts at exclusion of liability but also attempts to restrict liability. The 1977 Act is set out in *Cases and Materials* (14.1.1.2).

It is likely that the common law rule relating to incorporation of terms in contracts, and the *contra proferentem* rule of construction are applicable here. These are matters concerning the law of contract and works on that subject should be consulted for further information.

Section 29 of the Public Passenger Vehicles Act 1981 provides that an operator of public service vehicles cannot, by contract, negative or restrict liability for personal injury or death to his passengers. Under s. 149 of the Road Traffic Act 1988, any attempt by the user of a private motor vehicle to exclude or restrict the duty of care owed to a passenger by 'any antecedent agreement or understanding between them' is void. On the authority of *Pitts* v *Hunt* [1990] 3 All ER 344, s. 149 also catches voluntary assumption of risk (see 14.3.2.1).

In some cases, for example, attempts to avoid safety legislation, the courts will 'strike out' exclusion notices which are 'repugnant to statute'. **Chapter 7** deals in detail with the action for breach of statutory duty. The legal effect of 'exclusion' or agreement not to sue is the same as for consent and it is obvious that there can, ultimately, be no rigid and absolute dividing line between the two defences. Exclusion or agreement can, and does extend to liability for negligence and the claimant must be a party to the agreement. In contrast, 'consent' is traditionally associated with 'intentional' torts, and can arise by implication.

Where consent and voluntary assumption of risk are concerned, the defence turns on the question of whether the claimant has actually consented or agreed to accept the risk of injury, whereas exclusion or restriction of liability pivots merely on the question of whether the defendant has effectively brought the term to the notice of the claimant. In short, 'has the defendant effectively disclaimed liability?' It will not avail the claimant to plead that he has not read or taken note of the excluding term if he ought to have done so in the circumstances.

14.3.1.3 Voluntary assumption of risk

This is sometimes known as 'implied assumption of risk' (*Winfield*, p. 730) as contrasted with 'express assumption of risk'. It has just been argued, however, that express assumption of risk, where it takes the form of some contractual undertaking or agreement not to sue, is best regarded as a free-standing defence. In the case of some non-contractual agreements, it may be correct to describe it as a form of express assumption of risk.

? **QUESTION** 14.5

How does 'voluntary assumption' of risk differ from 'consent' and 'exclusion of liability' or 'agreement not to sue'?

It differs from 'consent' in that it has reference to the risk of injury occurring; consent refers to the certainty of some particular interference. It differs from 'exclusion' or 'agreement not to sue' in that it is a waiver of liability implied in the circumstances.

Voluntary assumption of risk is usually associated with the tort of negligence, although it is conceivable that a claimant could assume the risk of some intentional or deliberate interference, where his conduct is such that the defendant is led to the conclusion that he has consented to the interference. Support for this contention can be found in the judgment of Sir John Donaldson MR in *Freeman* v *Home Office (No. 2)*. Further reference to this case can be found in **Chapter 10** (10.4.3.5).

Risk

It is meaningless in legal terms to inquire whether a claimant has impliedly assumed a risk, where that risk is not even remotely tortious in nature. Confusion can arise when, for example, even judges sometimes refer to the fact that everyone runs the risk of injury when using the highway. Although modern traffic conditions are dangerous, it is only where someone is guilty of tortious behaviour that the question of whether the injured party has waived his right to sue arises. The same is true, for example, in relation to the ordinary, usual, and incidental risks that spectators have to face at dangerous sporting activities.

The defence is only relevant where either:

(a) it is established that the defendant is in breach of his duty to the claimant, that is, has apparently committed a tort against him. In this case, the effect of assumption of risk is to negate the breach of duty; or

(b) the waiver of his right to sue by the claimant prevents any duty arising in the first place. Of course, a duty can only arise in relation to conduct that could be tortious: if a traffic accident would have occurred however carefully a vehicle driver had conducted himself, the defence is hardly relevant. In the tort of negligence, the duty of a vehicle driver is to observe the standard of care of a reasonable man acting in the circumstances of the particular case.

Agreement

'Voluntary assumption of risk' is usually concerned with negligent behaviour on the part of a defendant.

? QUESTION 14.6

We examined the tort of negligence in **Chapter 1**. What difficulties might be encountered with a defence based on the implied waiver by a claimant of his legal right to sue if he is injured as the result of the defendant's negligence?

In many cases of negligence the form taken by the negligent behaviour is not known until after the relevant events have occurred, and liability is based on an ex post facto inquiry. In other words, liability is fixed retrospectively, by posing the question: 'How would a reasonable man have conducted himself in the circumstances of the defendant?' The driver of a car, for example, owes a duty to take care for the safety of all other road users; but the breach of duty can take a number of forms, because driving involves many functions of the brain and limbs. In the absence of some express provision, or consent, how can a court determine the extent of the claimant's waiver?

Implied *volenti* probably causes most difficulty and is often obscured by the 'standard of care' cases (below). In general, the courts are reluctant to accede to its use because it can so easily become a licence to commit negligence in those cases where consent precedes the act of negligence.

This reluctance was behind the decision in *Dann v Hamilton* [1939] 1 KB 509, in which the claimant accepted a drunken driver's offer of a lift in his car. The claimant was found not to be *volenti*. The court was reluctant to conclude that she willingly accepted the legal consequences of voluntary assumption, as opposed to realizing that she was doing something dangerous.

This decision was distinguished in *Morris v Murray* on the ground that the aircraft trip in that case 'served no useful social purpose'. In *Dann* the female claimant needed to get home, late at night, after a party.

Today, the argument on the applicability of *volenti* in the context of this would be superfluous because of s. 149 of the Road Traffic Act 1988.

The defence of contributory negligence was not raised in *Dann* although at that time it would have been a complete defence, but *Owens v Brimmell* [1977] QB 859 (and other cases) suggest that this defence might now succeed on such facts as a partial defence allowing responsibility to be apportioned.

As *Winfield* (p. 730) puts it: '. . . a quite extraordinary situation would have to exist for the court to be justified in holding that the claimant had consented generally to lack of reasonable care by the defendant'.

There is considerable authority for the proposition that even where implied assumption of risk is concerned, there should exist something in the nature of an agreement between the parties. The reasoning here is that the claimant has a detailed awareness of the particular risk(s) in question.

? **QUESTION** 14.7

Can you think of another reason why an agreement is thought to be necessary?

Acceptance of risk must be freely given; it must be a full, free, and unfettered acceptance, so an agreement will be good evidence that this is the case.

Jones (p. 388) defines *volenti non fit injuria*

> as . . . a voluntary agreement by the claimant to absolve the defendant from the legal conse-
> quences . . . of harm created by the defendant, where the claimant has full knowledge of both the
> nature and extent of the risk [involved in the particular case].

The decision in *Nettleship* v *Weston* [1971] 3 All ER 581, discussed in 1.7.3, is strong authority for the proposition that an agreement between the parties is necessary.

Some judges are prepared to accept implied assumption of risk without the need for an 'agreement'. In *Morris* v *Murray* [1990] 3 All ER 801 (CA), the claimant and the pilot of an air-craft had met in a pub and together consumed a large volume of alcohol. It was agreed after some hours of drinking that they would take a trip together in the aircraft. As a result of the negligence of the drunken pilot, the aircraft crashed. The pilot was killed and the claimant was badly injured. The claimant brought an action for damages against the pilot's estate.

At first instance, the defendant's alternative plea of contributory negligence was accepted, the claimant's damages being reduced by 20%, and the defence of voluntary assumption of risk was rejected. On appeal, however, the plea of voluntary assumption of risk succeeded. Fox LJ said that the drunken escapade

> was fraught with danger from the start. If the [claimant] had been sober at the time he must be taken
> to have accepted fully the risk of serious injury. The danger was both obvious and great . . . [he must
> have known] that the deceased . . . was [not] capable of discharging a normal duty of care.

Although the claimant had himself been drinking 'he was certainly not "blind drunk" and was capable of appreciating the risks involved in what was merely a form of "entertain-ment"'. This flight served no useful social purpose and there was no need or compulsion for the claimant to join in. By embarking upon the flight the claimant implicitly waived his rights in the event of injury consequent on the deceased's failure to fly with reasonable care. He accepted the risks and implicitly discharged the deceased from liability. The possibility of a claimant being able to plead that drunkenness prevented him from 'consenting' was left open.

In rejecting contributory negligence, his Lordship said that the wild irresponsibility of the venture was such that the law should not intervene to award damages. Flying with a drunken pilot was great folly. He pointed out that the defence of voluntary assumption of risk had been abrogated by statute for passengers in motor vehicles covered by insurance, although there did not exist any similar enactment relating to aircraft which was applicable to the present case. The court did not see any merit at all in the claimant's claim, and was loath to allow the defence of contributory negligence, because to do so would have given the claimant some compensation.

The claimant had implicitly waived his rights which means in legal terms that he had abandoned his legal remedy against the defendant. It was a crucial fact that the deceased pilot was very drunk indeed and incapable of performing the complex task of piloting an aircraft, and that the claimant must have been well aware of this state of affairs.

If this is a correct line of reasoning, it would seem to follow that it might only be contributory negligence on the part of the claimant to take a trip in an aircraft piloted by someone who was only slightly under the influence of alcohol. On this basis, the distinction to be made in such situations would be between degrees of foolhardiness on the part of a claimant: the greater the state of intoxication of the pilot, the greater the risk the claimant would be taking with his safety.

Morris seems to suggest that there comes a point at which the claimant must have abandoned all thought of self-preservation; or at least is being recklessly indifferent to the matter. At this juncture voluntary assumption of risk is appropriate as a defence. With respect, it must be dangerous to fly with someone who is subject to any degree of intoxication; no doubt, the greater the state of drunkenness the greater the danger of an accident. In which case, the defence of contributory negligence, to be discussed shortly, offers the court a means of judging the degree of a claimant's lack of care for his own safety.

The true situation in *Morris* is that the court did not want to award the claimant any compensation at all, on the ground that he had, in the circumstances, taken an unreasonable risk with his own safety. Unfortunately that is also the basis of the defence of contributory negligence, as we will soon discover, and it may be argued that the decision in *Morris* does little to clarify the distinction between the two defences. According to *Pitts* v *Hunt* (see 14.3.2.1), a claimant cannot be 100% to blame under the legislation governing contributory negligence.

? | **QUESTION** 14.8

Can you think of another reason for the dilemma facing the Court in *Morris*?

Contributory negligence applies where the claimant is partly to blame, with the defendant, for his own injury. In *Morris*, although there was no doubt that the claimant had been extremely careless for his own safety, it could not be said that the defendant was not also to blame. In fact, in this case, both parties were *in pari delicto*, i.e. equally to blame. They were engaged, jointly, in a grossly hazardous activity.

Do you think that the court would feel justified, if the defence of contributory negligence was applied, in finding that the claimant in this case was more to blame for his injury than the defendant? Probably not, hence the recourse to voluntary assumption of risk. In a case such as this the court's power to reduce the claimant's damages for contributory negligence is quite limited.

To define voluntary assumption of risk in such a way is to turn it into a blunt instrument of policy and to sever any link with the idea of consent. The defence, in this way, becomes very like the defence of illegality (see 14.3.2) which is a true creature of judicial policy.

The court in *Morris* side-stepped the 1945 legislation which applies where the claimant and the defendant are each partly responsible for the claimant's injury. The Law Reform (Contributory Negligence) Act 1945 is discussed at 14.3.4. *Morris* is not, however, the only case in which a court has expressed willingness to consider the use of voluntary assumption of risk as an instrument of policy to block completely the attempt of a 'willing' claimant to obtain compensation.

In *Kirkham* v *Chief Constable of Greater Manchester* [1990] 3 All ER 246 the deceased had hanged himself while in custody, and his estate sued the police for negligence, i.e. for failing to inform the prison authorities of the deceased's suicidal tendencies, contrary to official procedure. The Court of Appeal accepted an argument that voluntary assumption of risk might have been available as a defence, had the deceased not been suffering from mental illness at the time of his injury. As Lloyd LJ put it:

> So I would be inclined to hold that where a man of sound mind commits suicide, his estate would be unable to maintain an action against the hospital or prison authorities, as the case might be. *Volenti non fit injuria* would provide them with a complete defence. There should be no distinction between a successful attempt and an unsuccessful attempt at suicide. Nor should there be any distinction between an action for the benefit of the estate under the Law Reform Act and an action for the benefit of dependants under the Fatal Accidents Act. In so far as Pilcher J drew a distinction between the two types of action in *Pigney* v *Pointer's Transport Services Ltd* [1957] 2 All ER 807, I would respectfully disagree.
>
> But in the present case Mr Kirkham was not of sound mind. True, he was sane in the legal sense. His suicide was a deliberate and conscious act. But Dr Sayed, whose evidence the judge accepted, said that Mr Kirkham was suffering from clinical depression. His judgment was impaired. If it had been a case of murder, he would have had a defence of diminished responsibility due to disease of the mind.
>
> I have had some doubt on this aspect of the case in the light of Dr Sayed's further evidence that, though his judgment was impaired, Mr Kirkham knew what he was doing. But in the end I have been persuaded by counsel for the plaintiff that, even so, he was not truly *volens*. Having regard to his mental state, he cannot, by his act, be said to have waived or abandoned any claim arising out of his suicide. So I would reject the defence of *volenti non fit injuria*.

It might be preferable to block a claim for damages in these cases simply on the basis that the claimant caused his own injury, although this is not a convincing argument where the defendant is under a duty to prevent the claimant's act in the first place.

The circumstances in *Kirkham* were of a special kind, there was very close proximity between the parties and official procedures recognized the potential dangers inherent in those circumstances. Suicide committed in prison is a known risk of which the authorities are well aware. In this regard, a mentally unstable prisoner with known suicidal tendencies is a greater risk than the allegedly 'sane' prisoner with the same tendencies. The defendant was in close supervision of the potential suicide, and it is arguable that anyone who is contemplating suicide is probably in an unbalanced state of mind at the time, even if they are clinically 'sane'. It must, therefore, be very difficult, if not impossible, to distinguish between suicides or attempted suicides according to the state of mind of the actors.

Even if there is a duty, and that duty has been breached, it is still incumbent on the claimant (or his estate or dependants where death results) to prove cause and effect. In some circumstances, it may well be impossible for the claimant to convince the court that the most reasonable of precautions, if taken by the defendant, would have prevented the suicide or attempted suicide: a fortiori in the case of the 'sane' claimant. In that case, the court is free to conclude that the deceased or injured claimant was wholly responsible for his own injury. The defence of contributory negligence may also be available in appropriate circumstances (see 14.3.4).

The House of Lords considered these issues in *Reeves* v *Commissioner of Police of the Metropolis* [1999] 3 All ER 897. An action in negligence was brought by the estate of a man (found by the judge at first instance to have been sane at the relevant time) who had committed suicide while in police custody. It was held that where a defendant owed a duty to prevent damage resulting from a deliberate act, whether of a third party or of the claimant, the chain of causation was not broken by that act. The defendants admitted breach of duty and could not plead *novus actus interveniens*; nor could they plead *volenti non fit injuria*.

Their Lordships did, however, apply the Law Reform (Contributory Negligence) Act 1945 and reduced the damages payable by 50%: they said that the deceased should bear equal responsibility with the defendants for his own death.

In *Orange* v *Chief Constable of West Yorkshire Police* [2002] QB 347, it was held that while the police had a duty to assess the claimant as a suicide risk, a decision based on reasonable grounds that this was not the case would negate any further duty to guard the claimant against suicide.

Standard of care

Obfuscation is created in some cases of negligence where the courts are in fact setting appropriate standards of care, but the language of *volenti* is used to justify the decisions. 'Standard of care' is discussed in more detail in **Chapter 1**.

These decisions mainly concern injuries sustained by spectators and competitors at sporting and similar events. It is evident that spectators and competitors attending and participating in such events run the risk of injury; the more dangerous the event, the bigger likelihood of serious injury.

In normal circumstances injured parties cannot claim compensation from either the competitors or the organizers of the events. If, however, the injuries sustained were caused by the tortious behaviour of such persons, the question of compensation and, therefore, of defences would arise. Defences presuppose apparently tortious behaviour. We have seen that *volenti* can operate in both ways, that is, to negate the effect of a breach of duty or to prevent the duty arising in the first place.

The problem in the present context is that judges often talk of a claimant's willing acceptance of the risk inherent in some dangerous event or competition. With respect, if these risks are not the result of tortious behaviour it is pointless to express the absence of liability in terms of 'acceptance'. A tennis ball or soccer ball hit into the crowd, quite accidentally, during the normal course of play is not connected with any tort, so what is the point of claiming that the spectators take the risk of injury in such a case? A similar point has been adduced, earlier in this chapter, in relation to road accidents.

The following statement, by Sellers LJ in *Wooldridge* v *Sumner* [1963] 2 QB 43, is typical of this approach:

> There would, I think, be a difference, for instance, in assessing blame which is actionable between an injury caused by a tennis ball hit or a racket accidentally thrown in the course of play into the spectators . . . and a ball hit or a racket thrown into the stands in temper or annoyance when play was not in progress.

In similar vein is the observation of Diplock LJ in the same case:

> A person attending a game or competition takes the risk of any damage caused to him by any act of a participant done in the course of and for the purposes of the game or competition notwithstanding that such an act may involve an error of judgment or a lapse of skill, unless the participant's conduct is such as to evince a reckless disregard for the spectator's safety.

By 'reckless disregard' his Lordship must have meant 'negligence'. Negligence is not based on recklessness, but if his Lordship meant trespass to the person, which can be committed recklessly, he would merely be saying that a participant in the event could be liable in trespass in such circumstances. Since the action of the claimant was pursued in the tort of negligence, his Lordship must have had that form of liability in mind. This case has been interpreted as laying down a 'heat of the moment' standard of care for competitors, lower than might otherwise be expected.

In *Wooldridge*, the claimant was a photographer at a horse show. He was taking some close-up photographs at a jumping event, when he was struck by a horse ridden by the defendant, who had, according to the claimant, been negligent in the handling of his steed. It was found that the defendant had not, in fact, been negligent, because he had kept within the rules of the competition and had observed the standard of care appropriate to a competitor in such an event.

The Court of Appeal in *Wilks* v *Cheltenham Home Guard Motor Cycle and Light Car Club* [1971] 2 All ER 369, did not adopt an approach based on acceptance of risk but proceeded on the basis of what would be an appropriate standard of care for a competitor going all out to win. The event in question was a motorcycle scramble, and the claimant, a spectator, was injured when one of the cycles got out of control. An action was brought in negligence against the organizers of the event and the motorcycle rider who had lost control. The trial judge found that the organizers had fenced the track perfectly adequately and had not been negligent, but he found against the competitor who appealed. The Court of Appeal held that a competitor going all out to win in such a competition could not be expected to observe the standard of care of a careful, prudent driver of an ordinary vehicle in use on the public highway. In the circumstances, the defendant had observed the standard of care expected of him, within the rules of the event, and had not been negligent. It is interesting to note that while Lord Denning MR preferred to apply the 'reckless disregard' test from *Wooldridge*, Edmund Davies and Phillimore LJJ adopted a simpler 'negligence' approach, albeit adapted to the circumstances of the case. For their Lordships it was merely a question of whether this competitor had observed the standard of care expected of him in the circumstances.

These cases involve the duty of care owed in the tort of negligence by a competitor to a spectator. In *Harrison* v *Vincent* [1982] RTR 8, discussed in 1.7.1.1, the claimant was a fellow participant of the defendant in the event, which was a race for motorcycles with sidecars. The 'normal' negligence standard was said to be applicable to the maintenance of the vehicle, for which the defendant was responsible, but the 'reckless disregard' test was found to be appropriate to the riding of the machine.

The approach of Edmund Davies and Phillimore LJJ in *Wilks* (above) is preferable to this 'dual standard' analysis. It is difficult to see what 'reckless disregard' adds to the standard of care in negligence; it suggests merely that the court must adjust the standard according to the circumstances of the case.

In *Condon* v *Basi* [1985] 2 All ER 453, discussed in 1.7.2, the question of liability in negligence between competitors was also relevant. You may wish to refer to that decision at this stage. Sir John Donaldson MR observed, in that case:

> I have cited from those two judgments [from the Australian case of *Rootes* v *Shelton* [1968] ALR 33] because they show two different approaches which, as I see it, produce precisely the same result. One is to take a more generalized duty of care and modify it on the basis that the participants in the sport or pastime impliedly consent to taking risks which would otherwise be a breach of the duty of care . . . [the other approach suggests that the general *Donoghue* v *Stevenson* standard of care applies, adapted to the circumstances] . . .

His Lordship preferred the latter approach, but went on to say

> I do not think it makes the slightest difference in the end if it is found . . . that the defendant failed to exercise that degree of care which was appropriate in all the circumstances, or that he acted in a way to which the plaintiff cannot be expected to have consented. In either event, there is liability.

With all respect, the end does not always justify the means and the ordinary standard of care approach is much simpler than the implied consent approach. We have so far considered cases in which spectators have sued competitors, and competitors have sued fellow competitors, but the *volenti* approach has also been taken in cases where spectators have sued the organizers of the event. In *Murray* v *Haringey Arena Ltd* [1951] 2 KB 529, the claimant was 6 years old and a spectator at an ice hockey match held on the defendant's premises. He was injured when a puck was hit into the crowd. His claim for damages failed, because the organizers were not liable for risks ordinarily incidental to the game since spectators willingly accepted those risks. This decision must really be based on the fact that there was simply no negligence behind the incident, because it is hardly satisfactory to assert that such a young claimant had waived his legal right to sue.

As *Jones* says (p. 393):

> This is not an application of *volenti non fit injuria*. It is true that in a sport which necessarily involves some physical content the players can be taken impliedly to consent to those contacts which occur within the ordinary performance of the game. But this consent negatives what would otherwise be a battery, it is not consent to negligence by other competitors. Similarly, spectators do not assume the risk of negligence simply by being present at the event.

The consensual relationship between the parties in these cases determines the relevant standard of care. In this sense, it may be said that the claimant's consent as a matter of policy can set the relevant standard of care, appropriate to the circumstances; though 'consent' can hardly explain the decision in *Murray* (above).

You will find the decision in *Phillips* v *Whiteley* [1938] 1 All ER 566 discussed in Chapter 1. In this case the language of *volenti* was not employed, yet the claimant was only entitled to the standard of care expected of a jeweller, when piercing ears; she had consensually accepted a low standard of care. It could also be claimed, by analogy, that in *Morris* v *Murray* the claimant had accepted, and was only entitled to, the standard of care expected from a drunken pilot.

Ultimately, it is a question of policy whether consent determines the standard of care in any given set of circumstances.

Please note the following general points:

(a) competitors may also sue the organizers of the event;

(b) occupiers' liability may be relevant;

(c) exclusion of liability by way of contract may be relevant in some cases;

(d) the provisions of the Unfair Contract Terms Act 1977 may also be relevant.

We are now in a position to consider the remaining general features of *volenti non fit injuria*.

14.3.1.4 **The consent or agreement must be real**

It is a cardinal feature of the defence that mere knowledge of a risk or danger is itself not enough. Although knowledge is evidence of acceptance, a claimant must be shown to have waived his legal remedy. Section 2(3) of the Unfair Contract Terms Act 1977, says 'where a contract term or notice purports to exclude or restrict liability for negligence a person's agreement to or awareness of it is not of itself to be taken as indicating his voluntary acceptance of any risk'. The Act implicitly recognizes a defence of *volenti* **separate** from exclusion of liability by contract.

Employment cases

The acceptance of risk must be voluntary, so it will very rarely succeed in an action by an employee against his employer because the economic reality is that few employees have any real choice.

In *Smith* v *Baker* [1891] AC 325, the claimant was a quarryman working below a crane carrying loads of stone, and in *Burnett* v *British Waterways Board* [1973] 1 WLR 700, he was a lighterman working a barge, with knowledge of a notice purporting to exclude the defendant from liability for injuries. The plea of *volenti* failed in both cases, because the claimants, who were employees of the defendants respectively, had no real choice in the matter. They had to accept their working conditions. A plea of *volenti* by an employer was successful in *ICI* v *Shatwell* [1965] AC 656, but the circumstances in that case were somewhat exceptional. Two shot firers, who were themselves statutory safety officials subject to personal duties to maintain health and safety standards conspired together to pursue their work in an obviously dangerous and illegal way. They worked alone at the mine face and there was no real possibility of more senior officials finding out what they were up to. Each was held *volens* as regards the risk created by the other, with the result that the employer could not be vicariously liable.

It may be possible for an employer to use *volenti* where an employee has specifically agreed to undertake a particular task, fraught with danger, for extra payment, so-called 'danger money'. Consent would, however, as in all cases of *volenti* have to be specific; consent must relate to the risk or danger which occurs and not to some interference of a general nature, especially where consent precedes an act of negligence, because it cannot always be certain what form the negligence will take. It would also have to be considered whether the claimant had taken the danger money simply as consideration for agreeing to run the factual risk, or whether he was also accepting the legal risk. As Diplock LJ said in *Wooldridge* (above) the relevant consent 'is not consent to the risk of injury but consent to the lack of reasonable care that may produce that risk . . . [and] the [claimant] at the time [he gave his consent must have] full knowledge of the nature and extent of the risk that he ran'.

His Lordship went on to say that even if a danger, created by the defendant, was in existence at the time the claimants decided to run the risk (having full knowledge of the risk) the court would still enquire whether it was reasonably foreseeable by the defendant that the claimant 'would so act in relation to [the danger] as to endanger himself'.

> **?** **QUESTION** 14.9
>
> Is the test of knowledge of the danger, and its nature and extent, subjective or objective?

The test is subjective, that is, what the claimant actually knew, not objective, that is, what he ought reasonably to have known. It follows that the claimant must be capable of understanding the nature and extent of the risk in question. The decision in *Kirkham* (above) illustrates this point; and drunkenness was no excuse for the claimant in *Morris* (above). If a claimant ought to have known of a danger, the appropriate defence is contributory negligence.

Volenti is not, on the whole, a widely used defence. In the opinion of Fleming, *An Introduction to the Law of Torts*, 2nd edn, Oxford: Oxford University Press, 1985, the defence is moribund, for two main reasons:

• the difficulty of proving consent, as Fleming puts it (at p. 140): 'The life-cycle of the defence, indeed, is marked by the progressive displacement of *imputed* consent by nothing short of *real* consent as the basic requirement'; and

• the rise in popularity of contributory negligence, which has eclipsed *volenti*.

Rescue

Volenti has also been rejected in the so-called 'rescue cases'. If, as a result of the pressures of the moment (legal or moral), a person is injured in rescuing, or attempting to rescue, someone else who has been put in peril as the result of the defendant's wrongful behaviour, that injured person (the 'rescuer') has an independent cause of action in tort against the defendant. In short, if rescue is foreseeable in the circumstances, and danger invariably invites rescue, a duty of care is owed directly to the rescuer—the defendant's obligation to the rescuer is not based on any breach of duty to the person imperilled. It is not necessary that the person placed in danger should have been hurt or even that he was actually in danger, provided that the rescuer's conclusion that danger did exist was reasonable at the time of the emergency. This duty to rescuers is firmly established in the law, although there is no general legal obligation upon anyone to attempt a rescue.

> **EXERCISE** 14.2
>
> Consider *Videan* v *British Transport Commission* [1963] 2 All ER 860. What do you think would be the main outcome from this case in the present context?

A young child wandered on to the railway track and was exposed to the danger of being run down by a motor-trolley (used on the track for maintenance work) when he was saved by his father, the stationmaster. The latter was killed in the successful rescue of his son.

The Court of Appeal held that since a stationmaster's presence on the line was foreseeable, and the duty owed to a rescuer was of an independent nature, i.e. it was not derived from any duty owed to the person in danger, it was irrelevant that the boy in this case was a trespasser to whom the defendant owed no legal liability.

The decision emphasizes the independent nature of the duty owed to the rescuer. It was held that the defendant was in breach of its duty to the claimant, who had rescued a person, a trespasser on the defendant's premises, to whom at that time the defendant did not owe any legal duty. It was enough that the rescuer's presence on the premises was foreseeable at the relevant time; indeed it was sufficient that some emergency was foreseeable in the circumstances, not necessarily the actual emergency which materialized.

Although a duty to rescuers had earlier been recognized in other jurisdictions, notably that of the USA, it was not until the decision of the Court of Appeal in *Haynes* v *Harwood* [1935] 1 KB 146, that such an obligation became firmly established in English law. Here, the court cited with approval the following opinion of Cardozo J expressed in *Wagner* v *International Railway Co.* (1921) 133 NE 437:

> Danger invites rescue. The cry of distress is the summons to relief. The law does not ignore those reactions of the mind in tracing conduct to its consequences. It recognizes them as normal. It places their effects within the range of the natural and probable. The wrong that imperils life is a wrong to the imperilled victim; it is a wrong also to his rescuer.

In *Haynes*, a horse and cart took off along a busy street because the horse had been frightened as a result of a young boy throwing a stone; all this was put down to the defendant's negligence. The claimant, a policeman, was injured when he stopped the horse, so preventing injury to members of the public. He was awarded damages as a rescuer.

This decision was followed in *Baker* v *Hopkins and Son Ltd* [1958] 3 All ER 147, in which a doctor went to the rescue of workmen endangered by their employer's negligence. The men were working at the bottom of an open shaft, and had been overcome by carbon monoxide fumes leaking from a faulty compressor unit. Unknown to anyone at the time, the men were dead, but the doctor insisted on being lowered down the fume-filled shaft, secured only by a rope tied round his waist. No breathing apparatus was available, in fact firemen were waiting for it to arrive. The doctor, like the men, succumbed to the fumes and his widow was awarded damages against the men's employer for breach of its duty to the doctor as a rescuer.

? QUESTION 14.10

Can a person who places himself in danger owe a duty to a rescuer?

The answer is 'yes'. The point was discussed in *Baker* (above) and an affirmative opinion expressed at first instance, and in the Court of Appeal. In *Harrison* v *British Railways Board* [1981] 3 All ER 679, it was applied to the facts.

The defendant negligently attempted to board a train which was on the move and the claimant, who was a guard on that train, attempted to rescue him. It was found, by Boreham J, that the claimant, in failing to engage the train's emergency brake before setting out to rescue the defendant, had contributed to his own injuries. Accordingly, the claimant's damages were reduced by 20%.

> **?** **QUESTION** 14.11
>
> What are the two important features of this case?

Two important conclusions were drawn by the judge in this case:

(a) a person who puts himself in danger can be liable to his rescuer;

(b) a rescuer can be met by the plea of contributory negligence.

A rescuer who bungles the attempt could make matters worse, in which case the rescuer might find himself sued by the rescuee. No doubt, on the basis of ordinary *Donoghue* v *Stevenson*, 'neighbour' principles, the rescuer could well owe a duty of care in negligence to the rescuee. The rescuee would then have to prove breach of duty, that is actual negligence. Presumably, the relevant standard of care would be that of the reasonable man attempting a rescue, perhaps in extremely hazardous conditions, so the standard expected in the circumstances would reflect the court's assessment of the merits of the rescuer's action. The courts are not keen to find against a rescuer.

The decision in *Horsley* v *MacLaren* ('*The Ogopogo*') [1971] 2 Lloyd's Rep 410 (Canadian Supreme Court), raises some interesting and unusual points of argument.

This case dealt with a situation in which A had accidentally fallen overboard into the sea from a boat. B, the owner of the boat, stopped his craft and reversed it towards the spot where A had gone into the water. However, by this time A had apparently become unconscious.

C, another guest on B's boat, jumped into the water to rescue A. Unfortunately C was unsuccessful because A's body had disappeared by now, and C himself was in danger because of the cold.

D, who was also a guest of B, had by now got into the water to help in the rescue of A. Her husband took control of the boat, and D was rescued. B then resumed command of his boat and steered towards C, who was taken aboard. Tragically, he was dead—killed by the shock of having been in the bitterly cold water.

The claimant, who was C's widow, claimed damages from B for his negligence in executing the rescue of A, as a direct result of which C had attempted his rescue of A.

It was found that the defendant, B, had not been negligent on the facts. There was evidence that he was drunk at the time (the event was a 'pleasure' cruise and most of the people involved had consumed some alcohol) but he was not a professional captain, and thus was not expected to possess the highest degree of skill attainable. The claimant lost her case but the court did seem to accept the contention that in principle it is possible for a rescuer to be found liable for conducting a rescue carelessly. The court also accepted that B, as owner and operator of the boat, owed a duty to do his best to rescue a guest who had fallen into the sea: he had a duty to take reasonable care for the safety of his guests.

?   **QUESTION** 14.12

Why is the duty owed to rescuers important here?

'Rescue' is dealt with here because rescuers are volunteers. There is no general duty to rescue, so it might be said that rescuers can be met with a plea of *volenti*. This has been rejected in genuine rescue cases, because rescuers are not acting 'freely'; they are acting under the compulsion of the moment. They are not, in that sense, free agents. Defendants have sometimes argued, for example in *Baker* v *Hopkins* (above) that a *novus actus interveniens* (intervening act, coming between the defendant's wrong and the claimant's damage) applies in rescue cases, that is the rescuer's voluntary act causes his own damage. This argument can only be sustained where the rescuer's behaviour amounts, in the opinion of Willmer LJ in *Baker*, to a 'wanton disregard for his own safety'.

In *Harrison* v *British Railways Board* (above) the finding of 20% contributory negligence on the part of the rescuer was arrived at only very reluctantly, and the courts will be slow to accept criticism of a rescuer's behaviour from the person who created the emergency in the first place. See also *Crossley* v *Rawlinson* [1981] 3 All ER 674 at 2.5.1.1.

A 'rescuer' may not succeed at all where he intervenes after the danger has gone, because his conduct may be regarded as unreasonable in the circumstances. In *Cutler* v *United Dairies (London) Ltd* [1933] 2 KB 297, the claimant went into a field to calm the defendant's restive horse and was injured in so doing. The court accepted that he was a mere 'volunteer', because there was no real danger to person or property.

The duty to rescuers extends to those who attempt to, or actually save property and goods, whether they belong to himself or other persons. In *Hyatt* v *Great Western Railway Co.* [1948] 1 KB 345, the court said the ruling in *Haynes* (above) applied also to the rescue of property. A claimant/rescuer may not be justified in taking the same risks in relation to property that would be acceptable in 'saving' persons. Each case will, no doubt, be determined on its own facts.

A final point concerns the essential nature of the duty itself. It is often dealt with in the context of the tort of negligence, and is expressed in terms of the defendant's 'negligence' towards the rescuer; it is considered as an example of duty of care in negligence. While a defendant's negligence is often the reason for an emergency arising in the first place, the duty owed to the rescuer does not appear to depend on any *Donoghue* v *Stevenson* duty owed to the victim. In view of the fact that a defendant may be liable to a rescuer where he places himself in danger, a would-be suicide attempt would probably attract rescuer liability. The duty to rescuers, in fact, seems to be based on simple foreseeability of rescue in the circumstances: the defendant does not need to be 'at fault' beyond the requirement that 'danger invites rescue'. Claims for psychiatric damage suffered by rescuers are dealt with at 4.3.2.

14.3.2 **Illegality**

This general 'defence' is often expressed by reference to the Latin maxim *ex turpi causa non oritur actio*. This means that an action in law cannot be founded on an illegal act.

14.3.2.1 **Comparison with *volenti***

Illegality, like *volenti*, is a complete defence; that is if the defendant is successful in his plea the claimant gets nothing at all; and both defences are based very much on policy. Success in either defence is very hard to predict, although *ex turpi causa* is probably more difficult.

The two defences are very close. In *Morris v Murray* (see 14.3.1.3), Fox LJ, referring to *volenti*, said: 'It seems to me . . . that the wild irresponsibility of the venture is such that the law should not intervene to award damages and [should] leave the loss where it falls.' It seems that one or other of these defences will be accepted whenever the court feels that the claim of the claimant is without merit, in spite of the defendant's clear culpability.

The rationale for 'illegality' is that the claimant's cause of action is tainted with crime or immorality, will excite public distaste or opprobrium, or is an 'affront to the public conscience' (see *Kirkham* v *Chief Constable of Greater Manchester* discussed at 2.4.2.2). It rests on the premise that the court should not provide a forum for legal action in the particular circumstances of the case. *Volenti*, on the other hand, is based on the claimant's consent to injury.

Nevertheless, the sentiment expressed by Fox LJ in *Morris* does seem to explain the reasoning behind the application of these defences in some cases. In any event, it could be argued that the parties in *Morris* were engaged in an illegal joint enterprise. It must be illegal for an aircraft to be flown in the circumstances of that case. If a stranger to the venture, on the ground at the time, had been injured in the accident, would that person not have had a cause of action against both claimant and defendant in *Morris*, at least on the basis that the claimant was aiding and abetting the offence?

Megaw LJ in *Nettleship* v *Weston* [1971] 2 QB 691 (see 1.7.1.3) suggested that someone who went willingly on a journey with the drunken driver of a motor car could be regarded as jointly liable with the driver, in terms of aiding and abetting the illegal behaviour, and could be met with a plea of *ex turpi causa* should he be injured in an accident caused by the driver's negligence. It would not be sufficient, however, merely to be present or carried in a vehicle driven by such a person, or to be in an unroadworthy vehicle or in a vehicle which was not taxed and/or uninsured.

Another leading case on *volenti, ICI v Shatwell*, could also be explained on the basis of illegality. The brothers were obviously engaged in a joint, and deliberate, flouting of the law. It must be stressed that illegality, as such, was not pleaded in either *Morris* or *Shatwell* and Megaw LJ was expressing an obiter opinion in *Nettleship*. You will find further discussion of *Shatwell* in **Chapter 8** (8.2.1).

 EXERCISE 14.3

Read the facts of *Pitts* v *Hunt* [1990] 3 All ER 344. Why was *volenti* not relevant in this case?

After drinking alcohol together the defendant gave the claimant a lift home on his motor-bike. The defendant, whose alcohol level was twice over the legal limit, was encouraged by the claimant to drive too fast and to intimidate other road users. To the claimant's knowledge the defendant did not have a licence and was not insured. In a collision with an oncoming vehicle whose driver was not to blame, the defendant was killed and the claimant badly injured. He sued the defendant's estate for the deceased's negligence.

The defence was not relevant, because s. 149 of the Road Traffic Act 1988 prohibits exclusion of liability. According to the Court of Appeal that provision catches implied *volenti*, as well as agreements. The defendant in *Pitts* had to have recourse to *ex turpi causa*, which is unaffected by the 1988 Act.

In the absence of a provision such as that contained in the Road Traffic Act 1988, the opinion of Fox LJ in *Morris* v *Murray* should leave us in no doubt that *volenti* could well have been applicable in *Pitts*.

You will observe that the reasons given by the Court of Appeal in *Pitts* for finding that *ex turpi causa* applied differed. Dillon LJ found that the claimant's action arose directly *ex turpi causa*; Balcombe LJ held that the courts cannot set a standard of care for the circumstances where the parties are engaged in a joint criminal enterprise; and Beldam LJ said that public policy prevented the claimant from receiving compensation.

14.3.2.2 Public policy

In *Euro-Drain Ltd* v *Bathurst* [1998] 2 All ER 23, Kerr LJ said: 'The *ex turpi* defence ultimately rests on a principle of public policy that the courts will not assist a claimant who has been guilty of illegal (or immoral) conduct of which the courts should take notice.'

Authority on the subject is scanty and each case seems to be decided on its own merits. This defence is based on public policy, that is the courts will not help a claimant where it would be 'an affront to the public conscience' to do so and might encourage him or others to engage in illegal activities.

The 'public conscience' approach is criticized in *Pitts* v *Hunt* (below) and received a disapproving analysis in the House of Lords in *Tinsley* v *Milligan* [1993] 3 WLR 126. In *Tinsley*, which was concerned with the effect of illegality in contract and on claims to property between contracting parties, Lord Goff expressed the opinion that the 'public conscience' test in effect amounted to nothing more than a statement by the court that it had a discretion 'whether to grant or refuse relief'. This discretion, it is submitted, lies behind all the reasons given by the courts when refusing to assist the claimant on grounds of illegality. The House of Lords rejected the 'public conscience' test in the particular context of *Tinsley*. In *Kirkham* (above) the defence of *ex turpi causa* was held inapplicable to suicide, which is no longer a crime, certainly where the balance of the deceased's mind was disturbed.

In *Ashton* v *Turner* [1981] QB 137 two burglars were in a 'getaway' car. The claimant was the passenger and was injured by the defendant's negligent driving. The court refused to recognize a duty of care between participants in a crime, in relation to an act done in connection with the commission of that crime. This, said the court, was a matter of public policy.

The claimant's own illegal act was one of the issues in *Vellino* v *Chief Constable of Greater Manchester* [2002] 1 WLR 218. The claimant was someone known to the police and they had gone to his home on a number of occasions to arrest him but each time he had tried to escape by jumping from the second floor window of his flat. He was seriously injured on the last occasion and claimed damages from the police, alleging that since it was foreseeable he would try to escape, yet again, and that injury was foreseeable, the police had a duty to stop him escaping. The court dismissed his claim because at the time of the accident he was trying to escape from the police and was not under their control when he jumped. Also, since he had been lawfully arrested, and attempting to escape from police custody is a crime, the defence of *ex turpi causa* ('illegality') was available to the police and this blocked his claim.

The device of refusing to set a duty of care will only work where the tort of negligence is involved. In other cases, for example trespass to the person, *ex turpi causa* must be faced as a defence to a cause of action which has already formed. Again, where negligence is involved, some courts have said they will not set any standard of care for criminal activity, rather than set a lower standard. In *Pitts* v *Hunt* the court said it was 'impossible' to set such a lower standard, indicating a reluctance to distinguish between degrees of illegality.

It was held in *Marshall* v *Osmond* [1983] QB 1034, that police in pursuit of someone who has wrongly taken and driven away a vehicle do owe a duty of care in negligence to that person, but it is a duty to take such care as is appropriate in the circumstances. By analogy with sporting activities discussed above, in relation to *volenti*, the court will be able to adjust liability according to the facts of the case. In the *Nottingham Evening Post* of 29 March 1990, it was reported that a motorcyclist injured in 'a high speed chase' had been awarded £13,500 damages against the police, although the claimant's damages had been reduced because of his contributory negligence.

In these cases the following factors are important but not conclusive:

(a) were the parties equally at fault?

(b) was the tort an integral part of the illegal activity?

(c) in the opinion of Bingham LJ in *Saunders* v *Edwards* [1987] 2 All ER 651, the illegality must probably arise directly and not be incidental to what would otherwise be a genuine cause of action. His Lordship said he preferred to take a pragmatic approach to the solution of such problems;

(d) current moral standards play a part;

(e) it may be relevant that a claimant has to rely on an illegal contract;

(f) causation will be important, as are matters of time and space.

If the illegality is totally unconnected with the tort it may be ignored. In *National Coal Board* v *England* [1954] AC 403, Lord Asquith said:

> If A and B are proceeding to the premises which they intend burglariously to enter, and before they enter them B picks A's pocket and steals A's watch, I cannot prevail upon myself to believe that A could not sue in tort.

The more serious the offence, and the stronger the causal link between the offence and the tort, the more likely it is that *ex turpi* will apply.

In *Saunders* v *Edwards* (above) the claimants entered into a lease with the defendant which was designed to avoid stamp duty, i.e. to defraud the Inland Revenue. Afterwards, the claimants sued the defendant in the tort of deceit (which is another name for fraud) when they found that the lease did not include a roof terrace which the defendant had promised would be part of the rented premises.

The Court of Appeal held that the claimants were not barred from bringing an action in the tort of deceit by the *ex turpi* defence, because they did not have to rely on the illegal contract to prove their case in tort. The claim in deceit was an independent cause of action, which incidentally materialized during an illegal transaction. The claimant's fraud on the Inland Revenue did not affect the deceit of the defendant. The moral culpability of the defendant greatly outweighed that of the claimants. The court had to steer a middle course between aiding people seeking to pursue or enforce an illegal object, or agreement, and refusing assistance to a deserving claimant on the first indication of any unlawfulness.

14.3.3 **Necessity**

This general defence may be described as the deliberate or intentional commission of what might otherwise be tortious conduct, to avoid some greater evil, there being no reasonable alternative. However, its precise boundaries are unclear and there is some overlap with other defences such as defence of property and self-defence. According to *Street* (p. 90), the difference between these defences '. . . is that self-defence or defence of property pre-supposes that the claimant is prima facie a wrongdoer: the defence of necessity contemplates the infliction of harm on an innocent plaintiff'.

It is unlikely that necessity will provide a defence to actions for negligence, because the issue in such a case will simply be whether the person was negligent or not in the circumstances. In all cases of necessity there must be no reasonable alternative open to the defendant. It was said in *Esso Petroleum Co. Ltd* v *Southport Corporation* [1956] AC 218 that if he brought about the need for intervention by his own negligence, his plea must fail. There must be a danger (or what seems to be one in the perception of the reasonable man) and the action taken must be reasonable in the circumstances.

14.3.3.1 **Protection of the realm**

In the *Saltpetre* case (1606) 12 Rep 12, it was said that entry upon another's land by officers of the State to defend the Realm, by the construction of earthworks, would be protected 'but after the danger is over, the trenches and bulwarks ought to be removed . . .'

The extent to which this protects an ordinary individual seeking to utilize the defence and whether the status quo ante (i.e. the state in which things were) should be restored, or compensation paid as of right is doubtful.

In *Rigby* v *Chief Constable of Northamptonshire* [1985] 2 All ER 985, the police used CS gas to get a psychopath out of the claimant's premises and set them on fire. It was found that necessity protected the police from the claimant's action in trespass (to land), but there was liability in negligence because the police conducted the operation without the support of adequate fire prevention facilities.

14.3.3.2 **Protection of the person**

In *Esso Petroleum Co. Ltd* v *Southport Corporation (above)* it was said that jettisoning goods or, as in this case, discharging oil (which polluted the corporation's beaches) from a ship which was in danger of sinking to save those on board could be justified by necessity. The action in trespass to land failed.

Again, in *Leigh* v *Gladstone* (1909) 26 TLR 139, it was held that necessity justified the forcible feeding of the claimant, a suffragette who was on hunger strike in prison. The claimant's action in trespass to the person (battery) failed. It was held in *Re A* [2000] 4 All ER 961 (CA), that doctors were justified, on a principle of necessity and not emergency, in separating conjoined twins even though the death of the weaker twin was medically certain as a result of the separation. (Both twins could have survived for some months without the operation, though their deaths were certain within that timescale.) Necessity justifies the medical treatment, or nontreatment of those patients not competent to consent: *F* v *West Berkshire Health Authority*

[1989] 2 All ER 545(HL); *Frenchay Healthcare NHS Trust* v *S* [1994]. See also the discussion of *R v Bournewood Community and Mental Health NHS Trust ex parte L* [1998] 3 All ER 289 (HL), and *L* v *United Kingdom (Application No. 45508/99)* (2004), *The Times*, 19 October in 10.4.5.4.

14.3.3.3 **Protection of property**

In principle, necessity is available in this context, but it is not so readily acceptable as in protection of the person. In *Cope* v *Sharpe (No. 2)* [1912] 1 KB 496, the defendant was held not liable for having set fire to the claimant's land in the reasonable, though mistaken, belief that it was the only way to prevent a larger fire from destroying his employer's pheasant shoot. He had acted reasonably at the time, although it later transpired that the fire would not have spread.

In the earlier case of *Kirk* v *Gregory* (1876) 1 Ex D 55, however, the defendant removed a deceased person's valuables 'against the remote chance' that they might be stolen by servants who were having a 'jubilant feast', and his plea of necessity failed. It was also held by the Court of Appeal in *Southwark London Borough Council* v *Williams* [1971] Ch 734, that the defence could not be used as a 'mask for anarchy' by homeless squatters who were defending an action in trespass to land for occupying unoccupied council premises. In this form of defence, i.e. protection of property, it is arguable that compensation might be sought, for the effects of an act of necessity, on quasi-contractual grounds: *Winfield* (pp. 753–4).

The Court of Appeal in *Monsanto plc* v *Tilly* [2000] Env LR 313 held that campaigners against genetically modified crops and plants could not rely on necessity or public interest to justify trespass to land committed as part of their publicity campaign.

14.3.4 **Contributory negligence**

The burden of proof is on the defendant to show that the claimant did not take reasonable care of himself and contributed, by this want of care, to his own injury. This defence has no relevance to claims between co-defendants; these claims are governed by the provisions of the Civil Liability (Contribution) Act 1978, which have been discussed in the introduction to this book. According to *Fookes* v *Slaytor* [1979] 1 All ER 137, the defendant must specifically plead the defence of contributory negligence.

An issue of contributory negligence is, in essence, an issue of fact, to be determined according to the circumstances of the case. Damages are apportioned according to the degrees of fault of the claimant and defendant.

 QUESTION 14.13

What is the source of the basic principles of this defence?

 The law is laid down in the Law Reform (Contributory Negligence) Act 1945, as interpreted in the cases. The Act is set out in *Cases and Materials* (14.1.2).

The rules, according to s. 4 of the Act, are not confined to the tort of negligence. In s. 4, 'fault' is defined as: 'negligence, breach of statutory duty, or other act or omission which gives rise to a liability in tort, or would, apart from this Act, give rise to the defence of contributory negligence'.

In *Murphy* v *Culhane* (see 14.3) it was held that the defendant could plead this defence to a claim made in trespass to the person, which is a form of liability based on *intentional* interference. Contributory negligence was held not to be applicable to the tort of deceit in *Corporacion Nacional Del Cobre De Chile* v *Sogemin Metals Ltd* [1997] 2 All ER 917. Indeed the weight of opinion is that it does not apply to intentional torts in general, so *Murphy* is an exception to the rule. See the extracts from the judgments in *Cases and Materials* (14.1.2).

In *Gran Gelato Ltd* v *Richcliff (Group) Ltd* [1992] 1 All ER 865, the Court of Appeal held that the 1945 Act applied where there was concurrent liability in contract and tort on the part of the defendant, though the duty in tort had to be identical with the contractual obligation.

14.3.4.1 **Apportionment**

Before 1945, contributory negligence was a complete defence at common law.

The court is now given a discretion by the Law Reform (Contributory Negligence) Act 1945 to do what is 'just and equitable' in the circumstances of the case. The courts have not laid down rigid rules on this matter: they do not want to fetter their discretion unduly. There is no single principle governing apportionment in these cases.

In *Capps* v *Miller* [1989] 2 All ER 333, a motorcyclist, injured in a collision caused by the defendant's negligence, was wearing a crash helmet at the time of the accident, but he had not fastened the chin strap properly. It seems that had his helmet stayed on, the extent of his injuries would probably have been some 'incalculable degree less'. The trial judge found against contributory negligence because of the defendant's 'gross' negligence, and the fact that the claimant's responsibility was less than 10%. The Court of Appeal held that the claimant's carelessness should be taken into account, bearing in mind that he had committed a criminal offence, and breach of statutory duty, in failing to secure his helmet. Accordingly, the Court of Appeal ordered a 10% reduction in his damages.

14.3.4.2 **Claimant's contribution**

It is essential that the claimant and the defendant have contributed to the former's injury; both parties must be to blame. This is essentially a matter of establishing that the claimant's conduct had causative potency.

In *Stapley* v *Gypsum Mines Ltd* [1953] AC 663, a supervisor instructed Stapley and another coal miner, X, to make the roof of a mine safe. They could not do so but agreed to carry on working. The roof collapsed on Stapley, killing him. The House of Lords had to decide whether the accident was solely Stapley's fault, or partly X's fault.

It was held that the court must discriminate between those faults which are too remote and those which are not. One test was whether there was 'sufficient separation of time, place, or circumstances' between the respective negligence, in which case it was not contributory negligence, or whether X's fault was 'so much mixed up with the state of things brought about by Stapley that, on a common sense view, it must be regarded as having contributed to the accident'. These words are taken from Lord Reid's speech. In this case it was found that X's negligence had contributed to the accident, but the damages would be reduced by 80% because of Stapley's negligence.

In *Barrett* v *Ministry of Defence* [1995] 3 All ER 87, the claimant was a soldier aged 30. It was held by the Court of Appeal that the defendant could be regarded as having assumed responsibility for his safety because of its past behaviour towards him. He had choked to death after indulging in an excessive consumption of alcohol. The defendant was found liable in negligence, but only from the point at which the claimant's drunkenness had become apparent. Damages awarded to the estate of the deceased were reduced for his contributory negligence.

? **QUESTION** 14.14

Is it possible that a claimant could be found to be wholly to blame for his/her misfortune?

Apportionment under the 1945 Act is not automatic. On grounds of legal causation, the court may find a claimant to be wholly at fault and that he must bear the whole loss. There has been much debate about whether a claimant can be found 100% to blame under the 1945 Act. The balance of opinion is probably against this view, and it does not seem to accord with the wording of the Act, which speaks in terms of apportionment of blame between the parties.

In *Pitts* v *Hunt* (above) Beldam and Dillon LJJ expressed the opinion that there should be an apportionment of 50% contributory negligence in the case of a joint illegal enterprise. It was said that the provisions of the 1945 Act apply only where the claimant is partly to blame, and that a finding of 100% contributory negligence would not be appropriate.

There is, however, some authority for the proposition that the 1945 Act does allow a deduction of 100%. In *Jayes* v *IMI (Kynoch)* [1985] ICR 155 damages were reduced by 100% and Goff LJ said:

> there is no principle of law which requires that, even where there is a breach of statutory duty in circumstances . . . where the intention of the statute is to provide protection, inter alia, against folly on the part of a workman, there cannot be 100% contributory negligence.

In *Froom* v *Butcher* [1976] 1 QB 286, the Court of Appeal considered the consequences of a failure to wear a seat belt in a motor vehicle. The defendant's negligence was the sole cause of an accident involving the claimant's car; the claimant suffered injuries which would have been avoided had he worn a seat belt, and an injury to his finger which would have occurred even if he had been wearing a seat belt. It was held that, apart from cases where injury would not be eliminated by the wearing of a belt, and cases where wearing a belt might be dangerous in itself, for example, where an occupant of a vehicle was pregnant or obese, damages for injuries to the occupants of seats in the front of cars should be reduced, where no seat belt was worn though one was provided. The reduction should be 25% where a seat belt would have prevented the injury and 15% where it would have reduced the severity of the injury. The Court of Appeal reduced the claimant's overall damages by 20%.

The court said that the claimant need not have contributed to the accident; it was enough that he had contributed to the damage caused by the accident. As Lord Denning MR said: 'The accident is caused by the bad driving. The damage is caused in part by the bad driving of the defendant, and in part by the failure of the claimant to wear a seat belt.'

In *Condon* v *Condon* [1977] RTR 483, it was held that because the claimant suffered from a phobia of being shut in, there was a sufficient reason for not wearing a seat belt.

In *Clifford* v *Drymond* [1976] RTR 134, the Court of Appeal made a 20% reduction in the claimant's damages where, in contravention of Rule 13 of the Highway Code, he used a zebra crossing in such a way that he was struck by a car.

In *Gregory* v *Kelly* [1978] RTR 426, the claimant's damages were reduced by 40%, for not wearing his seat belt and knowing, from the start of the journey, that the foot brake in the vehicle was inoperative.

There are a number of cases in which claimants have had their damages reduced for contributory negligence in accepting lifts from drunken motorists. In *Owens* v *Brimmell* [1977] QB 859, for example, the claimant and the defendant went on a 'pub crawl' and got drunk. The defendant drove the claimant home and crashed the car. The claimant's damages were not reduced for his failure to wear a seat belt, because the defendant could not prove that such failure had made any difference to his injuries, but a reduction of 20% was made for his contributory negligence in riding with a drunken driver.

In 1973 statutory regulations were introduced providing that protective headgear must be used when riding motorcyles. Since 1981, it has been compulsory to use seat belts in the front seats of cars. Special provisions concerning seat belts relate to children under 14, and there are some exemptions relating to the use of headgear and seat belts. Since 1989 the use of seat belts in the rear seats of cars has also been compulsory in certain circumstances. Observance or non-observance of these regulations by a claimant would be evidence for or against the existence of contributory negligence.

Smoking

In *Badger* v *Ministry of Defence* (2005), *The Times*, 30 December, the claimant's husband, who had died of lung cancer, had been exposed to asbestos dust and fibres in the course of his employment with the defendant. He had also smoked. Both the exposure to asbestos, for which the defendant admitted liability, and his smoking were causative of his cancer. He was aged 63 at the time of his death and had started smoking in about 1955. Stanley Burnton J found that it was reasonably foreseeable by a reasonably prudent person after 1971, when the first health warning was put on cigarette packets, that if he or she smoked there was a risk of danger to health. Furthermore, the deceased had been specially advised about the damaging effects of smoking on his health in 1968, 1991, 1992, and 1995. His Lordship therefore reduced the damages payable to the claimant in respect of her husband's death by 20% because of his contributory negligence.

14.3.4.3 **Children**

Conduct which in the case of an adult would be regarded as contributory negligence is not necessarily so regarded when committed by a child. The test is 'did the child conform to the normal standard expected from his age group?' According to Salmon LJ in *Gough* v *Thorne* [1966] 1 WLR 1387, the child should be: 'not a paragon of prudence, nor a scatterbrained child'. In this case, a girl aged 13 was found not to be contributorily negligent in crossing the road without looking, when signalled to do so by a lorry driver unaware that he was being overtaken. The same reasoning was applied in *Jones* v *Lawrence* [1969] 3 All ER 267, to a boy aged 7, who ran out into the road without looking and was hit by a motor cyclist travelling at 50 mph in a 30 mph zone. In *Minter* v *D & H Contractors* (1983), *The Times*, 30 June, the defence was applied to a boy aged 9, when riding his bicycle in a busy street.

On the authority of *Oliver* v *Birmingham and Midland Motor Omnibus Co. Ltd* [1933] 1 KB 35, a child, an aged, or an infirm person, is not 'identified' with the negligence of the person in whose charge he happens to be at the time of the defendant's negligent act. In this case a young child was crossing the road in the charge of his grandfather whose negligence, together with the bus driver's, caused the child's injuries. It was found that the child's claim was not affected by the grandfather's negligence.

14.3.4.4 Emergencies

Where a claimant is faced with an emergency, or 'dilemma', as a result of the defendant's tort, he will not be contributorily negligent, even if, with hindsight, he did not make the best decision, provided that he acts reasonably at the time of the emergency or dilemma. This is the case for example, where the claimant is exercising some right and the question arises whether he acted reasonably in doing so in spite of the situation of danger created by the defendant.

As Patteson J put it, in *Clayards* v *Dethick* (1848) 12 QB 439: 'The whole question was, whether the danger was so obvious that the claimant could not with common prudence make the attempt.'

14.3.4.5 Scope of risk

The injury suffered by the claimant must also be within the broad scope of risk created by his negligence. In *Jones* v *Livox Quarries Ltd* [1952] 2 QB 608, the claimant, contrary to express instructions, rode on the back of a quarry vehicle. A dumper vehicle driven by another employee collided with the rear of the quarry vehicle, crushing the claimant. It was held that the injury was caused partly by the claimant's dangerous position on the vehicle. The argument that the claimant's negligence related to the foreseeable risk of falling off, but not to the risk of being crushed was rejected. His injury was within the scope of the risk which the claimant's conduct had created.

14.3.4.6 Reciprocity

The claimant often owes a duty of care in negligence to the defendant. In other words, there is reciprocity of duty, for example, in the case of two motorists who collide. It is not necessary, however, that the claimant owes such a duty. As Bucknill LJ put it in *Davies* v *Swan Motor Co. (Swansea) Ltd* [1949] 2 KB 291: 'It is not necessary to show that the [claimant's] negligence constituted a breach of duty to the defendant. It is sufficient to show lack of reasonable care by the plaintiff for his own safety.' On a practical point, in *Eagle* v *Chambers* (2003), *The Times*, 1 September (CA), it was held that since the law imposed on drivers of motor vehicles a high burden of care to reflect the fact that a car, or other vehicle, was a potentially dangerous weapon, it would be rare for a pedestrian to be found more responsible than the driver for injuries arising from a road traffic accident unless the pedestrian had suddenly moved into the path of the oncoming vehicle.

14.3.4.7 Nature of 'damage'

'Damage' in s. 4 of the Law Reform (Contributory Negligence) Act 1945 is couched in terms wide enough not only to include 'loss of life and personal injury', but also damage to property.

In *Drinkwater* v *Kimber* [1952] 1 All ER 701, the word 'damage' was found not to include liability to pay damages to a third party.

The court in *Maes Finance Ltd* v *A L Phillips and Co.* (1997), *The Times*, 25 March, had to consider whether contributory negligence could be raised for the first time at the assessment of damages stage, that is after the court had delivered its judgment. It was held that much would depend on the issues settled in the judgment. If the judgment had settled an issue on which a claim of contributory negligence would depend, the defence could only be pleaded if the judgment itself was set aside. If no such issue had been settled, e.g. where a defendant alleged that the claimant had himself caused a particular loss, contributory negligence could be raised at the assessment of damages stage.

■ SUMMARY

- Many defences are dealt with in the context of particular torts, for example, statutory authority in relation to nuisance and justification by law (or lawful authority) in relation to trespass to the person. The Police and Criminal Evidence Act 1984, amended by the Serious Organised Crime and Police Act 2005, confers powers of arrest, which may be used as a defence in cases of false imprisonment, and assault and battery.

- There are also a number of defences which relate to the criminal law which might be of relevance in some situations involving tortious conduct. For example, reasonable force may be used to resist unlawful criminal interference, although this is probably merely self-defence; in certain circumstances citizens are, at common law, entitled to take reasonable steps to prevent a breach of the peace; under s. 3 of the Criminal Law Act 1967, reasonable force may be used in the prevention of crime or apprehension of offenders, suspected offenders, or those 'unlawfully at large'.

- This chapter focuses on the main general defences:
  (a) consent/*volenti non fit injuria*;
  (b) illegality;
  (c) contributory negligence.

- Only contributory negligence is widely used. It is a versatile defence, in that it applies to most, if not all, torts, where appropriate, and it offers the courts a means of 'sharing the blame' between the parties.

- Illegality has always been an unpredictable and uncertain defence. Public policy is, a judge once said, 'an unruly horse'.

- The involvement of a criminal act is not a prerequisite for this defence. *Kirkham* is only one of several cases in which there has been some reference to the effect on the 'public conscience' should the courts provide a forum for actions tainted with illegality. It is, at best, a vague notion and it is unclear how the public reaction is to be gauged in any particular instance. Apart from the question of degree, it is uncertain whether emotional reactions or feelings of retribution on the part of the public should be incorporated in the 'test'.

- The court will sometimes refuse to set a duty where illegal activity is involved. This approach incorporates the factor of illegality into the argument on whether or not a duty of care ought to be imposed in particular circumstances. We have seen that *volenti* is often used in this way and that that distorts the picture of what is really happening. In both cases, that is of illegality and *volenti*, their pivotal roles as defences is obscured in such cases. In any event, this approach can only work where the tort of negligence is involved, because the duty is fixed in other torts. However, consent may be part of the duty equation in some cases of battery.

- This is also true of the standard of care rationale: the court will refuse to get involved in assessing degrees of illegality. It can only work where the standard has to be set in the particular circumstances of the case; that means it only applies where negligence or fault of some kind has to be proved.

- It is also claimed that the courts must not be seen to encourage the claimant and others in illicit activities. This is a difficult claim to substantiate because the deterrent effect of a refusal to assist the claimant is of dubious substance, particularly where, as is often the case, the issue before the court is essentially one of negligence.

- Illegality strongly resembles *volenti non fit injuria*. Both defences are based on public policy. *Volenti* is said to be based on the consent of the claimant, but the determination of that 'consent' by the courts is often influenced by considerations of policy as, for example in *Morris* v *Murray* and *ICI* v *Shatwell*. Both defences are complete defences and both defences are based on the merits of the claimant's claim.

- Most confusion occurs in the implied (or imputed) *volenti* cases. The expression *volenti non fit injuria* embraces the whole range of consent or agreement and whatever form it takes, it may be said that it all boils down to consent or no consent, but it has been suggested that:

  (a) consent, which may be express or implied, should be restricted to intentional torts (any specific consent given to an intentional interference, for example, the tort of battery, would not extend to an act of negligence);

  (b) contractual consent or similar agreements should be regarded as a specific defence, which can embrace both intentional torts and the tort of negligence;

  (c) the term 'voluntary assumption of risk' best expresses the notion of implied consent to negligence, and express (or specific) consent to negligence is best dealt with in terms of contractual, or similar agreements.

- Contributory negligence, which is based on the premise that the claimant either knew or ought to have known of the relevant danger, must be distinguished from *volenti* which is based on the claimant's full knowledge of the nature and extent of the risk, and both defences must be distinguished from *novus actus interveniens* and *nova causa interveniens*, the doctrine of intervening causes, which is discussed in **Chapter 2**. In practice, however, it may often be difficult to find the precise dividing line between them all, as cases like *Morris* v *Murray* demonstrate. All are means of defence, and the courts' task, in the final analysis, is to strike a balance between the interests of the litigants, taking into account, too, the public interest.

■ **FURTHER READING**

Giliker, P. and Beckwith, S., *Tort*, 2nd edn, London: Sweet & Maxwell, 2004, Chapter 14.

Hepple, Howarth, and Matthews, *Tort: Cases and Materials*, 5th edn, London: Butterworths, 2000, Chapter 7.

Jones, M., *Textbook on Torts*, 8th edn, Oxford: Oxford University Press, 2002, Chapter 14.

Kidner, R., *Casebook on Torts*, 9th edn, Oxford: Oxford University Press, 2006, Chapter 15.

Law Commission Consultation Paper No. 160: The Illegality Defence in Tort, 2001 (to result in a report).

Markesinis, B.S., and Deakin, S.F., *Tort Law*, 5th edn, Oxford: Oxford University Press, 2003, Chapter 8 (s. 1).

Murphy, J., *Street on Torts*, 11th edn, London: Butterworths, 2003, Chapters 6 and 15.

Salmond and Heuston on the Law of Torts, 21st edn, London: Sweet & Maxwell, 1996, Chapter 22.

Stanton, K.M., *Modern Law of Tort*, London: Sweet & Maxwell, 1994, Chapter 5.

Stauch, M., Wheat, K., and Tingle, J., *Sourcebook on Medical Law*, 2nd edn, London: Cavendish Publishing, 2002, Chapters 3, 4, 10, and 12.

Weir, T., *Casebook on Tort*, 9th edn, London: Sweet & Maxwell, 2000, Chapter 5.

Winfield and Jolowicz on Tort, 16th edn, London: Sweet & Maxwell, 2002, Chapter 26.

 CHAPTER 14 ASSESSMENT EXERCISE

Rex, and his fiancée, Portia, after drinking alcohol at lunchtime, stole a car for a joyride. Portia, not wearing her seat belt, drove the car at speed along a cliff top road, skidded on a bend and the car crashed into a boulder before coming to a stop hanging precariously over the edge of the cliff. Rex was injured but managed to get out of the car.

Sam, a passing motorist, stopped at the scene of the accident and, together with Rex, climbed into the car to help Portia. The car tipped up under the combined weight of them all and fell down the cliff. Rex and Sam were seriously injured and Portia was killed, but it transpired that she would in any event probably have died from her initial injuries.

Discuss the tortious issues arising from these events.

See *Cases and Materials* (14.3) for a specimen answer.

■ INDEX